# ORGANIZATIONAL COMMUNICATION

## Second Edition

Library of Congress Catalog Number: 87-13856
ISBN: 978-0-88738-699-2
Printed in the United States of America

Library of Congress Cataloging-in-Publication Data

Organizational communication.
    1. Communication in organizations.  2.  Communication in management.
  I. Ferguson, Sherry.  II. Ferguson, Stewart.

HD30.3.072      1987      658.4'5        87-13856
ISBN 0-88738-164-2
ISBN 0-88738-699-7 (pbk.)

# Organizational Communication

## Second Edition

*Edited by*
**Sherry Devereaux Ferguson**
**and**
**Stewart Ferguson**

Transaction Publishers
New Brunswick (U.S.A.) and London (U.K.)

*To*
*Leslie and Maureen*

# Contents

# Acknowledgments

Lesley A. Albertson, "Telecommunications as a Travel Substitute: Some Psychological, Organizational, and Social Aspects," by Lesley A. Albertson in *The Journal of Communication* (27:2). Reprinted by permission of *The Journal of Communication*.

Patricia Hayes Andrews, "Socialization in Groups and Organizations: Toward a Concept of Creative Conformity." Original essay prepared for *Intercom*, first edition of *Organizational Communication*.

Michael Burgoon, Judee K. Heston, and James McCroskey, "Communication Roles in Small Group Interaction." From *Small Group Communication: A Functional Approach*, by Michael Burgoon, Judee K. Heston and James McCroskey. Copyright © 1974 by Holt, Rinehart & Winston, Inc. Reprinted by permission of CBS College Publishing.

Ke-Lu Chao and William I. Gorden, "Culture and Communication in the Modern Japanese Corporate Organization." Reprinted with permission from "Culture and Communication in the Modern Japanese Corporate Organization," the *International and Intercultural Communication Annual* 5 (1979).

Olga L. Crocker, "Conflict: An Overview." Original essay prepared for *Intercom*, first edition of *Organizational Communication*. All rights reserved by author.

Keith Davis, "Management Communication and the Grapevine." Reprinted by permission of the *Harvard Business Review*. "Management Communication and the Grapevine" by Keith Davis (September/October 1953). Copyright © 1953 by the President and Fellows of Harvard College; all rights reserved.

Richard V. Farace, Peter R. Monge, and Hamish M. Russell, "Communicating in Micro-Networks." From *Communicating and Organizing*, by Richard V. Farace, Peter R. Monge and Hamish Russell. Reprinted by permission of Random House, Inc.

Gene D. Fowler and Marilyn E. Wackerbarth, "Audio Teleconferencing versus Face-to-Face Conferencing: A Synthesis of the Literature," *The Western Journal of Speech Communication* 44:3 (Summer 1980). Copyright © 1980 by the Western Speech Communication Association. Reprinted by permission.

Gerald Goldhaber and Donald Rogers, "Information Needs." From Goldhaber-Rogers: *Auditing Organizational Communication Systems*. Copyright © 1979 by Kendall/Hunt Publishing Co. Used with permission.

Gerald Goldhaber and Donald Rogers, "The ICA Audit (Questionnaire Survey)." From Goldhaber-Rogers: *Auditing Organizational Communication*

*Systems.* Copyright © 1979 by Kendall/Hunt Publishing Co. Used with permission.

Dennis S. Gouran, "Leadership in Small Groups." Original essay prepared for *Organizational Communication.*

Thad B. Green and Paul H. Pietri, "Using Nominal Grouping to Improve Upward Communication," pp. 37–43, *MSU Business Topics* (Autumn 1974). Reprinted by permission of the publisher, Division of Research, Graduate School of Business Administration, Michigan State University.

Susan A. Hellweg and Kevin L. Freiberg, "Corporate Quality Circles: Using Small Groups in Organizations." Paper presented to International Communication Association Convention, Organizational Communication Division, San Francisco, California, May 1984.

Bonnie McDaniel Johnson, "Characteristics of Effective Decision Building." From Bonnie McDaniel Johnson, *Communication: The Process of Organizing,* Copyright © 1977 by Allyn and Bacon, Inc., Boston. Reprinted with permission of the publisher.

Bonnie McDaniel Johnson, "Phases of Decision Building." From Bonnie McDaniel Johnson, *Communication: The Process of Organizing,* Copyright © 1977 by Allyn and Bacon, Inc., Boston. Reprinted with permission of the publisher.

Sandra M. Ketrow, "Nonverbal Communication in the Organization." Original essay prepared for *Organizational Communication.*

Richard B. Kielbowicz, "Leaks to the Press as Communication Within and Between Organizations." From "Leaks to the Press as Communication Within and Between Organizations," *Newspaper Research Journal* 1 (February 1980). Reprinted with permission.

Wilfred List, "When Workers and Managers Act as a Team: QWL in Canada." *Globe and Mail Report on Business Magazine* (October 1985). Reprinted with permission.

Norman R. F. Maier, "Assets and Liabilities in Group Problem Solving: The Need for an Integrative Function," *Psychological Review,* Vol. 74, 1967, pp. 239–49. Copyright © 1967 by the American Psychological Association. Reprinted by permission of the publisher and the author.

Barry J. McLoughlin, "Encountering the Media." Original essay prepared for *Organizational Communication.*

Barry J. McLoughlin and James R. McLoughlin, "The Consultant-Client Relationship and Organizational Change." Original essay prepared for *Organizational Communication.*

Robert L. Minter, "The Hiring Interview." Reprinted by permission of the publisher, from *Supervisory Management,* (December 1974) Copyright © 1974 American Management Association, New York. All rights reserved.

Maryruth K. Nivens, "Managing Conflict and Stress." From a speech delivered at "Up the Managerial Ladder, a Conference for Women," November

2, 1979, Auburn University at Montgomery, Montgomery, Alabama. Printed with permission.

William D. Richards, Jr., "Network Analysis in Organizations." Original essay, Printed with permission.

Fritz J. Roethlisberger, excerpt from *Management and Morale*. Reprinted by permission of the publishers from *Management and Morale*, by Fritz J. Roethlisberger, Cambridge, Massachusetts: Harvard University Press, Copyright © 1941 by the President and Fellows of Harvard College.

Carl Rogers and Richard E. Farson, "Active Listening." Reprinted by special permission of the author and the Industrial Relations Center, University of Chicago.

Stephen L. Ross, "Creative Problem Solving." Original essay prepared for *Organizational Communication*.

Alice Sargent, "Women and Men Working Together: Toward Androgeny." Copyright © 1983, *Training and Development Journal*, American Society for Training and Development. Reprinted with permission. All rights reserved.

Michael Z. Sincoff, Dudley A. Williams, and C. E. Tapie Rohm, Jr., "Steps in Performing a Communication Audit." Reprinted by permission of the authors.

Michael Stano, "Guidelines for Conducting the Performance Appraisal Interview: A Literature Synthesis," *Journal of Applied Communication Research*, 9:2, pp. 131–142. Reprinted with permission. William J. Starosta, "Intercultural Communication and the Organization." Original essay prepared for *Organizational Communication*.

Lea P. Stewart, " 'Whistle Blowing': Implications for Organizational Communication." From " 'Whistle Blowing': Implications for Organizational Communication," by Lea P. Stewart in *The Journal of Communication* 30:4. Reprinted by permission of *The Journal of Communication*.

Frederick Taylor, excerpts from *Scientific Management*, Copyright © 1947, Harper and Row Publishers, New York, New York, pp. 40–47. Reprinted with permission.

Richard J. Tersine and Walter E. Riggs, "The Delphi Technique: A Long-Range Planning Tool," *Business Horizons*, Vol. 19 (April 1976), pp. 51–56. Copyright © 1976, by the Foundation for the School of Business at Indiana University. Reprinted by permission.

Jacques Vallee, Robert Johansen, and Kathleen Spangler, "The Computer Conference: An Altered State of Communication," from *The Futurist* (June 1975), published by the World Future Society. Reprinted with permission of the publisher.

Norma M. Williams, Gideon Sjoberg, and Andree F. Sjoberg, "The Bureaucratic Personality: An Alternate View." From "The Bureaucratic Personality: An Alternate View," *JABS*. Vol. 16:3 (1980). Reprinted with permission.

# Introduction

Since the first edition of this book was published, communication in organizations has taken on a new meaning. The word processor, which only a few years ago was at the same time a promising and threatening innovation, has relegated the typewriter to the broom closet or the used office-equipment store. Similarly, even the smallest of business enterprises regard computers to be essential.

The new information-handling technology not only offers faster and more extensive data storage and processing capacity; it also introduces new problems, and raises some new questions about what we are trying to do. For example, word processors offer new levels of text editing that can result in more polished copy. But the ease with which editing can be done sometimes results in multiple rewrites to a point where time is not always saved. Computers have also been found to have an extraordinary capacity for storing garbage.

Many writers have dubbed the present time the information age, and they see the new information technology making a major impact on organizations. However, significant technological innovations have always required periods of adaptation. Old ideas and procedures have tended to impede the rational utilization of innovations. This is what Marshall McLuhan called the "horseless carriage" syndrome. McLuhan, using another automobile metaphor, said that we look at new things through old eyes and judge where we are going on the basis of where we have been, as if we were driving a car by looking in the rearview mirror.

We may indeed be into the information age in terms of the technological environment in which we live; however, the indications are that we are caught in the adaptation lag that characterizes periods of social transition; that is, we are operating on old terms in a drastically changed environment. During periods of transition, direction is established by reexamining or redefining goals and objectives and attempting to exploit new techniques to achieve them.

This book sets out to examine some dominant themes in organizational and communication theory and to use these as a base on which to build strategies for the efficient utilization of modern communication technology. The themes that we have noted reflect broad trends in the theory of society in general, which are characterized by a move toward democratization. This trend, sometimes described as a move from a top-down to a bottom-up approach, is not only motivated by social enlightenment but has become accepted as necessary for the efficient functioning of institutions within a modern complex society.

While the idea of democratic organizations is by no means new (for over twenty years, organizational theorists have been saying that people at all levels of the organization should make a greater contribution to the decision-making process), it is very much easier to recognize a need for democratic change than to bring about the change.

Communication scholars would say that historically such changes have taken place as a result of major innovations in communication technology. In traditional societies, communication took place through live interpersonal communication, and the patterns of communication were largely governed by proximity, which in turn reflected the hierarchy of authority in the society. Information moved from the top down and was presented in ways that served the interests of the authority system. Such an arrangement was not conducive to change; nor was change pursued, since it posed a threat to the existing order of things.

The development of mass communication techniques took information control away from the traditional authorities and bypassed their gatekeepers. If information is power, as the saying goes, then such a change in the proprietorship of information implies a considerable shift in the social-bargaining dynamic. As a consequence, more democratic concessions have to be made by those in authority.

Modern communication technology has further changed social interaction by manipulating time and space and by removing the body from the communication act. These changes have the potential to operationalize theories of democratic management in ways not possible in the days of Fayol or Roethlisberger.

Some of the factors inhibiting democratic change in organizations are the same ones that operate in the larger society. The hierarchical ordering in organizations is, if not more pronounced than in society at large, at least more obvious and immediate. As a result, conventions of what is considered to be appropriate communication between people of different status are deep set, even though certain superficial informalities such as the use of first names may be more common than in the past.

The computer promises to act as a catalyst for productive democratic change, not only in its potential to allow bypassing of authority structures, but also in its circumvention of the conventions of formal face-to-face interaction. The computer manipulates space in obvious ways by connecting terminals at opposite ends of the building or opposite ends of the world. It manipulates time in the same way by allowing immediate or delayed interaction between numerous dispersed terminals. In the computer conference, questions may be answered after a five-minute or a five-day consideration of the question. This new arrangement places a higher value on the thoughtful answer than on the facile one. The anonymity made possible by the use of passwords can at the same time remove the inhibitions of lower-status participants and discourage prejudgment of participants' ideas based on the status of the sender.

Although the new information technology can, and no doubt will, effect a major shift in interaction patterns within organizations, we will, based on past experience, continue to use today's technology on yesterday's terms until the adaptation lag has run its course. In other words, we have the alternative of accepting an electronic horseless carriage, or attempting to gain a better understanding of the social implications in the new technology so that appropriate application of the new tools can be accelerated.

In this book we have attempted to assemble various insights on organizational theory and practice and communication theory and practice to show the close relationship between the two disciplines. We have also pointed to areas in which the implications of the new communication technology seem to be most relevant, such as management theory, leadership theory, and conferencing.

The book is organized into twelve parts. Part One traces the development of the major schools of management theory, starting in the 1920s with Frederick Taylor's work on scientific management. This school of thought emphasized analysis and management of process, based on efficient production. Critics said that Taylor's was a top-down approach that assumed efficient management was largely a matter of making rational decisions and ensuring that orders were obeyed. The relationship of management to workers was said to be paternalistic. Motivation derived from an appropriate system of economic rewards or punishments. Taylor's approach was individual-centered, stressing personal, rather than group, accomplishments.

It is no longer fashionable to claim to be a proponent of stick-and-carrot motivation systems; nonetheless, most organizational specialists will admit that, in spite of a more enlightened body of organization theory, Taylorism remains a dominant part of the operational philosophy of many organizations.

In the 1930s the scientific management approach gave way to what came to be known as the *human relations school*, where the emphasis shifted toward a consideration of the psychological needs of workers. Although motivation was still considered to be largely a question of providing financial rewards, job satisfaction and self-esteem assumed new importance as factors that influenced improved production. The individual was now seen to be dependent on recognition and approval from the social and organizational groups with which he identified. This human relations approach, with its roots in extensive research carried out at the Western Electric Hawthorne plant, continued to evolve through to the 1960s. As the movement developed, more emphasis was placed on the need for workers to believe that they had a say in decisions that affected their welfare. Although the need for a more humane and democratic approach to managing organizations had become a significant part of management theory, critics maintained that the underlying philosophy was still paternalistic and manipulative.

The next major movement in organizational theory entailed a shift from the psychological to the sociological or anthropological approach. The *systems school* no longer saw the organization as an autonomous entity but rather as a subunit of the larger social environment, dependent on the communication networks that both laced together the subunits of the organization and connected it with the larger community. Some of the figures in the systems school were Herbert A. Simons, Robert L. Kahn, James G. Miller, and Daniel Katz.

This shift to a communication emphasis in organizational theory reflected a more general preoccupation of scholars with the processes of communication in society. An interest in communication networks in society was stimulated by the work of scholars such as Paul Lazarsfeld and Elihu Katz, who established that opinion was formed not through formal communication systems, but rather through informal networks controlled by opinion leaders. In other words, what passed through the formal channels was interpreted and disseminated by means of interpersonal networks.

The fourth school of theory included in Part One is the *human resources school*. In many regards, the human resources approach differed from the human relations approach in degree rather than in substance. Some writers tend to use the terms *human relations* and *human resources* interchangeably; others assert that the human resources school represents a shift from a nominal recognition of the psychological needs of the individual to a belief that the individuals who comprise the workforce of an organization are its most valuable resource. Proponents of the human resources approach maintain that all members of the organization not only should have token input into decision-making and goal determination; they should also *own* the

goals and personally identify with them. Personal and social identification, gratification, and motivation have become central issues in the
human resource approach. The work of Maslow, McGregor, and
Herzberg is frequently cited.

Designating schools of theory is more a matter of denoting different
centers of emphasis than denoting radically different paradigms. The
central ideas from which all the theories evolved were articulated by
some of the earliest workers in the field. Organizational theory has
developed parallel with social science, and both have been characterized in the last 25 years by a move from a micro systems approach to
a macro systems approach. In other words, a holistic view that
assumes interactions, interdependencies, and balances between all the
elements of the social environment has replaced a tendency to consider
subsystems in isolation. The increasing use of the term *culture* to
describe the complete organizational system recognizes a need to
consider the value systems of organizations in relationship to the
broader social systems.

In the past, organizations tended to be regarded as set apart from
the larger society, and in large part able to determine the nature and
extent of their interaction with the external environment. The modern
view assumes that a symbiotic interdependency exists between an
organization and the social and technological environment in which it
is set—what has come to be known as a sociotechnical systems
approach. Part Two of the text considers the way in which the social
and technological environment that generates management theory can
influence the extent to which the theory can be exported or imported.
It has been suggested that social theories that seriously question the
existing order often have to be transplanted into favorable alien climates; and if they become viable, they are sometimes reimported in
modified form. Some historians would say that the American revolution was conceived in France, transported to the United States, and
used as a model for the French revolution. In the same way, organizational approaches such as quality circles involve reimportation of
American concepts operationalized in Japan. These are some of the
considerations discussed in Part Two of the text.

The bottom-up approach to organizational and social interaction
becomes manifest in communication theory through a concentration
on interpersonal communication processes. Theories of communication in society have passed through stages of structural analysis similar
to those noted in the evolution of organizational and social science
theory. First, it was assumed that mass communication produced a
mass homogenous society. This approach was soon found to be inade-

quate, and the dominant theory manifested itself in various models of limited effect until it moved to the position that the policy maker was not pulling the strings that made society jump, but instead frantically trying to keep up with trends generated in and by society; hence the proliferation of public opinion polls and issue monitoring. It is sometimes implied that the early ideas in both organization and communication theory were limited and naïve. It may instead be true that the early theories were appropriate for the times in which they emerged, but as society became more complex and more sophisticated, more sophisticated models had to be created. Perhaps the initial effect of the truly mass media *was* to homogenize society, but the extraordinary increase in the size of the new information base caused different people to assemble reality in different ways. As a result, diversity grew out of massification.

This consolidation of ideas to form dominant trends, which generates more diversity, is a recurrent cycle in social evolution. The social scientist comes to realize that the truth is not locked in any macro or micro model; he must constantly alternate between the microscope and the wide-angle lens, modifying his models as his instruments improve and as he learns to use instruments more effectively.

The social scientist sometimes refers to such recurrent social cycles as pendular swings. But this metaphor does not consider that when the pendulum swings, it does not return to the same kind of homogeneity or diversity. At each transition, new levels of complexity have evolved. A more appropriate analogue may be seen in the cycle of mold development. When a nutritive medium is left exposed to the atmosphere, a mold will soon cover the surface. Eventually small colonies of various other molds, frequently of different colors, will appear. Over time, one of these new molds will dominate and take over. The cycle can be repeated several times. Presumably, given the right circumstances, something could eventually crawl out of the saucer, as each cycle from homogeneity to diversity evolved to a higher level of complexity than previous cycles.

For the social scientist attempting to understand and explain such social processes, a helical model may perhaps be more useful and appropriate than a pendular or cyclical model. Like a spiral staircase, each convolution in the helical model arrives at a new floor level. In political science terms, for example, the conservatism of the 1950s would be a different genre from that of the 1980s; references to pendular swings between conservatism and liberalism may be valid in only the broadest terms.

As organizations and organizational process have become more complex, there has been a move from an atomistic to a holistic perspective—a move that, rather than diminishing the importance of the individual in the organization, is placing new importance on processes of information exchange and opinion formation at the interpersonal level. In other words, a study of *macro* processes, for instance those manifested in the democratization of society through new levels of access to the mass media, is now leading to a renewed emphasis on *micro* processes, such as experimentation with quality circles and bottom-up decision making. This focus on the micro level represents, however, an emphasis very different from the atomistic perspective of Frederick Taylor in his time and motion studies in the 1920s.

In keeping with this contemporary, bottom-up perspective, Part Three of this book enters the area of organizational communication theory by reviewing some of the theoretical propositions relating to interpersonal communication. This section includes general theory relating to the effects of the physical environment on interpersonal interaction, the nonverbal components of interpersonal communication, and communication between individuals of different cultural backgrounds.

Part Four takes interpersonal communication theory into the organization, with chapters on interaction between women and men in the organization, organizational socialization processes, and the bureaucratic personality.

Part Five takes a wider-angle view, with a focus on formal and informal interpersonal networks, including chapters on management networks and the grapevine, leaks to the press as intraorganizational and interorganizational communication, and whistle blowing.

Some applied interpersonal communication concepts are discussed in Part Six, with chapters on active listening, the hiring interview, performance appraisal interviews, and the media interview. For the most part, the articles are written from the executive or management point of view.

Part Seven includes chapters on micro networks, stages of decision building, characteristics of effective decision building, communication roles, leadership in small groups, and quality circles as a popular form of small group communication used in organizations today.

Part Eight looks at advantages and disadvantages of various group problem-solving approaches, including face-to-face conferencing, audio and video teleconferencing, and computer conferencing.

Focusing on creative problem solving, Part Nine examines some of the group problem-solving techniques that are more structured, such as the *nominal group* and the *Delphi* approaches, as well as less structured techniques such as brainstorming and synectics.

Articles on conflict, stress, and change in the organization, as well as the role of the consultant in effecting organizational change, appear in Part Ten.

Part Eleven examines some of the research techniques and instruments available to individuals seeking to study communication processes in the organization, including the ICA Communication Audit, small-world research techniques, and network analysis approaches.

The last unit in the text, Part Twelve, offers a number of case studies designed to illustrate specific communication concepts discussed in earlier chapters. An appendix to the book lists selected films and videotapes that enhance the teaching of the units.

We would like to thank Irving Louis Horowitz of Transaction Books for his support and encouragement and editor Kimberly Jesuele of Transaction Books for her careful handling of our manuscript. We would also like to thank Anne Bertrand-May for her preparation of the graphics and our son Eric Ferguson for his help with typing.

# Part I

# ORGANIZATIONAL THEORY AND ITS COMMUNICATION IMPLICATIONS

# 1

# Scientific Management School

## Classical School

The first major school of organizational theory has been labeled the *classical* school. Major figures representing this school were an American, Frederick Taylor, father of scientific management; a German, Max Weber, father of bureaucracy; and a Frenchman, Henri Fayol, father of the first administration theory. Other contributors to the classical school were Luther Gulick, Lyndall Urwick, James Mooney, and Alan Reily. These scholars were all products of the last century, producing their greatest contributions in the early part of this century. Before them, no organized body of management theory existed.

## Scientific Management

The international scientific management movement originated in 1911 with the publication of Frederick Taylor's *Scientific Management*. Earlier known as "Taylorism" or as the "Taylor system," scientific management was devised as a solution to the tensions between labor and management in the late 1800s.[1]

Taylor first presented his system of management to the American Society of Mechanical Engineers in 1895. His paper, titled "A Piece-Rate System: A Step Toward Partial Solution of the Labor Problem," advocated what Taylor later called "a mental revolution."[2] He felt that the first step in this mental revolution was to stop fighting over how large a share of the pie labor and management should get and to concentrate instead on making the pie bigger.[3]

According to Taylor, the best way of achieving this end was to substitute science for rule-of-thumb management. Taylor's aim was to establish a scientific measure of what constitutes a fair day's work. By raising lagging productivity, management would profit; if management compensated workers for increased output, workers would likewise profit.

Scientific management was the outcome of twelve years Taylor spent at the Midvale Steel Company, first as an engineer and later as a manager. The most well known of his techniques for determining a fair day's work were his "time-and-motion" studies. These studies involved clocking with a stopwatch the time that it took to carry out various tasks. Different combinations of tools and techniques were applied to work tasks, and every motion made by the workers was analyzed and recorded. Eventually, one "best" method was identified, and detailed instructions for applying these techniques to specific tasks were put in writing and circulated to all relevant employees.

Exemplary of Taylor's time-and-motion studies were his experiments at Bethlehem Steel Company. Taylor found that a conscientious worker could load twice as much iron ore with a relatively small shovel as with a larger one. He identified fifteen different sizes and types of shovels for loading different kinds of materials. Within a few years, 140 workers were doing the work previously done by 400 to 600 workers.[4]

Through these experiments and others, Taylor sought to rationalize tasks and to eliminate as much as possible the need for discretionary judgments regarding the work accomplished. Just as management by objectives seeks to reduce a supervisor's subjective judgment regarding subordinate performance, Taylor sought to reduce the arbitrary power of supervisors and managers by giving concrete measures with which to gauge performance.[5] He believed that clarified job expectations would focus the attention of managers and workers on organizational goals and job-related behavior and thereby eliminate personality conflicts and labor-management strife.

Taylor's system included much more than the time-and-motion studies for which he has been severely criticized. He also developed much-needed systems for organizing storerooms, standardizing tools, charting work, providing written job descriptions, keeping books, selecting and training workers, and accounting. Some scholars credit Taylor with inventing the "rest break" or "coffee break," although others claim he never put the theory into practice.[6] Taylor's investigation of machine speeds for metal cutting led to his discovery of "high-speed" steel that could hold its cutting edge while red hot, which allowed a significant increase in machine speeds. It was this discovery that prompted Taylor to try to speed up the manual work process in order to utilize fully the increased machine speeds. Later he took advantage of the same discovery to require any company that bought patent rights for high-speed steel to adopt the Taylor system for speeding up work.[7]

Over a period of time, Taylor gained the devotion of an inner circle of friends and proponents of the scientific management approach. Some of these admirers made a substantial contribution to his work. Frank and Lillian Gilbreth, for example, developed the motion studies later incorporated by Taylor into his research. Henry Gantt contributed a managerial bonus system and the Gantt chart for planning work output, and Carl Barth developed the Barth slide rule for use in calculating machine speeds. Barth later convinced the newly opened Harvard Business School to accept Taylor's system as a management model.[8]

By 1917 at least twenty-nine firms had been "Taylorized," and scientific management theories were spreading with varying degrees of success through France, England, Germany, and the Soviet Union.[9] The influence of the school did not stop with these nations. Because many organizations and industries adapted Taylorism to their own structures and work cultures and not all admitted using the system, it is difficult to know with precision the complete extent of its popularity; however, some authors claim that scientific management has been underestimated and that, in fact, it is one of the most pervasive and invisible of the forces that have shaped modern society.[10] Even though other schools of theory have displaced scientific management, many claim that Taylorism approaches still typify practices in many organizations today.

### Criticisms

Scientific management has been termed an "efficiency evangelism" and "a faith designed for pragmatists."[11] Taylor's system was criticized for tolerating only "first-class men" and for being elitist and authoritarian.[12] Critics accused Taylor of offering a cynical view of economic man, exemplified by his advocacy of paying workers according to their individual output rather than their group performance. His theories were said to be mechanistic and atomistic, regarding man as a machine whose movements could be broken down, timed, and analyzed.[13] Taylorism was said to imply close supervision of workers, giving them little autonomy or potential for self-direction.[14]

Taylor's system transferred power from the traditional sources of foreman and manager to the new scientific managers, who most often came from the professional middle classes. For this reason, neither management nor the workers liked the system.

The transition to Taylorism was expensive, since it was typically marked by resistance, strikes, and sometimes violence. On more than one occasion, Taylor received death threats. Others sought to discount

Taylor's theories by proving him insane, and some hired detectives to follow him, observe his behavior, and question household servants and acquaintances. In 1911 Taylor had to defend his system before a special investigative committee of the U.S. Congress.[15]

The following dialogue taken from *Scientific Management* is the one for which Taylor has been most often criticized. Critics invoke this excerpt to demonstrate Taylor's advocacy of an oppressive work environment, Draconian supervision tactics, and an antihumanistic world view.

Our first step was the scientific selection of the workman. In dealing with workmen under this type of management, it is an inflexible rule to talk to and deal with only one man at a time, since each workman has his own special abilities and limitations, and since we are not dealing with men in masses, but are trying to develop each individual man to his highest state of efficiency and prosperity. Our first step was to find the proper workman to begin with. We therefore carefully watched and studied these 75 men for three or four days, at the end of which time we had picked out four men who appeared to be physically able to handle pig iron at the rate of 47 tons per day. A careful study was then made of each of these men. We looked up their history as far back as practicable and thorough inquiries were made as to the character, habits, and the ambition of each of them. Finally we selected one from among the four as the most likely man to start with. He was a little Pennsylvania Dutchman who had been observed to trot back home for a mile or so after his work in the evening about as fresh as he was when he came trotting down to work in the morning. We found that upon wages of $1.15 a day he had succeeded in buying a small plot of ground, and that he was engaged in putting up the walls of a little house for himself in the morning before starting to work and at night after leaving. He also had the reputation of being exceedingly "close," that is, of placing a very high value on a dollar. As one man whom we talked to about him said, "A penny looks about the size of a cart-wheel to him." This man we will call Schmidt.

The task before us, then, narrowed itself down to getting Schmidt to handle 47 tons of pig iron per day and making him glad to do it. This was done as follows. Schmidt was called out from among the gang of pig-iron handlers and talked to somewhat in this way:

"Schmidt, are you a high-priced man?"

"Vell, I don't know vat you mean."

"Oh yes, you do. What I want to know is whether you are a high-priced man or not."

"Vell, I don't know vat you mean."

"Oh, come now, you answer my questions. What I want to find out is whether you are a high-priced man or one of these cheap fellows here.

What I want to find out is whether you want to earn $1.85 a day or whether you are satisfied with $1.15, just the same as all those cheap fellows are getting.''

"Did I vant $1.85 a day? Vas dot a high-priced man? Vell, yes, I vas a high-priced man.''

"Oh, you're aggravating me. Of course you want $1.85 a day—every one wants it! You know perfectly well that has very little to do with your being a high-priced man. For goodness' sake answer my questions, and don't waste any more of my time. Now come over here. You see that pile of pig iron?''

"Yes.''

"You see that car?''

"Yes.''

"Well, if you are a high-priced man, you will load that pig iron on that car to-morrow for $1.85. Now do wake up and answer my question. Tell me whether you are a high-priced man or not.''

"Vell—did I got $1.85 for loading dot pig iron on dot car to-morrow?''

"Yes, of course you do, and you get $1.85 for loading a pile like that every day right through the year. That is what a high-priced man does, and you know it just as well as I do.''

"Vell, dot's all right. I could load dot pig iron on the car to-morrow for $1.85, and I get it every day, don't I?''

"Certainly you do—certainly you do.''

"Vell, den, I vas a high-priced man.''

"Now, hold on, hold on. You know just as well as I do that a high-priced man has to do exactly as he's told from morning till night. You have seen this man here before, haven't you?''

"No, I never saw him.''

"Well, if you are a high-priced man, you will do exactly as this man tells you to-morrow, from morning till night. When he tells you to pick up a pig and walk, you pick it up and you walk, and when he tells you to sit down and rest, you sit down. You do that right straight through the day. And what's more, no back talk. Now a high-priced man does just what he's told to do, and no back talk. Do you understand that? When this man tells you to walk, you walk; when he tells you to sit down, you sit down, and you don't talk back at him. Now you come on to work here to-morrow morning and I'll know before night whether you are really a high-priced man or not.''

This seems to be rather rough talk. And indeed it would be if applied to an educated mechanic, or even an intelligent laborer. With a man of the mentally sluggish type of Schmidt it is appropriate and not unkind, since it is effective in fixing his attention on the high wages which he wants and away from what, if it were called to his attention, he probably would consider impossibly hard work.

What would Schmidt's answer be if he were talked to in a manner which is usual under the management of "initiative and incentive"? say, as follows:

"Now, Schmidt, you are a first-class pig-iron handler and know your business well. You have been handling at the rate of 12½ tons per day. I have given considerable study to handling pig iron, and feel sure that you could do a much larger day's work than you have been doing. Now don't you think that if you really tried you could handle 47 tons of pig iron per day, instead of 12½ tons?"

What do you think Schmidt's answer would be to this?

Schmidt started to work, and all day long, and at regular intervals, was told by the man who stood over him with a watch, "Now pick up a pig and walk. Now sit down and rest. Now walk—now rest," etc. He worked when he was told to work, and rested when he was told to rest, and at half-past five in the afternoon had his 47½ tons loaded on the car. And he practically never failed to work at this pace and do the task that was set him during the three years that the writer was at Bethlehem. And throughout this time he averaged a little more than $1.85 per day, whereas before he had never received over $1.15 per day, which was the ruling rate of wages at that time in Bethlehem. That is, he received 60 per cent, higher wages than were paid to other men who were not working on task work. One man after another was picked out and trained to handle pig iron at the rate of 47½ tons per day until all of the pig iron was handled at this rate, and the men were receiving 60 per cent more wages than other workmen around them.[16]

After Taylor's death, his disciples softened the focus of the system, eliminating what had been perceived as some of the harshest penalties of the piecework system and shifting the emphasis of research from "work" studies to the more humanistic "fatigue" studies for which Lillian Gilbreth acquired a reputation.

### Defence of Taylorism

Admirers of Taylorism claim that for all its faults, scientific management was founded on honorable intentions: a desire for reconciliation between management and labor, with the hope of maximum gains for both and with science and rationality as cornerstones of the theory.

Taylor defended his work in much these same terms. He spoke of the desire to further "close, intimate, personal cooperation between management and workers." He summarized his approach as "Science, not rule of thumb; Harmony, not discord; Cooperation, not individualism; Maximum output, in place of restricted output; Development of each man to his greatest efficiency and prosperity."[17]

By the criteria of the 1980s, Taylor's theory may be wanting; however, in the 1880s when Taylor first formulated his ideas, they represented a large step forward over what had been in most cases total lack of system. In fact, scientific management has been termed the most comprehensive and detailed system of management ever developed.

Among those who feel that Taylor made a powerful and lasting contribution to Western thought is Peter Drucker, one of Taylor's staunchest advocates. Drucker claims that Taylor intended to meet the needs of individuals and organizations.[18] If you accept Drucker's view, Taylorism becomes "pro–organization," rather than "pro–management" in its orientation and can be regarded as a forerunner to later human-resource approaches. Moreover, Taylor's consideration of technological, as well as human, organizational factors suggests later sociotechnical systems approaches. David Whitsett and Lyle Yorks argue that Taylor had considerable insight into group influences long before the Hawthorne studies that heralded the beginning of a human relations era.[19] As an engineer and manager, Taylor saw workers restricting output and engaging in wage-setting behaviors. His theories grew out of a desire to overcome these negative influences. He also showed an early sensitivity to the problems created by the use of overqualified workers.

The Schmidt dialogue for which Taylor has been so criticized was said to have been designed to illustrate that the person best suited to perform a task may be ill equipped to understand the science of the task, that the basic responsibility for designing the task is management's, and that the older approach of simply urging workers to do more is inhumane and ineffective.[20] Taylor himself said that critics were inaccurately interpreting his work:

> This is the most serious accusation which has been made against scientific management, namely, that it is a system for merely speeding up workmen, causing them to overwork and finally leaving them with no more pay than they originally had. . . . It is the worst falsehood that has been told against scientific management because it is directly the opposite of the truth.[21]

Taylor felt that the managers needed to change before the workers changed. He also emphasized the importance of top management's commitment to changes that are being undertaken and the value of discussing proposed changes with workers. He felt change should be implemented gradually[22] and should take into account "the motives which influence man."[23]

Rather than representing an antihumanistic perspective, radically at variance with the later human relations, human resources, and systems approaches, scientific management could alternatively be regarded as the first stage in a management evolution toward more refined soci-otechnical systems approaches. To regard scientific management as pro-management, human relations as pro–worker, and systems and human resources as pro–organization is too simplistic. As Daniel Wren stated, "The emerging view has been that of less certainty and more variability in prescriptions for managerial practice. The conclusion should not be that Argyris, McGregor and Herzberg were wrong (nor were Fayol, Taylor, Mayo, et al.) but that their ideas were bound by time and place."[24]

## Bureaucracy

Max Weber, a German sociologist, worked in the same period as did Taylor and Fayol. A professor, editor, and consultant to government, he established himself as a leading academic of his time. His major contribution was his conception of *bureaucracy* as the ideal organiza-tional form. His work on bureaucracy was conceived in the early 1900s but not translated into English until 1947.[25]

### Major Tenets of Theory

Major characteristics of a bureaucracy, according to Weber, are (1) rules and regulations, (2) division of labor and specialization, (3) a hierarchy of responsibility, (4) professional qualifications, and (5) impersonal relationships. [26] Today the term "bureaucracy" has come to signify any organization with a "high degree of formal structure."[27]

Rules in organizations may be written or unwritten. To reduce the number of written rules, employees (usually called *professionals*) internalize the rules. Engineers, scientists, accountants, analysts, and legal employees spend many years training to learn what to do in organizational situations, which makes them effective bureaucrats, valuable to the organization. Often these professionals will be highly specialized, allowing them to achieve greater efficiency and productiv-ity.[28]

The principle of *hierarchy* that characterizes bureaucracies means that each organization member reports to one superior, and each superior also has one person to whom he is responsible until finally one reaches the top of the pyramid.

Weber believed that the average worker does more to harm than to further the goals of the organization, since his emotions cause him to react in irrational and unpredictable ways. This emotionalism inter-feres with the efficient operation of the organization. The impersonality characteristic of bureaucracy minimizes the effect of individuals on the organization and helps to control the negative aspects of personal-ity. At the same time, administration's impersonality and clear sets of rules and procedures protect the individual from abuse of power by those operating over him.[29]

Weber proposed that continuity is possible only with bureaucratic rule. The charismatic leader often leaves a void that is not easily filled. He prepares no one for power, and he rules in a loose and unstable way. The traditional leader inherits his power, and the transition from one leader to the next is usually smooth; however, personality charac-teristics vary from leader to leader, making the quality of the adminis-tration unpredictable. With bureaucratic rule, regulations decide the quality of the leadership, and individuals are easily replaceable. By limiting the freedom of individuals, the bureaucratic organization as-sures continuity.[30]

Many points in Weber's bureaucratic model mirrored Taylor's ideas regarding job specialization, subdivision of tasks, standardization of procedures, and written rule systems presided over by technical ex-perts who replace personalized coercive authority. Both men sought an efficiency model and ways of dealing with the more irrational and unintelligent aspects of employee behavior in organizations.

### Criticisms

The word "bureaucracy" conjures up many negative connotations. We associate the word with all the distasteful characteristics of large unwieldy organizations—red tape, inefficiency, waste, impersonality degenerated to the status of dehumanization, and lack of commitment. We expect bureaucracies to ignore us, waste our time, produce little at great cost, and to be inhabited by dull, faceless organization men and women. The very impersonality that Weber believed to be the great strength of bureaucracy has come to denote the lack of humanity in twentieth-century organizations.

### Defence

Those defending bureaucracy would claim as strong points its ration-ality, clear delineation of individual responsibility, standardization, efficiency in dealing with large-scale administrative tasks, reduction of friction, discretion, and lack of ambiguity.

## First Theory of Administration

A contemporary of Taylor and Weber, Henri Fayol articulated his first ideas of administrative theory in 1900 when he read a paper before the International Mining and Metallurgical Congress. In 1908 he first put forward his fourteen general principles of administration in a paper prepared for the Society of Mineral Industry, and in 1916 he published his five elements of administration in *Administration Industrielle et Générale*. Not until a 1949 translation by Constance Storrs did this work appear in America.[31]

Within Fayol's lifetime, his contributions were overshadowed by Taylor's work, as scholars such as Henry Le Chatelier and Charles de Freminville translated and popularized Taylor in France. Nonetheless, Fayol founded and presided over the Center of Administrative Studies, a group formed to advance "Fayolisme"; and shortly before Fayol's death, this group merged with the "Taylorisme" group to form the Comité National de l'Organisation Française. The merger brought together the two main schools of management thought prevalent in France in the first quarter of the twentieth century. Although early interpreters of Fayol's work stressed differences between his theories and those of Taylor, Fayol himself insisted that the two complemented each other in their efforts to advance management theory. Like Taylor, Fayol was a manager-engineer and derived his theories from his own experiences.[32]

The fourteen principles of management for which Fayol is best remembered include:

- *division of work* or specialization.
- *authority* or the right to give orders.
- *discipline* (based on obedience and respect).
- *unity of command* or one superior only.
- *unity of direction* or one head and one plan for a group of activities with the same objective.
- *subordination of individual to general interest*.
- *remuneration* (as a reward for work performed).
- *centralization* (with the degree varying according to different cases).
- *scalar chain* of command (from ultimate authority to lowest ranks of the organization).
- *order* or a place for everything and everyone.
- *equity* or fairness and justice in employee relations.
- *stability of tenure of personnel* or low turnover and orderly personnel planning.
- *initiative* (by individual members).
- *esprit de corps* or harmony and unity of spirit.[33]

Fayol intended these principles as guides to theory and practice but not as rigid rules or laws. For example, he observed, "Seldom do we have to apply the same principle twice in identical conditions; allowance must be made for different and changing circumstances. . . . Therefore, principles are flexible and capable of adaptation to every need; it is a matter of knowing how to make use of them, which is a difficult art requiring intelligence, experience, decision and proportion."[34] He derived these principles from those used "most frequently" in his own experience.

Fayol outlined five managerial functions: planning, organizing, command, coordination, and control. Of these five elements, Fayol stressed the first two. He advocated long-range planning and forecasting, important contributions to modern management theory. In terms of organizing, Fayol proposed a relatively narrow span of management—less than six under most conditions—and unity of command. He saw the function of staff as assisting the general manager, searching for better work methods, gathering information, assisting with correspondence and other personal duties of the manager, and engaging in long-term research.[35]

Like Weber, Fayol emphasized hierarchy, professionalism, and specialization; but unlike Weber who prescribed the ideal organization model, Fayol advocated principles based on his own experience and that of other practicing managers. Taylor, Weber, and Fayol all sought to add order to what had previously been rule-of-thumb management practices. The varying backgrounds of these scholars led them to approach the problem from different perspectives, but the principles put forward by all three very much conformed to the spirit of classical organization theory.

## Communication Implications

In general, the classical school ignored the role of communication in the organization. These theorists stressed instead organizational structure and its implication for individual roles and behavior. Concepts such as span of control dealt with the need to restrict the number of subordinates assigned to any one supervisor to avoid overloading the supervisor in terms of communication. The classical school implied a vertical downward flow of communication through line officials and upward or horizontal communication from staff to line officials and personnel.

In an organization governed by classical principles, the major types of communication flowing downward would be job instructions, job rationale, rules and procedures, appraisal information and indoctrination. Essentially, task-related information is transferred. The stress in classical theories is on implications in organizational structure and roles for formal communication. Nonetheless, classicists such as Taylor recognized the existence of informal communication between workers which manifested itself in work restriction and wage-setting practices. In his conception of functional authority, Taylor also acknowledged the possible benefits of bypassing certain individuals in the scalar chain in order to communicate with organization members having greater expertise in particular areas.[36]

The classical theorist who most directly addressed the role of communication in the organization was Fayol, who put forward a case for horizontal communication.[37] Recognizing the time element in passing information up and down the organization, Fayol proposed a *bridge* or *gangplank* to allow lateral transmission of messages by peers occupying the same level in the hierarchy but different departments. (See fig. 1-1)

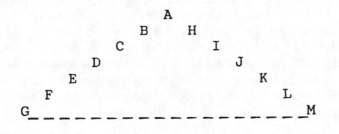

**Fig. 1.1**
**Fayol's Bridge or Gangplan**

Instead of G transmitting information to M by observing the formal communication chain—G to F to E to D to C to B to A and back down to H, I, J, K, L, and M—Fayol suggested that G should be allowed to communicate directly with M, with no intermediaries. Thus, Fayol explicitly sanctioned the bypassing of formal channels under certain conditions, particularly crisis conditions. Passing the information directly increases the speed of transmission and decreases the chances of distortion and omission.

In summary, it can be said that the classical school of organization theory *implies* more than states communication principles and leaves the development of these principles to later management theorists.

## Definition of Major Concepts
## Associated with Classical School

Numerous writers acknowledge that classical organization theory has as its foundation scalar and functional processes, division of labor, emphasis upon formal structure, and span of control.[38] Classical theory differentiates between *scalar* and *functional* processes, with scalar referring to the top-down chain of authority from board to president to vice-presidents to general managers, lower-level supervisors, foremen, and workers. Functional processes refer to specialized work performed at different layers of the authority pyramid. For example, sales and marketing, manufacturing, purchasing, finance, personnel, and public relations departments are designated on the basis of tasks or functions performed for the organization.

Within each of these functional units or departments, jobs can be further broken down on the basis of specialized tasks accomplished by members. For example, a public relations department may employ photographers, writers, graphic artists, and researchers. In a small firm with limited PR requirements, an individual may perform several functions and a small group of employees may report to one boss. In a larger firm, such as Revlon or Chase Manhattan Bank, which place a greater stress on PR, a PR department could potentially employ a number of people in each job category, with supervisors for each functional area. Thus, while scalar processes refer to the authority pyramid, functional processes refer to the nature of job functions.

Classical theorists also differentiate between *line* and *staff* organizational structures, with line management having direct responsibility for achieving the goals of the organization and staff having the job of advising and supporting line managers. Line managers are in the direct chain of command, linking one level with the next in the scalar-process model. Line authority refers to the relationship between superior and subordinate, with each subordinate knowing the person to report to, as well as who is lower in the line.

Staff refers to those who support and advise line managers. The primary function of a staff person is to assist and offer service to those operating in line positions. A department that serves and advises another department is referred to as a staff department. The line person has no obligation, however, to accept advice given by staff. An example of line departments would be manufacturing and sales. An example of staff departments would be PR and training. A legislative assistant to a U.S. Congressman, executive assistant to a corporation vice-president, or a speechwriter would be examples of staff functions. Unlike line departments, staff departments do not contribute directly to product output.

Another term frequently mentioned in classical theory is *span of control*, a term that denotes the number of workers managed by any one supervisor or executive. Military organizations probably first implemented this theory, and Lyndall Urwick was the first writer to apply the principle to organization theory.[39] Urwick stated that the optimal span of control was six.[40] Contemporary research indicates that the answer can be more variable, contingent on factors such as nature of the work supervised (whether routine or demanding), managerial skills, employee skills, and organization type. Organizations with short spans of control will have a "tall" structure with many layers of authority. Tall structures with few decision and power points are more centralized. Organizations with wide spans of control (more workers under each supervisor, but fewer levels) tend to have *flat* structures. Flat organizations are more decentralized. The organization has many decision points, and power is dispersed.

The term *division of work* refers to job specialization. The need for specialization can grow out of the size of a task or its complexity and the need to break the task into small units in order to understand and cope with its requirements. Breaking down a task into its component parts can also lead to greater efficiency.

In summary, it can be said that key words in the classical school were *formal organization, centralized, authority, science, rationality, structure,* and *order*. The classicists stressed delineation of organizational goals, division of labor, the scalar chain of command, and formal aspects of structure.

The major types of organizations studied by the classical theorists were industrial firms and public utilities. The dominant research methods included personal observation, participation, and sometimes surveys.[41] Many concepts discussed under the mantle of the classical school can still be seen today in military organizations and manufacturing establishments characterized by assembly-line operations. Weber's bureaucratic model is well exemplified by large government organizations.

In many office environments, consultants continue to carry out time-and-motion studies, tracking the time required for trips to the water fountain or to the filing cabinet, seeking to ensure that supplies and facilities are within the reach of employees. Company cafeterias reduce the time that workers must be away from the office and allow shortening of the lunch hour. Texts such as Braverman's *A Guide to Office Clerical Time Standards: A Compilation of Standard Data Used by Large American Companies,* published in 1974, detail the time required to open and close a drawer, giving evidence that classical theories are still alive and well in North America today.

## Notes

1. Judith A. Merkle, *Management and Ideology: The Legacy of the International Scientific Management Movement* (Berkeley, Calif.: University of California Press, 1980), p. 7.
2. Frank B. Copley, *Frederick W. Taylor: Father of Scientific Management,* vol. 2 (New York: Harper & Co., 1923), p. 404.
3. See discussion by David A. Whitsett and Lyle Yorks, *From Management Theory to Business Sense* (New York: AMACOM, 1983), p. 18.
4. Everett M. Rogers and Rekha Agarwala-Rogers, *Communication in Organizations* (New York: Free Press, 1976), p. 32.
5. Whitsett and Yorks, *op. cit.*, p. 223.
6. Merkle, *op. cit.*, p. 29.
7. *Ibid.*, p. 34.
8. *Ibid.*, p. 45.
9. *Ibid.*, p. 50.
10. *Ibid.*, p. 3.
11. *Ibid.*, pp. 2–3.
12. *Ibid.*, p. 13.
13. James G. March and Herbert A. Simon, *Organizations* (New York: John Wiley, 1958), p. 34; see also Rogers and Rogers, *op. cit.*, p. 32.
14. Oscar Grusky and George A. Miller, eds., *The Sociology of Organizations* (New York: Free Press, 1970), p. 2.
15. Merkle, *op. cit.*, p. 34.
16. Frederick W. Taylor, *Scientific Management* (New York: Harper & Row, 1911), pp. 30–48.
17. *Ibid.*, p. 140.
18. Whitsett and Yorks, *op. cit.*, p. 84; B.G.F. Cohen, ed., *Human Aspects in Office Automation* (New York: Elsevier Science, 1984), p. 132, notes that Drucker considers automation to be a logical extension of Taylor's scientific management theories.
19. Whitsett; *op. cit.*, pp. 68–69.
20. *Ibid.*, pp. 41–42.
21. *Ibid.*, p. 43.
22. *Ibid.*, p. 53.
23. Taylor, *op. cit.*, p. 119.
24. Daniel A. Wren, *The Evolution of Management Thought* (New York: John Wiley, 1979), p. 490.
25. *Ibid.*, p. 250.
26. Max Weber, *The Theory of Social and Economic Organization,* A. M.

Henderson, trans. and Talcott Parsons, ed. (New York: Free Press, 1947), pp. 329–33.

27. Rogers and Rogers, p. 83.
28. Richard H. Hall, "Professionalization and Bureaucratization," *American Sociological Review*, 33 (February 1968), pp. 92–104.
29. Hans H. Gerth and C. Wright Mills, eds. and trans., *From Max Weber: Essays in Sociology* (New York: Oxford University Press, 1946), pp. 196–204 and 214–16.
30. Weber, *op. cit.*, p. 328.
31. Wren, *op. cit.*, pp. 227–28.
32. *Ibid.*, p. 228.
33. Henri Fayol, *General and Industrial Management*, trans. Constance Storrs (London: Sir Isaac Pitman and Sons, 1949), pp. 19–42.
34. *Ibid.*, p. 19.
35. *Ibid.*, pp. 43–110. See Wren summary, pp. 240–48.
36. Taylor's concept of the functional foreman deviated from some of these classical principles. Taylor advocated that supervisors should have functional rather than scalar authority. In other words, one man could have different bosses for different aspects of his work, with managers giving orders to the persons best able to carry out the task rather than selecting the individuals on the basis of position in the scalar or authority chain. Managers would have authority in specific task areas. Taylor's functional authority concept is said to have been an early attempt at decentralization of authority. All authority would be based on knowledge, not position, and this would bring about a shift in the duties of the general manager.
37. Fayol, *op. cit.*, p. 34.
38. See, for example, Wren, *op. cit.*, p. 499; Joseph A. Littener, *Organizations: Structure and Behavior* (New York: John Wiley, 1963), p. 14; or Thomas R. Tortiello, Stephen J. Blatt, and Sue DeWine, *Communication in the Organization: An Applied Approach* (New York: McGraw-Hill, 1978), pp. 25–33.
39. Tortiello, Blatt, and DeWine, *op. cit.*, p. 31.
40. Lyndall F. Urwick, *Scientific Principles of Organization* (New York: American Management Association, 1938); an earlier paper in which Urwick stated this principle was "Executive Decentralization with Functional Coordination," *The Management Review* (December 1935) Vol. 13, pp. 356–59. His ideas regarding span of control were influenced by Sir Ian Hamilton, *The Soul and Body of an Army* (London: Arnold, 1921), p. 229.
41. Rogers and Rogers, *op. cit.*, p. 30.

# 2

# Human Relations School

The human relations period has been called a "social man era," but actually the emerging philosophy was born late in the scientific management era, only achieving recognition in the 1930s. Simultaneously, management thought was evolving in two directions: (1) research into industrial behavior, as represented by the Hawthorne studies and the emergence of a Mayoist philosophy, and (2) the development of a top-management view of organizations, as reflected in the writings of Chester Barnard.

## The Hawthorne Studies

Most organizational theorists agree that human relations concepts grew out of the Hawthorne studies, experiments conducted at the Western Electric Hawthorne plant in Cicero, Illinois. This plant was the equipment production and supply arm for the American Telephone and Telegraph Company. Although some speak of the human relations movement as a reaction to the mechanistic bent of the classical school, the studies that spawned human relations approaches were based on a scientific management approach. Moreover, the original incentives for these studies were economic.

### Origin of the Studies

The development of the tungsten lamp with more light per watt resulted in revenue losses for the electric companies, and in 1909 the hydro companies began campaigning for use of increased lighting levels in industry to compensate for the reduced levels of electricity consumption.[1] By 1918 the electric companies were sponsoring research to prove that better lighting would increase productivity, and in 1923 the General Electric Company funded a series of studies to be carried out by the Committee on Lighting in Industry (CLI) of the National Research Council.[2] The CLI selected Charles Snow to head the research at the Hawthorne plant of Western Elecric in Cicero, Illinois, a plant employing approximately 25,000 people.

The results of these first illumination studies conducted between 1924 and 1927, and reported by Snow in 1927,[3] were inconclusive, showing no direct relationship between lighting levels and productivity. The experiments did show an overall increase in production during the study period, but the increase occurred whether the test called for an increase or a decrease in illumination. Output also increased with both test and control groups; in other words, even if no changes in lighting levels were made, group productivity rose as if changes had been made.

By the end of 1925, Snow had concluded that factors other than illumination must be influencing production, and he suggested as possibilities social pressures, physiological and psychological factors, and the influence of the home environment.

The second series of tests in 1926 produced similar results and led Snow to decide that psychological factors were masking any effects of illumination on production. One of Snow's assistants, Homer Hibarger, followed up with a third illumination study based on the premise that even with almost no light, workers with a cooperative attitude could continue to produce. Hibarger reduced the levels gradually to 10, then to 3 footcandles, and finally to 0.06 of a foot candle. During the reduction, production continued to increase until the 0.102 level, at which time a slight decrease occurred. At the 0.06 level (approximately moonlight), a serious reduction in output was noted.

By the time these experiments were completed, the researchers had decided that illumination had little impact on productivity; however, Hibarger was convinced that supervisory style *did* affect productivity, and he wanted to study the work habits of a small group of employees in carefully controlled conditions to understand better the specific influences at work in the situation. George Pennock, Western Electric superintendent of inspection, agreed; and in the second major phase of experimentation that began in 1927, Pennock took control. These experiments came to be known as the Relay Assembly Test Room experiments. It was Pennock who was responsible for Mayo's later involvement in the Hawthorne studies.

These illumination studies preceded the active involvement of Harvard University professors Elton Mayo and Fritz Roethlisberger, the two men who later came to be known as the major figures associated with the Hawthorne studies. Mayo was not aware of the Hawthorne research until the second year of the Relay Assembly Test Room experiments. Thus, to this point in the research, the illumination experiments and the fatigue studies that followed very much reflected the physical bias of the scientific management school. Nonetheless, men such as Snow and Hibarger were beginning to see new implications in the data they had collected, and Pennock later wrote that the key factors influencing the increases in productivity were psychological—namely the interest being shown in the workers by the experimenters.[4] This idea, first articulated by Snow and Hibarger, was refined and developed by Mayo and his Harvard colleagues, called in to help interpret the results of the studies.

### Mayo and Colleagues Join the Hawthorne Research Team

During the winter of 1927–28, Mayo addressed a conference of personnel managers at the Harvard Club in New York City. George Pennock, who attended, told Mayo of the Hawthorne experiments and invited him to join the study as a consultant.[5] Subsequently T. K. Stevenson, a Western Electric Company executive, corresponded with Mayo and sent him copies of the first fatigue study results. As a result of this meeting and ensuing correspondence with Western Electric officials, Mayo paid his first visit to the Hawthorne plant in April 1928 and joined the research team.[6] Mayo later gave major credit in the Hawthorne researches to his collaboration with Pennock; to M. L. Putman, who later succeeded Pennock as leader of the experiments; to Fritz Roethlisberger, an industrial psychologist and Harvard University colleague involved in the studies; and to William J. Dickson, Chief of the Employee Relations Research Department of Western Electric, Hawthorne Works.[7] Roethlisberger and Dickson published in 1939 what came to be regarded as the most important book to detail these research efforts, *Management and the Worker*.[8] A less scholarly discussion summarizing the results of the studies appears in Roethlisberger's 1941 account *Management and Morale*.[9]Because of its more "folksy" and uninhibited style of presentation, this account allows insight into the sense of novelty and discovery that these early researchers were experiencing.

In reading Roethlisberger's description of the Relay Assembly Test Room experiments and Bank Wiring Room experiments, one becomes convinced that these men are disciples of their own theory—"true believers." The following excerpt is taken from Roethlisberger's 1941 description of research conducted between 1927 and 1932:[10]

#### Experiments in Illumination

The Western Electric researches started about sixteen years ago, in the Hawthorne plant, with a series of experiments on illumination. The purpose was to find out the relation of the quality and quantity of illumination to the efficiency of industrial workers. These studies lasted several years, and I shall not describe them in detail. It will suffice to point out that the results were quite different from what had been expected.

In one experiment the workers were divided into two groups. One group, called the "test group," was to work under different illumination intensities. The other group, called the "control group," was to work under an intensity of illumination as nearly constant as possible. During the first experiment, the test group was submitted to three different intensities of illumination of increasing magnitude, 24, 46, and 70 foot candles. What were the results of this early experiment? Production increased in both rooms—in both the test group and the control group—and the rise in output was roughly of the same magnitude in both cases.

In another experiment, the light under which the test group worked was decreased from 10 to 3 foot candles, while the control group worked, as before, under a constant level of illumination intensity. In this case the output rate in the test group went up instead of down. It also went up in the control group.

In still another experiment, the workers were allowed to believe that the illumination was being increased, although, in fact, no change in intensity was made. The workers commented favorably on the improved lighting condition, but there was no appreciable change in output. At another time, the workers were allowed to believe that the intensity of illumination was being decreased, although again, in fact, no actual change was made. The workers complained somewhat about the poorer lighting, but again there was no appreciable effect on output.

And finally, in another experiment, the intensity of illumination was decreased to .06 of a foot candle, which is the intensity of illumination approximately equivalent to that of ordinary moonlight. Not until this point was reached was there any appreciable decline in the output rate.

What did the experimenters learn? Obviously, as Stuart Chase said, there was something "screwy," but the experimenters were not quite sure who or what was screwy—they themselves, the subjects, or the results. One thing was clear: The results were negative. Nothing of a positive nature had been learned about the relation of illumination to industrial efficiency. If the results were to be taken at their face value, it would appear that there was no relation between illumination and industrial efficiency. However, the investigators were not yet quite willing to draw this conclusion. They realized the difficulty of testing for the effect of a single variable in a situation where there were many uncontrolled variables. It was thought therefore that another experiment should be devised in which other variables affecting the output of workers could be better controlled.

A few of the tough-minded experimenters already were beginning to suspect their basic ideas and assumptions with regard to human motivation. It occurred to them that the trouble was not so much with the results or with the subjects as it was with their notion regarding the way their subjects were supposed to behave—the notion of a simple cause-

and-effect, direct relation between certain physical changes in the workers' environment and the responses of the workers to these changes. Such a notion completely ignored the human meaning of these changes to the people who were subjected to them.

In the illumination experiments, therefore, we have a classic example of trying to deal with a human situation in nonhuman terms. The experimenters had obtained no human data; they had been handling electric-light bulbs and plotting average output curves. Hence their results had no human significance. That is why they seemed screwy. Let me suggest here, however, that the results were not screwy, but the experimenters were—a "screwy" person being by definition one who is not acting in accordance with the customary human values of the situation in which he finds himself.

### The Relay Assembly Test Room

Another experiment was framed, in which it was planned to submit a segregated group of workers to different kinds of working conditions. The idea was very simple: A group of five girls were placed in a separate room where their conditions of work could be carefully controlled, where their output could be measured, and where they could be closely observed. It was decided to introduce at specified intervals different changes in working conditions and to see what effect these innovations had on output. Also, records were kept, such as the temperature and humidity of the room, the number of hours each girl slept at night, the kind and amount of food she ate for breakfast, lunch, and dinner. Output was carefully measured, the time it took each girl to assemble a telephone relay of approximately forty parts (roughly a minute) being automatically recorded each time; quality records were kept; each girl had a physical examination at regular intervals. Under these conditions of close observation the girls were studied for a period of five years. Literally tons of material were collected. Probably nowhere in the world has so much material been collected about a small group of workers for such a long period of time.

But what about the results? They can be stated very briefly. When all is said and done, they amount roughly to this: A skillful statistician spent several years trying to relate variations in output with variations in the physical circumstances of these five operators. For example, he correlated the hours that each girl spent in bed the night before with variations in output the following day. Inasmuch as some people said that the effect of being out late one night was not felt the following day but the day after that, he correlated variations in output with the amount of rest the operators had had two nights before. I mention this just to point out the fact that he missed no obvious tricks and that he did a careful job and a thorough one, and it took him many years to do it. The attempt to relate changes in physical circumstances to variations in output resulted in not a single correlation of enough statistical significance to be recognized by any competent statistician as having any meaning.

Now, of course, it would be misleading to say that this negative result was the only conclusion reached. There were positive conclusions, and it did not take the experimenters more than two years to find out that they had missed the boat. After two years of work, certain things happened which made them sit up and take notice. Different experimental conditions of work, in the nature of changes in the number and duration of rest pauses and differences in the length of the working day and week, had been introduced in this Relay Assembly Test Room. For example, the investigators first introduced two five-minute rests, one in the morning and one in the afternoon. Then they increased the length of these rests, and after that they introduced the rests at different times of the day. During one experimental period they served the operators a specially prepared lunch during the rest. In the later periods, they decreased the length of the working day by one-half hour and then by one hour. They gave the operators Saturday morning off for a while. Altogether, thirteen such periods of different working conditions were introduced in the first two years.

During the first year and a half of the experiment, everybody was happy, both the investigators and the operators. The investigators were happy because as conditions of work improved the output rate rose steadily. Here, it appeared, was strong evidence in favor of their preconceived hypothesis that fatigue was the major factor limiting output. The operators were happy because their conditions of work were being improved, they were earning more money, and they were objects of considerable attention from top management. But then one investigator—one of those tough-minded fellows—suggested that they restore the original conditions of work, that is, go back to a full forty-eight-hour week without rests, lunches, and what not. This was Period XII. Then the happy state of affairs, when everything was going along as it theoretically should, went sour. Output, instead of taking the expected nose dive, maintained its high level.

Again the investigators were forcibly reminded that human situations are likely to be complex. In any human situation, whenever a simple change is introduced—a rest pause, for example—other changes, unwanted and unanticipated, may also be brought about. What I am saying here is very simple. If one experiments on a stone, the stone does not know it is being experimented upon—all of which makes it simple for people experimenting on stones. But if a human being is being experimented upon, he is likely to know it. Therefore, his attitudes toward the experiment and toward the experimenters become very important factors in determining his responses to the situation.

Now that is what happened in the Relay Assembly Test Room. To the investigators, it was essential that the workers give their full and whole-hearted coöperation to the experiment. They did not want the operators to work harder or easier depending upon their attitude toward the conditions that were imposed. They wanted them to work as they felt, so that they could be sure that the different physical conditions of work were solely responsible for the variations in output. For each of the experimental changes, they wanted subjects whose responses would be uninfluenced by so-called "psychological factors."

In order to bring this about, the investigators did everything in their power to secure the complete coöperation of their subjects, with the result that almost all the practices common to the shop were altered. The operators were consulted about the changes to be made, and, indeed, several plans were abandoned because they met with the disapproval of the girls. They were questioned sympathetically about their reactions to the conditions imposed, and many of these conferences took place in the office of the superintendent. The girls were allowed to talk at work; their "bogey" was eliminated. Their physical health and well-being became matters of great concern. Their opinions, hopes, and fears were eagerly sought. What happened was that in the very process of setting the conditions for the test—a so-called "controlled" experiment—the experimenters had completely altered the social situation of the room. Inadvertently, a change had been introduced which was far more important than the planned experimental innovations: The customary supervision in the room had been revolutionized. This accounted for the better attitudes of the girls and their improved rate of work.

### The Development of a New and More Fruitful Point of View

After Period XII in the Relay Assembly Test Room, the investigators decided to change their ideas radically. What all their experiments had dramatically and conclusively demonstrated was the importance of employee attitudes and sentiments. It was clear that the responses of workers to what was happening about them were dependent upon the significance these events had for them. In most work situations the meaning of a change is likely to be as important, if not more so, than the change itself. This was the great *éclaircissement*, the new illumination, that came from the research. It was an illumination quite different from what they had expected from the illumination studies. Curiously enough, this discovery is nothing very new or startling. It is something which anyone who has had some concrete experience in handling other people intuitively recognizes and practices. Whether or not a person is going to give his services whole-heartedly to a group depends, in good part, on the way he feels about his job, his fellow workers, and supervisors—the meaning for him of what is happening about him.

However, when the experimenters began to tackle the problem of employee attitudes and the factors determining such attitudes—when they began to tackle the problem of "meaning"—they entered a sort of twilight zone where things are never quite what they seem. Moreover, overnight, as it were, they were robbed of all the tools they had so carefully forged; for all their previous tools were nonhuman tools concerned with the measurement of output, temperature, humidity, etc., and these were no longer useful for the human data that they now wanted to obtain. What the experimenters now wanted to know was how a person felt, what his intimate thinking, reflections, and preoccupations were, and what he liked and disliked about his work environment. In short, what did the whole blooming business—his job, his supervision, his working conditions—mean to him? Now this was human stuff, and there were no tools, or at least the experimenters knew of none, for obtaining and evaluating this kind of material.

Fortunately, there were a few courageous souls among the experimenters. These men were not metaphysicians, psychologists, academicians, professors, intellectuals, or what have you. They were men of common sense and of practical affairs. They were not driven by any great heroic desire to change the world. They were true experimenters, that is, men compelled to follow the implications of their own monkey business. All the evidence of their studies was pointing in one direction. Would they take the jump? They did.

Some researchers have felt that Mayo, Roethlisberger, and Dickson got more than their share of the credit for the Hawthorne studies and that some of the early work done by Snow and Hibarger got insufficient notice.[11] In the preface to *Management and the Worker*, Mayo himself said that to name everyone who participated in the Hawthorne studies would read like "a telephone book."[12] Mayo, Roethlisberger, and Dickson were intimately involved in the experiments from 1928 to 1932, and it was during this period of time that the emphasis shifted to a new human relations bias, a phenomenon attributed primarily to Mayo, the most important interpreter of the Hawthorne researches. Moreover, the major works detailing the Hawthorne studies were written by Roethlisberger, Dickson, and Mayo.

### Contribution of Chester Barnard

Working in the same period as Mayo and the Hawthorne researchers, Chester Barnard published his influential book *The Functions of the Executive* in 1938.[13] A self-made scholar who contributed the first in-depth analysis of organizations as cooperative systems, Barnard has been called "a sociologist without portfolio."[14]

*The Functions of an Executive* draws on Barnard's personal experiences as president of the New Jersey Bell Telephone Company, as well as on the theories of men such as Kurt Lewin, Max Weber, and Alfred North Whitehead.[15]

Some of the concerns that were common both to the Hawthorne researchers and to Barnard were the importance of cooperation, the relationship between noneconomic motivation and productivity, and the relevance of the informal organization to the functioning of the formal organization.

Barnard said that the three functions served by the informal organization are (1) communication, (2) maintenance of cohesiveness in the formal organization, and (3) maintenance of feelings of personal integrity and self-respect. These functions, he said, help to make the organization more efficient and effective; in this regard, they are indispensable. These informal groupings arise out of personal contacts that are not governed by the formal organization.

Barnard stressed the importance of communication, both in the informal and the formal organization, as well as in terms of executive function. Barnard saw executives as "interconnecting centers in a communications system."[16] His acceptance theory of authority gave a "bottom-up" interpretation of authority. He said that authority didn't reside in those who gave orders, but in the acceptance or nonacceptance of authority by subordinates. To disobey was to reject authority.[17]

In a theme that would later be picked up by Chris Argyris, Barnard spoke of the disparity between individual and organizational motives. However, according to Barnard, the executive function modifies individual motives and acts to secure the cooperation required by the formal organization. Thus, all formal systems are characterized by (1) a willingness on the part of organizational members to cooperate, (2) common purpose, and (3) communication.

A major contribution to the human relations school was Barnard's delineation of principles of communication. Among the most important points he made were the following: (1) All organizational members should be acquainted with the channels of communication. (2) Formal channels of communication must connect all organization members, with every person reporting to or being subordinate to someone else. (3) Lines of communication must be as direct and as short as possible in order to increase the speed of communicating and to decrease distortions. No bypassing of formal channels should take place.

### Communication Implications in Human Relations Approaches

As a direct result of the Hawthorne studies and the influence of Mayo, communication assumed a new importance in managerial theory. Rather than seeing the worker as an economic man, human relationists saw the worker as a social being. The school had a strong psychoanalytic bias. Like the classical school, the human relations theorists believed that humans have an emotional nonrational side; but unlike the classicists, they believed that these attributes should be recognized and addressed, not ignored. They interpreted their studies to mean that manipulation of economic incentives or physical environment was not sufficient to harness the energies and commitment of workers. Rather than offering employees cash incentives, management should seek to identify and satisfy the deeper needs of workers. The assumption was that a satisfied worker would produce more and better.

This viewpoint led Mayo, Roethlisberger, Dickson, and their colleagues to concentrate on supervisory leadership style as a means of achieving satisfied employees.[18] The early illumination studies demonstrated that the attention paid to workers can be as important as environmental changes. Discussing the "Hawthorne effect," which many social scientists regard as the major finding of the studies, Roethlisberger observed: "In most work situations, the meaning of a change is likely to be as important as, if not more so, than the change itself. This was the great *éclaircissement*, the new illumination, that came from the research."[19] The Hawthorne effect has been defined as the "tendency for individuals to behave in an artificial way when they know they are subjects in an experiment."[20]

The Hawthorne studies influenced a switch in interviewing techniques from highly structured to nondirective questions. The basic premise of the extensive interviewing program developed by the Hawthorne researchers was that the new supervisory role should be one of openness, concern, and willingness to listen to employees.[21] They felt that employees would work harder if management paid attention to them, listened to their problems, answered their questions, and relied less on "rationalistic control systems."[22]

This philosophy had numerous communication implications. Listening came to be regarded as the core of all human relations-oriented training programs. Employee newspapers, house organs, and corporate magazines increased in popularity. In later years, senior-level executives turned to videotapes to deliver their annual messages and to encourage their employees to produce. Terms such as *job satisfaction, job enrichment,* and *worker morale* gained prominence.[23]

Group meetings were espoused as a means of opening the lines of communication between management and workers, allowing employees to raise questions and to vent their frustrations. Hotlines were installed in some organizations to cope with the proliferation of the grapevine and its negative effects on worker morale.

Working in the same period as Mayo and Roethlisberger, Carl Rogers was surprised to learn of the similarities between his own approach and that of the Hawthorne researchers. On more than one occasion, Rogers visited the Hawthorne plant.[24] The article "Active Listening," included in the interpersonal portion of this text, well illustrates the compatibility of Mayo's and Rogers' ideas.

The *Scanlon plan* was one of the earliest attempts to elicit worker participation and involvement. The Scanlon plan involves building a worker-union-management partnership to create greater employee commitment and identification with the firm. The plan, which consists of a suggestion system, joint discussion and screening committees comprised of management and workers, and a plant-wide bonus formula based on productivity increases, has been termed the "boldest attempt" at employee participation in the history of the United States.[25]

Joseph Scanlon instituted the first Scanlon plan at the financially threatened steel company where he worked as a laborer on an open-hearth blast furnace. In 1938 the LaPointe Steel Company was at the brink of bankruptcy. Union leader Scanlon, in consultation with management, worked out a productivity plan to reduce costs and to share with workers benefits of the savings.[26] Unlike traditional suggestion systems that rewarded the individual, the plan was group-oriented, with cooperation being stressed over competition.

The production committees, located throughout the plant or firm, were typically composed of one manager and a small number of elected workers. These committees screened the suggestions and decided which ones to implement. Except for high cost suggestions, the production committees had authority to implement immediately any suggestions assessed as viable ones. Suggestions requiring large expenditures were passed on to the company's screening committee, composed equally of top management and elected representatives from the workforce. This committee also computed monthly bonuses for all employees on the basis of decreased costs and increased productivity.[27]

The Scanlon plan is still popular today in many companies. A recent study examined the effectiveness of a 1983 effort to institute this plan in a large manufacturing establishment, more than forty years after Scanlon first proposed his plan.[28] Articles on the Scanlon plan continue to appear in the management literature,[29] and the basic idea advocating participatory decision making has more currency today than ever before.

Social scientists originally presumed that the Scanlon plan would work only in failing companies, but its introduction into healthy businesses has often yielded equally good results.[30] Empirical research shows that employees feel that the plan improves trust and confidence in a company, increases employee knowledge, and encourages organizational members to strive for excellence in their work. Researchers have found, however, that levels of employee participation vary in different organizations and that an employee's prior commitment and identification with the organization influences the extent of his participation. Management attitudes toward employee participation have also been shown to influence the success of the plan.[31]

The Scanlon plan very much exemplifies the most fundamental tenets of human relations philosophy. The emphasis on listening to workers, the bottom-up participatory decision making processes, the emphasis on upward communication flow, and the encouragement of cooperation between management and workers labels this program as one designed in the true spirit of human relations.

Yet another outgrowth of the Hawthorne studies, *opinion and climate surveys* were designed to identify and solve organizational problems.[32]

Some have felt that the most important contribution of the Hawthorne studies was to "rediscover" the primary group (defined by Rogers and Rogers as "a relatively small-sized group of individuals in intimate relationships, such as a family or friendship network").[33] Rather than placing importance on the formal structural relationships within the organization, human relations gave new recognition to informal group relations and peer pressure, or *horizontal communications*. To many, the term *human relations* came to connote communication.[34]

### Criticisms of the School

By the late 1950s the human relations school, like its predecessor scientific management, was under strong attack. Critics responded to Mayo in much the same fashion as they had to Taylor, calling human relations approaches insincere, syrupy, and superficial, and dubbing its advocates "the happiness boys."[35] These critics said that human relations approaches were promanagement and masked the true economic motivations of their proponents. Some claimed that calls for worker participation were ritualistic and symbolic, leading people to play games. An excerpt from a United Automobile Workers 1949 publication, *Ammunition*, is typical of these criticisms:

> The prophet is Elton Mayo, a Harvard University professor who has been prying into the psychiatric bowels of factory workers since around about 1925 and who is the Old Man of the movement. The Bible is his book, the *Human Problems of an Industrial Civilization*. The Holy Place is the Hawthorne Plant of the Western Electric Company (the wholly owned subsidiary of one of the nation's largest monopolies, the AT and T). At Hawthorne, Ma Bell, when she wasn't organizing company unions, allowed Professor Mayo to carry on experiments with a group of women workers for some nine years . . .

For these nine years about every kind of experiment a very bright Harvard professor could think of was tried on the women. Everything you do to white mice was done to them, except their spines and skulls were not split so the fluid could be analyzed . . .

What did make them produce and produce and produce with ever-increasing speed was the expression of interest in their personal problems by the supervisor; interviews by psychiatrically trained social workers and (later on) the way they were paired off with friendly or unfriendly co-workers.

Now obviously this is the greatest discovery since J. P. Morgan learned that you can increase profits by organizing a monopoly, suppressing competition, raising prices and reducing production.[36]

The U.A.W. cynics labeled the Hawthorne researchers as "cow sociologists" because contented cows give more milk.[37]

The most often-mentioned criticism was that human relations approaches were manipulative. As one critic asserted, managers seemed to have received the message that seduction is "preferable to rape in gaining the victim's cooperation."[38] Unions claimed that diversionary tactics such as gripe sessions, token rewards, and suggestion boxes shifted attention from real issues such as the need for better pay, enhanced benefits, and safe working conditions. Some declared that such techniques were attempts to coopt workers to support the status quo. These critics charged that the founders of the human relations school did not sufficiently appreciate the complexity of humans and their relationship to the work environment.

Probably because of its union connection, the Scanlon plan did not evoke the same negative reactions as did other human relations efforts. Nonetheless, the human relations movement as a whole was suffering the same recession as was the United States economy in 1957. Studies were clearly indicating that there is not necessarily a relationship between "happy" or satisfied workers and productivity. It became evident that a new approach integrating the goals of the organization with the goals and needs of its members was required.

The response to this expressed need was overwhelming. The 1960s saw a proliferation of management theories that led more than one organizational scholar to term the situation a "jungle."[39] One of the persons destined to lead these theorists into a new era was Keith Davis, sometimes called "Mr. Human Relations."[40] Davis' work marked the beginning of a modern, more sophisticated view of human relations that took into account both economic and psychological perspectives and stressed empirical investigation.[41] With Douglas McGregor, whose work is discussed in the subsequent chapters, Davis built a bridge between the early conceptions of human relations and the later human resource theories.

## In Defence of Human Relations

In defence of human relations, it can be said that this philosophical school explicitly recognized the importance of more than just economic incentives in the workplace. In so doing, these theorists laid the foundation for human resource and systems approaches. Some have classified the development of the social system viewpoint as a major contribution of the Hawthorne research.[42] The following excerpt from Roethlisberger and Dickson gives evidence to support this claim.

> The parts of the industrial plant as a social system are interrelated and interdependent. Any changes in one part of the social system are accompanied by changes in other parts of the system. The parts of the system can be conceived of as being in a state of equilibrium, such that if a small (not too great) modification different from that which will otherwise occur is impressed on the system, a reaction will at once appear tending toward the conditions that would have existed if the modification had not been impressed. . . . Some parts of the system can change more rapidly than others.[43]

Barnard likewise defined organizations as cooperative systems. In *The Functions of the Executive*, he defined his use of the term "cooperative systems":

> A cooperative system is a complex of physical, biological, personal, and social components which are in a specific systematic relationship by reason of the cooperation of two or more persons for at least one definite end. Such a system is evidently a subordinate unit of larger systems from one point of view.[44]

Barnard spoke of the need to maintain equilibrium in the organization, to examine external forces to which adjustments must be made, and to stay attuned to the internal environment or climate comprised of physical, biological, and social elements and forces within the organization.

## Organizational Development

Organizational development, or O.D., is an outgrowth of the human relations movement. Numerous writers see this movement as the consequence of insights gained in the benchmark studies carried out at the General Electric Hawthorne works.

Historically, the trend toward organizational humanism has passed through three broad phases. Originally, organizations sought to recognize the individual needs of workers and to attempt to meet these needs as a means of improving productivity. Implicit in this approach was the assumption that productivity was largely a matter of inducing workers to become more committed to improving production. Another implicit assumption was that management was already committed to organizational goals and knew how they could best be achieved.

In the 1950s, the emphasis moved towards a management development approach that assumed organizations could best be improved by improving managers. This approach still took for granted that organizations functioned as a consequence of management acting and subordinates being acted upon.

The third phase in the movement toward humanistic organizations, beginning in the 1960s, has come to be known as the human resources school; and this approach stresses improving the performance of all members of the organization. O.D. is one means by which the organization seeks to achieve this end. O.D. assumes that for an organization to function efficiently, all members must identify with the company goals and be committed to working as a team towards achieving these goals.

O.D. does not replace early managerial approaches but rather consolidates them into a general operational philosophy. Writers such as Likert, McGregor, Bennis, Maslow, and Argyris laid out most of the theoretical base upon which O.D. was built. All of these writers proposed a humanistic philosophy in organizations which could only be achieved through changes in attitudes and values within organizations. What O.D. sets out to do is to "develop strategies for bringing about planned change in organizations' value and attitude systems," or in the organizational culture.[45]

An important element in cultural groupings, either in organizations or in society in general, is the reference group with which the individual associates him- or herself. The O.D. approach attempts to optimize the individual's sense of belonging through team-building strategies. This team building is accomplished in three stages: Development of the individual, development of the group, and development of the whole organization.[46]

The practitioners of O.D. have adopted techniques used by social scientists, notably behavior-modification psychologists. Behavior modification is seen to be effected in three stages. The first stage involves the individual recognizing and confronting his or her present attitudes and behavior and becoming aware of the possibility of change.[47] Stage two involves attempting change, and stage three establishes the new attitudes and behavior as part of the individual's everyday repertoire. This cycle is termed *unfreezing, changing,* and *refreezing.*

Early work in O.D. drew on the consciousness-raising techniques of the late 1960s, such as encounter group or T-group activity. O.D. practitioners generally justify group and individual consciousness-raising methods on the grounds that most problems arise because of a reluctance to confront problems and a tendency to smooth over difficulties in attempts to save face.

Critics of the early O.D. work claimed the approach was largely individual-centered, taking place in contrived situations and involving artificial groups brought together only for the sessions. The members later returned to their normal work environment that had not changed; and if anything, they were less likely than before to fit in.[48] More recent work in O.D. has attempted to solve some of these problems by dealing with existing work groups in real-life situations.

In some ways, the awareness sessions that were an important part of O.D. work, particularly in the beginning of the movement, resembled the group therapy sessions run by psychologists. Advocates of O.D. would consider the parallel with group therapy to be positive, while skeptics would be most critical of this aspect of O.D. work. They regard the consciousness-raising sessions as dangerous psychological tinkering by amateurs.[49]

Other critics of the O.D. approach say that the uncompromising levels of honesty required in T-group interaction may be dysfunctional in the larger organizational setting. Rather than being able to adapt more readily to the organization and to become more productive in personal and organizational terms, the individual may become yet more alienated unless the organization also changes.[50]

Typical of those holding this last view is George Strauss, who said that it is easier for organizations to change to accommodate ordinary people than to change people to fit some hypothetically perfect organization. Strauss also warned that the O.D. approach could be abused when used as a means of eliciting behavior that conforms to existing organizational constraints.[51] This last point is also made by Warner Woodworth, Gordon Meyer, and Norman Smallwood in an article that takes a critical look at O.D. theory.[52] They suggest that it may not be appropriate to assume that organizational goals or interests correspond with the personal aspirations or interests of workers. They also suggest that more attention should be given to questioning the validity of organizational goals within the context of society at large than to devising strategies for achieving these goals. They view the O.D. consultants as, in large measure, part of the management culture and consequently prone to perpetuate the top-down approach to democracy.

The shift from a top-down to a bottom-up approach characterizes not only organizational theory, but social theory in general. However, history confirms that the process is a slow one. This is a point made by several organizational theorists, most notably by Robert Blake and Jane Mouton, whose managerial grid has been used as an O.D. model more frequently than has any other approach. Blake and Mouton maintain that it takes at least four years to initiate noticeable change in an organizational culture.

In summary, it can be said that the O.D. movement, which grew out of human relations theory, has developed in a fashion parallel to that of management theory in general, evolving from an individual-centered approach that stressed activities such as sensitivity groups to organization-centered approaches such as team-building. The progress of human relations theory is discussed in a subsequent chapter on human resource theory.

Some critics claim that O.D. has become a generic term that today is used to mean almost everything. Consequently, the term, they say, has little meaning anymore.

## Notes

1. Charles D. Wrege, "Solving Mayo's Mystery: The First Complete Account of the Origin of the Hawthorne Studies—The Forgotten Contributions of C. E. Snow and H. Hibarger," *Academy of Management Proceedings* (1976), pp. 12–16.
2. Elton Mayo, *The Human Problems of an Industrial Civilization* (Boston: Harvard University, 1933), p. 55.
3. C. E. Snow, "Research on Industrial Illumination," *Technical Engineering News* (1927), pp. 257–82.
4. See George Pennock, "Industrial Research at Hawthorne," *The Personnel Journal* (February 1930), vol. 8, pp. 296–313.
5. Daniel A. Wren, *The Evolution of Management Thought*, Second Ed. (New York: John Wiley, 1979), p. 299.
6. David A. Whitsett and Lyle Yorks, *From Management Theory to Business Sense* (New York: AMACOM, 1983), p. 157.
7. Elton Mayo, preface, in Fritz J. Roethlisberger and William Dickson, *Management and the Worker* (Cambridge: Harvard University Press, 1939).
8. Roethlisberger and Dickson, *op. cit.*

9. Fritz J. Roethlisberger, *Management and Morale* (Cambridge: Harvard University Press, 1941).
10. *Ibid.*, pp. 9–26.
11. Wrege, *op. cit.*, pp. 12–16.
12. In Roethlisberger and Dickson, *Management and the Worker, op. cit.*, preface.
13. Chester Barnard, *The Functions of the Executive* (Cambridge: Harvard University Press, 1938).
14. Wren, *op. cit.*, p. 335.
15. *Ibid.*
16. *Ibid.*, p. 342.
17. *Ibid.*, p. 341.
18. Whitsett and Yorks, *op. cit.*, pp. 168–69.
19. Roethlisberger, *Management and Morale, op. cit.*, p. 169.
20. Everett M. Rogers and Rekha Agarwala-Rogers, *Communication in Organizations* (New York: Free Press, 1976), p. 37.
21. Wren, *op. cit.*, p. 305.
22. Whitsett and Yorks, *op. cit.*, pp. 168–69.
23. *Ibid.*, pp. 170–80.
24. *Ibid.*, p. 158.
25. Michael Schuster, "The Scanlon Plan: A Longitudinal Analysis," *The Journal of Applied Behavioral Science* (February 1984), vol. 20, p. 23.
26. R. Davenport, "Enterprise for Every Man," *Fortune* (1950), vol. 41, pp. 51–58; cited in Schuster, *op. cit.*, p. 24; see also Wren, *op. cit.*, pp. 356–57.
27. Rogers and Rogers, *op. cit.*, pp. 40–42.
28. Schuster, *op. cit.*, pp. 23–38.
29. See, for example, J. W. Driscoll, "Working Creatively with a Union: Lessons from the Scanlon Plan," *Organizational Dynamics* (Summer 1979) vol. 8, pp. 61–80; M. Schuster, "Forty Years of Scanlon Plan Research: A Review of the Descriptive and Empirical Literature," *International Yearbook of Organizational Democracy* (1983), pp. 53–71; and J. Kenneth White, "The Scanlon Plan: Causes and Correlates of Success," *Academy of Management Journal* (June 1979) vol. 22, pp. 292–312.
30. Schuster, *op. cit.*, p. 24.
31. *Ibid.*
32. Whitsett and Yorks, *op. cit.*, p. 182.
33. Rogers and Rogers, *op. cit.*, p. 38.
34. Whitsett and Yorks, *op. cit.*, p. 180.
35. Wren, *op. cit.*, p. 475.
36. From "Deep Therapy on the Assembly Line," quoted by Loren Baritz, *The Servants of Power* (New York: John Wiley, 1960), pp. 114–15; cited by Wren, p. 321.
37. Wren, *op. cit.*, p. 321.
38. Whitsett and Yorks, *op. cit.*, p. 171.
39. See, for example, Harold Koontz, "The Management Theory Jungle," *Academy of Management Journal* (December 1961), pp. 174–188; and Lyndall F. Urwick, "Have We Lost Our Way in the Jungle of Management Theory," *Personnel* (May–June 1965) vol. 42, pp. 15–16.
40. Wren, *op. cit.*, p. 479.

41. *Ibid.*, p. 480.
42. *Ibid.*, p. 312.
43. Roethlisberger and Dickson, *op. cit.*, p. 567.
44. Barnard, in *A Sociological Reader on Complex Organizations*, Amitai Etzioni, ed. (New York: Holt, Rinehart and Winston, 1969), pp. 15–16.
45. See Anthony P. Raia, "Organizational Development—Some Issues and Challenges," *California Management Review* (Summer 1972) vol. 14, p. 13; also Stephen R. Michael, "Organizational Change Techniques: Their Present, Their Future," *Organizational Dynamics* (Summer 1982) vol. 11, pp. 67–80.
46. S. Jay Liebowitz and Kenneth P. DeMeuse, "The Application of Team Building," *Human Relations* (January 1982) vol. 35, pp. 1–18.
47. George Strauss, "Organization Development: Credits and Debits," *Organizational Dynamics* (Winter 1973) vol. 1, p. 6.
48. W. Warner Burke and Warren H. Schmidt, "Management and Organizational Development," *Personnel Administration* (March–April 1971), p. 54.
49. Stanley M. Herman, "What is This Thing Called Organization Development?" *Personnel Journal* (August 1971), p. 596; also Raia, p. 14.
50. Herman, *op. cit.*, p. 596.
51. Strauss, *op. cit.*, p. 12.
52. Warner Woodworth, Gordon Meyer, and Norman Smallwood, "Organization Development: A Closer Scrutiny," *Human Relations* (April 1982) vol. 35, p. 311.

# 3

# The Systems School

## General Systems Theory

The term "general system theory" was coined by biologist Ludwig von Bertalanffy in 1937 when he first presented his theory to a University of Chicago philosophy seminar. It was only after the war that he published this theory.[1]

Von Bertalanffy sought to develop a theory that would take into account interrelationships in the world around him. He wanted a model that could cross disciplines and see the world in a holistic rather than atomistic way. Whereas the mechanistic approach of scientific management had broken human phenomena into their smallest component parts, von Bertalanffy saw the whole to be greater than the sum of its parts. He believed that the complex interaction of parts makes it necessary to study total units as systems. In fact, von Bertalanffy defined general systems theory as "the science of wholeness."

In the 1920s only von Bertalanffy, fellow biologist Paul A. Weiss, and philosopher Alfred North Whitehead were interested in developing a general theory of complex phenomena.[2] Whitehead's work on "organic mechanism" appeared in 1925, and von Bertalanffy's statements on organismic biology date to 1925–26. After the war, however, what von Bertalanffy terms "a secret trend" developed in various disciplines, with a simultaneous appearance of similar ideas independently on different continents.[3]

In the 1940s and 1950s a small group of scientists at the University of Chicago and later at the Mental Health Institute at the University of Michigan began working together to evolve a general theory of behavior. Members of a working group dedicated to developing an interdisciplinary-based theory included physiologist and psychiatrist James G. Miller, economist Kenneth Boulding, mathematician Anatol Rapoport, sociologist Talcott Parsons, and other natural scientists such as Enrico Fermi.[4] Boulding and the others saw general systems theory as a means to develop a common vocabulary that would enable specialists to communicate across disciplines.[5]

In 1954 the advocates of a "general systems theory" formed a society to investigate the potential of the theory, and a few years later von Bertalanffy and Rapoport became the first joint editors of a yearbook devoted to the topic. Today the Society for General Systems Research has chapters and divisions in many parts of the world, attesting to the widespread popularity of this academic approach.[6]

Meanwhile other related developments were occurring. J. Von Neumann and O. Morgenstern's game theory appeared in 1947;[7] Norbert Wiener's *Cybernetics or Control and Communication in the Animal and the Machine* appeared in 1948;[8] and C. E. Shannon and W. Weaver's information theory was published in 1949.[9]

### Cybernetics

Wiener's *Cybernetics* resulted from then-current developments in computer technology, automation, and information theory.[10] By the early 1940s, physicists, electrical engineers, and mathematicians were working on servo-mechanisms; and the interdisciplinary study of self-regulation in the animal and the machine began at a Josiah Macy Foundation Conference on Cerebral Inhibition, May 1942, in New York City. It was at this conference that Norbert Wiener, Arturo Rosenblueth, and Julien Bigelow presented their paper titled "Behavior, Purpose and Teleology," later published in the 1943 *Philosophy of Science.*[11]

The term "cybernetics" derives from the Greek word *kybernētēs,* which means "steersman." Plato uses the term in his discussion of the art of government. The Latin word *gubernator* came from the Greek, and in turn, the English word *governor* from the Latin. The latter now has dual meanings "ruler" or "a self-adjusting mechanism on a steam engine, intended to keep the engine at a constant speed under varying conditions of load."[12] Involved in this steering or control behavior is a *feedback loop* linking the *output* of the system to its *input.* When the output varies from a preset norm, compensatory behavior will restore the system output to the norm. It was hypothesized that organisms subjected to disruptive internal or external changes will behave similarly, acting to restore internal equilibrium.[13]

Even before Wiener, at the turn of the century, some scientists hypothesized that organisms subjected to disruptive internal or external changes will behave similarly, acting to restore internal equilibrium. Physicist Claude Bernard wrote of such a process of homeostasis-seeking behavior; and Cannon's *Wisdom of the Body* is said to be "a classical exposition of these phenomena in the autonomic processes of men."[14]

According to von Bertalanffy, Wiener carried the cybernetic, feed-back, and information concepts far beyond the scope of technology, generalizing them into the biological and social realms.[15] Wiener said that all purposeful behavior requires negative feedback. For these reasons, some call *cybernetics* the effort to understand the behavior of complex systems. More recent definitions of cybernetics almost always include social organizations as one of the categories of relevant systems.

Von Bertalanffy attempted on more than one occasion to clarify what he saw to be the distinction between general systems theory and cybernetics. For example, he stated:

> Systems theory . . . is frequently identified with cybernetics and control theory. This . . . is incorrect. Cybernetics, as the theory of control mechanisms in technology and nature and feedback, is a part of a general theory of systems; cybernetic systems are a special case, however important, of systems showing self-regulation.[16]

Again, later in the same work, von Bertalanffy noted that whereas an open-system model involves dynamic interaction of components, a cybernetic model involves a feedback cycle. By means of feedback of information, a desired value is maintained or a target achieved. A feedback system, with its lack of metabolism, is closed thermodynamically and kinetically.[17] On the other hand, open-systems theory is a generalized kinetics- and thermodynamics-based theory. Von Berta-lanffy said his theory appeared prior to cybernetics, systems engineering, and other related fields.

Wiener's theory is said to be at the base of a "second industrial revolution." Whereas the first industrial revolution witnessed the machine replacing human energy, with man performing control functions, the second industrial revolution, involving automation, has relegated control to servomechanisms, with humans monitoring and maintaining the automated functions.[18] Cybernetics is regarded as part of general systems theory. In solving control problems, cybernetics often draws on information theories such as those of Shannon and Weaver, discussed in the following section.

### Information Theory

By the late 1920s, communications engineers were studying problems of interference, or noise, and channel capacity.[19] Representative of their work was a 1949 contribution by C. E. Shannon titled "The Mathematical Theory of Communication."

Shannon's so-called "information theory" has been called more a theory of communication than information, since the work is concerned with purely technical problems of data transmission involving source, transmitter, channel, receiver, and destination. Shannon did not deal with the semantic aspects of communication or information content. He was not concerned with problems of meaning.[20]

Two concepts developed by Shannon and related to systems theory were the idea that *uncertainty* is dispelled by information and the relationship of encoding to *transformation* processes.[21]

### Decision-Making Theory

According to von Bertalanffy, another related area developing simultaneously with the Systems School was decision-making theory.[22] Connected with this theory were men such as Herbert Simon, Richard M. Cyert, and James G. March.[23]

### Summary

General systems theory includes special system theories, such as the ones above. According to Erwin Laszlo, these special systems include "the cybernetic system theories of Wiener and Ashby; the information system theories of Shannon and Weaver; the biological system theories of von Bertalanffy, Weiss, and Miller; the mathematical system theories of Rapoport and von Neumann; the social system theories of Parsons, Merton, and Buckley; the political system theories of Easton, Taylor, and Deutsch; the management and organization theories of Churchmann and Ackoff; the psychological and psychiatric theories of Grinker, Menninger, Arieti, and Gray; the human communication system theories of Cherry, Vickers, and Thayer; and others."[24] Laszlo emphasizes that general systems theory is a *general* theory of systems, not a theory of *general systems*.[25]

## Organizations as Open Systems

According to Laszlo, seven principal types of systems are the physicochemical, biological, organic, social-ecological, sociocultural, organizational, and the technical.[26] The two men most often given credit for applying social systems thinking to the organization are Daniel Katz and Robert Kahn.[27] Rogers and Rogers, for example, said that publication of the Katz and Kahn book, *The Social Psychology of Organizations,* in 1966 marked "the real beginning of the application of systems thinking to organizations."[28]

Katz and Kahn in turn credit Talcott Parsons as the significant influence in moving sociological thought in general in the direction of *open systems* theory.[29] Sociologists such as Parsons and George C. Homans proposed that society is a system of interrelated parts marked by a boundary and maintaining an equilibrium.[30]

For communication scholars, the open system approach offers the most natural avenue for exploring organizational functions and relationships. This approach views the organization as a system composed of many subsystems whose interdependent and interlocking parts are held together by communication. A change in any part of the system affects the other parts. These subsystems function within a *boundary*.[31]

The same kind of communication exchanges that go on within the boundaries of the organization also take place between the organization and its larger *environment*. These transactional processes may involve transfer of energy, people, money, materials, or information.[32]

For example, a stockbroker receives *input* from the environment in the form of information about specific companies, world events, and general market trends. He transforms this input into *output* in the form of a telephone call or newsletter to clients considering new investments. A clothing manufacturer receives input from the larger environment in the form of human labor; raw material such as fabric, thread, and zippers; and equipment such as sewing machines. The manufacturer transforms this input into output in the form of products such as dresses, scarves, slacks, and shirts.

The outputs of one system are inputs for another. The stockbroker's telephone call is input to his client; the dress is input to the retail clothing distributor. In the case of a pilot-training program, the output of the training academy (certified pilots) becomes input for airlines, police, air-surveillance teams, and helicopter services. The output of a tuna-canning plant is input for wholesale grocers.

In social systems, there is also a cyclical return to the point of origin. For example, computer-product sales return capital to the organization, which uses the capital to pay its workers, to acquire new raw materials, and to replace worn equipment. These transactions between the organization and its environment, involving input of energies and conversion of output into further energic input, have caused organizations to be termed "flagrantly open systems."

This model of an energic input-output system derives from the work of von Bertalanffy. In summary, the terms *input* and *output* have been defined by Rogers and Rogers as the information, matter-energy, and other products that any system absorbs from or discharges into its environment.[33] The process by which input is transformed into output is sometimes called *through-put*.[34]

*Open vs. Closed Systems*

*System openness* refers to the degree to which a system is receptive to all kinds of inputs. Because the open system constantly imports energy, it does not run down. Thus, negative rather than positive entropy characterizes all living systems. According to Katz and Kahn, "the law of *negative entropy* states that systems survive and maintain their characteristic internal order only so long as they import from the environment more energy than they expend in the process of importation and transformation."[35]

Katz and Kahn further stated:

> To insure survival, systems will operate to acquire some margin of safety beyond the immediate level of existence. The body will store fat, the social organization will build up reserves, the society will increase its technological and cultural base.[36]

The term *homeostasis* refers to maintenance of balance in living systems.[37] *Stability* refers to the "ability of a system to maintain a given behavioral posture over time. The more sensitive a system, the less likely it is to be stable over a broad range of inputs and outputs."[38]

Unlike open systems, *closed systems* are subject to the second law of thermodynamics. According to this law, entropic processes move a system toward equilibrium, causing it to run down and eventually to die. Whereas an open system is connected to and interacts with its environment, reenergizing itself from sources in the dynamic, ever-changing external environment, a closed system fails to take from or give anything to its environment. The closed system is self-contained, isolated from the larger environment.[39]

Organizational environment has been defined as "the totality of physical and social factors that are taken *directly into consideration* in the decision-making behavior of individuals in the organization."[40] The *internal* environment, or those influential physical and social factors within the boundaries of the organization, is sometimes called *climate*.[41] Climate refers to the whole of an organization's communication-flow patterns, interpersonal relations, and other atmospheric factors. Before the 1960s organizational researchers tended to look inside the walls of the organization to explain the successful or unsuccessful operation of a firm or organization and the behavior of its members. The Hawthorne studies and the scientific management school, for example, stressed the organizational climate.

*External* environment refers to physical and social variables outside the organizational boundaries but still considered relevant to decision-making that goes on inside the boundaries. This concept of the *relevant* environment as distinct from the *total* environment is stressed by many who seek to apply open systems thinking to the organization.[42]

In the same way that the relevant external environment affects the functioning of the organization, the organization can exert an influence on the environment. For example, a slowing down of the economy may force a business or company to reduce the number of workers employed from the community; but if these unemployed workers have no income, the rest of the community will also suffer. Thus, just as the relevant external environment forced changes on the organization, the organization initiated change processes within the larger community. Less income means lower sales, fewer purchases, and fewer investments. In such a state of "dynamic" interaction, cause-effect relationships are difficult to determine.

*Boundary* refers to the conceptual division between a system and its environment.[43] The boundary of an organization may be regarded as its walls, the outer fence, the community in which the organization operates, or even beyond the community to a larger context. Concepts such as boundary and relevant environment are flexible ones, often to be pushed and shoved around. Even boundaries that would appear at first sight to be fixed and easy to discern, such as national territorial limits, often become the subject of vehement international debate. Several years ago, for example, Canada sent a scientific expedition to the Arctic to seek further information on the presence or absence of a land connection underneath the frozen waters. The discovery of such a connection to the Arctic would have territorial implications for Canada and for Russia, challenging previously accepted territorial boundaries. Another illustration of this same point was made in an article we wrote a few years ago titled "How High is Canada?"[44] The article discussed a dispute over the ownership of air waves.

Even physical limits are sometimes difficult to fix, and psychological ones even more so. If you define an organization as the building at 54 Winslow Street and all its occupants, how do you classify the company's assets in the local trust company, its activities in the community, the park that it built and maintains for the city? Are the regular customers of a bowling alley less a part of the organization than are the members of a private curling club? Does the payment of dues clearly establish the latter as part of the organization, and the failure to pay dues exclude the former? Are the lifeguards who work at a community pool a part of that organization, but not the public who pay the pool employees' salaries? These examples may illustrate the difficulty of setting boundaries.

Some authors such as H. Ulrich regard the boundary of a system to be "where relations are less concentrated than at other places. The higher concentration will be within the system boundary."[45] Most organizations, for example, will have more internal than external relations. Some theorists consider management of these boundary areas to be the most important objective of the executive.

### Relevant Communication Concepts and Organizational Information Needs

An important communication concept associated with open-systems theory is "feedback," described as the characteristic of a self-regulating system. Feedback loops allow a system to modify its performance on the basis of evaluative information inputs, comparing past performance with a criterion value. The control loops may be "closed loops" existing within the boundaries of the system or "open loops," where part of the information flow takes place outside the system boundary.[46] Open systems are typically characterized by open feedback loops that allow the social organism to perceive environmental changes and to transmit information about these changes to the decision-making part of the organism. On the basis of this information, the organism will adapt and thus survive.

Karl Deutsch says there are three kinds of information that can be transmitted and received as feedback: (1) information about the organism and its own parts, (2) information from the past, and (3) information about the world outside.[47]

Charles R. Dechert makes the interesting point that since social action normally involves a feedback loop, in some senses the socially controlled also control the controller.[48] No one knows the value of this statement more than the politician who ostensibly makes decisions from a position of power, but in fact, relies heavily on opinion poll results. To ignore the feedback from his constituency is to invite defeat at the next election. Rogers and Rogers use the term *external accountability* to refer to the "degree to which an organization is dependent on, or responsive to, its environment."[49]

Organizations constantly strive to obtain from their environments information or feedback that will help them to reduce their uncertainty. A buzz word in industry and government circles today is "proactive." Rather than waiting for events and circumstances to impact upon them, organizations plan ahead for contingencies. They set out scenarios that have some potential of coming into being; then they design for those contingencies.

For example, Tylenol was caught off guard with the first round of poisonings attributed to its capsule medication. The company was forced into a reactive stance, which it accommodated by immediately removing all Tylenol products from drug-store and supermarket shelves. As a consequence of its rapid and unreserved accommodation of a volatile environment, Tylenol survived the first assault.

Rather than waiting for a possible second incident, the company proceeded to repackage its product and to design a new capsule-shaped tablet. Tampering with the "caplet," as it was termed, would be much more difficult, since the medication was compressed into a tablet form with the brand name cut into the surface. When a second Tylenol poisoning occurred in 1985, Tylenol purchased time on national networks to announce that all capsules would be removed from the market and the new caplet would be sold in the place of the original capsule form. Tylenol's proactive approach proved invaluable, and the company survived.[50]

A more humorous example of contingency planning appeared in United States newspapers a few years ago. The newspapers reported that the U.S. government postal service had devised an elaborate scheme for rerouting all mail in the event of nuclear war. This would seem to be the ultimate in "thinking the unthinkable."

Environmental surveillance is another way in which organizations cope with uncertainties. John Naisbitt in *Megatrends* reported the growing popularity of trend-monitoring services.[51] These services attempt to keep government and industry leaders informed of trends in the socioeconomic environment. The services analyze and report significant shifts in issue coverage by the local press and on radio and television. In the same way, opinion polls attempt to track ever-shifting and elusive public opinion. The purpose of this trend analysis and polling is to warn people in decision-making positions of environmental shifts, soon enough that they can take "proactive" measures to deal with the potential future problems indicated. In other words, the information enables the organization facing a high level of uncertainty to cope. The organization is essentially stockpiling information that may help it to survive at some point in the future.

Stockpiling is not an easy task, however; for the rapid change processes make most information and products redundant almost before they are released. Whether it is micro-chips or guns, today's technology, like fashions, will notlong be in vogue. New ideas are equally ephemeral. Our turbulent and unstable external environment generates a high degree of uncertainty for people and for organizations.

Because openness to the environment is so important, the individuals who serve as boundary spanners are vital to the organization. These individuals have been termed *cosmopolites*.[52] Cosmopolites appear at the top and at the bottom in most organizations. The executive who appears in a speech-making capacity at the local Rotary Club, plays golf each Wednesday at the country club, or travels to a convention in a distant city, is acting out a cosmopolite role.

Similarly, the catalogue clerk at Sears or the door-to-door salesman for Avon products is a cosmopolite. According to Rogers and Roger, cosmopolites act as "the open doors and windows of an organization, allowing for a cross-ventilation of new ideas."[53] A consultant is a cosmopolite imported into the organization, specifically to allow the entry of an outside viewpoint. Rogers and Rogers commented on characteristics of cosmopolites:

> In one sense cosmopolites are a special type of gatekeeper as they control the communication flows by which new ideas enter the system. The cosmopoliteness of individuals is indexed by their wide travel, readership of nonlocal publications, national and international group affiliations, and membership in professional occupations with a high rate of migration, such as college professor, salesman, or minister. . . . Certain formal positions in organizations, such as market research analyst, ombudsperson, public relations officer, research and development scientist, and sales manager provide opportunities for wider contact with the environment. As a result these individuals are more likely than others to be cosmopolites.[54]

Rogers and Rogers report that a typical measure of a person's "cosmopoliteness" is his stated loyalty to the organization. For example, an employee may be asked: "In the long run, would you rather be known and respected (1) throughout the institution where you work, or (2) among specialists in your field in different institutions?"

While most organizations recognize the value of the executive or consultant acting as a cosmopolite and attach credibility to information acquired from these high-level employees, organizations rarely attach the same importance or credibility to information originating with lower-level cosmopolites. In organizations where little upward communication flow occurs, the environmental intelligence gained at lower levels is often lost to the organization.

Attaching importance to the cosmopolite function causes one to place correspondingly greater value on networking. Women seeking to assume executive status often say that the presence of all-male networks makes their life and jobs more difficult. If these networks are considered to be necessary links to the external environment, then membership in them may be not only desirable, but indeed vital to the continued viability of the organization. To function effectively in a cosmopolite role, a person must nurture connections, all connections possible with the outside environment.

An open systems view of the organization has many implications. For example, the role of each member of the organization assumes new importance, as does knowledge of all the other parts of the organization. The Japanese practice of job rotation, which has now become a part of management practice in some U.S. firms such as the Topeka Gaines plant, operationalizes this philosophy. The fast-track system initiates new employees into systems thinking by asking them in the first month of their employment to identify their major job objectives, as well as to identify people and units within the organization who hold the potential to influence or be influenced by these objectives.[56] Fulfilling such an assignment forces the new employee to discover how he fits within the whole and how the interrelated parts of the organization function.

In organizations with many subsystems comprised of diverse groups, the integrative function may be important. Studies by Paul Lawrence and Jay Lorsch found that the most effective of highly diverse organizations had specific formalized units to integrate the different groups.[57]

Well-placed bridge and liaison roles throughout the organization are essential in maintaining the necessary communication linkages between subsystems. This topic is pursued in later chapters on network and small-world theory. The gatekeeper role may be important in preventing information overload, a topic also later developed.

Another general principle brought out in open systems theory is that there is no one best way of accomplishing an objective. Whereas in a closed physical system, the same initial conditions must lead to the same final result, in open systems this is not true, either at the biological or the social level. The concept of *equifinality*, first suggested by von Bertalanffy, refers to the idea that there are more ways than one to produce a given outcome.[58] A company that is producing defective widgets can correct the situation by getting better machinery, by retraining unskilled employees, or by firing and replacing the quality-control person. There may be no one best solution; the solution will vary according to the circumstances. This aspect of systems theory will be pursued in the section on sociotechnical systems theory that follows.

Because of the difficulty of establishing boundaries, research into open systems can be extremely difficult. Traditionally, researchers tended to establish artificial boundaries—i.e., a particular branch of an organization or a laboratory setting. In other words, they adopted a closed-systems approach, one that does not well tap the dynamic interactions of open systems such as organizations. The researchers tended to ignore the relevant environments of organizations in order to avoid admitting too many variables into their studies. A desire to emulate the hard sciences by specifying and artificially limiting variables has produced much research not capable of being generalized. Nic Kramer and Jacob de Smit point out that in the early stages of research this approach can give quick insights, but its usefulness at later stages is limited.[59]

Essentially, when you choose to focus on a subsystem of a system, the rest of the system becomes the relevant environment. For example, most organizations have maintenance, managerial, innovative, and production subsystems. If a researcher chooses to study only the maintenance subsystem, the managerial, innovative, and production subsystems become part of the relevant environment. One writer compared this process to "raising the resolution level."[60] Extending the boundary to study entities that belonged at first to the relevant environment would be equivalent to "lowering the resolution." An example would be expanding a study from simple concentration on the maintenance subsystem to a network analysis of all the communication links between the maintenance, managerial, innovation, and production subsystems. In essence, you create a "supersystem." Deciding at what level to study a system will often be an arbitrary choice.

Some argue that social scientists rarely think in large-system terms. On the other hand, physical scientists who are well equipped methodologically often don't understand nuances of social systems. These physical scientists seem to have a strong "physicalistic" bias, preferring to think in terms of buildings, networks, vehicles, amounts of energy or money or labor; whereas social scientists often are concerned with organizational climates, values and attitudes, and cognitive styles, as well as with the physical elements with which people must interact. Study of such systems requires a more holistic approach that takes physical, biological, behavioral, and social properties into account.[61]

This approach must be expansive enough to take into consideration not only the transactions occurring within the boundaries of a system, but also those exchanges with relevant external environments. All social systems, including organizations, are *dynamic* systems, adapting to ever-changing forces in their environments. Systems thinking emphasizes the importance of feedback loops and constant circulation of ideas and information in the organization.

Rogers and Rogers summarize the implications of an open system approach to studying organizations as (1) elevating communication to a position of high authority, (2) bringing about a shift in focus from individualistic to relational variables, and (3) influencing researchers to look outside the organization's boundary for better understanding of what goes on inside.[62]

## Sociotechnical Systems

Some find systems theory too "elusive" and "abstract."[63] Managers often call for ideas that can be put in action. Academics want means of isolating variables and studying relationships. Systems theory causes problems for these people. As Wren noted, "Critics of general systems theory found it too crude for fruitful research, too abstract for organizational realities, and too complex for meaningful decision prescriptions."[64] Not all was lost, however, he observed, since from this debris came sociotechnical systems and contingency approaches. General systems theory underlies these approaches.

Sociotechnical systems theory emerged from systems theory and illustrates many facets of open systems thinking, but with a new emphasis on technology. The term "sociotechnical system" was coined by E. Trist and K. Bamforth in 1951 to describe "a method of viewing organizations which emphasizes the interrelatedness of the functioning of the social and technological subsystems of the organization and the relation of the organization as a whole to the environment in which it operates."[65] In other words, in any organization *people* interact with some form of *technology*.

Whereas many techniques aimed at improving organization effectiveness concentrate exclusively on the social system (or the *people* aspect), a sociotechnical approach suggests that we must also consider the means by which people produce services or products *(technology)*. Sociotechnical systems interventions examine people and technology to find ways of modifying each to better meet the needs of the other in the context of organizational goals and survival requirements. A sociotechnical systems approach attempts to shape behavior in ways that will improve organizational performance and at the same time redesign technical systems to enhance the quality of work life for the users of the system. A sociotechnical systems perspective examines the interactions between *social* and *technical* systems.[66]

William Pasmore, Carole Francis, Jeffrey Haldeman, and Abraham Shani define the social subsystem of an organization as "the people who work in the organization and the relationships among them . . . [including] the reasons that organizational members choose to work in the organization, their attitudes toward it, their expectations of it, patterns of supervisory-subordinate relationships, skill levels of employees, and the nature of the subgroups within the population.''[67] In summary, a social system approach encompasses all that is human in the organization. Many diagnostic tools exist for identifying the needs, motivations, skill levels, and interpersonal relationships of employees and managers. Some of these diagnostic tools are included in the final chapter of this book under the communication audit. Many thousands of instruments exist, so many that it is difficult to compare and assess the possibilities.

Sociotechnical theory assumes that identifying the needs that people bring to the workplace and seeking to meet those needs through effective design of work and technology is the best way of assuring that organizational members will work toward organizational goals. Thus, a sociotechnical systems theorist must also analyze the technical subsystem of the organization. Pasmore and colleagues define the technical subsystem as "the tools, techniques, procedures, skills, knowledge, and devices used by members of the social system to accomplish the tasks of the organization."[68] Historically, sociotechnical systems theorists have chosen to look primarily at organizations employing physical technologies. Much less frequently they have studied white-collar and service-oriented organizations.

In both blue-collar and white-collar settings, the technical system will place restraints on the social system by shaping the behaviors required to operate it. This view assumes that the degree of challenge and variety offered by a job and the potential for self-direction, input to decision-making processes, and integration into the work force will be governed by the nature and arrangement of the technology. The technology will produce particular kinds of movements and behavior, determine the location of workers, and influence the productivity of the worker.

Other second-order effects arise out of these influences. Work roles and relationships grow out of the demands of the technology, requiring some to operate the technology, some to service it, and some to supervise the operation and servicing. Employees develop psychological contracts with the organization that delineate how much freedom they will give up in exchange for specific rewards they will receive; they develop self-concepts in line with their roles and the way employers and fellow workers treat them. If an organization stresses the value of the individual and provides learning and personal-growth opportunities, the organization will maintain its ability to adapt to changing environmental demands. If the structure and the technology stabilize, and personal flexibility is discouraged, the organization will stagnate and move toward entropy.[69]

Sociotechnical theory assumes that organizations employing similar technologies will develop similar patterns that will in turn influence their relationships with other organizations and the larger society.[70]

The conclusion reached by sociotechnical systems theorists is that we must seek to redesign technologies to meet the needs of people, not only in order to improve the quality of working life, but also in order to ensure the survival of the organization. Yet Pasmore and colleagues point out that few sociotechnical experiments involve technological changes; most seek to rearrange the social system or people around an existing technology. These experiments, they say, do not well reflect the essence of sociotechnical systems thinking.[71]

Some of the assumptions of sociotechnical systems theory that mirror open systems theory are:[72]

1. Organizations, in both their social and technical spheres, must constantly adapt not only to each other but also to changing external environmental conditions, which makes flexibility in organizational design extremely important. The principle of *joint optimization*, which is the goal of any sociotechnical systems intervention, means that an organization will function optimally only if social and technical systems meet the demands of each other and the environment. To do so, organizational members and designers must constantly review and modify sociotechnical arrangements to better accommodate shifts in this environment.
2. The principle of *equifinality* suggests that there is more than one means to an end; in an organizational context, this principle suggests that more than one organizational structure can be appropriate to achieve a goal, and a range of technologies may be available. The choices made should reflect the needs of the members of that particular organization. Much of the design of an organization's operating system should in fact be left to the people who must interface with it. Except when absolutely necessary, people should not be bound by rigid sets of rules, regulations, and procedures. Rules should evolve over time as organizational members acquire more information about each other and about the technology. This aspect of sociotechnical design has been referred to as "minimum critical specification," encouraging experimentation and functional adaptation.
3. Larger systems will be least disrupted and least influenced by unprogrammed deviations from the norm in technical procedures when these deviations or "variances" can be controlled close to their sources. Therefore, operators involved in processing must be

able to identify and correct these variances when they occur. To have the capacity to do so, operators must receive training, information, and responsibility (autonomy). This principle implies that operators must be allowed to conduct their own maintenance, quality control, and other functions and that management must share any information it acquires regarding the operation of the system.

4. If workers assume responsibility for their own activities, supervisors can then concentrate on ensuring that necessary communication takes place with other subsystems outside the boundaries of their direct responsibility. In other words, supervisors can assume liaison roles, acting as links to other parts of the organization. As open systems, organizations must constantly exchange information across boundaries and communicate with other parts of the larger system.

5. Reward, training, selection, promotion, and appraisal systems must mesh with the philosophy of sociotechnical work design. Management must develop its philosophy and be consistent: "For example, if the system is to function as a collection of interdependent, autonomous work groups, individual rewards, externally imposed quality standards, and task-oriented management will interfere with the accomplishment of organizational goals."[73] Some sociotechnical systems experiments have attempted to eliminate all status differentials between management and labor.

6. Sociotechnical systems theorists argue that only through integration of human and organizational needs can an organization achieve the highest levels of productivity. What this means in practice is tasks that require an optimal level of variety, meaningful patterns, and skills worthy of respect; a work cycle of optimum length; employee involvement in setting standards; and adequate feedback of results obtained. The approach recognizes the need for adequate training. Job rotation, autonomous work groups, job design by organization members who will be performing the work tasks, quality circles, and internal training by peers represent some of the ways of operationalizing sociotechnical approaches.

In summary, some characteristics of such approaches include autonomous groups, status equalization, minimal critical specification, provision of feedback, pay for learning, and peer review.

Since the first classic studies of the British coal-mining industry were reported by Trist and Bamforth in 1951, interest in sociotechnical systems methods of redesigning work has grown tremendously. In 1982 Pasmore and his colleagues reported over 100 published reports of sociotechnical systems experiments, at least as many theoretical statements, and several major reviews of the literature. They noted that sociotechnical systems theory has become eclectic, drawing on many behavioral science theories and techniques. They fear that the approach is being applied indiscriminately today to organizations, often without outside expert guidance and with insufficient understanding of the principles, resulting in a growing number of failures.[74] One author attempted to summarize some of the field applications of sociotechnical systems theory:

> The benchmark studies were A. K. Rice's reports on new systems of working groups in the Ahmedabad Textile Mills in India and Eric Trist's studies of the Longwall system of coal mining. Jacque's book *The Changing Culture of a Factory* was a substantial contribution as well. More recent are Walton's reports on the Volvo and Saab production plants, all of which have become part of a general philosophy of work restructuring. Today these efforts are seen as prototypical examples of methods that contribute to the quality of work life, an umbrella concept for many of the practices that have evolved out of a behavioral science orientation to management.[75]

Rogers and Rogers claim that the study of anthropologist W. Lloyd Warner was one of the first organizational studies to take the environment into account. Warner studied the influence of community social-status variables on a factory strike.[76]

In 1958 British scholar Joan Woodward studied the relationship between organizational structure and technology in 100 manufacturing companies in South Essex, England. She found that the more successful firms in different technological areas had structures similar to others sharing their category—but different from those in other areas of technology. In her research, Woodward classified organizations as (1) unit and small-batch systems producing customized products, (2) large-batch and mass systems, involving a fairly standardized product, or (3) long-run continuous process, involving a standard product manufactured by means of a predictable series of steps. She found that the more successful organizations from the first and third groups deemphasized precise job descriptions, delegated more, and allowed more participation and autonomy. Successful organizations of the second group had line-staff organizations, emphasized closer supervision and tighter controls, and relied more on formal, written communications. These organizations did not need to adapt so rapidly to change in areas of customer need and technological advances as did the firms in groups one and three. Less flexibility was required. What Woodward's study demonstrated was that the above-average firms in each technological category adapt organizational structure to the demands of the technology.

Paul R. Lawrence and Jay W. Lorsch similarly found in studying ten American plastics, food, and containers companies that there is no one best way to organize.[77] They discovered that successful organizations adjusted to their relevant environments. Firms facing a more stable and certain environment tended to experience more success if they were centralized and relied on a formal management hierarchy of authority and on regulations and procedures. Those facing more unstable, uncertain environments were more successful if they were decentralized and flexible, relying on open communication, cross-functional teams, and influence based on knowledge and expertise rather than on formal authority. In other words, organizations experienced success when the organizational design was "consonant with the environment." More turbulent environments required more differentiated structures.

The work of researchers such as Woodward and Lawrence and Lorsch led to studies and books about the "contingency" approach to organizational design. Woodward's work is generally regarded as the starting point for contingency theory. In the leadership area, the contingency approach was developed by scholars such as Robert Tannenbaum and Warren H. Schmidt and Fred E. Fiedler. These theories are described in more detail in the chapter on human-resource approaches to motivation and leadership. The contingency approach suggests that no one type of organizational structure or leadership style is appropriate to all situations. Organizational goals, size, location, technology, and culture must be considered when the most appropriate organizational structure and communication behavior are specified. Scientific management may still be the best approach for some organizations and human relations, for others. Some people may want or require more structure and more formal relationships; some tasks may demand more rules and regulations. Contingency theory does not regard any one set of assumptions—Theory X or Y—to be best all the time.

Some say that contingency theory is a "new name for what has been observed, but not codified" for some time, and that organizations and people have always changed to accommodate shifts in their environment. Similarly, these scholars claim that the systems concept is an old one; modern developments represent an amalgam of many disciplines.[78]

Matrix management offers one of the best examples of sociotechnical systems theory and contingency thinking operationalized in organizations. Matrix organizations overlay the formal management hierarchy, as set out in the organization chart, with one or more secondary networks built around the needs of special project teams. In a matrix management arrangement, project managers who can report to more than one boss assemble the resources needed to carry out a job assignment. The project managers have expertise in the technical aspects of the special project and have powers of decision on all details of the project except on matters affecting the general policy of the organization. The project team is connected to the formal organization management in ways that use the resources of the organization as a support system.[79]

Proponents of the matrix approach reject the possibility of a neatly drawn formal hierarchy with one boss for each subordinate, neatly drawn lines of authority, and staff clearly separated from line. They would say that only in very small or undifferentiated organizations are such accommodations justified. Matrix managers see no clear boundaries between jobs or divisions. They consider allocating resources for single purposes or users as uneconomical and illogical in today's climate of multiple and sometimes-conflicting goals. Resources must be used for many and diverse ends. Change and uncertainty are the dominant characteristics of the time, according to these matrix management theorists, who call for new forms of organizational structure.[80] Leonard Sayles observed of the modern organization:

> There are just too many connections and interdependencies among all line-and-staff executives—involving diagonal, dotted, and other "informal" lines of control, communication, and cooperation—to accommodate the comfortable simplicity of the traditional hierarchy, be it flat [as in the decentralized organizatin] or tall [as in the bureaucratic organization].[81]

There is no doubt that the exponential growth in technological development over the past two or three decades has put a premium on organizational flexibility and ability to accommodate or adapt to change. Indeed, the most-often cited examples of matrix organization are research and development firms, spawning grounds for this management approach.[82] Such organizations often argue that the nature of their work makes conventional management controls inappropriate.

Along with these frontier industries, the whole industrial spectrum has experienced recent change. Computers, modems, and word processors have changed the way information moves and changed the speed at which it moves. History shows us that where a new way of handling information is developed, the impact is felt throughout society. This necessitates new structural forms and approaches.

The term *matrix management* is relatively new; but as with many other current concepts, the phenomenon that the term describes has been around for a long time. Although governments are not noted for innovativeness, they have long utilized the flexibility offered by project-management approaches. The committee of experts or commission of inquiry exemplify common devices that facilitate expert input on matters outside the areas of competence of members of government. Similarly all political systems, however democratic, have some mechanisms for exercising emergency powers capable of short-circuiting time-consuming due process in situations where immediate action is imperative.

Some industries have always adopted management approaches similar to those advocated by matrix management proponents. The nature of the work in these firms has determined management patterns. In the aircraft industry, for instance, a multilayered project approach has always been the norm. In an enterprise involving the orchestration of many highly specialized areas of expertise such as structures, aerodynamics, electronics, hydraulics, engines, and the standard array of engineering and production skills, no other approach is possible.

The coining of a new term to describe an old phenomenon has generated explanations to a point where one reacts like the Molière character who was surprised to learn he had been speaking prose all his life and didn't know it.

Some commentators regard the matrix management approach as institutionalized "adhocary".[83] Others call the matrix form of organization a structural crutch most commonly used when "two equally important but partially conflicting departments must cooperate on some task. Instead of appointing a committee, the manager in charge of the critical task is asked to report simultaneously to the two department heads who are in conflict."[84] This point of view tends to miss the most important justification for matrix organizations, a situation where the inertia and technical limitations of an organization's hierarchical system operate against the completion of desirable or necessary projects. In these situations, matrix structures allow for rapid assembly of project teams, who are given a high level of independent authority and allowed to draw on the organization's management and resources as support systems. In this way, the organization can react quickly to changing environmental conditions.

### Notes

1. Ludwig von Bertalanffy, *General System Theory,* rev. ed. (New York: George Braziller, 1968), p. 14.

2. Erwin Laszlo, *Systems Science and World Order: Selected Studies* (Oxford: Pergamon Press, 1983).
3. von Bertalanffy, *op. cit.*, pp. 11–14.
4. Laszlo, *op. cit.*, p. 4.
5. Daniel A. Wren, *The Evolution of Management Thought,* second ed. (New York: John Wiley, 1979), p. 521.
6. Laszlo, *op cit.*, p. 4.
7. J. Von Neumann and O. Morgenstern, *Theory of Games and Economic Behavior*, (Princeton, N.J.: Princeton University Press, 1944).
8. Norbert Wiener, *Cybernetics or Control and Communication in the Animal and the Machine,* second ed. (Cambridge: The M.I.T. Press, 1948).
9. C. E. Shannon and W. Weaver, *The Mathematical Theory of Communication* (Urbana: The University of Illinois, 1949).
10. Wiener, *op. cit.*, p. vii, points out that ideas relating to statistical information and control theory were novel and not well accepted during the period when he was first working.
11. Arturo Rosenbleuth, Norbert Wiener, and Julien Bigleow, "Behavior, Purpose and Teleology," *Philosophy of Science* (1943), vol. 10, pp. 18–24; cited in Charles R. Dechert, "The Development of Cybernetics," in *A Sociological Reader on Complex Organizations,* Amitai Etzioni, ed. (New York: Holt, Rinehart and Winston, 1969), p. 104.
12. *Ibid.*, p. 100.
13. *Ibid.*, pp. 100–03.
14. *Ibid.*, p. 104.
15. von Bertalanffy, *op. cit.*, p. 15.
16. *Ibid.*, p. 17.
17. *Ibid.*, pp. 149–150.
18. Dechert, *op. cit.*, p. 107.
19. *Ibid.*, p. 106.
20. Alec M. Lee, *Systems Analysis Frameworks* (New York: John Wiley, 1970), p. 153.
21. *Ibid.*, p. 154.
22. Herbert A. Simon, *Administrative Behavior* (New York: Free Press, 1945); see also James G. March and Herbert A. Simon, *Organizations* (New York: John Wiley, 1958).
23. Richard M. Cyert and James G. March, *A Behavioral Theory of the Firm* (Englewood Cliffs, N.J.: Prentice Hall, 1963).
24. Laszlo, *op. cit.*, pp. 17–18.
25. *Ibid.*, p. 17.
26. *Ibid.*, p. 20.
27. Daniel Katz and Robert L. Kahn, *The Social Psychology of Organizations* (New York: John Wiley, 1966).
28. Everett Rogers and Rekha Agarwala-Rogers, *Communication in Organizations* (New York: Free Press, 1976), p. 54.
29. Katz and Kahn, *op. cit.*, pp. 8–9.
30. Walter Buckley, *Sociology and Modern Systems Theory* (Englewood Cliffs, New Jersey: Prentice-Hall, Inc., 1967), p. 9.
31. Talcott Parsons, "Suggestions for a Sociological Approach to Theory of Organizations," in Etzioni, *op. cit.*, pp. 32–46.
32. Katz and Kahn, *op. cit.*, p. 16.

33. Rogers and Rogers, *op. cit.*, p. 65.
34. Katz and Kahn, *op. cit.*, p. 20.
35. *Ibid.*, p. 28.
36. *Ibid.*, p. 24.
37. von Bertalanffy, *op. cit.*, p. 43.
38. Dechert, *op. cit.*, p. 106; see also Norman D. Cook, *Stability and Flexibility: An Analysis of Natural Systems* (Oxford: Pergamon Press, 1980), pp. 1–2.
39. von Bertalanffy, *op. cit.*, pp. 39–43 and 143–44; see also Katz and Kahn, *op. cit.*, p. 19.
40. Gerald Zaltman, Robert Duncan, and Jonny Holbek, *Innovations and Organizations* (New York: John Wiley, 1973), p. 114.
41. Rogers and Rogers, *op. cit.*, p. 73.
42. Nic J.T.A. Kramer and Jacob de Smit, *Systems Thinking: Concepts and Notions* (Leiden: Martinus Nijhoff Social Sciences Division, 1977), p. 34.
43. Open Systems Group, The Open University, *Systems Behavior,* third ed. (London: Harper and Row, 1981), p. 17.
44. Stewart Ferguson, "How High is Canada?" *The Monitor,* University of Windsor, 1978; see also Kramer and de Smit, *op. cit.*, p. 30.
45. Cited in Kramer and de Smit, *op. cit.*, pp. 31–32.
46. Dechert, *op. cit.*, p. 105.
47. Cited in Buckley, *op. cit.*, p. 52.
48. Dechert, *op. cit.*, p. 115.
49. Rogers and Rogers, *op. cit.*, p. 70.
50. The Tylenol case is discussed in Fraser Seitel, *The Practice of Public Relations,* second ed. (Columbus, Ohio: Charles E. Merrill, 1984), pp. 492–97.
51. John Naisbitt, *Megatrends* (New York: Warner, 1984); see also Peter F. Bartha, "Tuning in on Issues Management," *The Canadian Business Review* (Summer 1984), pp. 25–27.
52. James D. Thompson, *Organizations in Action* (New York: McGraw-Hill, 1967); see Rogers and Rogers, *op. cit.*, pp. 67–68 and 140–41 for an excellent discussion of the role of the cosmopolite in the organization.
53. Rogers and Rogers, *op. cit.*, p. 68.
54. *Ibid.*, p. 140.
55. *Ibid.*, pp. 140–41.
56. Gerald M. Goldhaber, *Organizational Communication,* fourth ed. (Dubuque, Iowa: Wm. C. Brown, 1986), p. 50.
57. Paul R. Lawrence and Jay Lorsch, "New Management Job: The Integrator," *Harvard Business Review* (November–December 1967) vol. 45, p. 144.
58. von Bertalanffy, *op. cit.*, p. 40; see also Katz and Kahn, *op. cit.*, p. 27.
59. Kramer and de Smit, *op. cit.*, p. 33.
60. *Ibid.*, p. 35.
61. Kenyon B. De Greene, "Major Unanticipated Aspects of Societal Model-Building and Use," in *The Relation Between Major World Problems and Systems Learning,* ed. George E. Lasker, Proceedings of the 1983 Conference, Society for General Systems Research (Seaside, California: INTER-SYSTEMS, 1983), vol. 2, pp. 388–89.
62. Rogers and Rogers, *op. cit.*, p. 59.

63. Wren, *op. cit.*, p. 527.
64. *Ibid.*, p. 528.
65. E. Trist and K. Bamforth, "Some Social and Psychological Consequences of the Long Wall Method of Coal-Getting," *Human Relations* (February 1951) vol. 4, pp. 3–38; cited in William Pasmore, Carole Francis, Jeffrey Haldeman, and Abraham Shani, "Sociotechnical Systems: A North American Reflection on Empirical Studies of the Seventies," *Human Relations* (December 1982), vol. 35, pp. 1181–82.
66. Pasmore et al., *op. cit.*, p. 1182.
67. *Ibid.*, p. 1183.
68. *Ibid.*, p. 1184.
69. *Ibid.*, pp. 1184–85.
70. See Joan Woodward, *Industrial Organization: Theory and Practice* (London: Oxford University Press, 1965).
71. Pasmore et al., *op. cit.*, p. 1185.
72. *Ibid.*, pp. 1182 and 1186–89.
73. *Ibid.*, p. 1188.
74. *Ibid.*, p. 1180.
75. David A. Whitsett and Lyle Yorks, *From Management Theory to Business Sense* (New York: AMACOM, 1983), p. 230.
76. Rogers and Rogers, *op. cit.*, p. 62.
77. Paul R. Lawrence and Jay W. Lorsch, "Differentiation and Integration in Complex Organizations," *Administrative Science Quarterly* (June 1967), vol. 12, pp. 1–47; also Paul R. Lawrence and Jay W. Lorsch, *Organization and Environment* (Homewood, Ill.: Richard D. Irwin, 1968).
78. Wren, *op. cit.*, pp. 506–07 and 517.
79. Gerald R. De Maagd, "Matrix Management," *Datamation* (October 15, 1970), p. 47.
80. Leonard R. Sayles, "Matrix Management: The Structure with a Future," *Organizational Dynamics* (Autumn 1976), vol. 4, p. 17.
81. *Ibid.*, p. 3.
82. C. Ray Gullett, "Personnel Management in the Project Organization," *Personnel Administration/Public Personnel Review* (November–December 1972) vol. 35, p. 18.
83. Alvin Toffler, *Future Shock* (New York: Random House, 1970), p. 117.
84. William Ouchi, "Going from A to Z: Thirteen Steps to a Theory Z Organization," *Management Review* (May 1981), vol. 70, p. 11.

# 4

# Human Resources School: Theories of Motivation and Leadership

In the post-Hawthorne period, the study of organizations developed with two main areas of emphasis: macro analysis of social and technical systems, discussed in the previous chapter; and micro analysis of human behavior, as evidenced in motivation, leadership, and group-dynamics studies.

By the late 1950s, a new philosophy concerning people in organizations had emerged. This philosophy was termed by different people "industrial humanism,"[1] "organizational humanism,"[2] and "human resources."[3] The recession of 1957–1958 and the beginning of the space age served as benchmarks in this shift from social man to organizational humanism.

Human resource theorists believe that ideally the goals of the organization and the goals of the individual should be synonymous. The basic assumptions of such an approach are that people are self-actualizing, that they enjoy work and gain satisfaction from achieving goals, and that maximum commitment grows out of an organizational environment that challenges, supports, and involves its members and appropriately recognizes their contributions. Trust and commitment characterize this approach.

The major criticism of the earlier human relations school was its tendency to focus almost exclusively on social relations and to neglect the satisfaction that people derive from work itself. In the language of transactional analysis, the human relations approach can be said to have encouraged parent-child transactions, marked by unequal power and low respect. On the other hand, the organizational humanists, or human resources advocates, saw people as capable of adult-adult transactions and as the most important resource of the organization.

Important names associated with the human resources school were Abraham Maslow, Douglas McGregor, Frederick Herzberg, Keith Davis, Chris Argyris, David McClelland, and Rensis Likert. With the exception of Maslow, the first publications of these scholars' theories appeared between 1954 and 1961. Later significant contributions to human resources theory were made by Fred Fiedler, Robert Blake and Jane Mouton, Warren Bennis, and others already mentioned under systems theory, such as Herbert Simon. The first part of this chapter will focus on those contributions most relevant to the development of modern motivation theories; the second part of the chapter will discuss leadership theories which emerged as part of the human resources movement.

## Motivation

Many managers still believe that people want, more than anything else, good wages and job security. However, contemporary research and management theory suggests that traditional motivational incentives such as money, strict supervision, and the work ethic are inappropriate for nearly half of today's work force in the United States.[4]

One study that sampled over two hundred employees and their supervisors asked subordinates to rank their personal preferences from a list of ten job factors considered as motivators. The supervisors were asked to anticipate the rankings that would be made by their subordinates. The point of the exercise was to assess the accuracy of supervisor perceptions of what motivates their employees.[5]

The study revealed a strong discrepancy between supervisor perceptions of subordinate needs and needs actually stated by subordinates. For example, the supervisors rated "good wages" as the category that subordinates would rank as their highest priority; the subordinates, however, rated "interesting work" as their highest priority. "Job security" and "promotion and growth" were evaluated by supervisors as the second and third most likely priorities of subordinates. The subordinates rated "full appreciation of work done" and "feeling of being in on things" as their second and third choices. The fact that the subordinates' top three priorities were ranked fifth, eighth, and tenth by the supervisors suggests that management perceptions are out of line with organizational realities. Of additional interest is the fact that compared with the results of a 1946 study that used the same techniques and questions, almost no change occurred. The 1946 study revealed the same discrepancies as the recent study.[6]

Another study by Daniel Yankelovich found that while traditional incentives still work for 56 percent of the population, they fail to elicit the desired response for another 44 percent of the population. Young, highly educated middle managers and professionals comprise 17 percent of those who seek responsibility and challenge more than material rewards; and 27 percent of the unmotivated come from the poorly educated low-income, largely blue-collar workers. Yankelovich concluded:

> I can sum up what is happening in the American workforce today in a single phrase: a growing mismatch between incentives and motivations. The incentive system does not work as well as it used to. Formerly, management had the tools for motivating people adequately to insure ever-increasing productivity. This is no longer true. People's values and attitudes have changed faster than the incentive system—creating a mismatch.[7]

The four traditional motivators—money, fear of unemployment, strict supervision, and reliance on the work ethic—fail to motivate 44 percent of our work force today in a marketplace where productivity and competitiveness are deemed essential.[8]

Yankelovich suggests that more appropriate motivators may be flexible work schedules, more personalized feedback mechanisms, opportunities to develop one's mind and body, a fuller integration of lifestyle and workstyle, broader distribution of symbolic privileges and amenities, and job enrichment.[9]

The results of these studies suggest that the motivation theories of early human resource theorists such as Frederick Herzberg and David McClelland are not outdated and that Abraham Maslow's need hierarchy may indeed apply to individuals operating in a modern organizational context.

Douglas McGregor served as a bridge between the old human relations school and the new human resources view of the organization. In *The Human Side of Enterprise*, McGregor challenged the validity of both the classical principles of organization and human relations theory.[10] He said that both are founded on erroneous assumptions about human nature and claimed that managers who accept one or the other sets of assumptions will tend to manage accordingly.

McGregor labeled the first set of assumptions "Theory X"; Theory X represented a traditional view of the relationship of man to his work. These assumptions were as follows:[11]

1. The average person inherently dislikes work and will avoid it if possible.
2. Because of this characteristic dislike of work, most people must be coerced, controlled, directed, and threatened with punishment to assure that they work toward organizational objectives.
3. The average person prefers to be directed, wishes to avoid responsibility, has relatively little ambition, and above all desires security.

On the other hand, Theory Y assumptions imply the following:[12]

1. Expenditure of physical and mental effort in work is as natural as play or rest; the average person does not inherently dislike work.
2. External control and the threat of punishment are not the only means to bring about effort toward organizational objectives; people will exercise self-direction and self-control in working toward objectives to which they are committed.
3. Commitment to objectives is a function of the rewards associated with their achievement; the most important of such rewards, the satisfaction of ego and self-actualization needs, can be direct products of effort expended toward organizational objectives.
4. The average person learns under proper conditions, not only to accept but also to seek responsibility. Avoidance of responsibility, lack of motivation, and emphasis on security are generally consequences of experience, not inherent human characteristics.
5. The capacity to exercise a relatively high degree of imagination, ingenuity, and creativity in the solution of organizational problems is widely, not narrowly, distributed in the population.
6. Under the conditions of modern industrial life, the intellectual potential of the average person is only partly utilized.

McGregor maintained that Theory X assumptions characterized managerial behavior in most organizations. While he noted a shift from "hard" management (presumably scientific management) to "soft" management (human relations) practices, he felt both adhered to Theory X assumptions about human nature and believed that no fundamental change had taken place in management philosophy as it was operationalized in the organization. Accordingly, McGregor put Theory Y forward as a tentative beginning for a new school of thought. This new human resources movement would stress the development of self-control, encourage creativity, recognize people as the greatest asset of an organization, reward people on the basis of their performance and contribution toward the achievement of organizational objectives rather than on the basis of individual accomplishments, give people a stake in the organization by giving them a voice, and motivate through the challenge of work itself.

### Personal Needs

Abraham Maslow proposed that every individual has a staircase of needs—physiological, safety, love, esteem, and self-actualization.[13]

Physiological needs relate directly to survival and self-preservation, safety to security, love to need to belong, esteem to need for achievement and recognition, and self-actualization to self-fulfillment.

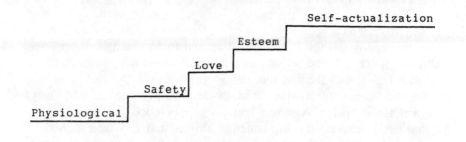

**Fig. 4.1**
**Maslow's hierarchy of needs**

Maslow suggested that only when the lower-level needs—physiological, safety, and love—are satisfied, will the higher-level needs become important. For example, a starving man may be obsessed by the thought of food; but once fed, other needs will emerge such as a desire for a safe predictable environment and for a loving companion and community status.

The higher-level needs, esteem and self-actualization, could be regarded in some senses as luxuries. The victim of an earthquake will be little concerned with satisfying esteem needs or engaging in self-actualizing endeavors. He or she will be too occupied with finding shelter for his or her family, attending to the injured, and helping to set up community support groups.

Even in the most favorable circumstances, few people may achieve self-actualization, marked by creativity, curiosity, independence, ambition, and freedom from restraint. According to Maslow, self-actualizing people are a rare breed.

Maslow has questioned the applicability of his need-priority model to the management field, noting in 1965 that much of the evidence on which McGregor based his Theory X, Theory Y model came from his own research and papers on motivation:

> But I of all people should know just how shaky this foundation is as a final foundation. My work on motivation came from this clinic, from a study of neurotic people. The carryover of this theory to the industrial situation has some support from industrial studies, but certainly I would like to see a lot more studies of this kind before feeling convinced that

this carryover from the study of neurosis to the study of labor in factories is legitimate.[14]

If Maslow's model isn't generalizable, the advertising field doesn't know it, because one of the easiest ways of illustrating the prevalence of the five need categories is to turn on television. The advertisements may be readily analyzed in terms of appeal to physiological, security, affiliation, esteem, and self-actualizing needs, with the emphasis of the appeals falling into the first four categories.

On the basis of extensive research into the attitudes of employees toward their work, Frederick Herzberg concluded that our motivational needs exceed the fundamental drives that can be satisfied by higher salaries, better working conditions, satisfactory interpersonal relations, and acceptable administrative practices. All these he terms "hygiene" factors or job *context* factors. If these hygiene factors are inadequate or deteriorate below a certain level, the result will be dissatisfied employees. For example, you will rarely find satisfied employees earning below-standard wages, spending long hours in dangerous polluted environments, or working in situations of high interpersonal conflict. However, removing these sources of dissatisfaction will not ensure the presence in a company of *motivated* employees. According to Herzberg, more than "hygiene" factors is required.[15]

In conducting his research, Herzberg asked his respondents to tell about "a time when you felt exceptionally good or a time when you felt exceptionally bad about your job, either a long-range sequence of events or a short-range incident." Herzberg found that when people reported unhappiness and job dissatisfaction, they attributed their unhappiness to their job context or hygiene factors such as inadequate salaries, bad administrative practices, inappropriate company policies, or poor benefits. When they reported feeling happy or satisfied in their work, they attributed this good feeling to the nature of the work itself or job *content*. Thus, Herzberg calls these job-content factors "motivators."[16]

Herzberg claims that hygiene factors are preventive, not curative. They may act to remove dissatisfaction and prevent problems, but they don't lead to positive attitudes. The factors that act as "motivators" derive from the nature of the work itself; for example, a challenging task, increased job responsibilities, opportunities for growth and development, achievement of goals, and recognition for accomplishments. These factors characterizing job content satisfy an individual's esteem and self-actualization needs and lead to superior performance. Herzberg says that people tend to "actualize themselves" in every area of life, including work, and only in performing a job can people reinforce their aspirations.

In this regard, Herzberg's theory draws heavily on Maslow's need hierarchy, with Herzberg's hygiene factors corresponding to Maslow's physiological, safety, and interpersonal-need categories and his motivators corresponding to Maslow's self-esteem and self-actualization categories.[17]

In *The Achieving Society,* David McClelland identified three need categories that influence our motivation to perform: need for achievement, need for affiliation, and need for power.[18] His research showed that people with a high need for achievement prefer and seek tasks that offer a high degree of autonomy; they set realistic goals with a carefully calculated risk factor; they plan ahead; they want frequent and accurate feedback on their successes and failures; they will choose a competent coworker over a personable one. People with a high need for affiliation value friendships and relationships over achievement and prefer teamwork to individual responsibility. People with a high need for power seek positions of authority and status that will allow them to control and influence others.

Some of McClelland's work involved comparing the manifestation of needs in different cultural contexts. He looked for evidence of felt needs in the content of children's stories. Through his content analysis of children's stories, McClelland set out to determine the strength of the need to achieve in different countries, and he established an achievement index. He concluded that in fact the achievement motive is stronger in some countries than in others, with the United States ranking especially high in achievement motivation.

In *Personality and Organization,* Chris Argyris proposed that employees' efforts to satisfy their needs within the organization often lead to a conflict between the goals of the organization and the goals of the individual constituents of the organization.[19] According to Argyris, four basic characteristics of the formal organization act to keep individuals from maturing and engaging in self-actualizing behaviors. These properties are (1) the specialization of labor, which stifles individual initiative and limits self-development; (2) the chain of command, which institutionalizes power and authority at the top of a hierarchy and increases passivity and dependency at the bottom; (3) unity of direction, which discourages definition of goals at lower levels and participation in decision-making processes; and (4) span-of-control, which decreases autonomy and encourages close supervision of employees, presupposing their immaturity. Thus, Argyris concluded that there is a basic incongruency between the needs of a healthy personality and the demands of a formal organization. He speculated that people respond to such situations by leaving the organization, daydreaming or becoming aggressive, becoming apathetic, trying to get ahead to achieve more autonomy, and creating and nurturing informal groups to decrease their sense of alienation. Management in the past has typically reacted to the defensive behavior of the workers by becoming more autocratic and more directive or by using pseudo-human relations in an effort to manipulate behavior. As will be discussed in the section under leadership, Argyris holds the view that participative, employee-centered leadership will decrease these feelings of apathy and resentment, while at the same time increasing the likelihood that the organization will be able to meet its goals.

### Personal Expectancies

Lyman W. Porter and Edward Lawler III suggested that a person's performance is linked to certain intrinsic and extrinsic rewards that come about as a consequence of the performance. Intrinsic rewards, like Herzberg's motivators, come from within, satisfaction at doing a job well. Extrinsic rewards come from the organization and, as in Herzberg's hygiene theory, are closely related to environment and the fulfillment of lower-level needs; these rewards include job security, pay, status, a pleasant work setting, and recognition for work in the form of promotion and tenure. If these extrinsic factors are to be related to performance, they must be *perceived* as being rewards. For example, a person who gains much enjoyment from sales work and makes a very high salary from commissions may not perceive a promotion to supervisor as a reward. Such a promotion could entail losses in both earnings and job satisfaction. Also, rewards must be perceived as being equitable or fair. If you get a $500 raise when you believe you deserve a $1500 raise, you may have little motivation to work hard in the coming year. Unlike Herzberg but like Victor Vroom, Porter and Lawler believe that external rewards may serve as motivators.[20]

Victor Vroom's expectancy model presents the view that the strength of our motivation depends on the attractiveness of a reward times our estimate of the probability that our efforts or behavior will enable us to receive the reward.[21] Vroom says that we have both first-level and second-level goals in most instances.

For example, in a job-related context, our first-level goal may be to complete a specific task successfully. If we perceive that the assignment is reasonable and the completion of the project is within our ability range, we will see our first-level goal as realistic and achievable—that is, successful completion of the project. Vroom refers to this assessment of whether or not we can reach our first-level goal as *expectancy*.

However, Vroom says that our second-level goals also influence our motivation to perform. For example, our second-level goal may be to achieve a managerial-level position in the organization. If we perceive that our superior will give us credit for our work, as in our next performance evaluation, and that our work will result in recognition and promotion within the organization, we will possibly be motivated to exert effort to carry out the project assignment as best we can. If, however, we perceive that our superior is unfair, or that we will not be credited with the work we do, it does not matter whether we think we can successfully complete the project; we will not be motivated to do so. Motivation to perform depends on the extent to which achieving a first-level goal may help us reach a second-level goal.

The third variable discussed by Vroom in his expectancy theory is the relative value that we place on any given goal. In other words, we all have many different goals, some more important than others. For example, if achieving status in the organization is relatively less important to us than time spent with family, we may choose to spend less time in the office on a project, regardless of the chances of being rewarded for efforts expended. We will work harder to achieve those goals of greatest importance to us. Vroom uses the term *valence* to refer to the relative value we attach to a particular goal. It is the interaction between *expectancy, instrumentality,* and *valence* that determines our motivation to accomplish a given goal.

Learning what people value most may not always be easy, however; and if the theories and research of Herzberg, Yankelovich, and others are correct, there may be a gap between what contemporary management and workers regard as appropriate rewards and motivators.

Management by objectives well exemplifies expectancy theory. In management by objectives, supervisors and subordinates together set goals that they regard as acceptable and achievable. Through the discussion of these goals, subordinates learn the expectations of management; and it is assumed that if the goals set seem appropriate and realistic, the employee will be motivated to attempt to achieve them in the coming year. At the end of the year, the performance appraisal process should allow the opportunity for both the employer and the employee to assess the degree of success experienced in these undertakings. The criteria by which the performance will later be measured must be set before the work begins. Both employer and employee must agree on the criteria. Research has demonstrated that employees perform best when asked to set their own goals. Periodic reviews, preferably at least semiannually, will allow the discussion of achievements, obstacles, future plans, and objectives.

### Expectations of Others

Studies also suggest that motivation may be related not only to needs and self-expectations, but also to the expectations that others have of us. A classic article by J. Sterling Livingston appearing in the 1969 *Harvard Business Review* indicated that expectations of superiors may influence the motivation of subordinates to perform. Livingston concluded that such expectations determine both the level and the quality of performance.[22]

In 1961, experiments with employees at Metropolitan Life Insurance Company showed that new insurance agents performed better in outstanding agencies, regardless of their sales aptitude. David E. Berlew and Douglas T. Hall of M.I.T. monitored the career progress of 49 college graduates who were management-level employees of AT&T; after five years the researchers decided that the relative success of the college graduates, as measured by performance evaluations and salary increases, depended largely on the company's expectations of them.[23]

A study of the careers of 100 insurance salespersons conducted by the Life Insurance Agency Management Association likewise found employees with average sales-aptitude test scores five times as likely to succeed under managers with good performance records as under those with poor records.[24] Employees with superior scores were twice as likely to succeed under the same conditions. Research into the performance of automobile salesmen in Ford dealerships in New England found ten of the top fifteen salespersons in one dealership, and four of these five had previously worked for other dealers without achieving notable sales records. The study concluded that the training and motivational skills of the managers were the critical factors making the difference. Having carefully selected their subordinates, the successful managers were slow to give up on them; to do so would be to admit failure. The less-effective managers selected more quickly and gave up more easily, choosing to place the blame for any inadequacies on others.

A series of experiments dating from Albert Mill's work almost seventy years ago and including the well-publicized studies of Robert Rosenthal of Harvard University demonstrated that the expectations of others can become self-fulfilling prophecies.[25] In the management field, what this means is that an employee may avoid any situation that carries even a minimal risk of failure. This refusal to engage in even low risk taking may have serious consequences for an organization. For example, in avoiding situations that could lead to failure, a salesman could lose sales. A bank manager would make only "safe" loans and lose business to competing banks. When these scenarios occur, they will confirm the low expectations of management.

Livingston concluded that the most critical element in communicating expectations to subordinates is not so much what managers say as what they do. Indifference, aloofness, and a noncommittal attitude communicate low expectations and result in feelings of inadequacy and low motivation to achieve. In the case of the Metropolitan Life Insurance Company, employees interpreted their assignment to low-performing groups as a request to resign.

At the same time, Livingston said that managerial expectations must be realistic; striving for the unattainable will cause people to give up. For example, studies have shown that setting production quotas too high will result in declining production. Research by David C. McClelland and John W. Atkins revealed that "the degree of motivation and effort rises until the expectancy of success reaches 50 percent, then begins to fall even though the expectancy of success continues to increase. No motivation or response is aroused when the goal is perceived as being either virtually certain or virtually impossible to attain."[26]

Livingston found that the difference between superior and weaker managers was confidence in their ability to develop their subordinates; high expectations were based on high self-image, the perception of their own ability to select, train, and motivate others. Because the superior manager often has a record of success, the subordinates perceive the manager's expectations as credible, realistic, and achievable.

Livingston cited the example of "Sweeney's miracle," where a Tulane faculty member taught an uneducated janitor to program and operate computers.[27] By 1969, the janitor was running the computer center and responsible for training new employees to program and maintain the system. Sweeney's expectations were based not on the janitor's previous history of school achievement but on his own knowledge of his teaching abilities: "What a manager believes about his own ability to train and motivate employees is the foundation on which realistically high managerial expectations are built."

Livingston's finding that managerial expectations have the strongest influence on the young[28] may confirm the wisdom of the Japanese practice of attempting to hire men and women directly out of school and of avoiding early promotions that would alert workers to the expectations of management. These findings also suggest that the fast-track system, which is presently used in many North American firms to identify and accelerate the progress of high-potential employees, may have weaknesses as well as strengths. The Japanese believe that it is important to maximize the contributions of all employees and that one of the ways of achieving this end is to allow a fair and reasonable time for assessment of the employees' work. They believe that the longer-term commitment and loyalty on the part of the many will more than compensate for any weakened enthusiasm on the part of high achievers thwarted in their desire to make rapid progress through the ranks. For every employee identified as fast-track potential, many others not so identified will enter the organization. Communicating low management expectations to the many could seriously damage the morale and productivity of employees who may not feel they have had adequate opportunity to prove their value.

The earlier study citing the work of Berlew and Hall found a 0.72 correlation between how much a company expected of an employee in the first year and how much that employee contributed in the next five years. The first year was deemed critical in setting standards, internalizing attitudes, and reinforcing the expectations of management. In that regard, the first boss may be the most important in a person's career.[29]

## Leadership

The literature on leadership in organizations could be characterized as being built around the answers to three questions: What is a leader? Is there one best leadership style for achieving results in the organization? To what extent should a leader involve others in his decision making?

### What is a Leader?

Numerous writers feel that it is important to distinguish between leaders and managers. They regard the manager to be most concerned with short-term problems of task completion. The leader, on the other hand, is involved in the management of ideas, with the ability to rise above the day-to-day humdrum of nuts and bolts, looking both backward and forward in order to establish direction and historical perspective. Some see the leader as philosopher, more concerned with asking why things should be done at all than with doing them efficiently.

These views characterize the writing of Warren Bennis, who worries that the characteristics of leadership most valuable to organizations are the very ones being eroded.[30] He sees this erosion as the result of pressures placed on organizations to respond to rapidly increasing numbers of special-interest groups. He says that leaders are victims of an unconscious conspiracy that threatens to prevent them from doing anything whatsoever to change the status quo. Leaders spend their time "consulting, pleading, temporizing, martyrizing, trotting, putting out fires, either avoiding or taking the heat, and spending too much energy in doing both. They've got sweaty palms, and they're scared. One reason is that many of them don't have the faintest concept of what leadership is all about. Like Auden's captain, they are studying navigation while the ship is sinking."

Bennis proposes that the most important priorities for all leaders should be (1) to lead, not manage; (2) to create an "executive constellation" capable of running the office of the presidency (this constellation may be comprised of some vice-presidents and some executive assistants); (3) to allow them to become "conceptualists," people with "entrepreneurial vision." Those surrounding the president should not be "yes-people" and should know more about their areas of competency than does the president. The president must not allow the bureaucratic machinery to sap his or her strength and initiative but must use creativity to the hilt and encourage others to do the same. Bennis says that nothing ensures the status quo so much as putting the best minds and best talents on task forces, for as "their reports continue to get better . . . our problems get worse." Bennis adds that we desperately need generalists, people capable of making the "right connections among scientific, humanistic, and sociocultural concerns."

Writing in the 1950s, Anshen, like Bennis, sees the shifts in the social and organizational environment as a call for a new definition of the role of the leader.[31] The most pressing factors in the new environment are the rapidly accelerating technology, enhanced information-handling capacity, and new social definitions of the role of business organizations in society. An environment that is characterized by rapid change calls for a leadership approach that transcends the pressures of the moment and anticipates long-range trends. The executives best equipped to meet this challenge are those who can think like philosophers, a quality not usually stressed in conventional training practices.

Like numerous other writers, Anshen sees the alleged shift from the management of things to the management of people, said to characterize the human-relations approach to organizations, as largely rhetorical. Similar to prior approaches, the object of people management was to better control the management of things. Anshen maintains that the central concern of management remains the fulfillment of short-term organizational goals.

Organizational parochialism characterizes business practices; and this characteristic, more than any other, impedes their adapting to the organization's new social and technological environment. Management's function should be to devise management approaches that are not organization-bound but are capable of being transferred across industries, across technologies, and across national boundaries. This new function involves the management of ideas, and this function, according to Anshen and others, is the role of the philosopher. This approach does not imply that the leader should become preoccupied with intellectual or esoteric speculation. The questions that leaders must address should be core questions tightly focused on long-range goals. The answers to these questions should give rise to a total scheme for operating a business.

Anshen suggested that revised management education approaches can produce this new breed of leaders. Such education programs should deemphasize the technical component and expand the education base to include studies in processes of social dynamics and the manipulation of ideas. His quest seems to be for a return to what at one time was known as a liberal education, a move that would be supported by Bennis, who likewise urges tomorrow's leaders to become generalists capable of making connections between many different specialized areas.

In many ways, the call for longsightedness expressed by both Bennis and Anshen echoes the concern that as society becomes more and more complex, most of a leader's time is spent in reacting to pressures of the moment. The quest for what has come to be known as a "proactive" approach is scarcely new. Henri Fayol was calling for long-range planning at the end of the nineteenth century. Anshen saw the 1930s call for management of people rather than things as stylistic rather than philosophical in its emphasis. The goals, he said, were still short-term and limited in function.

Numerous authors believe that the leader's role is concerned more with interpersonal relationships and the manager's with task-related functions. Abraham Zaleznik sees this distinction as the central idea in the study of leadership.[32] He concentrates on psychological factors that distinguish leaders from managers. Leaders, he says, differ from managers in motivation, in personal history, and in how they think and act.

Leaders tend to be characterized by a childhood and upbringing that sets them apart from their peers and fosters a high level of introspection. Although the leader's most valuable quality is his ability to empathize with the deeper feelings of others, he is likely to have acquired this quality through being apart from his fellows. What such a background gives the leader, according to Zaleznik, is a capacity for independent thinking and a high level of self-confidence. Such qualities in themselves, however, do not assure that a person will become a leader. What Zaleznik sees as a common experience in the history of leaders is a close relationship with a visionary mentor.

Like Bennis and Anshen, Zaleznik sees leaders as operating from high-risk positions, acting "to develop fresh approaches to long-standing problems and to open issues for new options." On the other hand, he views managers as acting to limit choices, with the instinct for survival generating low risk-taking behavior and enabling these individuals to tolerate mundane, practical work. The manager focuses the attention of others on procedure rather than on substance. According to Zaleznik, managers play for time, recognizing that with the passage of time and the delay of major decisions, compromises will emerge that "take the sting out of win-lose situations."

## Is There One Best Leadership Style?

The personalities of leaders become manifest in what is called leadership style. A large part of the literature on leadership is directed toward answering the question "Is there one best leadership style for achieving results in organizations?"

### Fiedler

According to Fred Fiedler's contingency theory of leadership, different situations call for different leadership styles. Determining the right match between leader and situation requires a good understanding of the leader's *personality* and an accurate diagnosis of the *situation* in which the person is operating.[33]

The leader's *personality* or *style* grows out of the system of values and needs that drive him or her. Fiedler accepts the broad distinction generally made between those who have predominantly relational styles, that is those who place the highest value on their relationships with their coworkers, and those who derive their satisfaction from the successful completion of a task.

*In order to match leaders to situations, Fiedler first attempts to discover the personality profile of the leader.* He acquires this profile from the leader's scoring on the test instrument shown in figure 4.2. This instrument asks subjects to think of everyone with whom they

**Fig. 4.2**
**Least preferred co-worker (LPC) scale.**

(From *Improving Leadership Effectiveness,* 2nd ed., by Fred E. Fiedler. Copyright © 1984 John Wiley & Sons, Inc. Reprinted by permission of John Wiley & Sons, Inc.)

have worked, presently or in the past, and then to describe the one person with whom they could work *least* well. The subjects rate this *least-preferred coworker* along an eight-point semantic differential scale involving polar opposites such as *helpful-frustrating* and *efficient-inefficient.*

Fiedler labels those individuals who describe their least-preferred coworkers in very negative and rejecting terms as low LPCs; and conversely, those who rate their least-preferred coworkers at the high end of the scale as high LPCs. In effect, the low LPC says, "If I can't work with you, you're no damn good." This pattern typifies the person who, forced to make a choice, opts for getting on with the job and leaving interpersonal considerations to be resolved at a later date. The high LPC leader, on the other hand, sees his least preferred coworker not only as a colleague, but also as an individual who may have other acceptable or even admirable qualities. The high LPC leader sees close interpersonal relationships as prerequisite to task accomplishment.

Fiedler has administered these tests to thousands of subjects over a period of more than twenty-five years. He has conducted his research in the private and public sector, in government, in industry, in universities, and in small business. His research confirms a strong correlation between *high-LPC* scorers and *relationship-oriented* leaders and between *low-LPC* scorers and *task-oriented* leaders.

Fiedler believes in differentiating between personality or leadership style and behavior. For example, the low-LPC leader may see that the accomplishment of a task demands very pleasant interpersonal behavior and act accordingly. On the other hand, the high-LPC leader may decide that driving a group to success may be the best way to foster close interpersonal relationships. In both of these cases, the leaders' motives are more important than their behavior. The behavior is only a means to an end. In the first instance, interpersonal relations (the means) facilitate task accomplishment (the end). In the second example, the leader derives his satisfaction from the quality of interpersonal relationships in his organization (the end), which he feels would deteriorate without successful task accomplishment (means to an end).

Fiedler says that a leader must satisfy his own needs as well as those of the organization; and where the two are incompatible, the needs of the leader will generally take precedence. As the leader may change his behavior for the convenience of the moment, observing behavior as a way of determining personality types is not reliable.

Unlike behavior, personality or leadership style remains relatively constant, as style reflects the underlying motivations of the leader. An individual acquires his values early in life; and these values are highly resistant to change at a later date, even where change can be seen to be desirable. Attitudes, particularly toward authority figures, peers, and subordinates are firmly set. Fiedler points out that even the most capable psychiatrists find it difficult to effect lasting personality changes in a client.

The second step in determining the possibility of a leader's success in a particular situation is to identify the situational "favorableness" or situational control. Having suggested a way of identifying the inherent style of a leader, Fiedler next sets out to categorize component parts of a situation that determine the extent to which a leader has influence and control. A high degree of influence and control means that the leader can predict with reasonably high certainty the results of decisions and actions that he can take in attempting to gratify his needs.

Establishing the extent of a leader's control of a given situation involves measuring three aspects of the situation: 1. *quality of leader-member relations*, 2. *degree of task structure*, and 3. *position power of the leader*.

The scale devised by Fiedler to measure the *quality of leader-member relations* is shown in figure 4.3. This scale replaces a semantic differential scale used in Fiedler's earlier work. The new scale measures not only the leader's relationship with his or her group, but also subordinate managers' relationships with their groups. Fiedler regards leader-member relations to be the most important of the three situational variables, as the leader must have confidence that he is not being undermined by his subordinates. This instrument indicates to what extent the leader enjoys the support and loyalty of group members.

The second scale designed to contribute to a measurement situational control relates to *task structure*. (See figure 4.4) The more explicit and detailed the regulations governing a task, the more likely subordinates are to follow out the assignment without challenging the

LEADER-MEMBER RELATIONS SCALE

| Circle the number which best represents your response to each item. | strongly agree | agree | neither agree nor disagree | disagree | strongly disagree |
|---|---|---|---|---|---|
| 1. The people I supervise have trouble getting along with each other. | 1 | 2 | 3 | 4 | 5 |
| 2. My subordinates are reliable and trustworthy. | 5 | 4 | 3 | 2 | 1 |
| 3. There seems to be a friendly atmosphere among the people I supervise. | 5 | 4 | 3 | 2 | 1 |
| 4. My subordinates always cooperate with me in getting the job done. | 5 | 4 | 3 | 2 | 1 |
| 5. There is friction between my subordinates and myself. | 1 | 2 | 3 | 4 | 5 |
| 6. My subordinates give me a good deal of help and support in getting the job done. | 5 | 4 | 3 | 2 | 1 |
| 7. The people I supervise work well in getting the job done. | 5 | 4 | 3 | 2 | 1 |
| 8. I have good relations with the people I supervise. | 5 | 4 | 3 | 2 | 1 |

Total Score------ ☐

**Fig. 4.3**
**Leader-member relations scale.**

(From *Improving Leadership Effectiveness,* 2nd ed., by Fred E. Fiedler. Copyright © 1984 by John Wiley & Sons, Inc. Reprinted by permission of John Wiley & Sons, Inc.)

leader or the organization. Leaders who are operating from a blueprint or step-by-step instructions will not have difficulty gaining the cooperation of their subordinates. The more structured a task, the more control the leader can exercise. An example of such a well-defined situation is an assembly-line operation, with routine and highly structured task expectations.

On the other hand, research and development work involves highly unstructured assignments necessitating creative input from group members. The outcome of decision-making processes in such environments is much more uncertain.

The scale measuring task structure asks four major questions: Is the goal clearly stated or known? Is there only one way to accomplish the task? Is there only one correct answer or solution? Is it easy to check whether the job was done right?

The third situation variable that Fiedler measures is *position power*, or the degree to which the leader can reward, punish, or otherwise control the compliance of subordinates. (See figure 4.5) Fiedler maintains that the leader is not always aware of the extent of his influence in these matters and suggests that the leader's superiors are better able to assess both position power and task structure. Self-assessments may be subject to distortion.

The relevance of discovering the quality of leader-member relations, the degree of task structure, and the position power of the leader relates to the following proposition put forward by Fiedler: In any situation, a leader has more control and influence if (1) members are supportive, (2) he or she knows exactly what to do and how to do it, and (3) the organization gives him or her the means to reward and punish subordinates. A situation is regarded as "high" control if all three conditions are positive or favorable to influence by the leader; as one of *moderate* control if conditions are mixed (at least one negative condition); and as one of *low* control if all three conditions act against leader influence and control.

Figure 4.6 allows the leader to total his scores on leader-member relations, task structure, and position power in order to arrive at a situation-control score.

Having identified the leadership style of the individual subject as relationship-oriented (high LPC) or task-oriented (low LPC) and having diagnosed the situation as one of high, moderate, or low control (based on an assessment of leader-member relations, task structure, and position power of the leader), *Fiedler says that the third step is to fit the leader to the situation.* Fiedler maintains that no one leadership style suits all situations, and extensive testing of his contingency model

TASK STRUCTURE RATING SCALE--PART 1

| Circle the numbers in the appropriate column | Usually True | Sometimes True | Seldom True |
|---|---|---|---|
| Is the Goal Clearly Stated or Known? | | | |
| 1. Is there a blueprint,picture,model or detailed description available of the finished product or service? | 2 | 1 | 0 |
| 2. Is there a person available to advise and give a description of the finished product or service,or how the job should be done? | 2 | 1 | 0 |
| Is There Only One Way to Accomplish the Task? | | | |
| 3. Is there a step by step procedure,or a standard operating procedure which indicates in detail the process which is to be followed? | 2 | 1 | 0 |
| 4. Is there a specific way to sub-divide the task into separate parts or steps? | 2 | 1 | 0 |
| 5. Are there some ways which are clearly recognized as better than others for performing the task? | 2 | 1 | 0 |
| Is There Only One Correct Answer or Solution? | | | |
| 6. Is it obvious when the task has been finished and the correct solution has been found? | 2 | 1 | 0 |
| 7. Is there a book,manual,or job description which indicates the best solution or the best outcome for the task? | 2 | 1 | 0 |
| Is It Easy To Check Whether the Job Was Done Right? | | | |
| 8. Is there a generally agreed understanding about the standards the particular product or service has to meet to be considered acceptable? | 2 | 1 | 0 |
| 9. Is the evaluation of this task generally made on some quantitative basis? | 2 | 1 | 0 |
| 10. Can the leader and the group find out how well the task has been accomplished in enough time to improve future performance? | 2 | 1 | 0 |

SUBTOTAL ☐

**Fig. 4.4a**
**Task structure rating scale—part I.**

(From *Improving Leadership Effectiveness,* 2nd ed., by Fred E. Fiedler. Copyright © 1984 John Wiley & Sons, Inc. Reprinted by permission of John Wiley & Sons, Inc.)

TASK STRUCTURE RATING SCALE—PART 2

Training and Experience Adjustment

NOTE: Do not adjust jobs with task structure scores of 6 or below

(a) Compared to others in this or similar positions, how much <u>training</u> has the leader had?

| 3 | 2 | 1 | 0 |
|---|---|---|---|
| No training at all | Very little training | A moderate amount of training | A great deal of training |

(b) Compared to others in this or similar positions, how much <u>experience</u> has the leader had?

| 6 | 4 | 2 | 0 |
|---|---|---|---|
| No experience at all | Very little experience | A moderate amount of experience | A great deal of experience |

Add lines (a) and (b) of the training and experience adjustment, then subtract this from the total given in Part 1.

Subtotal from Part 1.    ......................

Subtract training and experience adjustment.....

Total Task Structure Score......................

**Fig. 4.4b**
**Task structure rating scale—part II.**

POSITION POWER RATING SCALE

Circle the number which best represents your answer

1. Can the leader directly or by recommendation administer rewards and punishments to his subordinates?

| 2 | 1 | 0 |
|---|---|---|
| Can act directly or can recommend with high effectiveness | Can recommend but with mixed results | No |

2. Can the leader directly or by recommendation affect the promotion, demotion, hiring or firing of his subordinates?

| 2 | 1 | 0 |
|---|---|---|
| Can act directly or can recommend with high effectiveness | Can recommend but with mixed results | No |

3. Does the leader have the knowledge necessary to assign tasks to subordinates and instruct them on task completion?

| 2 | 1 | 0 |
|---|---|---|
| Yes | Sometimes or in some aspects | No |

4. Is the leader's job to evaluate the performance of subordinates?

| 2 | 1 |
|---|---|
| Yes | Sometimes or in some aspects |

5. Has the leader been given some official title of authority by the organization(e.g.,foreman,department head,platoon leader)?

| 2 | 0 |
|---|---|
| Yes | No |

**Fig. 4.5**
**Position power rating scale.**

(From *Improving Leadership Effectiveness*, 2nd ed., by Fred E. Fiedler. Copyright © 1984 John Wiley & Sons, Inc. Reprinted by permission of John Wiley & Sons, Inc.)

SITUATIONAL CONTROL SCALE

Enter the total scores for Leader-Member Relations
dimension,the Task Structure scale,and the Position Power
scale in the spaces below. Add the three scores together and
compare your total with the ranges given in the table below
to determine your overall Situational Control.

1. Leader-Member Relations Total

2. Task Structure Total

3. Position Power Total

GRAND TOTAL

| Total Score | 51-70 | 31-50 | 10-30 |
|---|---|---|---|
| Amount of Situational Control | High Control | Moderate Control | Low Control |

**Fig. 4.6**
**Situational control scale.**

(From *Improving Leadership Effectiveness*, 2nd ed., by Fred E. Fiedler. Copyright
© 1984 John Wiley & Sons, Inc. Reprinted by permission of John Wiley & Sons,
Inc.)

suggests marked differences in the performance of both high and low LPC leaders, depending on the characteristics of the situation.

As figure 4.7 shows, the performance graphs of the two are similar in shape but opposite in value. The high LPC leader functions best in situations of moderate or mixed control and performs poorly in situations of either high or low control. The low LPC leader, on the other hand, performs best in situations of high or low control but poorly in moderate or mixed-control situations.

Twenty-five years of research have led Fiedler to conclude that the notion of a "born leader" capable of leading in all circumstances is a myth. He used the terms "task-oriented" and "relationship-oriented"

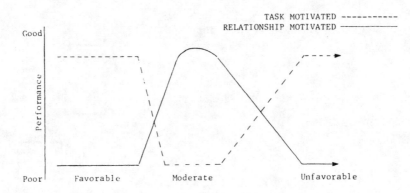

| Leader-member relations | Good | Good | Good | Good | Poor | Poor | Poor | Poor |
|---|---|---|---|---|---|---|---|---|
| Task structure | High | High | Low | Low | High | High | Low | Low |
| Leader position power | Strong | Weak | Strong | Weak | Strong | Weak | Strong | Weak |

**Fig. 4.7**
**Schematic representation of the performance of relationship- and task-motivated leaders in different situational favorableness conditions**

(From Fred E. Fiedler, "The Leadership Game: Matching the Man to the Situation," *Organizational Dynamics,* Winter 1976: 11. Reprinted with permission.)

in preference to the more common terms "autocratic" and "democratic," because the latter terms are value-laden, with a negative connotation for task-oriented approaches. Fiedler maintains that democratic approaches are absurd in some situations, as in the case of an airline pilot holding a committee meeting to decide how to make a tricky landing.

Fiedler claims that the most important principle to be drawn from his research pertains to the matter of responsibility. Organizations, Fiedler says, bear as much responsibility for the leader's successes or failures as do the leaders themselves. An organization can more readily change the situation in which the leader works than the leader can change his personality to fit a fixed situation.

Fiedler cites examples to illustrate this last point. An organization can modify a leader's position power, either strengthening or weakening it, to suit the operating style of the leader. A superior can assign the person a higher rank, or give subordinates equal or nearly equal rank. The superior can give the individual full executive authority or require him to consult with his group. The organization can syphon information through the leader or give information directly to the group.

The organization can also influence the task structure by giving the leader explicit instructions or by deliberately making goals and procedures vague. Those in positions of power can assign a leader to a group homogeneous in culture, educational background, or technical skills; or they can assign him to a group diverse in talents and background or with a history of conflict, thus manipulating leader-member relations. Fiedler claims that in certain cases, a leader's effectiveness can be improved by making the situation less favorable.

Another important way of assuring the leader's effectiveness is to teach him to recognize the situations that best fit his style. If the leader is aware of the situations in which he is likely to fail or succeed and seeks out those situations that favor his style of leadership, success is assured. Also if the leader is aware of his strengths and weaknesses, he can try to change the group situation to match his style. Fiedler says that we must train people "differentially." Failure to do so accounts for the lack of success of many training programs.

### Argyris

Argyris examined 50,000 samples of management behavior from 50 private and public organizations in order to identify the most common characteristics of chief executive officers (CEOs). He wanted to discover to what extent CEOs encourage their subordinates to be *frank, trusting,* and *willing to take risks.* He also wanted to discover to what extent there is congruency between stated philosophies of management and their actual practices.[34]

Argyris concluded that 1. Most CEOs are articulate, competitive, and persuasive, stimulating win-lose behaviors in their subordinates. 2. CEOs unconsciously encourage conformity and discourage risk taking in others. 3. CEOs claim to value the same attributes in their vice-presidents that they themselves manifest, such as frankness and forcefulness; but in actual fact, they discourage these qualities.

The CEOs studied by Argyris saw themselves as 1. being single-mindedly, almost "slavishly" committed to setting and achieving difficult goals, 2. needing continuous and immediate feedback, and 3. wanting their achievements to bear their personal stamp. When asked to describe other successful CEOs, they described these leaders as intelligent, exuding confidence and ambition, being opportunistic and single-minded, loving excitement and achievement, and seeking situations allowing them to be clearly identified with the results of their actions.

Subordinates' responses to questions on their CEOs reveal that although they generally regard the CEO as sincerely motivated, often they feel the CEO is unaware of the inconsistencies between his stated philosophy and behavior or is unwilling to discuss these inconsistencies. The vice-presidents react to the situation by carefully planning and measuring their statements, while at the same time trying to disguise their caution in order to appear forceful and confident. The vice-presidents give three reasons for exercising caution: 1. to protect the *boss,* because he would be upset if he knew his impact on others; 2. to protect the *organization,* which needs people with purpose and drive; or 3. to protect *themselves.*

Argyris found that CEOs like to be perceived as dynamic, intense, and aggressive, but not "overpowering" and "difficult to deal with." They don't like to think they've selected subordinates who are easily intimidated. Away from the subordinates, CEOs can look more objectively at the problems their leadership style generates, admitting that they tend to trespass on subordinates' ground when a crisis exists. They can admit that their tendencies to exercise tight managerial controls (particularly financial) and to make highly detailed plans encourages dependency, submissiveness, and lack of initiative in their subordinates. CEOs often admit that they couldn't themselves work for such leaders. Nonetheless, rarely do CEOs discuss these problems with subordinates, believing that such forthright discussion might be threatening to the VPs and might violate the organizational ethic.

Argyris found that the extent to which subordinates accept or resent the CEO's style will in large part be determined by the age of the company. In a young growing company, an aggressive leadership style will be tolerated by subordinates. As a company becomes more established, lower level executives will resent consistent interference from the CEO. Argyris found that those with leadership styles most similar to the CEO's style will often opt to leave the organization, seeking an environment in which they can more openly assert themselves. Those who stay may rationalize that the president is under great stress. Some VPs accept the behavior of the CEO because they believe that the CEO knows his own shortcomings but is unable to change. The majority of VPs design programs to try to confront the leadership issue, seeking to involve all levels of management through organizational development processes. Examples of such programs are management by objectives, experiential learning or sensitivity group sessions, encounter groups, and team building.

Argyris believes that all such programs are destined to failure because even if CEOs desire change, their inability to effect change in their own leadership style will undermine and subvert all efforts at broader organizational change. Top executives find themselves unable to behave in accordance with the new values. They have not been trained to put theories to work in real-life situations.

Chris Argyris argues the case for one best leadership style for achieving results in organizations and claims that training can produce leaders capable of achieving this style. However, he recognizes that the learning process is a long and difficult one.

In describing his approach to leadership, Argyris distinguishes between two types of theories of action.[35] The first Argyris calls *espoused* theories. Espoused theories are those articulated by people as important and as guiding their actions. In other words, espoused theories are based on *what people say.*

*Theories-in-use,* on the other hand, are based on *what people do.* By observing people's behavior, we are able to arrive at their theories-in-use. Argyris says that people vary considerably in their espoused theories, but very little in their theories-in-use. Observation of behavior patterns reveals that most people hold the same theories-in-use. Their actual behavior, or their theories-in-use, almost always conform to what Argyris calls a Model I theory in use.

According to Argyris, Model I behavior is governed by four guiding principles: 1. to achieve one's purpose by managing and controlling the environment; 2. to win, not lose, by controlling the task; 3. to suppress negative feelings by unilaterally protecting oneself; and 4. to emphasize rationality by unilaterally protecting others from getting hurt.

Trying to control the environment and the task, while trying to protect oneself and others, creates the following kind of behaviors: (1) People behave defensively and close themselves off from others. (2) People don't seek or receive valid feedback. (3) People don't publicly test their ideas, especially important or potentially threatening ones. (4) There is low freedom of choice, low internal commitment, and little risk taking. (5) Single-loop learning results, with the individual learning only within the confines of what is acceptable. The person may find out how well he or she is achieving a goal, but he or she never questions the goal or the values implicit in the goal. In the classroom, for example, single-loop learning results when the instructor asks the students very specific questions in order to control their responses. Argyris describes such learning patterns as similar to a thermostatically controlled heating system. As he puts it, the thermostat never questions the temperature setting.

Argyris claims that adhering to Model I behavior enables us to embrace the familiar and to avoid the novel. There is uncertainty in novelty and consequently a risk of failure. Model I behavior conforms to traditional authority configurations and regards admissions of uncertainty to subordinates or request for the input of subordinates as signs of weakness in the leader.

Argyris' Model II theory in use would have different governing principles: (1) to seek valid information, (2) to create a climate for free and informed choice, and (3) to encourage internal commitment to the choice. Adherence to these principles would result in a rejection of unilateral control; joint protection of self and others, oriented toward growth; minimally defensive interpersonal relations and group dynamics; high freedom of choice, internal commitment, and risk-taking; and double-loop learning.

Argyris believes that a healthy theory-in-use must allow for the possibility of questioning what is taken for granted. If this questioning is not possible, the system stagnates and does not adapt or evolve to meet the demands of a changing environment. Inviting others to confront one's views and possibly to alter them allows everyone involved to reach a position based on the most valid information and to become internally committed to a decision.

Individuals operating with Model II theories-in-use share power with anyone competent and relevant in deciding and implementing a decision. They see face saving, either one's own or someone else's, as defensive and nonproductive. If necessary, such face saving must be jointly planned.

Model II people evaluate their own and others' actions in terms of how well the actions generate useful information and solve problems so that they stay solved. These people try to build networks in which the contribution of all organization members are maximized, basing their decision on the widest possible exploration of views. By inviting others to confront their positions, Model II individuals eliminate oneupmanship and emphasize feedback and double-loop learning.

The end result should be enhanced decision-making and policy-making effectiveness, better monitoring of decisions and policies, and an increased likelihood that errors and failures will be communicated openly and that participants will learn from feedback. To return to the thermostat metaphor, the double-loop feedback system could be likened to a greenhouse climate-control system. Certain combinations of humidity and temperature will stimulate or inhibit the development of molds or parasites. In such a system, a second humidity feedback loop controls the setting of the temperature. Unlike the single-loop thermostat system mentioned earlier, the temperature setting is, in effect, questioned.

Argyris is uncompromising in his commitment to democratic leadership. However, he warns that what is frequently presented as democratic process may be little more than a ploy to gain old ends by new means. He says there is no point in paying lip service to democratic discussion unless we accept the possibility of being proved wrong. In the same way, it is pointless to go through the motions of discussing a problem with a subordinate on the pretext that "we must work something out together" if we have already reached a decision.

Argyris cites many examples drawn from his management training courses where those trained in Model II behavior consistently provided Model I solutions to set exercises. Even though the seminar participants claimed a commitment to the Model II approach and thought that they were applying this theory, analysis of their solutions, both by panels of their peers and by faculty running the seminar, showed a persistence of Model I values.

A typical exercise involved a mock interview with an employee whose performance had been consistently unsatisfactory. Although the interviewer often adopted a superficially democratic style in terms of the language used in the interview, analysis of his behavior showed that he engineered the development of the discussion in a Model I fashion.

Argyris also described the progress of six company presidents who had studied Model II theory for three years and had attended six seminar sessions varying in length from two days to one week. According to Argyris, these executives had managed to master the problems involved in inventing and reproducing in simulation sessions Model II solutions to set exercises. They accepted in principle the philosophy of Model II. They believed in the superiority of Model II behavior in terms of group goal achievement. They understood how to operationalize the theory. They were, however, still reluctant to try out the method in their own businesses. They feared the confusion and dissonance that could result from changing the game rules for their colleagues and subordinates. They worried about appearing to be ridiculous or weak, particularly since one of the important elements of the Model II approach is the need for honesty. Being honest entailed saying in effect, "This is what we have to do and I don't know if it's going to work." The Model II approach stresses the need to accept fear of failure and to confront the fear. The presidents were fearful of failure, but they were committed to a philosophy that said they had to transcend their fear.

Argyris reported that the presidents did eventually introduce Model II practices into their organizations; and although they reported varying levels of resistance and hostility, they also reported successes. In the case of some organization members, once they became accustomed to the new levels of openness on the part of their CEOs, they also became committed to the philosophy. In these organizations, changes began occurring at lower levels.

The evolution of a Model II organization is seen by Argyris to be, at least in the first place, a top-down process: "In those instances where subordinates responded positively, they in turn have taken the first painful steps toward creating a Model II world with their own subordinates."

Implicit in Argyris' approach is the proposal that only when all members of an organization become committed to a truly democratic organization will new levels of efficiency be achieved. He believes that democratization is achieved when the interests and goals of the organization are shared by all its members.

### Blake and Mouton

Blake and Mouton view leaders as highly adaptable, characterized by a dominant leadership style but able to assume other styles as well. To illustrate the range of possible leadership styles, Blake and Mouton developed a grid with four quadrants depicting the dominant style characteristics, with a compromise style located where the four quadrants meet.[36] (See figure 4.8).

Blake and Mouton accept a broad distinction between people-oriented and production-oriented leadership. Accordingly, their grid has two axes—one labeled *concern for people* and one titled *concern for production*. Each has nine gradations.

Position 1,1 on the grid is what Blake and Mouton term *Impoverished Management,* where minimum regard is given to both task and people. The 1,9 position, where production considerations are minimal and people concerns maximum, represents what the grid designers call *Country Club Management.* Position 9,1, where production concern is maximum and people concern minimal, is labeled *Authority-Obedience* style. The 9,9 position, where both people concern and production concern are at maximum levels, is termed *Team Management;* and the central position on the grid, 5,5, is termed *Organization Man Management.* This position denotes a "middle of the road" approach, giving of oneself but not overdoing it, being fair but firm, doing a job but finding a comfortable tempo.

Blake and Mouton subscribe to the idea that an ideal management style will include a high level of regard for interpersonal relationships.

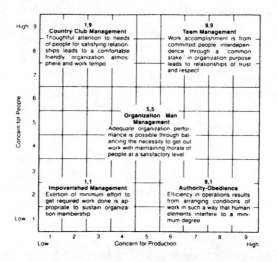

**Fig. 4.8**
**The Managerial Grid.®**

(From *The Managerial Grid III: The Key to Leadership Excellence,* by Robert R. Blake and Jane Srygley Mouton. Houston: Gulf Publishing Company, Copyright © 1985, page 12. Reproduced by permission.)

However, as their method of scaling suggests, they do not consider that a commitment to democratic principles necessarily involves de-emphasizing the concern for task fulfillment. This acceptance of the possibility of a 9,9 style with both task and human factors getting maximum concern is explained in terms of the correct emphasis on one set of concerns enhancing the contribution of the other concerns. As they put it, the result of the mix is not arithmetically determined. In other words, it is not a zero-sum situation.

Although the authors concede that a particular style may fall any-where in the Grid—for example, 3,3, 4,4, 6,6, or 7,7—they maintain that the five styles represented by the four corners and center of the grid are the most frequently observed styles.

Blake and Mouton offer the following explanation of contingency adaptation: Although individuals are characterized by a dominant style, they will also have one or even two back-up styles that they will use when their usual approach is frustrated. Such a back-up style is not necessarily a compromise style but may, for example, be a polar switch from a 1,9 to 9,1 position.

The designers see the successful application of the Grid approach as progressing through six phases aimed at moving organization members toward a 9,9 leadership style. Phase 1 involves introducing team members to basic concepts from which the Grid approach is built. Phase 2 sets out to develop the work team by establishing ground rules based on the concepts learned in Phase 1. All levels from the top down become involved. Phase 3 deals with the learning of techniques to bring about effective working relationships between different teams within the organization. Phase 4 is concerned with the building of an organizational policy blueprint. Phase 5 tackles the implementation of the blueprint, and Phase 6 establishes the new approach as the foundation of the organization's culture.

In the mid-1940s, workers at both the Bureau of Business Research of Ohio State University and at the Institute for Social Research at the University of Michigan carried out studies that are often identified as forerunners to the Blake and Mouton research.

In their work on leader behavior, the Ohio team, led by Ralph M. Stogdill and Carroll L. Shartle, isolated two dominant factors that characterized the dimensions across which leader behavior varied. These dimensions were titled *initiating structures* and *consideration*. *Initiating structures* described leader behavior designed to improve the efficiency of the work team by attending to the functions of individual team members, patterns of formal communication within the organization, and procedures for completing tasks. *Consideration* described behavior that was directed toward improving the interpersonal relationships within the group.[37]

The University of Michigan team, working independently at about the same time as the Ohio team, also isolated two factors that they called *production orientation* and *employee orientation*. Production orientation described behavior directed toward successful completion of the work task, and employee orientation described behavior emphasizing the welfare and feelings of the workers.[38]

Both the Ohio State and the University of Michigan studies concluded that the broad distinction between different kinds of leader behavior lies in the leader's primary orientation toward task or toward people. The University of Michigan studies are discussed in more depth in the section below dealing with the contributions of Likert.

### Leavitt and Lipman-Blumen

Like Fiedler, Harold J. Leavitt and Jean Lipman-Blumen also see leadership style in the two broad groupings of task orientation and relationship orientation.[39] They note the shift in management philosophy toward a more relational approach and see evidence of this trend at least as far back as the 1920s.

Leavitt and Lipman-Blumen acknowledge that changes in management philosophy, and more particularly changes in practice, are difficult to effect, in large measure because those charged with initiating and administering changes have often been selected for leadership because they embodied the very characteristics on which the new approach places a low value. In other words, to ask a leader chosen for his or her aggressive task-oriented personality to change the system so that interpersonal relationships take precedence over task completion is a tall order. Nonetheless, Leavitt and Lipman-Blumen think changing the system is possible, and they put forward "a modest how-to-do-it proposal for those managers who may want to edge their organizations toward a more relational posture." Their proposal includes a model of achieving styles and suggestions on what they regard to be the ideal mix.

The authors see social values moving away from competitiveness. They see a greater emphasis on quality of work and job satisfaction associated with skills, after the style of the preindustrial artisan. They recommend that those companies who want to change the organizational structure to accommodate the new values should hire flexible people who are willing to learn. The authors see United States values shifting from a central focus on the career to the career as part of a general life style. An emphasis on new levels of affectionate social relationships responds to the gap left by what many regard as the erosion of traditional social institutions.

Some management scholars believe that the success of Japanese industry grows out of a similar emphasis on relationships. The Japanese system rewards people for encouraging and facilitating the development of others, whereas the United States system rewards personal performance.

Leavitt and Lipman-Blumen's model attempts to explain relational behavior and to show how people differ, not only in what they want (motives), but in ways of getting it (achieving styles).

Their model identifies four direct achieving styles and five relational styles. The *four direct styles* are as follows:

1. Intrinsic Direct
2. Competitive
3. Power Direct
4. Instrumental Direct

People with *intrinsic direct* style select, initiate, and seek out activities that permit direct confrontation with the environment. They are challenged by tough tasks, the completion of which provides its own satisfaction. They work to solve a problem "because it's there."

The *competitive direct* person always looks for competition. Being good is being better than someone else.

*Power direct* types seek out situations where they can organize and control others to assure performance of tasks. They want to make sure things get done.

*Instrumental direct* describes a style manifested by people who use direct achieving (winning, gaining power, solving problems) as a means of achieving other ends.

The five relational styles are as follows:

1. Vicarious Relational
2. Contributory Relational
3. Collaborative Relational
4. Reliant Relational
5. Instrumental Relational

A person operating with a *vicarious relational* style fulfills a need for achievement by identifying with the success of others. This type can live off the reflected glory of others.

*Contributory relational* describes those who fulfill their achieving needs by contributing to the success of someone else.

*Collaborative relational* types prefer to work with groups in cooperative settings, sharing success and failure.

*Reliant relational* people get others to do their achieving for them. They are able to delegate and are often patient with subordinates, but this style also sometimes suggests weakness or helplessness.

*Instrumental relational* personalities use relationships as a means of achieving other ends. In this way, the lobbyist forms a relationship with a legislator.

Leavitt and Lipman-Blumen see their ideal leader type as a mix of leader styles that can be described as *Contributory-Collaborative/ Intrinsic/Power*. They term this style *CIP*. The ideal executive with such a style profile would:

1. actively search out challenging tasks and enjoy working hard to get them done (intrinsic direct);
2. enjoy working on these tasks as part of a team, willingly taking counsel and appropriately sharing responsibility and rewards (collaborative relational);
3. take a serious interest in others by encouraging them, bringing them along; and being proud of their success (contributory relational); and
4. make sure things are organized, on schedule, and under control (power direct).

Such a leader would not be strongly competitive (competitive direct) and would not play political games (instrumental direct, instrumental relational).

According to Leavitt and Lipman-Blumen, organizations have members with the personality characteristics corresponding with their ideal CIP, and many of them are women.

The authors describe the results of a study they completed that compared the achieving styles of second level R & D managers with high school boys and girls. The following chart shows the dominant styles that they found, ranked in order of emphasis:

SECOND LEVEL R & D

1. Competitive Direct
2. Vicarious Relational
3. Power Direct

| *High School Boys* | *High School Girls* |
| --- | --- |
| 1. Competitive Direct | Vicarious Relational |
| 2. Intrinsic Direct | Intrinsic Direct |
| 3. Power Direct | Contributory Relational |

Using a modified version of their achieving styles instrument that included a collaborative relational measure, the authors carried out a similar study involving managers and their wives, with the following results:

MANAGERS

| Middle | Senior |
|---|---|
| 1. Power Direct | Power Direct |
| 2. Intrinsic Direct | Competitive Direct |
| 3. Competitive Direct | Vicarious Relational |

WIVES OF

| Middle | Senior |
|---|---|
| 1. Vicarious Relational | Vicarious Relational |
| 2. Intrinsic Direct | Intrinsic Direct |
| 3. Contributory Relational | Contributory Relational |

The authors interpreted the first study as an indication that high school boys and male managers share competitive characteristics. In order to prepare for the CIP leadership role of the future, males should develop a more contributory style. The high school girls came closer to the CIP model.

In the second study, the managers' wives better matched the ideal CIP type than did their husbands. The authors suggested that these test results imply a need for male managers to adopt a more collaborative and contributory style, while their wives and women in general should become less vicarious and more power-directed to prepare for the future.

Could the CIP type survive in the real world of present day organizations? Maybe not, say the authors, because such people would probably be devoured by the high-powered movers of the present system. The choices then are as follows: (1) Forget it. (2) Modify the CIP recipe to include a stronger power component. (3) Change the culture of organizations.

The first alternative runs against current trends and pressures. The second choice of compromising by changing the mix makes short-term sense, but the best long-term alternative is to change organizational culture to match the new social values. This answer seems to be tautological and says in effect that the way to make a new set of values fit into an existing value system is to change the old value system. The obvious question is "How do you accomplish this end?" The authors suggest that doing so involves a commitment at the top to CIP principles and a system of rewards for behavior that supports the new philosophy.

### To What Extent Should Leaders Involve Subordinates in Decision Making?

The third question that characterizes a significant part of the literature on organizational theory asks "To what extent should leaders involve subordinates in decision making?" The following section examines the theories of some organizational scholars who address this question. These writers have also made contributions to other aspects of organizational theory, but they are selected for inclusion in this discussion because their theories exemplify the trend toward democratization of organizations.

#### Kurt Lewin

Kurt Lewin and his associates are generally given credit with being the first to view leadership as a range along a continuum from "laissez-faire" to "democratic" to "authoritarian." Lewin's work opened up and expanded the study of subordinate participation in decision making and emphasized the role of the group in achieving behavior changes. Research conducted in World War II on efforts to change food habits showed that changes were more easily effected through group discussion techniques than through individual measures. In 1945, Lewin founded the Research Center for Group Dynamics at Massachusetts Institute of Technology; after his death, the center was transferred to the University of Michigan.[40]

#### Tannenbaum and Schmidt

Tannenbaum and Schmidt, whose ideas are considered in more detail in this section, predate most writings included in our review of the leadership literature. Their work is presented out of historical order because their first concern relates to the question of desirable levels of participation in decision-making processes. The theories of these two scholars laid out the building blocks from which many subsequent writers assembled their theories of organizational leadership.

Tannenbaum and Schmidt saw the central question in the debate on organizational leadership to be "Should a manager be democratic or autocratic—or something in between?" They set up a continuum on which they plotted different kinds of leader behavior varying from highly autocratic to highly democratic. The kinds of leader behavior noted on their continuum related to "the degree of authority used by the boss and the amount of freedom available to his subordinates in reaching decisions."[41]

The range of possible leader behavior is as follows: manager makes decision and announces it; manager "sells" decision; manager presents ideas and invites questions; manager presents tentative decision subject to change; manager presents problem, gets suggestions, makes decision; manager defines limits, asks group to make decision; and manager permits subordinates to function within limits defined by superior (See figure 4.9). This continuum provided a basis on which much of the later organizational leadership theory was built and is most notably reflected in Rensis Likert's four systems of management.[42]

Tannenbaum and Schmidt describe the continuum as moving from the authoritarian toward the democratic in stages that shift the emphasis from what interests the manager and how he or she sees things toward subordinate-centered emphasis, which gives priority to the feelings and interests of subordinates.

The authors suggest that the new kinds of leader/subordinate relationships implicit in the move toward higher levels of democratic collaboration raise new questions that must be addressed, and they give four examples.

The first question they pose is "Can bosses ever relinquish responsibility by delegating it to someone else?" The answer to this question

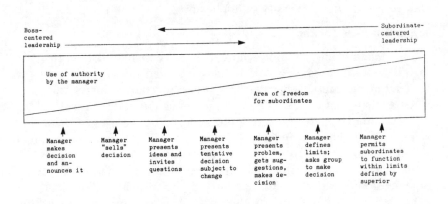

**Fig. 4.9**
**Continuum of leadership behavior.**

(From Robert Tannenbaum and Warren H. Schmidt, "How to Choose a Leadership Pattern," *Harvard Business Review,* March–April 1958, Copyright © 1958 by the President and Fellows of Harvard College; all rights reserved. Reprinted with permission of the publisher.)

is that delegation is not a way of "passing the buck." Risk taking is a part of management's responsibility, and managers should be prepared to answer for the quality of their decisions.

The next question is "Should managers participate with their subordinates once they have delegated responsibility to subordinates?" Not if the subordinates feel that the managers' presence will inhibit the problem-solving process, say the authors. If on the other hand, the subordinates feel that their leaders' contribution would enhance the quality of the decisions, then the leaders should by all means participate, but only as a *member* of the group, and then only if they clearly state to the group that they see themselves in *member* roles.

Question three asks "How important is it for the group to recognize what kind of leadership behavior the bosses are using?" It is very important, they say, and it is important also that the bosses do not adopt a "democratic" facade when they have already made choices. They should not attempt to convince the group that their decision is the group's decision.

The last question raised is "Can you tell how 'democratic' managers are by the number of decisions their subordinates make?" The answer to this question depends on the kinds of decisions subordinates are allowed to make, say Tannenbaum and Schmidt: "Obviously a decision on how to arrange desks is of an entirely different order from a decision involving the introduction of new electronic data-processing equipment."

Having set out different approaches to leadership and discussed the implications of each, the authors address the factors to be considered in choosing a course of action. The three factors they regard as particularly important are (1) forces in the manager, (2) forces in subordinates, and (3) forces in the situation.

The *forces in the manager* considered to be most relevant in determining his effectiveness relate to his personality characteristics. Tannenbaum and Schmidt group these forces under the headings (1) manager's value system, (2) his confidence in his subordinates, and (3) his own leadership characteristics.

The manager's value system will influence the importance he places on subordinate input into the making of decisions affecting subordinates. How the manager feels about the responsibility that his position imposes on him to carry the burden of decision making is also the product of his personal value system, as is the weight he places on organizational efficiency, personal growth of subordinates, and company profits.

The leader's confidence in his subordinates will depend on how he regards their qualification to deal with particular situations. It is likely, say Tannenbaum and Schmidt, that the manager may feel that he is more capable than his subordinates. The manager may or may not be justified in this belief.

The *manager's leadership tendencies* are categorized in terms of his inclinations towards a highly directive leadership style or toward a team approach. Much of the theoretical literature on leadership continues to distinguish between two dominant leadership styles.

Tannenbaum and Schmidt claim that an understanding of these personal characteristics can often enable the manager to become more effective.

*Forces in the subordinates* also refer to personality variables. The freedom that a manager can give to his subordinates will depend on (1) their need for independence, (2) their readiness to accept responsibility for decision making, (3) their ambiguity-tolerance level, (4) their understanding and interest in the problem, (5) their identification with organizational goals, and (6) whether or not they have the knowledge and experience to deal with the problem. The success of a collaborative approach is contingent on the presence of a climate of mutual confidence and respect.

*Forces in the situation* include such environmental variables as (1) type of organization, (2) the work group, (3) the nature of the problem, and (4) the pressures of time.

In dealing with type of organization, Tannenbaum and Schmidt concentrate on organizational values and traditions, or what subsequently has come to be termed "organizational culture." The style a manager, particularly a new manager, adopts will depend on how he reads the organizational culture. How the manager perceives the values of his superiors will influence his bias toward one or the other end of the behavioral continuum. Other more tangible factors such as size of working unit, geographical distribution, and organizational security needs may also impose restraints on the manager in terms of the alternative approaches open to him.

The nature of the work group as defined by their history as a team, their similarity of background and experience, their cohesiveness, and agreement on goals will also strongly influence the functioning of the group.

The nature of the problem itself will of course, in large part, determine the optimum level of group consultation. A problem that involves expertise or knowledge held only by the leader or another individual may not appropriately be handled through group consultation, and such a situation calls for unilateral decision making. However, the writers proposed that the final decision be made only after the work group is asked whether everyone having relevant knowledge has been consulted.

The factor that, more than any other, can determine how a manager behaves relates to the pressure of time. Some problems may be, or may seem to be, emergencies or crises; and the manager may feel that an authoritarian approach is warranted. Given the need to respond to pressures of the moment, a leader should move toward a long-range philosophy for achieving objectives. Tannenbaum and Schmidt offer as appropriate objectives raising employee motivation, improving the quality of managerial decisions, developing teamwork and morale, and furthering the individual development of employees.

Tannenbaum and Schmidt conclude that there is no best leadership style. There is instead a different best approach for different situations, and the leader's goal should be to improve his "batting average." He will be most able to do so if he improves his understanding of the forces acting on him, his subordinates, and his organization.

Fifteen years after laying out their major concepts, Tannenbaum and Schmidt reviewed this theory retrospectively. They felt that the dimension that was most lacking in their original model was the relationship of the organization to the larger social environment and the influence this relationship would have on the operation of the organization. The societal trend that they saw to have had the greatest effect on organizational philosophy was the move toward higher levels of democratic participation in social, political, and organizational institutions. They consequently added a social environmental component to their model.

### Likert

Although Tannenbaum and Schmidt developed a model of leadership behavior, theirs was largely a descriptive model. The development of techniques for conducting empirical research, based on this and similar social science descriptive models, was made possible by instruments evolved by Rensis Likert and others who followed him. These instruments offered techniques for measuring attitudes and behavior and made possible more scientific studies, not only in organizational theory but in the social sciences in general. Likert's greatest contribution to modern organizational theory was in the development of research instruments for classifying and measuring attitudes and behavior in organizations.

Likert was one of the earliest advocates of a participative-leadership style.[43] Working out of the Institute for Social Research at the University of Michigan, in the mid-1940s, he began a study of organizations that was to stretch over more than twenty years. His research examined a variety of organizational types in a quest to discover what principles and methods of leadership result in the highest productivity levels, the lowest turnover and absenteeism rates, and the greatest job satisfaction. As mentioned in an earlier section, his work led to the delineation of two leadership orientations—employee and production. He found that subordinates working under managers with a strong employee orientation were characterized by a greater team spirit, higher morale, less anxiety, and lower absenteeism and turnover rates. In these situations, the managers spent more time interacting with group members on matters of human relationships than on technical functions. This type of leadership assumes that the group performs best when the group members not only identify with the organizational goals but are instrumental in setting them. In order for team members to make the maximum contribution, they must first of all be motivated to do so; then they must be able to do so. The team members' ability to contribute will depend on their experience, the available information, and the organizational mechanisms for participative decision making.

Likert's studies supported his assertion of a distinct correlation between leadership characteristics or style and the productivity of a group, and his ideal organization is one where all members make the highest possible contribution to the decision-making process.

Likert identified four systems of management: (1) *exploitative-authoritarian*, (2) *benevolent-authoritarian*, (3) *consultative*, and (4) *participative*. Systems 1 and 2 have been likened to McGregor's Theory X and Taylor's scientific management. Systems 3 and 4 have been compared to McGregor's Theory Y.

System 1 *(exploitative-authoritarian)* organizations adhere to strict lines of authority and use punitive measures to exercise their authority. Workers are motivated by fear of dismissal. Lack of trust characterizes this management system. Although it is the least efficient of the four, System 1 management still dominates in most large organizations.

System 2 *(benevolent-authoritarian)* organizations are autocratic but allow a token level of input from the employees and limited control at middle levels of the organization. Nonetheless, this system is still basically paternalistic and manipulative and only superficially different from System 1.

System 3 *(consultative)* organizations encourage a more free exchange of information between management and workers. Management listens carefully to input from the workers and can indeed actively solicit comment. Although it takes into account the views of workers, this system still retains for management final powers of decision making, both in setting goals and in designing strategies for achieving these goals. Likert feels that System 3 organizations do not take the fullest advantage of the contribution the workers have to offer.

System 4 *(participative)* exemplifies Likert's ideal approach. A System 4 organization involves all members in decision making. Management consults with team members and keeps them informed on all aspects of task identification and goal attainment strategies.

As discussed earlier, Likert developed an instrument for determining where an organization falls along the continuum from exploitative-authoritarian to participative. He obtained his placement data by administering a questionnaire eliciting responses to questions on leadership, motivation, communication, interaction, decision making, goal setting, control, and performance. Likert's instrument had 51 questions, and he plotted the average score for each question on a 51-by-4 matrix. The four columns represented the four systems of management. The plotted scores for the questions were joined to yield a profile that generally fell predominantly in one or other of the four systems columns.

Because of Likert's belief in the value of interaction and collaboration, a large number of the questions in his instrument dealt with communication. Likert regarded communication to be of primary importance, as maximum involvement and contribution by all members of the organizations depend on a high level of interaction and a ready flow of information up, down, and across the organization.

To illustrate the need for an unimpeded information flow in all directions, Likert developed what he called the *linking pin model.* (See figure 4.10) This model breaks the organization down into small groups. The leaders interact with small groups of their peers and with the next level up the hierarchy, as well as with their own group subordinates. Ideally the individual becomes a nodal point in a network, passing information to and getting information from each point to which he or she is connected. Information moving in one direction is no more important than information moving in another. In communication terms, one could say that the model, and indeed the general philosophy of Likert, assumes that the efficiency of a system depends on the quality of its feedback circuits.

### Vroom

Vroom's approach to leadership resembles Fiedler's in the way he accepts that different situations will demand different approaches. However, unlike Fiedler, he assumes that individual leaders can and

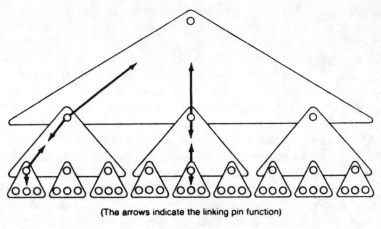

(The arrows indicate the linking pin function)

**Fig. 4.10**
**The linking pin.**

(From *New Patterns of Management* by Rensis Likert. Copyright © 1961 McGraw-Hill Book Company. Used with permission of McGraw-Hill Book Company.)

should adopt different approaches to suit the demands of different situations. Vroom claims that research demonstrates the ability of leaders to change their style to adapt to the demands of different situations.[44]

Tests involving a large number of leaders in different countries show little variation in the ability and willingness of these individuals to collaborate with subordinates. However, one leader may seek group participation only on important decisions while another may involve the group only in decisions that are of little consequence. Vroom says that the appropriate level of democratic involvement of subordinates in decision-making processes will vary from situation to situation.

Different situations will demand different approaches by leaders. In most cases, leaders will respond to these situations in different ways. Perhaps more important, leaders will sometimes respond to the same situation in different ways. Vroom regards this flexibility as a positive factor so long as the flexibility patterns of the leader fit the demands of a particular situation. In other words, nothing is gained if a leader substitutes one inappropriate approach for another inappropriate approach.

Vroom and Yetton developed the model shown in figure 4.11 to provide a checklist against which the leader can assess the characteristics of various kinds of situations and determine the most appropriate problem-solving approach. They call the model a decision tree. The first three steps on the decision tree (A through C) ask questions related to the problem situation, and the subsequent four steps (D through G) ask questions about the effect of the proposed solution on subordinates.

To use the tree, start at point A with the articulation of the problem and answer questions pertaining to the situation. A negative answer to any question directs the user of the model to a different subsequent question than would be the case with an affirmative answer. For example, if you answer "no" to question A "Does the problem possess a quality requirement?", further questions on quality become irrelevant; so the tree moves to question D. Steps D through G question the extent to which subordinate involvement will affect the solution of the problem. In the same way as with question A, if you answer "no" to question D "How important is it that subordinates accept the decision?", you can bypass E, F, and G. In this case, you move directly to the second part of the model, which involves classes of solutions.

The solutions are arranged along a scale from authoritarian to full participation of subordinates. In solution type AI the leader solves the problem alone, using whatever information is available. Solution AII requires the leader to seek whatever specific information he or she believes is necessary from his subordinates but still assumes that the leader will be making the decisions himself. C type solutions involve consultation with subordinates. The CI approach is to share the problem with appropriate subordinates, getting ideas and suggestions before making a decision. Approach CII is also consultative but takes place within the context of a group meeting. The final solution type, GII, describes a group decision through consensus.

In the example described above, where the answers to questions A and D are both negative, any of the solution types could be appropriate, depending on circumstances. Examination of the model shows that the more questions you must address on the decision tree, the more limited are your possible solutions.

Vroom points out that this decision-tree model should not be regarded as the sole basis for decision making. However, the model increases the likelihood of arriving at rational choices by requiring systematic examination of the nature of the problem, the consequences of alternative decisions, and the degree of collaboration necessary to guarantee the best solution.

Having set out the basis of his problem-solving approach, Vroom says that application of the approach will depend on certain predeter-

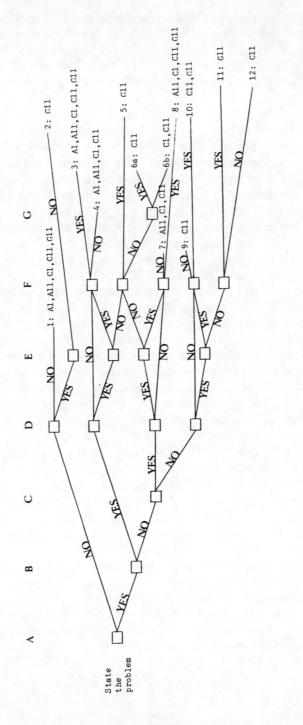

**Fig. 4.11**
**Decision process flowchart (feasible set).**

(Reprinted, by permission of the publisher, from "Can Leaders Learn to Lead?"
Victor Vroom, *Organizational Dynamics*, Winter 1976, p. 19, © 1976 American
Management Association, New York. All rights reserved.

mined criteria. One of these criteria is efficiency, and the major efficiency factor concerns use of time. Vroom's time-efficient *Model A* addresses this factor. Within the framework of the Model A approach, determination of the importance of acting expediently to cope with emergency or crisis situations governs the choices. Scarcity of time generally evokes autocratic solutions. Where time is not regarded as a critical factor, higher levels of group participation can be encouraged on the grounds that the time invested can result in greater commitment on the part of the team members. Committed team members are likely to behave in a more informed and responsible way in future situations. Vroom calls the time investment approach *Model B*. He sees no conflict between Model A and Model B approaches, since they are both designed to achieve optimum results in different kinds of situations.

Vroom does not claim that the models are more than heuristic devices. He says that a mechanistic application of his models or any other models will result in what Argyris calls "espoused theory." The intent is rather to provide leaders with a means of discovering more about themselves and to provide an opportunity to evaluate their own style as it compares with the styles of others. The models also provide an opportunity to evaluate the extent to which sharing of power with subordinates contributes to the quality of decisions made.

In summing up his approach to leadership training, Vroom admits he is not sure that training can bring about permanent changes in leaders. However, he says if leaders can acquire a more accurate picture of how they typically interact with subordinates, they can consequently better enter into dialogues with them. The results of such dialogue can be mutual understanding, mutual trust, and mutual commitment.

## Conclusions

Business and industry's quest for increased productivity and profitability has led many researchers to attempt to answer the question "What motivates employees?" and "What type of leadership offers the best results, taking into account the interests of both employees and the organization?"

While it is generally acknowledged that some workers will always be motivated primarily by money and material rewards, some of the most prominent people in the field such as Herzberg, McGregor, McClelland, and Maslow suggest that material benefits alone will not ensure a motivated employee.

Human resource theorists see work to be more than a means of earning money. Through work, people establish personal identity, self-respect, and a sense of personal value. When the work situation fills more of the worker's personal needs, he contributes more of himself than would be the case with less humanistic approaches. Unlike the human-relations school, human-resource proponents also place equal stress on organization goals. They claim that team members will have a much higher level of commitment to the successful completion of tasks where they have been involved in a democratic decision-making process.

The democratization of the workplace has been a theme around which much of the leadership discussion has revolved. Some theorists see the ideal leader as the personification of one or another of the leadership philosophies. To others, the ideal leader combines the various philosophies in some optimum mix, while yet others see the best leader moving from one philosophical approach to another, according to the dictates of various situations; or alternatively, modifying the situation to suit his own personality.

Whatever the differences between the various theorists, they all seem to subscribe to the idea of democratic organizations, varying only in their opinion of how much organizational democracy is possible or advisable, on the time required to change the organizational culture to accommodate democracy, and on the extent to which culture can be changed.

Communication scholars would say that some of the most significant changes in society have come about as a consequence of advances in communication techniques—the invention of the printing press, the influence of radio, the ubiquity of television in Western societies, and now the new computer technology.

This reasoning leads us to suppose that the introduction of the new electronic information-handling technology into organizations will bring about accompanying changes in organizational structure, demanding new interaction patterns to utilize fully the potential of the technology.

At the same time, the technology offers a means of attacking in a novel and exciting way the motivation problem faced by North American business and industry. Although computer conferencing has been a fact since the 1960s, only in recent years have organizations begun to take this medium of communication seriously. Even with today's growing interest in computer conferencing, organizations most often use the medium as a means of connecting people in different geographical locations and from different disciplines rather than as a means of communicating within an organization.

W. W. Simmons developed an instrument that he named the "Consensor," designed to facilitate decision-making processes within organizations, and several large corporations such as Xerox purchased his innovation; on the whole, however, few efforts have been made to apply such techniques to the internal functioning of organizations.[45]

There is a need to develop a better means of drawing on the human resources of organizations. The potential to involve employees at all levels of the organization in dealing with its most pressing problems not only guarantees an organization access to the full extent of its human resources in its problem-solving endeavors, but also aids the organization in identifying individuals capable of making the most creative contributions. Most important of all perhaps, this method of involvement holds a promise of creating motivated employees. The acceptance that an individual's presence in an organization can and does make a difference is a critical first step in dealing with the motivation problem. In this regard, computer conferencing offers an extremely valuble tool for management.

Other means of engaging employees on a large-scale basis in daily, weekly, or monthly problem-solving activities are not nearly so attractive. Face-to-face interaction has many liabilities, among which are the tendency for some individuals to dominate a discussion; status, age, and sex factors that may influence acceptance of ideas; time restraints; groupthink and social pressures to conform; and the tendency for winning the argument to become more important than finding the best solution. In a face-to-face situation, one frequently feels a need to take a stance, even if all the facts are not available.

The asynchronous nature of computer conferencing allows time for contemplation and fact finding and doesn't encourage hasty advocacy. The potential to exchange private messages encourages compromise (some studies show the number of private messages in a computer conference far exceeds public exchanges). Every person has the same chance to contribute and to have his or her ideas considered, without prejudice. Pseudonyms or code-numbered ideas means that an intelligent perceptive clerk may have his or her ideas evaluated on the same terms as the ideas of a senior corporation officer or a deputy minister in government. This is not to say that responsibility for making choices would shift from the senior administrators; however, the possibility for employees at all levels to contribute at the idea stage to delineating available choices would be greatly enhanced. Fear of ridicule and of rejection of ideas stifles creativity in any problem-solving forum. Computer conferencing presents a unique opportunity to elicit opinions and ideas and to give every person in the organization a chance to contribute. Consensus, which is the essence of the Japanese approach, becomes a possibility.

Studies of both face-to-face problem-solving groups and computer-conferencing groups have identified roles that are played by different individuals. Studies of face-to-face interaction have found that some individuals act in task roles, initiating, seeking information, giving information, elaborating, orienting, integrating, energizing the group. Others adopt maintenance roles—encouraging others, mediating differences, relieving tensions, controlling balance in the participation of others. Still others act in dysfunctional roles—blocking, acting as aggressor, telling irrelevant stories, disrupting with jokes, seeking recognition, or dominating. Such studies have found that some individuals tend to act consistently in moving the discussion forward, on to higher planes of development. Scheidel and Crowell's spiral model was developed to illustrate the process by which group thought progresses in "reach-test" types of motion, with subsequent clarification, substantiation, and verbalized acceptance. (See later chapters for development of these ideas).

Similarly, studies of computer conferencing have found that participants adopt roles. Some persons tend to introduce new ideas, while others are best at developing and refining the ideas; still others act as synthesizers. Studies by Vallee, Johansen, and Spangler have found the "provocative" and "synthesizing" roles to be complimentary.[46] The provoker pushes the discussion forward into new areas of thought, and the synthesizer ties the loose strands together. Identifying the functions that different people in the organization perform best could be valuable to management.

The problems that must be overcome in gaining the cooperation of people at the highest levels of the corporate or governmental structures grow out of management's fear of losing control, of being found wanting themselves, or adhering to a basically elitist philosophy founded in the belief that only those at the highest levels of authority have the knowledge and/or ability to assume decision-making responsibilities. In organizations controlled by these fears or philosophies, the motivated worker will be hard to find.

In the past, it was necessary to overcome the fears of employees at lower levels of the organization, employees faced with a new computerized environment, secretaries and clerks fearful of losing their jobs. Today the challenge to management is to accommodate the potential for positive change inherent in their new automated environments. More studies that encourage use of computers within the organization for creative problem solving would help to open up this area of experimentation within organizations.

As developed in the following chapters, researchers have looked to Japan with its high productivity levels and seemingly model examples of motivated workers for answers to their questions regarding what else is needed in the United States and Canadian systems. It has been suggested that quality circles, where an emphasis is given to shared responsibility and involvement of lower-level workers, account in large part for the high degree of motivation in Japanese workers. Ironically, the quality circle concept originated in North America. Now North Americans go to Japan to study the development of the concept.

Research relevant to the idea of quality circles has come out of the fields of sociology and communication. The study of small-group dynamics and decision making has repeatedly confirmed that although people may accept a decision and agree that the decision is worthy, they will not necessarily commit themselves to making the decision work. Their commitment depends on the degree to which they were involved in the decision-making process.

Management studies on employee resistance to change confirm these same ideas. Out of the acceptance of the importance of employee involvement in change processes came the suggestion box and the ombudsman. Computer conferencing seeks, in the spirit of sociotechnical systems theory, to operationalize systems thinking by examining the total environment and giving the same stress to the technical as to the human aspect of organizations.

## Notes

1. William G. Scott, *Organization Theory: A Behavioral Analysis for Management* (Homewood, Ill.: Richard D. Irwin, 1967); see also William G. Scott, *Organization Concepts and Analysis* (Belmont, Calif.: Dickenson, 1969), pp. 150–51.
2. Daniel A. Wren, *The Evolution of Management Thought,* second ed. (New York: John Wiley, 1979), p. 476.
3. See Wren, *op. cit.,* p. 544, for a discussion of what this term has come to connote; see also Everett M. Rogers and Rekha Agarwala-Rogers, *Communication in Organizations* (New York: Free Press, 1976), pp. 44–45.
4. Daniel Yankelovich, "Yankelovich on Today's Workers: We Need New Motivational Tools," *Industry Week* (August 6, 1979) vol. 202, p. 63.
5. Kenneth A. Kovach, "Why Motivational Theories Don't Work," *S.A.M. Advanced Management Journal* (Spring 1980), pp. 56–57.
6. *Ibid.*
7. Yankelovich, *op. cit.,* p. 63.
8. *Ibid.*

9. *Ibid.*
10. Douglas McGregor, *The Human Side of Enterprise* (New York: McGraw-Hill, 1960), pp. 33–57.
11. *Ibid.*, pp. 33–44.
12. *Ibid.*, pp. 45–57.
13. Abraham Maslow, *Motivation and Personality,* second ed. (New York: Harper and Row, 1954), pp. 80–92.
14. Abraham Maslow, *Eupsychian Management* (Homewood, Ill.: Richard D. Irwin, 1965).
15. Frederick Herzberg, Bernard Mausner, and Barbara Bloch Snyderman, *The Motivation to Work,* second ed. (New York: John Wiley, 1959), pp. 113–15; see also Frederick Herzberg, "One More Time: How Do You Motivate Employees?" *Harvard Business Review* (January–February 1968) vol. 46, pp. 53–62.
16. Herzberg et al., *op. cit.,* pp. 35 and 113–15.
17. Keith Davis, *Human Relations at Work* (New York: McGraw-Hill, 1967), p. 37.
18. David C. McClelland, *The Achieving Society;* see also David C. McClelland, J. W. Atkinson, R. A. Clark, and E. L. Lowell, *The Achievement Motive* (New York: Appleton-Century, 1953); and David C. McClelland, *Motives, Personality, and Society: Selected Papers* (New York: Praeger Special Studies, 1984), pp. 35–51.
19. Chris Argyris, *Personality and Organization* (New York: Harper & Row, 1957), pp. 232–237.
20. Lyman W. Porter and Edward E. Lawler III, *Managerial Attitudes and Performance* (Homewood, Ill.: Richard D. Irwin, 1968).
21. Victor H. Vroom, *Work and Motivation* (New York: John Wiley, Inc., 1964), p. 17.
22. J. Sterling Livingston, "Pygmalion in Management," *Harvard Business Review* (August 1969), pp. 81–89.
23. David E. Berlew and Douglas T. Hall, "Some Determinants of Early Managerial Success," Alfred P. Sloan School of Management Organization Research Program #81–64 (Cambridge, Mass.: The M.I.T. Press, 1964), pp. 13–14; cited in Livingston, *op. cit.,* p. 86.
24. Livingston, *op. cit.,* p. 87.
25. Robert Rosenthal and Lenore Jacobson, *Pygmalion in the Classroom* (New York: Holt, Rinehart, and Winston, 1968), p. vii.
26. Livingston, *op. cit.,* p. 85.
27. *Ibid.*, pp. 85–86.
28. *Ibid.*, p. 86.
29. David E. Berlew and Douglas T. Hall, "The Socialization of Managers: Effects of Expectations on Performance," *Administrative Science Quarterly,* Sept. 1966, pp. 219–22; cited in Livingston, *op. cit.,* p. 86.
30. Warren Bennis, *The Unconscious Conspiracy: Why Leaders Can't Lead* (New York: AMACOM, 1976; see also Warren Bennis, "Leadership—A Beleaguered Species," *Organizational Dynamics* (Summer 1976) vol. 5, pp. 3–16.
31. Melvin Anshen, "The Management of Ideas," *Harvard Business Review* (July–August 1969), pp. 99–107.
32. Abraham Zaleznik, "Managers and Leaders: Are They Different?" *Harvard Business Review* (May–June 1977) vol. 55, pp. 67–78.

33. Fred E. Fiedler, "The Leadership Game: Matching the Man with the Situation," *Organizational Dynamics* (Winter 1976), pp. 6–16; see also Fred E. Fiedler, "The Contingency Model and the Dynamics of the Leadership Process," *Advances in Experimental Social Psychology* (1978) vol. 11, pp. 59–112; Fred E. Fiedler, "Style or Circumstance: The Leadership Enigma," *Psychology Today* (March 1969), pp. 38–43; and Fred E. Fiedler, *A Theory of Leadership Effectiveness* (New York: McGraw-Hill, 1967).

34. Chris Argyris, "The CEO's Behavior: Key to Organizational Development," *Harvard Business Review* (March–April 1973), pp. 54–64.

35. Chris Argyris, "Leadership, Learning, and Changing the 'Status Quo,' " *Organizational Dynamics* (Winter 1976) vol. 4, pp. 29–43.

36. Robert R. Blake and Jane Srygley Mouton, "An Overview of the Grid," *Training and Development Journal* (May 1975) vol. 29, pp. 29–37; see also Robert R. Blake and Jane Srygley Mouton, "A Comparative Analysis of Situationalism and 9.9 Management by Principle," *Organizational Dynamics* (Spring 1982) vol. 10, pp. 20–42.

37. Ralph M. Stogdill, *Methods in the Study of Administrative Leadership* (Columbus, Ohio: Ohio State University, Bureau of Business Research, 1955); see discussion in Paul Hersey and Kenneth H. Blanchard, *Management of Organizational Behavior: Utilizing Human Resources*, second ed. (Englewood Cliffs: Prentice-Hall, 1972), pp. 73–74.

38. Hersey, *op. cit.*, p. 72.

39. Harold J. Leavitt and Jean Lipman-Blumen, "A Case for the Relational Manager," *Organizational Dynamics* (Summer 1980) vol. 9, pp. 27–41.

40. Kurt Lewin, Ronald Lippitt, and Ralph K. White, "Patterns of Aggressive Behavior in Experientially Created 'Social Climates,' " *Journal of Social Psychology* (1939) vol. 10, pp. 271–99. Also see Kurt Lewin, *Resolving Group Conflicts* (New York: Harper and Row, 1948); and Ralph K. White and Ronald Lippitt, *Autocracy and Democracy: An Experimental Inquiry* (New York: Harper and Brothers, 1960).

41. Robert Tannenbaum and Warren H. Schmidt, "How to Choose a Leadership Pattern," *Harvard Business Review* (May–June 1973) vol. 51, pp. 162–80; the original article was published in 1958 in volume 36 of the *Harvard Business Review*, pp. 95–101. The continuum of leadership behavior derives from p. 167 of the original article.

42. Rensis Likert, *New Patterns of Management* (New York: McGraw-Hill, 1961).

43. *Ibid.*

44. Victor H. Vroom, "Can Leaders Learn to Lead?" *Organizational Dynamics* (Winter 1976), pp. 17–28; see also Victor H. Vroom, "A New Look at Managerial Decision-Making," *Organizational Dynamics* (Spring 1973), pp. 66–80; for a comparison of the theories of Vroom, Fiedler, and Argyris, see Lyman W. Porter, "Leadership Symposium: Introduction," *Organizational Dynamics* (Winter 1976), pp. 2–5.

45. W. W. Simmons, "The Consensor: Tool for Decision Makers," *Futurist* (April 1979) vol. 13, pp. 91–94.

46. See later chapter on computer conferencing; see also Robert Johansen, Jacques Vallee, and Kathleen Spangler, *Electronic Meetings: Technical Alternatives and Social Choices* (Reading, Mass.: Addison-Wesley, 1979).

# Part II

# TRANSPLANTING MANAGEMENT THEORIES ABROAD

# 5

# Technology and Culture as Determinants of Management Theory

Geert Hofstedte, a Dutch psychologist and management researcher, administered psychological inventories to 116,000 employees of a multinational corporation based in forty countries around the world. As a result of statistical analysis of this data, Hofstedte identified four dimensions that he then used to describe and differentiate the national cultures of the forty countries. His study took six years to complete.[1]

Hofstedte's population sample included representatives of the wealthy countries of the West and the larger, more prosperous Third World countries. Out of the socialist block, he looked only at Yugoslavia.

His basic premise was that our culture influences us to see the world in a certain unique way. He found the following four dimensions of culture that seemed to vary from country to country:

1. *Power Distance*—the extent to which hierarchical power and structure set people psychologically apart from one another; i.e., those in power should look and act powerful
2. *Uncertainty Avoidance*—the extent to which ambiguity is perceived as threatening and anxiety-arousing; i.e., how much we accept and need rules, bureaucracy, clear delineation of responsibilities
3. *Individualism-Collectivism*—the extent to which individuals or groups are regarded as primary resources for work and problem solving; i.e., the United States vs. the Japanese system
4. *Masculinity-Femininity*—the extent to which those values and behaviors that seem to be stereotypically masculine traits (such as assertiveness, independence, and achievement) are valued in contrast to more stereotypically feminine values and behaviors (such as nurturance and sympathy)

Hofstedte believes that you can consider these four dimensions of national culture as personality characteristics of a country. He rated a country on each of these four dimensions by averaging how employees scored on their responses to questions eliciting these cultural characteristics.

Some examples will illustrate the nature of his findings. Scandinavia scored high on femininity on the *masculine-feminine* dimension. Scandinavian management stresses consensus-based, intuitive decision making and informal personal contacts. This management style is regarded as a more feminine one.

In contrast, the United States scored high on the masculinity dimension, placing much emphasis on fact-based management and fast decisions based on clear delineation of responsibilities. The United States consultant going in to solve a Scandinavian organizational problem would criticize the executive decision-making style as "intuitive" and "consensus-based."

Hofstedte found that the French are most comfortable with large power distances. They don't like to decentralize power. For this reason, management by objectives was never really accepted by the French. Another example of how this affinity for large power distances affects organizational practices can be seen in the example of a United States-based multinational corporation with a worldwide policy that salary increase proposals be initiated by an employee's direct supervisor. The French modified this policy to mean that the *superior's superior's* superior, three levels above, should initiate the salary proposals.

Germans scored high on the need for *uncertainty avoidance,* requiring formal rules, specialization, and assignment of tasks to experts. In this context, it should be no surprise that Max Weber, the father of bureaucratic theory, was a German. Bureaucracy makes possible order even in conditions of change. Power exists in the role, not in the person; and rules protect the lower-ranking organizational members from abuse by higher-ranking members. German managers believe that matrix organizations frustrate this need for clarity in organizational relationships by creating dual and sometimes ambiguous reporting obligations. Responsibility is diffused in the matrix organization.

The United States offers the best example of a country rating high on the *individualism* scale, followed closely by Australia and Great Britain. To nationals of these countries, enlightened self-interest is extremely important. Strong historical and cultural links exist between individualism and capitalism. The U.S. Bill of Rights well exemplifies this focus on the individual, as does Canada's *Charter of Rights and Freedoms*. In collectivist societies, on the other hand, such as Japan and Iran, loyalty is toward the clan, the organization, or society, which in turn assumes responsibility for protecting its members. Japan, which regards "hire and fire" policies as poor ones, stresses lifetime employment and employee loyalty. In the United States *collectivism* is a bad word; in China under Mao, *individualism* was for many years a word with negative connotations, although recent trends indicate that some changes are occurring in the traditional cultural values of that country.

The United States scored slightly below average on cultural value placed on power distance, well below average on uncertainty avoidance, highest out of forty countries on individualism, and well above average on the masculinity dimension. Canada scored close to the United States on all dimensions; and strong similarities between the national cultures of the United States, Ireland, New Zealand, Great Britain, Canada, and sometimes India were manifested, indicating that the English-speaking world may share more in common than just language.

In the light of these results, Hofstedte considers the implication that this research can have for attempts to import and export management theories between national cultures. Specifically, he looks at Maslow's hierarchy of needs; Herzberg's job enrichment theories of motivation; the participative management theories of McGregor, Likert, and Blake and Mouton; and Fiedler's contingency model.

Hofstedte does not regard Maslow's theories to have high universal application. For example, countries scoring high on *uncertainty avoidance* are likely to stress security motivation much more than will low scorers on this dimension. On the other hand, countries scoring high on the *feminine* dimension are likely to stress social relationships over esteem. Yet on Maslow's scale, security needs are on the lower end of the scale, and love and social needs fall below esteem and self-actualization. In all fairness to Maslow, however, he never claimed that his theories were generalizable to other countries.

Herzberg's job-enrichment theories of motivation aim at restructuring individual jobs to give greater satisfaction to the individual. Hofstedte claims this theory reflects the *individualism* and *masculinity* of United States values, and humanization takes the form of encouraging personal goal accomplishment. Collectivist societies, on the other end of the continuum, restructure work into group assignments, forming semiautonomous teams. The Japanese exemplify this style. In societies with more feminine values, the emphasis is on interpersonal relationships with competition deemphasized.

The participative management theories of Likert,[2] Blake and Mouton,[3] and Argyris[4] advocate democratization of the workplace and involvement of employees at all levels in decision making, with managers taking the initiative in instigating participation. Representatives of countries with large power distances would feel uncomfortable with this model, desiring more distance between management and employees; those from lesser power-distance countries may believe that workers, not managers, should be initiating the change processes.

Hofstedte believes that of these leadership theories, Fieldler's proposition best takes into account cultural differences, allowing for cultural adaptation.

David McClelland's earlier studies of achievement needs in different national cultures offer further insights into the results obtained by Hofstedte.[5] McClelland found that countries scored differently on need to achieve. (McClelland points out that the word "achievement" is scarcely translatable into any language other than English.)

The results of these studies lead us to conclude that we must proceed cautiously when we attempt to apply management theories grown in one national culture to another culture with very different values and ethics. Even within one country, adaptation of theories may sometimes be necessary, as when an organization employs large numbers of minority racial or ethnic groups. The dilemma for the organization, according to Hofstedte, is always whether to adapt to a local culture or to try to change it. Where technologies run counter to traditional values, attempts to modify the local culture may be the only answer; in other instances, the organization will need to adapt by training managers for assignments abroad.

Leonard Goodstein wrote a follow-up article to Hofstedte's in which he agreed that significant differences exist between national cultures but said that United States theorists have not been guilty of the cultural imperialism implied by Hofstedte.[6] He said that the people of this country have not been interested in exporting their theories; however, many other countries with high uncertainty avoidance and low masculinity needs have chosen to import theories from the United States. Goodstein concludes that the international presence and success of multinationals such as IBM, Citicorp, Xerox, and Mobil Oil attest that "American management behavior, modified to some greater or lesser degree to meet the demands of the host country culture, is transplantable."[7] He states further that if a country imports United States management the country should expect United States management theory to follow. Nonetheless, he feels that Western management theorists have indeed shown a sensitivity to cultural diversity. The fact that many United States and Canadian organizations now subscribe to Japanese principles of management suggests two-way flow between some of the more developed countries, with adaptations manifested in Theory Z organizations.

Extending Hofstedte's and Goodstein's discussion, we would like to suggest another scenario. John Naisbitt in *Megatrends* as well as numerous other writers suggest that the United States and other Western countries have already left the industrial age behind and entered the information age.[8] Older, more authoritarian management models, appropriate to earlier periods in Western development, may now be inappropriate, as much because of the demands of the information age as because of growing concern for humanitarian principles. On the other hand, newly developing societies face a dilemma because of the disjunction between their stage of industrial development and the international communication systems to which they are becoming increasingly exposed.

Changes in information-flow patterns as a consequence of technological advances in information handling is illustrated by the following models. These show a dramatic shift in information access, from the top-down flow of the pre-mass media traditional society to the simultaneous access afforded by modern information media. (See Figure 5.1)

The *traditional model* is characterised by an essentially dualistic society with an elite separated from the mass of "have-nots" by a small entrepreneurial middle class. The flow is predominantly top-down with limited feedback.

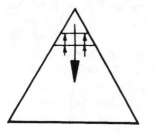

The traditional model is characterized by an essentially dualistic society with an elite separated from the mass of don't-haves by a small entrepreneurial middle class. The flow is predominantly top-down with limited feedback.

INFORMATION FLOW IN TRADITIONAL SOCIETIES

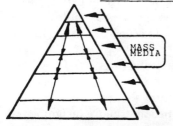

MASS MEDIA

The contemporary social structure is highly diversified and the information flow patterns are such that those at the bottom of the pyramid may access information directly, at the same time or even before those at the top.

INFORMATION FLOW IN MODERN SOCIETIES
(With simultaneous access to mass media)

**Fig. 5.1**
**Traditional and simultaneous access models**

The *contemporary social structure* is highly diversified and the information-flow patterns are such that those at the bottom of the pyramid may access information directly, at the same time or even before those at the top.

Advanced communications potential and the new computer technology demand egalitarianism and information sharing, characteristics of systems and human resource theories, not scientific management or human relations theory. The success of the Japanese in the information age may be the direct result of the natural fit between the management systems they have evolved and the characteristics of current information technology. The people of the United States have been moving toward an acceptance of this match as they modify the shape and style of their organizations to incorporate features of the Japanese model. Other nations are likely to do the same as they join the United States, Canada, and other Western nations in the information age.

Goodstein wonders why so few Europeans or Third World countries have evolved their own management theories. Using this logic, the answer may be clear: There may have been no need, since these nations have typically followed rather than led in technological development. If technology determines the nature and character of a country, as writers such as Jacques Ellul suggest, the early management theories developed by Britain and the United States may well be the most appropriate ones for countries still a stage behind technologically.

Most Third World nations do not presently have the human or economic resources to support research and development in areas of advanced technology. Many still have high levels of illiteracy and the inability to educate large numbers of their population. Without a literate and educated work force, no country can hope to enter the information age. A growing number of these countries are able to compete, however, in the industrial area, offering a cheap labor market and sometimes abundant natural resources. With this industrialization will come literacy and probably many Western values as multinational corporations offer their expertise and financial resources to the underdeveloped countries.

Technological determinism assumes that technology carries with it its own ethic and that this ethic will be more powerful and influential than any cultural value system. If you accept this perspective, Hofstedte's delineation of cultural differences becomes more insignificant, since these values are destined to change over time. Just as the United States embraced Taylorism in the 1920s, human relations in the 1950s, and sensitivity training and MBO in the 1960s, the country will continue to modify its management theories, its institutions, and its value systems. It could be argued, for example, that many Americans discarded the Protestant work ethic as early as the 1960s in favor of quality-of-life considerations. A recent national survey in Canada showed that Canadians value environmental considerations over even jobs. The maxim "Big is better" is being replaced in many aspects of our lives by "Small is beautiful." In the same way, cultural manifestations of power distance, uncertainty avoidance, individualism-collectivism, and masculinity-femininity will change over time.

Eastern and Third World countries demonstrate the same flexibility. After many years of socialism, Mainland China is said to be moving toward capitalism. Japan developed its present management model following World War II. What makes the Japanese model and Theory Z appropriate to both Japan and the United States today is not their cultural similarities but the corresponding stage of development they have both reached in terms of levels of education in their population and level of technological sophistication. These characteristics call for the egalitarianism and stress on communication that must distinguish all information societies. On the other hand, Taylorism and authoritarian leadership styles may be more appropriate in some countries today, regardless of the cultural profile of the country, than are participative management approaches. To those who believe in technological determinism, the academic argument over whether management theories can be transplanted abroad is an inconsequential one in which the wrong questions are being asked and answered.

## Notes

1. Geert Hofstedte, "Motivation, Leadership, and Organization: Do American Theories Apply Abroad?" *Organizational Dynamics* (Summer 1980), vol. 9, pp. 42–53.
2. Rensis Likert, *New Patterns of Management* (New York: McGraw-Hill, 1961).
3. Robert R. Blake and Jane S. Mouton, *The Managerial Grid* (Houston, Texas: Gulf Publishing Co., 1964).
4. Chris Argyris, *Inner Contradictions of Rigorous Research* (New York: Academic, 1980).
5. David McClelland, *The Achieving Society* (New York: Van Nostrand Reinhold, 1961).
6. Leonard D. Goodstein, "Commentary: Do American Theories Apply Abroad?" *Organizational Dynamics,* (Summer 1981), vol. 10, pp. 49–54.
7. *Ibid.,* p. 53.
8. John Naisbitt, *Megatrends* (New York: Warner Books, 1982).

# 6

# The Japanese Management Model: An Example for the United States

Statistics comparing Japanese and United States management systems tell us that relative to the United States, Japanese productivity growth rates are high, absenteeism is low, turnover rates average about half the United States figures, unemployment is low (only 2 percent in 1983), employee commitment to the company is high, and industrial strife is rare.[1]

Contemporary Japanese management and employment systems originated in the post-World War II period. Poor economic conditions and severe labor-management conflict, coupled with the United States occupation, created a need for new human-resources approaches to management. The emergent systems were often based on United States ideas but applied in a manner congruent with traditional Japanese values. Today Japan is a major producer in international markets, and Western countries are looking to the Japanese management model for answers to present problems.

Most Japanese organizations regard human assets as their most valuable resource. Examples of policies that reflect this bias are stress on the *long-term,* on *group membership,* and on *communication.*

## Stress on the Long-Term

Many aspects of the Japanese system reflect this emphasis on the long-term. Lifetime employment for regular employees, seniority-based pay increments, the *zaibatsu* influence, and slow promotion through the ranks exemplify this characteristic of the system.

The Japanese company sees its first responsibility to be providing employment and security for its regular employees.[2] These employees will most often be males, hired directly out of school. This is true for both white- and blue-collar workers. High school graduates comprise the blue-collar work force and university graduates, the white-collar.

124

Because the best companies hire directly from the best schools, competition to enter the preferred programs is intense.

Companies hire on the basis of personality, intelligence, and company "fit" more than on the basis of specific skills, since most firms have their own training programs and expect employees to be generalists, capable of changing jobs frequently. These "school-leaver" men comprise the company "elite," or the "virgin workforce." They receive preferential treatment, not only in terms of hiring practices, but also in terms of training and promotions.[3] This elite group of employees are offered employment security to age 55. Upper-level positions are most often filled from these ranks, and hiring from outside into such positions is extremely rare. It is believed that these school-leaver men will be most easily assimilated into the company. Because this population of employees is expected to remain with the company for life, careful selection is important.

The second-ranked employee group in the Japanese system are the male midcareer entrants, those who worked for one or more firms after graduation before joining their present organization.[4] Included in this group are both blue- and white-collar workers. These midcareer men will be less sought after, receive less training after hiring, and will be promoted more slowly (if at all) than the school leavers. They are viewed as "rejects" from other firms, even if the choice to leave was their own. Because the Japanese system is seniority-based, they will receive lower pay even if they do work similar to that done by the school leavers. Although not guaranteed job security to age 55, this group will be the last to be laid off or fired.

Women, both blue- and white-collar, comprise the third group of regular employees. While receiving the same starting wage as men, they earn less over time because they are rarely promoted and generally have fewer years of service than do male employees. They also receive fewer benefits, not generally being eligible for company housing. Women are expected to join a firm upon graduation, to work for a few years, and then to marry and leave the company.[5]

The above three categories of employees are all regarded as "regular" employees, to be protected as much as possible from layoffs and termination.

Next in the Japanese system come the "temporary" employees, men or women hired for a set term, usually six months to a year. At the company's option, their contracts may be renewed. Temporaries often work for a company for many years.

The lowest-ranked employees of any firm are the day laborers, renewed on a day-to-day basis, but often employed for many years by the same firm. Obviously, the privileges enjoyed by these last two groups are much less than privileges granted to the regular employees. If the company experiences financial difficulty, the day laborers and temporary workers are the first to be discharged.

The pay of these two groups is based on what they do, not on seniority; and they do not qualify for training, supplementary benefits, retirement bonuses, or other social extras. They have been termed the "dismissable slack" of Japan's labor force, second-class citizens most often represented by women, blacks, the unskilled, and the disadvantaged.[6]

Rodney Clark described a typical Japanese firm of 1200 as employing 500 male school leavers, 300 midcareer men, 100 women, and 300 temporary and day workers. Midcareer men tend more often to be present in small firms; the more prestigious large firms employ more male school leavers.[7]

Japanese managers believe that job security contributes to high morale and productivity, low turnover and training expenses, and increased cohesiveness. Consequently, they try to protect their regular employees as much as possible. Faced with economic difficulties or a recession, the Japanese will employ all other means of coping before considering layoffs or terminations. For example, they may institute across-the-board wage cuts that affect not only employees, but also management. They may cut dividends, reduce investment in equipment, borrow money, or put pressure on suppliers for better terms. They may shift employees from their regular positions to other areas of higher demand. Typically, they will retrain or transfer poor performers, rather than terminate them, trying to find an organizational fit for every employee, even in the most difficult of circumstances.[8]

Slow promotion practices characterize the Japanese system; however, informal assessments of an employee's abilities at an early stage in his career may result in more select job assignments. Some jobs are more critical than others to the organization, and experience in these positions allows the acquisition of skills important to future promotions. Also, small salary differentials may alert an employee to his unofficial ranking in the organization.[9]

Some critics argue that deferred promotions discourage the most promising and ambitious of employees, but others disagree. The personnel director of one Japanese firm commented: "The secret of Japanese management, if there is any, is to make everybody feel as long as possible that he is slated for the top position in the firm— thereby increasing his motivation during the most productive period of his employment."[10] Such practices are based on the premise that "the increased output of the losers, who are striving hard to do well and still hoping to beat the odds, more than compensates for any lags in the motivation of the impatient winners."[11]

In contrast to the United States system, which attempts to identify and reward early the most promising organizational members, the Japanese system claims to place more emphasis on the morale of the much larger numbers of people who will never reach the top, but who nonetheless help tosustain and move the organization toward fulfillment of its goals.

A complex appraisal system attempts to measure both individual and group performance, including technical competence, leadership skills, and judgment. The system also attempts to assess social and personality factors such as creativity, emotional maturity, and cooperative behavior. Bottom-line performance is not the sole, or even the most important, factor in job appraisals. Attitude and behavior are considered equally important. Occasional mistakes are accepted and tolerated as part of the learning process.[12]

Such criteria encourage employees to engage in easily observable behavior such as voluntary overtime or helping colleagues who are experiencing difficulties with a problem.[13] Frequent, regular evaluations enable focusing on means as well as ends. In such appraisals, employees are ranked in comparison with other members of an appropriate group, taking age and status into consideration. Comparative rankings are not, however, made known to the employees.

Assuming that the early rankings employees receive do not decide their future in the organization, one could argue that the slow promotion system practised in the Japanese firm allows the time necessary for careful judgments to be made.

As already stated, the Japanese incentive system is seniority-based; it is also need-centered. For example, an older janitor will make more than a young engineer. The assumption is that the man's productivity will have increased as a consequence of his years with the firm, and his needs will be greater as he grows older.

In Japan, status derives from factors over which one has little or no control, such as age, sex, and group size and power. These factors determine hierarchical relationships in Japanese firms. The Japanese see all individuals as superior to, subordinate to, or occasionally equal to each other:

> Hierarchy is established on the basis of age (older is superior), sex (male is superior), organizational status (higher rank is superior), and organizational power and size (large, more powerful organizations are supe-

rior). Only when all these attributes are identical are the individuals on an equal plane. The concept of hierarchy pervades every aspect of the culture—even the language (it is impossible to speak with another person without recognizing their hierarchical position over, or under, one).[14]

Since age, rank, and organization size increase with time, status, like other benefits of the Japanese system, grows with longevity.

Another group of employees indirectly dependent on the larger firms are those working for subcontracting or satellite firms.[15] In Japan, small firms often ally themselves with a major parent firm, performing specialized services such as fabrication of small parts, maintenance, or shipping. Reliance on the small firms for such services allows the parent firms to limit the number of regular staff employed and to restrict its superior wage-and-benefit packages to its elite employees. The smaller firms benefit from such arrangements so long as the parent firm does well; but in difficult economic times, the amount of work contracted out may be less than at other times. These alliances, as well as the ability to expand and contract their work force, make it possible for larger firms to guarantee lifetime employment to the limited number of workers comprising its regular workforce. This guarantee of employment exists, in many ways, at the expense of the temporaries, day workers, and employees of satellite firms.

It is said, however, that the parent firms attempt to sustain these satellite firms, even under worsened economic conditions, to the extent that the survival of the allied firms is not threatened.[16] Sometimes the larger firms transfer employees to the subcontractor, and many hold shares and board positions with the smaller companies. A large firm may have commitments to many smaller firms, and some of these firms in turn have their own subcontracting companies that perform still more specialized services.

The term *zaibatsu* refers to coalitions of several large firms tied to each other by interlocking directorates. An example would be an alliance of a major bank, a major manufacturing firm, a major export company, and a major chemicals corporation. Each of these firms would purchase shares in the other firms and give preferred status to these corporations in purchasing and sales.[17]

Thus, the major Japanese firms are largely controlled by other firms such as banks and insurance companies, who are at the same time the corporations' creditors. Considered in conjunction with the stress on debt financing and market size and share rather than on profits, this system removes the pressure to think in the short-term and to respond to short-lived fluctuations in the financial market. This long-term perspective is passed on in benefits to the regular employee, both in the form of lifetime employment, in time and money spent on intensive training programs, and in a toleration for the employee who makes mistakes as he or she is learning to assume a place in the corporation or acquiring new skills through job rotation. In this environment, short-term losses will not necessitate layoffs or terminations, as might be the case in the United States or Canada.[18] In the West, reward systems and performance-monitoring focuses on and reinforces the short-term. Yoshiya Ariyoshi, chairman of Japan's largest shipping firm, once said, "American managers are judged by their stockholders on the basis of how big a profit they turned in the last quarter and what they can be expected to turn in the next quarter."[19]

### Stress on Group Membership

Every Japanese organization adheres to a philosophy articulated by management and internalized by all organizational members. The Japanese believe that integration of employees into a company is not possible unless the employees know and accept the philosophy and goals of the organization. Management believes that familiarity with company goals will help direct an employee's actions, place constraints on his or her behavior, and make the employee more motivated and productive. Most Japanese philosophies place a strong emphasis on teamwork, group membership, and cooperation, stressing the uniqueness of the firm and its existence as a corporate family. In many corporations, Japanese employees begin their day by repeating in unison a pledge of loyalty to the firm and singing a company song.[20]

First and foremost the Japanese regard themselves as members of a group. When the Japanese introduce themselves, they will often give not only their own name, but also the name of the firm employing them. The employee is "section manager X in department Y in company Z." At the Marysville, United States of America, Honda plant, every associate including President Irimajiri wears a white smock bearing the "Honda of America" name and the employee's first name.[21] The Japanese see the groups in which they hold membership as interrelated and interdependent. They value harmonic coexistence and avoid conflict-ridden independence. When an individual holds membership in more than one group at the same time, he ranks his priorities in order to avoid conflict. Typically a man places company over family, and a woman, family over company.

Many of the Japanese practices are geared toward integrating the individual into the group. Job rotation allows the regular employee to make lateral moves that acquaint the person with functions and people throughout the organization. These career moves, often planned well in advance, give both white- and blue-collar workers many valuable learning experiences, and also help the employees to better understand and feel a part of company goals and operations. Job rotation encourages flexibility and creates generalists rather than specialists. The individual develops loyalty to the organization rather than to particular departments. These interdepartmental transfers promote the development of informal communication networks useful in cooperative problem solving and help to alleviate boredom.

The job selection process itself favors those with moderate views and a harmonious personality, facilitating socialization into the organization. Japanese organizations look for individuals willing to endorse their values. They believe that a homogenous population can more easily cultivate the friendship networks important to information transfer and cohesiveness of purpose.[22]

Extensive benefit packages available to regular organizational members and their families encourage identification with the company. These benefit options include subsidized housing, company nurseries, educational scholarships for family members, savings plans, medical insurance, sponsored loan programs, and cafeteria privileges. For the average employee, more than 50 percent of his monthly pay can come from special family and age allowances and pay for good attendance.[23]

Firms often sponsor cultural, athletic, and other recreational activities, in which the employees are encouraged to participate. They sponsor softball teams, office parties, company picnics, and overnight trips. To the Japanese, individual skills are only important if they contribute to group success; so membership on a sports team, for example, gives the talented individual a chance to gain recognition for his skills. The office party and the company picnic give him a chance to become integrated into the company. Frequent letters sent out by management to family members accomplish this same end, encouraging affiliation with the purposes and goals of the organization by fostering group membership and identity.

### Stress on communication

The Japanese system stresses open and frequent communication, "bottom-up" decision making, and group autonomy. Failing to rely on outside experts for problem solving encourages group autonomy. In many Japanese firms, group-based quality control circles deal with day-to-day problems encountered by individual members. For example, at Honda's Marysville, United States of America plant, department managers meet each day at 8:00 A.M. These meetings are chaired by a different manager each day, and the agenda ranges from quality control, repair, assembly, and welding, to the plant expansion plans. Managers outline any problems experienced and tell how they solved them. Group members call on outside experts only when they require specialized technical services or training in problem-solving techniques.[24] Informal lateral networks that cross department boundaries allow the exchange of much job-related information.

Even in Japanese-owned U.S. companies, plant managers spend a minimum of two hours a day in the shop and make themselves readily available at other times. Personnel managers likewise spend two to four hours each day on the floor with the workers, discussing issues and meeting the company's employees on their own territory.[25] Much stress is placed on face-to-face communication. Even high-ranking company executives rarely have private offices but share open work spaces with individuals at different hierarchical levels. In one Japanese-owned television company located in the United States, the top manager has an office adjacent to the receptionist at the entry to the building; he is open and visible to anyone who comes into the building, whether employee, customer, or business associate.[26]

The Japanese evaluate organization members on their communication and interpersonal skills. Decision making in a Japanese context is consultative, with proposals often originating at lower- or middle-management level, and after informal discussion with peers and supervisors, moving up the organization. The "ringi" process, whereby employees affix their seals of approval to a symbolic document, legitimizes decisions by documenting consensus on issues. The document implies unanimous consent, if not unanimous approval of decisions.

Negotiations are primarily lateral between departments concerned with any particular decision, and those outside the main decision-making group simply acknowledge the chosen course of action. Nina Hatvany and Vladimir Pucik explained the rationale behind this very formalized and sometimes ritualistic decision-making process that characterizes the Japanese system:

> Those outside the core of the decision making group . . . do not participate; they do not feel ownership of the decision. On the other hand, the early communication of the proposed changes helps reduce uncertainty in the organization. In addition, prior information on the upcoming decisions gives employees an opportunity to rationalize and accept the outcomes.[27]

Managers generally wait to implement decisions until those outside the decision-making caucus have had the opportunity to express their views, believe that they have been heard, and have indicated willingness to support the decision, even if they personally would not have made the same choice. It is said that the Japanese prefer to agree on a general direction to follow and to leave the details to be worked out later.

Stephen Marsland and Michael Beer discuss this bottom-up decision-making process as an illustration of the division of labor between management levels.[28] Once a problem has been identified by the organization, low-level managers in the related area assume responsibility for developing and implementing a solution or plan to cope with the identified need. They have the time to assume this responsibility because they are not responsible for evaluating or developing their immediate subordinates. This latter task falls to middle managers, who must review all subordinate plans and attempts at implementation, along with reviewing training and development needs of all beneath them. The duty of the top managers is to maintain consensus within the firm, develop company policies, and maintain good public relations. These individuals review decisions made at lower levels of the organization but do not directly concern themselves with company operation. Marsland and Beer note the positive aspects of this system:

> This pattern of delegation tends to encourage decision making at the lowest level consistent with available information and knowledge—a pattern too seldom found in American firms. Japanese management systems are, therefore, information intensive; rely on people at all levels to take responsibility for the firm's goals; and require teamwork. To gain superior information flow, a network of relationships and contacts is built up over time—thus the need for managers to remain with the firm for a long time to build those information networks and thus the need for permanent employment. To allow bottom-up decision making, lower-level managers and blue-collar workers alike must be experienced in their jobs and in the organization's ways—another argument for long tenure and slow promotion. Moreover, a heavy investment in selection, training, and development—which extends to blue-collar workers as well as white-collar staff—further develops the competencies required in bottom-up decision making. Teamwork among managers and implementation of bottom-up plans is enhanced by a spirit of cooperation and commitment to the firm—thus lifetime employment, company housing, company vacations, company cafeteria, and company-sponsored club activities. These create a "closed society" that reinforces cooperation within management and labor.[29]

All of these factors influence how the Japanese interact with one another. The following excerpt from Ke-Lu Chao and William I.

Gorden, "Culture and Communication in the Modern Japanese Corporate Organization," expands on some of the communication practices within Japanese organizations.[30]

## Communication Tends to be Vague

Japanese tend to express themselves ambiguously. They hesitate when they have to say "no," and they may say "yes" but mean "no." The Japanese language structure is conducive to ambiguity. Their verbs come at the end of sentences and therefore, one is not able to understand what is being said until the whole sentence is uttered. In addition, the Japanese language is quite loose in logical connection. One can talk for hours without reaching the point. Akira Suzuki, a leading scholar, considers the ambiguity of his country's language as a manifestation of the need to get along with one another. Even in ordinary conversation, Japanese will say *"Ah so, des ne,"* or *"Honto des yo,"* (gratifying response) whereas an American conversation might be more apt to include "No, I don't think so." Intuitive understanding or *haragei,* which can be translated as "belly art or abdominal performance" is more important because, as many Japanese proverbs remind one, verbal language is not worthy of trust and in fact is even a dangerous thing. The need for maintenance of harmony and avoidance of conflict carry over into the Japanese business organization, and therefore, Japanese communication practices tend to be vague and general. Half our sources report this phenomenon.

## Communication Emphasizes Harmony

The emphasis within the organization is often upon the ability of the individual to work cooperatively with his group, rather than upon one's ability to lead or to work as an individual. The concern for group harmony frequently is evident in company mottos. For example, the Hitachi Corporation motto reads: "The spirit of harmony is one which has always been most highly valued in our firm."[31]

In Japan, relationships are very important. Therefore, there is much attention to gift-giving and to politeness. The sense of public consciousness, however, is not so strong. One's responsibility is quite weak to those whom one does not know. For example, a person probably will say *"Sumimasen"* (Excuse me) upon stepping upon the foot of a stranger on a train, but if it is the foot of a friend or an acquaintance, he definitely will say *"Sumimasen."* The cultural concern for harmony in one's relationships, of course, carries over into an individual's behavior within his work organization. Seven of the ten sources report the high value Japanese place upon harmony.

Perhaps the tendency of Japanese to speak with very little gesticulation, and a general sobriety, (not to be confused with restraint when it comes to consumption of alcoholic beverages, for heavy drinking is common) and the value of hard work, order, security, training and good manner, all coalesce into a unique concern of this culture for secure and harmonious relationships.

### Ritualistic Communication is Important

The Japanese love for ritual may be observed within the Japanese business organization. The Matsushita Electric Company, for example, begins its working day with a hymn to country and company. All the employees assemble to sing:

> For the building of a new Japan
> Let's put our strength and mind together.
> Doing our best to promote production,
> Sending our goods to the people of the world,
> Endlessly and continuously,
> Like water gushing from a fountain,
> Grow, industry, grow, grow, grow!
> Matsushita Electric![32]

At Toyota and many other companies, the day opens with five minutes of supervised calisthenics. Half of our sources report on group rituals such as company motto, song, and physical exercise.

### The Japanese Businessman Primarily Depends Upon Face-to-Face Communication

When communicating with the business organization, one is expected to start with face-to-face discussion. Not to do so is to show disrespect. According to Kosuke Miyoshi, a letter is rather sort of a record or conclusion.[33] If one sends a letter to a company, he most probably will not get an answer, but after talking face-to-face, a letter serves as a record or confirmation. The contrary is true in the United States. Only one of our sources, however, mentions this practice as still true in today's Japanese business organization.

### The Japanese Firm Utilizes Open-Space Offices

In the traditional Japanese home, a large single room serves multiple functions. At night, it is the bedroom, at one time in the day, it is the dining room, and yet another time the living room. This sense of open-space, likewise, is characteristic of Japanese aesthetics expressed in the business organization.

A typical Japanese office is located in a large open area filled with desks and tables. There are only a few private offices for senior executives. In the open-space office, the middle manager usually sits at the head of a long table with his work team seated around it. Each manager thus can easily turn to another manager and discuss a common problem. Consequently, individual conferences in a very real sense are open for others to hear. As one might expect, the open-space office arrangement facilitates calling small group conferences. Individual secrecy and the grapevine are minimized and internal communication is facilitated. One of our sources reports on the Japanese open-space office setting.

## Communication is Group-Oriented

The Japanese are racially homogeneous and they are extremely group oriented. The anthropologist Ruth Benedict stressed the Japanese denial of individualism in favor of collectivity orientation.[34] Similarly, Fukutake indicates that group membership is considerably more important to the Japanese than to citizens of the United States.[35] In an empirical study of Japanese values, Caudill and Scarr reported strong collectivity orientation in Japan.[36] It is not unusual, for example, for large numbers of newlyweds to enjoy a *group* honeymoon trip, and when Japanese businessmen travel, they most frequently travel in small delegations.[37] Japanese culture lays great stress upon acting properly. The "shame" of the group and "losing face" in the eyes of others holds great control over one's behavior. Consequently, the words "I" and "you" tend to be missing in daily conversation. Group centeredness carries over into the Japanese organization.

Japanese workers wear their firm's uniform. They appear to have less autonomy in the work situation. In a survey which asked whether an employee should work at his own pace, 78 per cent of a British Engineering sample, as compared to only 25 per cent of the employees at the Hitachi Corporation, said that they preferred to work at their own pace.[38] Japanese employees often cheer each other when changing shifts, like baseball players applauding a team-mate who has just hit a home run.[39] This is yet another instance of the Japanese unique emphasis on the group. One very able executive described the traditional organization in Japan as "Management by Omikoshi."[40] The *omikoshi* is the portable shrine carried on the shoulders of perhaps a dozen men. The fun of it is to carry the shrine, shout *"washoi, washoi"* in unison, and add one's weight to the weight of the other pole carriers. All ten of our sources report the group-oriented character of the Japanese.

## Leadership and Responsibility are Diffused

Since in Japanese business a task is performed by a group rather than by individuals, responsibility is not located in any one person. The responsibilities of each organizational unit also are defined only in very general and broad terms. Job descriptions are vague. The organizational chart is drawn in terms of divisions rather than departmental heads. For example, "The export department shall take charge of exportation and necessary investigations and negotiations."[41]

There is a tendency to reduce the role of a top manager to a figurative one, even to an ornamental role *(kazarimono)*. Very often, the top executive has grown up with a group, knows its members and has a talent for keeping communication flowing. A manager's primary responsibility in the company is to create a proper atmosphere and to maintain harmonious interpersonal relationships. Because there is no clear-cut delineation of individual authority and function, a Japanese leader's power is relatively uncertain and tacit. All ten studies report this characteristic.

## Decision-making Practices are Consensual

*Ringi* is composed of two parts: *rin* means that subordinates submit a proposal to their peers and request their input and approval; *gi* means deliberation and discussion. A proposal is usually initiated by a lower-level employee when confronted with a problem common in the conduct of day-to-day business. The document drafted is known as a *ringisho*. The *ringisho* states the problem and a suggestion for its solution with reasons for accepting it. The formal *ringisho* must be passed around various divisions and departments to all concerned. Each person receiving the paper places his name-seal on the document as evidence that he has seen and approved it, or he may add a modification. If he disapproves, he will return the document to the initiator for revision of the proposal. After a revision, the initiator may again circulate the document on the same route up through different levels of management to top management, eventually reaching the president. If the president stamps his seal, the *ringisho* is returned to the originator for implementation.

The larger the organization, the more complicated is the decision process because it involves reviewing proposals from dozens of people whose major concerns naturally are their own and those of their division. When a decision to be made is of major importance, the initiator first will consult informally with the parties involved rather than only circulating a formally prepared proposal.[42] In this manner, the initiator will minimize the possible disagreement and conflict which might occur when his document is circulating. The top executive seldom will disapprove the *ringisho* because the lower-level initiator intuitively will have considered the top executive's viewpoint before writing the formal document.

*Ringi* is consistent with Japanese culture. The system has definite advantages. Proposals are initiated by those closest to a problem or an area which needs attention. Thus, *ringi* offers lower-level employees a chance to demonstrate their capabilities and also make fresh inputs into a highly-structured and hierarchical organization. Furthermore, by circulating the proposal *(ringisho),* all those concerned in the firm will become informed, and acquire ownership in the decision-making.

Opponents of the *ringi* mode of decision-making argue that it is too slow for today's rapidly changing technology and markets. They also contend that a lower-level employee lacks a company-wide perspective. He tends to see things in short-range rather than long-range terms. Under *ringi,* authority is diffuse and responsibility ill-defined. Giving one's seal of approval to proposals piled high may become perfunctorily bureaucratic rather than a matter of critical evaluation. Finally, because the system depends upon middle and lower level managers to generate proposals, top managers tend to be followers rather than movers and shapers.

In a few Japanese business organizations, efforts are underway to revise or even to eliminate the consensual system. In them, the *ringi* format has been simplified by reducing the number of individuals who must examine a proposal. Instead of circulating a proposal, companies have the *ringishos* brought to executive meetings. In others, the *ringishos* may be submitted directly to top management in urgent cases. Furthermore, delegation of authority is becoming more common. Although somewhat reformed, the system of *ringi* continues to be in the mainstream of decision-making in today's Japanese organization. Almost all recent studies cited the current use of *ringi*, and seven of these mention modern modifications.

Consensual decision-making also is the norm within a meeting of managers. In a meeting, the Japanese use a method of reaching agreement called *matomari*, or adjustment.[43] Preliminary to discussion, a senior member usually makes an opening statement dealing with factual information pertaining to the issue. A statement may provide hints of a manager's preference, but it does not commit him to a specific idea or course of action. Gradually, the members begin to sense the direction of the group and adjust their own views accordingly. Most commonly, they have worked together long enough to know what are the others' attitudes toward a certain issue. Thus, it is relatively easy to limit the conflict and reach a consensus, if not unanimity. If an argument does emerge, the leader usually suggests a follow-up meeting, or one of the more prestigious members may try to reconcile the two sides. Occasionally, one of the middle or lower status members tries for some sort of comic relief.[44] Together they will work toward a compromise which takes into consideration the desire and feelings of both the majority and minority. However, until approximately 70 per cent of the members are in agreement, minority members may support their own points of view.

The real power is in the hands of the men of influence. There is an "old boy network" in Japanese business. They tend to stay behind the scenes. Informally, they share important information. Usually, before a meeting is held they have reached a decision and a meeting proceeds exactly as was informally planned.

The Japanese economy is directed toward a national goal, and almost everyone feels a sense of participation in it. This may be traceable to the historic and geographic fact that scratching out a living on those mountainous, typhoon-prone islands has been tough and requires a consensual commitment. There is a norm akin to the Protestant ethic. Subordinates greet superiors with *o-iso-gashii-desho,* which translates "You must be in an honorably busy state of affairs."[45] There is a spirit of cartel in spite of the fact that under U.S. occupation the cartels of Mitsui, Mitsubishi and Sumitomo were broken up. In the seventies, however, the presidents of the 27 Mitsubishi companies meet on Friday every month to plan a common strategy. The 17 Mitsui presidents meet once a month on Thursday and the 17 Sumitomo presidents one Monday per month. The big borrowers have a council, and unusually large bank debts in Western terms are permitted these firms. Engineers from competing firms swap technological ideas.[46] There is a club atmosphere and a consensus building practice which helps the Japanese nation function as one giant corporation.

In summary, Japanese organizations place a stress on the long-term, on integrating employees into the organization and fostering cooperative behaviors, and on communication and participatory decision making.[47] Typical United States organizations, on the other hand, stress short-term orientation, reward people for competitive rather than cooperative behaviors, and encourage personal rather than group responsibility for decision making.

### Notes

1. Stephen Marsland and Michael Beer, "The Evolution of Japanese Management: Lessons for U.S. Managers," *Organizational Dynamics* (Winter 1983), vol. 11, pp. 49–67.
2. *Ibid.*, p. 55.
3. *Ibid.*, p. 58.
4. *Ibid.*
5. *Ibid.*, pp. 60–61.
6. William D. Torrence, "Blending East and West: With Difficulties Along the Way," *Organizational Dynamics* (Autumn 1984), vol. 13, p. 25.
7. Cited in Marsland and Beer, *op. cit.*, p. 59.
8. Nina Hatvany and Vladimir Pucik, "Japanese Management Practices and Productivity," *Organizational Dynamics* (Spring 1981), vol. 9, pp. 9–10; see also Torrence, *op. cit.*, pp. 23–24, for an example of such a philosophy operationalized in North America.
9. *Ibid.*, pp. 12–13.
10. *Ibid.*, p. 13.
11. *Ibid.*
12. *Ibid.*, pp. 13–14.
13. *Ibid.*, p. 14.
14. Marsland and Beer, *op. cit.*, p. 54.
15. *Ibid.*, pp. 56–57.
16. *Ibid.*, p. 57.
17. *Ibid.*
18. *Ibid.*
19. Richard S. DeFrank, Michael T. Matteson, David M. Schweiger, and John M. Ivanevich, "The Impact of Culture on the Management Practices of American and Japanese CEOs," *Organizational Dynamics* (Spring 1985), vol. 13, p. 64.
20. Lawrence E. Kostoff, *A Yen for Harmony: Japanese Managers Try Their Style in North America* (videorecording) (Toronto, Ont.: Ontario Educational Communications Authority, 1979).

21. Christopher Waddell, "The Drive to Catch Japan," *Globe and Mail Report on Business Magazine,* (November 1985), p. 32.
22. Hatvany and Pucik, *op. cit.,* p. 12. See also DeFrank et al., *op. cit.,* pp. 63–64.
23. *Ibid.,* p. 18.
24. Waddell, *op. cit.,* p. 32.
25. Hatvany and Pucik, *op. cit.,* p. 16.
26. *Ibid.*
27. *Ibid.,* p. 17.
28. Marsland and Beer, *op. cit.,* pp. 52–53.
29. *Ibid.,* p. 53.
30. Ke-Lu Chao and William I. Gorden, "Culture and Communication in the Modern Japanese Corporate Organization," *International and Intercultural Communication Annual* (1979), vol. 5, pp. 27–33.
31. Ronald Dore, *British Factory-Japanese Factory, The Origins of National Diversity in Industrial Relations,* (Berkeley and Los Angeles: University of California Press, 1973), p. 51.
32. T.F.M. Adams and N. Kobayashi, *The World of Japanese Business,* (Tokyo: Kodansha International Ltd., 1969), p. 92.
33. William Bowen, "Japanese Managers Tell How Their System Works," *Fortune,* (November 1977), p. 128.
34. Ruth Benedict, *The Chrysanthemum and the Sword,* (Boston: Houghton Mifflin, 1946).
35. T. Fukutake, *Man and Society in Japan,* (Tokyo: University of Tokyo Press, 1962).
36. William Caudill and H.A. Scarr, "Japanese Value Orientations and Culture Change," *Ethnology,* (1962), Vol. 1 pp. 53–59.
37. John Condon and Keisuke Kurata, *In Search of What's Japanese about Japan,* (Tokyo: Shufunotomo Company Ltd., 1974), p. 89.
38. Dore, p. 231.
39. *Time,* "Japan, Inc.: Winning the Most Important Battle," (10 May 1971), p. 87.
40. Miller, p. 66.
41. Yoshino, p. 203.
42. Yoshino, p. 255.
43. Boye De Mente, *How to do Business in Japan: A Guide for International Businessmen,* (Los Angeles: Center for International Business, 1972), p. 21.
44. Sethi, p. 98.
45. *Time,* pp. 86–87.
46. *Time,* pp. 86–88.
47. See also Randy Y. Hirokawa, "Improving Intra-Organizational Communication: A Lesson from Japanese Management," *Communication Quarterly* (Winter 1981), vol. 30, pp. 35–40.

# 7

# Japanese Mutations: Theory Z and QWL Organizations

Both Theory Z and QWL illustrate shifts in North American management theory that bring the countries' organizations a stage closer to the Japanese model.

## Theory Z

In the process of studying Japanese and United States organizations, William Ouchi, a University of California at Los Angeles management scholar, saw that each country had developed its own unique approach to management. He also saw, however, that a hybrid organization had evolved, one that combined both Japanese and United States characteristics. Ouchi labeled these hybrid organizations "Theory Z" organizations.[1]

Examples of firms that he found to manifest these characteristics were IBM, Intel, Hewlett-Packard, Eastman Kodak, and Eli Lilly. These firms also rank among the most consistently successful United States corporations. Long before Americans began to look to the Japanese for management models, organizations such as Eli Lilly evolved their own company philosophies that blended effectively the best of the two systems.[2] Ouchi suggests that Eli Lilly represents a different kind of organization, distinct both in structure and process. The company is not simply "well managed," or more than usually devoted to good human relations practices, but is a unique organization type. In the following passage, Ouchi argues that there is a clear need for more Western firms to follow Eli Lilly and IBM in adopting a new organizational paradigm:

> Our Western management paradigm argues that we should maximize plant size, but the Japanese attempt to minimize plant size, expecting always that new production technologies will call for changes in plant design; we believe that organizational efficiency is maximized when individuals specialize their careers and pursue those careers by moving

from one firm to another, yet the Japanese pursue their careers across a single firm; we believe that automation should be undertaken for the purpose of increasing productivity while the Japanese believe that automation should be undertaken only when the task is so fine and requires tolerances so close that human hands cannot reliably produce high quality. We believe that if we hew to our normal paradigm, then productivity and efficiency will be maximized. Yet we observe that productivity increases each year at a lower and lower rate, and recent years have shown a net decline in productivity of the American economy. A reasonable observer can hardly conclude that our organizational paradigm is adequate.[3]

Ouchi observes that the high rates of mobility and turnover in American firms mean that we have organizations composed of strangers, aggregations of specialists who do not understand each other's language. He says that strangers cannot be subtle with each other; they are "reduced to those forms of agreement, of measurement, and of control that are so contractual, so straightforward, and so simple, that any stranger can instantly understand them."[4] In this process, however, we remove all that is capable of subtlety, the complex, or the long-term.

The existence of organizations composed of strangers creates other problems also, according to Ouchi. Typical American bureaucracies, characterized by high rates of turnover, offer no guarantees that if rewards are not received immediately, they will ever be received. In the same way, in organizations composed of specialists, no one is ever sure what the person in the next office, let alone the next department, is doing; and consequently, employees cannot feel confident that rewards are being equitably distributed in the organization.

On the other hand, in a Type Z organization, people are willing to make short-term sacrifices because they know that most parties will be around for the long run and that offsetting adjustments will eventually be made and credit will be given. In other words, in the long run, equity will be restored. As a generalist who operates in many capacities over the years, an organization member is able to assess the contributions of people throughout the organization and to judge the fairness of the reward system. Ouchi summarized these points in the following way:

> Over a period of years . . . it will become evident which members of a team contribute the greatest value, and which contribute the least. If team members know that all of them will be there in the long run, an equitable outcome is assured. In addition, there is little incentive to goldbrick or to cheat under these conditions, since such "free riding" will be discovered and punished with equal certainty in the long run.[5]

Familiarity on its own, however, is not sufficient to yield better coordination or higher productivity. The development of a unique philosophy of management, as typified by every Type Z organization, is also necessary. Where no such philosophy, or common understanding of organizational goals and acceptable methods of management exists, you can only justify making decisions on the basis of financial considerations. Only by explicitly stating a philosophy of management can you legitimize considering more subtle, complex, and long-run concerns.

For such a philosophy to be interpreted the same by all employees, the organization should have long-term employment, promote slowly so that managers can learn and internalize this philosophy, develop an appraisal system sufficiently complex to reflect the complexity of the philosophy, and encourage job rotation so that organization members get a sense of total organization purpose and contribute a point of view "to complete the common understanding."[6]

Ouchi says that if it is true that the progress of industry leads to transactions of an increasingly complex and ambiguous nature, it may be necessary to change our organizational paradigm. Instead of stressing expertise and specialization, perhaps we should be stressing instead coordination and integration.

Ouchi says that organizations governed by a philosophy are not capable of tight control. Type Z organizations have weak monitoring capacities and must rely on employees internalizing and acting on the organizational philosophy. Employees bring a larger cultural value system with them to the organization; and since changing this value system is rarely feasible, Type Z organizations generally tend to manifest the values of the larger system. Unable to convert new employees to a "firm-specific culture deviant from the surrounding society," the organization adopts values identical to those of the larger culture in which it resides.[7] For this reason, American Type Z firms such as Eli Lilly reflect a strong commitment to values such as egalitarianism, job security, and participatory democracy.[8]

Ouchi suggested thirteen steps an organization could take in progressing to Theory Z status. These steps entail:

1. educating managers in Theory Z and leading them to understand that egalitarianism and integrity form the foundation of the theory;
2. auditing the company's philosophy to discover inconsistencies between stated philosophy and operational philosophy;
3. involving the CEO at an early stage in stating just how far he is prepared to go in supporting egalitarian participation (In the beginning, he may wish to place limits on the extent of decision-making

powers shared with subordinates, and it is important that he be honest in saying so.);

4. creating appropriate structures and incentives that will force individuals to work together to share information and resources;
5. instructing organization members in interpersonal skills such as recognizing patterns of interaction in group decision-making processes and in developing leadership skills;
6. testing the organization's progress informally by asking whether managers are being called on less often and having their authority challenged more frequently (the answer should be "yes" to both) and formally by administering evaluation questionnaires to subordinates;
7. involving the union by encouraging management-union seminars and meetings and contributing to union-sponsored workshops;
8. stabilizing employment and building an experienced and committed work team by adopting policies that offer alternatives to layoffs, such as more part-time employment opportunities, hiring and travel freezes, shortened workweeks and pay checks, and lower profits for shareholders during difficult economic periods;
9. slowing down evaluation and promotion to underscore the importance of long-run performance, while offering challenging assignments in a cooperative atmosphere that will develop the person, assuring future career progress;
10. broadening career paths and encouraging generalization through job rotation, allowing employees to gain a better understanding of other departments;
11. implementing changes from the top-down, with the full involvement and commitment of senior management, with emphasis on long-term results;
12. soliciting suggestions from workers as a group rather than as individuals; and
13. developing holistic relationships between managers and their employees through open and frank discussions and question-and-answer sessions.[9]

Ouchi predicts that these steps will take between ten to fifteen years for the typical organization but that, once begun, they will be self-sustaining because they appeal to the basic values of all employees. He says that the outgrowth of these processes will be greater productivity and efficiency, as well as more satisfied organization members.

## Quality of Work Life

Another example of the move toward more egalitarian organizational structures and work practices in the United States can be seen in quality-of-work-life projects being undertaken in many United States and Canadian firms. Like environmental and lifestyle issues, the term "quality of work life" was a byproduct of the 1960s, a period when many Americans questioned traditional assumptions and values. In a generally affluent society, United States academics, government leaders, and union representatives began expressing concern about the effects of employment on the health and well-being of workers. "Job satisfaction" became a buzz word. The University of Michigan, through a series of national attitude surveys conducted in 1969 and 1973, drew attention to "quality of employment." The Department of Health, Education, and Welfare sponsored similar studies, including the publication of *Work in America* in 1973. Inflation pressures resulted in a federal productivity commission which sponsored a series of labor-managed QWL experiments jointly managed by the University of Michigan Quality of Work program and the National Quality of Work Center.[10]

This flurry of interest in QWL continued through the mid-1970s but diminished in the late 1970s as a consequence of more pressing national concerns such as energy shortages and inflation. In 1979, however, a new cycle of interest in QWL emerged. This interest grew out of an increasing awareness of the challenge posed in international markets by Japan, combined with the maturation of many quality-of-work-life projects initiated in the early 1970s. Programs such as those developed by General Motors received national publicity and were lauded as illustrating creative new approaches to management.[11]

David A. Nadler and Edward E. Lawler III make the point that the term *quality of work life* has been much maligned, used in so many different contexts by so many different people that no one really knows what the term means anymore. For example, these authors say that *quality of work life* has been defined as a *variable* (meaning an individual's reaction to a work experience or the quality of an individual's work life), as *an approach* (joint labor-management cooperative projects, but with the focus still primarily on the individual rather than on organizational outcomes), as *methods* (experiments with autonomous work groups, job enrichment, or design of new plants as sociotechnical systems), as a *movement* (an ideological statement about the nature of work and one's relationship to the organization, with terms *participative management* and *industrial democracy* often being used and most people being either "for" or "against" the movement), as *everything* (organizational development, internal consulting, etc.), or as *nothing*.[12] Nadler and Lawler make the following observation about the last definitions above:

So the chairman decides that there is a need to improve QWL; he sends out memos or makes speeches discussing this concern. While everyone agrees, no one is sure exactly what it means, and typically there is some passive resistance from senior management, who are uncertain about this new development. Finally, the chairman decides that the firm will have a QWL program and sends out instructions to implement one or puts QWL into the objectives of senior management. Senior managers turn to managers in the next level down and say, "We need some QWL." In turn, those folks turn to their subordinates and convey the same message, until a human-resources manager is told by his operating manager, "We need QWL. They're very interested in it upstairs. Get me some."

Faced with this situation, the human-resources manager has several choices. One is to go out and buy some. (Indeed, there are an array of vendors willing to sell "QWL packages"—witness the current quality circle fad.) Another approach is for the human resources manager to survey the various activities that are going on, including organizational development work, internal consulting, organizational effectiveness, and so forth, and then go back to his supervisor and say, "Boss, we already got some. We just didn't know we had it."[13]

This view sees QWL as a global concept and a panacea for all that is wrong in the organization. Interpreting QWL to mean all organizational development efforts leads eventually to the final definition of QWL as being equivalent to nothing. Nadler and Lawler believe that the term and what it represents are worth preserving, and they offer the following definition: "Quality of work life is a way of thinking about people, work, and organizations. Its distinctive elements are (1) a concern about the impact of work on people as well as on organizational effectiveness and (2) the idea of participation in organizational problem solving and decision making."[14]

By this definition, all Theory Z organizations would qualify as having QWL programs, but not all organizations committed to QWL would qualify as Theory Z organizations. For example, a Theory Z organization will always have a human resource emphasis and participatory decision making; but organizations hosting QWL initiatives may or may not manifest Theory Z characteristics such as long term employment, slow evaluation and promotion, and cross-functional career paths.

Some of the ways of operationalizing QWL include quality circles, restructuring work, creating innovative reward systems to promote a different organizational climate, and improving the work environment.

Some writers claim that not all organizations can successfully initiate quality-of-work-life programs. They state that certain prerequisite favorable conditions are necessary, requiring the firm to manifest the following composite characteristics: (1) a history of financial success, (2) high employment stability, (3) advanced personnel policies, espousing human development goals at corporate and lower levels, (4) significant internal QWL resources such as an organizational-development or human-resources department, and (5) management commitment to top-down change.[15] In other words, by this logic, only the enlightened and well-endowed firms should undertake QWL programs.

Others such as Robert W. Keidel argue that a growing number of studies have demonstrated that QWL can "take root and flourish in a wide range of organizational settings." He cites studies he carried out for the U.S. Office of Personnel Management indicating that QWL can "take root and flourish in a wide range of organizational settings." He cites studies he carried out for the U.S. Office of Personnel Management indicating that QWL often reflects markedly different starting conditions and follows divergent process paths.[16]

Keidel studied QWL activity in fifteen different United States firms and in one article reported three representative cases: Polaroid Corporation's ABC plant, furniture manufacturer Corry Jamestown, and Donnelly Mirrors. The initial conditions under which these QWL programs were started varied greatly—with Polaroid offering highly favorable conditions and Corry Jamestown, highly negative conditions. Donnelly Mirrors faced a crisis situation. All encouraged plant-wide participation in the program. In the case of Donnelly, the company set in place a plant-wide bonus system called the Scanlon plan, based on experiments originally conducted at the LaPointe Steel Company. In some cases, the changes were bottom-up, and in other cases, top-down, but in all cases management moved toward a greater appreciation of the intrinsic value of QWL approaches. All personnel involved increasingly referenced their change activities to a larger organizational context, drawing on all levels of the organization. Each organization chronicled the progress of its programs, maintaining documented records. All had setbacks but overcame these temporary difficulties. In all three instances, the firms drew on outside consultants and expertise, while at the same time opening up to other organizations and sharing their experiences. In only one case was work redesign attempted and then only after fifteen years.

In concluding, Keidel warns of the importance of being consistent, ensuring that authority patterns, reward systems, and personnel procedures reflect and reinforce QWL values.

Nadler and Lawler also offer cautions, saying the last twenty-five years of research have demonstrated consistently that job satisfaction can lead to decreases in turnover and absences and sometimes to increases in commitment but will not necessarily result in increased productivity. It is naïve to assume that QWL will lead to higher productivity. Nor should management assume that lower-level projects unsupported at higher levels will succeed or that pilot projects will spread throughout an organization. The two authors suggest that too much emphasis in QWL has been put on lower-level workers and too little on middle management: "QWL has been described as something the top tells the middle to do to the bottom at organizations."[18]

Leonard A. Schlesinger and Barry Oshry discussed the particular dilemma faced by middle managers who often receive no support from top management in their efforts to set in place QWL projects, who do not believe that their efforts are recognized or rewarded by management, and who see their prior power base slipping away as lower-level workers gain new decision-making powers.[19] Formerly charged with disseminating information in the organization, these middle managers see QWL programs as institutionalizing means of bypassing their authority and redistributing control of information and resources. Computerization of the workplace, as discussed in previous chapters, likewise diminishes their power and takes away their offices and status symbols. Deadlines imposed by upper management and production quotas are sometimes at odds with time-consuming participative-decision processes involving large numbers of workers. Both top management and workers may see middle managers as blocking progress in QWL programs and blame the middle managers for problems that are generic to the system. When middle managers do delegate, they still retain responsibility for results; so in essence, they may correctly perceive that under QWL programs they have responsibility without authority.

While middle managers are charged with developing and planning the careers of their subordinates, no one at a higher level may be assuming responsibility for planning career progress for middle managers. Workers may be pushing for more and better training opportunities that entail absences from work, while senior management may be pushing for short-term immediate goal accomplishment. One middle manager is cited as saying, "There is a top-management point of view and a workforce point of view, but none for middle managers."[20] Middle managers often find themselves in a reactive position, "for or against" the plans of senior management or the workforce. Explaining away the problems, senior management may be tempted to say, "We have weak middle management." Middle management may feel that quality-of-life perspectives have relevance only for lower-level organization members, not for them.

Schlesinger and Oshry suggest that the answer to helping middle managers to cope with their present feelings of alienation and ambiguity may be integrating groups.[21] These groups would be comprised solely of middle managers, who would meet with the intent of sharing information and offering support and encouragement to each other. The collective group would offer a solid data base for decisions that the managers must make as individuals. Because most middle managers are accustomed to operating as loners, some may have negative feelings about collective actions. For this reason, Schlesinger and Oshry propose several progressive levels of integration activity, with the first level being limited to information sharing. At the second level, middle managers begin to assimilate information, diagnose organizationwide issues, and use each other as resources to help in problem solving and in identifying coping strategies. At higher levels of integration, group control replaces individual decision making.[22]

It is important that top management become aware of and support these middle management attempts at integration. This awareness may generate its own problems, however. As Schlesinger and Oshry point out, top managers may begin to ask the same questions that middle managers presently ask, "What is the base of our power?" and "What is our function in the organization?";

> In the same way that the empowerment of workers may be slowed down by middle managers' feelings of powerlessness, the empowerment of middle managers may be slowed by top managers' fears. Just as middle managers are frequently perceived as the villains in QWL programs, top managers may become the villains as middle managers begin to establish a power base. Yet blaming top managers is as much nonsense as blaming workers or middle managers. Each level has its role in the organization— top managers are shapers, workers are producers, and middle managers are integrators—and each layer also has problems that hinder its work.[23]

To make a positive contribution to quality-of-life projects, middle managers need training as much as do their subordinates. Schlesinger and Oshry specify that some of the most vital skill requirements are in the area of communication, group skills, conflict resolution, and diagnosis and problem-solving skills. Through career-development programs, pay systems, organizational structure, and job design, organizations must develop support systems for middle managers that are capable of yielding positive results.

The idea that more thought needs to be given to the problems and dilemmas experienced by middle managers is increasingly invading the management literature, not only regarding quality-of-life issues but also in terms of technological change and environmental concerns. This topic is addressed in a subsequent chapter on the physical environment.

The following chapter on QWL illustrates some of the positive aspects of quality-of-life projects that have succeeded in the Canadian workplace.

## Notes

1. William D. Ouchi, "Organizational Paradigms: A Commentary on Japanese Management and Theory Z Organizations," *Organizational Dynamics* (Spring 1981), vol. 9, pp. 36–43.
2. *Ibid.*, p. 37.
3. *Ibid.*, pp. 38–39.
4. *Ibid.*, p. 39.
5. *Ibid.*, p. 42.
6. *Ibid.*, p. 40.
7. *Ibid.*
8. Based on William G. Ouchi, *Theory Z: How American Business Can Meet the Japanese Challenge* (Reading, Mass.: Addison-Wesley, 1981), pp. 58, 71–72, 78–79.
9. William Ouchi, "Going from A to Z: Thirteen Steps to a Theory Z Organization," *Management Review* (May 1981), vol. 70, pp. 8–16.
10. David A. Nadler and Edward E. Lawler III, *Organizational Dynamics* (Winter 1983), vol. 11, p. 21.
11. *Ibid.*
12. *Ibid.*, pp. 21–23.
13. *Ibid.*, p. 24.
14. *Ibid.*, pp. 24 and 26.
15. Robert W. Keidel, "QWL Development: Three Trajectories," *Human Relations* (September 1982), vol. 35, pp. 743–44.
16. *Ibid.*, p. 744.
17. Nadler and Lawler, *op. cit.*, p. 26.
18. *Ibid.*, p. 25.
19. Leonard A. Schlesinger and Barry Oshry, "Quality of Work Life and the Manager: Muddle in the Middle," *Organizational Dynamics* (Summer 1984), vol. 13, pp. 5–19.
20. *Ibid.*, p. 10.
21. *Ibid.*, pp. 12–19.
22. *Ibid.*, p. 15.
23. *Ibid.*, p. 16.

# 8

# When Workers and Managers
# Act as a Team:
# QWL in Canada

*Wilfred List*

The universe of Ford Motor Co. of Canada's Windsor casting plant is a combination of ear-shattering noise, floating grit from huge furnaces, the glow of molten metal spilling from immense cauldrons, and temperatures that can reach 45 degrees Celsius during the summer. Three years ago, the fiery process of turning out cast-metal parts was often matched by the heat with which Ford and its unionized employees at the plant hammered out their conflicts. Productivity was low, absenteeism high, product quality poor, and operating losses large enough to threaten the survival of the plant.

Now, however, the Windsor factory is a model of labor-management co-operation. Confrontational attitudes have been replaced by shared responsibility and respect. Absenteeism and grievances have dwindled, productivity and profits have soared, and once-cynical employees talk of a new sense of job satisfaction. More than a quarter of the plant's 1,050 blue-collar workers take time from the production line for meetings of 16 plant committees at which they discuss matters ranging from improving the work environment to more efficient production methods and the annual golf tournament.

A visitor steeped in the older style of hierarchical management might wonder about the cost of such a proliferation of workplace democracy. The answer, according to both managers and union leaders who recall the Windsor operation's bad old days, is that without the more egalitarian atmosphere the plant might well be closed today.

The new look in the Ford plant at Windsor is a product of "quality of working life" (or QWL, as its practitioners call it), a catchall term coined in the 1970s to describe more democratic ways of organizing and managing work. The specific forms that QWL programs have taken are as diverse as the companies in which they have sprouted: Along with Ford, Canadian General Electric, Shell Canada, Eldorado

Nuclear and a score of smaller Canadian firms are experimenting with new, innovative work arrangements. But the universal goal is to make work more satisfying to those who do it and more valuable to the employer for whom it is done. The general strategy for achieving the goal is to give workers more of a say in decisions affecting their work.

Among employers, a major push for QWL has come from a recognition that companies in North America must gain the commitment of their workers to remain competitive with Japan and other countries. According to the QWL proponents, only by enabling workers to directly participate in the organization and management of their daily jobs and assume broader responsibility can North American industry meet the sharpened competition from abroad.

From the employees' side, the attraction of QWL has been its promise of more freedom and dignity in their daily lives. As one government-sponsored publication on QWL put it, "A democratic society cannot be built upon non-democratic institutions and organizations."

Not all QWL projects have been as successful as those at the Ford casting plant or at Shell and CGE. Many died on the vine. Some were superficial and lacked commitment or an understanding by management that employees are not something to be manipulated merely to increase productivity. A number of projects fell victim to lack of trust, hard times or internal politics. (Nor is a company's success with QWL in one workplace any assurance of similar success elsewhere in its operations. A QWL project covering only a small number of workers at Ford's Oakville assembly plant foundered in 1982 amid disagreements between the union and local management. More recently, a company-designed "employee involvement plan" was voted out at a Ford engine plant in Windsor.)

The process of moving from an adversarial relationship toward a cooperative one is neither easy nor painless. Building a new model of participatory-style management requires time, effort and money to train workers and supervisors in new work systems, and work schedules have to be reorganized so employees can attend team meetings or plant-wide sessions.

QWL at its most ambitious encompasses not only problem-solving and self-managing roles for workers, but also job rotation, multi-skill training, pay for skills and full communication between the company and its employees (with a major role for the union if the workplace is organized). Dividends for individuals and for the company have varied from firm to firm. For example, at CGE's Bromont plant in Quebec, at Shell's Sarnia chemical plant in Ontario and at Eldorado Nuclear in

Port Hope, Ont., the emphasis on multiple skills has increased the skill level of the entire work force.

At Bromont, there are monthly plant-wide meetings at which workers receive reports on production, quality and profits. So pervasive is the egalitarian principle in the CGE plant that members of senior management take a regular shift at a production job every three months. The Bromont workers are divided into self-supervising teams, are trained in a variety of jobs and even have a voice in the hiring of new team members. Although there is no union at CGE in Bromont, similar practices prevail in some union plants, including Shell Canada's chemical plant in Sarnia.

While the QWL scheme at the Ford casting plant lacks some of the features found at Bromont and other state-of-the-art workplaces, its success in the bitter soil from which it sprang represents a minor miracle of human creativity. How it survived and grew—bringing more satisfaction to the lives of plant workers and smiles to the faces of Ford accountants—is a story that reveals a great deal about what can make a QWL program work and what can scuttle it.

Management and leaders of the United Auto Workers at the casting plant had for years lived their daily lives by the adversarial credo. The plant was closed in 1980 when the auto industry went into an economic tailspin. When it was reopened in 1981 after a 10-month shutdown, the future was precarious. Workers were bitter and dissatisfaction was rife. The general attitude, in the pungent summary of one worker, was "screw you before you screw me." So divided were the union and management camps that Tom Schlotz, the man who had been running the plant since 1978, had never spoken to the UAW's plant chairman.

The changes brought about by QWL are impressive. Production manager Mitch Puklicz, who admits frankly that in 1982 the casting plant had the reputation of "junk peddlers," says that now has changed to "best in class." Quality has climbed by 40%, measured by the product reject rate. There has not been a grievance arbitration since the inception of QWL, and the few grievances that surface are minor. Plant and eating facilities have been improved, time clocks have been removed, and the absenteeism rate is the lowest of any of Ford's five Windsor plants and the lowest among the corporation's four North American casting plants. At the same time, the balance sheet has gone from a $5-million loss the year the plant reopened to a $55-million profit last year.

Puklicz, who has spent most of his working life in the 50-year-old casting plant (including 10 years as a UAW member), attributes the financial turnaround to improved productivity and quality brought about by QWL. He does not hesitate to criticize Ford's previous labor relations practices, conceding that he himself is from the old school of Ford management that believed in a regimented work force. "If you were a supervisor, the union was your natural enemy," Puklicz says. "We were trained for confrontation from day one. . . . I was boss and expected the workers to do what I told them without asking why." It was hard for him to change, he says, but "today there's mutual trust. If we had continued with the old Ford philosophy, it's possible the plant would have been closed down by now."

As at Eldorado Nuclear, whose QWL plan emerged from a period of labor turmoil, the turnabout in philosophy at Ford stemmed from a recognition by both management and union that the old ways were no longer tolerable. Ford's senior management was convinced that only a better way of operating would assure survival. Dick Poirier, then the UAW plant chairman, felt that unless there was some change in the relationship the jobs of his members could disappear. But the union and the workers in the casting plant were skeptical of Ford's corporate-wide employee involvement program, especially since it had its genesis across the border in Detroit.

Instead, Ray Wakeman, then president of the UAW local that included the casting plant and now a staff representative at union headquarters in Toronto, approached the Quality of Working Life Centre in Toronto for advice. The centre, financed by the Ontario Government to promote QWL in unionized companies, assigned consultant Hugh Auld to help Ford and the union develop a plan. Poirier, who had been plant chairman for 10 years, knew he was taking a political risk in agreeing to shed his traditional adversarial role: If the plan went sour he could expect to be tossed from office.

At the Ford plant, as at most other workplaces where QWL exists, the first step in the difficult process of change was to create a joint steering committee (initially six members, but later expanded to nine from management and eight from the union). That committee set goals for the program, with the ultimate long-term objective being a fundamental change in the social culture of the entire plant.

Along the way, the committee had to develop a participatory style of management in which employees at all levels—including those in non-unionized areas—would have a role in decision-making. Important to winning the union's confidence was an agreement that any matter related to collective bargaining would be outside the scope of the plan and that no one would lose a job as a result of any QWL-related productivity improvements.

Good communications are essential to the success of QWL. Workers want to feel involved rather than be treated as an unwelcome necessity. At the Ford plant, workers are made aware of every facet of the company's operation, the good news as well as the bad—and it has been almost all good ever since QWL was introduced. Employees have responded to their new sense of involvement with a rash of ideas for making their work more efficient as well as more enjoyable or at least less stressful. One result is a cool room that gives workers relief from the heat of the furnaces during their rest break. Another is the enclosing of work areas to muffle noise. A joint team has been planning a physical fitness centre for the plant.

In the quest for efficiency, one QWL team developed a method of storing 1,500-pound metal slugs that saved the company more than $300,000 a year. Another saved $150,000 annually by modifying the way crankshafts are cleaned. Other proposals for redesign of equipment saved thousands more. That sort of achievement is common in workplaces where QWL has taken root (though perhaps some sort of record was set when Eldorado Nuclear workers, in a brainstorming session over a hitch in part of the new plant at Port Hope, identified 28 problems that needed correction).

Although the level of employee commitment to QWL varies from workplace to workplace, it is particularly strong at the Ford casting plant. "Sure there are always some guys who will say it sucks," says UAW member Frank Kotow. "But most agree with the program." Praise for QWL's achievements from rank-and-file workers has the flavor of testimonials at a religious revival meeting. "Before, all I cared about was getting my cheque each week," confesses Kotow, who has worked in the plant since 1976. "But now that I know management is listening and I can improve the job, I give it my best." And when workers speak, production manager Puklicz listens. He went along with a committee proposal to add three men to a work crew to reduce excessive overtime, although at one time, he says, his response would have been, "Screw it, we've got a budget."

Not all problems are solved by QWL, however, and some new ones are created. At Ford as at other QWL plants, foremen have felt threatened by any move to give their subordinates greater power in determining how work is to be performed. In plants where traditional foremen are an extinct breed of management, new-style team leaders, who coach rather than direct workers, are also apprehensive that they may become obsolete in the future.

One particular problem for foremen at Ford is the interruption in work when employees leave to attend team meetings. If a foreman refuses a worker permission because he can't be spared from the job, the worker goes higher up the management line. "The next thing the foreman knows, he's had his ass chewed and been told the worker has to get to the meeting," plant manager Schlotz says, acknowledging that the foreman is caught in the middle. If it's not meetings that upset foremen, it is requisitions from employees for changes or additions to equipment that one of the QWL committees has decided are needed to improve efficiency. All that has meant that Schlotz has to spend more time stroking supervisors than motivating rank-and-file workers.

While some foremen remain disgruntled, most workers who have experienced the change under QWL like their new freedom. At the Shell chemical plant, where employees work in self-managing teams, one sums up the difference between over-the-shoulder supervision before he came to Shell and the new approach: "The foreman handed out orders and everyone got away with as much as possible. When I started at Shell, I could feel the openness. You had freedom but you had to be responsible. I figure that's a lot better way to operate."

Nevertheless, QWL is not a quick fix or a panacea. Hans van Beinum, executive director of Ontario's Quality of Working Life Centre, makes the point that each QWL project must take into account the history and environment of the company. There is no over-all pattern to serve as an easy formula, and the opportunities for autonomy on the job, variety in work and for working together will differ for each plant. Some companies, like CGE at Bromont, carefully screen job applicants to select those the company feels can adapt to the greater responsibilities required of them than would be the case in a traditional plant.

For some companies, the primary goal of QWL has been productivity improvement. But union leaders, who favor such programs, see them first as a way of improving the lives of workers. Neil Reimer, former president of the Energy and Chemical Workers Union, which has been in the forefront of union support for QWL, says that if a more democratic system also increases productivity "that's all right with us."

Many Canadian union leaders, though, are suspicious or hostile toward QWL. Partly, that is a defensive reaction against change, a concern about being perceived as soft on management, or a lack of knowledge of what QWL is all about. But there is also fear that QWL may undermine workers' loyalty to the union if they identify with management goals. UAW Canadian director Robert White is ambivalent about QWL, neither overtly opposing nor supporting it. He is undoubtedly right in feeling that it is easier to start from scratch in a new plant than to change existing attitudes in an old one. Gerard

Docquier, Canadian director of the United Steelworkers of America, is more positive about QWL, as long as it does not infringe on the collective agreement.

William Westley, president of McGill Human Resource Associates, a Montreal firm that has served as consultant on the introduction of QWL systems, says union leaders who oppose such programs are acting irresponsibly. "A unionized plant is one of the best environments for QWL because it combines the strength and assurance of the protection a union brings with the dignity QWL gives workers."

Is QWL the way of the future, a quiet revolution in the workplace, or merely another fad that will fade away? QWL specialist Harvey Kolodny, of the University of Toronto's Faculty of Management Studies, is convinced that it represents a philosophy of managing work that will be as indispensable in the future as the assembly line is today. "Any manager of manufacturing who builds a plant and operates it in a traditional, autocratic way will very quickly find he has an obsolete plant on his hands," Kolodny says. At the Ford casting plant, manager Schlotz agrees. "Even if the union dropped out, we wouldn't return to the old ways," he says.

Individual QWL plans may atrophy and die, but a philosophy of work that enhances the dignity of the worker and leads to improved productivity and quality is clearly an idea whose time has come.

### A Study in Workplace Innovation

When Richard Pelletier took a day from his executive office to work on the production line, it barely raised an eyebrow. At the Canadian General Electric plant that Pelletier manages in Quebec's Eastern Townships, innovation is a way of life. Senior managers at the CGE plant in Bromont, Que., work at least one day every three months on production jobs to help bridge the gap between the executive offices and the workers on the line. That work-about approach to managing underlines the departure from the traditional organization of jobs at the Bromont plant, whose program to enhance the quality of working life is state-of-the-art. Highly sophisticated technology is matched by an equally advanced social system that emphasizes worker participation in decision-making and problem-solving.

The $80-million Bromont plant, opened in August, 1983, is one of the first in the GE system to incorporate the latest in computer-integrated manufacturing, including robotics, voice control and computerized controllers. The wide responsibility workers have been given to manage their own jobs has produced a flood of ideas for operating the factory more efficiently.

The plant manufactures airfoils for jet engines, a process that requires a precision that permits virtually no room for error. Tolerances on airfoils are measured to the thousandth of an inch. Yet the workers who prepare the metal also have the responsibility for quality control. There are no foremen breathing down the backs of the 175 production workers, who operate in semi-autonomous teams, with each member trained to perform many or all of the tasks for which the team is accountable. "We really have to take a fresh look at how business is run," Pelletier says. "The values of people in the work force are a lot different than they were 30 years ago. They're better educated and they expect to participate more." At Bromont, team meetings are held weekly to deal with production problems or individual difficulties as well as with expenditures needed to enable the team to do its work efficiently. Periodic plant-wide meetings—bringing together the more than 300 members of the production, administrative, professional and support teams—keep workers well briefed on production costs and schedules, new technology and market developments.

Pelletier, who has worked for CGE and its U.S.-based parent for 18 years, says that "10 years ago in creating new plants, the company retained the traditional management system because it didn't know better. Today, we are beginning to recognize that workers have to be treated as individuals and that authoritarian management does not lead to either worker satisfaction or commitment."

There are no time clocks in the plant, but a worker knows that if he is late he is letting his team down. "Team members are the first to take a shot at the latecomer," Pelletier says.

All employees are on salary and can arrange for time off with pay for medical appointments or other pressing matters. Perhaps it is the peer pressure and the responsibility workers have accepted for self-management that account for the fact that absenteeism is a mere 1.5% of all time worked—one of the lowest in the GE corporation, which employs 500,000 workers worldwide.

Huzon Grenier, 43, who operates a carousel that moves material through the plant, explains the low absenteeism rate. "If you are interested in your job, you don't want to stay home. Here at CGE you can express your own personality. In most shops you hate to get up to go to work. Here it's different. There's no one cracking the whip."

One of Grenier's tasks in his first job in the plant was to tally the number of metal cylinders in a four-foot-high drum. That meant bending over to pull out the pieces one at a time, a job that took several hours. "I figured there had to be a better way," Grenier says, so he came up with the idea of a tilting device for the drum that would make it easier to extract the pieces. The engineering staff drew a blueprint and had the tilter manufactured in nearby Granby. As well, Grenier suggested that weighing a sample of pieces from the top of each drum would allow the total contents to be projected mathematically, instead of having everything tallied manually. That allowed the counting job to be done in a fraction of the time.

René Decelles, 28, agrees that increased responsibility encourages creativity. "It keeps you alert. I find it challenging. It's a little like operating your own business because you have responsibility in your area of work." For some workers, though, there is a price to pay for replacing the traditional authoritarian system of management with one that gives employees a large measure of autonomy and opportunities to learn new skills.

A report on the Bromont experience by McGill Human Resource Associates, which helped CGE to implement the program, cites the comment of one worker: "You've got to be on the ball all the time. You can't really afford to have an off day or just muddle through. We can't depend on a foreman to fix our mistakes, to tell us what to do. This job really uses up everything I've got. It's very demanding. We're always learning new things. The company has a great deal of confidence in us, trusts us, and that's very gratifying. But they expect a lot too."

The level of training in the Bromont plant is high, with experienced production workers teaching less-qualified employees new and more complex jobs, such as how to use computer technology in production. There is no union at Bromont and the eight-member senior management team would undoubtedly prefer it that way, although workers at most CGE plants in Canada and GE plants in the United States are covered by union contracts. A union with agreements at other CGE plants tried a year ago to organize the Bromont workers by distributing leaflets, but it quickly abandoned the effort when it drew no response.

The company plans to introduce a system by year's end under which grievances are heard by a review team of three workers from the production areas and two from the professional or administrative group. There is, however, no provision for binding third-party arbitration, as is the case where there is a collective agreement.

The Bromont system gives work teams a significant role in hiring, and in rare cases firing, team members. One day members of a production team called on senior management member Norman Lockwood. "You've got to get rid of X," he was told. "He's not pulling his weight." Lockwood was reluctant to step in, saying, "You have to sort out your own problems." The team members left but returned a week later and told Lockwood that X would have to go because he would not co-operate by doing the variety of jobs, including sweeping the floor, that other team members did in rotation. "The employee had a hearing," Lockwood said of X. "But we finally had to let him go."

At Bromont, as in some other plants with quality-of-working-life schemes, employees are expected to acquire a variety of skills, and their pay increases as they master each skill. Employees also share in savings created through reduction of controllable costs. Gains-sharing payouts, which are paid quarterly, totalled $1,000 for each employee last year and could be more than twice that figure this year.

New skills are demanded of supervisors as well—skills in managing more democratically. Jacques Gauthier, 40, who has been a supervisor in traditional plants, says that at CGE he is more of a coach. "You have to discard the idea that you run the department. You have to regard workers as collaborators rather than as subordinates. I had some difficulty at first. But I adjusted." Though QWL is under fire in some other plants, at Bromont its future seems secure. Says Pelletier: "The employees wouldn't let us drop it."

### Breakdown of Trust

Hard times that lead to cost-cutting can be a lethal threat to quality-of-working-life programs, as union and management are finding at American Cyanamid Co.'s fertilizer and chemical plant in Niagara Falls, Ont. The plant has a quality-of-working-life plan, named Partichange, covering 95 employees in three production departments. But after nearly five years the program has failed to expand to any of the nine other areas in the plant, which has a total of 400 unionized and 225 non-unionized workers. In fact, the QWL program is losing the confidence of many employees.

The growing disaffection does not stem from any lack of support from Al Wood, the 58-year-old president of Local 21 of the Energy and Chemical Workers Union, or from 53-year-old Walter Secen, the intense and dedicated manager of the QWL program and former plant manager, whose service with Cyanamid is only three years short of Wood's 34.

Current plant manager Bob Dartnell, who came to Niagara Falls from the company's plant in Hannibal, Mo., in 1981, says he is committed to the quality-of-working-life plan, which also has the blessing of Cyanamid's president and chief executive officer, George J. Sella Jr., at the corporate headquarters in Wayne, N.J.

During the 1970s, the parent corporation had milked the 45-year-old Niagara plant and allowed it to run down. By Secen's own account, grievances multiplied, tension was high and there was a complete breakdown of trust. QWL was introduced at the initiative of Secen and Wood in an attempt to repair the damage. Despite early progress and enthusiasm for QWL, however, economic factors have left the program struggling for survival. Because of poor market conditions for its products, Cyanamid has laid off workers and deferred plans for a training program that would have meant more pay as workers acquired new skills.

Secen, who had been plant manager for 10 years, says, "QWL has become the scapegoat for employee frustrations." Wood, a quiet-spoken, fatherly person, says QWL has led to impressive changes for the better, "but the people in the plant don't want to attribute it to QWL." Employees agree that communications between the company and workers are better, relations with most foremen have improved, and there is a team spirit among workers that had been previously lacking. Working conditions are better, they say, and the number of grievances is down by half.

But for many of the employees, QWL has not lived up to its promise. Evan Bines, 28, who has worked in the nitrate department for four years, sums up the view of many of the employees: "The concept of QWL is fantastic. But austerity and layoffs have created a lot of hostility and are destroying trust."

Dan Sirianni, who was QWL committee chairman in the nitrate department for nearly three years, agrees such programs are "the best thing that's ever hit the labor force." But he too is disillusioned with the way Cyanamid's program has worked out and feels the company is only giving lip service to the principle of consultation. Clearly, retrenchment and budget paring have set back QWL. Dave Hall, present chairman of the business committee in the nitrate department, also praises QWL, but says the elimination of jobs is jeopardizing its survival.

The problem of winning over the foremen is as great at Cyanamid as in other plants, and has led to a no-win situation. To convert foremen to the QWL concept, the company created a foremen's task force. But in the perception of rank-and-file workers, that has sharpened the demarcation between workers and supervisors.

Despite all the problems, Secen is still optimistic that the entire plant will eventually become involved in QWL. "We are trying to change a system of management that has been with us since the Industrial Revolution—the only system we knew," he says. "It's not a short-term project, but rather a continuous effort."

**Part III**

# INTERPERSONAL COMMUNICATION IN THE ORGANIZATION: THEORETICAL PERSPECTIVES

# 9

# The Physical Environment and Communication

Physical systems create a context within which social interaction takes place, influencing the nature and frequency of the interaction. Fred Steele has coined the term "environmental competence" to refer to awareness of one's physical environment and its impact and "the ability to use or change that environment to suit one's ends."[1]

Too often management has failed to recognize the relevance of setting; and when it has acknowledged the influence of the physical environment on workers, it has looked for a single "right" solution to the arrangement of the setting. This attitude on the part of management results in fashion trends in office design, as evident in the move from private cubicles to bull pen to office landscape systems.[2] More often than not, no one researches the effects of these settings on the individuals who must operate within them.

Commenting on this problem, Franklin Becker stated: "The role the physical setting plays as a medium of communication, as well as how it structures interaction and communication patterns, remain largely overlooked."[3]

## Lack of Control of Employees over Setting

Traditionally, advisers to management have been plant location and layout experts (primarily concerned with cost factors in building design) and space-planning firms (skilled in the areas of economic analysis, engineering, and interior design, but with little training in the social sciences).[4] Recent trends in human-factors engineering, or ergonomics, show a broadened focus on how people interact with machines and technology in a working environment.

Ergonomics takes into account not only physiological, but also psychological factors that can generate stress, headaches, and other complaints.[5] Nonetheless, the emphasis in ergonomics has been on safety and comfort in using technology in automated offices. Studies

165

exemplifying this emphasis have as their concern the design of secretarial chairs, visual factors related to VDU screens, radiation exposure, and workstation design.[6] These studies have tended to stress the influence of environmental factors on our sense of well-being rather than on how these factors structure and determine our communication behavior and relationships.

The standards by which we judge our physical environment are also often at odds with our needs. The architect who designs a building that "stands out" is frequently rewarded over the one who creates a structure that "fits in."[7] The bold impressive building will often be a hard monumental one. Frequently the basis of architectural rewards will be the presumed lack of popular appeal of the design. Boards of specialists acting on behalf of the public, but not necessarily in their interests, make the awards. An example in point is Paul Rudolph's Art Architecture building at Yale,[8] a building that won a citation for good design but was described in the following way:

> It is . . . not an easy building to live with.
>
> Physically, it is often uncomfortable. It gets hot when the sun pours in. Security controls are difficult. Offices are cramped. The spaces are not perfect for twenty-foot high paintings or intimate conversation or classroom study. The lighting is inadequate. There are great difficulties in manipulating one's personal environment.[9]

Some architects specify in their contracts that their written permission is required to make any changes to the building, including such minor adjustments as moving partitions and changing the drapes. In many public buildings, long lists of regulations governing employees' behavior can include prohibitions against hanging pictures on the walls, rearranging furniture, bringing live plants into the building, and even placing a family portrait on one's desk. In many such buildings, where the architects do not hold such rigid control, the office furnishings will be standard ones, selected by business agents out of catalogues.

Typically, in such hard office buildings, employees do not control the temperatures of their own work areas; rather they must adjust to that preferred by the building custodians or maintenance engineer.

Similarly, janitors make most decisions on day-to-day spatial arrangements, placing chairs and tables in accordance with their own norms and expectations and for ease of maintenance.[10] In some institutional settings, furnishings are bolted to the floor. From the point of view of the organization, many see the company's physical facilities as the most visible and concrete representation of the organization, and they see these facilities as the most direct way of projecting an image to the public. This concern with appearances may override the issue of suitability of a structure in favor of what is to happen within its walls. Using sociologist Edgar Friedenberg's analogy, Sommer stated the problem in this way: "Institutional architecture is like the pet food business—the consumer is not the purchaser and unless the consumer becomes ill or bites the purchaser, there isn't going to be much change."[11]

It is difficult to complain about a building. It is existent, often at great cost or for long periods of time. If the building falls into the category of hard architecture, change is expensive. Sommer uses the term "hard architecture" to refer to structures that are designed to be "strong and resistant to human imprint."[12] The most accessible persons, the custodians and one's coworkers, may have the least interest or the least power to effect changes. The administration has other priorities.

Social psychologists tell us that an important aspect of fulfilling individuals' self-esteem needs, as well as contributing to their ability to perform tasks successfully, is giving them control over work design, pace, physical layout, and furnishings. Such researchers say that we must not only consider what people are physically capable of doing, but also what they are willing to do, given the conditions of the workplace and society in which they live. For a growing number of employees, quality of life ranks over material gain as a motivator. Elaine Cohen and Aaron Cohen agree with Herzberg that good conditions or facilities will not ensure motivation, but poor conditions and facilities will inhibit the performance of even the simplest tasks.[13] Studies have likewise found that companies placing employees in underground facilities have higher turnover rates and lower employee morale than do those offering more agreeable settings.

Franklin Becker proposes that in many regards workplace settings are self-governing, self-regulating systems, with their own mechanisms for bringing behavior into line. Such behavior settings impose their agenda on the persons operating within them. Social pressure from other organizational members, deadlines imposed from outside, etc., act as maintenance mechanisms, assuring that the program will be carried out. Becker suggests that the people who enter and become a part of such behavior settings will behave in ways compatible with its program. For example, assembly line workers facing a fast-moving line may quite accurately see that they are expected to produce large quantities of work. The pace of the line may also lead the workers to decide that they need not try to do particularly high-quality work, since the organization obviously values quantity over quality.[14] If you accept such a deterministic, setting-biased viewpoint, you will probably also accept that in such environments, rigid controls over details of timing, design, and equipment are unnecessary and indeed inappropriate.

In the same way, research studies have determined that the more successful equipment installations occur when the workers are able to structure their own work and time and arrange their environments in the way they regard as most comfortable and effective.[15] An experiment at Morse Chain Division of Borg-Warner in Ithaca, New York, encouraged machinists who use heavy equipment in the shop to take time off to paint their machines in colors of their choice.[16] In a situation of poor labor-management relations, inadequate pay, or poor safety (in other words, where basic hygiene factors are lacking), such a move would be viewed with cynicism and would only serve to worsen the tensions. However, where workers are encouraged to participate in decision making and see such a move as an active effort to involve them, the results may be positive. Workers see decisions about office size, locations, degree of enclosure, and storage space as important issues that exemplify management's attitude toward them.[17] For some workers, the opportunity to personalize their work setting may make the difference between commitment and disinterested apathy.

Studies by Yvonne Clearwater report that resentment and anger typify the response of employees to management policies that prohibit personalization of their working environment. She cites examples of such employees flaunting organizational rules by papering walls with posters, notices, and photographs.[18]

Likewise, studies reported in the housing literature suggest a relationship between personalization and neighborhood pride, personalization and satisfaction with dormitory living, and personalization and group cooperation. One study even found personalization related to dropout rates among college freshmen.[19]

Operating on this premise, many banks and nightclubs have attempted to humanize and soften their settings in an effort to make their customers feel less out of place and less intimidated by a hard, cold environment.

## Buildings Communicate

Harvard School of Design faculty member and architect John Seiler made the following observation regarding the communication function of buildings:

Buildings influence behavior by embodying messages. They tell people how the company operates, what it values, and where it has been and is going. They do these things with or without integrity, with or without accuracy. Buildings may, unfortunately, like an ill-designed advertisement you can't get rid of, send messages that are garbled, specious, or monotonic.[20]

Some buildings are designed to make people feel their own unimportance. The Kramberg building in West Germany is a twelve-tiered structure, broadest at the base where the lowest-echelon workers are housed, and visibly narrowing in stairstep fashion at each additional floor level until finally, at the highest level, the top administrators occupy only a fraction of the floor space used at the lower levels. The building is a strong symbolic representation of the very limited numbers of employees who will realize their aspirations to reach the highest echelons of the organization. The Kramberg building typifies the tendency of management to set aside the top floors of its buildings for the president of the company, the chairman of the board, and other top-line executives.[21]

In older buildings, the location of the offices will reflect the dominance of the hierarchy, with corner offices with windows housing senior executives and heads of departments. The most powerful executive will have the office with the greatest square footage and the most windows. Also, the higher-status offices will be less accessible, with secretaries and receptionists acting as gatekeepers.[22]

Buildings and their furnishings can tell the prospective employee much about the organization, its values, and how open the organization is to the newcomer. Law firms wanting to attract wealthy clients have found that dark woods, muted colors, deep reds, leathers, and antiques have the best drawing power—better than glass, chrome, and electric blue interiors.[23] Extremes of office decoration may point to the fact that no power is available to the outsider.[24] The following has been cited as exemplary of such a case:

One company I know of has its senior executives segregated on the top floor of the building, in a kind of garden-penthouse overlooking New York's harbor, reached by a small private elevator which is simply but expensively decorated by a Renoir landscape. The floors below look like any other office, the usual mixture of shabby and modern. The penthouse is full of English wood paneling, French eighteenth-century furniture, enormous hunt tables, breakfront libraries, chinoiserie commodes, paintings, and furniture gathered from every salesroom and antiques shop in Paris and London. Adams fireplaces have been hacked out of ancestral walls to be recessed into offices without chimneys. Regency wine coolers which once held bottles of champagne now serve as telephone tables. At one corner of the office stands a carved and gilded horse from an old fairgound carrousel, the rest of which, together with its machinery, is packed away in crates somewhere. An office like this one as good as warns you that you aren't going to get any power until you get the key to that private elevator, and the people up there in the penthouse are not likely to want to see you have one. Indeed, sharp echelons like this one are partly *intended* to keep the lower echelons in their places, and to make the access to power mysterious, difficult, and impressive.[25]

It has been said that where the offices of senior executives are located at the upper levels of a building, a tight control and supervision of day-to-day activities of the organization is implied. The residence of senior executives on the ground floor, on the other hand, implies an abdication of responsibility for the routine functioning of the organization.[26]

The size of offices, the quality and color of the carpets, even the floor on which an employee works, speak of a person's place in the hierarchy and of the options available to him. The lower his position, the more limited will be his range of choices.

The same building may communicate different messages to different people. For example, Becker discussed the case of a business school containing five different lounges, each with a closed door and a sign indicating "faculty lounge," "staff lounge," "PhD lounge," "MBA lounge," or "undergraduate lounge." According to Becker, access to the lounges reflects Guttman-type scaling. Anyone qualifying for entry to the lounge at the top of the hierarchy (the faculty) can also enter all lounges falling below that level. If, on the other hand, you have membership at the bottom of the hierarchy, you can only access that level and nothing higher. There is the unspoken expectation that no one will enter anyone else's territory. Becker indicated that conversations with faculty members revealed that they indeed felt as uncomfortable talking with students in the undergraduate lounge as the students felt in faculty territory.[27]

While such an environment can communicate a sense of status and group membership to the people at the top of the scale, those at the bottom receive a different message. It is true that a greater sense of social cohesiveness among individual groups can result from the stratification, and possibly some undergraduates will be motivated to strive for later membership in the higher ranks, but many will acquire feelings of indifference or even alienation.[28]

It is not uncommon for institutions such as a school or a nursing home, managed by one group for the "good" of another, to convey "paternalistic and negative images" to the inhabitants, causing them to feel neglected and ignored. In the same way, an institution can transmit equally well a sense of caring and concern. Through color, graphics, and lighting, a hospital can communicate progress and modernity rather than sterility and impersonality. A study of renovations at one hospital, for example, found that even small-scale changes to the physical environment increased patients' feelings that the hospital was friendly, less bureaucratic, and caring. Yet the changes observed in the study cost the hospital less than $3,000.[30]

A summary of some of the major points made in the literature dealing with status and setting follows.

"The higher one's position in the hierarchy, the greater and better one's space allotment will be."[31] The president of a corporation will command a larger office and higher-quality furnishings than will the middle manager or the junior clerk. Executive offices will often be on the top floors of a building, and the most important offices will be located at the corners. In traditional offices, the further one is from the physical center of an office, the more powerful one is. Michael Korda claims that power tends to emanate in an X-shaped pattern, leaving certain central areas as "dead" space.[32] Secretaries, technicians, and clerks typically occupy these interior spaces. Americans in particular seem to prefer corners that protect their backs and sides. In some organizations, this preference results in much wasted central space.[33]

"The higher one's position in the hierarchy, the less one is likely to need or to use the space."[34] In the majority of organizations, there is an inverse relationship between the amount of space occupied by an individual and the time spent in the office. The executive who spends the majority of his day in board meetings, at lunches with clients, and on tours of the plant gets the oversized office with windows and an elaborate filing system. The secretary, who is responsible for doing the filing and being available on a nine-to-five basis to answer the telephone and greet visitors, gets the small office with no windows.

"The higher one's position in the hierarchy, the better protected one's space will be."[35] The president of a firm and upper management members will be protected by secretaries, outer offices, doors, and protocol from those wishing to see them. The lowest-ranking members of the organization such as secretaries and filing clerks will be the most visible and the least protected.

"The higher one's position in the hierarchy, the more ambiguous will be the setting provided." Franklin Becker explains this principle in the following way:

> Higher-status persons, in nonpublic locations in older buildings are likely to be allowed to treat their work setting as highly ambiguous, open to change, flexible and unique. A low-status employee in a highly visible public location in a new building should experience administrative pressure to treat his or her work setting as unambiguous, inflexible, unchangeable, and standardized. The front receptionist in the main lobby of the headquarters building provides a familiar image. Persons with intermediate status working in different locations in buildings of different age and condition should experience levels of ambiguity in their work setting that fall somewhere between these two extremes.[36]

The more ambiguous one's setting, the more discretionary activities become possible. Less-ambiguous settings limit the options available to workers and deny them control over their working environment. Providing an ambiguous setting implies trust in the occupant; and conversely, an unambiguous setting implies lack of trust.

"The higher one's position in the organization, the easier it is to invade the territory of lower-ranked individuals."[37] A manager can enter a subordinate's office in person or by telephone, whenever he wishes; but the subordinate will hesitate to phone too often and will probably make an appointment, inquire from the secretary as to the availability of the supervisor, or will knock before entering the supervisor's office. More often than not, the subordinate will pause at the door of the supervisor's office, waiting for a verbal or nonverbal invitation to enter.

"Power diminishes with distance from the source of power."[38] Those located closest to sources of power gain status from the proximity, as in the case of an executive secretary or assistant. Aides or colleagues located on another part of the floor or in another building do not benefit in the same way from the proximity to power. It is said that whereas executives prefer secluded protected territory, secretaries regard their offices as having more status if they can see in many directions, maintaining visual control over territory.[39]

### Relationship of Setting to Communication

Seiler stated well the relationship between setting and communication:

> Buildings influence behavior by structuring relationships among members of the organization. They encourage some communication patterns

and discourage others. They assign positions of importance to units of the organization. They do these things according to a plan that fits the company's strategic design, or to a nonplan that doesn't. They have effects on behavior, planned or not.[40]

The physical environment inside which communication takes place has a profound effect on the nature of the communication. We speak of some places having a warm, friendly atmosphere and of other places being cold and oppressive. These kinds of folksy observations are far from being superficial. Indeed, there is abundant evidence that the psychological impact of setting can be extremely powerful. The history of urban planning in London offers one such example. Much original work in city planning and development took place in London following the Second World War. This occurred for several reasons. London was one of the largest cities in the world. England had been involved in a war for seven years, during which time normal ongoing construction projects had been stopped. The older slum sections of the city had further deteriorated, and added to this natural decay was a considerable amount of bomb damage.

The London County Council built up a team of young, competent, and enthusiastic architects and town planners, many of whom had grown up in the areas where new concentrated development was proposed. In many regards, these men understood the problem; in other regards, they only thought they understood the problem. People living in overcrowded conditions in slum areas tend to regard the problems of development as largely a matter of providing adequate, sanitary accommodation with a high level of privacy. In the case of the London city-planning project, these objectives were met by well-constructed high-rise developments. Care was taken in the design of the projects to ensure that the apartment windows did not overlook other apartments and that the occupants of each apartment had direct access to the apartments from the elevators.

What had been conceived to be utopian apartments for the working class turned out to be isolation cells where people became so depressed after a few months that many gave up their new residences to return to slum areas in other parts of the city. The chief cultural characteristic of the lifestyle of the east-end Londoner, by necessity, was gregariousness. To remove such a man from virtually all social intercourse was to guarantee neurosis.

In fairness to the early designers, they learned by their mistakes and built subsequent complexes so that there were clusters of families who did share common space in the hallways and whose balconies overlooked each other. The planners also brought back some of the street culture to the antiseptic lots on which the apartments were set. They did so by accommodating street-vendor stalls, which played an important part in the traditional lifestyle of the Londoners.[41] In many ways, the London development story is similar to the children's story of the rich man who built a castle with a high wall surrounding his garden to ensure his privacy. After a time, he found himself to be poor company and knocked a hole in the wall so that the children and the wildlife could come back into the garden.

In an organizational-communication context, the physical environment has for some time been recognized as an important factor. The classic Hawthorne studies examined different aspects of the effects of the work environment on employees and production. Humphrey Osmond identified the "sociopetal" and "sociofugal" functions of settings and the tendency for the physical setting to bring people together or to push them apart.[42] In sociopetal layouts, people constantly see each other and make eye contact. In such settings, avoiding conversation is difficult. For example, people will feel obliged to respond to those seated across from them, as in cross-table and cross-corner arrangements.[43] Eye contact signals an opening for conversation; so the closer a visitor's chair is to the receptionist, the more likely conversation will ensue.[44]

Americans like to minimize eye contact, and the contemporary concept of the open plan is designed to do so. In earlier bull-pen arrangements with large undefined areas of space, eye contact with coworkers was unavoidable, but four-to-five-foot-high partitions in some landscaped offices cut down on eye contact and give low-level workers a sense of protected territory. This type of open plan assumes that to an American, visual privacy is more important than acoustical privacy.[45]

The arrangement of chairs, desks, and sofas directly influences the quality and quantity of interaction. Placing chairs in straight rows, back to back, as is common in airports and institutional waiting rooms, discourages communication between those occupying the chairs. Sociofugal space discourages interaction. Out-of-the-way offices reached by "single-loaded" corridors give the privacy necessary for carrying out jobs requiring intense concentration, but such spatial arrangements do not provide sociopetal meeting space. For individuals occupying these offices, the only central meeting spaces that encourage interaction may be elevators, cafeterias, and front lobbies.[46] A modified sociopetal arrangement is exemplified in the ordering of workstations around central corridors "like spokes in a wheel."[47] The corridors allow people to make contact as they pass each other.

Even where an organization provides sociopetal settings, however, status differences and socialization processes may override the determinist aspects of spatial arrangements.[48] For example, the aspiring junior executive may cross the length of the room to sit and converse with another young executive rather than cultivate a friendship with a lower-ranked individual. On the other hand, he or she may hesitate to join a corporate executive engaged in conversation with the president of the firm. A subordinate will usually seek permission to sit at the table or desk of a superior, but the reverse does not apply.

The nature and size of rooms will also influence the degree to which people tend to be drawn together and to interact. Glass is used by many designers to keep activities in the open and to encourage interaction in a friendly and democratic atmosphere.[49] Studies by Abraham Maslow and Norbett Mintz suggest that more positive exchanges between people will occur in "beautiful" rooms, surroundings that are visually and aesthetically pleasing to the eye.[50] Studies by Griffitt and Veitch found that ambient temperatures are likewise related to interpersonal attraction and acceptance. They found that in uncomfortable settings, people made harsher interpersonal judgments.[51] Other studies have found environmental conditions such as level of noise, lighting, colors, privacy, and location can affect organizational decisions such as salary recommendations, performance appraisals, and negotiation of grievances.[52] The design and furnishing of some meeting rooms may serve to discourage rather than encourage interaction. In a typical conference room, the president or the group leader sits at the head of the table, and his associates flank him or her on either side. In such meetings, the president generally dominates, and little interaction or exchange of ideas occurs. Such seating arrangements facilitate one-way communication and stimulate little feedback. It has been found that persons occupying the corners of rectangular tables contribute least to the discussions.[53]

Comparing some corporate headquarters to cold and unresponsive airports, Sommer discusses the fact that the hard architecture used in such settings tends to limit severely the interaction that goes on there:

> The board room contains a long rectangular table with twelve to twenty chairs on each side and the chairman's place at the head. Everything is dark brown, royal blue or black to suggest dignity and responsibility. Common sense dictates that meetings in these rooms are largely ceremonial. All the real work of the company is done beforehand. . . . The hard conference room is designed to restrict interaction to prescribed

patterns. Most often this means statements from the chair followed by brief requests for clarification from the wings and by replies from the chair. *Robert's Rules of Order* or frequent votes do little to enhance discussion. Except for the person at the head of the table who addresses everyone, the other people talk only to the Chair. At a long conference table, side-by-side interaction would be impolite and distracting. Most votes taken at this kind of meeting are unanimous. Interaction within this type of room can be made polite, superficial, and restricted to prearranged channels. Older hard furniture was wood-stiff and straight-backed. Modern hard wood is steel, plastic, and glass but still cold, stiff, and unresponsive and if not permanently fixed, at least pseudo-fixed.[54]

A squared circle that maximizes eye contact and minimizes distance between group members encourages more participation than the long conference table discussed above. Such a table also serves to equalize power.[55]

The importance of seating arrangements was well recognized in negotiations that took place in the 1960s between the United States and Viet Nam. James McCroskey, Charles Larson, and Mark Knapp described the eight months of negotiation over the shape of the bargaining table:

> The United States and South Viet Nam wanted a seating arrangement in which only two sides were identified. They did not want to recognize the National Liberation Front as an "equal" partner in the negotiations. North Viet Nam and the NLF wanted "equal" status given to all parties—represented by a four-sided table. The final arrangement was such that both parties could claim victory. The round table minus the dividing lines allowed North Viet Nam and the NLF to claim all four delegations were equal.[56]

In the office situation, people will be more responsive to those whom they can easily see. Those whose desks are in close proximity will probably interact more frequently. On the other hand, those who wish to maintain social distance may use desks to act as barriers, preventing encroachment into personal space. Business and social discourse conducted at seven to twelve feet has a more formal character than that which occurs at four to seven feet.[57]

Closed doors are viewed in the United States as suspicious, communicating unfriendliness. People who choose to work behind closed doors are regarded as less approachable. A recent study showed that male executives are much more likely than are their female counterparts to close their office doors. In the same spirit, women are more likely to describe their offices as "friendly," while men tend to describe theirs as "functional."[58]

The relative location of facilities and people will affect the level of interaction. The best meeting places are those centrally located with resting places that allow people to stop and converse without obstructing the way.[59] Some studies indicate that degree of contact is correlated negatively with the amount of difficulty encountered "by way of corners to be turned, indirect paths to be followed, etc.,"[60] explaining why people who live near mailboxes, entrance ways, and stairways have a much more active social life.[61] Other typical studies reveal that people in departments that share space on the same floor interact more than those who have offices on different floors. The Hawthorne studies have been interpreted as a demonstration of how a single room can increase group interaction and influence the appearance of cliques.[63]

Bureaucratic buildings are often sociofugal in design, separating those who work in different departments and at different levels of the organization. Persons isolated by floors and buildings will have very restricted communication patterns.[64] As discussed in later chapters, a communication audit may be used to help identify patterns of office interaction. Such an audit may involve (1) having employees fill out questionnaires about their interactions with other organizational members, (2) interviewing representative sample of employees to learn about their communication activities, or (3) having employees keep a log or tally sheet of their communication with others inside or outside the organization over a specified period of time, usually two weeks. Totaling the results and preparing interaction matrices will show the combined total of telephone calls, documents, visits, conferences, and electronic mail for each employee unit.[65]

Studies such as these are concerned with information flow and communication networks and facilitate the planning of space layout. What these studies do not show, however, are the needs for privacy and accessibility felt by people at different levels of the organizational hierarchy.[66] Implicit in some such studies is the assumption that existing patterns of communication are the right ones, an assumption that is not necessarily valid.

An example of a firm that involved employees at all levels in the planning of a new building was Teradyne Connection Systems (TCS), a New Hampshire firm manufacturing circuit-board backplanes.[67]

In TCS's old facilities, departments were scattered randomly throughout the plant. Members of the different departments rarely saw or communicated with each other. Assembly areas were located "out back" in an uninviting part of the plant, away from the areas that housed the specialists responsible for helping assembly workers with problems. The engineers, salespeople, production controllers, quality assurers, materials suppliers, and production people were rarely available to assist in solving problems encountered by assembly line workers, and the consequent delays in meeting delivery deadlines sometimes resulted in unhappy customers.

TCS President Windsor Hunter believes that buildings influence behavior by structuring relationships among organization members, encouraging some communication patterns and discouraging others, and that buildings likewise convey messages. In this case, Hunter and his management associates felt that the "assembly crisis problem" should guide the considerations of the architects designing the new building. They also wanted the building to make a statement about the value that they placed on their employees.

The result of extensive consultations with workers, foremen, and upper management was a building that met the human-recognition needs of its occupants and at the same time guaranteed the involvement of the specialists in assembly line concerns. The assembly area was made a focal point of the building, like the hub of a wheel, surrounded on three sides by specialist departments and leaving a fourth side open for possible later expansion. Working so close to the final assembly point, the specialists began to adopt a stronger customer orientation as well.

To contribute to the message that the company cared about the physical and psychological well-being of its employees, the architect located the building in a wooded area beside a historic canal, used warm artificial lighting and an effective ventilation and air conditioning system, built pleasant lounging and lunch facilities, and provided convenient tree-screened parking lots for the employees. A gallery built around the assembly area was designed to permit visitors to see through glass walls onto the assembly floor and down into a wide two-story corridor serving as the major walkway of the building. This vantage point allowed the visitor to observe the diversity of complex custom-designed products being put together out of standard subcomponents, and thus to gain insight into both plant functions and relationships between functions.

## The Automated Office and New Status Symbols

As the previous discussion indicates, spatial arrangements and physical-support systems serve three different kinds of functions—activity, authority, and recognition.[68]

An example of how physical facilities may encourage the performance of specific tasks or activities is evident in the presence of the conference room, designed to permit the privacy necessary in conducting job appraisal interviews or the intimacy important to management-client consultations. On the other hand, the laboratory in a research firm will be planned to facilitate quick easy exchanges between lab workers involved in joint endeavors.

Components of the physical setting may likewise establish or reinforce authority in an organization by communicating hierarchy of responsibility, typically through use of nameplates, office size and location, and quality of the furnishings.[69] Authority can also be communicated by who wears the white hat in a mining operation or a three-piece suit in the office.

The "recognition" function refers to the way in which the physical environment legitimizes, rewards, and supports status differences based on achievement (rather than on authority or supervisory functions, which may or may not be performed outstandingly) and the extent to which the physical setting fulfills basic human recognition needs.[70] Psychologists argue that such status distinctions are legitimate and will surface, whether sanctioned by the organization or not. Organization members will set themselves apart by a special kind of desk, by a plaque or certificate on the wall, or by the presence or absence of a briefcase. Many senior government workers and consultants in Washington and Ottawa, for example, carry a briefcase; but a recent survey by a Canadian television reporter found that many briefcases carried nothing more significant than the owner's lunch, a novel, or an umbrella. Nonetheless, the briefcases served an important status function, transmitting a seriousness of purpose and status in the organization or work culture in which the professionals moved.

Not all members of an organization will have the same recognition or status needs. The clerical worker with fifteen years of experience may have needs of a different intensity from those of the junior clerk. All organization members will have fundamental human-recognition needs that must be met, however, and one way of meeting these needs is through appropriate ordering of the physical environment. Thus, beyond the activity, authority, and status functions, organizations also serve a fourth human-recognition function, rewarding organization members for achievements but also giving at least minimum recognition to employees' needs for identity, physical comfort, variety, and beauty by providing work surroundings that accomplish this end.[71] Becker proposes that the landscaped office design may be the most satisfactory way of meeting these basic human recognition needs for the majority of employees, even if middle management reacts with more ambiguity to the changes.[72] Some of the pros and cons of the landscaped office will be discussed in a later section of this article.

Franklin Becker puts forward the argument that rather than using the physical environment to satisfy activity and human-recognition needs, the organization too often allocates space and resources in such a way as to satisfy authority and status needs, defending these allocations on the basis of activity rationales. He says that authority and status needs are legitimate ones, but he suggests that it is becoming increasingly inappropriate for space, equipment, and furnishings to be used to satisfy authority and status functions. For example, the advertising executive who spends more time in the air than on the ground should not have three times the space of the graphic artist with his numerous stacks of cardboard, art supplies, drafting table, and finished sketches.

Becker says that we need to identify new environmental nonverbal cues or symbol systems to satisfy the authority and status needs of organizational members.[73] For example, nurses, who do not occupy private offices or a single desk but move around an entire nursing unit, wear badges of rank. The same is true of the military. The mining supervisor wears a different colored hat from his subordinates. A high school senior wears a class ring, a sorority or fraternity member a special pin, and a priest special outer vestments that can denote not only rank but also order. These nonverbal symbol systems will most often be used in situations where other kinds of environmental support systems are unavailable to establish authority and status. Mobility characterizes all of the former classes of people—the student who moves from classroom to classroom, the priest who visits parishioners and transfers often from church to church and diocese to diocese, the mining operator who stays in one location only long enough to complete a job.

Becker proposes that the new mobility stimulated by portable electronic microcomputers and remote teleconferencing and telecommunications facilities suggests that status symbols should likewise become more mobile. The use of office size as a badge of distinction is a holdover from days of relatively inexpensive space and limited mobility and is no longer appropriate. For example, workstations are often shared now by individuals on different shifts. Even the workstation itself is highly movable.[74]

Eleanor Tedesco and Mitchell suggest that when an organization renovates or moves to new facilities, the firm should evaluate and redistribute status symbols. The flexibility of a new open plan will be hampered by employees taking old status symbols, such as a favored bookcase or lamp, with them. To mitigate employee fears that old status symbols will not be replaced, management may poll organizational members to ascertain the value attached to existing symbols and then attempt to choose other, more flexible and appropriate symbols.[75]

Becker's discussion recognizes that attempts to substitute apparel and other artifacts for the more traditional indicators of location and office size will generate suspicion and resentment among those at higher levels of the organization, and these are the people most important to the implementation of the new multiple symbol systems. Today's standards derive from work ethics and practices of the 1950s and have been fashioned largely by management, without input from workers or unions, who traditionally have been more concerned with wages, job security, and safety factors in the environment than with psychological factors.[76]

The primary purpose of current office-standards practices has been to reinforce authority, to reduce operating costs where possible, and to provide standards that legitimize unequal distribution of space and environmental resources across organizational levels while ensuring equity at any one level. Such practices are counterproductive, Becker contends, rarely contributing to satisfaction except at higher levels of management and acting as negative motivators at lower levels.[77] Although involvement of those at all levels of the organization is important in deciding the nature of the new systems, initiation of changes must be from the top down.[78]

Differences in office standards are greatest where those high in the organizational hierarchy are totally separated physically from those beneath them. For example, miners work in settings completely removed in location and quality from those of the mine owners and managers. The factory worker is in the same building but probably not on the same floor or sharing the same conditions as upper management. The office worker inhabits an environment more closely similar to that of his boss, but not so similar as that of the executive secretary. The landscaped office diminishes differences still more. Environmental conditions will be most common in the case of a person employed as a personal maid or valet.[79] In other words, the closer the proximity, the higher the environmental standards.

Becker speculates that this proximity and similarity factor will be a positive future influence on the lot of the average worker. With increasing use of the same electronic equipment and work stations by persons at very different levels of the organization, and with the push toward democratization and elimination of status symbols, the most proximate environments of the manager, the secretary, the engineer, the accountant, and the information officer will begin to merge. Such trends in office design and equipment are likely to result in improved environmental conditions for the lower-level employee and slightly poorer ones for middle management, as the physical setting for work becomes more uniform and standardized. Where managers use the same equipment as do their employees, the status of the lower group is enhanced.[80]

The open-plan office and electronic word and data processing equipment were originally introduced to cut costs, but today they promise to improve the workplace for the average employee, not only in terms of environmental conditions, but also in terms of work definition. Strassman predicts that in the next fifteen years more than 200 million electronic workstations will be placed in offices around the world. As the professional worker and the manager access information banks directly, engage in networking, utilize electronic message and filing systems, and rely more often on the enhanced problem-solving capabilities of computers, typists and secretaries may be freed to take on organizational duties of a less routine and more interesting nature. Two-thirds of a middle manager's time is currently spent in a liaison function, passing intraorganizational information to others;[81] however, as a consequence of automation and increased interaction between people at varying levels of the organization, this role is becoming redundant.

The concentration in studies to this point has been on how physical setting affects lower-echelon and assembly line workers rather than on how it affects managers, executives, and professionals. Whereas past advances in automation affected clerical and factory workers, present technological advances demand new skills and attitudes of professional workers and middle and upper management. In such a situation, those most likely to feel insecure in the new environment are the professionals and middle managers.[82] This insecurity is aggravated as their offices are taken away from them and traditional authority and status distinctions become blurred. As the numbers of clerical workers shrink, the numbers of technicians, professionals, and managers grow. These groups see enclosed offices as badges of success, and they resent the doorless workstations with movable partitions and a temporary look that seems to confirm that people, like objects, are replaceable. Many argue that these open-plan settings grew out of a desire to enhance the workplace for clerks operating in a bull pen layout and do not meet the needs for quiet and privacy required by professionals and managers.[83] To compensate for other lost privileges, managers may request and press for additional space, using scarce environmental resources to support authority and status instead of activity functions. Reducing the size of some workstations to give unnecessary space to others can have serious negative implications for the organization.[84]

For these reasons, it is important to develop and nurture new multiple-symbol systems before the old values also dominate the new computerized workplace. Becker says that once set in place, such systems are self-perpetuating, becoming part of the culture of the organization.

## Bürolandschaft

The justification for open-office landscaping has been the assumption that lowering of physical barriers will increase interaction between task partners. Office landscaping, or bürolandschaft, was developed in Germany and brought to the United States by the Quickborner team in 1964. Bürolandschaft involves mapping out the already-existing communication and work-flow patterns in a system and then attempting to facilitate those exchanges through appropriate spatial arrangements. Shoulder-level partitions, file cabinets, bookcases, and greenery replace fixed walls and allow employees to designate individual and group territories.[85]

Many offices use a mix of open-plan workstations and traditional offices. In the more "democratic" arrangements, the enclosed areas and conference rooms are in the central core; and the landscaped areas are on the periphery.[86] Access to windows helps to compensate for more negative environmental features such as reduced space.

In less democratic settings, upper management continues to prefer and demand completely enclosed private offices with an exterior view; middle management uses tall or ceiling-high partitions; and clerical and technical employees occupy open or partitioned space in the middle of the office area.[87]

Another alternative to the combination of private offices and open-plan workstations is exemplified in Herman Miller's "Action Office," a plan that provides individual work areas for everyone from corporation head to bookkeeper. The plan employs movable panels, modular components and attachable drawers, shelves, storage bins, work surfaces, and lateral files, as well as wiring outlets for office equipment.[88] The Herman Miller Company manufactures automated office furniture.

Because no one can predict facility requirements ten years in advance, such flexible and modular design offers ways of coping. In large corporations, departments and project teams are constantly being created and dissolved; in some businesses, the work force expands and contracts on a regular basis; still others rely on an ever-shifting supply of temporary workers. For this reason, many renowned office structures are vast, empty shells, with only their cores fixed in place. Modularity of design and furnishings allow assembling, rearranging, demounting, and storage of units. The key feature of workstations is movability.[89]

At one time, office furniture was made to last, but not so today. The U.S. Congress gives better tax depreciation rates on movable than on immovable materials and gives investment tax credits for remodeling, causing systems furniture designers to plan seven- to ten-year life spans for their products. All of these factors have influenced the development of open-plan offices, promoting the idea of flexible work spaces that favor change rather than stability.[90]

Justifications most often cited for office landscaping are that this environmental approach encourages greater communication between work teams, acts as a stimulus to those involved in routine work requiring low concentration, facilitates information exchange in high-traffic parts of the organization, gives a greater sense of privacy and territoriality to those employees previously working in bull pen arrangements, gives increased opportunity to supervise employees, and reduces the costs of renovating. The low cost of change means the organization will more readily change. Walter Kleinschrod suggests that the open plan is most efficient and appropriate to conditions of changing work patterns.[91] Some claim that the success of the new office automation systems is tied to the ability of firms to break down the divisions characterizing traditional office systems, a task made easier by the introduction of open-plan landscaping arrangements.

The Chicago headquarters of the MacDonald Corporation has been cited as an example of successful office landscaping. It is said that staff efficiency improved 35 percent after bürolandschaft was introduced. Turnover rates, which had been averaging 100 percent every two years in the old offices, dropped to 25 to 30 percent.[92] At Eastman Kodak, researchers studied the reactions of employees over a four-year period to office landscaping. The responses from over 700 persons in seven different departments showed that the employees liked the change from the conventional office environment. Later studies of another 494 employees supported the early test results.[93]

Even where offices are completely landscaped, however, some degree of privacy is still required for certain office functions such as the personnel one. Private offices and small meeting rooms are provided to meet these needs. The MacDonald Corporation headquarters has set aside one room with a giant waterbed as a "think tank."[94]

Those critical of the office-landscaping method claim that (1) few studies have demonstrated improvements in morale, efficiency, or work habits attributable to bürolandschaft; (2) it can be distracting and dysfunctional for upper management to be drawn into the details of day-to-day functioning of the organization when their main tasks necessitate making judgments based on a larger view of the system; (3) some studies indicate that while increasing general interaction, open office landscaping decreases intimate contacts that can be important in completing work tasks; (4) workers are frequently interrupted while engaged in work-related activities; (5) untidiness and noise are cited as major problems that even carpeting and acoustical tiles cannot completely alleviate; (6) supervisors find that the loss of privacy makes confidential conversations, job interviews, and performance appraisal meetings difficult; (7) security is difficult to assure in the open office; and (8) bürolandschaft assumes that the existing communication patterns are the most appropriate ones. Taking a different approach could mean setting up goals aimed at bringing the system up to what it should and potentially could be, with physical change as a facilitator.

A number of studies suggest that after the introduction of open-plan offices, communication actually deteriorates, with fewer friendships formed, less-frequent interaction between superiors and subordinates and between divisions, and poorer-quality interactions.[95] Some studies indicate that although more information is circulated, people's perceptions of functional efficiency decrease.[96]

Yvonne Clearwater found that the subjects she studied viewed landscaped offices as less democratic, which caused them to feel more "insecure, unsettled, alienated, passive, and vulnerable." This research obtained the same negative response to the open office from all categories of workers—clerical, technical, and supervisory. The people in Clearwater's study evaluated all items related to communication as being significantly worsened by the move to the landscaped office.

Clearwater concluded that the results of her study didn't support the intentions underlying the move; that is, improvement of flexibility, information flow, communication, and the elimination of internal barriers. She found no proof for claims of increased productivity, improved staff morale, or lower absenteeism.[97] Studies by Greg Oldham and Daniel Brass demonstrated that employee transfer to open-office design resulted in significant decreases in job satisfaction and motivation, with employees indicating they had trouble concentrating on their work in the open-plan office.[98]

Other studies have demonstrated that once employees move into an open-plan office, they are better able to observe the whole work process; consequently, some may come to the conclusion that their work has less impact on others and less significance than they previously thought.[99]

A study of an open-office design at the headquarters of the American Institute of Architects found that two-thirds of those interviewed said they preferred working in a conventional closed-office plan. The strongest negative reaction to the open plan came from professionals.[100] Researchers have found that those who most resent the open plan and who experience the keenest loss of privacy are the middle-level employees, the supervisors and administrators who have been forced from their closed offices. Secretaries and lower-echelon workers often like the landscaping arrangements, which they find colorful and appealing.[101] Typical of middle management's response to the open-landscape arrangements was the following:

> I don't know if the arrangement makes communications within the department better. I do know there are constant interruptions, that everything you say is overheard, which means you can't talk to an employee about poor performance unless you parade him or her into a conference room, and then everybody can see what's happening. For some reasons, nobody exercises common rules of courtesy here; the arrangement has brought out different—and worse—patterns of behavior than I've been accustomed to, even when working in a totally open space.[102]

In another case, an architect convinced company management to replace its conventional full-partitioned offices with an open-plan office system. Five-and-a-half foot high opaque panels supported shelves, desks, terminals, and lab benches. A week after the system was installed, the engineering manager called the system a disaster, claiming that he could not possibly operate within it. He said that no partitions at all would be better than the new arrangements.[103]

The old offices had contained three glass interior windows that gave occupants a 180-degree view of their surroundings. With the new opaque walls, the manager said he could never be sure when a customer, visitor, or someone with whom he would not want to share specific information was nearby.

In open-plan offices, middle- and low-level managers can substitute human for physical barriers, locating their workstations so that someone approaching must walk past many other workers before reaching them. Other officers can place their desks facing the door in order to maintain visual control over those entering the office. In many managerial or executive workstations, a freestanding oval conference table acts as a barrier to the door, and some individuals choose to use the table as a desk, rather than sit with their back to the door.[104] Mazelike entrances to workstations may serve to minimize visual and acoustical distractions[105] and offer psychological security to occupants of the workstations.

Cynics note that top management rarely relinquishes its private offices. They say that while landscaped offices are often justified on the basis of improving the quality of work life, communication, and efficiency, the real reasons have more to do with reducing the total amount of space per employee, lowering the costs of rearranging the office furniture, and maintaining an "image of modernity" in a highly competitive marketplace. They claim that the other justifications are symbolic, not substantive.[106]

## Overconcentration

Some feel that the open plan is a "people squeezer," creating overcrowded and mazelike effects. Whereas the original idea behind the open plan was to add unnecessary corridor space to work areas, over time the criterion became accommodating larger numbers of people in smaller amounts of space.[107] Those concerned about over-crowding say that rather than increasing communication or social contact, crowding may "strengthen a social order that discourages communication in order to prevent overstimulation from too many people in too little space."[108]

Issues related to density, crowding, and privacy have most often been studied in nonoffice environments—hospitals, schools, psychological laboratories, and housing complexes. The major finding of such studies has been that high density is not synonymous with crowding. For high-density situations to be perceived as crowding, a negative stressful state, an individual must feel unable to control the nature and type of his or her interaction with others. The experience of crowding reflects a failure to achieve a balance between the desired level of interaction and the obtained level of interaction.[109] Architectural design elements such as degree of enclosure, visibility levels, and means of controlling noise bear a significant relationship to perceptions of privacy. Studies by Eric Sundstrom have found that such perceptions characterize not only administrators, but clerks as well, who experienced increased levels of job satisfaction in circumstances where they had control over their environment.[110]

Some studies have demonstrated that an environment perceived as crowded may contribute to competitive and aggressive behaviors. In other circumstances, such conditions may result in social-withdrawal behaviors.[111] The concept of territoriality is an important one as relates to crowding. Animals and people mark out spaces that they defend against trespassers. Among humans, a potted plant or a storage cabinet or an ashtray may mark "home" territory. The act of moving a chair or park bench psychologically cancels out the right of the previous occupant to the chair. Spreading papers or books on a desk similarly establishes the space as occupied. Americans dislike sitting on the same side of the table as another, for they are entering the personal space of the other person.[112]

Employees who feel that their territory has been violated may well attempt to defend it. For the same reasons, workers may flee a bureaucratic environment over which they have no personal control and take their work to the more private territory of the home.[113] In forbidding members of the organization to bring personal furnishings or effects to their work environments, bureaucratic organizations act against very strong (albeit culturally influenced) employee needs.

When people complain of not having privacy, they are saying that they cannot control their relation to their social surroundings, for privacy is a relative term.[114] Steele agrees with other authorities on this subject when he says that crowding is in large part a psychological and social phenomenon, not an engineering measure. Whether a layout seems crowded will depend on the norms and needs of the people who use it. For instance, it has been found in Canadian university dormitories that room densities preferred by French-speaking students seem too crowded to English-speaking students.[115] Conversational distances will vary from culture to culture, with Arabs preferring much closer physical proximity than Americans. By the same token, Americans set physical barriers between themselves and others, whereas the English set psychic barriers, retreating into themselves for privacy.[116]

The same principles apply to organizational settings. Sommer prefers, however, to differentiate between the term "overcrowding" and the term "overconcentration." He says that when we talk about high-rise office buildings, the problem to which we are making reference is more one of overconcentration than overcrowding. "Overconcentration" refers to too many people in one place, regardless of size.[117] An example would be two advertising executives sharing the same office. While the office floor space may be sufficient for two people, ringing telephones and client visits would make the situation an untenable one for both parties. Similarly, our personal space requirements, which are for the most part culturally based, make some spatial arrangements intolerable.[118] For that reason, standard office settings are not appropriate for international companies who must house people of many cultural origins.

Overconcentration can occur easily in any organization that attempts to base its space-layout calculations on "purely mechanistic notions of the amount of space taken up by bodies and movement."[119]

### Future Trends: From Office to Home

Computerization of the workplace favors transfer of many tasks from the office to the home, causing many to predict a growing cottage industry.

Advantages to working at home include elimination of time wasted in commuting; lower rates of absenteeism; improvement in family life; and enhanced potential for retired knowledge workers, young mothers, and those with health problems and disabilities to participate in the work force.[120]

Those who support the move from the office to the home claim that the majority of secretarial, clerical, and professional jobs can be carried out at home, as most information-intensive tasks are best completed in isolation. Enthusiasts predict that equipping workers with office workstations for home use will result in more time devoted to productive work, while at the same time contributing to morale and job satisfaction.[121]

In such circumstances, the function of the office changes from a place where routine work occurs to a place for sharing experiences and ideas and for socializing. Strassman summarized this point of view in the following way:

> The office is a difficult place for generating creative thoughts or for serious concentration on documents. In the long run I see the role of the office building as emphasizing the socializing needs of the business. The purpose of getting people together in a building will be much more to stimulate inspiration, cooperation, motivation, and the sharing of complex experiences with members of a team than actually to complete creative work. This is why conference rooms, recreational and meeting facilities may become much more important in the future office architecture than is currently the case.[122]

Critics of the transfer of work from the office to the home claim that the home may contain many elements that mitigate against task accomplishment such as uncontrolled noise, demands by other family members, poor lighting, and interruptions such as the ringing of a doorbell or telephone calls from friends and neighbors. Home and work roles in such a setting may become confused and create dissonance for the individual faced with conflicting demands. The absence of daily contact with coworkers may generate a feeling of isolation and foster lack of commitment. Frequent change of employers can characterize the situation of workers employed at home, and unions fear that the availability of such a temporary work force may eliminate the supplementary benefits and job security for which the unions have worked hard.[123]

## Conclusions

Buildings should not require office workers to "live up" to an environment and change their behavior to fit the architecture. Instead, physical structures should accommodate as well as possible the people they were designed to house. The architect's focus should not be on novelty and private expression. Office buildings, airport terminals, and banks should not be evaluated by the same sculptural standards as are national monuments; and prisons should not be a model for schools, housing projects, or commercial buildings.[124] The emphasis should be on the comfort and satisfaction of the occupants and on encouraging the kind of communication patterns most appropriate to the activities going on inside the structure. As Latham has noted, utilitarian aspects of design cannot be separated from the aesthetic, for we experience the total.[125] Sommer made this same point when he said:

> There can be no dichotomy between good design and usable design or between beauty and function in architecture. To look beyond the physical structure of a building to its social consequences, to the sorts of activity it will contain, and to its effect upon the surrounding community is a necessary aspect of good design.[126]

Hard architecture is expensive and difficult to change, has no connection with the surrounding environment, clearly differentiates status levels, and restricts activities and people to specified locations. If Churchill was right when he said that the buildings we shape will eventually shape us, then "the inevitable result of hard buildings will be withdrawn, callous, and indifferent people."[127]

In recent years, many banks and nightclubs have attempted to humanize and soften their settings in an effort to make their customers feel less out of place and less intimidated by a hard, cold environment.[128]

Organizations should place as much importance on the image that they project to their employees as on the one they project to the public. The "backstage" areas where members of social systems carry out their "performances" should rank in importance with the "front stage" areas.[129] The offices of lower-echelon workers and of personnel departments no more belong in underground quarters or in windowless buildings or in drab, out-of-the-way locations than do those of the administrators; and ugly, depersonalized buildings and rooms cannot be justified on the basis of economy. An environment that contains inadequate stimuli will produce bored, apathetic, and disinterested employees who eventually "tune out" their environment or who flee to their homes in an effort to get something accomplished.[130]

Studies have found that companies placing employees in underground facilities have higher turnover rates and lower employee morale than do those with more agreeable settings.[131] Where placement of computers and other technology necessitates that workers be housed in underground facilities, management should look for ways to relieve the dullness of such an environment. An atrium from the higher to the lower floors, surrogate windows in the form of tropical fish tanks, posters, and profusion of plants and flowers have been used by some firms to counteract the negative features of basement quarters. Astute management will make every effort to try to counter the numbness that people may develop toward disagreeable surroundings:

> To survive he [man] accepts very quickly, almost subserviently, the pressures of his environment. His brain is apparently designed so that when intolerable signals come in over the circuits, the perceptive systems themselves shut down and do not perceive. A man can live and even be happy in the environment of a garbage heap. This is demonstrated (in the extreme) during wartime, when the human mind and perceptive system survives massive continuous shock. Most of man's ability to use his brain for emotional and aesthetic purposes must be cut off, and in some cases it is never regained.[132]

Settings should serve to reinforce a sense of the value of the individual in the organization, rather than to underscore and point to his insignificance, as does the Kramberg building of Germany. Offices and conference rooms should be flexible and capable of being personalized, humane and attractive, giving occupants the feeling that they have an investment in their surroundings and that modification of the undesirable is possible.[133] Settings should draw out the creativity that resides in the individual. Variety in color, lighting, humidity, and temperature will help to eliminate the feelings of boredom and restlessness that are created by a homogeneous environment.[134] It has been proposed that the best situation is "some novel stimuli in a familiar setting."[135]

Organizations need to realize that universal solutions applied to all settings will be inappropriate as often as not and that settings must vary with the people concerned and with the activities that go on inside them.[136] Schweitzer's hospital at Lambarene is said to represent such an attempt to take into account the cultural and individual identities of the people who were to be accommodated within its walls. Schweitzer made modifications in the design of the hospital, changes that would not be acceptable to modern Western institutions, in order not to frighten away the bush people whom he was serving.[137]

There is no single best arrangement of furniture or artifacts. The work task may demand increased or decreased social contact, or the employee may prefer to work in private or in cooperation with others. There are certain kinds of work activity that traditionally have involved open-plan interaction, and it is difficult to see how some of these work tasks could be performed in any environment other than an open arena. The newsroom with its frequent and rapid communication exchanges would slow to a costly halt if its reporters and editors were segregated in private offices with secretaries to act as gatekeepers. In the same way, the stock exchange is an open activity, and it is appropriately called the stock "market."

Design offices of highly complex technologies such as aircraft manufacturing are usually very large open areas, with rows of draftsmen and designers working at and walking around drawing boards. So many different skills must come together in the design of anything so complex as an aircraft that work environment must reflect and stimulate easy interaction.

Other instances where a "cabbage-patch" arrangement may be most appropriate involve what Mehrabian terms "low-load" tasks, jobs that do not demand high levels of concentration and mental input.[138] In such cases, the open office or work area can provide stimulation and allow the work experience to be enhanced by the social overtones. The high degree of interpersonal contact can compensate for other environmental inadequacies. It has been observed that "high density makes other people a more important stimulus."[139] In general terms, Mehrabian states that "the lower the load of a task, the more it requires a high-load setting for optimum performance."[140] He does also note, however, that certain complex jobs can become so familiar as to reduce their loads to moderate or low and allow the parties to benefit from an open work environment.[141] Other studies have found that for workers who are "outer-directed," the noise of others may be motivating.[142]

On the other hand, some kinds of work would be difficult, if not impossible, in an open arena. This would be the case when the work is of a contemplative nature or when too intimate a level of contact with processes could impair the capacity to understand or to administer systems as a whole. The top-level policymaker of the aircraft company or the newspaper will rarely choose an open office in which to carry out his duties. Decisions on spatial arrangements should be made in accord with the need to bring people together (sociopetal) or to keep them apart (sociofugal). The most important decisions should be based on activity and human recognition functions, not on status and authority functions.

If the open plan is considered to be the appropriate one for a particular person or business (and new experiences are sometimes needed to make employees aware of their range of alternatives), it should also be remembered that man is a territorial being. Not only walls, but also furniture and artifacts can be used to designate personal and group territory. Allowing employees to bring personal belongings to their work environments recognizes the very real nature of these socio-psychological needs. New nonverbal symbol systems that do not sap the resources of the organization must be devised to satisfy status needs of organization members.

Out of the open plan was born the room divider, the function of which was to return the open plan to a more psychologically closed one. The outside environment and adjacent inside environments can be distracting, and movable partitions and dividers may be highly practical, not only for the individual but also for the organization. The worker who can give total attention to a task when a high level of concentration is required will contribute more than does the frustrated employee who attempts to engage in problem solving in an atmosphere that he finds distracting and disorienting. Even the lowest-level clerk should have access to a closed facility when he feels the need for such a setting. Overcrowding, or overconcentration, can be as serious a problem as that of inadequate contact between members of an organization.

The ideal situation is probably one where an employee, whether low level or top line, has easy access to both open and closed work environments. While performing pleasant and easy or pleasant and complex (but very familiar) tasks, a worker could select to be with others and to discuss as he works. Under pressure to meet a deadline or working on a project demanding high concentration, the same worker could retreat behind closed doors.[143]

While not all office buildings can afford the same space for individual options, most buildings can incorporate private conference and work rooms and central lounge areas and coffee shops. Such areas can be especially effective when placed in the center of a cluster of offices and can serve a function not filled by conference rooms placed "deep in executive territory."[144] The coffee shop or the lounge is neutral territory and encourages cross-status exchanges important to the vitality of any system.

Such common lounging areas are especially important in academic settings and business settings involving information transfer. Faculty members and administrators need the opportunity to exchange ideas and to merge the findings of their different disciplines. Similarly, office buildings shared by different companies can benefit from such central socializing areas where cross-fertilization occurs.

Mehrabian proposes a design for such a social area that departs from the traditional coffee-shop format and uses limited numbers of "conversation pits." Strangers are forced into the same pit, thus enriching the "impersonal, alien, and sterile atmosphere of many office buildings, especially the new high-rise variety."[145]

In the future, organizations may give employees the option to transfer their work from office to home. If such options become commonplace, organizations must not forget the socialization function that is also a part of what any organization offers its workforce.

A similar trend toward moving the office from fifty-story skyscrapers to suburban shopping complexes closer to home may be seen in many communities.[146]

Cohen and Cohen call skyscrapers "totalitarian architecture" that disregards the individuality of its inhabitants and places them in cells of steel, glass, and concrete.[147] Many such structures, which take as much as five years to build, are already outdated before they are ever used, sometimes because their layouts have been based on passing fads and sometimes because they cannot accommodate advances in the equipment and technology that they must house. Inadequate wiring and ventilation capabilities, for example, can mean that a building is unable to support more than a limited number of computers.

To cope with these kinds of problems, contemporary builders are moving toward more flexible interiors, furnishing their offices with systems furniture and modular walls that "presuppose that people and things are interchangeable." Cohen and Cohen say that this philosophy is the basis of the modern bureaucratic structure, wherein organized work relies on the interchangeability of not only objects, but also people.[147] Max Weber, the father of bureaucratic studies, maintained that "a bureaucratic system increased efficiency to the extent that it

*depersonalized* the performance of official tasks. . . . But the impersonality that was the antidote to favoritism, nepotism, and arbitrariness,
when transferred to the area of design, resulted in faceless buildings in
which no one feels at home."[148]

The concern generated by this combination of hard impersonal
buildings and temporary interiors has caused social scientists to urge
"that the people who study human behavior and the people who plan
the human environment should join forces."[149] There is today a greater
awareness than twenty years ago of environment-related issues, and
some claim that a "fragile bridge" is already being built between the
social sciences and the design professions. To make further progress,
environmental consultants should work in collaboration with architects
and space planners, and management in general should seek to become
more "environmentally competent."[150]

To encourage this trend, rewards for outstanding architectural design
should be based on three-dimensional attributes of structures and not
on two-dimensional photographs that meet media, but not human,
standards.[151]

## Notes

1. Fred Steele, *Physical Settings and Organization Development* (Reading,
   Mass.: Addison-Wesley, 1973), p. 8.
2. *Ibid.*, p. 15.
3. Franklin D. Becker, *Workspace: Creating Environments in Organizations*
   (New York: Praeger, 1981), pp. 8–9.
4. Steele, *op. cit.*, p. 17.
5. Malcolm Peltu, *Successful Management of Office Automation* (Manches-
   ter, England: The National Computing Center Ltd., 1984), p. 25.
6. Paula B. Cecil, *Office Automation: Concepts* (Menlo Park, Calif.: Benja-
   min/Cummings, 1984), pp. 288–91. See also Rudy A. Hirschheim, *Office
   Automation: Concepts, Technologies and Issues* (Reading, Mass.: Addison-Wesley, 1985), pp. 229–32.
7. Francis D. Lethbridge, "The Honors Awards Program in Retrospect,"
   *A.I.A. Journal* (May 1973), p. 22; cited in Robert Sommer, *Tight Spaces:
   Hard Architecture and How to Humanize It* (Englewood Cliffs, N.J.:
   Prentice-Hall, 1974), p. 129.
8. Sommer, *op. cit.*, pp. 129–30.
9. Henry Wollman, "Calendar for the Yale School of Architecture," 1971;
   cited in Sommer, *op. cit.*, p. 130.
10. Sommer, *op. cit.*, pp. 104–5 and 112.
11. Robert Sommer, *Design Awareness* (San Francisco: Rinehart, 1972), p.
    85.
12. Sommer, *Tight Spaces, op. cit.*, p. 2.
13. Elaine Cohen and Aaron Cohen, *Planning the Electronic Office* (New
    York: McGraw-Hill, 1983), p. 106.

14. Becker, *op. cit.*, pp. 126–27, also pp. 77 and 97.
15. *Ibid.*, pp. 71 and 76.
16. Cited in Becker, *op. cit.*, p. 120.
17. *Ibid.*
18. Yvonne A. Clearwater, *Comparison of Effects of Open and Closed Office Design on Job Satisfaction*, unpublished Ph.D. dissertation, University of California, Davis, 1980; cited in Becker, *op. cit.*, p. 142.
19. Becker, *op. cit.*, p. 120.
20. Seiler, "Architecture at Work," *Harvard Business Review* (September–October 1984) p. 120.
21. Steele, *op. cit.*, p. 49. Also see Albert Mehrabian, *Public Places and Private Spaces* (New York: Basic Books, 1976), p. 145.
22. Michael Korda, "Office Power—You are Where you Sit," in Lawrence B. Rosenfeld and Jean M. Civikly, *With Words Unspoken: The Nonverbal Experience* (New York: Holt, Rinehart and Winston, 1976), p. 183.
23. Cohen and Cohen, *op. cit.*, p. 121.
24. *Ibid.*, p. 183.
25. *Ibid.*, pp. 183–84.
26. *Ibid.*, p. 183.
27. Becker, *op. cit.*, p. 100.
28. *Ibid.*
29. Franklin Becker, *Housing Messages* (Strondsberg, Penn.: Dowden, Hutchinson and Ross, 1977), p. 3.
30. F. D. Becker, S. Ashworth, D. Poe, and D. Beaver, *User Participation, Personalization, and Environmental Meaning* (Ithaca, N.Y.: Program in Urban and Regional Studies, Cornell University, 1978); cited in Becker, *op. cit.*, pp. 100–01.
31. Gerald M. Goldhaber, *Organizational Communication*, fourth ed. (Dubuque, Iowa: Wm. C. Brown, 1986), p. 204. According to *Northeast Training News*, March 1980, p. 7, 270 square feet is regarded as minimum workspace for a top-level executive, 196 square feet for a mid-level executive, and an average of 72 square feet for staff specialists.
32. *Ibid.*, p. 182.
33. Cohen and Cohen, *op. cit.*, pp. 114–16.
34. Becker, *Workspace, op. cit.*, p. 144–51.
35. Goldhaber, *op. cit.*, p. 206.
36. Becker, *Workspace, op. cit.*, pp. 51 and 68–69.
37. Goldhaber, *op. cit.*, p. 206.
38. Korda, in Rosenfeld and Civikly, *op. cit.*, pp. 182–83.
39. *Ibid.*
40. John A. Seiler, *op cit.*, p. 120.
41. Numerous other examples of city planning efforts that failed in the same way and for the same reasons exist. Some of these examples are discussed by William H. Ittelson, Harold M. Proshansky, Leanne G. Rivlin, and Gary H. Winkel, *An Introduction to Environmental Psychology* (New York: Holt, Rinehart and Winston, 1974), pp. 267–84; also by Norman W. Heimstra and Leslie H. McFarling, *Environmental Psychology* (Monterey, Calif.: Brooks/Cole, 1974), pp. 87–114.
42. Humphrey Osmond, "Function as a Basis of Psychiatric Ward Design," *Mental Hospitals* (1957), vol. 8, pp. 23–29.

43. Some of the most-often cited studies supporting these conclusions were by Robert Sommer. According to Edward Hall, "The Anthropology of Space: An Organizing Model," in *Environmental Psychology: Man and His Physical Setting* H. M. Proshansky, W. H. Ittelson, and L. G. Rivlin, ed. (New York: Holt, Rinehart and Winston, 1970), p. 19, Osmond was the person responsible for Sommer's initial interest in the relationship of furniture to conversation. Sommer has published this research in numerous articles and books; one of his earliest was "Studies in Personal Space," *Sociometry* (1959), vol. 22, pp. 247–60.
44. Cohen and Cohen, *op. cit.*, pp. 117–18.
45. *Ibid.*, p. 118.
46. *Ibid.*, p. 125.
47. *Ibid.*
48. *Ibid.*, p. 106.
49. *Ibid.*, p. 125.
50. Abraham H. Maslow and Norbett L. Mintz, "Effects of Esthetic Surroundings: I. Initial Effects of Three Esthetic Conditions Upon Perceiving 'Energy' and 'Well-Being' in Faces," *Journal of Psychology* (1956), vol. 41, p. 253; see also Norbett L. Mintz, "Effects of Esthetic Surroundings: II. Prolonged and Repeated Experience in a 'Beautiful' and 'Ugly' Room," *Journal of Psychology* (1956), vol. 41, pp. 465–66.
51. See William Griffitt, "Environmental Effects on Interpersonal Affective Behavior: Ambient-Effective Temperature and Attraction," *Journal of Personality and Social Psychology* (1970), vol. 15, pp. 240–44. Also W. Griffitt and R. Veitch, "Hot and Crowded: Influences of Population Density and Temperature on Interpersonal Affective Behavior," *Journal of Personality and Social Psychology* (1971), vol. 17, pp. 92–98.
52. W. J. Sauser, C. G. Arauz, and R. M. Chambers, "Exploring the Relationships Between Level of Office Noise and Salary Recommendations: A Preliminary Research Note," *Journal of Management* (1978), vol. 4, pp. 57–63.
53. Fred L. Strodtbeck and L. Harmon Hook, "The Social Dimension of a Twelve Man Jury Table," *Sociometry* (1961), vol. 24, pp. 397–415.
54. Sommer, *Tight Spaces, op. cit.*, p. 108.
55. William E. Spaulding, "Undiscovered Values in Meetings," *Journal of Systems Management* (1978), vol. 29, pp. 24–27.
56. James C. McCroskey, Carl E. Larson, and Mark L. Knapp, *An Introduction to Interpersonal Communication* (Englewood, N.J.: Prentice-Hall, 1971), p. 97.
57. Edward T. Hall, *The Hidden Dimension* (Garden City, N.Y.: Doubleday, 1966), p. 115.
58. Cohen and Cohen, *op. cit.*, pp. 109–10 and 123.
59. Steele, *op. cit.*, p. 38.
60. T. Allen, "Meeting the Technical Information Needs of Research and Development Projects," MIT Industrial Liaison Program Report, no. 13-314, November 1969; cited in Steele, *op. cit.*, p. 65.
61. Leon Festinger, Stanley Schacter, and Kurt Back, *Social Pressures in Informal Groups: A Study of Human Factors in Housing* (Stanford, Calif.: Stanford University Press, 1950).
62. Sommer, *Tight Spaces, op. cit.*, p. 12; see also Steele, *op. cit.*, p. 36.

63. George C. Homans, *The Human Group* (New York: Harcourt Brace & World, 1950), pp. 88–89.
64. Sommer, *Tight Spaces, op. cit.,* p. 102.
65. Eleanor Hollis Tedesco and Robert B. Mitchell, *Administrative Office Management: The Electronic Office* (New York: John Wiley, 1984), pp. 216–17.
66. Becker, *Workspace, op. cit.,* p. 70.
67. Seiler, *op. cit.,* pp. 111–20.
68. Becker, *Workspace, op. cit.,* pp. 144–48.
69. *Ibid.,* p. 145.
70. *Ibid.*
71. *Ibid.,* pp. 145–46.
72. *Ibid.,* p. 139.
73. *Ibid.,* pp. 148–51.
74. Cohen and Cohen, *op. cit.,* pp. 16–17.
75. Tedesco and Mitchell, *op. cit.,* p. 219.
76. Becker, *Workspace, op. cit.,* pp. 111 and 138.
77. *Ibid.,* p. 150.
78. *Ibid.,* pp. 132 and 136–39.
79. *Ibid.,* pp. 77 and 140–41.
80. *Ibid.*
81. Paul A. Strassman, *Information Payoff: The Transformation of Work in the Electronic Age* (New York: The Free Press, 1985), pp. xvii and 196.
82. Becker, *Workspace, op. cit.,* p. 69. Also see Harry J. Otway and Malcolm Peltu, "The Challenge of New Managerial Roles," in *New Office Technology: Human and Organizational Aspects* (Norwood, N.J.: Ablex, 1983), pp. 1–2.
83. Cohen and Cohen, *op. cit.,* pp. 121 and 133.
84. Becker, *Workspace, op. cit.,* p. 148.
85. Phillip Howard, "Office Landscaping Revisited," *Design and Environment* (Fall 1972), pp. 40–47.
86. Tedesco and Mitchell, *op. cit.,* p. 215.
87. *Ibid.*
88. Cecil, *op. cit.,* pp. 42–43.
89. Cohen and Cohen, *op. cit.,* pp. 11–13.
90. *Ibid.,* pp. 127–32 and 141.
91. Walter A. Kleinschrod, "The Case for Office Landscape," *Administrative Management* (October 1966), pp. 19–20.
92. Everett M. Rogers and Rekha Agarwala-Rogers, *Communication in Organizations* (New York: Free Press, 1976), p. 104.
93. Tedesco and Mitchell, *op. cit.,* p. 214.
94. *Ibid.*
95. Becker, *Workspace, op. cit.,* pp. 59 and 106.
96. Malcolm J. Brookes and Archie Kaplan, "The Office Environment: Space Planning and Affective Behavior," *Human Factors* (1972), vol. 14, pp. 373–91.
97. Clearwater study cited in Becker, *Workspace, op. cit.,* pp. 106–07 and 111. Numerous other studies are also cited by Becker.
98. Greg R. Oldham and Daniel J. Brass, "Employee Reactions to an Open-Plan Office: A Naturally Occurring Quasi-Experiment," *Administrative Science Quarterly* (1979), vol. 24, pp. 267–84.

99. Becker, *Workspace, op. cit.*, p. 106.
100. A. O. Dean, "Evaluation of an Open Office Landscape: AIA Headquarters," *A.I.A. Journal* (1977), vol. 66, pp. 32–39.
101. Sommer, *Tight Spaces, op. cit.*, p. 109.
102. Cited in Becker, *Workspace, op. cit.*, p. 107.
103. Seiler, *op. cit.*, p. 118.
104. Cohen and Cohen, *op. cit.*, pp. 115–16.
105. *Ibid.*, pp. 116 and 132.
106. Becker, *Workspace, op. cit.*, p. 68.
107. Cohen and Cohen, *op. cit.*, pp. 132–33.
108. Sommer, *Tight Spaces, op. cit.*, p. 122.
109. Becker, *Workspace, op. cit.*, pp. 122–24.
110. Eric Sundstrom, Robert E. Burt, and Douglas Kamp, "Privacy at Work: Architectural Correlates of Job Satisfaction and Job Performance," *Academy of Management Journal* (1980), vol. 23, pp. 101–17.
111. Becker, *Workspace, op. cit.*, p. 124.
112. See Cohen and Cohen, *op. cit.*, pp. 11 and 109; see also Jonathan L. Freedman, *Crowding and Behavior* (New York: Viking, 1975), pp. 24–40.
113. Proshansky, Ittelson, and Rivlin, "Freedom of Choice and Behavior in a Physical Setting," in *Environmental Psychology, op. cit.*, p. 179. See also Hall, *Hidden Dimension, op. cit.*, p. 31.
114. Proshansky, Ittelson, and Rivlin, "Freedom of Choice," *op. cit.*, pp. 175–83.
115. Steele, *op. cit.*, p. 29.
116. Hall, *Hidden Dimension, op. cit.*, p. 131.
117. *Tight Spaces, op. cit.*, p. 122. Also see Proshansky, Ittelson, and Rivlin, *op. cit.*, pp. 181–83.
118. Hall, *op. cit.*, p. 32.
119. Steele, *op. cit.*, p. 29.
120. Strassman, *op. cit.*, pp. 7 and 46–49. Also see Peter F. Eder, "Telecommuters: The Stay-at-Home Work Force of the Future," *The Futurist* (June 1983), vol. 18, p. 30; and Frank W. Schiff, "Flexiplace: Pros and Cons," *The Futurist* (June 1983), vol. 18, pp. 32–33.
121. *Ibid.*, p. 46. Also Becker, *Workspace, op. cit.*, p. 151.
122. Strassman, *op. cit.*, pp. 45–46.
123. Eder, *op. cit.*, p. 30, and Schiff, *op. cit.*, p. 33.
124. Sommer, *Tight Spaces, op. cit.*
125. Richard S. Latham, "The Artifact as a Cultural Cipher," in *Who Designs America?* Laurence B. Holland, ed. (Garden City, N.Y.: Doubleday Anchor, 1966), p. 262.
126. Sommer, *Design Awareness, op. cit.*, p. 4.
127. Sommer, *Tight Spaces, op. cit.*, pp. 24–26.
128. Mark L. Knapp, *Nonverbal Communication in Human Interaction* (New York: Holt, Rinehart and Winston, 1972), p. 30.
129. Erving Goffman used these terms in *The Presentation of Self in Everyday Life* (Garden City, N.Y.: Doubleday Anchor, 1959).
130. John Platt, "Beauty, Pattern and Change," in *Functions of Varied Experience* Donald W. Fiske and Salvatore R. Maddi, ed. (Homewood, Ill.: Dorsey, 1961), pp. 402–30.

131. Sommer, *Tight Spaces, op. cit.,* pp. 114–19.
132. Latham, *op. cit.,* p. 264.
133. Sommer, *Tight Spaces, op. cit.,* p. 107.
134. Heimstra and McFarling, *op. cit.,* p. 67. Also Rosenfeld and Civikly, *op. cit.,* p. 178.
135. Rosenfeld and Civikly, *op. cit.,* p. 179.
136. Steele, *op. cit.,* p. 15.
137. Sommer, *Tight Spaces, op. cit.,* p. 105.
138. Mehrabian, *op. cit.,* pp. 143–45.
139. Freedman, *op. cit.,* p. 105.
140. Mehrabian, *op. cit.,* p. 143.
141. *Ibid.*
142. Cohen and Cohen, *op. cit.,* p. 118.
143. *Ibid.,* p. 146.
144. *Ibid.*
145. *Ibid.,* pp. 147–48.
146. Robert A. Russel, *The Electronic Briefcase, The Office of the Future,* Institute for Research on Public Policy, September 1978.
147. Cohen and Cohen, *op. cit.,* p. 103.
148. Sommer, *Tight Spaces, op. cit.*
149. *Ibid.,* pp. 106–07, and Sommer, *Design Awareness, op. cit.,* pp. 86–87. Other persons supporting this view include Steele, *op. cit.,* p. 17, and C. M. Deasy, "When Architects Consult People," *Psychology Today* (1970), vol. 3, pp. 54–57 and 78–79.
150. Becker, *Workspace, op. cit.,* p. 2.
151. Cohen and Cohen, *op. cit.,* p. 102.

# 10

# Nonverbal Communication in the Organization

*Sandra M. Ketrow*

The Chinese ideogram for the verb "to listen" incorporates characters that represent *ear, eyes, heart,* and *undivided attention,*[1] emphasizing the point that the words or language which we hear comprise only a part of any message and that messages can be nonverbal as well as verbal.

What is nonverbal communication? Nonverbal communication is usually defined as all those behaviors or cues that are *not* verbal. Almost any voluntarily manipulated, intentional act or signal that is not words and is consistently interpreted by those on the receiving end qualifies as nonverbal communication.[2] Thus, in the employment interview your greeting smile is considered nonverbal, but the actual verbal statement, "I'm pleased to meet you," is not.

Estimates for the level of contribution that nonverbal cues provide for the meaning of a given message range from 60 to 93 percent. Burgoon says that the most reasonable estimates lie in the range of 60–70 percent. Furthermore, adults rely more heavily on nonverbal than verbal cues in communication.[3] In other words, nonverbal signals carry more weight or importance than do verbal symbols in human communication in organizations.

Meaning is conveyed by the interrelationship of words and nonverbal systems. Birdwhistell pointed out that "linguistics and kinesics are infra-communication systems, within the larger communication system comprising all the senses. Language is only one part of a communication process, just as the metabolism is only one aspect of the process of living."[4] Many sensory cues are available, some of which we notice at the conscious level, while others influence us subconsciously.

## Domain and Functions of Nonverbal Communication

What "counts" as nonverbal communication? First, a receiver orientation suggests that any behavior or act that a receiver interprets as intentional should be considered communication.[5] Alternatively, a message orientation sees communications as "those behaviors that form a socially shared coding system; that is, they are behaviors that are typically sent with intent, used with regularity among members of a social community, interpreted as intentional, and have consensually recognizable interpretations."[6] The absence as well as the presence of nonverbal signals can also influence the interpretation of meaning.

Nonverbal communication serves several functions in relationship to verbal communication. Nonverbal cues can *repeat, contradict, complement, substitute for, accentuate,* or *regulate* verbal symbols.[7]

*Repetition.* In this case, verbal meaning is reinforced through redundancy. When a shipment of office supplies comes in, the shipping clerk says, "Put it down there," and points down to the floor. Meaning is thus fairly clear.

*Contradiction.* Nonverbal cues may negate a message by indicating the opposite of the verbal meaning. This may be intentional, such as when we engage in sarcasm. A customer may say on the telephone, "Sure, I'd love to see your display on Thursday!" while rolling his eyes and shaking his head. On the other hand, contradiction may occur in the form of unconscious cues, such as nervously tapping a pen during an interview. Research suggests that when lack of congruency between the verbal and nonverbal exists, nonverbal cues are more likely to determine the total or particular meaning of the message.[8] Possibly this greater reliance on the nonverbal signals is tied to the apparent processing of nonverbal communication as an automatic response, while verbal cues tend to require more analysis.[9] Perhaps because we react on reflex to nonverbal communication, we trust it more.

*Substitution.* This term describes nonverbal acts that replace verbal messages. In a noisy factory or processing plant, getting a worker's attention by waving or gesturing with a "Come here" hand signal may be more effective than screaming to be heard over noisy machinery. Nonverbal messages are culture-specific. For example, a North American displaying an open hand to indicate the number "five" would shock a Greek, since this gesture is a vulgar one in Greece.

*Accentuation.* Using nonverbal signals to emphasize a verbal message results in a stronger meaning being conveyed. While giving a sales presentation to a client, a computer sales representative may use a two-key-stroke demonstration on the personal computer to support her point about its ease of use and its capacity to facilitate task accomplishment. In this example, underaccentuation makes the case. Generally, accentuation brings to mind an exaggerated display, with loud volume and large gestures accompanying the verbal communication.

*Complementing.* While thanking his subordinate for timely completion of a project, a manager smiles warmly and pats him on the shoulder. He has supplemented the verbal message with the nonverbal cues. That is, the nonverbal signals "fill in" the rest of the picture.

*Regulation.* The final function of nonverbal cues allows us to control a communication transaction. Afraid of dissent, the chairman of the board will not allow anyone to speak during an important policy-making board meeting. How? Rather than stating the "rule" explicitly, he simply avoids eye contact with anyone, or does not point to those who are leaning forward or raising their hands in their attempt to gain the floor. Thus, we regulate the flow of the communication. While we follow certain rules of turn-taking in our interactions, such regulative cues differ from culture to culture.

There is reason to believe that we process nonverbal communication differently from verbal communication. Research in brain functions has resulted in knowledge about which hemisphere processes communication. Although both right and left can process language, the left hemisphere of the brain processes most verbal communication. It is the right (or "minor") hemisphere that seems to control the "spatio-temporal, gestalt, and emotive forms of communication for which nonverbal is best suited."[10] We respond to and produce nonverbal signals at a direct, rather than abstract level.[11] For instance, pupil dilation occurs often as a result of interest. Since we lack conscious control over this nonverbal "message" cue, it could be regarded as less ambiguous than voluntary signaling.

## Categories of Nonverbal Communication

Communication specialists provide many different ways to classify nonverbal cues and acts, creating different taxonomies. A message orientation simplifies this proliferation of different codes and categories because of its assumption that a coding system should include signals that are intentionally and voluntarily encoded, capable of being consistently interpreted by receivers. Thus, seven classes of nonverbal communication behavior qualify as codes:

1. *physical appearance;*
2. *artifacts,* or personal objects that communicate some message;
3. *paralanguage,* or vocal features other than words;
4. *kinesics,* or body movement;

5. *proxemics,* or use of space and distance in human interaction;
6. *haptics,* or touching;
7. *chronemics,* or the use of time in interaction.[12]

Note that while we can separate these cues or signals artificially, just as we can letters and words, it is their patterns and sequences that may be more significant in determining meaning. That is, discrete behaviors (such as a handshake or a direct eye gaze) may be examined, but it is the total context that assigns meaning to communication. It is difficult, however, to determine set structures for nonverbal communication, since its rules vary from context to context. A frown in one case may indicate that an employee does not understand instructions, whereas a frown in another instance may signify lack of approval. Nonverbal codes, in the same way as languages, are culturally determined.

### Physical Appearance & Artifacts

*Physical appearance* is the first nonverbal dimension to affect us in any relationship with others. Appearance may even dictate whether we engage in communication at all. What comprises physical appearance is everything that is visible; that is, primarily what others see. Those with visual impairment or blindness may experience physical presence differently. Appearance includes such nonverbal cues as the body, physical attractiveness, clothing, and body adaptors (e.g., hair, skin color, cosmetics). Artifacts, or those personal items we select and keep on or close to our bodies, will also be discussed in this section, since these too communicate messages to others.

It is possible to believe that you cannot judge someone until you know the person well. However, two points should be made. First, physical appearance may dictate whether or how much you interact with another person. Individuals will not spend time talking to someone they perceive as unattractive. Not getting the job as a result of an interview can very well result from the interviewer's decision that the physical appearance of a person does not fit the company image. Second, impressions about personality, character, and attitudes are formed quickly and are based primarily on physical appearance. Estimates for this impression formation range from ten seconds to four minutes. A well-qualified job candidate arrives on time for his interview with a conservative, traditional engineering firm. Wearing a conservative navy suit, white shirt, and tasteful tie, he is fifty pounds overweight and has shoulder-length hair pulled back in a ponytail. His appearance screams and warns the interviewer that he may like to operate outside the "rules." In this case, the interviewer stated that he "would never hire this hippie."[13]

Some components of physical appearance we can control or manipulate. Others are inherited and although we cannot control them, they influence the response of others. Sex is one of these components, as is race. Traditionally, females and those of racial origins other than Caucasian have been perceived to be of lower status, power, and intelligence, and lacking in other characteristics needed for success in organizations.

Generally, body shape and size may be controlled only to a small degree. Body type is classed by weight, muscularity, and height. Those with rounder and softer bodies are often stereotyped more negatively than those who have taller, thinner bodies, or those with trim, muscular bodies. Research indicates that obese persons will have more difficulty in making friends as well as obtaining jobs. Additionally, taller persons have the advantage in everything from presidential elections to job promotions and even perceived status.[14] As a result of their greater height, many males have the edge in organizations.

Physical attractiveness is one dimension of appearance that is judged quite subjectively. While there seems to be a high level of agreement about those we judge attractive, differences of opinion occur as a result of age, sex, and race. However, according to Mark Hickson and Don Stacks in *NVC: Concepts and Perspectives,* "physical attractiveness influences our perceptions of social interaction and how we structure that interaction."[15] Attractiveness influences the amount of time spent in social interaction, as opposed to task interactions. Insofar as attractiveness impacts the organization, those who are judged attractive can be seen as better liked and more intelligent. Such assessments can result in greater immediate and future success. For males, hard work and personality can compensate for lack of attractiveness. However, females should expect difficulty when judged unattractive. Those with moderate or great attractiveness can expect easier communication and success in organizations.

According to Hickson and Stacks, body adaptors are defined as "those changes involving the hair and/or the skin which affect the appearance of the individual."[16] There is often little we can do to alter skin color as racial genes set it. Because of long-held racial prejudices, having skin that appears anything but Caucasian may result in perceptions of limited attractiveness. Also, certain skin colors and types evoke stereotyped responses. However, tanning has gained in popularity and serves as a cue that we have the money and leisure to go where the sun is hot and bright. We seem to associate people in power and wealth with a tanned complexion.

Hair styles are judged positively or negatively, depending on color, texture, cut, and length. Any manipulations of hair on the face or head are perceived as messages we provide to others. In general, for both males and females, shorter (but not too short!) and neat hair is essential for successful judgments in the organization. Facial hair for males, perhaps with the exception of a neatly trimmed short mustache, does not usually result in successful interviews or lead to promotions. As for cosmetics, men in organizations who use makeup are likely to be viewed negatively. The exception is for television interviews. Women are expected to use makeup, but those who underuse or overuse makeup are perceived negatively.

We infer many characteristics about people from their clothing: sex, socioeconomic status, group and occupation, and extent of social (and organizational) conformity. Many studies indicate that clothing affects credibility, persuasiveness, and compliance. This area has received so much attention in the current quest for success in organizations that "wardrobe engineers" like John Molloy can tell us precisely what to wear in order to make sales, get promotions, and achieve positions of leadership.[17] Males and females in major corporations wear similar clothing, with differences according to sex and particular function. For example, factory workers probably are "allowed" to dress in unisex coveralls or pants and shirts. On the other hand, managers wear suits, and women are expected to wear skirts.

Deciding whether multinational corporations or whether John Molloy established today's "corporate uniforms" is not important. It is important to distinguish what a particular company, industry, or occupation considers acceptable. IBM, for example, used to require its marketing and management employees to wear only white shirts with dark, conservative business suits (most still wear white shirts). On a busy city street, we can pick out attorneys and bankers, advertising executives, secretaries, physicians, and even sanitation or street workers. What an individual wears marks his or her occupation and class, as well as status. In any organization, clothing influences who talks to whom. A person's dress may affect whether someone else wants to be seen and associated with the person. One last point to emphasize is that clothing will also affect whether a person is perceived as competent, credible, persuasive, or influential. For example, a pediatrics physician can choose to wear street clothes rather than a white laboratory coat in order to project an aura of greater approachability and to encourage open communication with his or her small patients.

In regard to *artifacts*, a number of objects provide information about individuals. Some examples include eyeglasses, jewelry, smoking materials, and occupation markers. In some occupations, such as medicine or law, heavy horn-rimmed eyeglasses can promote an image of intelligence and competence. Too much jewelry (rings, necklaces, earrings, etc.) in almost any occupation or organization establishes a negative image. For most males, one or two rings and a watch may be the limit. An earring might be acceptable for rock stars; but in many companies, even for lower-level positions, males who wear chains around the neck or an earring can expect not to be promoted. Females tend to be bound by different rules, but excessive displays of jewelry are still considered in poor taste. Similarly, many companies are banning smoking entirely because of the health impact and loss of productivity. As a result, the use and display of smoking artifacts can increasingly create a division of status and even influence employability. Occupational markers such as firefighters' or military hats, a "professional's" briefcase, and a chef's tall white cap serve to set their owners apart by identifying their group. These too can affect such outcomes as credibility and influence.

Another type of artifact communicates but is not attached to one's body. If supplied by the organization, furnishings and objects used to decorate are generally considered part of the physical environment. However, when supplied or chosen by the individual, these artifacts should be considered an extension of the person's physical appearance. For example, a publishing company for which this author worked allowed employees to select an art print and have it framed. The company paid for the print and the framing, but individuals certainly communicated their personalities in the choice, framing, and display of the art. Most people feel the need to "personalize" their work areas with small objects or photographs, even humorous posters. When organizations forbid their employees to express themselves in this way, they are cutting off an important channel of communication. Studies have found that, in fact, display of some objects may enhance performance.[18] Along this line, Hickson and Stacks raise a significant issue regarding the use of automobiles. As they point out, hundreds of thousands use cars (or trucks or vans) to conduct business.[19] Yet we know little about how this particular extension of the individual and organization creates impressions or influences transactions.

Key visibility positions in organizations require individuals to pay great attention to appearance. While it seems to be true that appearance can help or harm individual success in organizations, it is even more true for those who represent the company to the outside world: company chairpersons, presidents, principal managers, receptionists, and sales representatives. These people can directly create success or disaster for their organizations, since they are perceived to reflect the company image. Next to context or environment, appearance is a key point of communication contact between people.

### Paralanguage

Vocal features that accompany oral messages also serve to provide information about the individual and about the meaning of the message. Trager divided these vocal cues related to the production of sound into four types: (1) voice qualities, which include *pitch* (high or low), *range* (monotone or varied), *quality of articulation* (distinct or slurred), *rate* (fast or slow), and *rhythm* (smooth or jerky); (2) vocal characteristics, or vocalized noises such as laughs, yells, or groans; (3) vocal qualifiers, which include *intensity* (loudness), *pitch range* and *duration* of sound, and which depend on situational variables that affect sound such as room size; and (4) vocal segregates, rhythmic factors that affect the flow of speech, such as *disfluencies* and other noises that fill pauses.[20] Other vocal cues that influence interpretation of meaning and the relationship between speaker and listener include silence, interruptions, duration of speaking, and the cues used to end speaking turns—for example, questions (upward inflection) or "periods" (downward inflection).

Based on these vocal cues, people make three types of judgments about others. One judgment associates personality characteristics with certain vocal-cue combinations.[21] For example, some years ago, only a low-pitched, resonant, and well-articulated male voice would be chosen by major broadcasting companies to deliver "serious" news.[22] As a result, women were not taken "seriously" by such organizations. As we have moved toward less sex discrimination, women's higher-pitched voices are now used frequently for "hard" news. On the other hand, when an organization must make an announcement of a major mishap, a male is still likely to be chosen, partly because we associate the lower-pitched male voice with power, authority, and credibility. We make a second judgment about the emotional state of the speaker,[23] and thus, intended meaning of the message. An angry employee will probably speak in a loud voice, at a fast rate, and with high pitch. Third, we are able to recognize speakers from vocal cues. From vocal cues alone (such as over the telephone), most individuals are able to identify accurately the sex, age, race,[24] and possibly even socioeconomic status or regional origin of the other party. Those who possess the so-called "broadcaster's" Midwestern dialect are most likely to be perceived positively.[25] Other regional or linguistic influences, such as a Latino-American or Black dialect or accent, may result in discrimination without conscious intent. Some research indicates, for instance, that individuals with such dialects receive lower ratings in employment interviews.[26] One other consideration centers around the rate of speaking. Those who speak at a fast rate may be seen more positively, perceived as competent and persuasive.[27]

The last set of vocal cues serve to set the parameters of communication, acting to frame and regulate interaction and perceptions. *Duration* of speaking (whether single word or the entire turn), *interruptions,* and *silences* (including pauses and hesitations) all function to regulate interaction. Those who dominate, or control, the floor are more likely to be perceived as leaders.[28] This association of leadership with "talkativeness" seems to hold true regardless of the quality of the comments or the actual function in which the speaker engages.[29] Males tend to interrupt more and be interrupted less often than females. Thus, one might note that those who interrupt and talk frequently in pairs or groups (such as company meetings) have much influence over the outcome of the discussion.

It may very well be true that it is not what we say, but rather how we say it that dictates the outcome of decisions in a discussion, who exerts influence in that discussion, and even whether we are selected to belong to a particular organization.

### Kinesics

Suppose that you wish to ask your manager for a salary raise. You enter the office with a confident stride, stand directly facing her as she sits in her chair, and look her straight in the eye as you smile. When you ask for the salary increase, it is likely that she will respond to you in some positive or supportive manner. Contrast this manner of self-presentation with the person who slinks into the manager's office, stands with shoulders slumped and head and eyes down, with lips pressed tightly together. The manager will not make the same inference about confidence and self-image, or assertiveness. It is the use of kinesics that distinguishes these two different scenes and defines direction of the interaction.

*Kinesics* is defined as the study or classification of movements of the body, including posture, facial expression, eye movement, and gestures. This area of nonverbal communication has long been a subject of study.

Ray Birdwhistell developed a system to study kinesics through observation, and he outlined some general principles. First, he indicated that the five body senses (sight, hearing, taste, smell, and touch) all provide information for the interpretation of meaning of a message; however, one sense may be the most prominent, or control the interpretation. In the case of the confident employee asking for a raise, the heads-up stride can set the interpretation. Second, interpretation of movement and gesture is subjective, differing from culture to culture or setting to setting. In order to accurately infer meaning, we must know whether the employees or the business are Japanese or North American. In Japan, eyes down indicates deference or respect; in North America, failure to make direct eye contact may indicate: (1) lack of confidence, or (2) deception. Third, similar to other researchers, Birdwhistell posits that kinesic behavior is interpreted and used less consciously than is verbal communication.[30]

*Facial Displays, Gestures, and Posture.* Ekman and Friesen have catalogued five different expressive body behaviors: emblems, illustrators, regulators, adaptors, and affect displays.[31] One advantage to their system is that it allows us the flexibility to interpret different nonverbal cues and combinations according to the situation or culture. That is, the meaning for a gesture may be subjective. The signal for OK (three fingers held up straight, thumb and index finger forming a circle) is used extensively by professional SCUBA divers. However, it is possible that the same gesture displayed across a noisy computer complex might be interpreted as representing the number zero (0).

In general, *emblems* commonly substitute for verbal expressions. As in the above example, there is a direct counterpart of a word for the gesture.

*Illustrators* form the second category. These gestures complement and support the verbal message. Because they are redundant, they serve to emphasize the message. A supervisor may point to the far corner of the warehouse when he tells a forklift operator to move a stack of crates to that area.

*Regulators,* the third category, control turns in the flow of communication. Leaning forward, direct body orientation, head nods, eye-gaze direction, and gestures can regulate whether you talk or the other person gets his or her turn.[32] In a company meeting, these crucial communication behaviors will dictate who can become leader of the group,[33] or even whether a dissenting opinion will be expressed.

Fourth, *adaptors* have the specific purpose of adjusting or satisfying the body or emotional needs in some way. Doodling with a pen during a conversation (handling the pen is a compensator), cleaning finger-nails, or smoking cigarettes all illustrate the use of adaptive gestures.

The last category is *affect displays*. Although some facial displays vary from culture to culture, Ekman and Friesen found support for the universal expression of six emotions: fear, anger, surprise, disgust, sadness, and happiness.[34] These nonverbal cues indicate the emotions or feelings of the person displaying them. An employee who is repri-manded severely may raise the inner corners of his eyebrows, squint his eyes, and turn down the corners of his mouth in displaying sadness or unhappiness. In combination with body posture, pupil dilation, and other nonverbal cues, we can generally interpret these displays accu-rately.

Finally, it is possible to have *affect-display blends* or even a *neutral* expression. Thus, a company officer involved in negotiating the sale of her company might display a "poker face" and a rigid posture in order to conceal her true response to any offer. Still, the face is the most visible indicator of emotions and feelings. Split-brain research pro-poses that the left side of the face displays emotion most accurately, and because of hemisphere processing, looking at the left side of the other's face with one's left eye will provide the most accurate assess-ment of emotional state.[35]

*Eye Behavior.* The eyes are as important as the face in regulating communication and displaying emotion. Visual cues provide much information about the individuals who are interacting, as well as about their relationship. These cues let us know whether we have made contact with the other person and inform the other party that the lines of communication are open. We do not feel obligated to talk to someone with whom we have not made eye contact. As the old saying goes, "The eyes are the window of the soul," indicating the type of relationship shared and our need for inclusion or affiliation with others.[36] Eye behavior includes several components: eye contact, eye gaze, eye direction, and pupil size.

*Eye contact* can be described as the point at which the eyes of one person consciously meet, or "contact," those of another. The pres-ence or absence of this particular nonverbal cue is particularly impor-tant. Appropriate presence or absence is dictated by culture, sex, race, and ages of the interactants. Not meeting someone's eyes may signal deference to status, discomfort or shyness, or even deception. This nonverbal act can also be a strategic move to retain control of the speaking turn. Law enforcement officers who fail to remove sunglasses during communication strip this vital set of cues from the information available for interpretation.

*Eye gaze* represents the length of the visual contact. Gazing at someone too long can be interpreted as a violation of individual barriers. Too short may be akin to the absence of eye contact. A gaze longer than four to five seconds could be interpreted as a challenge, a display of dislike or displeasure, or even sexual approach. The interpretation, of course, is tempered by other cues present in the situation, such as body posture. In general, however, eye contact of "appropriate" length is positive, since we seek and give eye contact when we want to communicate, when we like people (or are hostile toward them), and when we seek feedback or feel physically distant from others.

Verbal messages sent with eye contact will be more positively interpreted than those without or with limited eye contact, increasing satisfaction and impressions of competence, credibility, and indicating involvement and helpfulness;[37] and high-status persons usually will receive more eye contact than those of low status.[38] Thus, a sales representative who is trying to make a sale or a clerk at a cash register trying to keep the customer happy should be attentive to giving and getting eye contact. Those managers who wish to be evaluated as more considerate and involved should give rather than avoid eye contact.[39]

*Eye direction*—or the movement/shift of the eyes to the left, right, down, or up—can signify attitude, comfort, deception, or turn regulation. Hickson and Stacks summarized research regarding the direction of looking behavior. This research sought to relate sex to direction of glance and to explain the results in terms of dominant brain hemisphere theory. First, males who were asked questions (four categories: verbal, numerical, spatial, and musical) tended to look to the right no matter what type of question was asked. That is, they seemed to use the left side of the brain, which is related to analytical or numerical-objective functions. Females generally looked to the left, apparently consulting the right or more abstract brain hemisphere. Perhaps the stereotypes of males and females related to task have some substance. For those who must judge ability, noting which direction someone looks when asked questions can indicate how well that person may respond to a particular problem. Unconscious judgment of performance may hinge on which direction you look when asked a task-related question. Second, another study reported that left-dominant persons (they look right) would engage in more verbal and active defense mechanisms than those who look left (more passive and nonverbal). When approached with an accounting error, for example, someone with left dominance would be more likely to project or turn on others. Someone with right dominance would repress or deny the error.[40] Finally, looking down indicates deference, deception, discomfort, or concession of conversational turn. Typically, in giving up the floor, Caucasians briefly look away from their receivers, then give eye contact again as they finish speaking.[41] Looking up is usually associated with reflection, perhaps disbelief or annoyance, but usually not a concession of conversational turn.

In regard to *pupil size,* researchers report that larger pupil size is associated with greater attractiveness and trustworthiness, as well as indicating higher levels of interest in the surrounding environment. Also, according to Hickson and Stacks, "pupillary dilation reflects the amount of mental effort required to perform a task."[42] An accurate judgment of deception or effort might be critical to the customer or client in a business transaction involving large amounts of money.

In short, the presence and quality of visual cues provide vital information to organizational members, since credibility, involvement, and control are integral features of most organizational transactions.

### Analysis of Kinesics and Organizational Relationships

Burgoon presented a modified version of Mehrabian's functional approach to categorizing kinesics that is useful in analyzing kinesics behavior and relationships in the organization. The four dimensions of the model are: (1) *intimacy and similarity;* (2) *immediacy;* (3) *emotional arousal, lack of composure and formality;* and (4) *dominance.*[43] These categories allow the integration of the various nonverbal cues that form patterns and sequences. This system is helpful, since some nonverbal signals are difficult to interpret without the presence or absence of others, or without noting the sequence in which they occur.

In the *intimacy* and *similarity* dimension, degree of liking (positive or negative), attraction, and trust are displayed. We seem to relax more easily with persons we like, trust, or find otherwise attractive, but relax very little with those we dislike, mistrust, or find unattractive. We display our attitude through *body orientation* or *axis.* Orientation is the alignment between the shoulders and legs of two interactants. While there are some differences between males and females, in general a more direct orientation will be used with someone well-liked, with more body lean toward the other person, more gesturing, and greater eye contact.

*Immediacy* focuses on attention and level of involvement. Burgoon associated more direct orientation, forward body leans, and greater eye contact with greater immediacy or greater attentiveness. On the other hand, such cues as backward leans, averted gaze, and increased distance express detachment. High degrees of involvement can often be seen in mentor relationships where higher-status/powerful individuals "help" select subordinates who show promise.

The third category focuses on *arousal* versus nonarousal, or degree of emotional involvement, as well as *composure* and *formality*. People become more active and physiologically excited as their emotional state increases. That is, when they are aroused, they will move more, show greater muscular tension, and their pupils will dilate. The converse is true of a lack of or limited emotional response.[44] Rigid or erect postures and restrained gestures can indicate anxiety or a high degree of formality.

Finally *dominance,* or status and power relationships, can be inferred from kinesics. Generally, a more direct body orientation is used in interaction with persons of higher status; head position is lowered more often by the person of inferior status; and the higher-status individual will display more relaxed leg and hand positions. As noted in the discussion on eye behavior, high-status persons generally receive more and give less eye contact. In many organizations, as with our friend who comes in to ask for a raise, interactants provide clear kinesic indicators of the relationship between or among themselves. We "know" who is in charge, or who is not, who is cooperative, who is influential, who has special relationships, and who is involved or honest.

### Nonverbal Cues and Organizational Relationships

The next three sections bear less on the nonverbal signals associated with the individual, and more on how the nonverbal cues structure the relationship with another person.

#### Proxemics

While this area is examined in the chapter on physical environment, it is traditionally considered an integral subcode of nonverbal communication. Since this dimension combines in particular with kinesics and haptics to produce perceptions of dominance, immediacy and involvement, it should be reviewed. Proxemics is how we use space in relationship to other people.

Just as language varies from culture to culture, so do nonverbal signals, including proxemics. This was an important principle established by anthropologist Edward Hall in the 1950s as he studied the influence of culture on interpersonal distance, time, and other factors. He suggested that some cultures place more importance on certain sensory modalities than do others.[45] For example, in the United States it is the visual and auditory cues that are deemed critical; whereas other cultures place greater stress on touch. Thus, we might expect "touch" cultures to stand or sit closer in communication than we would expect of cultures that do not emphasize the haptic sense.

In this section, we will examine primarily the type of interpersonal space referred to as informal space. This is the so-called personal territory or "bubble" that surrounds the body and moves with the person, determining the appropriate interpersonal distance between individuals. In the United States, comfortable interaction distances range from 0–18" (intimate); 18"–4' (personal); 4'–12' (social); to over 12' (public). For other cultures, however, these "marker points" differ.

Imagine a first encounter between a Japanese and an American. Because the Japanese have less physical space available to them, they may require less informal space to feel psychologically comfortable. However, one might guess that they also have a rigid code about violating that smaller space. The Japanese have strict social codes of formality governing who may touch whom and how. We are far more casual about touch in the United States. While the Japanese bows formally to greet the American, the American returns the greeting with a handshake. Both may feel cheated or violated.

The differing requirements for seating arrangements create difficulties as well. For example, desks that force their occupants to face one another have interesting effects: the encouragement of frequent communication, ideal for some types of business and working relationship, but terrible for those requiring quiet to perform their tasks. Seating patterns that we traditionally view as conducive to "good business" can change as we orient more to other cultures, including where we place the so-called "head" of the table and the height and type of seats. To encourage effective communication, we will need to do more than replace "four-person round tables in the company dining room" with army mess tables.[46] As we engage in more and more international business, moving closer to what social critic Marshall McLuhan called the "global village," the study of proxemics will become more important.

### Haptics

As proxemics established the interpersonal distance barriers for each person, haptics allows us to bridge those territories. Haptics, or the study of touch and touching, is also known as "zero proxemics."[47]

Anthropologist Ashley Montagu emphasized how crucial touch is. His research on tactile deprivation among children demonstrated that those touched less in their early years were not as "healthy" as those who experienced more tactile contact.[48] Touching is essential to our mental, emotional, and physical health. Again, however, culture dictates how and when people can touch. Specifically, Hickson and Stacks propose that people living in agrarian societies tend to be more "touch-oriented" than do people in industrial or service societies.[49] This could explain difficulties in crosscultural or international business transactions in situations where representatives from a predominantly agrarian- or industrial-oriented culture meet with those from a service-oriented culture (even within one country).

Aside from the cultural influences that include sex, race and age, other norms such as function and intent also exert pressure. For example, touch can be regarded as falling into five related categories: (1) *functional-professional* touches, such as in a medical examination, which serve a clear function and are relatively impersonal; (2) *social-polite* or ritualistic behavior such as handshakes or other "socially prescribed" touches; (3) *affectionate-intimate* touching that requires closer proximity (or intrusion of personal space) and involves touches in areas reserved for those in more personal (interpersonal) relationships;[50] (4) *relational-dominant* touching that can violate all boundaries, both personal and social, and is used to establish or reinforce superior-inferior relationships; and (5) *relational-manipulative* touching between equals or unequals in relationships, used by one person to aid an intended outcome. The function and intent of the first three categories of touching are clear. For example, a light touch on the back of the shoulder from one's supervisor acts as an expression of "good job." The fourth category includes the supervisor who deliberately squeezes the upper arm of the subordinate while giving instructions. The final type of touching is exemplified by the hand-pressings of political candidates.

### Chronemics

In United States organizations, "time is money." We treat time as a commodity, to be spent, saved, or squandered. Consequently, *chronemics,* or the use and structuring of time, takes on great importance in the organization. Nonverbally, we structure our interactions in relation to time: now, tomorrow, by 5 p.m., next week, two weeks ago. Hall examined time perceptions (as well as proxemics) in cultures, noting that cultural expectations and values dictate how we function.[51] An agrarian society places a much lower value on punctuality than does a society geared to precise machine operations and production lines (although this is beginning to change, and we see time clashes frequently between those who grew up with a more traditional time-orientation and those who have adopted the more relativistic time perceptions of the information age). However, two other time perceptions also affect us in organizations: how the individual perceives and uses time, and the influence of our biological time "clocks."

In individual *psychological-time orientations,* perception of time centers around one's notion of time flow and cycles—generally, past, present, and future. Theorists suggest that we tend to focus predominantly on one of these orientations that predisposes us to structure our lives based on that orientation.[52] It is argued that men, for instance, are conditioned to be future-oriented and that women are present-oriented. Thus, men may be goal-oriented and plan well, examining the past and present to see how each affects the future. Women, on the other hand, have a less "gestalt" and more "atomistic" view of time, taking each moment as it comes. This is a decided disadvantage for women in organizations that value planning and future orientation.

Second, *biological-time orientation* or circadian rhythms (internal time "clocks") definitely influence our behavior. We sleep, work, and play in a relatively set daily pattern. Changing these phases can have a devastating effect on work performance; this happens, for instance, when an executive or sales representative flies around the world for a meeting. Furthermore, there are some longer time cycles that affect us: (1) the physical cycle, which lasts approximately 23 days; (2) the emotional cycle, which is 28 days, and (3) the intellectual cycle, 33 days long.[53] Generally, the first half of each cycle is the strongest, where the person feels and functions best physically, emotionally, and intellectually. Contrary to the popular folk belief, women are not the only ones who "have their periods." The obvious implication is that these cycles differ in length; thus, you might be physically strong and alert, but intellectually be a disaster waiting to happen. That might be barely acceptable for a factory assembly-line worker, but for a subway train controller it could have terrible consequences.

Finally, our cultures condition us with a *cultural-time system.* According to Hall, three time systems function simultaneously to establish norms of interaction using time. The first one is *formal time,* which has the components of order, cycle, value, tangibility, and depth (duration). In the United States, for example, we view events as linked, and this short-unit sequencing can negatively affect our ability to conduct long-range planning.

The second time system is *informal time,* which builds in some of the individual or psychological orientations. One variable that affects time perceptions is duration, or the length of an event or interaction. North Americans seem to require shorter time periods for activity than do Arabs, for example. For an appointment at 4:00 p.m., we would also set the duration at less than an hour and probably have a precise ending time designated. Arabs or South Americans, though, might not keep that appointment punctually, nor would it disturb them if it lasted longer than the allotted half hour. Hall says that there are four factors, or isolates, that allow us to distinguish duration: urgency, monochronism, activity, and variety. Cultures are either *monochronic* (arbitrary, individually set and learned) or *polychronic* (multiple events or no events may occur). This is controlled by an attitude about activity. Americans are typically monochronic, with only one major event occurring at a time and taken in sequence. Many other cultures, however, are quite content to allow one event to precede another "planned" one (what happens "later" is not necessarily important), or even to just sit. North Americans have difficulty with just sitting and not "doing anything." On the other hand, we possess a need for urgency ("Time is passing us by!") and for variety ("doing" several actions at once, like talking to a coworker and reading a report at the same time).

Then there is *technical time*. Such precise measurements of time as the astronomer's sidereal year (365 days, 6 hours, 9 minutes, 9.54 seconds) versus the solar year (365 days, 5 hours, 48 minutes, 45.51 + seconds) add to how we arrange our relationships with others. In some ways, global time zones reflect this. When a district manager must call the central office, he or she must know the zone time (or no one may answer the telephone).

As a nonverbal message in organizations, there are three major effects of these time influences: (1) on relational structures, (2) on performance perceptions, and (3) on control of outcomes. Relational structures and performance perceptions are set or reinforced by the use of time, such as length of meetings or punctuality. Higher-status individuals can be late for a meeting, or hold or continue one later than planned. A lower-status person who is late for a meeting with a superior, however, can be considered incompetent or rude. In fact, one of the cardinal rules of employment interviewing is that the candidate must always be punctual, or be assured of not being hired. How long it takes one to complete a report, or in some service establishments, to answer the ringing telephone can be a measure of performance competence. Such time behavior projects a message about competence and attitude or about company image and performance. Last, the amount of time one takes to respond to a request for action (whether it is several moments or several days of silence that follow) indicates the attitude of the individual regarding the importance of the request and the sender, and also determines the outcome. Delaying time of response can well end in the action being too late. Thus, the perception and use of time becomes critical in and between organizations and their members.

A final issue remains. In some respects, we should also consider that organizations are themselves subcultures. For example, a large public university will possess very different qualities and characteristics than does a small private one, and in fact, different colleges within the university will vary. The organizational members will, therefore, interact very differently as well. Business units "expect" their members to present a business-like physical appearance, including grooming and clothing. That means suits, ties, etc. However, typical liberal arts units are very casual about their expectations. It comes as no surprise to see professors or even clerical staff dressed in jeans or other casual attire. Furthermore, the performance evaluations for these professors may be a function of how they "fit" their unit image. We must, therefore, view culture and subculture as a nonverbal communication dimension that must be added to the others.

It should be apparent that the seven nonverbal dimensions—physical appearance, artifacts, paralanguage, kinesics, proxemics, haptics, and chronemics—have a dramatic impact on the functioning of organizations and their members. The relative prominence of nonverbal cues over verbal messages stands out as we consider all the possible levels at which we process them. While words are important, nonverbal messages frame the meaning we attach to those verbal symbols. Neglecting to "read" as many nonverbal signals as possible can result in a lost deal or promotion; paying attention to these signals can make the difference in organizational survival and success.

## Notes

1. Ronald B. Adler and Neil Towne, *Looking Out/Looking In* (New York: Holt, Rinehart, & Winston, 1984), p. 233.
2. Judee K. Burgoon, "Nonverbal Signals," in *Handbook of Interpersonal Communication* ed. Gerald R. Miller and Mark L. Knapp (Beverly Hills: Sage Publications, 1985), pp. 348–49.
3. Burgoon, *op. cit.,* p. 346.
4. Ray Birdwhistell, "Some Body Motion Elements Accompanying Spoken American English," in *Communication: Concepts and Perspectives* ed. Lee Thayer (Washington, D.C.: Spartan Books, 1967), pp. 71–72.
5. Mark L. Hickson III and Don W. Stacks, *NVC: Nonverbal Communication (Studies and Applications)* (Dubuque, Iowa: Wm. C. Brown, 1985), pp. 9–10.
6. Burgoon, "Nonverbal Signals," *op. cit.,* p. 348.

7. Paul Ekman, "Communication Through Nonverbal Behavior: A Source of Information About an Interpersonal Relationship," in *Affect, Cognition, and Personality* ed. Silvan Solomon Tompkins and Carroll E. Izard (New York: Springer, 1965); also Judee K. Burgoon and Thomas J. Saine, *The Unspoken Dialogue: An Introduction to Nonverbal Communication* (Boston: Houghton Mifflin, 1978).

8. Albert Mehrabian, *Silent Message* (Belmont, California: Wadsworth, 1971). See Burgoon, "Nonverbal Signals," *op. cit.*, pp. 358–59, for a summary of research regarding the relative contribution of specific nonverbal features to judgments about meaning.

9. Hickson and Stacks, *op. cit.*, pp. 13–14.

10. *Ibid.*

11. Paul Watzlawick, Janet Helmick Beavin, and Don D. Jackson, *Human Communication: A Study of Interactional Patterns, Pathologies, and Paradoxes* (New York: W.W. Norton, 1967).

12. Burgoon, *op. cit.*, pp. 349–50.

13. Personal conversation, unpublished interviewing research, Gainesville, Florida, January 1983.

14. Hickson and Stacks, *op. cit.*, p. 64; see also Nancy Henley, *Body Politics: Power, Sex, and Nonverbal Communication* (Englewood Cliffs, N.J.: Prentice-Hall, 1977) for more detailed information.

15. Hickson and Stacks, *op. cit.*, p. 70.

16. *Ibid.*, p. 78.

17. John T. Molloy, *Dress for Success* (New York: Warner Books, 1975); Molloy, *The Woman's Dress for Success Book* (New York: Warner Books, 1978).

18. Edward W. Miles and Dale G. Leathers, "The Impact of Aesthetic and Professionally Related Objects on Credibility in the Office Setting," *The Southern Speech Communication Journal* (1984), vol. 49, pp. 361–79.

19. Hickson and Stacks, *op. cit.*, p. 198.

20. George L. Trager, "Paralanguage: A First Approximation," *Studies in Linguistics* (1958), vol. 13, pp. 1–12.

21. David W. Addington, "The Effect of Vocal Variations on Ratings of Source Credibility," *Speech Monographs* (1971), vol. 38, pp. 242–47; "The Relationship of Selected Vocal Characteristics to Personality Perception," *Speech Monographs* (1968), vol. 35, pp. 492–503.

22. See, for example, Burgoon, "Attributes of the Newscaster's Voice as Predictors of His Credibility," *Journalism Quarterly* (1978), vol. 55, pp. 276–81, 300.

23. Patricia Hayes Andrews and John E. Baird, Jr., *Communication for Business and the Professions* (Dubuque, Iowa: Wm. C. Brown, 1986), p. 144.

24. Andrews and Baird, *op. cit.*, p. 144.

25. Judee K. Burgoon and Michael Saine, *The Unspoken Dialogue: An Introduction to Nonverbal Communication* (Boston: Houghton-Mifflin, 1978), pp. 182–3.

26. Sandra M. Ketrow, "The Effects of Interview Skills Training on Employment Interview Outcome," unpublished research, Gainesville, Florida, February 1983.

27. Gerald Goldhaber, *Organizational Communication* (Dubuque, Iowa: Wm.

C. Brown, 1986), p. 202; W. Barnett Pearce and Bernard J. Brommel, "Vocalic Communication in Persuasion," *Quarterly Journal of Speech* (1972), vol. 58, pp. 298–306; Pearce and Forrest Conklin, "Nonverbal Vocalic Communication and Perception of Speaker," *Speech Monographs* (1971), vol. 38, pp. 235–41; and Richard L. Street, Jr., and Robert M. Brady, "Speech Rate Acceptance Ranges as a Function of Evaluative Domain, Listener Speech Rate, and Communication Context," *Communication Monographs* (1982), vol. 49, pp. 290–308.

28. John A. Daley, James C. McCroskey, and Virginia P. Richmond, "Relationships Between Vocal Activity and Perceptions of Communicators in Small Group Interaction," *Western Journal of Speech Communication* (1977), vol. 41, pp. 175–87; Mehrabian, "Communication Length as an Index of Communicator Attitude," *Psychological Reports* (1965), vol. 17, pp. 519–22; and Henry W. Riecken, "The Effect of Talkativeness on Ability to Influence Group Solutions of Problems," *Sociometry* (1958), vol. 21, pp. 309–21.

29. Sandra M. Ketrow, "Valued Leadership Behaviors and Perceptions of Contribution," paper presented at the Speech Communication Association Convention, Washington, D.C., November 1983.

30. Birdwhistell, *Kinesics and Context: Essays on Body Motion Communication* (Philadelphia: University of Pennsylvania Press, 1970).

31. Paul Ekman and Wallace V. Friesen, "The Repertoire of Nonverbal Behavior: Categories, Origins, Usage, and Codings," *Semiotica* (1969), vol. 1, pp. 49–98.

32. John M. Wiemann and Mark L. Knapp, "Turn-taking in Conversations," *Journal of Communication* (1975), vol. 25, no. 2, pp. 75–92.

33. John E. Baird, Jr., "Some Nonverbal Elements of Leadership Emergence," *Southern Speech Communication Journal* (1977), vol. 42, pp. 352–61.

34. Charles Darwin, *The Expression of the Emotions in Man and Animals* (London: Murray, 1872); Paul Ekman and Wallace V. Friesen, "Constants Across Cultures in the Face and Emotion," *Journal of Personality and Social Psychology* (1971), vol. 17, pp. 124–29; Paul Ekman, Wallace Friesen, and Paul Ellsworth, *Emotion in the Human Face* (New York: Pergamon Press, 1972); Carroll E. Izard, *The Face of Emotion* (New York: Appleton-Century-Crofts, 1971); Izard, *Patterns of Emotions* (New York: Academic Press, 1972).

35. Harold A. Sackheim, Ruben C. Gur, and Marcel A. Saucy, "Emotions Are Expressed More Intensely on the Left Side of the Face," *Science* (October 27, 1978), vol. 202, pp. 434–36.

36. Teri Kwal Gamble and Michael Gamble, *Contacts: Communicating Interpersonally* (New York: Random House, 1982), p. 159.

37. J. G. Amalfitano and N. C. Kalt, "Effects of Eye Contact on Evaluation of Job Applicants," *Journal of Employment Counseling* (1977), vol. 14, pp. 46–8; Judee K. Burgoon and Lynn Aho, "Three Field Experiments on the Effects of Violations of Conversational Distance," *Communication Monographs* (1982), vol. 49, pp. 71–88; Ralph V. Exline, "Psychology: An Approach to Human Communication," in *Approaches to Human Communication* ed. R. W. Budd and B. D. Ruben (Rochelle Park, N.J.: Hayden, 1972), pp. 334–55; Kathleen Perkins and Sandra M. Ketrow,

"Operator Eye Contact and Client Satisfaction in Computer-Assisted Transactions," unpublished research, February 1986.

38. Mehrabian, "The Significance of Posture and Position in the Communication of Attitudes and Status Relationships," *Psychological Bulletin* (1969), vol. 71, pp. 365.
39. Hickson and Stacks, *op. cit.*, pp. 202–03.
40. *Ibid.*, p. 106.
41. Starkey Duncan, Jr., "Some Signals and Rules for Taking Speaking Turns in Conversations," *Journal of Personality and Social Psychology* (1972), vol. 23, pp. 283–92; "On Signalling That It's Your Turn to Speak," *Journal of Personality and Social Psychology* (1974), vol. 10, pp. 234–47.
42. Hickson and Stacks, *op. cit.*, pp. 105–06.
43. Burgoon, "Nonverbal Signals," *op. cit.*, p. 375; Judee K. Burgoon and Jerold L. Hale, "The Fundamental *Topoi* of Relational Communication," *Communication Monographs* (1984), vol. 51, pp. 193–214; Mehrabian, *Silent Messages;* Mehrabian, *Nonverbal Communication* (Chicago: Aldine-Atherton, 1972).
44. Mehrabian, "Relationship of Attitude to Seated Posture, Orientation, and Distance," *Journal of Personality and Social Psychology* (1968), vol. 10, pp. 26–30; Mehrabian and M. Williams, "Nonverbal Concomitants of Perceived and Intended Persuasiveness," *Journal of Personality and Social Psychology* (1969), vol. 13, pp. 37–58.
45. Edward T. Hall, *The Silent Language* (New York: Anchor Books, 1973).
46. Thomas J. Peters and Robert H. Waterman, Jr., *In Search of Excellence* (New York: Warner Books, 1982), p. 220.
47. Hickson and Stacks, *op. cit.*, p. 47.
48. Ashley Montagu, *Touching: The Human Significance of the Skin* (New York: Columbia University Press, 1971).
49. Hickson and Stacks, *op. cit.*, pp. 54–55.
50. *Ibid.*, p. 52.
51. Hall, *Silent Language, op. cit.;* Hall, *Beyond Culture* (Garden City, N.Y.: Doubleday, 1976).
52. Hickson and Stacks, *op. cit.*, pp. 126–28; Thomas J. Cottle, *Perceiving Time: A Psychological Investigation with Men and Women* (New York: John Wiley, 1976); Thomas J. Cottle and Stephen J. Klineberg, "Temporal Orientation, Integration, and Imaginings: The Influence of Sex-Role Learning," in *The Present of Things Future: Explorations of Time in Human Experience* (New York: Free Press, 1974), pp. 102–23; Gerard Groos and Serge Daan, "The Use of Biological Clocks in Time Perception," in *Time, Mind, and Behavior* ed. John A. Michon and Janet L. Jackson (Heidelberg, Germany: Springer-Verlag, 1985), pp. 65–74.
53. *Ibid.*

# 11

# Intercultural Communication and the Organization

*William J. Starosta*

### Culture

Persons who associate with each other learn how members of their group act in private and public settings. As association continues with persons of the same group, norms become apparent for the use of space and time, for preference of style and dress, for the use of language or dialect, for method of showing respect, for getting tasks done without giving offense, and for the structuring of leisure time, among other factors. Persons who associate with each other over the course of generations begin to feel that their way of viewing the world, the assumptions that their group members share about the necessity for change or the need not to give offense while interacting, are written as natural laws. They find it hard to imagine that other ways of eating, dressing, believing, or of structuring activity could have merit.

The sense of identity and common outlook that characterizes group members over generations permeates all of life's activities. The group comes to share and to transmit to future generations a set of cultural rules. No one person will exemplify all of the rules, but most members of the group will endorse most of the practices and beliefs of the culture. Not all of the rules for cultural preference or behavior will be played out at a conscious level. Some behaviors that are culturally influenced will be more visible than others; some will be played out more consciously than others; some will be more readily negotiable than others. The penalties that accrue to violators of cultural rules can range from ignoring behaviors that differ, to instructing wrongdoers, to scolding the violator or taking her to task, to punishing or banishing uncooperative members from the culture completely.

Each person is a member of many groups. Some of the groups are the gift of birth and upbringing, including national identity, region, ethnicity, language, and dialect. Other membership groups are based on voluntary affiliation, such as place of employment, sexual preference, community, political party, or institution of higher learning. While the most profound influences on a person's identity emanate from earlier identifications, groups entered into later in life also exert an impact upon the individual. They do so with greatest force when certain conditions apply: (1) the person is a member of only a few groups; (2) the individual interacts frequently with the members of the group; (3) membership in the group is important to the individual; and (4) the group is a source of rewards.

### Corporate Culture

Entry into a workplace can introduce the worker to a set of rules of conduct and behavior that touch as many facets of life. A worker may adopt a set of jargon words in common with those that are used within the company. He or she may tend to express a preference for the political party that seems to be favored by others in the company. The educational backgrounds of those who work for the company can be very similar to those of the new employee. Workers may be from the same region of the country or can be drawn from the same social stratum. The institution can be structured according to the norms of the management. That management can often be dominated by persons of a single gender, nationality, and ethnicity, and rewards can be given out in accordance with conformity to rules that are comfortable to such managers.

Rules of conduct will be enforced by the pressures of the workplace. If the worker is an active member of few other significant groups, if the worker values membership in the organization, if the rewards that come from the agency cannot be found elsewhere, and if the worker interacts frequently with other members of the group, the agency's norms are more compelling than if interaction is more limited. The Japanese company, as one example, is likely to act as the center of the worker's life, providing recreation, assistance with marriages, and counseling. Such companies perform many roles that, in North America, might be left to the family.

The place of work is a conglomeration of cultures. It is a macroculture, comprised of separate departments and units and quality circles, each of which in turn can be viewed as a distinctive (socio)cultural level. An open-systems model is appropriate for the analysis of cultural behavior: The individual is a member of various systems, each embedded within others. The individual interacts with others of his or her nation, region, language group, ethnicity, corporation, specialization, management level, gender, university, quality circle, assembly line, or task. The hierarchy of groups that influence behavior extends on every side of the worker. No individual is totally excepted from normative pressures at any level. Some corporations incorporate the norms of society at large, while other agencies, especially those transplanted to other national settings, fail to achieve agreement between the cultural expectations of the individual and those of the host nation. These cultural *"mismatches,"* the various areas where the person by habit would speak in a language or perform a task in a way that is not practiced within the local setting, can meet with any of the responses that are applied to culturally normed behaviors. The violator can be ignored, or given idiosyncrasy credit to perform in an alien manner. He or she can be taken aside and told, "We do not usually break the chain of command in this culture. You should be more aware of our ways." (S)he can be offered enticements or threatened with sanctions: "If you do not perform as expected, you can find another job (United States)" or "Is there a problem that can be dealt with to improve the manner of your performance (Japan)?" Or dismissal may follow the failure to abide by a dress code or to act according to other corporate expectations for behavior.

### Microcultures

The businessplace is a collection of groups. Each of these groups, in turn, stands to influence the conduct of individuals. The company seeks to harmonize the activities of these groups and their members within the business overculture. The ideal situation is one within which each individual pools unique skills and insights to create a product that surpasses the abilities of individuals and of individual corporate microcultures. This end state, *"synergy,"* represents the combining of a variety of outlooks and perspectives, in a transcendent process that is personally and professionally fulfilling. Too little attention has been given to the understanding of how individuals who are shaped by the dictates of many microcultures can collectively achieve a state of harmony. The simple corporate answer has tended to be to ask the individuals to sacrifice their sense of differentness and to merge with the corporate macroculture. Such a demand works more successfully in East Asia than it does in North America.

### Conflict

The potential exists for negative outcomes when a company sets up activities abroad, or when the company allows the hiring of significant numbers of persons from different national or cultural backgrounds without due preparation to manage the differing cultural expectations of the distinctive populations. Middle-level Black American managers are expected to adapt to the cultural expectations of the three-martini lunch, the notions of punctuality, and the dress codes of the corporate overculture. They must deal with prevalent beliefs that they are not as competent as White counterparts: They are asked "Can you" where their White counterpart would simply be expected to be able to perform the task. Women and Black Americans, along with other workplace minorities, learn to "read between the lines" within the workplace for messages that are stated without being stated. This manner of differential treatment, even when subtle and unintended, is a source of strain not faced by majority workers. The minority worker must outbelong the existing workers, outperform them, take on additional responsibilities to be perceived as being merely adequate, and otherwise face differential expectations and treatment.

A parallel challenge awaits managers in a company that has foreign subsidiaries. The manager has learned a set of skills for conducting business and for managing personnel that have worked well at home. These skills have been internalized and recognized by the parent company. They have been the basis for advancement within the home office. But the worker who is transferred abroad encounters *"role shock."* The government plays an unfamiliar role in expediting business or plays a ready scapegoat role for business deals that the company has completed but does not wish to honor. The keeping of appointments differs. It is unclear at which level of management certain requests are to be initiated. The manager has perhaps learned to intimidate a nonperforming worker, and to praise the achiever and to give him or her bonuses. Now, however, the preferred style is to treat nonperformance as an illness, which can be cured, not as a dead limb that must be severed. The assumption is that the worker is always part of the company, once hired. Further, the singling out of an individual for praise and merit bonuses can antagonize the coworkers of that person's work group, and they might then turn on the honoree. What was offered as a gesture that would facilitate performance and productivity in North America can lead to a work slowdown or stoppage, and to the early quitting of the recognized person.

### Intercultural Communication and the Organization

It would be presumptuous to attempt to relate the full range of intercultural communication concerns that face both the domestic and the international business concern. It must suffice to acquaint the reader with a sampling of types of questions that have been researched or should be studied further to obtain a fuller sense of how to minimize intercultural mismatches and conflict and to promote intercultural synergy.

1. International marketing: Products must be marketed in a place that is not the setting in which products were developed. With each product comes a set of values or an outlook that centers on what is "needed" by the targeted audience. To match the product with genuinely felt needs is a task to be undertaken by intercultural business communicators, by means of marketing analysis, product design, and alert management. Many advertising agencies now function abroad as well as domestically.

2. Culture-specific training: It is possible to be trained about the way in which business is conducted in a particular nation or region of the world. Language training, area studies, and other cognitively oriented approaches can now be supplemented with critical incidents, simulations, culture assimilators, role plays, and other forms of experiential training.

3. Communication skills training: Because the person who will be stationed abroad experiences anxieties over the availability of familiar fixtures such as physicians or toothpaste, sometimes the need to learn new methods of communication can be overlooked. Communication, verbal and nonverbal, is one of the things that can be taken for granted in a society: It seems "natural" for everyone to speak either of one or two languages. More natural still is the expectation that the standards for punctuality are universal; that under eighteen inches of space is placed between persons who are either intimate or ready to fight; or that angry words mean that a "fight" is or is not in progress. The transferee and his or her family should learn that their culture poses only a single set of answers to the questions of life. Other answers are possible and, within a given environment, are likely to make more sense than the answers imported from abroad. Differences are to be expected in the use of symbols and symbolic behaviors. The worker should learn to accept the differences as being valid, valid within their sphere, or dislikable but necessary within the new environment.

4. Human relations training: Interpersonal communication can suffer in the multicultural business environment. Information can flow within one language group at the expense of another. Certain groups can be privy to information that is denied to others. Persons within the organization can use their own standards of what constitutes a legitimate use of a lunch hour, what is a suitable style of dress, whether it is more acceptable to deal with one task at a time or rather to do parts

of numerous tasks simultaneously, and the like, in a manner that shows preference for their own habitual modes of operation. They can create a negative and oppressive atmosphere for those who are culturally different, without even recognizing they have created such an atmosphere. The turnover rate can be excessive for cultural minorities; women may not be promoted to upper levels of management basically because they do not communicate as men; and other evidence can be offered for the existence of patterns that breed conflict rather than synergy.

### The Intercultural Corporate Mandate

It will prove necessary for the intercultural corporate communicator to learn that differences exist between ways of living and experiencing life, and in ways of conducting business. The intercultural corporate communicator must become familiar with options in communication, belief, value, and business norms that are applied within different national settings. He or she must learn that the local culture will specify whether the individual or the group is the focus of concern, whether the boss or the manager sets the time schedule for completion of projects, and which other variables affect the conducting of business. The intercultural corporate communicator must adopt a flexible attitude and must take the time to become acclimated to the new cultural setting. He or she should take the advice of other homeside nationals about matters of survival and of style, about which practices are preferences and which are obligations. It is crucial to learn to view differences as *opportunities* if synergy is to be maximized. It is important that corporate employees be made to feel welcomed within the business setting, regardless of cultural background. The intercultural managers must make membership in the particular corporate culture assume greater importance to the culturally different employee by fulfilling individual needs, so that all members of the corporate macroculture will willingly work together without undue frustrations or reservations to achieve the purposes of the corporate culture.

## Part IV

# DEVELOPING INTERPERSONAL RELATIONSHIPS IN THE ORGANIZATION

# 12

# Women and Men Working Together: Toward Androgyny[1]

*Alice G. Sargent*

The movement of women into the managerial work force has created a new culture in organizations, changing men's and women's relationships and generating pressure to find new ways for them to relate.

This calls for a synthesis, a blending of the best of two existing polarities—in this case, the masculine and feminine styles of instrumental and expressive behavior. In organizational leadership, this blend is often called androgynous management—a management approach that blends the best each gender offers.

Such changes do not come easily. The movement of women and of feminine values into organizations raises numerous issues for women and men. They include:

- Exercising power and control in organizations and relationships;
- Creating support systems to facilitate change;
- Learning to deal with emotions;
- Resolving over- and under-dependency issues;
- Redefining competency in management to include women's skills;
- Granting permission to deal with sexual attraction between men and women.

Both men and women pay heavily for trying to conform to a management style that reflects mostly masculine values. This style emphasizes rationality and solving technical tasks. It accents competition, the use of power to gain the ends of the organization and an external reward system. People's needs often get lost; the organization has top priority. Anger and frustration are the emotions most often expressed in the masculine world of management.

Students of management—and some practitioners—increasingly recognize that focusing on task alone produces ineffective management. The results are isolation and alienation which are among the major problems confronting organizations today. Managers are learning to deal with relationships among people and to foster cooperation across bureaucratic levels, instead of taking the top-down approach.

The needs of organizations for a model of managerial effectiveness converge with the needs of women and men for different ways of behaving as managers. Women face a discrepancy between how they have been socialized and how they are expected to act as managers. Others see women as bringing "female" qualities to the office when "male" qualities are considered characteristic of good management. Hence, femininity and competence seem in conflict. Acting feminine may mean a woman is not taken seriously. If her ideas are not listened to, her effectiveness as a manager is impaired.

Women have been socialized to be compliant, particularly with males, yet risk-taking is valued and necessary in management. Women in management also experience a conflict between autonomy and learned helplessness. The polarities of passivity and aggressiveness, dependence and independence frequently conflict with managerial expectations.

Research shows that managers of both sexes believe successful managers possess characteristics, attitudes and temperaments ascribed more commonly to men than to women. The impact of such perceptions can be severe for women. They may try to suppress feminine behaviors and enhance or adopt masculine behaviors, or they may seek to preserve their feminine self-image and suppress attributes deemed essential for management. They may lose even if they exhibit behaviors regarded as necessary for effective management: Assertiveness is regarded highly in a male manager, but may be seen as pushiness in a woman.

A Navy study on preferred coworkers found that both men and women, when asked directly, said they prefer to work with men. Men are considered, often correctly, to have more access to information and to people with power. It is believed, and often true, that men are listened to more by others. Such expectations show the long road ahead in altering stereotypes and making women full citizens in the work place.

Men, seeming to be in the favored position, pay less obvious penalties than women for adopting and expressing the dominant management style. Men often do not know they are acting "masculine" and do not realize how liberating it might be to have other choices.

Some men, however, see the disadvantages and costs of the masculine style. Stress and related diseases can shave 10 years off a man's life. Unwillingness to express a full range of emotions can impoverish relationships; many men will no longer sacrifice close relationships with members of both sexes.

Fortunately, men and women no longer need to penalize themselves with old behaviors if they are willing to change and to risk some awkwardness and uncertainty.

## Blending Old and New

Androgynous management is not really new at all; it is born out of the old. Androgynous management embraces instrumental and expressive behavior, vicarious and direct achievement styles, collaboration and confrontation behavior, a proactive and a reactive style and compliance- and alliance-producing skills.

Each sex may need to accentuate the behaviors of the other sex in order to be androgynous. Women need to discuss issues in a linear, systematic style as well as use intuition; to deal with power as well as emotion; to assert themselves and compete, where appropriate, as well as to foster collaboration

For men, of course, it is the reverse. Men need more than power and competitiveness in order to have a full repertoire of effective behavior. They need to learn to express and deal with emotions other than anger and frustration. They need to engage less in joking and jockeying to establish a position and more in sharing and nurturing to build a team. Thus, a synthesis is necessary, a blending of strong masculine and strong feminine characteristics.

## Support Systems and Networks

Any environment can be lonely during change. This may be especially true of organizational, bureaucratic environments, where managers often think they must deal with issues by themselves. When powerful changes overturn management styles and expectations, both women and men may experience uncertainty, self-doubt and fear. Managers of both sexes need support systems through which to share these doubts and networks to provide information, examples for comparison and access to power.

Women, working for effectiveness and acceptance, need support from men and women, without charges of so-called feminine overdependence.

Some support networks already exist for men through avenues such as business lunches, business travel and sports. But men have little support for change in precisely those areas where they feel most uncomfortable. Men lack structures that support being sensitive, expressing feelings, being vulnerable or comforting others. They need feminine competencies of empathy, dealing with emotion and relating to others to be able to provide support.

Support systems could be built into the organizational structure so that men and women could share experiences and strategies for coping with change.

### How Do You Recognize a Competent Woman?

Competent women and men may not act alike. Women gain a sense of identity both through the development of themselves and of others, sometimes too much in the direction of others. Organizations, however, expect effectiveness to be shown through taking action, giving advice, influencing others and having leadership presence.

Many women expect a higher level of expertise from themselves than from others. They won't speak up until completely sure of the facts. They may overuse the power of expertise and underuse the power of their position. Women often express feelings before they arrive at solutions. This may make them appear to be "hysterical" or to lack sufficient problem-solving skills.

Coaching a new manager who was a woman, a male manager said, "You're just not thinking fast enough or putting your ideas out quickly enough for our culture here." The male manager failed to question an organizational style which was competitive, lacking in introspection and reflection—one that devalued feelings and was probably oriented to crisis. The competent woman may not appear able to respond rapidly to new ideas, but her style may work better in certain situations.

### Barriers to Women and Men Working Together

It is useful to use the transactional analysis model to conceptualize the barriers to adult/adult relationships between male/male, female/female and male/female. If we simply exchange the terms parent, adult and child for father, man and boy and mother, woman and girl, we see the fireworks inherent in adult relationships. Adult relationships that are male/male or female/female require reducing competition to become more collaborative and interdependent. Adult male/female relationships face a variety of barriers, including differing approaches to power and control, dealing with emotions, dependency and sexuality. (See fig. 12-1)

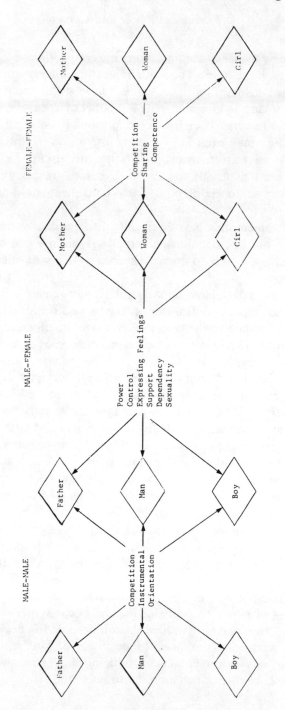

**Fig. 12.1**
**Barriers to adult/adult communication between men and women**

## Exercise of Power and Control

In the new management environment, cooperation needs to replace competition more often. The old, autocratic management style may be used for fire-fighting, but more consultative styles should be used for decision making and for managing human resources.

Women often draw back from competition or confrontation in policy-making; they may even fail to recognize a power struggle, although power dynamics are rampant (and frequently useful) in every organization. Women managers sometimes give away their power, fail to take power when appropriate and overuse collaboration when inappropriate.

Unlike women, men have been taught to emphasize power, slipping easily into one-up, one-down interactions, even when it is unnecessary. They use power to create distance in many business and social relationships.

Research studies have demonstrated the gender differences surrounding power and control issues. Bartol and Butterfield asked managers and graduate students to rank managerial effectiveness in different situations. The researchers reversed the names of men and women managers in several case studies. A male manager was rated highly effective when he entered an organization, interviewed employees for three weeks and then developed a plan that dictated how employees would operate. When a female manager did exactly the same thing, she was rated ineffective for being too directive and pushy.

But gender prejudice cuts both ways. A woman manager was rated effective for showing consideration for others when she spent time dealing with an employee's personal problems, while a male manager who showed the same behavior was rated as wishy-washy for getting too involved in employee needs.

A woman manager in a federal agency budget department first adopted more masculine approaches and then relaxed into androgynous behavior. It was five years, she said, before she felt comfortable "showing some of my feminine behaviors instead of just focusing on task." Having proved herself in the masculine arena she could reintegrate some of her feminine behavior and become more androgynous. She said, "One reason I've finally been accepted is because I'm high on collaboration. There used to be a lot of staff and line power struggles. I was instrumental in introducing joint accountability. People are working together much more harmoniously."

## Dealing with Emotions

In general, women do not find a receptive climate for the expression of emotions in organizations, except anger or frustration. Some women believe men use anger as a weapon, while men sometimes think women use pain and fear in the same manner.

If men and women are to work together effectively, emotional expression is essential. Emotional data is critical to effective problem-solving; feelings are present and have an effect whether expressed or not.

Frequently, men and women differ on how they see interpersonal issues. Women tend to view these issues in the context of a total relationship, consisting of interactions between two people. Many men have learned an organizational style that responds to the message more than the messenger. Therefore, men may be more likely to feel isolated at work and to withdraw from expressions of feelings.

## Challenging Dependency

Women are allowed dependency, but men are punished for expressing it. Hence, learned helplessness has been primarily a woman's issue. Dependency has become so closely aligned with femininity that women must work now to overcome this expectation. Often, women give away their independence, seeking help when they do not need it. Indeed, women may run into resistance in the managerial world when they try to be independent.

On the other hand, men often insist on independence, even when it might benefit them or their organization to seek help. Men also tend to resist talking about problems, isolating themselves out of fear of dependency and cutting themselves off from behaviors essential to being fully effective managers. Working through dependency can be important for both men and women, as well as organizations, but it often means taking risks.

## Defusing Sexuality

As organizations begin to value androgynous behavior, the feminine behaviors of expressing feelings and touching can become potent issues. Touching needs to be openly negotiated so as not to be misinterpreted. Henley and Mayo point out that when a man touches a women, it is often regarded as dominance, whereas when a woman touches a man, it is regarded as warmth.

Common business practices may be misinterpreted when they cross gender lines. A lunch invitation may be seen as something other than an act of colleagueship. A man may feel rejected if a woman turns down a dinner invitation because she is too tired or busy, but he may not feel the same if a male colleague gives the same reasons.

Men in one organization felt uncomfortable when they were traveling with women colleagues. The men withdrew, and the women were cut out of an important information and support network.

Issues of sexual attraction are frequently ignored, when simply acknowledging attraction can do much to defuse it. Generally, men and women want and need to relate to each other as colleagues and professionals. Sexuality, if acted out, can complicate a professional relationship and interfere with work effectiveness. Furthermore, the motives for sexual attraction may range from curiosity to a need to impose power.

### Conclusion

We are moving slowly toward an androgynous identity for managers. The androgynous manager can deal with power and control in a balanced way; is comfortable with the full range of emotions; can seek support and give it to others; can be independent without becoming isolated; and can acknowledge attraction and choose whether to act on it or not. Such a person is better equipped to face the challenges of these complex, ambiguous times.

### Note

1. Portions of this article are taken from Sargent's book *The Androgynous Manager*. AMACOM, 1981.

### Bibliography

Bartol, K.M. and D.A. Butterfield, "Sex Effects in Evaluation Leaders." *Journal of Applied Psychology* vol. 61, No. 4, 1976.

Bartolome, F. "Executives as Human Beings." *Harvard Business Review*, Nov.–Dec. 1972. pp. 62–69.

Mayo, C. and N. Henley. *Gender, Touch and Non-Verbal Behavior*. New York: Springer-Verlag, 1981.

Sargent, A.G. *Beyond Sex Roles*. St. Paul: West Publishing Co., 1977.

Sargent, A.G. *The Androgynous Manager*. New York: AMACOM, 1981.

# 13

# Socialization in Groups and Organizations: Toward a Concept of Creative Conformity

*Patricia Hayes Bradley*

The reasons individuals become members of groups and formal organizations are divergent and often multi-dimensional. For one person, group membership represents security and belonging; for another, it connotes prestige and power; and for still others, organizational affiliation offers the opportunity to exert concerted effort toward the common goal of creating a qualitatively better, safer society. However selfish or altruistic an individual's motives might be, whether they are riveted on private financial gain, oriented toward public service, or perhaps more commonly, projected toward a combination of these two goals (and many, many more), William Whyte's notion that we are all "organization men"[1] and women is a commonplace observation of American life during the last decades of the twentieth century. Yet, many have decried the homogenizing effects of organizational membership.[2] In fact, attacks levied against bureaucracy, the most prominent organization form, often center on the tendency of bureaucratic structures not only to dehumanize and alienate but also to give birth to dull, gray organization beings, persons stripped of their individuality and creativity, nonthinkers, conformers.

Yet, it is almost a paradox that the society that bewails bureaucracy for its alleged robbery of personal assertiveness and independence, at the same time anguishes over those who perch on the opposite end of the conformity-anticonformity continuum—the deviates, persons who seem always to be offering contrary views, those who jumble the apples with unceasing predictability, the hapless souls who seem never to fit into the role models and opinion molds fashioned for them. This paper considers the social influence phenomenon as it operates within groups and organizations by (1) *exploring some of the theories that seek to explain why groups exert pressure for uniformity and why individuals comply;* (2) *examining some of the major research findings relating to conformity, deviation, and social influence;* (3) *considering the consequences of and reactions to opinion deviation;* and (4) *developing a concept of creative conformity as an appropriate approach to human and organizational behavior.* First, however, it is important to define some of the terms central to a thoughtful consideration of social influence, particularly *organizations, norms, conformity, anticonformity,* and *independence.*

## Basic Definitions

Basic to the concept of organization is the notion that individuals alone are often unable to fulfill all of their needs and wishes. Moreover, as several people coordinate their efforts toward common goals, they usually find that they can do more with relative effectiveness than any one of them could have done alone. To achieve efficiency within organizations, most are structured to divide labor and to differentiate responsibility. Thus, an organization is, as Schien has noted, "the rational coordination of the activities of a number of people for the achievement of some common explicit purpose or goal, through division of labor and function, and through a hierarchy of authority and responsibility."[3] As organizations go about the task of coordinating the efforts of individual members, norms develop. Typically, the term "norm" refers to a set of expectations held by group members concerning how one ought to behave. As such, norms exist on such evaluative scales as appropriate-inappropriate, good-bad, just-unjust, and moral-immoral. An individual's compliance with a norm is most readily measured by public behavior; but implicit in a broader understanding of norms is the notion that they are often *assumed* to extend to private feelings and attitudes.

While some norms apply to all persons at all levels of a given organization, others differ according to the position or role of a particular person. Thus, all employees of an industrial organization might be expected to show up for work regularly, but assembly-line workers would normally wear work clothes and managers might typically wear more formal ("white collar") attire. In every organization some norms are *explicit,* that is, formally stated. *Implicit* norms, on the other hand, are generally unstated, but among enduring members of groups and organizations, they are known and understood. Together, implicit and explicit norms constitute a potentially powerful regulatory mechanism for achieving uniformity of opinion and behavior among those who aspire to maintain or perhaps even enhance their group membership.

If norms refer to expectations regarding behavior, then clearly the conforming individual is one who fulfills these expectations. Even so, several distinctions must be made. First, there are those who conform because they desire reward from others, primarily their approval. Deutsch and Gerard refer to this type of behavior as *normative social influence*, that is, conformity to the "positive expectations of another"; and they distinguish it from *informational social influence* where the conforming person simply accepts information obtained from others as being correct, that is, as supportive "evidence about reality."[4] In the latter case, the person conforms because, having considered alternative views, s/he is actually convinced that the majority is correct. Pleasing the group is not the point; supporting a correct decision is. We often find, not surprisingly, that normative social influence is associated with public compliance, and informational influence, with private acceptance. Nevertheless, the two often work together, and there is some evidence to demonstrate that public compliance may eventually lead to private acceptance. Festinger and his colleagues have found that whenever a person's attitude is discrepant with his/her overt behavior, there is a tendency for the attitude to change toward closer agreement with the behavior.[5] Thus, while we normally assume that behavior is a reflection of a felt belief, it is also possible for an action to alter an attitude.

A final conceptual issue worth exploring is the distinction between *independence* and *anticonformity*. Hollander and Willis have pointed out that *pure conformity* exists when there is a great deal of movement toward greater agreement with the majority view.[6] There is no *one* opposite to pure conformity, for the nonconformist may be demonstrating either independence or anticonformity. According to Hollander and Willis, the truly independent person is well aware of what is expected of him or her. These expectations, however, do *not* function as guidelines for the individual's behavior; in fact, often the independent person is completely indifferent to them. The anticonformist, on the other hand, is quite another matter. This person is also cognizant of the group's norms and consistently reacts by moving away from these social expectations. In a very real sense, then, the group does guide the anticonformist's behavior, for anyone who knows the norm can predict the person's behavior with precision. While independents give no weight to the norm in making a judgment, both pure conformists and anticonformists notice the group's norm to an unusual degree:

the conformist, in order to accept the norm and the anticonformist, to disagree with it.[7]

## Theories of Social Influence and Conformity

Before considering the individual and situational factors most likely to encourage or inhibit conformity behavior, two important theoretical issues should be addressed: (1) *why do groups exert pressure for uniformity?* and (2) *why do many individuals conform to existing norms?* One approach to providing an answer to the first question can be found in Festinger's *group locomotion hypothesis.*[8] Organizations (and certainly small groups within them) have any number of goals to which they are committed. If these groups are unable to achieve their goals, they are likely to have difficulty maintaining themselves as a unit. Festinger points out that groups typically try to function so as to facilitate goal achievement. If it is assumed that this can best be accomplished when members conform to certain norms, and such is often the belief, then majority members become motivated to pressure deviates into conforming. In some situations, continued deviance may be only irritating, but on other occasions, it may become totally disruptive of the group's completion of its task. If, for example, a religious organization has a minister who decides to grow long hair and a beard, this behavior could cause a variety of reactions ranging from wild enthusiasm on the part of the youth to mild disapproval among the general congregation to actual withdrawals of church membership and financial support. In the latter instance, where goal achievement is clearly hindered, the deviating minister will undoubtedly experience pressure for uniformity toward what is probably an implicit church norm: Only conservative hair styles are appropriate for preachers!

Another interesting approach to understanding group pressure may be drawn from Festinger's *social comparison theory.*[9] Most individuals do not need to consult the views of others to validate their perceptions of physical reality. A stove is hot; an elephant is big; a car is red. With matters of opinion and belief, however, the individual often finds comfort and reassurance in knowing that other persons share his/her views. Whenever members of a group or organization share common beliefs, values, or opinions, they create a kind of social reality for the validation of those views. This social validation process works best when group members are uniform in their beliefs; that is, according to social comparison theory, deviance destroys or seriously weakens the social reality that allows for opinion validation.

Finally, a number of theorists have advanced *balance theories,* parts of which may be relevant in explaining the group pressure phenomenon.[10] According to this perspective, groups prefer to exist as balanced systems. Consider the following example where imbalance or inconsistency has become a problem. A small group of executives meets regularly to make policy decisions. The groups is close-knit, and there is a feeling of shared liking. Suppose further that member A strongly opposes the other four members on an important policy decision. Among the several options available to the majority members are (1) avoiding discussion of the issue, (2) deciding that the issue is not as important as they had first believed, (3) deciding that member A must not really understand the policy or has been misinformed, or (4) deciding that member A is not as likable as they had once believed. Either of the last two approaches are particularly relevant to social pressure, for if the third interpretation is made, the result would be a number of attempts to inform, elaborate, and persuade the deviate. If this strategy fails, then another way to create balance is to choose alternative four and direct negative sentiments toward the deviate while reinforcing all conforming others. Research has shown that both of these approaches are common occurrences, particularly among highly cohesive groups who are making important decisions.

In addressing the second major question concerning why individuals often conform, two of the theoretical perspectives already discussed are of relevance. First, the *group locomotion hypothesis* is important in that if the individual group member is committed to helping the group attain its goals, and if the person further believes that his/her conformity will facilitate goal achievement, then s/he should be internally motivated to conform. Organizations that demand unanimous votes for major policy decisions often inspire individuals to feel that a dissenting vote would not simply indicate symbolic protest, but would prevent the organization (here represented by the group's majority) from moving forward toward a generally desired goal. Also potentially useful in understanding motivations toward conformity behavior is *balance theory*. Like the group, the individual strives for consistency throughout his/her life. If group or organizational membership is valued, then the knowledge that one does not agree, fit in, or meet the expectations of others is potentially dissonance producing. Thus the individual is often motivated to agree, to conform, and to become more similar to other group members in order to achieve a personal sense of balance or consistency.

Not unlike social comparison theory, Campbell's *epistemological weighting hypothesis* focuses on the extent to which individuals rely on others for validating their perceptions.[11] Campbell believes that knowledge may be acquired through either personal modes (such as trial and error or the observation of inanimate objects) or social modes (for example, observation of others or receiving instructions regarding appropriate and inappropriate behavior). From this perspective, what determines an individual's conformity is the relative weight given to the personal and social modes of knowledge acquisition. It should be noted, however, that Campbell's theory only works with informational social influence. Moreover, Campbell himself is quick to point out that on some occasions the individual conforms because of desired rewards or in an attempt to escape the costs of nonconformity. As a result, knowledge acquisition may not be terribly relevant.

A final approach to explaining conformity behavior is the *social-exchange view*, which construes conformity as a social process in which positive effects are brought about in interactions with others by manifestations of expected behavior.[12] Thus conformity becomes either a deserved reward to others that smooths the path of interaction and provides for further prospects of rewarding exchange or as a payment in advance for anticipated rewards. Conformity then might be thought of as a technique of ingratiation[13] or perhaps as a way to amass credits in one's status "bank."[14]

### Research Findings: Personal and Situational Variables

The area of social influence has suffered from no paucity of empirical investigations. Taylor was one of the earliest organizational researchers to be concerned with norms and their effects on industrial productivity.[15] Studies contributing to the human relations movement later pointed to the salience of informal work groups in establishing norms, sometimes at variance with the organization's notion of acceptable quantities of output.[16] Within the laboratories of social psychologists, the earliest experiment on social influence was conducted in the 1930's by Muzafer Sherif whose research with the autokinetic effect demonstrated that in a *group* situation, individual judgments soon converged over a number of trials.[17] One of the most extensive investigations of social influence was conducted by Solomon Asch.[18] He confronted naive subjects with the unanimous and erroneous opinions of several confederates on tasks involving simple perceptual judgments and discovered marked movement in the direction of the majority. In fact, only one fourth of Asch's naive subjects remained *completely* independent, but one third of the subjects displaced their estimates toward the majority judgment in half or more of the trials. It is important to note, too, that these line discrimination tasks were of no intrinsic importance to the subjects, the naive subject was unacquainted with the other group members, and they, in turn, made *no overt* attempts to influence his views.[19]

One of the implications of Asch's research is the seeming dichotomy between the independent subjects and the conformists. In an attempt to differentiate these two basic "types" of individuals, a number of investigators have sought to discover personality characteristics that might be associated with yielding behavior. Crutchfield's research was one of the earliest to unearth a kind of differential character profile.[20] He found that the independent person demonstrated great intellectual effectiveness, ego strength, leadership ability, and maturity of social relations. At the same time, s/he seemed to lack inferiority feelings, rigid and excessive self-control, and authoritarian attitudes. Finally, the independent was free from a compulsion to follow rules and was adventurous, self-assertive, and high in self-esteem. In contrast, Crutchfield reported that "the overconformist had less ego strength, less ability to tolerate ambiguity, less ability to accept responsibility, less self-insight, . . . less productive originality, more prejudiced and authoritarian attitudes, . . . and greater emphasis on external and socially approved values."[21]

The quest for personality characteristics that might be predictive of yielding behavior has received less attention in recent years. Although individuals do possess more or less enduring attributes, research has demonstrated that these attributes are modifiable by situational or contextual factors. It is not uncommon to find that the same individual is confident and self-assertive in one situation and reticent and uncertain in another. Thus so-called "universal traits" are extended or extinguished, depending upon the nature of the task being performed, the kind of people who surround the person, the nature of their interpersonal relations, and even other factors totally external to the group itself (such as the existence of an emergency or a particular political climate).[22] The point is that situational factors can prove so powerful that they break through the habitual response patterns and intensify or weaken the enduring attributes of personal character.

What are the situational variables that seem salient in affecting social influence processes? What, for example, are the contextual factors that seem most likely to produce conformity? Previous research points to the importance of a *unanimous majority*. Asch found that the inclusion of a single person who disagreed with the naive subject reduced the conformity rate by thirty percent.[23] In explaining this finding, Asch hypothesized that a fellow dissident both lowered the group consensus and provided the deviant member with social support for his/her private views. Follow-up research by Allen and Levine found, however, that unanimity was not necessary with subjective judgmental tasks where complete consensus was not anticipated or needed for significant social influence to occur.[24]

The *size of the majority* needed to achieve optimum pressure has also received a good deal of attention. Varying the size of the incorrect majority from one to fifteen, Asch found the effects of group pressure more pronounced when the unanimous opposition consisted of either three or four persons.[25] Other researchers, however, have failed to find a significant relationship between group size and conformity. Goldberg reported no significant difference between majorities of one, two, and three.[26] At the other extreme, Gerard and others found the most group-influenced judgments in a group of eight.[27] It is highly probable that group size is not nearly so important as the role relations among the members of the group. *One* powerful organizational executive exerting pressure for uniformity may be more influential than several lower-level employees in changing the publicly stated views of a would-be deviate.

Yet another important variable is *situational* or *stimulus ambiguity*. If an individual initially disagrees with a group's judgment on an issue that is unclear, uncertain, ambiguous, or difficult to understand, s/he is more likely to accept the group's position than if s/he perceives the issue to be more clear-cut and certain. After all, ambiguous matters are always open to interpretation; that is, they inherently involve degrees of correctness and incorrectness rather than absolutes of right or wrong. Thus especially on matters of opinion, belief, and attitude, the group's interpretation could easily be correct—or, at least, no more incorrect than the individual's.[28]

One final situational variable focuses on the nature of the interacting group and has to do with its degree of *cohesiveness*. Shepherd defines cohesiveness as "the quality of a group which includes individual pride, commitment, and meaning, as well as the group's stick-togetherness, ability to weather crises, and ability to maintain itself over time."[29] Highly cohesive groups demand, and usually get, great loyalty and conformity from their members. As a social-emotional quality of small groups, cohesiveness has been both lamented and applauded. People who belong to highly cohesive groups are usually there for positive reasons, often associated with their genuine liking for other group members, their feeling that the group's task is important, or perhaps their sense of pride in being affiliated with the group. If the highly cohesive group demands positive behavior, attitudes, or outcomes, its chances of getting them are better than are those of a group

lower in cohesiveness. On the other hand, the highly cohesive group
that establishes less positive standards or attitudes (such as low productivity, racial prejudice, or intolerance of divergent views) is also
more likely to maintain its norms and achieve its goals. Thus cohesiveness is neither good nor bad per se. Rather, it is a quality that enhances
the potency of the group's norms and goal achievement potential,
whatever they happen to be.[30]

The personality and situational variables discussed in this section
are not exhaustive but only suggestive of some of the significant
personal and contextual factors associated with social influence and
conformity behavior. But what of the deviate? How specifically do
groups exert pressure for uniformity? How does the deviant member
respond? Finally, what happens to the person who ultimately fails to
conform?

### The Deviate: Treatment and Impact

One interesting observation noted by the human relations researchers was the tendency of small informal work groups to develop verbal
and non-verbal methods of getting deviating members "back in line."
Tactics such as teasing, ridiculing, or punching and shoving the deviate
were not uncommon.[31] Perhaps the first systematic investigation of the
characteritics of pressure for uniformity was conducted by Schachter
who found that groups may exert forces for uniformity through increases in the *quantity* of communication.[32] He noted that communication quantity interacted with task relevance and group cohesiveness
such that communication attempts increased throughout the discussions in all groups *except* for the highly cohesive groups dealing with
important tasks. In those latter groups, communication to the deviate
reached a peak midway through the session and then proceeded to
decline steadily, leading ultimately to rejection. Subsequent research
by Taylor focused on the verbal behavior of majority members facing
an opinion deviate.[33] He found their communication was characterized
by dominance, reasonableness, and hostility.

Of all the variables that might affect a deviate's treatment, none is
more important than his/her position within the group. An individual's
group position is often measured on a scale reflecting status, usually
thought of as the significance, value, or prestige associated with a
given role. In most instances, we know that high status persons can
"get away with" more in terms of deviant behavior; that is, given the
performance of identical deviant acts (ranging from opinion deviation
to illegal behavior), the low status deviate is usually more severely

sanctioned than his/her high status counterpart.[34] And intriguing explanation for these findings has been advanced by Hollander whose "idiosyncrasy credit" model looks upon conformity as one input to the accumulation of status in the form of positive impressions or "credit" awarded by others.[35] This credit then permits greater latitude for nonconformity under certain conditions. A basic feature of this model is that there is *not* a fixed norm or set of norms to which all must comply equally. Rather, nonconformity behavior is defined differently by the group *depending upon how the individual group member is perceived*. Thus the same behavior is seen as deviant (in the negative sense) when performed by member A and as creative innovation when performed by member B. In this sense, conformity becomes person-specific and functionally related to status. Of course, this model is of great relevance to leadership. Leaders are usually great conformers to group norms,[36] but, at the same time, they are often initiators of change (reflected in seemingly nonconforming behavior). What often happens is that early conformity to group norms combined with such attributes as perceived competence may serve to enhance the acceptance of a leader's later nonconformity.

Yet, high status roles do carry with them high expectations. While there are wider latitudes of deviation for the high status person in some areas, there are greater restrictions in others. Extremely serious deviation, for example, may be more severely sanctioned when attributed to a high status actor than to a low status person.[37] There are, according to Hollander, at least two reasons why the role obligations of high status persons are so severely delimited.[38] First, high status is believed to hold greater self-determination; therefore, those in high status positions are assumed to be more responsible for their actions. Second, and perhaps just as important, high status carries with it role demands that are more likely to affect important outcomes for the members of the group. So long as norm violations can be construed as instances of "productive nonconformity,"[39] then the high status deviate's behavior will be accepted and perhaps even welcomed. If, however, his/her actions are seen to hurt the group or organization, the high status person will be held *more* responsible than would a low status member. As Hollander puts it, "It is true that acts of the high status person are less likely to be perceived negatively than those of a low status person, but given that the evaluation of acts is equally unfavorable, the high status person will pay the higher social price."[40]

Responses of the deviate to group pressure vary. But for most, being in a position of opposition to other group members is accompanied by uneasiness. As early as 1936, Smith demonstrated that college students become emotionally aroused when they learn that their peers disagree with them.[41] This arousal is greatest when the disagreeing peers challenge opinions that are strongly believed. Assuming the arousal is unpleasant, it should motivate attempts to lessen the disagreement; and one way to do this is to accept the majority position. Asch, too, was interested in discerning why yielding behavior occurred. Through post experimental interviews, he discovered that the frequent yielders reported three types of reactions: (1) they actually "saw" the majority estimates as correct (perceptual distortion); (2) they believed, contrary to what they saw, that their perceptions were probably incorrect and that the majority was probably right (distortion of judgment); and (3) they yielded because of a desire not to seem different from the other group members (distortion of action). Among those who remained totally independent, there were also several reactions: (1) complete, vigorous confidence; (2) withdrawn, introverted independence, and (3) doubtful, tension-ridden nonconformity. It should be noted, however, that no one of these groups (including the so-called "completely confident" category) was immune from some tension and experience of conflict. Finally, Bradley's study of the verbal behavior of deviates undergoing pressure for uniformity revealed some interesting patterns.[42] She found, for example, that opinion deviates made few early attempts at influence or leadership. As the discussions progressed, however, they expressed their ideas in a more assertive, influential manner. When this strategy proved futile, dominance tendencies regressed rapidly. In addition, deviate emotionality increased from the beginning to the end of the discussion sessions while reasonableness declined. Bradley speculated that when the discussion has progressed to the stage where the deviate sees that the exhibition of sound judgment and well-balanced thought is proving futile, s/he abandons them as useful persuasive tools. Even so, emotional involvement continues to rise.

There are situations, of course, in which the expression of deviant views may influence the ideas of the rest of the group. Grove found that the attitudes of both deviates *and* majority members are affected by the presentation of opposing views during group discussions. Moreover, while both majority group members and deviant group members appreciably changed their positions as a result of mutual interaction, majority convergence was greater than deviate convergence.[43] A recent study by Bradley, Hamon, and Harris further revealed that an articulate, intelligent deviate is capable of influencing the publicly expressed views of majority group members; that is, in group discussion settings, majority group members will use a significant number of the deviate's arguments, actually reciting them as their own.[44]

Group members who are valued by the group and/or are in positions of leadership may find it possible to engage in constructive deviation without sanctioning. Dittes and Kelley found, for example, that subjects believing they had high acceptance in their groups felt great freedom to express deviant views.[45] Certainly there is something to be said for the democratic assertion that all opinions, however deviant, should be aired. The old notion of playing the "devil's advocate" clearly implies that ideas will be better for having stood the test of argument. Many approaches to group problem-solving recognize the importance of gathering a divergent sampling of views *prior* to interpretation or evaluation; thus, they variously employ brain-storming, nominal grouping, and other techniques to encourage the expression of unstifled thought. One of Irving Janis' advocated solutions to *groupthink* was to bring in different points of view (often from outside the group), to expect *each* group member to play the role of critical evaluator, and to avoid overly directive leadership, particularly the statement of personal preferences. Thus in overcoming the natural "ingroup" tendency to agree, it is important to welcome and respect the freedom to disagree.

So far, we have looked at theories and research of the past in an attempt to assess the nature, kinds, strategies, processes, and outcomes associated with the social influence phenomenon. The last section of this work will focus on an approach to using this knowledge for the effective functioning of organizations and the fulfillment of individuals within them.

## Creative Conformity

All organizations engage in socialization. They have goals, values, norms, and preferred ways of doing things that are taught rather systematically, both overtly and covertly, to all new members. Schein differentiates *pivotal norms* (required for organizational membership, such as belief in the free enterprise system) from *peripheral norms* (desirable but not essential, such as holding conservative political views). He believes that organizations should seek creative individualists, persons who accept all pivotal norms while rejecting all others.[46] Schein's view is close to the one espoused in this work, but it differs in some important respects.

First, it is not possible to delineate a model organization person. There are simply too many kinds of skills involved, jobs to be performed, individual personalities to consider, and so forth. The kind of creativity needed among top level executives is clearly not the same as that desired among factory workers or even among leaders in different executive divisions (for example, the vice president for finance as opposed to the vice president for research and development). Even so, we can *begin* to discern an effective approach for organizations to pursue with many of their employees. And the approach originates with an assessment of the organization's norms and expectations. What are the values to which the organization is committed at a *behavioral level?* How are these made manifest? What are the implications for workers who spend their lives trying to be fruitful and fulfilled within this formal structure? Is the organization honest with itself about its values, and does it attempt to honestly communicate those values to employees at a time when such knowledge could make a difference, such as during the selection interview? The interviewing department chairman who tells a would-be assistant professor that "teaching and research are equally valued at this university" should probably ask him/herself, "*if* they are equally valued, why are they not equally rewarded?" In short, the organization must recognize the nature of its goals, expectations, and values before it can critically assess them and communicate them to employees.

Likewise, workers need to undergo a specific process of self-assessment prior to entering the organization and continuously throughout their productive lives. This assessment should focus on education, work experience, and developed skills as well as goals, expectations, and values. Only when both parties have evaluated themselves with directness and candor can a good "fit" between organization and individual occur. It is my view that the creative conformity suggested in the title of this work can only occur when there exists just such a "fit."

Consider the notion of the psychological contract. It implies that individual and organization have a variety of mutual expectations. These expectations not only cover the amount of work to be performed for a certain amount of money, but also the whole pattern of rights, privileges, and obligations between workers and organization. Many of these expectations are never written into formal agreements between employee and organization, but they continue to operate as powerful determinants of behavior.[47] From the organization's point of view, the psychological contract is implemented through the concept of *authority*. A decision to join the organization implies a commitment to accept its authority system.[48] Authority in this sense is *not* the same as pure power, for the former implies the willingness on the part of subordinates to obey *because* they *consent;* that is, because the employees understand the organization's expectations, they *agree* to accept certain roles or positions within the organization. It is crucial to note, however, that from employees' points of view, the psychological contract is implemented through their perception that they *can* influence the organization of their own immediate situations sufficiently to insure that they will not be taken advantage of. The mode of influence is not so important as the fundamental belief that the power to influence exists. The psychological contract, then, is based on acceptance of mutual influence, an understanding of mutual expectations, and a willingness to behave reasonably and fairly within the confines of the agreement.

If this contract is to be mutually satisfying, extensive agreement must exist between the standards of the individual and the expectations of the organization. This is to say that individual creativity can most meaningfully occur within an organizational context where individual needs and values and organizational goals are congruent. Thus for the most part, the individual does conform and quite probably in more than the pivotal areas—but s/he does so because it is natural. The person behaves as s/he normally would behave, and that behavior *is* in keeping with organizational expectations simply because employee and employer are well matched. Etzioni writes of three types of involvement that individuals may have as they approach their organizational responsibilities: (1) *alienative* (where the person is coerced into belonging); (2) *calculative* (where the person works to achieve a valued personal end—usually money, security, or prestige); and (3) *moral*.[49] This latter involvement concept is central to the discussion of creative conformity, for it means that the person intrinsically values the mission of the organization and his/her job within it and performs the job, not for reward, but because s/he values it!

Early in the history of our nation, one of the most valued of personal characteristics was "rugged individualism." While independence is clearly important in many contexts, in recent years the American value trend has moved in the direction of *interdependence*.[50] Thus the emphasis is upon cooperatively striving for common goals with a respect for the person's individuality and a simultaneous recognition of the strength of concerted effort.

But there is still another implication to the notion of interdependence that takes us beyond the organization's boundaries. For most organizations, the ability to grow is commensurate with adaptability to and management of change.[51] Every organization exists in a dynamic environment. As technological change proceeds at an incredible rate, organizations face constant problems of obsolescence. Moreover, social-political changes throughout the world are creating an undiminished demand for new services as well as the expansion of existing products. Organizations have changed further with the advent of computers and automation—needing highly educated managers, far exceeding the present supply.

The relationship between every organization and its environment is one of interdependence. Without reciprocal exchanges, adjustments, and mutually influencing interactions, neither can benefit the other. Given the dynamic state of the organization's surroundings, then, perhaps the most critical capacity to be developed by organizational members is the ability to meet a variety of new problems with creativity and flexibility. More important, this quality is not merely an attribute to be possessed by management, but by all of the organization's human resources. Flexible managers may alter the structure, policy, or even the goals of the organization in order to adjust to environmental changes. But if the employees themselves are inflexible, then altering the company's blueprint will have but minimal impact on the actual operation of the organization.

When organizations become committed to such "norms" as creativity, innovation, and flexibility, it is not only possible, but more highly *probable*, that organizational members can practice creative conformity in a personally fulfilling and professionally productive way. Given the presence of normative social influences, a virtual fact of group and organizational life, there is every reason to attempt to use these powerful social stimuli for the encouragement of positive group and individual goals. Deutsch and Gerard were among the first to recognize that social influence might be used to buttress, as well as undermine, individual integrity! They stated: "Groups can demand of their members that they have self-respect, that they value their own experience, that they be capable of acting without slavish regard for popularity. Unless groups encourage their members to express their own, independent judgments, group consensus is likely to be an empty achievement."[52]

In some senses, the creative conformity perspective represents an ideal. To apply it at all levels of all organizations would be an impossibility. But movement in the direction of the approach seems warranted in view of 1. the survival demands placed on the organization for adaptation and innovation and 2. the internal needs of the individual for self-actualization through organizational affiliation. Creative conformity, not unlike Schein's concept of creative individualism, stresses the acceptance of major organizational policies, goals, and values. But creative conformists are also free to accept most of the organization's relevant peripheral norms since their commitment to the organization is rooted in *value congruence*. They know what the organization stands for, accept it, and are committed to it at a personal level. Their relationship to this particular organization is simply one major manifestation of their over-all value orientation. And it is a mutual commitment, for the organization pledges to encourage innovation, to reward creativity, to applaud adaptability, and to nurture human growth in a context of organizational development.

## Notes

1. William Whyte, *The Organization Man* (New York: Doubleday and Company, Inc., 1956).
2. See, for example, J. Bensman and B. Rosenberg, "The Meaning of Work in Bureaucratic Society," in *Readings on Modern Organizations* ed. E Etizioni (Englewood Cliffs, N.J.: Prentice-Hall, 1969).
3. Edgar H. Schein, *Organizational Psychology,* second edition (Englewood Cliffs, N.J.: Prentice-Hall, Inc., 1970), p. 9.
4. Morton Deutsch and Harold B. Gerard, "A Study of Normative and Informational Social Influences upon Individual Judgment," *Journal of Abnormal and Social Psychology* (1955), vol. 51, p. 629.
5. Leon Festinger, *A Theory of Cognitive Dissonance* (Stanford, California: Stanford University Press, 1957).
6. Edwin P. Hollander and Richard H. Willis, "Some Current Issues in the Psychology of Conformity and Nonconformity," *Psychological Bulletin* (1967), vol. 68, pp. 62–76.
7. *Ibid*. It is important to note here that these distinctions do not connote a typology of persons, but rather a differentiation of responses.
8. Leon Festinger, "Informal Social Communication," *Psychological Review* (1950), vol. 57. pp. 271–282.
9. Leon Festinger, "A Theory of Social Comparison Processes," *Human Relations* (1954), vol. 7, pp. 117–40.
10. See, for example, Fritz Heider, "Attitudes and Cognitive Organization," *Journal of Psychology* (1946) vol. 21, pp. 107–12; Festinger, *A Theory of Cognitive Dissonance;* and Charles E. Osgood and Percy H. Tannenbaum, "The Principle of Congruity in the Prediction of Attitude Change," *Psychological Review* (1955) vol. 62, pp. 42–55.
11. Donald T. Campbell, "Conformity in Psychology's Theories of Acquired Behavioral Dispositions," in *Conformity and Deviation* ed. Irwin A. Berg and Bernard M. Bass (New York: Harper and Row, 1961), pp. 101–42.
12. For example, see J. Stacy Adams, "Inequity in Social Exchange," in *Advances in Experimental Social Psychology* Vol. 2, ed. Leonard Berkowitz (New York: Academic Press, 1965), pp. 267–99; Peter M. Blau, *Exchange and Power in Social Life* (New York: Wiley, 1964); George C. Homans, "Social Behavior as Exchange," *American Journal of Sociology* (1958) vol. 63, pp. 597–606; and John W. Thibaut and Harold H. Kelley, *The Social Psychology of Groups* (New York: Wiley, 1959).

13. Edward E. Jones, "Conformity as a Tactic of Ingratiation," *Science* (1965) vol. 149, pp. 144-50.
14. Edwin P. Hollander, "Competence and Conformity in the Acceptance of Influence," *Journal of Abnormal and Social Psychology* (1960) vol. 61, pp. 361-65.
15. Frederick W. Taylor, *The Principles of Scientific Management* (New York: Harper and Row, 1911).
16. F. Roethlisberger and W. Dickson, *Management and the Worker* (Cambridge, Mass.: Harvard University Press, 1939).
17. Muzafer Sherif, "A Study of Some Social Factors in Perception," *Archives of Psychology* (1935), vol. 27, no. 187.
18. Solomon E. Asch, "Studies of Independence and Conformity: A Minority of One Against a Unanimous Majority," *Psychological Monographs* (1956), vol. 70, no. 416.
19. See Dorwin Cartwright and Alvin Zander, "Pressures to Uniformity in Groups: Introduction," *Group Dynamics*, third edition (New York: Harper and Row, 1968), pp. 139–60.
20. Richard S. Crutchfield, "Conformity and Character," *The American Psychologist* (1955), vol. 10, pp. 191–98.
21. *Ibid.*, p. 196.
22. L. B. Rosenfeld, *Human Interaction in the Small Group Setting* (Columbus, Ohio: Charles Merrill, 1973).
23. Asch, *op. cit.*, no. 416.
24. See, for example, Vernon L. Allen and J. M. Levine, "Social Support, Dissent, and Conformity," *Sociometry* (1968), vol. 31, pp. 138–49 and V. L. Allen and J. M. Levine, "Social Support and Conformity: The Role of Independent Assessment of Reality," *Journal of Experimental Social Psychology* (1971) vol. 7, pp. 48–58.
25. Solomon E. Asch, "Opinions and Social Pressure," *Scientific American* (1955), vol. 193, pp. 31–35.
26. Samuel C. Goldberg, "Three Situational Determinants of Conformity to Social Norms," *Journal of Abnormal and Social Psychology* (1954), vol. 49, pp. 325–29.
27. Harold B. Gerard, R. A. Wilhelmy, and E. S. Conolly, "Conformity and Group Size," *Journal of Personality and Social Psychology* (1968), vol. 8, pp. 79–82.
28. Stimulus ambiguity is clearly not reserved to matters of attitude and opinion. Sherif's autokinetic situation, for example, is extremely ambiguous, and as Sherif has demonstrated in subsequent research, the group's judgment may be accepted for as long as a year.
29. C. Shepherd, *Small Groups* (Scranton, Pa: Chandler Co., 1964).
30. Irving Janis' work on "groupthink" is one of the best contemporary examples of the negative outcomes historically associated with highly cohesive groups, such as the development of an illusion of invulnerability, excessive rationalization, shared stereotypes, and a tendency toward self-censorship.
31. Roethlisberger and Dickson, *op. cit.*
32. Stanley Schachter, "Deviation, Rejection, and Communication," *Journal of Abnormal and Social Psychology* (1951), vol. 46, pp. 190–207.
33. K. Phillip Taylor, "An Investigation of Majority Verbal Behavior toward

Opinions of Deviant Members in Group Discussions of Policy," unpublished Ph.D. dissertation, Indiana University, 1969.

34. See, for example, Leonard Berkowitz and J. R. Macaulay, "Some Effects of Differences in Status Level and Status Stability," *Human Relations* (1961), vol. 14, pp. 135–48; Edwin P. Hollander, "Some Effects of Perceived Status on Responses to Innovative Behavior," *Journal of Abnormal and Social Psychology* (1961), vol. 63, pp. 247–50; and J. A. Wiggins, F. Dill and R. D. Schwartz, "On 'Status Liability,' " *Sociometry* (1965), vol. 28, pp. 197–209.

35. Edwin P. Hollander, "Conformity, Status, and Idiosyncrasy Credit," *Psychological Review* (1958), vol. 65, pp. 117–27; and E. P. Hollander, *Leaders, Groups, and Influence* (New York: Oxford University Press, 1964).

36. George C. Homans, *The Human Group* (New York: Harcourt-Brace, 1950).

37. Ralph Wahrman, "Status, Deviance, and Sanctions: A Critical Review," *Comparative Group Studies* (1972), vol. 3, pp. 203–24.

38. Hollander, *Leaders, Groups, and Influence*, p. 277.

39. Pauline Pepinsky, "Social Exceptions That Prove the Rule," in *Conformity and Deviation* ed. Irwin A. Berg and Bernard M. Bass. (New York: Harper and Row, 1961), pp. 424–434.

40. Hollander and Willis, *op. cit.*, p. 243.

41. C. E. Smith, "A Study of the Autonomic Excitation Resulting from the Interaction of Individual Opinions and Group Opinion," *Journal of Abnormal and Social Psychology* (1936), vol. 30, pp. 138–164.

42. Patricia Hayes Bradley, "Pressure for Uniformity: An Experimental Study of Deviate Responses in Group Discussions of Policy," *Small Group Behavior* (1978), vol. 9, pp. 149–60.

43. Theodore G. Grove, "Attitude Convergence in Small Groups," *Journal of Communication* (1965), vol. 15, pp. 226–38.

44. Patricia Hayes Bradley, C. Mac. Hamon, and Alan M. Harris, "Dissent in Small Groups," *Journal of Communication* (1976), vol. 26, pp. 155–59.

45. J. E. Dittes and Harold H. Kelley, "Effects of Different Conditions of Acceptance upon Conformity to Group Norms," *Journal of Abnormal and Social Psychology* (1956), vol. 52, pp. 100–07.

46. Edgar H. Schein, "Organizational Socialization and the Profession of Management," *Industrial Management Review* (1968), vol. 9, pp. 1–6.

47. Chris Argyris, *Understanding Organizational Behavior* (Homewood, Ill.: The Dorsey Press, 1960).

48. Schein, *Organizational Psychology*, pp. 12–13.

49. Amitai Etzioni, *A Comparative Analysis of Complex Organizations* (Glencoe, Ill.: Free Press, 1961).

50. E. L. Trist, "Urban North America: The Challenge of the Next Thirty Years," in *Organizational Frontiers and Human Values* ed. W. H. Schmid (Belmont, California: Wadsworth, 1970).

51. Schein, *Organizational Psychology, op. cit.*, p. 19.

52. Deutsch and Gerard, *op. cit.*, p. 635.

# 14

# The Bureaucratic Personality: An Alternate View

*Norma M. Williams*
*Gideon Sjoberg*
*Andrée F. Sjoberg*

During the past four decades, a number of social scientists have examined the "bureaucratic personality." But they have failed to come to terms with a crucial, as well as pervasive, feature of bureaucracy— its "hidden side." Specifically, they have failed to recognize that hidden arrangements are an inherent factor in shaping the bureaucratic personality. We present herein a quite different conception of bureaucracy, and we seek to highlight the impact of the bureaucratic structure, especially its hidden side, upon the personality of its members.

Our conclusions are mainly anchored in the personal experiences of the senior author, who worked for extended periods for a medium-sized public bureaucracy, a large labor union, and a major corporation. This work experience brought her into contact with still other bureaucratic organizations. In addition, the published accounts of members of various bureaucratic structures, especially during the 1970s, provide supporting documentation for our generalizations.

Our conceptualization of the bureaucratic personality is based upon the American experience and applies primarily to the managerial sector of bureaucracy and its immediate supportive structure, including administrative or senior secretaries. Selected aspects of our "constructed type," however, are applicable to all ranks of bureaucratic personnel.

### Existing Theoretical Orientations

Merton, taking Weber's classical analysis of bureaucracy as his point of departure, wrote a widely influential essay on the personality of bureaucrats.[1] In Merton's view, bureaucracies demand formality and clearly defined social distance between the occupants of different positions in the system. In this way, people can predict the actions of others, and stable sets of mutual expectations can emerge. "The structure is one which approaches the complete elimination of personalized relationships and nonrational considerations (hostility, anxiety, affectual involvements, etc.)"[2] Members of the bureaucracies are also expected to exercise prudence and self-discipline.

Merton devoted most of his attention to the dysfunctions of bureaucracy and the implications of these for personality. For example, although rules are essential, many bureaucrats come to view them as ends in themselves. Similarly, an obsession with discipline leads to rigidity, overconformity, trained incapacity, and resistance to change. Moreover, the emphasis on impersonality leads to the pigeonholing of persons and to neglect of compelling particularistic considerations. By inference the bureaucrat who allows personal considerations to influence his/her decisions is courting widespread disapproval.

A number of social scientists associated with the human relations school have also devoted attention to the bureaucratic personality.[3] By and large they have contended that the individual plays a more creative role in bureaucracies than is generally recognized. Argyris is a major representative of this school. Relying upon the work of Maslow and others, he emphasizes the need for recognition of the feelings of failure and frustration that result when one's self-fulfillment is blocked by the organizational environment.

Responding to the critics of his view, Argyris writes:

> The issues of dependence, submissiveness, expression of feelings, and defenses and their relevance to problem solving and decision making have been ignored. Because of these omissions, these theories would have difficulty in predicting certain trends.[4]

He further observes that most organizational theorists are unable to deal with the hostility and aggression displayed by an increasing number of young people who reject the notion that the individual is little more than a cog in the wheels of an organization. Thus, Argyris's perspective could help to account for certain kinds of absenteeism.

Perhaps the most important recent work on the bureaucratic personality is that by Hummel, who sees bureaucracy and society today as separate worlds in cultural conflict, with the bureaucratic realm inexorably taking society's place as the prime shaper of personality.[5] To state Hummel's argument in adumbrated form: When such replacement occurs, we find that on the social level, people become cases; culturally, means replace ends as ultimate norms; psychologically, the role replaces the person; linguistically, command replaces dialogue; and politically, pseudopolitics replaces politics.

Merton, Argyris, and Hummel have contributed to our understanding of the bureaucratic personality, but they have overlooked the far-ranging impact upon personality of bureaucracy's hidden dimensions. Merton mentions the existence of secrecy in bureaucracy, but he has not incorporated it into his theoretical framework. Although a full-fledged theory of bureaucracy lies beyond the scope of this essay, we do set forth the dominant characteristics of the hidden side.[6]

## An Alternative Theoretical Orientation

Perrow rightly observes that "organizations are tools for shaping the world as one wishes it to be shaped."[7] But neither he nor other organizational theorists have acknowledged the significance of secrecy systems, or hidden arrangements, in the struggle for power. Admittedly, a number of social scientists[8] have discussed informal structures and informal groups. And others have analyzed military and paramilitary structures whose operations are by definition geared to secrecy.[9] (Ungar, 1975; U.S. Senate, 1976) But until recently the pervasiveness of influence emanating from the hidden side of bureaucracies, even in democratic societies, in both the public and the private sectors, has generally gone unrecognized. Some of these arrangements, for example informal social circles, may be benign; others, such as structures serving to protect confidentiality, are essential to the functioning of a democratic order. But many hidden arrangements are associated with the acquisition and manipulation of social power, and these are the foci of our attention.

It is clear that Simmel's secrecy system[10] must be placed within Weber's bureaucratic "iron cage."[11] Secrecy systems exist both within and among bureaucratic structures. Bureaucracies assume that they can advance their goals by concealing at least some of their activites from competitors and from the public at large. This holds true in both the public and the private arenas.

The crisis surrounding the Vietnam War and Watergate heightened people's awareness of the means that governmental bureaucracies employ to advance their goals. In the public sector bureaucracies construct hidden social worlds in which other organizations—legislative bodies, lobbying groups, etc.—are seen as potential threats. A good deal of effort goes into warding off possible attacks from without, and a common defense is concealment of certain organizational activities. The manner in which the U.S. military "constructed" official statistics in Vietnam is a case in point. If we accept Adams's[12] contention, the military fabricated the size of the enemy forces, as well their casualties and number of deserters, in an apparent effort to demonstrate the success of the U.S. in the war. In addition, the political and military activities in Cambodia during the Nixon era have engendered intense controversy, for many significant bureaucratic decisions are still shrouded in secrecy. The accounts of Shawcross, Kissinger, and Wicker[13] all underscore the difficulties of determining the facts in this regard.

There are hidden dimensions to activities in the nonmilitary realm as well. Much has been written about Watergate[14] and its culmination in the resignation of President Nixon. Thus, the spillovers from Watergate have led to disclosures of a wide variety of hidden activities on the part of corporations seeking to enhance their overall position in the marketplace.[15]

As an example, we can point to the recent research on grain operators by Morgan,[16] an investigative journalist. His study documents the activities of five private grain companies which have through complex hidden arrangements come to control much of the world's grain trade and therefore its food supply. These grain companies have developed a superstructure that has long been concealed from the public, social scientists included. So secret have been their operations that in 1972, when the Soviet Union was able to purchase grain from these companies, apparently none was aware of the actions of the others. (In this situation, secrecy may have reduced the competitive advantage of each company.)

Viewed more generally, the economy has its subterranean, or "other," side which includes illegal, quasi-legal, and legal activities.[17] One subsector of this other economy is hidden from the ghetto or barrio economy, wherein drug trafficking and other illegal activities abound, as well as semi-legal and legal pursuits such as barter. Another subsector is built into the large corporations and in recent years has received considerable attention. We now know that a number of major economic activities are carried out within the hidden sphere of corporate structures. In the business world, where the goal is to maximize profits, legal manipulation of the books, pay-offs, cutting corners on contracts, and so forth all add to the profits. Moreover, pay-offs to public officials are a means of co-opting the latter and making them active participants in the hidden economy.

Implicit in our commentary up to this point is the fact that secrecy is enhanced by "jurisdictional overlaps." Where, for instance, extensive exchange of money or information takes place between the public and the private sectors, the boundaries between the two become blurred and considerable discretion is afforded persons who participate in both domains. Or where multinational corporations span several countries, managers can rather freely shift monies in their accounts without effective scrutiny by any national or international body.

Moreoever, the very nature of bureaucratic structures tends to foster hidden arrangements. The well-developed hierarchy of authority and division of labor that characterize the structure, as well as the use of universalistic criteria for employment and advancement, all help to enhance efficiency and a kind of rationality, but these same factors also generate subsurface activities within the structure. If managers are to sustain rationality, they must delegate considerable responsibility to subordinates who perform the more mundane chores of bureaucracy. Yet the delegation of responsibility, particularly to individuals who command highly specialized skills and technical knowledge, tends to undermine the hierarchical arrangements, including the positions of the immediate superiors of these specialists.

To avoid erosion of their power and authority, managers create their own hidden world. They protect themselves by delegating "blamability" under the guise of responsibility,[18] for the responsibility accorded underlings incurs more potential for blame than for rights and privileges. Organizational theorists who overlook this pattern have simply not come to terms with the internal workings of bureaucracy. While conceding that a high concentration of authority may increase the delegation of responsibility, theorists such as Perrow (1979) fail to grasp the implications of such delegation of responsibility within a bureaucratic setting. In practice this pattern means that higher-ups shift onto subordinates the blame for their own failures and inadequacies. John Dean, in *Blind Ambition*[19] makes it clear that his superiors in the White House delegated certain responsibilities to him for the express purpose of making him the scapegoat for some of their mistakes. Dean's account also dramatizes how "deniability" forms part of the pattern of avoiding blamability: He alleges that his superiors simply denied any responsibility for, or indeed any knowledge of, the activities they had assigned to him.

Not surprisingly, the threat of blamability leads underlings to attempt to protect themselves by creating a hidden system of their own. One way to escape punishment, to control one's circumstances to a degree, is to selectively disseminate information to superiors. Often this means telling superiors what they want to hear and avoiding the role of bearer of bad tidings. Other time-honored techniques are resorted to when the situation demands: work slowdowns, "misplacing'' crucial documents, and so on. Such tactics signal managers' dependency upon lower level personnel, particularly specialists who possess crucial information or command unusual skills.

The foregoing discussion is admittedly an oversimplification of the hidden side of bureaucracy; the situation is actually more complex. Sometimes hidden arrangements cut across hierarchical lines. Such is the case where higher status personnel must enlist the support of subordinates in order to attain a particular objective. A bureaucratic coup, where the ruling faction is overthrown by a rival element from within, necessarily depends upon the cooperation of strategic persons farther down the status ladder. Moreover, it may happen that secrecy systems in one organization have links to counterparts in another bureaucracy. We alluded to such arrangements earlier when we referred to pay-offs by corporations to elements of public bureaucracies.

We return to our initial postulate: Bureaucracies are a tool that human beings employ to acquire and sustain social power and thereby shape their internal and external environments. Throughout we have reasoned that hidden arrangements are a central means toward attaining this goal. But another aspect of bureaucracy requires special mention: This is the nature of bureaucratic rules. Rules or norms, far from being objective facts, require interpretation. Although the upper ranks of personnel are hemmed in by fewer restrictions than the lower, all bureaucrats, whether high or low, must use discretion in applying the rules of a bureaucracy.[20] Thus external pressures, as well as internal considerations such as hierarchy and division of labor, must be viewed within the context of the use of discretion, which then makes possible the creation of hidden arrangements. Effective bureaucrats learn to bend, to reinterpret, the formal rules to their own advantage.

In sum, our brief discussion focuses attention on the role of hidden arrangements in the struggle for power and authority.

### Hidden Arrangements and the Bureaucratic Personality

It is apparent that multiple hidden systems are an integral part of large-scale organizations. And this structural context has deep-seated consequences for the personality of members of bureaucracies.

One product of these hidden arrangements is the emergence of the ''bureaucratic face.'' This face has certain distinguishing characteristics. It must mask emotion and at the same time transmit both verbal and nonverbal cues. A skilled bureaucrat presents to the public a generally flat effect, all the while conveying information to persons within and external to the structure. Indeed, a single cue may need to be interpreted in different ways by persons in different secrecy systems, and the sender is well aware of this. In turn, the ability to send and receive messages is predicated upon a keen social memory—of what one said and what others said in different situations in the past.

Persons who are effective also learn to speak in a neutral and elliptical manner in delicate situations, especially those involving hidden arrangements. Often information is conveyed through indirection. For example, the investigator of leaks in the FBI's bribery probe (ABSCAM) observed that as a federal prosecutor he had not leaked information to reporters but had "provided guidance" by steering them away from false leads.[21] He had "let them know by tone of voice or general attitude" that the stories they were pursuing were valid. Under these circumstances, the prosecutor could deny that he had leaked any specific information.

The written word must also be accommodated to the hierarchical structure and its various secrecy systems. Here, as in face-to-face encounters, subordinates must learn how to make requests of superiors. One basic principle is to leave the latter room to say "no" if necessary. In fact, both parties must be allowed to "save face," a matter we will discuss further.

The bureaucratic face exudes an air of formal cordiality. Dean refers to adopting the "plastic smile."[22] A cordial, yet somewhat distant, demeanor fosters the image of one who is in harmony with the organization and its goals. And in times of political upheaval, formal cordiality serves to reduce tensions and facilitates the shifting of loyalties from one hidden group to another.

Side by side with formal cordiality is the demand for toughness. "Macho talk" is typical of the managerial face.[23] In frequent use are phrases such as "We have to make some tough decisions," or "We can't let sentiment influence our judgment." The senior author, in her capacity as a manager within a certain organization, was often told by her superiors to rework her reports on subordinates so as to make them more critical and thus more intimidating.

In light of this concern with toughness and the elimination of sentiment, bureaucrats must be wary of discussing their personal problems. Difficulties associated with family life, mental health, and so on do become subjects of conversation at work. And while the secrecy systems associated with informal groups provide some protection for the individual's personal struggles, superiors may demonstrate their toughness by discrediting personnel whose frailties leave them open to attack (or to demands for even greater loyalty). After all, personal weaknesses may well mean that one is making less than a maximum contribution to the organization.

Nevertheless, when disciplining, firing, or re-assigning employees, formal cordiality on the part of superiors comes to the rescue. Any harsh actions against an employee, especially one above the level of unskilled worker, tend to be accompanied by buffers such as "Please don't take this personally," or near-disclaimers such as "It's out of my hands; the decision came from higher up," or "I have to do this for the good of the organization" (an appeal to the generalized other). Indeed, superiors who accept their social world uncritically may find it impossible to express "human concern" in situations involving disciplinary action.

Another feature of the bureaucratic face is sensitivity to hierarchical status patterns.[24] In most bureaucratic settings personnel are deeply concerned with perks, with status symbols, with differential treatment accorded persons of unequal statuses. Thus, underlings learn to stroke the boss's ego, and higher-ups bestow small favors upon subordinates. As indicated above, in situations involving special requests or the meting out of discipline, an effort is made by both parties to let the other "save face." This helps to cover up the exchange of favors as well as avoid retribution for harsh decisions. After all, underlings have their own hidden arrangements enabling them to strike back against superiors who engage in overkill.

As we indicated, subordinates in a hierarchy will say and do things to make the boss feel important. A secretary will ask the boss's advice concerning which brand of coffee to buy for the office, where to go for auto repairs, and so on. Or there may be other small requests demonstrating employees' reliance upon superiors. So obvious is this pattern at times that the senior author has overheard secretaries discussing which of them was going to stroke the boss that day.

In turn, the effective manager is one who compliments subordinates on aspects of their daily work and tries to remember birthdays and other events of social significance to them. Permitting occasional rearrangement of working hours, overlooking certain kinds of errors—these and other concessions make it clear that the boss really cares and serve to strengthen the bonds of loyalty of inferior to superior. It should hardly be surprising that Marvin Watson, who served in President Johnson's administration, was viewed by some as ruthless, yet stoutly defended by others as a caring person because, for one thing, he always remembered the birthdays of his immediate subordinates.[25]

Ritual activities of this sort, along with a tacit understanding of the nature of the reciprocity involved, act to sustain loyalty in the face of the fact that both superiors and subordinates are engaged in activities that are somewhat hidden from each other. By occasionally letting down the status barriers, by demonstrating, albeit in a stylized manner, that one is human, the manager reduces some of the tensions associated with hierarchical authority and mutual secrecy systems.

The relationship between superiors and subordinates is further complicated by the fact that the latter need to give the appearance of abiding by the rules. Yet, breaking or bending the rules is at times essential if certain tasks are to be accomplished—for example, where corporate executives charge middle managers with responsibility for achieving almost impossible goals.[26] A good deal of creativity with respect to the use of discretion is called for under these circumstances. Bureaucrats need to learn how far they can go and what precautions they must take in restructuring the norms (there are particular rules that cannot be broken).

In many instances top officials can honestly say they had no knowledge of certain activities of subordinates, although there are instances where violations occur with the tacit, even the explicit, collusion of superiors. It is the purpose of secrecy systems to cloak the activities of underlings from persons above and the activities of higher-ups from those below.

These various underground activities generate the need for loyalty, for loyalty often binds together persons involved in somewhat disparate hidden arrangements. Because of the ever-present possibility of political contests and the resulting loss of perks and power, loyalty serves to protect superiors. And it is more than an abstract idea—it involves personal fealty to a particular person who in turn comes to represent the organization.

An important aspect of loyalty is dependency. The personal bond of loyalty does not involve emotions such as arise from intimate attachments within family or close friendship groups. Rather, we are talking about an environment wherein loyalty demands a studied commitment. Even when ties of loyalty are established, shifting political tides may require a person to transfer allegiance to another superior if he/she is to survive in the organization.

Financial dependence upon superiors obviously forges bonds of loyalty, but other factors operate as well. Specific personality traits play a salient role. For example, they influence the choice of executives in large-scale organizations.[27] Frequently, top-level managers actively seek a dynamic and aggressive individual who, nonetheless, is somewhat less dynamic and aggressive than themselves. To ensure loyalty, managers also tend to surround themselves with persons having similar personal tastes and interests.

While some sacrifice of efficiency is associated with loyalty, far more threatening to managers is the possibility of losing control over the resources they command. They therefore recognize that some loss of productivity is a small price to pay in order to protect and preserve their power base.[28]

Another reason loyalty looms large is the incompetence of many managers. The attainment of a high-echelon position in a bureaucracy does not necessarily require a high degree of competence in carrying out specific tasks or solving particular problems. Under these circumstances, managers know that if they are to succeed they must surround themselves with dedicated personnel who will not upstage them—who will work hard in their behalf and not leak information to rival factions. Moreover, the loyal subordinate must be ready to cover up the boss's errors and even accept the blame for mistakes not of his or her own doing.

Little wonder that "whistleblowers" pose such a threat to bureaucracy. Whatever their motives—ranging from high-minded moral concern to vindictiveness—they may be in a position to expose the inner workings of the organization which typically are protected from public scrutiny. If they are able to obtain support from the press of legislative bodies, whistleblowers can readily undermine certain high-level personnel as well as individuals loyal to them. Whistleblowers, however, pay a price for their efforts. They are seen as disloyal, as not being team players, and they must be prepared to sacrifice their position in the bureaucracy and possibly find themselves blacklisted from future employment.

Loyalty, being crucial to bureaucrats, is often enhanced by rituals of various kinds. The senior author experienced a ritual called a "donkey barbecue," also termed "eating ass." Shortly after she was hired as a manager in a large corporation, her immediate superior came to her office and announced in a loud voice: "Tomorrow we are going to a donkey barbecue." Early the next morning the boss informed her that they were to visit the sites under her supervision. He then began lecturing her about managers fulfilling their duties to their utmost ability and in the best interests of the organization.

At the first site the supervisor pointed out minor details that needed attention but did so in a loud voice that everyone could hear. Whenever she attempted to say something, he immediately cut her off and said in effect, "I don't care what you have or haven't been told. This is your job.'' And when they were around other managers or persons she supervised, he would raise his voice even more.

Rituals of this sort make it clear who is in charge. The process is meant to intimidate and embarrass new managers and emphasize their subordination to higher level individuals. The pattern is analogous to what Goffman terms ''mortification,''[29] a process whereby persons are stripped of their identity and forced into conformity with the demands of superiors and the organization as a whole.

Because bureaucracies tend to be fraught with political maneuvering, and because of the hidden arrangements that exist, employees are often uncertain of their positions in the organization—a condition leading to ''social paranoia.'' De Lorean, a former executive with General Motors, alludes to it.[30] John Dean's biography dramatizes the existence of social paranoia in the upper reaches of governmental bureaucracies. And Morgan mentions its presence among managers of grain companies.[31] The senior author of this paper also has personally observed this phenomenon. Many are the individuals who have displayed this personality trait. Obviously, paranoia is heightened during periods of crisis, but it is never far beneath the surface.

There are sound reasons for this pattern of social paranoia. Even when a member of a bureaucracy has filled all its demands, including loyalty to superiors, there is the ever-present danger of demotion or reassignment because of shifting political tides. The superiors with whom one has forged ties of loyalty may themselves be stripped of power, so that one slides downward in the system, at least in terms of prestige and perquisites. Nor can one ever fully trust other persons; you never know who is aligned with whom.

In addition, many managers and their immediate subordinates are placed in double-bind situations. Perhaps impossible goals have been set—as in a business organization where a manager may be expected to have his/her unit meet some targeted figure for sales, profit, or whatever. To achieve this objective rules may have to be bent or broken; on the other hand, violation of the rules can lead to retribution from above. Moreover, subordinates are expected to protect the boss. In many instances persons below fear sending up negative information. But this protective stance can itself lead to subordinates being blamed for whatever has gone wrong.

For the person who adheres to broader moral standards, the double-bind situation is acute. The bureaucracy's demands for attainment of an unrealistic, perhaps an amoral, goal not only places that individual in jeopardy of possible punishment by superiors but leaves him/her with a sense of guilt. Then too, one observes persons who have been "destroyed" by superiors, and these incidents reinforce existing feelings of paranoia.

The anxieties that typically assail members of bureaucratic organizations should not be minimized. After all, employees depend upon the organization for their livelihood and status, not to speak of special privileges. Often persons who have worked for an organization for many years find they have no real opportunity for employment elsewhere without accepting serious loss in pay, prestige, and accumulated retirement benefits. Unless one has some external sources of financial and emotional security, at least mild paranoia would seem to be a reasonable response to the harsh realities of the situation.

## Conclusions

We have surveyed the salient features of the bureaucratic personality. This personality is a product of the way in which modern bureaucracies are organized and the methods its members use to acquire and protect power and prestige. Our analysis is grounded in an alternative conception of the nature of bureaucracy, for we devote special attention to hidden arrangements. In some instances these are of little import; in others they may, through protection of confidentiality, actually advance the cause of human dignity. Often, however, they are associated with the struggle for power and privilege, and this is the area which commands our attention.

Although we recognize that variations exist in the personality patterns of bureaucrats, our "constructed type"[32] captures an essential aspect of social reality. Bureaucratic personality patterns include the ability to simultaneously take the role of others in several divergent or overlapping hidden arrangements and also read cues and convey subtle messages across these different social worlds. Essential here is a keen social memory and the presentation of oneself to the public with generally flat effect.

Successful bureaucrats display formal cordiality, yet talk and act tough when subordinates fail to (or even when they are expected to) carry out designated tasks. Bureaucrats are highly sensitive to status and to the differential treatment accorded persons occupying different positions in the hierarchy. They must learn how to bend or reinterpret rules as the occasion demands.

Loyalty to superiors is another key characteristic of the bureaucratic personality. Because loyalty is associated with dependency, it results in underlings being chosen in accordance with (or learning to emulate) the personality of their superiors. These loyalty patterns, the presence of hidden arrangements, as well as the struggle for power within and among bureaucracies all serve to foster social paranoia.

Admittedly, our view of personality theory differs considerably from that of most psychologists and sociologists. We think it essential to discuss the intimate tie between roles and personality. In addition, we must examine these within a broader structural context—one of hidden arrangements and power struggles.

We have also proceeded on the premise that the personality patterns (including the bureaucratic face) we have described reflect a bureaucratic social self and social mind. The self must, for instance, be attuned to taking the role of multiple audiences—audiences that may have divergent or contradictory expectations. Also, a keen social memory and the ability to speak elliptically are expressions not merely of the self but of a social mind which must of necessity be reflective in the manner we have outlined.

With this background in hand, we shall briefly consider the consequences of bureaucracy for personality patterns in the society as a whole. We are convinced that the bureaucratic personality has certain pervasive effects, and not just in the occupational setting. Tentatively, we can isolate three main personality types in modern society:

1. Some individuals have incorporated the bureaucratic personality as a way of life. It comes to dominate all spheres of their existence. A well-defined conception of self and mind, along with particular emotional, motivational, and cognitive patterns are associated with this personality type. And from these peoples' own perspective, they are authentic, even when this means a lack of intimate human bonds as well as the emotions associated with them.
2. Other persons separate their bureaucratic personality from their more intimate self or selves. Many such persons recognize the bureaucratic personality as a mask that they don in order to carry out their work. On the other hand, there are those persons who see both of their personalities as authentic—as parts of a broader whole.
3. A third type includes those individuals who, because of social paranoia at work and the tensions or conflicts resulting from the separation between the occupational sphere and other areas of life, have a fragmented or distorted self and mind. These are among the casualties of a bureaucratized society.

Still, that aspect of the social mind associated with critical reflection is generally suppressed in all three personality types.[33] Critical reflection poses a threat to existing loyalty ties and to the bureaucratic structure itself—a fact that accounts for the punishment of such deviants as whistleblowers. This is not to imply that members of bureaucracy are simply passive agents. The very existence of hidden arrangements bears witness to reflection and purposive action and demonstrates that persons do construct a particular kind of social reality. Yet, hierarchical arrangements and the potential for coercion seriously constrain the efforts of individuals to restructure fundamentally their work environment. With rare exceptions, students of personality have not acknowledged the impact of powerful organizations upon the personality of their members.[34]

As we have indicated, the influence of bureaucracy upon personality is not limited to the work situation. We shall reason that the suburban family in America—where the husband is a cog in the wheels of bureaucracy and the wife cares for the home and also functions as carrier of the more intimate emotions and reinforcer of her husband's proper bureaucratic face—has been ideally suited to the demands of bureaucracy. But today, as increasingly greater numbers of married women are gainfully employed outside the home, and especially with the impact of women's liberation, more women are searching for autonomy and freedom from the pressures to enhance and reflect their husbands' bureaucratic personality. These trends do, however, undermine the family, at least the family as envisaged a decade or so ago. Concomitantly, there are social pressures upon husbands today to involve themselves more fully in the emotional needs of the family— for example, to share the role of parenting with their wives.

Even more specific practical or policy implications can be drawn from our analysis. Social scientists urgently need to examine the impact of the bureaucratic personality upon the quality of goods produced and, especially, services performed in modern society. A strong case can be made for the argument that the bureaucratic personality seriously undermines the quality of human services. If so, we must rethink—indeed, reshape—the structure of bureaucracies if we are to improve the way in which bureaucrats deliver services.

Next we come to certain patterns in modern society which demand qualifications in our argument. Consider the area of negotiations. It is apparent that hidden arrangements may enhance the resolution of differences among competing parties in a democratic order (all the while making it difficult to establish accountability for the conduct of negotiations). The important point here, however, is that skilled negotiators may differ in significant respects from the bureaucratic personality we have delineated. At the very least, students of the negotiated order[35] need to pay more attention to hidden arrangements and to the personality type associated with brokering in bureaucratic settings.

We must also recognize the impact of tenure and strong seniority systems upon the bureaucratic personality. For example, the existence of tenure in higher education is a counter-force to the emergence of the bureaucratic personality in academia. Professors who hold tenured positions can exercise greater freedom of expression. Where faculty members also have external constituencies such as links to professional associations—as is the case at research universities—considerable deviation from the bureaucratic personality comes to exist. If tenure were abolished in academia, professors would become more dependent upon university administrators and would have to display greater loyalty to them.[36] The possibility of doing creative work and publishing on controversial intellectual issues would greatly diminish.

Finally, we need to examine the bureaucratic personality on a cross-cultural level. Just how does the personality of individuals staffing the bureaucracies of Japan differ from our type? What about the nations of Eastern Europe? Many features of the bureaucratic personality delineated herein seem to be more sharply etched in totalitarian orders.[37] Also, we need to explore the impact of a growing phenomenon—the multinational corporation—upon personality patterns in the managerial sector.

In general, the nature of bureaucracy and its impact upon the personalities of its members demands serious rethinking. If we are truly concerned with the quality of life—with making it possible for people in modern society to lead a more humane existence—then we must restructure bureaucracies in such a way that individuals can develop and sustain meaningful human relationships within and without the organizational context. It is because of the lack of critical examination of the nature of bureaucracy that social theorists have so far been unable to provide us with an adequate understanding of how personalities are formed, or indeed of the particular structural changes that are required if we are to achieve a truly moral context in which human beings can live with dignity. The implications of bureaucracy for personality in modern society are a compelling issue now and in the future.

## Notes

1. R. Merton, "Bureaucratic Structure and Personality," *Social Forces* (1940), vol. 18, pp. 560–68.
2. *Ibid.*, p. 561.
3. C. Perrow, *Complex Organizations: A Critical Essay,* second ed. (Glenview, Ill.: Scott, Foresman, 1979).

4. C. Argyris, "Personality and Organizational Theory Revisited," *Administrative Science Quarterly* (1973), vol. 18, pp. 141–67.
5. R.P. Hummel, *The Bureaucratic Experience* (New York: St. Martin's Press, 1977).
6. Herein we build on G. Sjoberg and P.J. Miler, "Social Research on Bureaucracy: Limitations and Opportunities," *Social Problems* (1973), vol. 21, pp. 129–43; and especially Sjoberg, "Social Research, Social Policy, and 'the Other Economy,' " in *Issues in Social Policy*, eds. W.B. Littrell and G. Sjoberg (Beverly Hills, Ca.: Sage Publications, 1976), pp. 215–30.
7. Perrow, *op. cit.*, p. 13.
8. M. Dalton, *Men Who Manage* (New York: John Wiley, 1959); and D. C. Miller and W. H. Form, *Industrial Sociology Work in Organizational Life*, third ed. (New York: Harper & Row, 1980).
9. S.J. Ungar, *FBI* (Boston: Little, Brown, 1975); and U.S. Senate, *Final Report of the Select Committee to Study Governmental Operations with Respect to Intelligence Activities*, Ninety-fourth Congress, Second Session, Books I and III, April, 1976 (Washington, D.C.: U.S. Government Printing Office, 1976).
10. K.H. Wolff, ed. and trans., *The Sociology of George Simmel* (New York: Free Press, 1950).
11. A. Mitzman, *The Iron Cage* (New York: A.A. Knopf, 1969).
12. S. Adams, "Vietnam Cover-up: Playing War with Numbers," *Harper's* (1975), vol. 250, pp. 41–73.
13. W. Shawcross, *Sideshow* (New York: Simon & Schuster, 1979); H. Kissinger, *The White House Years* (Boston: Little, Brown, and Co., 1979); T. Wicker, "The Reluctant Reality of Henry Kissinger," *Rolling Stone* (1980), vol. 311, pp. 47–51.
14. J.A. Lukas, *A Nightmare* (New York: Viking Press, 1976).
15. See for example, U.S. Senate, *Hearings Before the Subcommittee on Multinational Corporations*, Committee on Foreign Relations, Ninety-fourth Congress (Washington, D.C.: U.S. Government Printing Office, 1975); and S. Rose-Ackerman, *Corruption: A Study in Political Economy* (New York: Academic Press, 1978).
16. D. Morgan. *Merchant of Grain* (New York: Viking Press, 1979).
17. Sjoberg, *op. cit.*, 1976.
18. V.A. Thompson, *Modern Organization* (New York: A.A. Knopf, 1961).
19. J. Dean, *Blind Ambition* (New York: Simon & Schuster, 1976).
20. R.B. Stewart, "The Reformation of American Administrative Law," *Harvard Law Review* (1975), vol. 88, pp. 1669–1813.
21. R.J. Ostrow, "Abscam Leak Investigator Says Disclosures Punishable," *Austin American-Statesman*, Feb. 13, 1980, p. A-3.
22. Dean, *op. cit.*
23. Differences exist between men's and women's smiles. Some women adopt the patterns of "macho talk," but they are likely to intimidate or alienate the men around them. More effective women adopt a more neutral style.
24. Compare E. Goffman, *International Ritual* (Garden City, N.Y.: Doubleday, 1967).
25. M. Barrineau, "Marvin Watson, a Man Accustomed to Taking the Heat," *Dallas Times Herald*, Feb. 10, 1980, pp. J1, J6.

26. G. Getschow, "Some Middle Managers Cut Corners to Achieve High Corporate Goals," *Wall Street Journal,* Nov. 8, 1979, Sec. 1, p. 26.
27. R. Ricklefs, "Executive Recruiters Say Firms Tend to Hire Our Kind of Person," *Wall Street Journal,* Sept. 9, 1979, Sec. 1, P. 18.
28. Perrow, *op. cit.*
29. E. Goffman, *Asylums* (Garden City, N.Y.: Doubleday, 1961).
30. J.P. Wright, *On a Clear Day You Can See General Motors* (Grosse Pointe, Mich.: Wright Enterprises, 1979).
31. Morgan, *op. cit.*
32. For a discussion of this methodological tool, see G. Sjoberg and R. Nett, *A Methodology for Social Research* (New York: Harper & Row, 1968).
33. Compare G. Sjoberg and T.R. Vaughan, "Human Rights, Reflectivity, and the Sociology of Knowledge," in *Contemporary Issues in Theory and Research,* eds. W.E. Snizek, E.R. Guhrman, and M.K. Miller (Westport, Conn.: Greenwood Press, 1979), pp. 235–50.
34. Compare C.S. Hall and G. Lindzey, *Theories of Personality,* third ed. (New York: John Wiley, 1978); S. Stryker, "Developments in 'Two Social Psychologies': Toward an Appreciation of Mutual Relevance," *Sociometry* (1977), "The Three Faces of Social Psychology," *Sociometry* (1977), Vol. 40, pp. 161–77.
35. A. Strauss, *Negotiations: Varieties, Contexts, Processes, and Social Order* (San Francisco: Jossey-Bass, 1978).
36. Compare S. Arons, "The Teachers and the Tyrant," *Saturday Review* (1980), vol. 7, pp. 16–19.
37. Compare R. Bahro, *The Alternative in Eastern Europe,* trans. D. Fernback (London: NLB, 1978); and G. Konrad and I. Szelényi, *The Intellectuals on the Road to Class Power,* trans. A. Arato and R.E. Allen (New York: Harcourt Brace Jovanovich, 1979).

## Part V

# INTERPERSONAL COMMUNICATION NETWORKS IN THE ORGANIZATION

# 15

# Management Communication
# and the Grapevine

*Keith Davis*

Communication is involved in all human relations. It is the "nervous system" of any organized group, providing the information and understanding necessary for high productivity and morale. For the individual company it is a continuous process, a way of life, rather than a one-shot campaign. Top management, therefore, recognizes the importance of communication and wants to do something about it. But what? Often, in its frustration, management has used standard communication "packages" instead of dealing situationally with its individual problems. Or it has emphasized the means (communication techniques) rather than the ends (objectives of communication).

One big factor which management has tended to overlook is communication *within its own group*. Communication to the worker and from the worker is dependent on effective management communication; and clearly this in turn requires informal as well as formal channels.

## The Grapevine

A particularly neglected aspect of management communication concerns that informal channel, the grapevine. There is no dodging the fact that, as a carrier of news and gossip among executives and supervisors, the grapevine often affects the affairs of management. The proof of this is the strong feelings that different executives have about it. Some regard the grapevine as an evil—a thorn in the side which regularly spreads rumor, destroys morale and reputations, leads to irresponsible actions, and challenges authority. Some regard it as a good thing because it acts as a safety valve and carries news fast. Others regard it as a very mixed blessing.

Whether the grapevine is considered an asset or a liability, it is important for executives to try to understand it. For one thing is sure: Although no executive can absolutely control the grapevine, he can *influence* it. And since it is here to stay, he should learn to live with it.

*Perspective*

Of course, the grapevine is only part of the picture of communication in management. There is also formal communication—via conferences, reports, memoranda, and so on; this provides the basic core of information, and many administrators rely on it almost exclusively because they think it makes their job simpler to have everything reduced to explicit terms—as if that were possible! Another important part of the picture is the expression of attitudes, as contrasted with the transmisson of information (which is what we will be dealing with in this article). Needless to say, all these factors influence the way the grapevine works in a given company, just as the grapevine in turn influences them.

In this article I want to examine (a) the significance, character, and operation of management communication patterns, with particular emphasis on the grapevine; and (b) the influence that various factors, such organization and the chain of procedure, have upon such patterns. From this analysis, then, it will be possible to point up (c) the practical implications for management.

As for the research basis of the analysis, the major points are

1. *Company studied*—The company upon which the research is based is a real one. I shall refer to it as the "Jason Company." A manufacturer of leather goods, it has 67 people in the management group (that is, all people who supervise the work of others, from top executives to foremen) and about 600 employees. It is located in a rural town of 10,000 persons, and its products are distributed nationally.

   In my opinion, the pattern of management communication at the Jason Company is typical of that in many businesses; there were no special conditions likely to make the executives and supervisors act differently from their counterparts in other companies. But let me emphasize that this is a matter of judgment, and hence broader generalizations cannot be make until further research is undertaken.

   As a matter of fact, one of the purposes of this article is to encourage businessmen to take a close look at management communication in their own companies and to decide for themselves whether it is the same or different. In many companies, men in the management group now follow the popular practice of examining and discussing their problems of communicating with workers, but

rarely do they risk the embarrassment of appraising their communications with each other.
2. *Methodology*—The methods used to study management communication in the Jason Company are new ones. Briefly, the basic approach was to learn from each communication recipient how he first received a given piece of information and then to trace it back to its source. Suppose D and E said they received it from G; G said he received it from B; and B from A. All the chains or sequences were plotted in this way—A to B to G to D and E—and when the data from all recipients were assembled, the pattern of the flow of communication emerged. The findings could be verified and developed further with the help of other data secured from the communication recipients.

This research approach, which I have called "ecco analysis," is discussed in detail elsewhere.[1]

### Significant Characteristics

In the Jason Company many of the usual grapevine characteristics were found along with others less well known. For purposes of this discussion, the four most significant characteristics are these:

1. *Speed of transmission*—Traditionally the grapevine is fast, and this showed up in the Jason Company.

For example, a certain manager had an addition to his family at the local hospital at 11 o'clock at night, and by 2:00 p.m. the next day 46% of the whole management group knew about the event. The news was transmitted only by grapevine and mostly by face-to-face conversation, with an occasional interoffice telephone call. Most communications occurred immediately before work began, during "coffee hour," and during lunch hour. The five staff executives who knew of the event learned of it during "coffee hour," indicating that the morning rest period performed an important social function for the staff as well as providing relaxation.

2. *Degree of selectivity*—It is often said that the grapevine acts without conscious direction or thought—that it will carry anything, any time, anywhere. This viewpoint has been epitomized in the statement that "the grapevine is without conscience or consciousness." But flagrant grapevine irresponsibility was not evident in Jason Company. In fact, the grapevine here showed that it could be highly selective and discriminating.

For example, the local representative of the company which carried the employee group insurance contract planned a picnic for company executives. The Jason Company president decided to invite 36 executives, mostly from higher executive levels. The grapevine immediately went to work spreading this information, but it was carried to *only two of the 31 executives not invited*. The grapevine communicators thought the news was confidential, so they had told only those who they thought would be invited (they had to guess, since they did not have access to the invitation list). The two uninvited executives who knew the information were foremen who were told by their invited superintendent; he had a very close working relationship with them and generally kept them well informed.

Many illustrations like the above could be gathered to show that the grapevine can be discriminating. Whether it may be *counted on* in that respect, however, is another question. The answer would of course differ with each case and would depend on many variables, including other factors in the communication picture having to do with attitudes, executive relationships, and so forth.

3. *Locale of operation*—The grapevine of company news operates mostly at the place of work.

Jason managers were frequently in contact with each other after work because the town is small; yet grapevine communications about company activities predominantly took place at the plant, rather than away from it. It was at the plant that executives and supervisors learned, for instance, that the president was taking a two weeks' business trip, that the style designer had gone to Florida to study fashion trends, and that an executive had resigned to begin a local insurance business.

The significance of at-the-company grapevines is this: Since management has some control over the work environment, it has an opportunity to influence the grapevine. By exerting such influence the manager can more closely integrate grapevine interests with those of the formal communication system, and he can use it for effectively spreading more significant items of information than those commonly carried.

4. *Relation to formal communication*—Formal and informal communication systems tend to be jointly active, or jointly inactive. Where formal communication was inactive at the Jason Company, the grapevine did not rush in to fill the void (as has often been suggested;)[2] instead, there simply was lack of communication. Similarly, where there was effective formal communication, there was an active grapevine.

Informal and formal communication may supplement each other. Often formal communication is simply used to confirm or to expand what has already been communicated by the grapevine. Thus in the case of the picnic, as just described, management issued formal invitations even to those who already knew they were invited. This necessary process of confirmation results partly because of the speed of the grapevine, which formal systems fail to match, partly because of its unofficial function, and partly because of its transient nature. Formal communication needs to come along to stamp "Official" on the news and to put it "on the record," which the grapevine cannot suitably do.

### Spreading Information

Now let us turn to the actual operation of the grapevine. How is information passed along? What is the relationship among the various people who are involved?

Human communication requires at least two persons, but each person acts independently. Person A may talk or write, but he has not *communicated* until person B receives. The individual is, therefore, a basic communication unit. That is, he is one "link" in the communication "chain" for any bit of information.

The formal communication chain is largely determined by the chain of command or by formal procedures, but the grapevine chain is more flexible. There are four different ways of visualizing it, as Fig. 15.1 indicates:

1. *The single-strand chain*—A tells B, who tells C, who tells D, and so on; this makes for a tenuous chain to a distant receiver. Such a chain is usually in mind when one speaks of how the grapevine distorts and filters information until the original item is not recognizable.
2. *The gossip chain*—A seeks and tells everyone else.
3. *The probability chain*—A communicates randomly, say, to F and D, in accordance with the laws of probability; then F and D tell others in the same manner.
4. *The cluster chain*—A tells three selected others; perhaps one of them tells two others; and then one of these two tells one other. This was virtually the only kind of chain found in the Jason Company, and may well be the normal one in industry generally.

#### Active Minority

The predominance of the cluster chain at the Jason Company means that only a few of the persons who knew a unit of information ever transmitted it—what Jacobson and Seashore call the "liaison" individuals.[3] All others who received the information did not transmit it; they acted merely as passive receivers.

For example, when a quality-control problem occurred, 68 percent of the executives received the information, but only 20 percent transmitted it. Again, when an executive planned to resign to enter the

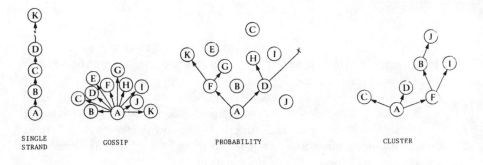

**Fig. 15.1**
**Types of communication chains**

insurance business, 81 percent of the executives knew about it, but only 11 percent passed the news on to others. Those liaison individuals who told the news to more than one other person amounted to less than 10 percent of the 67 executives in each case.

These active groups varied in membership. There was no evidence that any one group consistently acted as liaison persons; instead, different types of information passed through different liaison persons. However, as will be shown later, some individuals were invariably communication "isolates"; they received and transmitted information poorly or not at all.

The above findings indicate that if management wants more communication, it should increase the number and/or effectiveness of its liaison individuals. This appears to be a large order, but it is entirely possible. Liaison individuals tend to act in a predictable way. If an individual's unit of information concerns a job function in which he is interested, he is likely to tell others. If his information is about a person with whom he is associated socially, he also is likely to tell others. Furthermore, the sooner he knows of an event after it happened, the more likely he is to tell others. If he gets the information late, he does not want to advertise his late receipt of it by telling it to others.

In other words, three well-known communication principles which are so often mentioned in relation to attitudes also have a major influence on the spread of information by liaison individuals:

1. Tell people about what will affect them (job interest).
2. Tell people what they want to know, rather than simply what you want them to know (job and social interest).
3. Tell people soon (timing).

## Organizational Effects

The way an organization is divided horizontally into organizational levels and vertically into functions, such as production and sales, obviously has effects on management communication, for it cuts each company's over-all administrative function into small work assignments, or jobs, and sets each management person in certain relationships to others in his company.

### Horizontal Levels

Organizational levels are perhaps the more dramatic in effect because they usually carry authority, pay increases, and status. From the communication point of view, they are especially important because of their number. In a typical firm there are usually several management levels, but only one or two worker levels; furthermore, as the firm grows, the management levels increase in number, while the worker levels remain stationary.

Communication problems are aggravated by these additional levels because the chain of communication is lengthened and complicated. Indeed, just because of this, some companies have been led to try to reduce the number of intermediate management levels. Our concern here is with the patterns of communication among individuals at the different levels.

At the Jason Company, executives at *higher* levels communicated more often and with more people than did executives at *lower* levels. In other words, the predominant communication flow was downward or horizontal. When an event happened at the bottom level, usually the news did reach a high level; but a single line of communication sufficed to carry it there, and from that point it went downward and outward in the same volume and manner (cluster chain) as if it had originated at the top.

Accordingly, the higher an executive was in the organizational hierarchy (with the exception of nonresident executives), the greater was his knowledge of company events. This was true of events which happened both above his level and below his level. Thus, if the president was out of town, a greater proportion at the fourth level knew of it than at the sixth level. Or—and this is less to be expected— if a foreman at the sixth level had an accident, a larger proportion of executives at the third level knew of it than at the fourth level, or even than at the sixth level where the accident happened. The more note- worthy the event, of course, the more likely it was to be known at upper levels—but, in a company of this size, it had to be quite trivial indeed before it failed to reach the ears of top executives.

The converse follows that in terms of communications transmitted and received the sixth and lowest level of supervision, the foreman level, was largely isolated from all other management. The average foreman was very hesitant to communicate with other members of management; and on the rare occasions when he did, he usually chose someone at his own level and preferably in his own department. Members of this group tended to be the last links in management communication, regardless of whether the chains were formal or informal.

A further significant fact concerns the eight departmental superin- tendents at the fourth level. Six of them supervised foremen directly; two others, with larger departments, each had a single line assistant between him and his foreman. The two who had line assistants were much more active in the communication chains than were the six others; indeed, all but one of the six appeared to have little do to with their foreman except in a formal way.

Perhaps the clue is that, with increased organizational levels, those at the higher (and hence further removed) levels both recognize a greater need for communication and have more time to practice it!

*Functional Groups*

Functionalization, the second important way in which an organiza- tion is "cut up," also has a significant impact on communication in management. The functions which are delegated to a manager help to determine the people he contacts, his relationships with them, his status, and, as a result, the degree to which he receives and transmits information. More specifically, his role in communication is affected (a) by his position in the chain of command and (b) by his position in the chain of procedure, which involves the sequence of work perform- ance and cuts across chains of command, as when a report goes from the superintendent in one chain of command to the chief engineer in another chain of command and to the controller in still another.

In the Jason Company, the effects of functionalization showed up in three major ways:

1. *Staff men "in the know"*—More staff executives than line men usually knew about any company event. This was true at each level of management as well as for the management group as a whole. For example, when the president of the company made a trip to seek increased governmental allotments of hides to keep the line tannery operating at capacity, only 4 percent of the line executives knew the purpose of the trip, but 25 percent of the staff men did. In another case, when a popular line superintendent was awarded a hat as a prize in a training program for line superintendents, within six days a larger proportion of the staff executives than of the line executives knew about this event.

   The explanation is not just that, with one staff executive to every three line executives, there were more line executives to be informed. More important is the fact that the *chain of procedure* usually involved more staff executives than line executives. Thus, when the superintendent was awarded his hat, a line executive had approved the award, but a staff personnel executive has processed it and a staff accounting executive had arranged for the special check.

   Also the staff was more *mobile* than the line. Staff executives in such areas as personnel and control found that their duties both required and allowed them to get out of their offices, made it easy for them to walk through other departments without someone wondering whether they were "not working," to get away for coffee, and so on—all of which meant they heard more news from the other executives they talked with. (In a larger company staff members might be more fixed to their chairs, but the situation in the Jason Company doubtless applies to a great many other businesses.)

   Because of its mobility and its role in the chain of procedure, the staff not only received but also transmitted communications more actively than did the line. Most of these communications were oral; at least in this respect, the staff was not the "paper mill" it is often said to be. It seems obvious that management would do well to make conscious use of staff men as communicators.

2. *Cross-communication*—A second significant effect of functionalization in the Jason Company was that the predominant flow of information for events of general interest was between the four large areas of production, sales, finance and office, and industrial relations, rather than within them. That is, if a production executive has a bit of news of general interest, he was more likely to tell a

sales, finance, or personnel executive than another production executive.

Social relationships played a part in this, with executives in the various groups being lodge brothers, members of the same church, neighbors, parents of children in the same schools, and so on. In these relationships the desire to make an impression was a strong motivation for cross-communication, since imparting information to executives outside his own area served to make a man feel that the others would consider him "in the know." Procedural relationships, discussed earlier, also encouraged the executives to communicate across functional lines.

Since communications tended not to stay within an area, such as production, they tended even less to follow chains of command from boss to sub-boss to sub-sub-boss. Indeed, the chain of command was seldom used in this company except for very formal communications. Thus Fig. 15.2 reproduces a communication chain concerning a quality control problem in production, first brought to the attention of a group sales manager in a letter from a customer. Although it was the type of problem that could have been communicated along the chain of command, the exhibit shows that, of 14 communications, only 3 were within the chain of command and only 6 remained within one functional area—sales—where the information was first received.

The fact that the chain of command may affect management communication patterns less than procedural and social influences—which has shown up in other companies too[4]—means that management needs to devote considerably more attention to the problems and opportunities of cross-communication.

3. *Group isolation*—The research in the Jason Company revealed that some functional groups were consistently isolated from communication chains. Also, there were other groups which received information but did not transmit it, and thus contributed to the same problem—the uneven spread of information through the company. Here are three examples at the foreman level illustrating different degrees of failure to participate in the communication process and different reasons for this failure:

(a) The foremen in one group were generally left out of communication chains. These men were of a different nationality from that of the rest of the employees, performed dirty work, and worked in a separate building. Also, their work fitted into the manufacturing process in such a way that it was seldom necessary for other executives to visit their work location.

(b) Another group often was in a communication chain but on the tail end of it. They were in a separate building some distance from

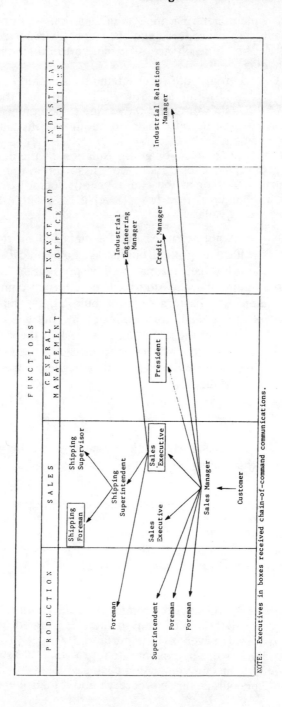

NOTE: Executives in boxes received chain-of-command communications.

**Fig. 15.2**
**Communication chain for a quality-control problem**

the main manufacturing area, their function was not in the main manufacturing procedure, and they usually received information late. They had little chance or incentive to communicate to other executives.

(c) A third group both received and transmitted information, but transmitted only within a narrow radius. Although they were in the midst of the main work area, they failed to communicate with other functional groups because their jobs required constant attention and they felt socially isolated.

In sum, the reasons for group isolation at the Jason Company were: geographical separation; work association (being outside the main procedures or at the end of them); social isolation; and the organizational level (the lower level of a group, the greater its tendency to be isolated).

Obviously, it is not often feasible for management to undertake to remove such causes of group isolation as geographical or social separation. On the other hand, it may well be possible to compensate for them. For example, perhaps the volume of formal communication to men who happen to be in a separate building can be increased, or arrangements can be made for a coffee break that will bring men who are isolated because of the nature of their work or their nationality into greater contact with other supervisors. In each situation management should be able to work out measures that would be appropriate to the individual circumstances.

### Conclusion

The findings at the Jason Company have yet to be generalized by research in other industries, but they provide these starting points for action:

1. If management wants more communication among executives and supervisors, one way is to increase the number and effectiveness of the liaison individuals.
2. It should count on staff executives to be more active than line executives in spreading information.
3. It should devote more attention to cross-communication—that is, communication between men in different departments. It is erroneous to consider the chain of command as *the* communication system because it is only one of many influences. Indeed, procedural and social factors are even more important.
4. It should take steps to compensate for the fact that some groups are "isolated" from communication chains.
5. It should encourage further research about management grapevines

in order to provide managers with a deeper understanding of them and to find new ways of integrating grapevine activities with the objectives of the firm.

6. "Ecco analysis," the recently developed research approach used at the Jason Company, should be useful for future studies.

If management wants to do a first-class communication job, at this stage it needs fewer medicines and more diagnoses. Communication analysis has now passed beyond "pure research" to a point where it is immediately useful to top management in the individual firm. The patterns of communication that show up should serve to indicate both the areas where communication is most deficient and the channels through which information can be made to flow most effectively.

In particular, no administrator in his right mind would try to abolish the management grapevine. It is as permanent as humanity is. Nevertheless many administrators have abolished the grapevine from *their own minds*. They think and act without giving adequate weight to it or, worse, try to ignore it. This is a mistake. The grapevine is a factor to be reckoned with in the affairs of management. The administrator should analyze it and should consciously try to influence it.

### Notes

1. Keith Davis, "A Method of Studying Communication Patterns in Organizations," *Personnel Psychology* (Fall 1953).
2. For example, see National Industrial Conference Board, *Communicating with Employees,* Studies in Personnel Policy, No. 129 (New York: 1952), p. 34.
3. Eugene Jacobson and Stanley E. Seashore, "Communication Practices in Complex Organizations," *The Journal of Social Issues* (1951) vol. 7, no.3, p. 37.
4. See Carroll L. Shartle, "Leadership and Executive Performance," *Personnel* (March 1949), pp. 377–78.

# 16

# Leaks to the Press as Communication Within and Between Organizations

*Richard B. Kielbowicz*

Contrary to the myth that has grown up around investigative journalism, few major political scandals have been uncovered solely by the persistent digging of the press. Most such stories have been broken only after someone in government leaked crucial details. The wholesale leak of classified documents, for example, brought the Pentagon Papers to the attention of the world. And unraveling the Watergate scandal—a feat generally credited to the industry of two reporters—would have been incomplete or impossible if it were not for leaks by government investigators.[1] Leaks have become a principal means by which the inner workings of bureaucracies are exposed to the scrutiny of the press and public.

Paradoxically, much information leaked to the press—and thereby entered into the mass communication system—is released primarily to communicate with a fairly narrow audience. The intended receivers can work in other agencies or even the organization from which the leak sprang. Some leaks to the press can thus be viewed as a form of organizational communication.

## The Nature of Leaks to the Press

Anonymous communications have long been used as a means of transmitting messages among elites, much as leaks do today. Before newspapers became the principal forum of political discourse, commentators offered their views on public affairs in pamphlets published anonymously or under pseudonyms. Some politicians disguised their identity to avoid retribution for unpopular comments; others resorted to classical pseudonyms to enhance their authority.[2] In seventeenth century England and eighteenth century colonial North America, newspapers gradually displaced pamphlets as the preferred channel of political communication, but the use of pseudonyms remained common. In many cases, the small, elite audience of readers probably knew the identity of some contributors.

The practice of leaking news is largely a twentieth century phenomenon, though it was not unknown earlier. For example, in 1844 a senator arranged for anonymous publication of a treaty that President John Tyler hoped to sneak through the Senate in executive session.[3] President Theodore Roosevelt, however, first recognized the general utility of leaking news to the press and regularly used it to advance his political objectives.[4]

The term "leak" originally applied to inadvertent slips by sources,[5] but it has since acquired a broader, more active meaning—a calculated release of information to reporters with the stipulation that the source remain unidentified.[6] A variety of contacts between reporters and officials have institutionalized leaking. Background briefings permit attribution to a veiled source (e.g., "high official," "informed source"). Information obtained from press conferences conducted on "deep background" cannot be ascribed to any source; the reporter assumes authority for the story. Backgrounders, then, are simply leaks to a group of reporters.

Veiled attributions pervade news writing today. Culbertson[7] found at least one unidentified source in 54 percent of the stories in the *New York Times* and *Washington Post,* in 36 percent of the stories in four other metropolitan dailies, and even in 30 percent of the articles in small Ohio dailies. Leaked information also appeared in 70 percent of *Newsweek's* articles and in 75 percent of the stories in *Time* magazine.[8]

Dahlan[9] and Hess[10] have catalogued myriad kinds of leaks. The major ones serve four general purposes:

1. Leaks for personal reasons. *Ego leaks* affirm the source's own importance by demonstrating his or her access to confidential information. An *animus leak* involves the release of information calculated to hurt someone the source dislikes.
2. Leaks for reasons of source-reporter relations. The *goodwill leak,* where a source bestows a "scoop" on a favorite reporter, earns credit that might later prove valuable. In a *diversion leak,* the source makes an innocuous story seem tantalizing so it will preoccupy the reporters, distracting them from more important developments.
3. Leaks for policy reasons. *Preparatory leaks* pave the way for later policy proposals. A *reaction-testing leak,* better known as a trial balloon, arises when policy options are being considered; the leaker wants to gauge the reaction of key agencies, clientele organizations, or the public before openly committing to a policy. *Deceptive leaks*

stem from various motives but share one characteristic—they aim to create a false impression. A *promotional leak* is the release of information deemed favorable to a policy or action, while the *crippling leak* discloses information that undermines a policy. The diplomatic establishment has its own subspecies of policy leaks: Leaks to *signal* or *clarify* intentions, *induce* discussions, and *alter* the course of negotiations. Policy leaks of various sorts are the type most likely to involve intra- or interorganizational communication.

4. Leaks for ethical reasons. *Whistle blowing,* at least when the source remains confidential, can be considered a form of leaking news. Whistle blowers turn to the press when their organization fails to correct serious abuses.

Since Rosten's pioneering study of reporters and their work,[11] scholars have increasingly studied leaks as an important form of political communication. Most investigators have interpreted leaks largely if not exclusively in terms of news management (see, e.g., the works of Cater,[12] Halperin,[13] Hess,[14] Ladd,[15] McGaffin and Knoll,[16] Rivers,[17] Roshco,[18] Rourke,[19] Sigal,[20] and Strentz.[21] Similarly, journalists who recount their experiences as recipients of leaked information typically view these experiences as political maneuvers, if they reflect on the reasons for the leaks at all (see, e.g., accounts by Anderson,[22] Rather and Gates,[23] Schorr,[24] and Wicker[25]).

Understanding the political motives that lie behind leaks is undeniably important, but the dominance of this explanation has overshadowed another valuable perspective. Except for the first two (and relatively inconsequential) types discussed above, most leaks to the press can be considered communication within and between organizations. In this view, anonymous disclosures of information through the mass media serve some of the same purposes as messages transmitted through the formal channels of intra- and interorganizational communication. Just as formal messages travel through organizations in three directions—upward, downward and horizontally[26]—a sender can relay a message through the mass media to a receiver working in the same, or any other, organization.

Leaks overcome some failings of organizational communication. Various characteristics of organizations (a) constrain the volume of messages that can be transmitted in different directions, (b) determine the speed with which messages are relayed, and (c) to some extent distort the message as it is conveyed from source to receiver.[27] As a form of organizational communication, leaks can supplement inadequate internal channels, bypass obstacles, and serve as an antidistortion device. Additionally, information leaked to the press can be more persuasive than that sent through formal organizational channels.

Transmitting organizational intelligence through the mass media, however, entails risk. The sender loses control of the message once it has been transferred to the reporter and news organization; the writer or editor can misinterpret it or add details that dilute the impact the sender hopes to create. Furthermore, the story may never be used. Finally, the receiver might overlook a particular message buried in the mass media, misinterpret it, or fail to accurately guess the source's identity, which can be crucial in properly decoding it. Such are some of the pitfalls anonymous sources face in using the mass media for messages aimed at organizations or particular receivers in organizations.

### Leaks as Upward Communication

Bureaucrats sometimes leak information to the press in order to communicate with the upper echelons of their own hierarchy. Leaks of this type are meant to overcome two failings of organizational communication: 1. that messages transmitted upward often escape the attention of superiors because of an information overload, and 2. that intermediaries in the chain of command hesitate to relay subordinates' reports to higher levels if they reflect poorly on the performance of a bureau.[28] Leaks as upward communication most often spring from tall or attenuated bureaucracies—that is, institutions comprised of many departments arranged vertically in the organizational scheme. With such a structure, the channels for vertical communication are most likely to become overloaded, or with the many intermediaries, messages will not be relayed because of the bureaucratic self-interest.

"Communicating out of channels" is a common response to the "dilemma of hierarchy vs. intelligence," Wilensky notes.[29] Communicating out of channels takes many forms, only one of which involves releasing information to the press. Because such messages are sent out of channels, sources typically seek anonymity. Thus, from leaks, the President or even a corporate executive "may learn of issues which would otherwise remain buried in the bureaucracy."[30] "Middle-rank officials" routinely leak information to "attract the attention of their superiors," a *New York Times* reporter with several decades of experience in covering the federal governmnet asserted in an affidavit filed in the Pentagon Papers case.[31] Administrators, including those working for state governments, learn to scan the press for information about their own agencies. They realize that important information may fail to reach them because it embarrasses underlings, or simply because communication within the bureaucracy is fragmentary.[32]

Leaks even convey information upward in relatively flat bureaucracies. Miller found that congressional aides who have relatively easy access to members of Congress nevertheless leaked information to attract their bosses' attention.[33] A formal report passed to a lawmaker might literally lie buried in a stack of documents, or at best compete for attention with other pressing issues. An informal communication sent via the press, however, would probably appear more salient, especially if it were carried in one of the prestige media. Similarly, leaked information in a concise, sprightly journalistic report might be more digestible for executives than an unabridged document working its way up through channels.

Whistle blowing, which sometimes takes the form of leaks to the media, arises from frustrated upward organizational communication.[34] (Many whistle blowers, though, publicly acknowledge their role in disclosing the information and therefore do not leak it.) Typically, whistle blowers first try to correct problems by appealing for reform through internal channels, but find that their message cannot clear bureaucratic hurdles. A leak, or even an on-the-record communication to the media, can be used to bypass an obstacle in reaching the upper levels of an agency. And public disclosure can pressure leaders to act decisively if they were not eager to do so.

### Leaks as Downward Communication

At first glance, agency heads would seem unlikely to leak information to the press as a means of communicating with their subordinates. Much less distortion occurs in information flowing from superior to subordinate than that flowing in the opposite direction. But even when ample channels exist for downward communication, leaks can be useful in carrying information to subordinates. Information leaked to the press probably reaches the lower levels of a large bureaucracy faster than it takes to percolate through formal channels, and in some cases it passes through fewer filters. A message prominently displayed in the prestige media appears more significant to subordinates than the same information outlined in a memorandum. A deputy press secretary observed that bureaucrats are especially impressed with information that "appears to have been pried loose rather than officially communicated."[36]

Sitting atop a huge bureaucracy, various Presidents have found leaks to the press a useful mechanism for communicating their wishes to those who formulate and implement policy.[37] For example, when Lyndon Johnson wanted the State Department to tone down its efforts to promote use of a multilateral force (MLF) in 1964, he drafted a memo for internal circulation *and* leaked the story to the *New York*

*Times.* "Unlike an internal memorandum with limited circulation inside the Executive Branch, a press clipping could be cited as proof of the President's wishes by opponents of the MLF on both sides of the Potomac and the Atlantic.[38] A leak signaling the President's (or other executive's) preferences serves as a "hunting license" to subordinates who share the same goals. Leaks can also direct subordinates to ignore public pronouncements. A President who has adopted a public posture to appease some interest group can, via a leak, signal the bureaucracy to discount the public statement.[39]

Presidents have used leaks to inform aides that they should resign. In 1958, Sherman Adams, White House chief of staff, embarrassed the administration by taking gifts from a Boston industrialist in return for influencing regulatory proceedings. To hasten Adams' departure without forcing a public confrontation, President Dwight Eisenhower authorized a leak that Adams' days in the White House were numbered.[40]

### Leaks as Horizontal Communication

Bureaucrats use leaks to convey information to other departments of their own agency, to other agencies, to another branch of government, and even to foreign governments. In a sense, all such messages are horizontal intra- or interorganizational communications, and they seem to be much more common than leaks transmitting information upwards or downwards. Such leaks occur frequently because of their utility in persuading receivers who can help or hinder the formulation and implementation of policies.

### Horizontal Communication Within an Agency

Bureaucrats occasionally leak information to communicate laterally with other bureaus in the same organization. This probably does not occur frequently in institutions where the formal lines accommodate messages rapidly and with little distortion. Sometimes, however, two related bureaus are isolated from one another (perhaps geographically) and rely upon subformal channels such as the press for communication.[41]

Compared to most Executive agencies, legislatures have many centers of decision making. With few formal channels for the exchange of information about their own institution. In Wisconsin, Dunn found that "legislative leaders, more than other officials, rely on newspapers for intraorganizational information."[42] Likewise, the communication channels in Congress are poorly developed, with inadequate coordinated information exchange between the two houses.[43] Senators and representatives keep abreast of developments in Congress by following news reports;[44] leaks from congressional committees which appear in the press doubtless provide valuable intelligence for members of Congress who do not obtain information directly from their colleagues.

## Communication Between Divisions of Government

Leaks are well suited to convey information between different divisions of the same government. Leaks provide a necessary shortcut to the tortuous path messages follow if transmitted through formal channels. For a middle-level official to communicate formally with his or her counterpart in another agency, a message must be relayed upward to the first's superior, laterally to the second's superior, and finally downward to the receiver.[45] (Of course, a number of strategies other than leaking information to the press can be used to bypass the intermediaries.) Not only does this delay receipt, but it also increases the chances for the message to be distorted during transmission.

By design, power in the U.S. federal government is fragmented and shared. Major policy actions ultimately involve both the Executive branch and Congress. Yet these two branches sometimes fail to coordinate the activities because their information exchange is so haphazard. The media "serve as a means of supplementing the internal lines of communication of the sprawling federal establishment."[47] Congressmen and women, for example, have few opportunities to question the President directly; they must rely on reports in the press—many of which have been leaked—to obtain clues as to the President's position on some matter.[47] Conversely, leaks alert the President to the directions congressional investigations might take.

Because federal agencies must justify their funding requests in Congress, appropriation hearings are preceded by preparatory leaks. Such leaks aim to shape the information environment in which Congress makes funding decisions. The Pentagon is especially adept at preparatory leaks. A surprising number of supposedly secret estimates of Soviet military prowess appear in print when Congress is considering the Defense Department's budget.[48] A related but more Machiavellian example: One military service leaks information disparaging another service's proposed weapons system so that its competing system is approved.[49]

## Communication Between Governments

Countries sometimes signal one another through leaks to the press. Such leaks originate from heads of government as well as the foreign policy and defense establishments. According to Dahlan, intergovernmental communication by anonymous sources has several advantages over messages sent through formal channels: Leaks can transmit intelligence outside the often-rigid international bureaucracies or link the lower bureaucratic levels of two countries; leaks can be efficient and fast; leaks in publications commonly serving as vehicles have high credibility among some elites; leaks signal intentions without committing a government to a particular proposal; leaks can provide a common set of facts on which parties base negotiations; leaks enable governments not party to negotiations to participate on the periphery; leaks can substitute for formal talks when parties are deadlocked; and leaks afford some means of communication between states that have no diplomatic exchanges.[50]

While some leaks simply communicate information to another country, most combine elements of communication and persuasion. When the 1919 Paris Peace Conference became deadlocked over French demands, Woodrow Wilson attempted to communicate his frustration and apply a little pressure. He leaked the news, which was published in the *New York Times,* that he had summoned a ship to take him home.[51] Since then, many U.S. foreign policy initiatives have been preceded by leaks designed to test reactions (i.e., float trial balloons) and to prepare both domestic leaders and foreign governments for some action the administration has in mind.[52] The European Economic Community also uses leaks as an accepted means of relaying information among its members.[53]

During crises, governments send messages through an array of formal and informal channels to prevent misunderstandings that can have catastrophic consequences. Negotiating with the Soviet Union during the Cuban Missile Crisis, President Kennedy was acutely aware that a garbled message could trigger a nuclear exchange. He supplemented the direct, formal contacts between Washington and Moscow with indirect communications through the press, including some leaked information.[54] Negotiations too heavily dependent on leaks, however, can create confusion. In the midst of the Cuban Missile Crisis, the eminent commentator Walter Lippmann published a column suggesting a way out of the confrontation. He advised that the United States should withdraw its missiles from Turkey if the Soviet Union would do likewise in Cuba. Lippmann's intimate connections with the Kennedy Administration were well known to the Kremlin, and Moscow interpreted this proposal as an authentic offer tendered by the White House. Although Lippmann's column had often carried Administration leaks in the past, this time the ideas were solely his own, and the Kremlin's misinterpretation created some consternation.[55]

## Conclusions

Leaks are one means by which the media of mass communication have been annexed to perform some of the functions of organizational and interorganizational communication. Information leaked to the press becomes available to a mass, heterogeneous audience, though it is aimed at a narrow, attentive audience. Ironically, newspaper readers inadvertently eavesdrop on semi-private conversations when they peruse some stories laden with disclosures from anonymous sources.

Information leaked to the press can in some circumstances travel to the intended recipients more rapidly, accurately, and completely than that relayed through internal channels. Leaked information, however, is subject to garbling by the press just as by organizational gatekeepers. Furthermore, the cryptic nature of news leaks means that some of the intended receivers never see them, and, if they do, they can misinterpret the message and guess the wrong source.[56] Not all leaks, of course, are a form of organizational communication. Many are intended to test or arouse general public opinion. Because many leaks are designed more to persuade than to communicate unadulterated information, Presidents since Theodore Roosevelt have taken measures—largely unsuccessful—to stanch their flow. But as long as government or any large organization operates with less than perfect internal communication channels, intelligence relayed externally by the press serves a vital function.

## Notes

1. E.J. Epstein, "Did the Press Uncover Watergate?" *Commentary* (July 1974), vol. 58, pp. 21–24.
2. W.P. Courtney, *The Secrets of Our National Literature: Chapters in the History of Anonymous and Pseudonymous Writings of our Countrymen* (London: Archibald Constable & Co., 1908), ch. 8.
3. A. Schlessinger, Jr., "The Secrecy Dilemma," *New York Times Magazine,* Feb. 6, 1972, p. 38.
4. G. Juergens, *News From the White House: The Presidential-Press Relationship in the Progressive Era* (Chicago: University of Chicago Press, 1981).
5. D. Schorr, *Clearing the Air* (Boston: Houghton Mifflin, 1977), p. 179.
6. See M.A. Dahlan, "Anonymous Disclosure of Government Information as a Form of Political Communication," Ph.D. dissertation, University of Illinois, 1967, pp. 19–38, for various definitions.
7. H.M. Culbertson, "Veiled News Sources—Who and What Are They?" *American Newspaper Publishers Association News Research Bulletin* (1975), no. 3, May 14, 1975, p. 9.

8. Culbertson, "Veiled Attribution—An Element of Style?" *Journalism Quarterly* (Autumn 1978), vol. 55, p. 460.
9. M.A. Dahlan, "Anonymous Disclosure of Government Information as a Form of Political Communication," Ph.D. dissertation, University of Illinois, 1967, pp. 77–83; 99–109.
10. S. Hess, *The Government/Press Connection: Press Officers and Their Offices* (Washington, D.C.: Brookings Institution, 1984), pp. 77–78.
11. L. Rosten, *The Washington Correspondents* (New York: Harcourt, Brace, 1937).
12. D. Cater, *The Fourth Branch of Government* (New York: Vintage, 1959).
13. M.H. Halperin, *Bureaucratic Politics and Foreign Policy* (Washington: Brookings Institution, 1974).
14. Hess, *op. cit.*
15. B. Ladd, *Crisis in Credibility* (New York: New American Library, 1968).
16. W. McGaffin and E. Knoll, *Anything but the Truth* (New York: G.P. Putnam's Sons, 1968).
17. W.L. Rivers, *The Opinionmakers* (Boston: Beacon Press, 1965).
18. B. Roshco, *Newsmaking* (Chicago: University of Chicago Press, 1975).
19. F.E. Rourke, *Secrecy and Publicity* (Baltimore: The Johns Hopkins Press, 1961).
20. L.V. Sigal, *Reporters and Officials: The Organization and Politics of News Making* (Lexington, Mass.: Lexington Books, 1973).
21. H. Strentz, *News Reporters and News Sources* (Ames, Iowa: Iowa State University Press, 1978).
22. J. Anderson, *The Anderson Papers* (New York: Random House, 1973).
23. D. Rather and G.P. Gates, *The Palace Guard* (New York: Harper & Row, 1974).
24. D. Schorr, *Clearing the Air* (Boston: Houghton Mifflin, 1977).
25. T. Wicker, *On Press* (New York: Viking, 1978).
26. H.A. Simon, *Administrative Behavior,* second ed. (New York: Free Press, 1957), p. 155.
27. A. Downs, *Inside Bureaucracy* (Boston: Little, Brown, and Co., 1967), pp. 112–31.
28. *Ibid.*
29. H.L. Wilensky, *Organizational Intelligence: Knowledge and Policy in Government and Industry* (New York: Basic Books, 1967), p. 46.
30. Halperin, *op. cit.*, p. 180.
31. S.J. Ungar, *The Papers and the Papers* (New York: E.P. Dutton, 1972), p. 173.
32. D.D. Dunn, *Public Officials and the Press* (Reading, Mass.: Addision-Wesley, 1969), p. 102.
33. S.H. Miller, "Reporters and Congress: Living in Symbiosis," Journalism Monograph No. 53, Jan. 1978, p. 4.
34. L.P. Stewart, "'Whistle Blowing': Implications for Organizational Communication," *Journal of Communication* (Autumn 1980), vol. 30, p. 97.
35. See R. Nader, P.J. Petkas, and K. Blackwell, *Whistleblowing* (New York: Grossman, 1972) and C. Peters and T. Branch, *Blowing the Whistle* (New York: Praeger, 1972).
36. M.B. Grossman and M.J. Kumar, *Portraying the President: The White House and the News Media* (Baltimore: Johns Hopkins University Press, 1981), p. 31.

37. Halperin, *op. cit.*, p. 286.
38. Sigal, *op. cit.*, pp. 136–37.
39. Grossman and Kumar, *op. cit.*, p. 31; Sigal, *op. cit.*, p. 136.
40. Grossman and Kumar, *op. cit.*, pp. 172–73.
41. C. Weiss, "What America's Leaders Read," *Public Opinion Quarterly* (Spring 1974), vol. 38, pp. 17–18.
42. Dunn, *op. cit.*, p. 12.
43. H.W. Fox, Jr., and S.W. Hammond, "The Growth of Congressional Staffs," in *Congress Against the President,* ed. H.C. Mansfield, Proceedings of the Academy of Political Science, vol. 32, no. 1, p. 120.
44. D.D. Dunn, "Symbiosis: Congress and the Press," in *Congress and the News Media,* ed. R.O. Blanchard (New York: Hastings House, 1974), p. 243.
45. Downs, *op. cit.*, pp. 115–116.
46. V.O. Key, *Public Opinion and American Democracy* (New York: Alfred A. Knopf, 1961), p. 405.
47. Rosten, p. 82; D. Cater, *Power in Washington* (New York: Vintage, 1964), p. 14.
48. Ungar, *op. cit.*, p. 92.
49. R. Hilsman, *The Politics of Policy Making in Defense and Foreign Affairs* (New York: Harper & Row, 1971), p. 7.
50. Dahlan, pp. 94–128; W.P. Davidson, "News Media and International Negotiation," *Public Opinion Quarterly* (Summer 1974), vol. 38, pp. 174–91.
51. G. Juergens, *News from the White House: The Presidential-Press Relationship in the Progressive Era* (Chicago: University of Chicago Press, 1981). pp. 242–43.
52. Dahlan, *op. cit.*, pp. 101–03.
53. R.A.R. Maclennan, "Secrecy and the Right of Parliament to Know and Participate in Foreign Affairs," in *Secrecy and Foreign Policy,* ed. T.M. Franck and E. Weisband (New York: Oxford University Press, 1974), p. 141.
54. P. Salinger, *With Kennedy* (Garden City, N.Y.: Doubleday, 1966), pp. 285–302; see also G.T. Allison, *Essence of Decision: Explaining the Cuban Missile Crisis* (Boston: Little, Brown and Co., 1971).
55. M. Kern, P.W. Levering, and R.B. Levering, *The Kennedy Crises: The Press, the Presidency, and Foreign Policy* (Chapel Hill: University of North Carolina Press, 1983), p. 129.
56. Dahlan, *op. cit.*, pp. 130–93.

## References

Allison, G.T. (1971). *Essence of Decision: Explaining the Cuban Missile Crisis.* Boston: Little, Brown and Co.
Anderson, J. (1973). *The Anderson Papers.* New York: Random House.
Cater, D. (1959). *The Fourth Branch of Government.* New York: Vintage.
———. (1964). *Power in Washington.* New York: Vintage.
Cohen, B.C. (1963). *The Press and Foreign Policy.* Princeton: Princeton University Press.

Courtney, W.P. (1908). *The Secrets of Our National Literature: Chapters in the History of Anonymous and Pseudonymous Writings of Our Countrymen.* London: Archibald Constable & Co.

Culbertson, H.M. (1975). "Veiled News Sources—Who and What Are They?" American Newspaper Publishers Association News Research Bulletin, No. 3, May 14.

———. (1978). "Veiled Attribution—An Element of Style?" *Journalism Quarterly* 55 (Autumn): 456–65.

Dahlan, M.A. (1967). "Anonymous Disclosure of Government Information as a Form of Political Communication." Ph.D. dissertation, University of Illinois.

Davidson, W.P., (1974). "News Media and International Negotiation," *Public Opinion Quarterly* 38 (Summer): 174–91.

Downs, A. (1967). *Inside Bureaucracy.* Boston: Little Brown.

Dunn, D.D. (1969). *Public Officials and the Press.* Reading, Mass.: Addison-Wesley.

———. (1974). "Symbiosis: Congress and the Press." In *Congress and the News Media,* R.O. Blanchard (ed.). New York: Hastings House. Pp. 240–49.

Epstein, E.J. (1974). "Did the Press Uncover Watergate?" *Commentary* 58 (July): 21–24.

Fox, H.W., Jr. and Hammond, S.W. (1975). "The Growth of Congressional Staffs." In *Congress Against the President,* H.C. Mansfield (ed.). Proceedings of the Academy of Political Science, vol. 32, no. 1. Pp. 112–24.

Grossman, M.B. and Kumar, M.J. (1981). *Portraying the President: The White House and the News Media.* Baltimore: Johns Hopkins University Press.

Halperin, M.H. (1974). *Bureaucratic Politics and Foreign Policy.* Washington: Brookings Institution.

Hess, S. (1984). *The Government/Press Connection: Press Officers and Their Offices.* Washington, D.C.: Brookings Institution.

Hilsman, R. (1971). *The Politics of Policy Making in Defense and Foreign Affairs.* New York: Harper & Row.

Juergens, G. (1981). *News from the White House: the Presidential-Press Relationship in the Progressive Era.* Chicago: University of Chicago Press.

Kern, M., Levering, P.W., and Levering, R.B. (1983). *The Kennedy Crises: The Press, the Presidency, and Foreign Policy.* Chapel Hill: University of North Carolina Press.

Key, V.O. (1961). *Public Opinion and American Democracy.* New York: Alfred A. Knopf.

Ladd, B. (1968). *Crisis in Credibility.* New York: New American Library.

McGaffin, W. and Knoll, E. (1968). *Anything but the Truth.* New York: G.P. Putnam's Sons.

Maclennan, R.A.R. (1974). "Secrecy and the Right of Parliament to Know and Participate in Foreign Affairs." In *Secrecy and Foreign Policy,* T.M. Franck and E. Weisband (eds.). New York: Oxford University Press. Pp. 132–43.

Miller, S.H. (1978). "Reporters and Congress: Living in Symbiosis." Journalism Monograph No. 53, January.

Nader, R., Petkas, P.J., and Blackwell, K. (1972). *Whistleblowing.* New York: Grossman.

Peters, C. and Branch, T. (1972). *Blowing the Whistle.* New York: Praeger.

Rather, D. and Gates, G.P. (1974). *The Palace Guard*. New York: Harper & Row.

Rivers, W.L. (1965). *The Opinionmakers*. Boston: Beacon Press.

Roshco, B. (1975). *Newsmaking*. Chicago: University of Chicago Press.

Rosten, L. (1975). *The Washington Correspondents*. New York: Harcourt, Brace.

Rourke, F.E. (1961). *Secrecy and Publicity*. Baltimore: Johns Hopkins University Press.

Salinger, P. (1966). *With Kennedy*. Garden City, N.Y.: Doubleday.

Schlesinger, A., Jr. (1972). "The Secrecy Dilemma," *New York Times Magazine* (February 6): 12–50.

Schorr, D. (1977). *Clearing the Air*. Boston: Houghton Mifflin.

Sigal, L. V. (1973). *Reporters and Officials: The Organization and Politics of Newsmaking*. Lexington, Mass.: Lexington Books.

Simon, H.A. (1957). *Administrative Behavior*. 2nd ed. New York: Free Press.

Stewart, L.P. (1980). " 'Whistle Blowing': Implications for Organizational Communication," *Journal of Communication* 30 (Autumn): 90–101.

Strentz, H. (1978). *News Reporters and News Sources*. Ames, Iowa: Iowa State University Press.

Ungar, S.J. (1972). *The Papers and the Papers*. New York: E.P. Dutton.

Weiss, C. (1974). "What America's Leaders Read," *Public Opinion Quarterly* 38 (Spring): 1–22.

Wicker, T. (1978). *On Press*. New York: Viking.

Wilensky, H.L. (1967). *Organizational Intelligence: Knowledge and Policy in Government and Industy*. New York: Basic Books.

# 17

# "Whistle Blowing": Implications for Organizational Communication

*Lea P. Stewart*

There is a growing tendency for employees of organizations, especially scientists and engineers, to challenge management decisions,[1] either protesting within the organization or to the public. This latter avenue of protest, often called "whistle blowing,"[2] is occurring more frequently or at least is being more widely reported.[3] But researchers have been slow to focus upon the determinants, forms, or outcomes of whistle blowing incidents.

There appear to be three reasons for this neglect. First, organizational phenomena have typically been looked at from the point of view of management[4]; whistle blowing is, by definition, an anti-management act. Second, there are no specific or well-developed treatments of whistle blowing from which to draw generalizations and conclusions.[5] Third, information about specific whistle blowing events is difficult to obtain. Although some cases, such as A. Ernest Fitzgerald's exposure of Air Force cost overruns[6], are well-documented, many are described very briefly in general discussions of organizational problems.[7]

This article examines whistle blowing as an organizational phenomenon, and analyzes 51 reports of actual incidents to derive a model of the steps through which whistle blowing incidents progress. From this model it is possible to generalize about the nature of whistle blowing incidents and how they fit into patterns of communication in organizations.

Americans do not have the same rights, such as freedom of the press, freedom of speech, and due process, at work as they do at home.[8] This lack of rights is most conspicuous for employees who do not belong to unions, such as scientists and engineers,[9] and stems, in part, from the idea that the employer and employee are, as Ewing notes[10] "equal partners to the employment agreement. Just as the employee is free to resign whenever he/she wants, so the employer is free to show him/her the door whenever it [sic] desires." The assumption behind the "legal notion of freedom of contract" is that an employee can leave a firm and find comparable employment with little difficulty.[11] Nonetheless, as Blades points out, "it is the fear of being discharged which above all else renders the great majority of employees vulnerable to employer coercion."[12] He maintains that "only the unusually valuable employee has sufficient bargaining power to obtain a guarantee that he will be discharged during a specified term of employment only for 'just cause.' "[13] Employers view the great majority of employees as expendable. Thus, an employee's threat to quit his/her job has little power in effecting change in an organization.

Nonetheless, society depends on the professional integrity of the experts in an organization to ensure that management decisions will not harm society.[14] Professionals are often bound by an explicit code of ethics such as that of the National Society of Professional Engineers, which states that the engineer "will regard his duty to the public welfare as paramount." The engineer is instructed to "notify the proper authority of any observed conditions which endanger public safety and health" if "his engineering judgment is overruled by non-technical authority." Thus, as Morse notes, "engineering ethics, from the viewpoint of industry, will rise or fall on the decisions of the engineer himself."[15] Application of engineering ethics in actual cases may, however, result in "gray-areas"[16] since engineers are also technically bound to uphold their clients' best interests in all cases.[17] Such a resulting dilemma would be especially acute for older engineers who might find job security in competition with ethical interests.[18]

According to Nader et al., whistle blowing is "the act of a man or woman who, believing that the public interest overrides the interest of the organization he serves, publicly 'blows the whistle' if the organization is involved in corrupt, illegal, fraudulent, or harmful activity."[19] Thus, whistle blowers challenge organizational heads "who appear to be engaged in illegal, immoral or irresponsible activity."[20] A whistle blower is "the muckraker from within, who exposes what he considers the unconscionable practices of his own organization,"[21] or the insider who feels compelled to tell all to the outsiders."[22] In general, the whistle blower "believes he can best rectify the unethical behavior in business or government by making his charges and identity public."[23] According to Walters, the whistle blower, "having decided at some point that the actions of the organization are immoral, illegal, or inefficient, . . . acts on that belief by informing legal authorities or others outside the organization."[24] Thus whistle blowers, whether federal employees[25] or employees of corporate organizations, put their duty to the public above their loyalty to the organization.[26] Whistle blowing is an indication that "the rules and guidelines for resolving disputes and failures within an organization have been insufficient"[27] and that the situation is so serious it demands public attention.

A large number of whistle blowing cases have involved professionals employed by industry and government.[28] In a survey of 800 members of the National Society of Professional Engineers, von Hippel found that most of the respondents had at one time or another felt obliged to question some of the activities in which their organizations were involved. "When asked to work on a product or project they believed not to be in the public interest," seven percent of the respondents said they had sought transfer within the organization and another seven percent said they had resigned. Over 20 percent refused to work on a project or on a client's commission or to accept a job offer for this reason; and 60 percent had "expressed their disapproval of a project to their employer or client."[29] The force of this disapproval is unknown.[30] Von Hippel and others[31] believe that known cases of whistle blowing may only be the tip of a rather large iceberg.

In the spring of 1975 the Committee on Scientific Freedom and Responsibility of the American Association for the Advancement of Science (AAAS) issued a report urging scientists and engineers to blow the whistle on their employers when they saw their work being used for "morally dubious ends."[32] In the same year, Senator Edward Kennedy "sponsored hearings . . . to publicize the cause of government employees who spoke out against illegal or immoral actions in their agencies."[33]

Although the AAAS and the Kennedy hearings encouraged conscious acts of whistle blowing, Dudar maintains that "most people who wind up in the fraternity [of whistle blowers] begin almost accidentally, expecting gratitude and encountering, instead, a stone wall of either indifference or hostility."[34] Apparently, much of the whistle blowing which does occur is a result of organizations' unresponsiveness to employees.[35] In a study of university students, Turner reports students "believed their freedom of expression was impaired, not because anyone actively prevented them from speaking, but because no one would listen, understand, or care."[36] Similarly, whistle blowers feel that management will not listen to what they view as legitimate concerns. There is some evidence to substantiate this belief. For example, Silver claims most employee complaints are "insubstantial,"[37] while Thompson claims most managers feel employees will see that management is "right" if they are given "the facts."[38] Walters believes managers should respect employees' rights to disagree with organizational policy not because it is the employees' fundamental right, but because it is in the best interest of the organization.[39]

In an often-quoted statement, James M. Roche, Chairman of General Motors Corporation, claims:

> Some of the enemies of business now encourage an employee to be disloyal to the enterprise. They want to create suspicion and disharmony and pry into the proprietary interests of the business. However this is labeled—industrial espionage, whistle blowing, or professional responsibility—it is another tactic for spreading disunity and creating conflict.[40]

Even when managers recognize the legitimacy of blowing the whistle, they may note how difficult it often is "to distinguish between those who are blowing the whistle and those who are crying wolf"[41] and maintain that employees who make a "public attack" on their organization should be willing to resign.[42]

Thus, Boulden warns engineers that "any effort to . . . speak out against company practices, will be interpreted by your employers and fellow workers as disloyalty and near treason."[43] He maintains whistle blowing almost never has a positive effect on an engineer's career, and the "odds are that management will not only attempt to brand your statements as falsehoods, but may also attack your veracity and competence"[44]. Peters and Branch describe the "typical" response to a whistle blowing attempt:

> A whistle blower's antagonists will probably do something like the following: hand the press a 2,000 page, computer-blessed study by experts in support of their position; cite national security, job protection, or economic emergency as the justification for their actions; impugn the person with the whistle as an unqualified, self-seeking, disloyal, and moderately unbalanced underling who just doesn't understand the complexities that converge at the top; call for further study of the problem; and retire to dinner with their lawyers.[45]

An article in *Time* notes that most employees who oppose corporate policy are fired, demoted, or forced to resign.[46]

D'Aprix maintains that "in a highly traditional organization, . . . there is considerable emphasis on communication up and down a chain of command. The worker is not permitted to air his grievances to his boss's boss without first seeking permission and approval.[47] Boulden warns engineers that they should always speak first to their supervisor when they have information about an unsafe product or condition within the company.[48] Most employees usually do seek such approval first,[49] but they are most likely to go directly to the public with their concerns when their criticisms have met with "bureaucratic runa-rounds, deaf ears, or hostility" in the past.[50]

Often, the whistle blower will be subjected to what Blades terms "abusive discharge" in which the employee is "discharged as a result of resisting his employer's attempt to intimidate or coerce him in a way which bears no reasonable relationship to the employment."[51] The "abusive discharge" is apt to be malicious because, as Ewing notes: "When a competent employee with years of service is fired for refusing to submit to a boss's improper or over-reaching demands, the boss feels guilt in a way not experienced when firing an employee for incompetence or laziness."[52] Stone suggests: "People who feel . . . threatened by whistle blowing will inevitably seek to 'make an example' of the whistle blower: by firing, demotion, or harrassment."[53] The whistle blower is seen as a threat to the hierarchical organization.[54] An organization may pay some price for the loss of an employee, but an employee is likely to pay a still higher price. Ewing cites a sociologist who has called "abusive discharge" the "organizational equivalent of capital punishment."

As a result of such attitudes, Nader *et al.* maintain the most vulnerable whistle blower is the one who speaks out from within an organization.[56] Accordingly, most whistle blowers are those who have reached what Peters and Branch call a "career plateau,"[57] because blowing the whistle may lead to expulsion from the organization, and often the end of a career.

Thus the potential whistle blower must call for help loudly enough to receive public attention, without appearing to be seeking ego gratification.[58] Whistle blowers are more likely to be heard and believed if they appear clearly to lose from their act. Some whistle blowers may find comfort in the fact that nearly all whistle blowers who have been punished for their views win their cases when they challenge their punishment in court.[59]

Although information on specific whistle blowing events is limited, I was able to collect information on 51 separate incidents.[60] The amount of information available on these events ranged from one paragraph descriptions in general overviews of whistle blowing[61] to extensive discussions of cases which were well-publicized (cf. accounts of the Goodrich air brake problem in 35 and 54.)

In pure whistle blowing incidents, the events occur in the following order (although some steps may be omitted.):

Step 1. An organizational member becomes aware of an organizational product or policy which he/she feels is unethical, immoral, or illegal and/or will endanger the public.

Step 2. The organizational members expresses his/her concerns to his/her immediate superior(s). The member perceives that his/her superior(s) is not going to act upon his/her concerns.

Step 3. The organizational member expresses his/her concerns to administrators higher up in the corporate or governmental hierarchy. The member perceives that the administrators are not going to act upon his/her concerns.

Step 4a. The organizational member takes his/her concerns to the regulatory body (such as a Congressional subcommittee, the courts, the Atomic Energy Commission) which is charged with overseeing the organization or government agency. This step, by definition, makes the member's concerns public.

and/or

Step 4b. The organizational members takes his/her concerns to the public press, which then publicizes them.

Step 5. The organizational member is isolated by his/her superiors (for example, his/her assistants are taken away and other organizational members are instructed to avoid him/her).

Step 6. The organizational member is expelled from the organization; he/she is either fired or forced to resign.

In the 25 cases of pure whistle blowing examined, only two deviated from this pattern. In one case, Step 5 occurred before Step 4b; in the other case, Step 5 occurred between Steps 4a and 4b.

There are two types of alumnus whistle blowers: those who voluntarily resign from an organization before blowing the whistle and those who are expelled (fired or forced to resign) and then blow the whistle. The following stages typically occur in alumnus whistle blowing incidents (although some steps may be omitted):

Step 1. An organizational member becmes aware of an organizational product or policy which he/she feels is unethical, immoral, or illegal and/or will endanger the public.

Step 2. The organizational member expresses his/her concerns to his/her immediate superior(s). The member perceives his/her superior(s) is not going to act upon his/her concerns.

Step 3a. The organizational member resigns voluntarily. His/her resignation may or may not be publicized.

and/or

Step 3b. The organizational member is expelled. He/she is either fired or forced to resign.

Step 4a The organizational member takes his/her concerns to the regulatory body (such as a Congressional subcommittee, the courts, the Atomic Energy Commission) which is charged with overseeing the products or services offered by the organization or government agency This step, by definition, makes the member's concerns public.

and/or

Step 4b. The organizational member takes his/her concerns to the public press, which then publicizes them.

There may be a lapse of time between Step 3a and Steps 4a or 4b. In one case, an organizational member voluntarily resigned and waited 21 years before completing Step 4a.

In the 26 cases of alumnus whistle blowing examined, only two exceptions to the above order were noted. One case occurred in the following sequence: Steps 1,2,4a,3a,4b. In the other case, the organizational member was isolated before Step 3b.

It is commonly believed that communication in organizations can be "improved" by increasing the *amount* of communication that occurs. But some restrictions on communication are inherent in organizations.[62] To be in an "organized state," random and diffuse communication must be restricted so that various groups and specialists will receive the information that is most relevant.[63]

Communication overload occurs when there is "an excess of 'input' over the ability of the message-receiver to 'handle' such input."[64] One mechanism to reduce overload is the "exception principle" which holds that "only significant deviations from standards, procedures, and policies should be brought to the attention of the superior; [that is, only] matters of exception and not of standard practice [are brought to the attention of superiors]."[65]

Procedures and practices such as the exception principle create problems for organizations, however. Too much information cannot be allowed to travel up the organizational hierarchy; yet decision makers must receive the information they need.[66] March and Simon posit the concept of "uncertainty absorption" to indicate that there are progressively increasing omissions of detail as a message travels up an organizational hierarchy.[67]

All complex organizations, by definition, involve superior-subordinate relationships,[68] and the communication occuring at these crucial junctions has received much research attention. One area of superior-subordinate communication that is relevant to whistle blowing is upward communication. When potential whistle blowers attempt to take their concerns[69] through an organizational hierarchy, they may be attempting to increase, or at least alter, the upward flow of information. They express their concerns directly to the public when they feel they cannot alter the flow of information or get a suitable response from the organization. This feeling may result because their superiors will not pass their conccerns to the next level of the hierarchy or because their superiors do not respond to the concerns as the subordinates wish them to. Thus, the crucial concern becomes the superior's decision to transmit information through an organizational hierarchy, to act upon the information in the way the subordinate wishes.

Subordinates are likely to pass information to their superiors if the information is seen as important and favorable to themselves.[70] Potential whistle blowers often consider their information to be favorable because they feel they have discovered an organization problem which needs to be remedied; thus their concern shows that they are conscientious employees. Their information is unlikely to be passed up the organizational hierarchy by their superiors, however, because this information, by definition, is unfavorable to their superiors.[71] Superiors are also unlikely to pass such information upward because they view messages which are favorable to subordinates as less accurate than messages which are unfavorable.[72]

The problem of passing information upward may be confounded by a large "semantic/information distance," Tompkins' term for the "gap" in information and understanding which exists between superiors and subordinates on specified issues.[73] Minter notes that serious semantic differences between superiors and subordinates are quite frequent, occurring approximately 60 percent of the time.[74] Such a gap might exit, for example, when the superior is a non-technical manager or an engineer with a different specialty than the subordinate.[75]

Given this framework, there is a potential for whistle blowing any time a subordinate communicates to a superior information perceived to be unfavorable to the superior. Of course, in many instances, when a superior stops a subordinate's message, the subordinate decides the information was unimportant and gives up. Occasionally, however, the subordinate feels that he/she has discovered something immoral, unethical, or illegal and refuses to keep silent. A subordinate who feels this way is likely to bypass the communication channels normally associated with the organizational hierarchy—sometimes by going directly to the public. Members of the organizational hierarchy are likely to react against such a person, in part, because he/she has publicly demonstrated the ineffectiveness of the organizational communication system.

The dilemma of the potential corporate whistle blower thus stems from one of the dilemmas faced by all complex organizations—how to restrict the flow of information up the organizational hierarchy and, at the same time, ensure that *all* the necessary information reaches the organizational decision makers. This dilemma could perhaps be eased first by encouraging communication "openness."

An "open" communication relationship exists between superiors and subordinates when "both parties perceive the other interactant as a willing and receptive listener, and refrain from responses which might be perceived as providing negative relational or disconfirming feedback."[76] Openness is an essential element for an effective organizational climate.[77] Employees are more satisfied with their jobs when communication openness exists between superiors and subordinates.[78]

Whistle blowing often occurs in research laboratories which employ scientists and engineers. Sanders maintains that a combination of technical ability and judgment with administrative ability and judgment is rare in scientists, but essential for managers of scientists.[79] Organizational communication specialists can help managers of engineers develop administrative ability and judgment and perhaps, thereby, obviate the need for whistle blowing.

A second principle that might help alleviate the whistle blower's dilemma involves a special technique for accomplishing more efficient upward communication—the use of ombudsmen. According to Silver, a political ombudsman is "a person of some eminence, learned in law, who is appointed by a legislative body to inquire into complaints against administrative officials and to make periodic reports about his findings."[80] A corporate ombudsman would hear an employee's complaint, decide whether or not the complaint was warranted, investigate the dispute, and suggest a solution. Silver maintains that an ombudsman could explain to an employee why the employee's complaint was unwarranted. He contends that

> one of the great problems of corporate life, and a cause for frequent grievance, is not the unfairness of management action, but the inexplicability of it. . . . Often . . . decisions appear to be arbitrary when in fact they are not. Equally often, work discontent is caused by a lack of understanding as to reasons for such apparently unfavorable decision.[81]

On the other hand, a corporate ombudsman will not be successful in answering the grievances of professional employees if he/she automatically assumes that decisions made by management are correct, especially when those decisions affect professional employees.

Dissent in organizations has not been studied from a communication perspective. Dissent occurs, at least in part, through the communication of information which organizational members consider negative. More systematic research needs to be conducted to determine the nature of this information and how it is acted upon by organizational members.

Whistle blowing is both a constructive and a destructive phenomenon. It is constructive because whistle blowers often reveal unethical practices or defect which would cause danger to the public, and it is destructive because whistle blowers often suffer personal and professional harm and/or create suspicion within organizations. As a result, the public may begin to distrust the motives of all complex organizations. Understanding whistle blowing may make it possible to reduce its destructive effects while at the same time protecting public safety and encouraging ethical behavior in organizations.

## Notes

1. David W. Ewing, "Multiple Loyalties," *Wall Street Journal,* May 1, 1978, p. 18.
2. According to Charles Peters and Taylor Branch, in their book *Blowing the Whistle: Dissent in the Public Interest* (New York: Praeger, 1972), pp. 18–19. While whistle blowing is a flippant term, this flippancy may be useful because it avoids the connotation of treason: "Whistle-blowing is severely hampered by the image of its most famous historical model, Judas Iscariot. Martin Luther seems to be about the only figure of note to make much headway with public opinion after doing an inside job on a corrupt organization."
3. Christopher D. Stone, *Where the Law Ends: The Social Control of Corporate Behavior* (New York: Harper & Row, 1975).
4. Thomas F. Carney, "Currents in Organizational Communication," *Journal of Communication* (Spring 1979), vol. 29, no. 2, pp. 200–211.
5. See Peters and Branch, *op. cit.*
6. Helen Dudar, "The Price of Blowing the Whistle," *New York Times Magazine,* Oct. 30, 1979, pp. 41–54; Ralph Nader, Peter J. Petkas, and Kate Blackwell (eds.), *Whistle Blowing: The Report of the Conference on Professional Responsibility* (New York: Grossman Publishers, 1972); and Kenneth D. Walters, "Your Employees' Right to Blow the Whistle," *Harvard Business Review* (1975), vol. 53, no. 4, pp. 26–34 and 161–62.
7. See, for example, David W. Ewing, *Freedom Inside the Organization* (New York: McGraw-Hill, 1977).
8. See Philip I. Blumberg, "Corporate Responsibility and the Employee's Duty of Loyalty and Obedience: A Preliminary Inquiry," *Oklahoma Law Review* (1971), vol. 24, pp. 279–84; rpt. in *The Corporate Dilemma,* eds. Dow Votaw and S. Prakesh (Englewood Cliffs, N.J.: Prentice-Hall, 1973), pp. 82–113; and David W. Ewing, *op. cit.*
9. Ewing, *op. cit.*; G. March and H. A. Simon, *Organizations* (New York: Wiley, 1958); C. O'Reilly and K. Roberts, "Information Filtration in Organizations: Three Experiments," *Organizational Behavior and Human Performance* (1974), vol. 11, pp. 253–65; and Nicholoas Wade, "Protection

Sought for Satirists and Whistle Blowers," *Science,* Dec. 7, 1973, p. 1002–03.

10. Ewing, *op. cit.,* p. 33.
11. Ewing, *op. cit.*
12. Lawrence E. Blades, "Employment at Will vs. Individual Freedom: On Limiting the Abusive Exercise of Employer Power," *Columbia Law Review* (1967), vol. 67, pp. 1404–35.
13. *Ibid.,* pp. 1411–12.
14. Frank Von Hippel, *"Protecting the Whistle Blowers,"* Physics Today, October 1977, pp. 9–13.
15. Gerry E. Morse, "Engineering Ethics—From the Viewpoint of Industry," *Journal of Engineering Education* (1954), vol. 45, pp. 214–19.
16. Robert J. Baum and Albert Flores, *Ethical Problems in Engineering* (Troy, N.Y.: Center for the Study of the Human Dimensions of Science and Technology, Rensselaer Polytechnic Institute, 1978).
17. Robert T. Howard, "A Bill of Professional Rights for Employed Engineers?" *American Engineer,* October 1966, pp. 47–50.
18. *Ibid.*
19. Nader et al., *op. cit.,* p. vii.
20. *Ibid.,* pp. 76–77.
21. Peters and Branch, *op. cit.,* p. 4.
22. Les Whitten, "The Whistle Blowers," *Harper's Bazaar,* September 1972, p. 168.
23. Joann S. Lublin, "Spilling the Beans: Disclosing Misdeeds of Corporations Can Backfire on Tattlers," *Wall Street Journal,* May 1976. p. 1; see also Ewing, *op. cit.*
24. Walters, *op. cit.,* p. 56.
25. Dudar, *op. cit.*
26. Julius Duscha, "Stop! In the Public Interest!" *New York Times Magazine,* March 21, 1971, pp. 4–19; Wade, *op. cit.* In the United States, political conservatives may date the beginning of whistle blowing as 1963 when Otto Otepka gave classified documents to a Senate subcommittee claiming that the Kennedy adminstration was harboring Communists in the State Department. Otepka, fired by Dean Rusk, defended his actions by claiming he had a "higher loyalty" to the nation and felt it should be protected from Communists. Liberals would probably date the first occurrence of whistle blowing as 1966 when James Boyd revealed Senator Thomas Dodd's unethical campaign finance practices to the public through the columns of Drew Pearson and Jack Anderson.
27. Peters and Branch, *op. cit.,* p. 291.
28. Von Hippel, *op. cit.*
29. *Ibid.,* p. 9.
30. See James Olson, "Engineer Attitudes Toward Professionalism, Employment, Social Responsibility," *Professional Engineer,* vol. 42, no. 8, p. 32.
31. Compare Ewing, *op. cit.,* and Louis V. McIntire and Marion Bayard McIntire, *Scientists and Engineers: The Professionals Who Are Not* (Lafayette, La.: Arcola Communication Co., 1971).
32. Ewing, *op. cit.,* p. 184.
33. *Ibid.,* p. 77.
34. Dudar, *op. cit.,* p. 52.

35. Walters, *op. cit.*
36. Ralph H. Turner, "Unresponsiveness as a Social Sanction," Sociometry (1973), vol. 36, p. 1.
37. Isidore Silver, "The Corporate Ombudsman," *Harvard Business Review* (1967), vol. 45, no. 3, pp. 77–87.
38. Kenneth M. Thompson, "Human Relations in Collective Bargaining," *Harvard Business Reivew* (1953), vol. 31, no. 2, pp. 116–26.
39. Walters, *op. cit.*
40. Jerry M. Flint, "G.M.'s Chief Scores Critics of Business," *New York Times,* March 26, 1971, p. 52.
41. Ewing, *op. cit.*, p. 227.
42. John Noble Wilford, "Scientists Discuss Dual Loyalty on Job," *New York Times,* Feb. 22, 1976.
43. Larry L. Boulden, "The Perils of Integrity," *Automation* (1975), vol. 22, no. 3, p. 43.
44. *Ibid.*, p. 44.
45. Peters and Branch, *op. cit.*, pp. 15–16.
46. "The Whistle Blowers," Time, Apr. 17, 1972, pp. 85–86.
47. Roger M. D'Aprix, *The Believable Corporation* (New York: AMACOM, 1977), pp. 29–30.
48. Boulden, *op. cit.*
49. Walters, *op. cit.*
50. *Ibid.*, p. 30.
51. Blades, *op. cit.*, p. 1413.
52. Ewing, *op. cit.*, p. 200.
53. Stone, *op. cit.*, pp. 214–15.
54. Ewing, *op. cit.*, p. 48.
55. *Ibid.*, p. 38.
56. Nader et al., *op. cit.*
57. Peters and Branch, *op. cit.*
58. *Ibid.*
59. Walters, *op. cit.*
60. For information on those whistle blowing events not cited elsewhere in this article, see Philip M. Boffey, "Vaccine Imbroglio: The Rise and Fall of a Scientist Critic," *Science,* Dec. 3, 1976, pp. 1021–25; John T. Edsall, "Scientific Freedom and Responsibility," *Science,* May 16, 1975, pp. 687–93; Timothy H. Ingram and Jerry W. Finefrock, "General Telephone's Fickle Finger," *The Progressive* (1969), vol. 33, no. 9, pp. 37–40; and Priscilla S. Meyer, "Blowing the Whistle Ends in Book, Movie and $500,000 a Year," *Wall Street Journal,* Feb. 15, 1978, pp. 1, 13.
61. Compare Ewing, *op. cit.*
62. Cecil Gibb, "Leadership," in *Handbook of Social Psychology,* vol. 4 (second edition) eds. G. Lindzey and E. Aronson (Reading, Mass.: Addison-Wesley, 1968), p. 241; and W. Charles Redding, *Communication Within the Organization: An Interpretive Review of Theory and Research* (New York: Industrial Communication Council, 1972).
63. Compare Daniel Katz and Robert L. Kahn, *The Social Psychology of Organizations* (New York: Wiley, 1966), p. 225; and Redding, *op. cit.*, p. 97.
64. Redding, *op. cit.*, p. 87.

65. William G. Scott, *Human Relations in Management* (Homewood, Ill.: Irwin, 1962), p. 201.
66. D. Ronald Daniel, "Management Information Crisis," *Harvard Business Review* (1961), vol. 39, no. 5, pp. 111–21; and Redding, *op. cit.*, p. 75.
67. G. March and H. A. Simon, *Organizations* (New York: Wiley, 1958).
68. See Freric M. Jablin, "Superior-Subordinate Communication: The State of the Art," paper presented at the Annual Convention of the International Communication Association, Philadelphia, 1978, p.2.
69. See Redding, *op. cit.*; for more information on upward communication and the determinants of its accuracy, see John Baird, "An Analytical Field Study of 'Open Communication' as Perceived by Superiors, Subordinates and Peers," unpublished Ph.D. dissertation, Purdue University, 1973; H. H. Kelly, "Communication in Experimentally Created Hierarchies," *Human Relations* (1951), vol. 4, pp. 39–56; N.R.F. Maier, R.L. Hoffman, and W. H. Read, "Superior-Subordinate Communication: The Relative Effectiveness of Managers Who Held Their Subordinates' Positions," *Personnel Psychology* (1963), vol. 16, pp. 1–11; W. H. Read, "Upward Communication in Industrial Hierarchies," *Human Relations* (1962), vol. 15, pp. 3–15; and A. Vogel, "Why Don't Employees Speak Up?" *Personnel Administration* (1967), vol. 30, no. 5, pp. 18–24. More complete reviews of general organization literature are contained in Redding, *op. cit.*, and Gary M. Richetto, "Organizational Communication Theory and Research: An Overview," in Brent D. Rugen (ed.), *Communication Yearbook I* (New Brunswick, N.J.: Transaction Books, 1977), pp. 331–46.
70. O'Reilly and Roberts, *op. cit.*
71. Kelly, *op. cit.*; and Read, *op. cit.*
72. L. Sussman, "Upward Communication in the Organizational Hierarchy: An Experimental Field Study of Perceived Distortion," unpublished Ph.D. dissertation, Purdue University, 1973.
73. P. K. Tomkins, "An Analysis of Communication Between Headquarters and Selected Units of a National Labor Union," unpublished Ph.D. dissertation, Purdue University, 1962.
74. R. L. Minter, "A Comparative Analysis of Managerial Communication in Two Divisions of a Manufacturing Corporation," unpublished Ph.D. dissertation, Purdue University, 1969. See also C. G. Browne and B. J. Neitzel, "Communication, Supervision, and Morale," *Journal of Applied Psychology* (1952), vol. 36, pp. 86–91; Maier et al., *op. cit.*; and H. Rosen, "Managerial Role Interaction: A Study of Three Managerial Levels," *Journal of Applied Psychology* (1961), vol. 45, pp. 30–34.
75. See Royden C. Sanders, Jr., "Interface Problems Between Scientists and Others in Technically Oriented Companies," in *The Management of Scientists,* ed. Karl Hill (Boston: Beacon Press, 1964), pp. 75–86.
76. Jablin, *op. cit.*, p. 4.
77. W. V. Haney, *Communication and Organizational Behavior,* second ed. (Homewood, Ill.: Irwin, 1967); and R. Likert, *The Human Organization* (New York: McGraw-Hill, 1967).
78. Baird, *op. cit.*; R.J. Burke and D.W. Wilcox, "Effects of Different Patterns and Degrees of Openness in Superior-Subordinate Communication on Subordinate Job Satisfaction," *Academy of Management Journal* (1969), vol. 12, pp. 319–26; and Jablin, "An Experimental Study of Message-

Response in Superior-Subordinate Communication," unpublished Ph.D. dissertation, Purdue University, 1977. For more information on communication openness in organizations, see Baird, *op. cit.*; Jablin, "Experimental Study," *op. cit.*; Jablin, "Superior-Subordinate," *op. cit.*; Redding, "The Empirical Study of Human Communication in Business and Industry," in *The Frontiers in Experimental Speech-Communication Research,* ed. Paul E. Ried (Syracuse, N.Y.: Syracuse University Press, 1966), pp. 47–81; J. Stull, "Openness in Supervisor-Subordinate Communication: A Quasi-Experimental Field Study," unpublished Ph.D dissertation, Purdue University, 1975; and P. Watzlawick, J. H. Beavin, and Don D. Jackson, *Pragmatics of Human Communication* (New York: W. W. Norton, 1967).

79. Sanders, *op. cit.*; see also A. F. Siepert, "Creating the Management Climate for Effective Research in Government Lavoratories," in *The Management of Scientists,* ed. E. Mendelsohn et al. (Boston: Beacon Press, 1976), p. 92.

80. Silver, *op. cit.*, p. 77.

81. *Ibid.*, p. 79.

# Part VI

# INTERPERSONAL COMMUNICATION: APPLIED PERSPECTIVES

# 18

# Active Listening

*Carl Rogers* and *Richard E. Farson*

## The Meaning of Active Listening

One basic responsibility of the supervisor or executive is the development, adjustment, and integration of individual employees. He tries to develop employee potential, delegate responsibility, and achieve cooperation. To do so, he must have, among other abilities, the ability to listen intelligently and carefully to those with whom he works.

There are, however, many kinds of listening skills. The lawyer, for example, when questioning a witness, listens for contradictions, irrelevancies, errors, and weaknesses. But this is not the kind of listening skill we are concerned with in this booklet. The lawyer usually is not listening in order to help the witness adjust or cooperate or produce. On the other hand, we will be concerned with listening skills which *will help* employees gain a clearer understanding of their situations, take responsibility, and cooperate with each other.

### Two Examples

The kind of listening we have in mind is called "active listening." It is called "active" because the listener has a very definite responsibility. He does not passively absorb the words which are spoken to him. He actively tries to grasp the facts and the feelings in what he hears, and he tries, by his listening, to help the speaker work out his own problems.

To get a fuller picture of what is meant by active listening, let us consider two different approaches to the same work problem.

### Example No. 1

*Foreman:* Hey, Al, I don't get this production order. We can't handle this run today. What do they think we are?

*Supervisor:* But that's the order. So get it out as soon as you can. We're under terrific pressure this week.

*Foreman:* Don't they know we're behind schedule already because of that press breakdown?

*Supervisor:* Look Kelly, I don't decide what goes on upstairs. I just have to see that the work gets out and that's what I'm gonna do.

*Foreman:* The guys aren't gonna like this.

*Supervisor:* That's something you'll have to work out with them, not me.

### Example No. 2

*Foreman:* Hey, Ross, I don't get this production order. We can't handle this run today. What do they think we are?

*Supervisor:* Sounds like you're pretty sore about it, Kelly.

*Foreman:* I sure am. We were just about getting back to schedule after that press breakdown. Now this comes along.

*Supervisor:* As if you didn't have enough work to do, huh?

*Foreman:* Yeah. I don't know how I'm gonna tell the guys about this.

*Supervisor:* Hate to face 'em with it now, is that it?

*Foreman:* I really do. They're under a real strain today. Seems like everything we do around here is rush, rush.

*Supervisor:* I guess you feel like it's unfair to load anything more on them.

*Foreman:* Well, yeah. I know there must be plenty of pressure on everybody up the line, but—well, if that's the way it is . . . guess I'd better get the word to 'em.

There are obviously many differences between these two examples. The main one, however, is that Ross, the supervisor in the second example, is using the active-listening approach. He is listening and responding in a way that makes it clear that he appreciates both the meaning and the feeling behind what Kelly is saying.

Active listening does not necesarily mean long sessions spent listening to grievances, personal or otherwise. It is simply a way of approaching those problems which arise out of the usual day-to-day events of any job.

To be effective, active listening must be firmly grounded in the basic attitudes of the user. We cannot employ it as a technique if our fundamental attitudes are in conflict with its basic concepts. If we try, our behavior will be empty and sterile and our associates will be quick to recognize this. Until we can demonstrate a spirit which genuinely respects the potential worth of the individual, which considers his rights and trusts his capacity for self-direction, we cannot begin to be effective listeners.

### What We Achieve by Listening

Active listening is an important way to bring about changes in people. Despite the popular notion that listening is a passive approach, clinical and research evidence clearly shows that sensitive listening is a most effective agent for individual personality change and group development. Listening brings about changes in people's attitudes toward themselves and others, and also brings about changes in their basic values and personal philosophy. People who have been listened to in this new and special way become more emotionally mature, more open to their experiences, less defensive, more democratic, and less authoritarian.

When people are listened to sensitively, they tend to listen to themselves with more care and make clear exactly what they are feeling and thinking. Group members tend to listen more to each other, become less argumentative, more ready to incorporate other points of view. Because listening reduces the threat of having one's ideas criticized, the person is better able to see them for what they are, and is more likely to feel that his contributions are worthwhile.

Not the least important result of listening is the change that takes place within the listener himself. Besides the fact that listening provides more information than any other activity, it builds deep, positive relationships and tends to alter constructively the attitudes of the listener. Listening is a growth experience.

These, then, are some of the worthwhile results we can expect from active listening. But how do we go about this kind of listening? How do we become active listeners?

### How to Listen

Active listening aims to bring about changes in people. To achieve this end, it relies upon definite techniques—things to do and things to avoid doing. Before discussing these techniques, however, we should first understand why they are effective. To do so, we must understand how the individual personality develops.

### The Growth of the Individual

Through all of our lives, from early childhood on, we have learned to think of ourselves in certain, very definite ways. We have built up pictures of ourselves. Sometimes these self-pictures are pretty realistic but at other times they are not. For example, an overage, overweight lady may fancy herself a youthful, ravishing siren, or an awkward teenager regard himself as a star athlete.

All of us have experiences which fit the way we need to think about ourselves. These we accept. But it is much harder to accept experiences which don't fit. And sometimes, if it is very important for us to hang on to this self-picture, we don't accept or admit these experiences at all.

These self-pictures are not necessarily attractive. A man, for example, may regard himself as incompetent and worthless. He may feel that he is doing his job poorly in spite of favorable appraisals by the company. As long as he has these feelings about himself he must deny any experiences which would seem not to fit this self-picture, in this case any that might indicate to him that he is competent. It is so necessary for him to maintain this self-picture that he is threatened by anything which would tend to change it. Thus, when the company raises his salary, it may seem to him only additional proof that he is a fraud. He must hold onto this self-picture, because, bad or good, it's the only thing he has by which he can identify himself.

This is why direct attempts to change this individual or change his self-picture are particularly threatening. He is forced to defend himself or to completely deny the experience. This denial of experience and defense of the self-picture tend to bring on rigidity of behavior and create difficulties in personal adjustment.

The active-listening approach, on the other hand, does not present a threat to the individual's self-picture. He does not have to defend it. He is able to explore it, see it for what it is, and make his own decision as to how realistic it is. And he is then in a position to change.

If I want to help a man reduce his defensiveness and become more adaptive, I must try to remove the threat of myself as his potential changer. As long as the atmosphere is threatening, there can be no effective communication. So I must create a climate which is neither critical, evaluative, nor moralizing. It must be an atmosphere of equality and freedom, permissiveness and understanding, acceptance and warmth. It is in this climate and this climate only that the individual feels safe enough to incorporate new experiences and new values into his concept of himself. Let's see how active listening helps to create this climate.

### What to Avoid

When we encounter a person with a problem, our usual response is to try to change his way of looking at things—to get him to see his situation the way we see it, or would like him to see it. We plead, reason, scold, encourage, insult, prod—anything to bring about a change in the desired direction, that is, in the direction we want him to travel. What we seldom realize, however, is that, under these circumstances, we are usually responding to *our own* needs to see the world in certain ways. It is always difficult for us to tolerate and understand actions which are different from the ways in which we believe we should act. If, however, we can free ourselves from the need to influence and direct others in our own paths, we enable ourselves to listen with understanding, and thereby employ the most potent available agent of change.

One problem the listener faces is that of responding to demands for decisions, judgments, and evaluation. He is constantly called upon to agree or disagree with someone or something. Yet, as he well knows, the question or challenge frequently is a masked expression of feelings or needs which the speaker is far more anxious to communicate than he is to have the surface questions answered. Because he cannot speak these feelings openly, the speaker must disguise them to himself and to others in an acceptable form. To illustrate, let us examine some typical questions and the type of answers that might best elicit the feeling beneath it.

| *Employee's Questions* | *Listener's Answer* |
|---|---|
| Just whose responsibility is the tool room? | Do you feel that someone is challenging your authority in there? |
| Don't you think younger able people should be promoted before senior but less able ones? | It seems to you they should, I take it. |
| What does the super expect us to do about those broken-down machines? | You're pretty disgusted with those machines, aren't you? |
| Don't you think I've improved over the last review period? | Sounds as if you feel like you've really picked up lately. |

These responses recognize the questions but leave the way open for the employee to say what is really bothering him. They allow the listener to participate in the problem or situation without shouldering all responsibility for decision-making or actions. This is a process of thinking *with* people instead of *for* or *about* them.

Passing judgment, whether critical or favorable, makes free expression difficult. Similarly, advice and information are almost always seen as efforts to change a person and thus serve as barriers to his self-expression and the development of a creative relationship. Moreover, advice is seldom taken and information hardly ever utilized. The eager young trainee probably will not become patient just because he is advised that, "The road to success in business is a long, difficult one, and you must be patient." And it is no more helpful for him to learn that "only one out of a hundred trainees reach top management positions."

Interestingly, it is a difficult lesson to learn that positive *evaluations* are sometimes as blocking as negative ones. It is almost as destructive to the freedom of a relationship to tell a person that he is good or capable or right, as to tell him otherwise. To evaluate him positively may make it more difficult for him to tell of the faults that distress him or the ways in which he believes he is not competent.

Encouragement also may be seen as an attempt to motivate the speaker in certain directions or hold him off rather than as support. "I'm sure everything will work out O.K." is not a helpful response to the person who is deeply discouraged about a problem.

In other words, most of the techniques and devices common to human relationships are found to be of little use in establishing the type of relationship we are seeking here.

### What to Do

Just what does active listening entail, then? Basically, it requires that we get inside the speaker, that we grasp, *from his point of view,* just what it is he is communicating to us. More than that, we must convey to the speaker that we are seeing things from his point of view. To listen actively, then, means that there are several things we must do.

*Listen from Total Meaning.* Any message a person tries to get across usually has two components: the *content* of the message, and the *feeling* or attitude underlying this content. Both are important, both give the message *meaning*. It is this total meaning of the message that we try to understand. For example, a machinist comes to his foreman and says, "I've finished that lathe set-up." This message has obvious content and perhaps calls upon the foreman for another work assignment. Suppose, on the other hand, that he says, "Well, I'm finally finished with that damned lathe set-up." The content is the same but the total meaning of the message has changed—and changed in an important way for both the foreman and the woker. Here sensitive listening can facilitate the relationship. Suppose the foreman were to respond by simply giving another work assignment. Would the employee feel that he had gotten his total message across? Would he feel free to talk to his foreman? Will he feel better about his job, more anxious to do good work on the next assignment?

Now, on the other hand, suppose the foreman were to respond with, "Glad to have it over with, huh?" or "Had a pretty rough time of it?" or "Guess you don't feel like doing anything like that again," or anything else that tells the worker that he heard and understands. It doesn't necessarily mean the the next work assignment need be changed or that he must spend an hour listening to the worker complain about the set-up problems he encountered. He may do a number of things differently in the light of the new information he has from the worker—but not necessarily. It's just that extra sensitivity on the part of the foreman which can transform an average working climate into a good one.

*Respond to Feelings.* In some instances the content is far less important than the feeling which underlies it. To catch the full flavor or meaning of the message one must respond particularly to the feeling component, if, for instance, our machinist had said "I'd like to melt this lathe down and make paper clips out of it," responding to content would be obviously absurd. But to respond to his disgust or anger in trying to work with his lathe recognizes the meaning of this message. There are various shadings of these components in the meaning of any message. Each time the listener must try to remain sensitive to the total meaning the message has to the speaker. What is he trying to tell me? What does this mean to him? How does he see this situation?

*Not All Cues.* Not all communication is verbal. The speaker's words alone don't tell us everything he is communicating. And hence, truly sensitive listening requires that we become aware of several kinds of communication besides verbal. The way in which a speaker hesitates in his speech can tell us much about his feelings. So too can the inflection of his voice. He may stress certain points loudly and clearly, and may mumble others. We should also note such things as the person's facial expressions, body posture, hand movements, eye movements, and breathing. All of these help to convey his total message.

### What We Communicate by Listening

The first reaction of most people when they consider listening as a possible method for dealing with human beings is that listening cannot be sufficient in itself. Because it is passive, they feel, listening does not communicate anything to the speaker. Actually, nothing could be farther from the truth.

By consistently listening to a speaker you are conveying the idea that: "I'm interested in you as a person, and I think that what you feel is important. I respect your thoughts, and even if I don't agree with them, I know that they are valid for you. I feel sure that you have a contribution to make. I'm not trying to change you or evaluate you. I just want to understand you. I think you're worth listening to, and I want you to know that I'm the kind of person you can talk to."

The subtle but most important aspect of this is the *demonstration* of the message that works. While it is most difficult to convince someone that you respect him by *telling* him so, you are much more likely to get this message across by really *behaving* that way—by actually *having* and *demonstrating* respect for this person. Listening does this most effectively.

Like other behavior, listening behavior is contagious. This has implications for all communications problems, whether between two people, or within a large organization. To insure good communication between associates up and down the line, one must first take the responsibility for setting a pattern of listening. Just as one learns that anger is usually met with anger, argument with argument, and deception with deception, one can learn that listening can be met with listening. Every person who feels responsibility in a situation can set the tone of the interaction, and the important lesson in this is that any behavior exhibited by one person will eventually be responded to with similar behavior in the other person.

It is far more difficult to stimulate constructive behavior in another person but far more profitable. Listening is one of these constructive behaviors, but if one's attitude is to "wait out" the speaker rather than really listen to him, it will fail. The one who consistently listens with understanding, however, is the one who eventually is most likely to be listened to. If you really want to be heard and understood by another, you can develop him as a potential listener, ready for new ideas, provided you can first develop yourself in these ways and sincerely listen with understanding and respect.

### Testing for Understanding

Because understanding another person is actually far more difficult than it at first seems, it is important to test constantly your ability to see the world in the way the speaker sees it. You can do this by reflecting in your own words what the speaker seems to mean by his words and actions. His response to this will tell you whether or not he feels understood. A good rule of thumb is to assume that one never really understands until he can communicate this understanding to the other's satisfaction.

Here is an experiment to test your skill in listening. The next time you become involved in a lively or controversial discussion with another person, stop for a moment and suggest that you adopt this ground rule for continued discussion: Before either participant in the discussion can make a point or express an opinion of his own, he must first restate aloud the previous point or position of the other person. This restatement must be accurate enough to satisfy the speaker before the listener can be allowed to speak for himself.

This is something you could try in your own discussion group. Have someone express himself on some topic of emotional concern to the group. Then, before another member expresses his own feelings and thought, he must rephrase the *meaning* expressed by the previous speaker to that individual's satisfaction. Note the changes in the emotional climate and the quality of the discussion when you try this.

## Problems in Active Listening

Active listening is not an easy skill to acquire. It demands practice. Perhaps more important, it may require changes in our own basic attitudes. These changes come slowly and sometimes with considerable difficulty. Let us look at some of the major problems in active listening and what can be done to overcome them.

### The Personal Risk

To be effective at all in active listening, one must have a sincere interest in the speaker. We all live in glass houses as far as our attitudes are concerned. They always show through. And if we are only making a pretense of interest in the speaker, he will quickly pick this up, either consciously or unconsciously. And once he does, he will no longer express himself freely.

Active listening carries a strong element of personal risk. If we manage to accomplish what we are describing here—to sense deeply the feelings of another person, to understand the meaning his experiences have for him, to see the world as he sees it—we risk being changed ourselves. For example, if we permit ourselves to listen our way into the psychological life of a labor leader or agitator—to get the meaning which life has for him—we risk coming to see the world as he sees it. It is threatening to give up, even momentarily, what we believe and start thinking in someone else's terms. It takes a great deal of inner security and courage to be able to risk one's self in understanding another.

For the supervisor, the courage to take another's point of view generally means that he must see *himself* through another's eyes—he must be able to see himself as others see him. To do this may sometimes be unpleasant, but it is far more *difficult* than unpleasant. We are so accustomed to viewing ourselves in certain ways—to seeing and hearing only what we want to see and hear—that it is extremely difficult for a person to free himself from his needs to see things these ways.

Developing an attitude of sincere interest in the speaker is thus no easy task. It can be developed only by being willing to risk seeing the world from the speaker's point of view. If we have a number of such experiences, however, they will shape an attitude which will allow us to be truly genuine in our interest in the speaker.

### Hostile Expressions

The listener will often hear negative, hostile expressions directed at himself. Such expressions are always hard to listen to. No one likes to hear hostile action or words. And it is not easy to get to the point where one is strong enough to permit these attacks without finding it necessary to defend himself or retaliate.

Because we all fear that people will crumble under the attack of genuine negative feelings, we tend to perpetrate an attitude of pseudo-peace. It is as if we cannot tolerate conflict at all for fear of the damage it could do to us, to the situation, to the others involved. But of course the real damage is done to all these by the denial and suppression of negative feelings.

### Out-of-Place Expressions

There is also the problem of out-of-place expressions, expressions dealing with behavior which is not usually acceptable in our society. In the extreme forms that present themselves before psychotherapists, expressions of sexual perversity of homicidal fantasies are often found blocking to the listener because of their obvious threatening quality. At less extreme levels, we all find unnatural or inappropriate behavior difficult to handle. That is, anything from an "off-color" story told in mixed company to seeing a man weep is likely to produce a problem situation.

In any face-to-face situation, we will find instances of this type which will momentarily, if not permanently, block any communication. In business and industry any expressions of weakness or incompetency will generally be regarded as unacceptable and therefore will block good two-way communication. For example, it is difficult to listen to a supervisor tell of his feelings of failure in being able to "take charge" of a situation in his department because *all* administrators are supposed to be able to "take charge."

### Accepting Positive Feelings

It is both interesting and perplexing to note that negative or hostile feelings or expressions are much easier to deal with in any face-to-face relationship than are truly and deeply positive feelings. This is especially true for the business man because the culture expects him to be independent, bold, clever, and aggressive and manifest no feelings of warmth, gentleness, and intimacy. He therefore comes to regard these feelings as soft and inappropriate. But no matter how they are regarded, they remain a human need. The denial of these feelings in himself and his associates does not get the executive out of the problem of dealing with them. They simply become veiled and confused. If recognized they would work for the total effort; unrecognized, they work against it.

### Emotional Danger Signals

The listener's own emotions are sometimes a barrier to active listening. When emotions are at their height, when listening is most necessary, it is most difficult to set aside one's own concerns and be understanding. Our emotions are often our own worst enemies when we try to become listeners. The more involved and invested we are in a particular situation or problem, the less we are likely to be willing or able to listen to the feelings and attitudes of others. That is, the more we find it necessary to respond to our own needs, the less we are able to respond to the needs of another. Let us look at some of the main danger signals that warn us that our emotions may be interfering with our listening.

*Defensiveness.* The points about which one is most vocal and dogmatic, the points which one is most anxious to impose on others—these are always the points one is trying to talk oneself into believing. So one danger signal becomes apparent when you find yourself stressing a point or trying to convince another. It is at these times that you are likely to be less secure and thus less able to listen.

*Resentment of Opposition.* It is always easier to listen to an idea which is similar to one of your own than to an opposing view. Sometimes, in order to clear the air, it is helpful to pause for a moment when you feel your ideas and position being challenged, reflect on the situation, and express your concern to the speaker.

*Clash of Personalities.* Here again, our experience has consistently shown us that the genuine expression of feelings on the part of the listener will be more helpful in developing a sound relationship than the suppression of them. This is so whether the feelings be resentment, hostility, threat, or admiration. A basically honest relationship, whatever the nature of it, is the most productive of all. The other party becomes secure when he learns that the listener can express his feelings honestly and openly to him. We should keep this in mind when we begin to fear a clash of personalities in the listening relationship. Otherwise, fear of our own emotions will choke off full expression of feelings.

*Listening to Ourselves.* To listen to oneself is a prerequisite to listening to others. And it is often an effective means of dealing with the problems we have outlined above. When we are most aroused, excited, and demanding, we are least able to understand our own feelings and attitudes. Yet, in dealing with the problems of others, it becomes most important to be sure of one's own position, values, and needs.

The ability to recognize and understand the meaning which a particular episode has for you, with all the feelings which it stimulates in you, and the ability to express this meaning when you find it getting in the way of active listening, will clear the air and enable you once again to be free to listen. That is, if some person or situation touches off feelings within you which tend to block your attempts to listen with understanding, begin listening to yourself. It is much more helpful in developing effective relationships to avoid suppressing these feelings. Speak them out as clearly as you can, and try to enlist the other person as a listener to your feelings. A person's listening ability is limited by his ability to listen to himself.

## Active Listening and Company Goals.

"How can listening improve production?"

"We're in business, and it's a rugged, fast, competitive affair. How are we going to find time to counsel our employees?"

"We have to concern ourselves with organizational problems first."

"We can't afford to spend all day listening when there's a job to be done."

"What's morale got to do with production?"

"Sometimes we have to sacrifice an individual for the good of the rest of the people in the company."

Those of us who are trying to advance the listening approach in industry hear these comments frequently. And because they are so honest and legitimate, they pose a real problem. Unfortunately, the answers are not so clear-cut as the questions.

### Individual Importance

One answer is based on an assumption that is central to the listening approach. The assumption is: The kind of behavior which helps the individual will eventually be the best thing that could be done for the group. Or saying it another way: The things that are best for the individual are best for the company. This is a conviction of ours, based on our experience in psychology and education. The research evidence from industry is only beginning to come in. We find that putting the group first, at the expense of the individual, besides being an uncomfortable individual experience, does *not* unify the group. In fact, it tends to make the group less a group. The members become anxious and suspicious.

We are not at all sure in just what ways the group does benefit from a concern demonstrated for an individual, but we have several strong leads. One is that the group feels more secure when an individual member is being listened to and provided for with concern and sensitivity. And we assume that a secure group will ultimately be a better group. When each individual feels that he need not fear exposing himself to the group, he is likely to contribute more freely and spontaneously. When the leader of a group responds to the individual, puts the individual first, the other members of the group will follow suit, and the group comes to act as a unit in recognizing and responding to the needs of a particular member. This positive, constructive actions seems to be a much more satisfying experience for a group than the experience of dispensing with a member.

### Listening and Production

As to whether or not listening or any other activity designed to better human relations in an industry actually raises production—whether morale has a definite relationship to production is not known for sure. There are some who frankly hold that there is no relationship to be expected between morale and production—that production often depends upon the social misfit, the eccentric, or the isolate. And there are some who simply choose to work in a climate of cooperation and harmony, in a high-morale group, quite aside from the question of increased production.

A report from the Survey Research Center[1] at the University of Michigan on research conducted at the Prudential Life Insurance Company lists seven findings relating to production and morale. First-line supervisors in high-production work groups were found to differ from those in low-production work groups in that they:

1. Are under less close supervision from their own supervisors.
2. Place less direct emphasis upon production as the goal.
3. Encourage employee participation in the making of decision.
4. Are more employee-centered.
5. Spend more of their time in supervision and less in straight production work.
6. Have a greater feeling of confidence in their supervisory roles.
7. Feel that they know where they stand with the company.

After mentioning that other dimensions of morale, such as identification with the company, intrinsic job satisfaction, and satisfaction with job status, were not found significantly related to productivity, the report goes on to suggest the following psychological interpretation:

> People are more effectively motivated when they are given some degree of freedom in the way in which they do their work than when every action is prescribed in advance. They do better when some degree of decision-making about their jobs is possible than when all decisions are made for them. They respond more adequately when they are treated as personalities than as cogs in a machine. In short if the ego motivations of self-determination, of self-expression, of a sense of personal worth can be tapped, the individual can be more effectively energized. The use of external sanctions, or pressuring for production may work to some degree, but not to the extent that the more internalized motives do. When the individual comes to identify himself with his job and with the work of his group, human resources are much more fully utilized in the production process.

The Survery Research Center has also conducted studies among workers in other industries. In discussing the results of these studies, Robert L. Kahn writes:

> In the studies of clerical workers, railroad workers, and workers in heavy industry, the supervisors with the better production records gave a larger proportion of their time to supervisory functions, especially to the interpersonal aspects of their jobs. The supervisors of the lower-producing sections were more likely to spend their time in tasks which the men themselves were performing, or in the paperwork aspects of their jobs.[2]

### Maximum Creativeness

There may never be enough research evidence to satisfy everyone on this question. But speaking from a business point of view, in terms of the problems of developing resources for production, the maximum creativeness and productive effort of the human beings in the organization are the riches untapped source of power still existing. The difference between the maximum productive capacity of people and that output which industry is now realizing is immense. We simply suggest that this maximum capacity might be closer to realization if we sought to release the motivation that already exists within people rather than try to stimulate them externally.

This releasing of the individual is made possible first of all by sensitive listening, with respect and understanding. Listening is a beginning toward making the individual feel himself worthy of making contributions, and this could result in a very dynamic and productive organization. Competitive business is never too rugged or too busy to take time to procure the most efficient technological advances or to develop rich raw material resources. But these in comparison to the resources that are already within the people in the plant are paltry. This is industry's major procurement problem.

G.L. Clements, president of Jewel Tea Co., Inc., in talking about the collaborative approach to management says:

> We feel that this type of approach recognizes that there is a secret ballot going on at all times among the people in any business. They vote for or against their supervisors. A favorable vote for the supervisor shows up in the cooperation, teamwork, understanding, and production of the group. To win this secret ballot, each supervisor must share the problems of his group and work for them.[3]

The decision to spend time listening to his employees is a decision each supervisor or executive has to make for himself. Executives seldom have much to do with products or processes. They have to deal with people who must in turn deal with people who will deal with products or processes. The higher one goes up the line the more he will be concerned with human relations problems, simply because people are all he has to work with. The minute we take a man from his bench and make him a foreman he is removed from the basic production of goods and now must begin relating to individuals instead of nuts and bolts. People are different from things, and our foreman is called upon for a different line of skills completely. His new tasks call upon him to be a special kind of person. The development of himself as a listener is a first step in becoming this special person.

## Notes

1. "Productivity, Supervision, and Employee Morale," *Human Relations,* Series 1, Report 1 (Ann Arbor, Mich.: Survey Research Center, University of Michigan).
2. Robert L. Kahn, "The Human Factors Underlying Industrial Productivity," *Michigan Business Review* (November 1952).
3. G.L. Clements, "Time for 'Democracy in Action' at the Executive Level," the A.M.A. Personnel Conference, February 28, 1951.

# 19

# The Hiring Interview

*Robert L. Minter*

"She's a nice person, likes to ski, has good feelings about her father—I think she'd be a good addition to our staff."

Preposterous? Yes. But too often, employment interviews yield a lot of peripheral information about an applicant and fail to delve into such important areas as work background, experience, and career aspirations. Regardless of size, purpose, or function, all organizations use some type of interview-screening process in recruiting personnel. But despite its wide use, the hiring interview is one of the most misunderstood and misused methods of communication.

Too often, people responsible for hiring receive little or no formal training in interviewing job applicants and so are unaware of the ways in which their interviewing styles influence an applicant's behavior. Organizations that do train their interviewers may give them only general information on company manpower requirements and personnel-placement policies. Rarely is an interviewer trained in the specific communication skills he needs to be effective.

Some personnel interviewers apparently feel that communication skills go along with common sense. They refuse even to consider special training. "I don't need training! I've been interviewing for years and the company has been satisfied." Part of this statement may be true (i.e., he has been interviewing for years), but whether he has been successful depends on the criteria used.

When an organization has high turnover and absenteeism, or when it must give new employees more on-the-job training than initially contemplated, its interviewing success must be termed something less than successful. Of course, not all problems with absenteeism, turnover, and on-the-job training stem from ineffective interviewing, but a large portion of such problems *can* be traced back to improper use of interview-screening procedures. (Communication problems are frequently created by interviewers who lack dialogue training or who are insensitive to the communication sins listed in Table 1.)

**TABLE 19.1**

**Common Sins of the Employment Interviewer**

1. The interviewer talks a lot and listens only a little—so gets sketchy information from which to assess the applicant's potential.

2. The interviewer fails to tell the applicant the major aim of the interview.

3. The interviewer wastes time by asking irrelevant questions. He may, for example, request information that is already on the application form or ask questions that range far afield from the job skills and attitudes needed for the vacancy.

4. The interview is disorganized because the interviewer has vague interview objectives and talks about whatever he is in the mood to.

5. The interviewer biases applicant responses by providing job information too early in the interview.

6. The interviewer "plays" psychologist by atttempting an in-depth personality assessment.

7. The interviewer believes that the best way to assess an applicant's potential is to observe his behavior under stress—and then provides the necessary stress.

8. The interviewer overreacts to body language, permitting first impressions to stereotype the applicant.

9. The interviewer doesn't have enough information about the problems of the particular job (e.g., reasons for turnover, absenteeism, low morale, specific job duties and responsibilities not covered in the job description).

10. Because he screens too many applicants within a short period of time, the interviewer falls prey to fatigue—fatigue that influences his assessment and attitude toward applicants.

11. The interviewer overemphasizes or otherwise misues the applicant's test results.

12. The interviewer attempts to conduct a thorough interview in ten to fifteen minutes.

13. The interviewer misinterprets letters of reference.

14. The interviewer oversells the job and the company—thus building false hopes and expectations that are very likely to end up in turnover statistics.

If any bells are ringing or if you are wondering how you and your company shape up, compare your procedures with those outlined here. Most effective interviewing procedures can be broken down into three distinct sequences—each with specific goals and appropriate methods for achieving them.

### Screening Procedures

If an organization is interested in a particular applicant, he may be given a battery of selection tests to assess such things as skills, aptitudes, and achievement. Some organizations (and some jobs) require only that an application form be completed in this first sequence.

If the applicant "passes" these initial tests, he usually moves on to a more thorough interview.

However, two basic facts should be established before thorough selection-interviewing techniques are used.

1. The applicant has met basic selection criteria (such as appropriate work experience, education, test scores, letters of reference, training, and skills) required for the position.
2. The interviewer is well informed about existing job requirements and demands of the vacant position.

If the interviewer believes the applicant is underqualified or over-qualified for the position, or has questionable letters of reference, then conducting a lengthy interview could waste time and motion for all concerned.

### In-Depth Interviewing

The second sequence, in-depth interviewing, is designed to get information about the applicant's work experience, work attitudes, and motivation for applying for a particular position. It is also used to clear up any hazy information the applicant gave on the application form and to fill in any omissions. Several interview stages could be involved in this sequence, depending on the recruitment policy and size of the organization. Here are the major interview stages of this second sequence.

#### First-Stage Interview

This interview is quite short if the applicant does not seem to meet the job requirements. The interviewer tries to tell the applicant, tactfully, why he does not qualify for the position. In some instances, the interviewer may briefly counsel the applicant on firms in the area that have openings appropriate for him.

But if the first-stage interviewer believes on the basis of general exploratory questioning that the applicant has the necessary qualifications, he will then recommend considering the applicant for a second-stage interview. Of course, if the first-stage interviewer may decide whether to hire or not, further interviews are not necessary.

#### Subsequent Interviews

The number of interviews scheduled for a particular applicant will often depend on the type of job in question. The interview schedule can usually be cancelled anywhere along the interview chain if an interviewer believes the applicant to be unqualified.

Before seeing applicants, interviewers who are not familiar with the vacant position must bone up on its requirements. Job descriptions help, but they do not provide all the information required to develop meaningful position-related questions. Most job descriptions do not and cannot include the many day-to-day duties and problems inherent in the job.

Suppose you are responsible for screening applicants for the position of administrative secretary, and you have several applicants to interview. You are given the following job description

> Position Title: Administrative Secretary
> Responsibilities: The administrative secretary supervises a secretarial pool of approximately ten stenographer-typists who are responsible for taking dictation, typing, filing, and general clerical work. The administrative secretary reports directly to the manager of the commercial office. On occasion, the administrative secretary will be asked to do personal secretarial work for the vice-president of the commercial office. The major responsibility of the incumbent is to be responsible for the entire clerical and secretarial function of the commercial office. The incumbent must have at least a high-school diploma along with several years experience as a private secretary; must be a proficient typist; and must demonstrate the ability to supervise others.
> Salary: Salary will be commensurate with experience ($9,000 to $11,000)

What additional information would you need before interviewing the applicants?

First, you would want to know how many interviewers will be involved and who will cover what areas. Once you know this, you can begin planning the areas to cover and the questions to ask each applicant.

You should also know something about the history of the job you are trying to fill. The following are examples of the kinds of information you should have at hand before you begin interviewing:

1. The rate and reasons for employee turnover and/or absenteeism.
2. The difficulties, if any, that the manager or vice-president of the commercial office has had with past administrative secretaries.
3. The problems inherent in the secretarial pool that the administrative secretary will have to cope with.
4. Any unusual demands of the position that are not stated in the job description.

5. The current expectations of the manager and vice-president regarding the qualities they look for in the administrative secretary.

Now suppose you talk to the manager and vice-president of the commercial office and learn that:

1. Absenteeism and turnover are extremely high in the secretarial pool. Consequently, if a backlog of work builds up, the administrative secretary will be expected to pitch in and help with work normally done only by secretaries. Unexpected absences and turnover in the secretarial pool have frequently required the administrative secretary to work as much as ten to fifteen hours of overtime per week.
2. Within the past year and a half, three administrative secretaries have worked in the commercial department. The new administrative secretary will be the fourth. The average time of the job for each administrative secretary has been approximately six months. Some of the past incumbents have quit because of job pressure. The combination of serving as personal secretary for two administrators and shouldering supervisory responsibilities for the secretarial pool created most of the stress.
3. Because some of the former administrative secretaries did not have cars, they had to depend on public transportation. Working overtime often made it quite difficult for them to catch the last bus of the evening and created baby-sitting problems for some.

Based on what is know from the job analysis, the following position-related questions could be pursued with individual applicants during the interview:

1. What is the applicant's philosophy of supervision?
2. How does the applicant feel about assuming the many role responsibilities required of a supervisor in this position?
3. What type of on-the-job pressure does the applicant appear to dislike? Like?
4. What does the applicant consider to be the greatest number of employees he feels comfortable in supervising?
5. How does he feel about training new secretarial personnel and working with a relatively inexperienced staff caused by a high turnover rate?
6. What is the applicant's opinion on the way to manage a secretarial pool?
7. How does the applicant feel about having to work for more than one boss?
8. What is the applicant's attitude toward "pinch-hitting" for some of the secretaries when they are absent?
9. What would be the applicant's mode of transportation?

10. What is the applicant's attitude toward overtime? Even if he appears to be enthusiastic, it pays to probe a bit.

During each stage, interviewers should avoid playing psychologist. Employment interviewers are usually not professionally qualified to assess anything more than surface personality attributes and social skills. Samples of questions that should be avoided follow (notice that these questions are clinically oriented and would require psychological expertise in analyzing the applicant's responses):

"How do you feel about your family?"
"To what degree can you take instructions without feeling upset?"
"Which of your parents has had the most profound influence on you?"
"What is the most difficult personal decision you've had to make?"
"Tell me about your home life during the time you were growing up."
"Who are your best friends? Why?"
"Tell me a story."

## Improving Procedures

Regardless of the number of stages involved in the interview-screening process, several guidelines can improve its overall effectiveness and efficiency. One is to make sure that each interviewer has specific responsibilities and objectives for his interview—without much overlap or duplication of effort among interviewers.

The role of the first-stage interviewer, for example, might be to assess the completed application form for omissions, vagueness, and innuendoes that require clarification. This interviewer might also explore the applicant's aspirations, job expectations, career objectives, and likes and dislikes for specific types of work. If the first-stage interviewer is impressed with the interviewee's credentials, he may recommend the applicant to someone else for a second-stage interview.

The responsibilities of the second-stage interviewer might be to assess the applicant's training and job experience and to explore his abilitiy to apply these to problem solving. (This would assume that the second interviewer has more experience with the particular job vacancy and is able to develop more task-relevant questions than the previous interviewer.)

The responsibilities of the final-stage interviewer might be to discover questions the interviewee has but did not ask earlier interviewers. He could also explore information the applicant obtained from previous interviewers and try to clear up any misunderstandings for the applicant. Salary negotiations could also take place here.

Communication among interviewers before the interview process begins, as well as discussion before and after each interview, will enhance the planning and effectiveness of the over-all screening sequence. This kind of interaction can give interviewers insight into the questioning strategy each should emphasize.

However, interviewers should avoid communicating impressions and feelings that will bias those who have not yet interviewed the applicant. Potential bias can be controlled if earlier interviewers limit comments to areas of information that require further exploration.

Specific job information should not be given to the applicant too early in the interview chain. Providing premature job information usually tempts the applicant to answer questions in terms of what he thinks the interviewer wants to hear. Interviewers should try to discover as much as possible about the applicant's background and work attitudes before filling him in on job specifics.

Recruiters in the interview chain should decide on the point at which to give the applicant job specifics. The deductive method (general to specific questioning) should be used to obtain applicant information as well as to give job information.

### TABLE 19.2

#### Checklist for the Interviewing Process

1. What pre-interview selection criteria will be used?

2. How many interviews will be involved in the interview chain for qualified applicants?

3. How knowledgeable are the interviewers about the job vacancy?

4. What are the reasons for turnover, absenteeism, low morale, and/or grievances for the job vacancy? Are the interviewers familiar with these reasons?

5. Do the interviewers know their specific roles in the interview chain?

6. Do the interviewers' roles overlap too much?

7. Should any interviewers be omitted or added to the interview chain to improve the efficiency and effectiveness of the process?

8. How are the test results, letters of reference, and interview results to be weighed?

9. Have past employers and references been checked?

10. What minimum standards have to be met in the first interview stage to qualify an applicant for further interview stages?

11. What channels of communication have been established to transmit information from one interviewer to the next without biasing the latter?

12. How much job information is to be given to the applicant in various interview stages, and by whom is it to be given?

13. Do the interviewers know the restrictions placed upon them by job discrimination and civil-rights laws?

14. How are the interviewers going to explore the job knowledge and work attitudes of applicants?

15. How are interviewers attempting to guard against in-depth personality assessment?

After each applicant has completed the interview chain, the interviewers can pool their information and make a decision on whether to hire. Often, however, the decision-making process is simple. Interviewers may have mixed opinions about the applicants. And some will inevitably believe that additional information is required before a final decision can be made.

# 20

# Guidelines for Conducting the Performance Appraisal Interview: A Literature Synthesis

*Michael Stano*

Much has been written regarding the complex, multidimensional process of performance appraisal interviewing. Despite the plethora of treatises on the subject, little synthesis has been attempted; no single source draws the wealth of literature together to form a comprehensive set of guidelines for conducting interviews. The intent of this article is to correct this deficiency by presenting a list of directives for assessment sessions, based on an extensive review of the appraisal literature. In addition, recommendations will be offered for future investigations of evaluation discussions and a set of references will be provided which should guide the researcher.

## Interview Guidelines

*1. Plan the Interview.*

With an employee's performance rating in hand, managers are advised to spend some time preparing for the interview. Often, the quality of the interview is dependent on the extent and nature of the preparation.

Specifically, managers ought to review all information in the worker's personnel file including not only data tied to the relevant performance period but past accomplishments and problems as well. Based on these accumulated facts, the supervisor can formulate flexible objectives for the pending interview and determine the means by which these objectives can best be achieved.

The interview focus should be narrow rather than broad; its aims modest rather than elaborate. Further, in its best form, the interview ought to be confined either to the objective of development or to the objective of performance-salary review. It is almost universally agreed that it is deleterious to combine the development and salary discussions in one interview.

Whether or not the employee does any advance work is largely dependent on the type of interview the manager intends to conduct. If the discussion is to be totally directed by the supervisor, little planning on the part of the subordinate is required. If, on the other hand, the employee is to be more than just a reactor, he/she needs to take the same preliminary steps as the employer. The nature and value of a participative interviewee role is discussed later.

*2. Set an Appropriate Time.*

The principle concern in scheduling the interview is determining the amount of time that should be allocated for it. No hard and fast rules governing this facet of the process can be laid out.

*3. Choose an Appropriate Setting.*

Appraisal interviews are often held in the manager's office and too few people realize the threat this can introduce. The best place for the discussion is in neutral territory where neither subordinate nor supervisor feel uncomfortable.

Wherever the interview is located, the manager should try to guarantee complete privacy and freedom from even the most minor interruptions such as telephone calls and uninvolved persons.

Once isolated in the chosen room, the manager ought not allow barriers to fill the space between him/her and the employee. An interceding expanse of desk, especially if it is cluttered with papers, can serve to distance the worker physically and psychologically. Side-to-side or corner seating is preferred.

*4. Concentrate on Results rather than Personality.*

Manager and employee ought to discuss job outputs or results rather than personality issues because trait analysis often leads to unproductive defensiveness:

> In companies where people are judged on the basis of the results of their work and where an attempt is made to orient the appraisal discussion to the jobs, rarely if ever is a healthy relationship between supervisor and subordinate destroyed. . . .
>
> On the other hand, in companies whose rating forms focus on personality traits, appraisal interviews are usually carried out half-heartedly, in an atmosphere of mutual embarrassment, and with little success.[1]

Recent court decisions regarding EEOC requirements suggest another reason for concentrating on results. Employers who base appraisals on vague or subjective data are liable to litigation; to be legal and nondiscriminatory, ratings of performance must stem from job analyses, and it is doubtful that many personality variables could survive the validation procedures.

## 5. Consider Variables outside the Employee's Control.

If a subordinate fails an assigned task it may be due to his/her own negligence. Alternatively, other forces in the organization could have so hindered the employee's ability to work that he or she cannot be held responsible.

## 6. Discuss the Employee's Future with the Company.

Whether development or salary oriented, the appraisal interview should explore the subordinate's future within the company. Workers want to know not only where they have been but also where they are going, and a discussion of career opportunities is therefore both desirable and appropriate.

## 7. Explore the Requirements of the Job.

The performance review session should be viewed as a time to exchange and refine job descriptions and to communicate and clarify evaluation criteria.

## 8. Outline Goals for Future Performance.

In the salary review, a consideration of future performance goals is not usually relevant, but this subject will most likely occupy more time than any other in developmental sessions. Perhaps the most important criterion for quality goals is that they be clear and specific rather than "do your best" in nature.

In addition to being specific, goals should focus on concrete, observable, and measurable behaviors. To the extent possible, the level of attainment or performance targets ought to be assessable by quantifiable means, for goals centering on countable phenomena force appraisals to deal with results and discourage analyses of personality.

Goals should also be challenging to the individual. This is not to say that goals should be impossibly difficult; it should be feasible for the employee to achieve the target. By necessity, goals must be matched to the capabilities of each individual.

Finally, selected objectives should be prioritized by the supervisor and subordinate. Since it is not feasible for the worker to concentrate at once on all aspects of development, it is necessary to devote some discussion time to determining which goals should be tackled immediately and which should be deferred.

In sum, goal-setting is an important activity which should be included in most nonsalary performance appraisal interviews. Whether goals are established by the manager alone, the employee alone, or the two jointly, they should be specific, prioritized, measurable, challenging, and satisfactory to both worker and company.

## 9. Give Appropriate Praise and Criticism.

Professional managers disagree regarding the form feedback on performance should take. Some contend that employees truly like criticism while others argue that negative comments inherently arouse feelings of embarrassment, hostility, and defensiveness, and ultimately lead to a breakdown of communication, excuse making, resentment of the appraisal process, and lower levels of production. At the opposite end of the evaluation continuum the same dilemma is present. It is said that workers need to be praised for their achievements but praise can also generate defensiveness, and the presence or absence of it has little bearing on later job efforts.[2]

Supervisors cannot simply refuse to deal with this subject because the interviewee's reaction is so unpredictable. The topic must be discussed because, at least in some instances, it has the potential of providing a foundation for learning. The key to the problem seems *not* to lie in skirting the issue entirely but rather in circumventing the debilitating effects of evaluation. Difficulties may be avoided a number of ways. First, the proper balance should be struck between praise and criticism. Frequently, appraisers provide negative feedback in overkill doses; it is *excessive* criticism, not criticism per se, which is disruptive.[3] If Farson and Bordonaro[4] are correct in their argument that praise can be threatening too, workers may have a "tolerance level" for positive evaluation as well and managers should, as a result, be wary of appearing overly supportive. In the final analysis, it would be wise to attempt to establish an appropriate ratio between comments of approval and of condemnation.

A second method of minimizing hard feelings during evaluation concerns the time placement of praise and criticism. Common to older "how-to" appraisal interview manuals is the suggestion that criticism be "sandwiched" by praise. This technique involves placing a negative statement between two positive ones and allegedly the pro-con-pro sequence makes the discussion of failings easier to accept. Most employees, however, quickly become aware of the manager's attempt to be clever and consequently the strategy usually falls short of its intended purpose. A more highly recommended procedure is to dispense supportive feedback almost exclusively at the beginning of the interview. This tactic helps establish an initial positive climate and once aware that his/her supervisor is duly appreciative of past successes, the subordinate becomes more receptive to a thorough analysis of those areas in which there is room for improvement.

Giving the proper kind of criticism can also reduce the defensiveness workers so often experience. Criticism should be based on objective evidence, observed examples, and factual information rather than on subjective impressions. In addition, criticism ought to be constructive in nature; instead of dwelling on past failures, the focus should be on what specific actions can be taken to eliminate future performance deficiencies.

## 10. Stay on the Subject.

Managers must exert control to prevent needless detours, escapes, and irrelevant exchanges. While some deviation from the point is allowable, the supervisor and subordinate have a well defined job to do during the session and they should not aimlessly wander into subject areas outside the theme of the meeting.

## 11. Utilize Summaries.

For clarity, it is important that interviewers make use of initial and final discussion summaries. A preview of where the interview is going builds trust in the supervisor, allows the subordinate to organize his/her thoughts, upgrades the quality of employee contributions, and generally improves session efficiency. A recapitulation of main ideas expressed better assures mutual agreement on specified plans of action.

## 12. Establish the Proper Climate.

The climate present in an appraisal interview is affected by a complex array of interlocking and intangible variables. Overall, communication will be more open and honest and problem solving will be facilitated if the manager can genuinely consider the employee as equal and can appear spontaneous, friendly, supportive, sensitive to and interested in the difficulties of the worker, understanding, cooperative, nonjudgmental with regard to feelings revealed, nonmanipulative, concerned for the dignity and worth of the individual, trusting, and confident of the employee's abilities. Obviously, the tone of the interview is dependent not only on what occurs within its confines but also on the day-to-day working relationship of supervisor and subordinate. To establish the proper discussion climate requires ongoing, continuous effort.

### 13. Allow Subordinate Participation.

Most commonly, subordinates are drawn into the appraisal process in one of two ways. First, employees may be required to prepare their own set of future performance objectives. A second method of drawing in the worker, often used in conjunction with the first, is to have him/her do a self appraisal of performance.

It is crucial that subordinate goal setting and evaluation does not totally absolve the manager of responsibility for what happens in the interview or make obsolete any of the substantive or style guidelines previously mentioned. The supervisor must still plan, schedule, give praise and criticism, etc., as he/she would if the discussion were nonparticipative, but accountability for session quality becomes a mutual concern and the position of the manager shifts from that of a dictator to that of a counselor who guides and assists more subtly. This altered function, instead of removing obligations, places new demands on the supervisor. He/she must be more open minded with regard to discussion organization and content, more flexible in terms of solutions to work problems, and more willing to negotiate changes in the management-made rating of performance should the employee provide reasons for doing so. Furthermore, the supervisor must acquire new skills aimed at encouraging the subordinate to talk. Optimally, the interviewee should monopolize from 40% to 60% of the discussion time in the participative interview,[5] and this goal is accomplished only when the manager has been taught to listen carefully and accurately, to give reflective feedback, and to ask appropriate, open-ended, nondirective questions.

Even though there are added burdens to be shouldered by the interactants when this style of interviewing is employed, the potential dividends are significant. Discussions tend to be more productive, meaningful, constructive, and satisfying. Defensiveness and other hostile reactions are quelled, and attitudes regarding the quality of supervision and the overall value of the entire appraisal process shift in the positive direction. Supervisors and subordinates are better able to pool their resources and the two-way flow of communication can be enlightening and educational for both. Worker involvement in the interview results in mutually set and agreed upon goals which, compared to manager-set objectives, are simultaneously more reasonable and difficult, better accepted and internalized by the subordinate, more highly

motivating, and achieved with greater frequency. Finally, self appraisals are often fairer and in other ways superior to supervisor appraisals.

All of the advantages stemming from participation seem to accrue
whether or not the subordinate actually becomes involved in the
interview. Employee knowledge that he/she can contribute if he/she
wants to is sufficient to obtain the desired result.[6]

The participative approach to interviewing is not a panacea and
although some studies have shown that it can be used equally well by
all supervisors with all employees in all circumstances,[7] it would be
more realistic to contend that it should be applied with some degree of
selectivity. Some managers may be more successful utilizing subordinate participation than others; and some interviewees, especially those
with experience and those with high independence needs, may respond
more favorably to the active role than do job novices low on authoritarianism.

### Summary of Guidelines

Based on the material available, it may be concluded that appraisal
discussions approach the ideal when an effort is made to:

1. Plan the interview.
2. Set an appropriate time.
3. Choose an appropriate setting.
4. Concentrate on results rather than personality.
5. Consider variables outside the employee's control.
6. Discuss the employee's future with the company.
7. Explore the requirements of the job.
8. Develop goals for future performance.
9. Give appropriate praise and criticism.
10. Stay on the subject.
11. Utilize summaries.
12. Establish the proper climate.
13. Allow subordinate participation.

### Recommendations for Future Investigations

An examination of the foregoing directives and literature might cause
one to believe that no need exists for additional research on performance appraisal interviews. Such is not the case; the individual who
wishes to delve into the process of assessment sessions might follow
any number of avenues.

Scholars might attempt to document empirically the relationship
between specific guidelines and productive interviews. While some of
the concepts mentioned, such as participation, goal setting, and the

effects of criticism, have been tested in quasi-experimental settings, the literature is, on the whole, rather anecdotal and of the "folklore" variety. Until more substantial and reliable data is gathered, caution is advised when applying the guidelines.

The situationality of the guidelines could also be probed. Currently, most directives are treated as more or less universally applicable. It is reasonable to contend, however, that some variables might be relevant in one context and not relevant in others. Keeley (1977), for example, has suggested that results-centered appraisals are not appropriate in certain occupations. Efforts aimed at determining the relative weight or importance of other suggestions for the appraisal discussion would seem useful.

The interviewee's role in the appraisal discussion deserves further definition. Most published material is designed for consumption by the manager, and the subordinate is infrequently provided with solid, explicit guidelines for his/her behavior.

A final recommendation for research is that we begin to examine the impact of sex roles on appraisal. Thus far, investigators have ignored the effects of the sex of the participants on assessment discussions.

*Conclusion*

This paper has attempted to integrate the literature concerning appraisal interviews. While the list of topics is comprehensive, the set of references which follows may be incomplete; the appraisal literature is broad and forever proliferating and to provide total coverage is an impossible task. Nevertheless, managers, consultants, and teachers of courses in organization behavior, organizational communication, and interviewing should find in the guidelines and references stimulus for reflection, training, or research.

### Notes

1. R.K. Stolz, "Can Appraisal Be Made Effective?" *Personnel*(1961), vol. 38, no. 2, p. 32.
2. F.P. Bordonaro, "The Dilemma Created by Praise," *Business Horizons*(1976), vol. 19. no. 5, pp. 76–81; and R.E. Farson, "Praise Reappraised," *Harvard Business Review*(1963), vol. 41, no. 5, pp. 61–66.
3. H.H. Meyer, E. Kay, and J.R.P. French, Jr., "Split Roles in Performance Appraisal," *Harvard Business Review*(1965), vol. 43, no. 1, pp. 123–29.
4. Farson, *op. cit.*; and Bordonaro, *op. cit.*
5. H.E. Crawford, "A Descriptive Analysis of the Employee Appraisal Interview in an Industrial Organization," Ph.D. dissertation, University of Minnesota, 1974; *Dissertation Abstracts International*(1974), vol. 35, no. 1266a(University Microfilms No. 71–17, 237), p. 49; N.R.F. Maier, *The*

*Appraisal Interview: Objectives, Methods, and Skills*(New York: John Wiley, 1958), p. 169; H. Mayfield, "In Defense of Performance Appraisal," *Harvard Business Review*(1960), vol. 38. no. 2, pp. 81–87; R. Parkinson, "Recipe for a Realistic Appraisal System," *Personnel Management*(1977), vol. 9, no. 11, pp. 37–40.

6. M.M. Greller, "Subordinate Participation and Reactions to the Appraisal Interview," *Journal of Applied Psychology*(1975), vol. 60, pp. 544–49.

7. R.J. Hayden, "Performance Appraisal: A Better Way," *Personnel Journal* (1973), vol. 52, pp. 606–13; G.P. Latham and G.A. Yuki, "Effects of Assigned and Participative Goal Setting on Job Satisfaction," *Journal of Applied Psychology* (1976), vol. 61; pp. 166–71; A.L. Patz, "Performance Appraisal: Useful But Still Resisted," *Harvard Business Review*(1975), vol. 53, no. 3, pp. 74–80; H.A. Tosi, "A Re-examination of Personality as a Determinant of the Effects of Participation," *Personnel Psychology* (1970), vol. 23, pp. 91–99; and K.N. Wexley, J.P. Singh, and G.A. Yuki, "Subordinate Personality as a Moderator of the Effects of Participation in Three Types of Appraisal Interviews," *Journal of Applied Psychology*(1973), vol. 58, pp. 54–59.

# 21

# Encountering the Media

*Barry J. McLoughlin*

**Why is communication through the media so important?**

In one appearance on the CBS program *Sixty Minutes,* a corporate executive, union leader, or government representative would reach more people than if he or she gives a speech to 20,000 people every night of the week for five years.

Realizing the extent of media's impact, thousands of North American executives are flocking to media consultants to learn how to "survive" and indeed maximize the potential of media encounters.

Many companies have realized the financial benefits of media exposure. The spiraling cost of paid media makes it prohibitive for smaller companies to advertise extensively; thus, they are increasingly turning their attention to attracting media interest to their products or services.

Political candidates have long recognized the value to their campaigns of exposure on the six o'clock news. Indeed, many campaign events are designed solely for that purpose!

In recent years the media have realized the enormous audience appeal of the business person as media celebrity. Witness the emergence of Lee Iacocca, T. Boone Pickens, Victor Kiam, Mary Kay, or countless other executives who have been firmly placed in the consciousness of millions of North Americans as a consequence of media exposure.

Executives in organizations of all kinds are now recognizing the value of learning how to communicate their issues and concerns more effectively through the media.

### Learning To Communicate

In order to communicate effectively through the media, the organization must place articulate communicators in the front lines. In order to be effective, the spokespersons must know some fundamental techniques for getting across the message and becoming more assertive in their communications.

Maximizing effectiveness means learning how to

- be succinct
- focus on the message
- deflect side issues and hostility
- stay in control of responses
- project a full three-dimensional personality

Those who are strongly opposed to an organization or its policies or plans will have their opinions reinforced by negative stories and will ignore the positive ones. Those who are strong supporters will tend to look askance at negative stories. Therefore, it is the public in the middle (the "don't know's" and "undecided's") who must be the focus of attention during an encounter with the media. It is important to reach this group and to communicate to them, through the interviewer or the reporter.

It is easy to associate the reporter with the opponents or critics. Reporters tend to ask questions that critics would normally be expected to ask. In this way, they sharpen up the "two sides to the story." It is essential that the interview subject does not ignore the thousands listening, watching, or reading who would like more information before making up their minds.

Comments must be addressed to this audience *through* the media. The executive's goal should not be to convince the reporter, but to communicate to the public.

## The Negotiation

### Whether Or Not To Go On The Record?

One can negotiate the interview to be

1. "on the record": where everything that is said can be quoted and attributed
2. "off the record": where nothing can be used and the source can't be identified in any way
3. "not for attribution" or "background": wherein content can be quoted but source can't be identified.

A reporter should not be tempted beyond journalistic endurance. He or she can repeat an "off the record" tidbit to colleagues at the Press Club bar; and since those colleagues were not party to any prior "negotiated arrangement," they can feel free to use that information in a subsequent story.

In summary, the interviewee must never provide a reporter with information that cannot withstand the glare of publicity in the media. In short, there are no guarantees.

### The Key to Effectiveness

Very few people give any thought to the structure of their answers when asked a question. Yet here the seeds of effectiveness or, conversely, ineffectiveness are planted.

### Unstructured Answers: The Traditional Response

Let's examine a typical response to a reporter's question:

Q. "Why is your organization changing its mind on this issue?"

A. "Well in order to understand the present you've got to go back to the past. Our organization began examining this issue . . . oh back in 1962. And at that time we adopted an analytical approach to the policy. So it wasn't until oh . . . about . . . 1968 . . ."

Q. (Interrupting) "But what about today?"

A. "Yeah well I'm coming to that. So anyway in 1968 our basic approach was to take a little more aggressive . . ."

This response is boring, filled with historical but useless information and, most importantly, leaves the interviewee totally vulnerable to the reporter's interruption at any point.

Unity of thought in a lengthy response is difficult. Combined with nervous apprehension, the two offer a prescription for a major blunder. Besides, it is difficult for the casual viewer or listener to absorb more than one bite-size chunk of information at a time. Each new piece of information tends to cancel out the memory and impact of the one preceding it. The result is a mass of words with an obscured message.

The recommended approach involves visualizing a wedge pattern in the mind while formulating a response (see fig. 21-1).

### Notes on the "Wedge" Structure (Ref. fig. 21-1)

### Initial Brief Answer

Notice that the initial answer is brief. This deliberate brevity forces the reporter to pursue the idea further in order to avoid an awkward pause. The answer should contain the essential theme or message.

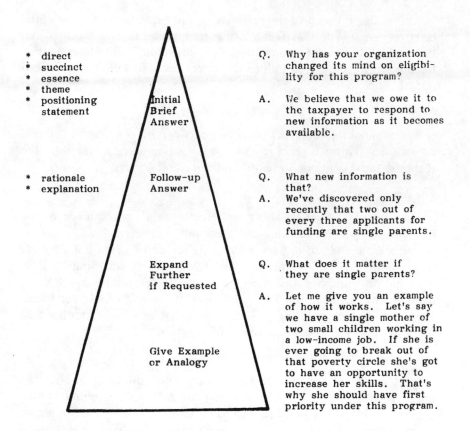

Q. Why has your organization
changed its mind on eligibility for this program?

* direct
* succinct
* essence
* theme
* positioning
  statement

Initial
Brief
Answer

A. We believe that we owe it to
the taxpayer to respond to
new information as it becomes
available.

* rationale
* explanation

Follow-up
Answer

Q. What new information is
that?
A. We've discovered only
recently that two out of
every three applicants for
funding are single parents.

Expand
Further
if Requested

Q. What does it matter if
they are single parents?

A. Let me give you an example
of how it works. Let's say
we have a single mother of
two small children working in
a low-income job. If she is
ever going to break out of
that poverty circle she's got
to have an opportunity to
increase her skills. That's
why she should have first
priority under this program.

Give Example
or Analogy

**Fig. 21.1**
**The McLoughlin wedge**

Thus the interviewee sets the agenda of the interview, and the unclut-
tered message registers clearly with the viewer or listener.

This brevity has an additional benefit in that it gives the interviewee
more time to formulate directional strategy, whereby each response
promotes a desired supplementary follow-up question.

Another way to begin is with a "positioning statement" that puts
the question or issue in a broader context. In other words, you or your
organization is positioned properly on the subject before getting into
the specifics: For example, "We're opposed to any measure that will
restrict our ability to respond quickly."

### Follow-Up Answer

At this stage, you give the rationale or the explanation for the initial brief response. You may feel a strong temptation to give the explanation at the outset, but you must make a conscious effort to resist this temptation if you are to induce the interviewer to follow the desired line of logic.

### Expanded Further

At this juncture, sidetracks and tangents can be perilous and should be avoided. Through graphic examples, analogies, or metaphors, the response must continue to reinforce the essential message.

### The News Message

This message must be short and simple as a consequence of the extreme competition for time and space in the news media.

The message is *not* the seven-point policy or program but why the seven-point program is needed and what it will accomplish. It is essential to compose the message in advance and to couch it in newsworthy terms. Is it a "wrinkle" or a "spin-off" of a larger trend, event, or news story? Can your news message be framed in a "quotable" way that will encourage reporters to use it?

### The Quote or the Twelve-Second Clip

Print reporters are looking for a "quotable" quote of one to two lines. Television reporters are looking for a "clip" of about twelve seconds in length. A radio reporter is seeking a voice "clip" eight to twelve seconds in length. The remainder of any interview will be used for background information or to help compose the narrative portion of an article.

### Criteria for Choosing a Quote or Clip

The following are unwritten criteria reporters employ for choosing one clip or quote over another:

- self-contained; i.e., it stands on its own merits
- sums up succinctly the point of view
- colourful or metaphorical
- passionate or energetic
- uses everyday language rather than "bureaucratese" or jargon
- active—not passive
- direct—not indirect
- personal—relates to the individual in the audience

## EXAMPLES

| *Poor Clip* | *Good Clip* |
|---|---|
| "There are a number of alternative approaches which we might consider. The first one being that . . ." | "We came here to listen to people—not to make pronouncements." |
| "It's not apparent at this stage whether or not we can proceed. On one hand, it appears simple but on the other . . .". | "We want to do not only what's right—but what's fair." |
| "There exists a supposition that an in-depth analysis might reveal several options . . .". | "It's time we faced the music." |

### Bridges: Getting Your Message Across

If the interviewer is shifting the interview into uncomfortable areas, refocus the interview agenda by using bridging phrases or "bridges" to the essential message that has been prepared.

*Bridges*

> "Let's not deal with the symptoms; let's look at the underlying problem . . .".
>
> "Let's look at it from a broader perspective . . .".
>
> "Another way to approach it is . . .".
>
> "There's another more important concern and that is . . .".
>
> "Have you considered a more important question and that is . . .".
>
> "That's not the real issue! The real issue is . . .".
>
> "Let's set that argument aside . . .".

### The Television Interview: Right Brain vs. Left Brain

When we watch television, we are engaged in a nonlinear communication process that scientists tell us involves the right hemisphere of the brain. The right hemisphere houses our feelings and emotions. It is the illogical side—poetry, music, and fantasy are all experienced in an apparently unorganized (nonlinear) fashion through the right side.

Television is an electronic medium that projects a picture in a series of concentric circles with no beginning and no end. This, of course, is contrary to the process involved in reading. That process involves the left hemisphere of the brain that functions in a linear, logical fashion.

With print, one must read the words sequentially and absorb them in order to understand their meaning. With television, the process is holistic: We form our impressions as the information is being processed. That is why television is very effective in stimulating impressions, rather than providing detailed information.

People can think much faster than words can be spoken. While an individual is speaking on television, the viewer has ample time to think about how the speech is delivered, clothes, hair, grooming, and finally whether posture and appearance are impressive. None of these observations can be made in the process of reading the same quotation in the newspaper.

In summary then, it is important to concentrate not just on the *what,* but on the *how* of the message.

### Suggestions for a Television Interview

Feel free to suggest to the reporter a more interesting backdrop for the interview. Executives should avoid being interviewed behind their desk. The viewer will instinctively think of them as "bureaucratic" or out of touch with the "real world." An interview that takes place outside the office reinforces the image of an active involved individual, in touch with the external environment.

If this alternative is not possible, suggest that the interview take place in a more comfortable location, such as a sitting room with a sofa and coffee table. The person will look less austere and aloof, and, most importantly, feel more comfortable.

Remember, television has its own logic. If, for example, an interview about the fishing industry takes place on a wharf, the setting produces far greater credibility and impact than a videotaped office interview. The individual seems connected to the issue being discussed.

### The Reality Of The Television Interview

Television is an intimate medium. Do not think of it necessarily as a "mass" medium. At the forefront of the mind should be the image of one person watching in his or her living room. The task is to connect with that one individual.

Therefore, it is important to identify with that person on a one-to-one basis.

A "one-to-one" rapport with an interviewer will be transmitted and recreated with the viewer. Keep the tone conversational.

Maintain eye contact with the interviewer, while talking and listening. Do not look around the studio or at the camera. Talk with the interviewer, focus complete attention on him or her.

There is one exception to this rule, however. On programs such as ABC's *Nightline,* when the interview is by distance via a television camera (known as a "double-ender"); look directly into the camera lens as if the lens itself is the interviewer's eyes. Do not look at the television monitor. Imagine the person is in the studio. The need to attain intimacy is even greater in this situation in order to counter the impersonal nature of the format.

Television accentuates mannerisms. A quick pace seems even quicker. If a pause is too long, it seems like an eternity. If one's nonverbal communication is distracting, it's far worse than would be the case in an ordinary conversation.

## Some Personal Do's and Don't's

### Perception

Like it or not, in television perception is reality. If you are perceived to be in control or to have answered the question, then to all intents and purposes you have done so.

### Getting Started

The first minute of the interview is critical:

- you are not certain of what to expect;
- you are in unfamiliar surroundings;
- you have to "get in step" or "slip into the groove."

Try to be brief and light. It's not up to you to order the flow or to bear the burden of the interview dynamics. That's the interviewer's responsibility.

Don't rush your responses; the interviewer feels pressure also. Keep your answers brief, usually one or two sentences. Then cease. Lean on your answer with silence. The pressure thereby is passed to the interviewer. The worst sins on television are answers that are too long, convoluted, jargon-filled, and flat!

Project energy and interest. Think to yourself: "I'm having this interesting dialogue with a fascinating person." It will show in voice and face. It's called "psyching yourself up."

### The Stand-Up Interview

A common scenario for an interview immediately following a speech is a hallway or lobby. One, two, or more reporters can be gathered in a designated interview room, or even inside the main meeting room itself.

Because each reporter is looking for a clip or quotation, the sequence of your answers is not important. This logic implies the following points:

1. Be succinct; otherwise your essential messages get buried.
2. Do not be afraid to repeat the substance of your message in response to a later question. Try not to say, "I repeat."
3. Avoid referring to an earlier answer; it's irrelevant and spoils the cohesion of the clip.
4. When several reporters are present, don't use an individual reporter's name in your answer; it discourages other broadcast reporters from using the clip.
5. Don't number or letter the points made in your answers. This makes for an awkward clip. Besides, people frequently get numbers and letters confused (i.e., "one . . . two . . . c . . ." or "a . . . b . . . three").
6. Don't be slavishly addicted to responding to every aspect of the question asked. The question is rarely included in the news clip, only the answer.
7. Answer only that aspect of the question with which you feel comfortable, or respond to the general thrust of the question. Don't blatantly ignore a question.
8. In a group situation, look directly at the interviewer addressing you. Don't look from one to the other, or you'll appear shifty and uncertain on a camera close-up.

The following are some suggestions for being interviewed "on the run":

1. Practice putting your head down when listening to a question. Keep it down until you think of an answer. Pause and then look up and deliver a clean self-contained "clip."
2. Slow down the pace. Pause before you begin to answer. Don't let the reporter hurry you.
3. If you suddenly remember a key point, say "I want to stress a very important point" (pause) and then deliver. Don't wait for the appropriate lead-in question. You might wait forever.

### Dealing With Hostility Or Perseverance

If you lose your temper in response to a loaded hostile question, you will probably be characterized as childish, petty, and out of control.

Instead, suppress the extreme emotion and politely but firmly challenge the interviewer's premise:

"I don't agree with your underlying premise . . ."

Your goal should be to get off the defensive and on to your positive message. Accomplish this end by dividing your answer into two elements: The first sentence is a quick clean disclaimer, such as: "Quite the contrary!", "Not at all," "That's a common misconception," "You couldn't be further from the mark." Then move to your message.

Remember, don't get into a sparring match! Show you have a sense of humour.

### Succeeding With The Interview

If you agree to be interviewed, buy yourself thirty to sixty minutes of time to think. Say you'll be glad to cooperate, but you would like some time to consult your files or colleagues. Then call back as promised. Never fail to return such a call.

Prepare properly by thinking of all possible questions and answers. The more precise and cogent, the better. Try out responses to the supplementary questions that might be invoked by your answers. Role-play with a colleague.

Think of the twelve-second clip you would like to appear on the news. This clip should sum up the message you want to put across. Practice appropriate responses to one or more probable questions.

Think of some concise examples to illustrate your message.

It's essential that you enter the interview with a high energy level and project this energy through your body language. If you project boredom, how can you expect the viewer or the listener to be interested? If you sound defensive, the audience will think you have something to hide or that you don't seem appropriately self-possessed.

If the interviewer is struggling for words, help out. Resist the opportunity to be condescending. With television or radio interviews, you must project an image of being helpful and fair. As a result, the reporter will respond better to you on a human level. This attitude can positively affect the tone of the ensuing story.

Finally, remember that the viewers, readers, and listeners appreciate honesty and sincerity. If you don't know the answer to a question, say so.

# Part VII

# DYNAMICS OF SMALL GROUP DECISION MAKING

# 22

# Communication in Micro-Networks

*Richard V. Farace, Peter R. Monge,*
and *Hamish M. Russell*

When people in social systems talk with one another on a regular basis, the patterns created by the messages they exchange are called communication networks. If the communication occurs in small groups the resultant patterns are called "micro-networks." If the communication patterns occur in large organizations they are called "macro-networks." This distinction is important because books on communication frequently discuss communication networks, but almost exclusively in terms of micro-networks. Large organizational macro-networks receive scant attention.

Knowledge about micro-networks developed out of research on whether different kinds of communication networks affected group performance. The question makes sense from an organizational viewpoint because organizations can exercise some degree of control over how members are organized and who may talk to whom.

The initial work that described micro-networks was published by Bavelas[1] and Leavitt[2], who developed procedures for studying communication networks in the small-group laboratory. Using a laboratory setting the researchers positioned people (initially five) around a table that was partitioned off so that each person was physically isolated. The only way group members could communicate was by sending messages through slots in the partition walls. The group was then assigned a task which required the participation of all group members. The specific network was imposed upon the group by controlling the slots each member could use to transmit messages. Some slots were open and some were closed, depending upon the network pattern.

Several types of networks were studied, utilizing both symmetrical (two-way) and asymmetrial (one-way) channels. Leavitt employed the circle, chain, Y, and wheel patterns. These four, as well as other networks that have been studied, are presented in Fig. 22.1.

The theoretical position articulated by Bavelas suggested that two

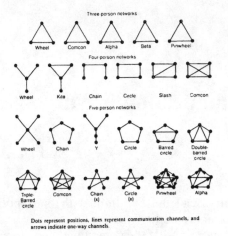

Dots represent positions, lines represent communication channels, and arrows indicate one-way channels.

**Fig. 22.1**
**Communication networks used in experimental investigation. Dots represent positions, lines represent communication channels, and arrows indicate one-way channels.**[1]

kinds of descriptors should be developed for networks. 1. those for individual positions within a network, and 2. those for the network as a whole. In general, indices for the network as a whole are simple sums of the individual measures. Leavitt argued that two concepts, centrality and peripherality, were of prime interest in the study of networks; he presented metrics for each.[4]

Subsequent investigation has examined the influence of several other variables. Shaw organizes these under three categories:

1. *Network-related variables:* group size, changes in network, opportunity to organize;
2. *Information-input variables:* noise, information distribution, reinforcement; and
3. *Group-composition variables:* ascendance, authoritarianism, leadership style, and popularity.[5]

These variables have been studied in relation to their effects on problem-solving efficiency, communication activity, organizational activity, and member satisfaction. They are typically measured by observational or questionnaire techniques.

Of the several dozen studies that have been conducted over the past two decades, only one consistent finding has emerged; it pertains to the concept of centrality. Centralized nets (e.g., wheel, Y) are more efficient—they permit faster problem solution with fewer errors—when dealing with simple tasks. Decentralized nets (e.g., circle, comcon) are more efficient when the task is complex. Decentralized nets, however, are more satisfying to group members, regardless of whether the task is simple or complex. The effects of other variables listed above have been reviewed, summarized, and tabled by Glanzer and Glaser,[6] Shaw,[7] and Collins and Raven.[8]

Unfortunately, there are several problems in attempting to apply the findings from small-group studies to larger organizations. First, the findings of the various studies are inconsistent and often contradictory. Nearly a quarter of a century of research has produced surprisingly little agreement among scientists as to the role that networks play in group processes.

Second, it is difficult to generalize the findings to small groups actually existing in large organizations, because the behavior of groups in the laboratory differs considerably from groups *embedded* in an organizational setting.[9] The point that Cohen and his associates make is that groups in an organization usually have a history, are clearly aware of power and status relations, and operate within the norms of the organizational context. Most small-group laboratory research, on the other hand, has used ad hoc, randomly formed groups without histories or a normative operating context.

Third, it is difficult to generalize the findings to groups larger in size than that used in the experimental design, since the findings seem to change as group size changes. Differences occur in the performance of three-, four-, and five-person groups, a fact which makes it unsafe to extend the findings to larger groups. This problem is all the more important if one considers that many if not most of the groups which operate within large organizations are larger than, say, the typical laboratory small group.

A fourth problem stems from the fact that virtually all studies have been designed to examine networks as a causal variable; i.e. they examine the effects that networks have on some aspect of group performance. Because virtually no research has been conducted to determine those factors which produce alternative network formations, little is known about the conditions which lead to the development of a circle or chain or Y or wheel network, or even to a more centralized (versus decentralized) network.

This problem of the evolution, or emergence, of group networks focuses not on the end-state of network formation, but on the process itself. The issue is change in communication patterns—how fast, through what intermediate states, and to what stabilization points? This point is well illustrated in a chapter on group structure and performance by Davis. He says:

> One strategy for the study of group structure under controlled conditions is to *impose* a structure upon a small group. Structure is thus treated as an independent variable, and the consequences of a particular structure may be observed with regard to group performance, interpersonal responses, and the personal reactions of members. A second strategy is to regard group structure as an *emergent* phenomenon—the interpersonal consequence of a set of persons' interaction over a period of time. Group structure is thus regarded as a dependent variable.[10]

While Davis's chapter, like the other available literature, does treat imposed structures, it does *not* deal with emergent structure.

Fifth, it is apparent that the micro-networks (such as the circle, chain, wheel, and Y) are highly atypical networks for real groups. Granted that an organization could arrange its work groups in one or more of these particular configurations, the fact remains that they are not "typical" organizational networks. Other arrangements are possible, occur more frequently, and are perhaps even more desirable.

Finally, previous micro-network research differentiates networks by creating discrete, private links between people. But differentiated patterns of interaction also exist in small groups where everyone talks *openly* in front of everyone else (called the *com*pletely *con*nected micro-network, or comcon). Even though everyone could talk to everyone else, not everyone does. Discussion typically centers around one or two persons; several may say almost nothing at all; others may maintain their own private dialogue (perhaps under their breath) throughout the entire discussion. Thus, people are not equally connected and a more highly differentiated structure would appear to exist.

Recognition of these problems forces us to raise serious questions regarding the usefulness of the entire network concept, at least as studied in the laboratory, for organizational analysis. Were our knowledge of networks limited to what has been provided by the micro-network research, the conclusion would most likely be that little is known and even less is useful. Here is where the distinction between micro- and macro-network becomes helpful, however, for macro-network analysis can and has been a highly useful tool for organizational analysis even though micro-network research has not.

## Notes

1. A. Bavelas, "A Mathematical Model for Group Structures," *Applied Anthropology* (1948), vol. 7, pp. 16-30; and Bavelas, "Communication Patterns in Task-Oriented Groups," *Acoustical Society of America Journal* (1950), vol. 2, pp. 725-30.
2. H. J. Leavitt, "Some Effects of Certain Communication Patterns on Group Performance," *Journal of Abnormal and Social Psychology* (1951), vol. 46, pp. 38-50.
3. M. E. Shaw, "Communication Networks," in *Advances in Experimental Social Psychology*, vol. 1, ed. I Berkowitz (New York: Academic, 1964), p. 113; reprinted with permission.
4. Leavitt, *op. cit.*
5. Shaw, *op. cit.*
6. M. Glanzer and R. Glaser, "Techniques for the Study of Group Structure and Behavior: II. Empirical Studies of the Effects of Structure in Small Groups," *Psychological Bulletin* (1961), vol. 58, pp. 1-27.
7. Shaw, *op. cit.*
8. B. E. Collins and B. H. Raven, "Group Structure: Attraction, Coalitions, Communication, and Power," in *The Handbook of Social Psychology*, vol. 4, second ed. eds. G. Lindzey and E. Aronson (Reading, Mass.: Addison-Wesley, 1969), pp. 102-214.
9. A. M. Cohen, E. L. Robinson, and J. L. Edwards, "Experiments in Organizational Embeddedness," *Administrative Science Quarterly* (1969), vol. 14, pp. 208-21.
10. From J. H. Davis, *Group Performance* (Reading, Mass.: Addison-Wesley, 1969), p. 88.

# 23

# Phases of Decision Building

*Bonnie McDaniel Johnson*

When Robert Bales wrote *Interaction Process Analysis* in 1951, he observed that the process of human interaction in groups had largely been ignored. Instead of looking at what people say to one another, researchers had been content to relate personality traits of individual members to outcomes of the group process such as the quality of decisions. His research was among the first to investigate how people actually communicate in the process of deciding. This section presents four descriptions of the phases which groups go through in building decisions. Unlike the normative theories developed for this process, these theories of decision building are empirical. They are theories of how groups have been observed to decide; they do not prescribe how groups should decide.

### Bales's Three-Phase Process

Bales and Strodbeck[1] have observed several hundred groups. They found that the category of talk varied by time. Early in the discussion people tend to give and ask for orientation. They called this first phase the "orientation phase." Then the conversation shifts and most of the talk involves the giving and asking of opinions. This constitutes the "evaluation phase." Finally, people begin to give and receive suggestions. They called this the "control phase." They also found patterns of positive and negative reactions. In the control phase, for example, negative reactions characterize the beginning; positive reactions characterize the end. This analysis of three phases of group development was one of the first descriptions of how people actually do solve problems.

### Janis's Cumulative Process

Irving Janis, in his study *Victims of Groupthink,* approached the task of describing group decision making in a different way. His intent was not simply to describe how groups decide. Rather, he sought to describe how integrative processes—especially pressures to conform—can affect decision making. His claim is that "The more amiability and esprit de corps among the members of a policy-making in-group, the greater danger that independent critical thinking will be replaced by groupthink."[2] Groupthink refers to a mode of thinking in which members' strivings for unanimity override their motivation to realistically appraise alternative courses of action.

In the process of describing the manifestations of groupthink, Janis indirectly presents a description of how any group builds decisions. Although his concern is not with "phases," he is concerned with the chronological development of ideas or "themes" in a discussion. The description following is largely my abstraction and extrapolation of ideas about group decision building from Janis's description of groupthink.

The process of reaching a final decision involves many subdecisions. Group members explicitly or implicitly decide upon what kinds of information are relevant and valid. Group members decide which "experts" are credible and relevant to the problem at hand. They arrive at some kind of consensus to be used to evaluate proposed decisions. Any group member who criticizes the group's assumptions about information, criteria, or possible proposals risks censure and exclusion. The process of excluding a person may happen so subtly that group members do not realize what they are doing. When members of a group fall into the groupthink syndrome, they simply censure their own comments to avoid the risk of group censure. They refrain from making remarks contrary to commonly held assumptions of the members. Janis describes the kind of group process which results from groupthink:

1. The group's discussions are limited to a few alternative courses of action (often only two) without a survey of a full range of alternatives.
2. The group fails to reexamine the course of action initially preferred by the majority of members from the standpoint of non-obvious risks and drawbacks that had not been considered when it was originally evaluated.
3. The members neglect courses of action initially evaluated as unsatisfactory by the majority of the group. They spend little or no time discussing whether they have overlooked non-obvious gains or whether there are ways of reducing the seemingly prohibitive costs that had made the alternatives seem undesirable.
4. Members make little or no attempt to obtain information from

experts who can supply sound estimates of losses and gains to be expected from alternative courses of action.
5. Selective bias is shown in the way the group reacts to factual information . . . Members show interest in facts and opinions that support their initially preferred policy and take up time in meetings to discuss them, but they tend to ignore facts and opinions that do not support their initially preferred policy.
6. Members spend little time deliberating about how their chosen policy might be hindered by bureaucratic inertia, sabotaged by political opponents or temporarily derailed by common accidents that happen to the best of well-laid plans. Consequently, they fail to work out contingency plans.[3]

Implicit in this description of the groupthink syndrome are four behavioral tendencies of people engaged in decision building. Janis was concerned with "faulty" decision methods. The principles discussed below must be inferred from what he says. I have labeled the four principles:

• The Rabbit in the Hat Principle: Version 1
• The Rabbit in the Hat Principle: Version 2
• The Rich Get Richer Principle
• The Ala Kazam! Principle

The *Rabbit in the Hat Principle* reminds us that problem solvers are not magicians. Unlike magicians, the only rabbits which problem solvers can pull out of a hat are those which they put into the hat. Version 1 states that a group chooses its solution to a problem from among those alternatives it discusses. This means that people in the group must communicate the ideas they have to others. Groups do not choose from among all possible alternatives. Before a possible alternative becomes an actual possibility in a discussion, it must first occur to a member of the group. Furthermore, the person to whom it occurs must risk describing the proposal to others. Any number of interpersonal factors such as "groupthink" may cause an individual to be unwilling to risk offering a particular proposal for consideration. Limitation of group discussion to only a few alternatives results from such individual members censuring their own ideas.

Version 2 of the Rabbit in the Hat reminds us that problem solvers do not use all relevant information to solve a problem. The only information they use is what they obtain and perceive to be important. Thus, the quality of group solutions depends on the aggressiveness of members in searching for information. (Again, information is not a rabbit which appears by magic. Rather, it must be searched out and then shared.)

The *Rich Get Richer Principle* states that ideas are not "born equal" or given equal consideration. Ideas initially preferred by the majority, as Janis observes, are given preferential treatment throughout the discussion process. Information which confirms the majority's original position is more likely to be considered by the group than information which reflects badly on the majority's position. Likewise, ideas originally frowned upon by the majority are disadvantaged. When a group member offers a proposal, the initial reactions (though often unreflective) result in a biased treatment of the proposal. Group members selectively interpret information in favor of proposals which they initially found attractive. The "rich get richer."

The final principle is concerned with the nature of the group "product." An important characteristic of a collective decision is that it is "announced," either formally or informally. Distinction should be made between the announcement of a decision (which is a set of symbolic displays and/or documents) and the actions which people take in interpreting the announcement. Implementation of a decision is part of the decision itself because it is the interpretation of the announcement in the form of actions. When group members think of desirable "products" of their deciding process, therefore, they must think of implementation as well as announcement.

The *Ala Kazam! Principle* is concerned with the confusion of implementation and announcement which characterizes much decision building. In Janis's words, "group members spend little time deliberating about how the chosen policy might be hindered by bureaucratic inertia, sabotaged by political opponents, or temporarily derailed by common accidents." The process of deciding is inevitably directed toward producing some kind of message (announcement) as the solution. Decision building is symbolic activity (talk). The only direct output of symbolic activity is symbols. Decision-building groups therefore can directly produce only symbols. But the goal of such groups is seldom to produce only symbols. They want to have an impact on the problems they discuss.

The Ala Kazam! Principle states that a group in producing a symbolic message (statement of a solution) does not ipso facto solve the problem. The solution can result only from actions taken in interpreting the message. This principle obviously has implications for how groups should go about building decisions.

Underlying Janis's conceptions of how people decide collectively, there is the notion of decision building as a cumulative process. Decisions are built as ideas occur to people, as they share ideas, evaluate ideas, announce decisions, and implement decisions in action.

The talk which occurs at each phase influences what happens in the next. The expectations of a group—the roles, norms, agenda, and intention—can either encourage or discourage unusual ideas and frank evaluation of ideas in a group.

## Scheidel and Crowell's Spiral Model

Thomas Scheidel and Laura Crowell have developed a "spiral model" to describe the process of decision building.[4] They criticize classical models such as reflective thinking as grossly "inaccurate in portraying the reasoning process in small groups." The reflective thinking model insists that for rational thinking to take place group members must proceed in a linear fashion. Members "complete" one step and then proceed to the next. In the reflective decision-making model, the topic is introduced; the problem is defined, possible solutions are offered, the best solution is selected, and finally the action is determined.

Scheidel and Crowell support their argument that ideas are not developed in a linear fashion with analysis of talk from several small groups. Their data indicated that only 22 percent of all talk in sample groups was devoted to the initiation, extension, modification, and synthesis of an idea. By contrast, 33 percent of the talk was spent substantiating and accepting an idea already under discussion. They interpret this to mean that:

> Group-thought seems to move forward with a "reach-test" type of motion, that is, one participant reaches forth with an inference which seems to be elaborated at length with movements of clarification, substantiation, and verbalized acceptance. Little wonder that group thinking often proceeds slowly when the anchoring of thought takes up practically half of the time.[5]

The spiral model of idea development suggests that when people collaborate to build decisions, one person "moves" the discussion to a "higher" level and then the talk of several people solidifies group consensus about that idea. The "movement" comments are those which initiate, modify, and synthesize ideas. The solidifying comments accept and substantiate. A spiral is a good metaphor for the "building" of decisions. It emphasizes the cumulation of group consensus through a process of "anchoring" thought. The announced decision results from a group's resolving its position on many lesser ideas.

### Fisher's Four Phases of Decision Emergence

Aubrey Fisher, in his theory of "decision emergence," combined features of the spiral model and models of "phases" of decision making into a more sophisticated conception of decision building. According to Fisher, there are four phases in "decision emergence." These phases can be identified by the kinds of talk which people engage in. The first phase is orientation. Much of the talk in this phase is "clarifying" and "agreement." People are trying to understand what the others are saying. The talk is generally "first encounter style;" people stick to safe topics, so there is little disagreement.

The second phase is conflict. After members of a group have talked enough to get to know one another, there are attempts to confront their differences. When this happens, conflicting opinions are voiced. People feel freer to respond unfavorably to ideas they do not like. Also there are more comments which are intended to substantiate an idea being debated. In groups such as those described by Janis, the conflict phase is brief. Groupthink suppresses conflict. In other groups, the conflict may be so bitter that the group dissolves before any decision emerges. According to Fisher, however, most groups move from conflict to a phase which he calls emergence.

The emergence phase is characterized by: 1. a decline in the proportion of unfavorable comments, 2. an increase in comments which modify the speaker's previously dissenting opinion, and 3. an increase in the proportion of comments indicating some change in stance toward what proposals should be accepted. Fisher says that during this phase people emphasize differences of opinion. They use their talk to make clear their individual points of view. In order for a group of people to agree to a common set of symbols as their "decision," they typically begin to describe their position in more general terms.

For example, two people may be in conflict because a particular proposal would cause immediate benefit to one and immediate harm to the other. During the conflict phase they argue strongly the pro and con of the proposal. As they realize that they must come to an agreement, they search for alternative ways to define the problem as well as for alternative proposals. They find that if the proposal is modified slightly, it will serve the long-run interests of both. Thus, they redefine the nature of the problem in light of a desirable solution. (Note that this is in contrast to the linear description of problem solving, in which the problem is defined only at the very beginning.) They say that "after all" the immediate costs will not be so great. By concentrating on the ambiguous "long-run" and by talking about mutual benefits, each is able to get out of being locked into his or her conflicting positions. Each saves face. A collective decision is possible. In the emergence phase, talk becomes more ambiguous, proposals get modified, and people modify their objections.

The final phase is reinforcement. The comments of group members are more favorable; typically there is little or no dissent. People talk about their unity and how "really good" their decision is. In the emergence phase, people modify proposals being considered. In the reinforcement phase, people recognize that they have reached agreement on how to solve the problem being discussed. Fisher describes the building of decisions like this:

> A specific point in time at which decisions are made is not apt to be found. In fact, the emergence process presupposes that groups achieve consensus on their decisions *after* those decisions appear to have been made. The very final stage of interaction then fulfills the purpose of procuring members' public commitment, the essence of consensus, to decisions already reached.[6]

Goals may be described as "retrospective." This means that while we have some idea about what we want, we do not have a very clear idea until after we get it. This same idea applies to Fisher's description of how groups solve problems. Members of a group have some general ideas about what they want to accomplish. They can set down in the beginning of a discussion some general criteria which any solution to a problem must meet, but specific criteria become evident and agreed upon during the discussion. Only during the final, or reinforcement phase, can the goals be made explicit. In the process of telling one another what is "good" about the decision, group members are practicing how to sell the idea to others, and they are convincing themselves that it is a good idea. They are "announcing" the decision to themselves.

### Notes

1. Robert F. Bales and F. L. Strodbeck, "Phases of Group Problem-Solving," *Journal of Abnormal and Social Psychology* (1951), vol. 46, pp. 485-95.
2. Irving Janis, *Victims of Groupthink* (Boston: Houghton Mifflin, 1972), p. 13.
3. *Ibid.*
4. Thomas Scheidel and Laura Crowell, "Idea Development in Small Discussion Groups," *Quarterly Journal of Speech* (1964), vol. 50, pp. 140-45.
5. *Ibid.*
6. Aubrey B. Fisher, *Small Group Decision Making: Communication and the Group Process* (New York: McGraw-Hill, 1974), p. 140.

# 24

# Characteristics of Effective Decision Building

*Bonnie McDaniel Johnson*

Empirical theories of how groups solve problems are helpful in understanding the general process of decision building. They suggest the cumulative nature of the decision-building process. They point to the role of talk in constructing the set of symbols which is the "collective decision," but for those of us who have sat through hours of unproductive conferences, empirical theories do not seem to be of much immediate benefit. What we want to know is how can we improve our meetings, not simply what is likely to happen in these meetings.

Empirical theories are not directly informative about what people should do. For example, if an investigator finds that in most groups there is a concentration of disagreement in the middle of a discussion, what are the pragmatic implications? We cannot conclude that talk should be concentrated in the middle. We would hardly want to train people not to make any statements of disagreement until one third of the discussion is completed.

Some researchers have investigated factors in group discussions which seem to be related to more effective decision building. Jay Hall suggests that group effectiveness results from four factors: commitment, conflict, creativity, and consensus.[1] Note that the first three refer to feeling states or climates. I describe each factor and its relationship to decision construction in informal groups below.

## Commitment

Commitment, according to Hall, is a feeling of "attraction, belonging, and ownership of the group ethos"; it is the "unifying force which holds the group together."[2] Commitment is what some people call motivation because it is a personal feeling which leads people to take actions because they want to do so. People who are committed to a group are actively involved in the talk which goes into the announced decision and then actively attempt to translate the words into actions.

In the group decision phase which Bales and Fisher have called "orientation" members attempt to secure commitment of people to one another and to the common task. Fisher says that there is a high proportion of talk classified as "clarifying" and "agreeing." Clarifying talk enables people to understand what is happening. When people state their agreements with one another, they build some foundation for commitment to one another.

The need for commitment is not concentrated in the opening of a discussion, though it is necessary throughout the decision-building process. We have all been in groups in which people seemed highly committed at first. All the members were actively participating; all were looking at one another; no one was doodling or engaging in other activities "on the side." Then as the discussion progressed, one by one people "dropped out." Most of them stayed in their seats, but only two or three people did the talking. Some of the non-talkers still watched. Occasionally, one would attempt unsuccessfully to break into the conversation. Some others seemed not to listen to what was being said. Members of such a group have lost their commitment. They display their lack of commitment by their failure to participate actively in what is happening.

Hall investigated the relationship of acts of verbal participation and feelings of involvement. His study involved approximately four hundred people participating in small group discussions. About two-thirds of the people reported they were "active participators" in the discussion. Hall instructed one hundred people (one or two in each group) to remain silent throughout the discussion unless someone extended to them a direct invitation to participate. About forty people who had not been so instructed reported that they were largely silent during the discussion. After the discussion, the people completed questionnaires which asked them to describe their feelings about the group and its decisions.

Two of the questions are of particular importance here. Item three asked, "How much responsibility for making the decision work would you feel?" Those who perceived themselves as active participators felt much more responsible for the decision they helped to construct than those who felt they did not participate. The relationship of commitment to participation is also evident in answers to question four: "How committed do you feel to the decision your group made?" Those who reported high participation also reported feeling committed to the decision. It should be noted, however, that members who did not participate rated the *quality* of the decision about as high as those who did participate.

According to Hall, this rating indicates that nonparticipators may be silently saying to the others: "We have heard your arguments, and they are sound. On the basis of facts—which we all heard and assessed—the decision you reached is a good one. But don't expect me to be satisfied with it, feel responsible for its success, or be committed to it." Hall continues: "The feeling tones associated with noninvolvement would seem to overshadow the logical appeal of decision content. The data from this exercise clearly reveals a paradox of human systems. What may be logically acceptable is not necessarily psychologically acceptable."[3]

In other words, decisions we "accept" in the sense that we are willing to take action are those decisions we feel we have helped to create. The most logical decision created by other people is their decision. Let them do what is necessary to make it work! Securing commitment, then, is a continuing problem of all decision-building groups. Special attempts are made during the first few minutes of a discussion to secure initial commitment, but initial commitment does not insure its continuation. People must be motivated to participate throughout the discussion. In this sense, the task of group members is analogous to that of interviewers or public speakers. All must secure initial commitment and then continuously motivate integration of all members of the group.

### Conflict

Conflict is Fisher's term for the second phase of decision emergence.[4] After an initial period in which group members stick to safe topics about which they can agree, they begin to offer proposals for solving the problem. Because these proposals are usually controversial, conflict ensues. Janis stresses that conflict is essential to the effective functioning of a decision-making group.[5] According to Janis, those groups who develop norms which suppress conflict are not capable of critically evaluating ideas presented to the group. As the result, they are led toward poorer decisions.

It is not simply the presence or absence of conflict, but the meaning of a conflict situation which distinguishes ineffective from effective groups. According to Hall, members of ineffective groups tend to believe that conflict is necessarily unhealthy. He states: "The earmark of the ineffective group is often the unarticulated feeling that speedy resolution of task demands is the sine qua non of effective functioning, and that anything, particularly dissenting points of view, which frustrates closure is seen as detrimental to the group.''

Conflicts are seen as impeding the "efficiency" of a group. When people voice disagreeing opinions it means that others must take time to answer the objections. It is easier to agree on a solution if people do not voice their objections. When people define their job as getting to a group decision as quickly as possible, anything which slows them down must be seen as bad. Conflict, then, is necessarily defined as a bothersome disturbance. Conflict can also cause hard feelings among group members. Members of ineffective groups tend to view interpersonal relationships as fragile. People must like one another if the group is to do its job. Therefore, they tend to define conflict as bad because it may damage the good interpersonal relations among group members.

Maier and Hoffman investigated the relationship of a discussion leader's attitude toward a dissenting member and the quality of the decision constructed by the group.[6] Some leaders reported that they appreciated the contributions of the dissenter. The dissenter reminded the group of risks they had overlooked. He or she made members explain the logic of their position. In short, for some leaders, the dissenter was a positive force helping the group construct a better decision. For other leaders, dissenters were "troublemakers" who did not really care about the group. Dissenters kept the group from being more effective.

Maier and Hoffman found that those groups led by people who saw dissenters as positive contributors were much more effective than the other groups. Their decisions were better than the other groups. The researchers conclude that the leader's perceptions have a powerful influence on how group members define their situation. Leaders who see dissenters as troublemakers create (with others' help) a set of expectations in which people are reluctant to disagree. Leaders who see the value of conflict subtly reward people for disagreeing and thus contribute to a norm which encourages open expression of doubts and disagreements. Thus, the meaning which the leader has is related to the meaning the group adopts to define conflict.

In effective groups, according to Hall, conflict means that

> there is less than optimal sharing of the group frame of reference; conflict is treated as a symptom of unarticulated rationales or latent feelings from which, once they are verbalized, the group may be able to profit. Getting to the bottom of conflicts, drawing out deviant opinions so that they may be tested for feasibility, and seriously attending to far-out member insights have more often than not sparked a reappraisal of group thinking to such an extent that group positions are revised and perform-

ance enhanced. . . . Differences are encouraged and handled by the effective group in a "clearing the air" working-through manner which increases the likelihood that end products will reflect the contributions of all.[7]

People act in a situation according to how they define it. Groups who establish a collective definition of conflict as detrimental not only develop expectations which discourage conflict, they also develop methods for suppressing and circumventing those conflicts which do arise. In some groups, one or more people develop the role of "peace maker." People learn to acquiesce to the compromises suggested by this person. Other groups use majority rule to prevent open conflict. Whenever a conflict arises, the matter is immediately put to a vote. Those in the minority are expected to remain silent.

Another method might be called "reciprocal payoffs." It is the expectation that if a person "gives in" on one issue, he should be allowed to win on a later issue regardless of how unreasonable an argument he presents. Conflict is avoided because people simply take turns in influencing what the collective decision will be. It is like two people deciding about a vacation. One wants to go a thousand miles away and fly. The other wants to go two hundred miles and drive. They compromise. They go a thousand miles and drive!

A final method groups use to avoid controversy is changing the subject. When debate over an issue gets under way, one person brings up an issue which may be largely unrelated to the debate. Group members drop the controversial topic; everyone then speaks in favor of (or opposed to) the new idea and the appearance of agreement is maintained.

Successful handling of group conflict is not easily achieved. People must express their doubts and disagreements. In order for this to happen, they must expect that others will try to understand their position. The expectation that others will try to understand does not mean that others will agree. Successful handling of conflicts results in people developing equivalent meanings for common symbols (and symbolic actions). It is a process of coorientation.

## Creativity

According to Hall, creativity is dependent upon conflict. Groups without conflict over ideas are not as likely to produce "creative" ideas as those who must talk out differing opinions in order to reach a collective decision. In order to measure the creativity of discussion groups, Hall had research subjects list possible solutions to a problem before engaging in a discussion. These prediscussion judgments were rated for quality. The higher their quality, the higher the group's "average resources" for problem solving. After the group discussion, the collective decision was rated for quality and also to determine whether one or more group members had listed it as a suggested answer prior to discussion. Decisions which had not been suggested by anyone were termed "emergent."

Hall found that those groups in which the prediscussion suggestions were diverse more often produced emergent decisions. He calls this the "high conflict condition"; there is little initial agreement on what must be done, and therefore, people must present and discuss differing ideas. These groups were more creative because they had to do more than merely accept a decision which several people felt to be best before the discussion began.

All emergent decisions are not equally "creative." Hall found a difference in quality between groups of strangers meeting for a brief period only (ad hoc groups) and established groups.[8] The collective decisions of *ad hoc* groups were consistently inferior to the members' average predecision judgment under conflict conditions. However, the emergent decision of established groups were vastly superior to their prediscussion judgments. One inference from these findings is that the established groups had more stable procedures for handling conflicts when they arose. Groups of strangers are unlikely to have worked out consensual expectations for managing conflict. Their relationship is more fragile than relationships in established groups. They are more uncertain about how to talk to one another when there is conflict.

Hall states two ways in which conflict, if adequately managed through supporting group norms, can facilitate creativity. First, "one effect of conflict in groups may be to achieve a more tentative opinion stating among members which, in turn, facilitates decision flexibility of the type needed for creativity."[9] This reason is similar to Fisher's description of what happens in the "conflict" and "emergent" phases of discussion. Group members state opinions and disagreement ensues. This disagreement is followed by more ambiguous, or in Hall's words, "tentative" statements of opinions. Group members become more flexible. It is this flexibility or ambiguity which allows group members to find creative decisions. A second way in which conflict facilitates creativity is through subjecting ideas to examination and modification. Hall states:

> Effective groups seem to recognize intuitively that where there is a conflict there is a need for both more data and a closer examination of

existing inputs. Out of such additions and re-examinations frequently come those "aha" kind of insights which not only have a compelling quality of logic once articulated, but which underlie and lead to creativity as well.[10]

Creativity, then, is a third factor in group effectiveness. Creativity results when group members question one anothers' assumptions (often their unrealized assumptions). When disagreements force people to justify their ideas to one another, when people thus force one another out of comfortable paths of thought, they may hit upon less obvious but better solutions to problems. They may construct decisions more acceptable to everyone. If the norms and roles of a group allow the expression of conflict without personal defensiveness, the result can be collective decisions which are better than the best individual judgments.

## Consensus

According to G. M. Phillips consensus is the distinguishing characteristic of small groups.[11] Consensus is often thought of as perfect agreement, but consensus does not mean that everyone in a group holds the same values or sees the world the same way. When a small group reaches a "consensus," it means that every person in the group accepts the collective decision as his or her own with understanding of what the decision means to others. Any person might have really preferred another decision, but all people feel committed to the group decision.

Hall explains consensus as both a set of expectations which constitutes a "decision rule" and a performance goal for which members strive. As a performance goal, consensus is the idea shared by group members that their final collective position or decision will reflect (at least) the tacit approval of every member. "Tacit approval" is not disgruntled silence. All members must "say"—in words or silent symbolic displays—"Yes, I can live with that decision."

Consensus as a decision rule means that all members actively seek out the opinions of other members. The job of constructing a collective decision is one of putting together many smaller decisions. At each decision point members of a group operating under a decision rule of consensus ask one another to express opinions.

I saw consensus work best as a decision rule with a group of "Outreach Workers" employed by metropolitan New York City Y.M.C.A. The group's task was to suggest some organizational goals.

The discussion lasted several hours before they produced a set of goals on which they could all agree. In the process, however, they scrupulously attended to each others' attitudes and feelings. The most common comments I heard them use were questions to one another such as, "What do you think about that idea?" "Are we all agreed?" "How would that go in your district?" "You're not saying anything, what's the matter?" Thus, they not only reached consensus on their announced decision in the end, they secured consensus on the validity of each idea they discussed. They would not proceed until everyone agreed he understood what was being said at that time and until they all had an equivalent sense of how relevant the issue was to the decision they were constructing.

Consensus as a decision rule is a means for accomplishing group effectiveness through commitment, conflict, and creativity. When group members' opinions are actively sought, they are more likely to participate, and therefore to feel commitment. By insisting on consensus, those who disagree are invited to express their opinions and feelings.

Consider the expectations of people who have learned that consensus is a decision rule in their group. First, they expect to be supported when they raise objections. Being "supported" does not mean others will necessarily agree with their ideas. Rather, it means that they will not be personally censured as a troublemaker for having said them. Everyone's opinions will be seen as contributing to a better decision in the end. Also, group members can expect that regardless of how much conflict there is over ideas, they will resolve the conflict. A person does not have to worry that in introducing conflict he may be destroying the group because the expectation is that people will talk about their disagreements until a consensus is reached. Such expectations are sure to lead to people being more willing to disagree and more able to sustain conversation until a creative solution is found.

## Notes

1. Jay Hall, *Toward Group Effectiveness* (Conroe, Texas: Teleometrics International, 1971).
2. *Ibid.*, p. 2.
3. *Ibid.*
4. Aubrey B. Fisher, *Small Group Decision Making: Communication and the Group Process* (New York: McGraw-Hill, 1974).
5. Irving Janis, *Victims of Groupthink* (Boston: Houghton Mifflin, 1972).
6. Norman R. Maier and L. R. Hoffman, "Acceptance and Quality of Solutions as Related to Leaders' Attitudes Toward Disagreement in Group

Problem Solving," *Journal of Applied Behavioral Science* (1965), vol. 1, pp. 373–86.

7. Hall, *op. cit.*, p. 4.
8. Jay Hall and M. Williams, "A Comparison of Decision-Making Performances in Established and Ad Hoc Groups," *Journal of Personality and Social Psychology* (1966), vol. 3, pp. 214–22.
9. Hall, *Toward Group Effectiveness, op. cit.*, p. 6.
10. *Ibid.*
11. Gerald M. Phillips, *Communication in the Small Group* (Indianapolis: Bobbs Merrill, 1973), p. 15.

# 25

# Communication Roles in Small Group Interaction

*Michael Burgoon, Judee K. Heston,*
and *James McCroskey*

Within a group, there are several roles or functions that need to be fulfilled if the group is to complete its task and maintain its cohesiveness. These are classified as task and maintenance roles. A third category are dysfunctional, self-centered roles that need to be avoided. These three categories include the range of constructive and destructive functions that group members may perform.[1] We will discuss each of these individually.

## Group Task Roles

These roles involve the communication functions necessary for a group to accomplish its task, whether it is decision making, problem solving, education and information exchange, or conflict resolution. Not all, but most, roles are required in each situation. No roles should be played by a single individual; each person should perform multiple functions. The good participant will fulfill most, if not all, of these roles.

1. *Initiator*—proposes new ideas, procedures, goals, and solutions. He gets the group started. Since getting started on any task is usually difficult, his is an important role. New ideas and perspectives are also essential to the continued life of a group.
2. *Information giver*—supplies evidence, opinions and relates personal experiences relevant to the task. We have discussed earlier the necessity of an abundance of information. In addition to quantity, quality information is needed. The quality of a decision or solution can be no better than the information that produced it. No information may be better than erroneous or biased information.
3. *Information seeker*—asks for information from other members and seeks clarification when necessary. This role is equally as important

as giving information; if we fail to ask others for their information, relevant evidence may be overlooked.

4. *Opinion giver*—states his own beliefs, attitudes, and judgments. Usually, there are a few people in a group who are more than willing to present their opinions. The concern is that everyone, including the introverts and communication apprehensives, give their views. Group effort has an advantage over individual efforts; it produces both a wider range of ideas and more creative contributions. This principle presupposes that all members participate. The ineffective participant withholds his opinions out of fear of criticism; the effective member expresses them.

5. *Opinion seeker*—solicits the opinions and feelings of others and asks for clarification of positions. Too often, we are so concerned with presenting our own views that we neglect to ask the opinions of others. The effective participant actively seeks others' attitudes and convictions, especially those of members who are hesitant to speak. Questioning for both opinions and information can play a vital role in group communication. It should not be overlooked as an effective discussion technique.

6. *Elaborator*—clarifies and expands the ideas of others through examples, illustrations, and explanations. As long as his elaborations are relevant to the task, this role is valuable. It is especially useful with others who are unable to express their own ideas adequately.

7. *Integrator*—clarifies the relationship between various facts, opinions, and suggestions and integrates the ideas or activities of other members. The integrator ties together elements that might otherwise seem unrelated and disjointed. This linking function makes contributions as useful as possible by incorporating ideas that might otherwise be disregarded.

8. *Orienter*—keeps the group directed toward its goal, summarizes what has taken place and clarifies the purposes or positions of the group. Essentially, he insures that the group has a direction and that it heads in the "right" direction. Without orientation, a group may easily "get off the track" onto trivial or irrelevant issues. This role is necessary to define or clarify continually the group's intermediate and ultimate goals so that the group's activities can be checked, at any given time, for consistency with the desired outcomes.

9. *Energizer*—stimulates the group to be energetic and active. By this person's communication and example, he motivates the group to reach a decision or to be more involved. The energizer's drive contributes to greater group efficiency and productivity.

## Group Maintenance Roles

These roles build and maintain the group's interpersonal relationships. They determine the socioemotional atmosphere of the group. If these roles are not performed, conflict may arise and group cohesiveness is reduced; if they are performed, the group interacts more smoothly, with greater satisfaction as an outcome.

1. *Encourager*—praises and agrees with others, providing a warm, supportive interpersonal climate. The accepting orientation, discussed as an input, is evidenced by how well a person shows encouragement and support for others. This function is valuable in producing solidarity in the face of conflict.
2. *Harmonizer*—attempts to mediate differences, introduce compromises, and reconcile differences. The harmonizer's conciliatory communication is directed toward reducing conflict and encouraging a pleasant socioemotional atmosphere.
3. *Tension reliever*—introduces a relaxed atmosphere by reducing formality and interjecting humor. This role, like the harmonizer, must be filled when conflict arises. This is not an easy assignment; when tension increases, people become less flexible and more emotionally involved. The effective participant attempts to suppress his own emotional reactions while trying to deemphasize the conflict for others. If he is good at telling jokes or making others see the humor of a situation, his intercession may go a long way in relieving tension.
4. *Gatekeeper*—controls the channels of communication, providing proper balance in the amount of participation of each member. The gatekeeper encourages those to talk who might otherwise not speak, while cutting off those who tend to monopolize the discussion. In conflict situations, he attempts to reduce the amount of communication by highly dissident or argumentative members, while increasing participation by more moderate, conciliatory members. However, if the situation warrants a confrontation, the gatekeeper opens up channels to the opponents so that the catharsis can take place. His overall purpose is the satisfactory continuation of the group. By his attention (or lack of it), by his body orientation and eye contact, and by the members he addresses, he can control the flow of communication.
5. *Follower*—acquiesces to the wishes of others. Although we do not generally recommend the follower role, in circumstances where the group's cohesion is disintegrating, this role is constructive in furthering maintenance of the group, because it does not contribute to conflict. It serves, rather, as a neutralizing element. The good participant may be advised, therefore, to adopt this role under stress situations, as long as he is following a leader who is trying to resolve conflict. If he is following one of the disruptive members, this role becomes a destructive one.

## Dysfunctional Roles

We have recommended that the effective participant function in as many of the task and maintenance roles as possible. The roles that are about to be discussed are ones that the good participant should avoid. They are self-centered roles played by a person who is more concerned about personal needs than the group's interest. These roles reduce group productivity, cohesion, and satisfaction.

1. *Blocker*—constantly objects to others' ideas and suggestions and insists that nothing will work. He is totally negative. As the name implies, the blocker prevents progress. He may belabor points that the group has finished discussing or repeatedly oppose recommendations. The blocker is always complaining, always dissatisfied. He is the type you forget to inform about meetings or plan them during times when he is busy.
2. *Aggressor*—insults and criticizes others, shows jealousy and ill will. Like the blocker, the aggressor is discontented and disapproving. His malevolence is evidenced by jokes at others' expense and efforts to deflate others, whom he distrusts and dislikes. He may have alienated or anxious personality traits.
3. *Anecdoter*—tells irrelevant stories and personal experiences. He is a little like the elaborator, only he gets carried away with irrelevant anecdotes. He is motivated by a need for attention (as are the others who take disruptive roles). While the stories and jokes may be entertaining, they retard group progress.
4. *Recognition seeker*—interjects comments that call attention to his achievements and successes. He boasts while trying to appear not to do so. For example, the recognition seeker might say, "When I won the state swimming meet, I noticed that that problem was occurring . . ." He needs the sympathy and recognition of others.
5. *Dominator*—tries to monopolize group interaction. He wants to lead the group and will use whatever tactics he feels necessary, such as flattering, interrupting, and demanding to get his own way. He has the "spoiled brat" syndrome: he is not happy until he is running things his way.
6. *Confessor*—uses the group to listen to his personal problems. The confessor seems compelled to reveal his shortcomings, fears, and needs to the group. He involves the group in his problems, using it for catharsis. Unless the group is intended to be therapeutic, this role is disruptive, side-tracking the group from its goals.
7. *Special-interest pleader*—represents the interests of a different group. He pleads for favors or attention for the group whose interest he represents. The special-interest pleader's loyalties lie outside the group.

8. *Playboy*—distracts the group with antics, jokes, and comments. He is uninvolved with the group's purpose, preferring to entertain himself and the other members through his horseplay or sarcasm. The label "playboy" does not derive from his flirtatious behavior, although this may be part of it, but for his affinity for "play" rather than "work." Nor should the label imply that only males are guilty of this behavior; females can be playboys just as easily.

Each of us may recognize within ourselves some tendencies toward these dysfunctional behaviors. If we are to be effective participants, we must consciously control these inclinations, while striving to perform the more constructive task and maintenance roles.

### Notes

1. K. Benne, and P. Sheats, "Functional Roles of Group Members," *Journal of Social Issues* (1948), vol. 4, pp. 41–49.

# 26

# Leadership in Small Groups

*Dennis S. Gouran*

### Introduction

If you were to ask the next person you meet if he or she could tell you what a leader is, the individual's nonverbal response most likely would convey an impression like, "What a ridiculous question! Everyone knows what a leader is." Yet, if you were to continue the inquiry by asking for a definition, you might also find the person in question quite hesitant and unsure of his or her answer. The respondent might even retreat to the sort of definition we have all been taught to avoid; for example, "A leader is a person who leads," or, "A leader is a person who exercises leadership." If you were to press still further by asking what it means "to lead" or "to exercise leadership," quite likely, the response would be less than precise. Among the definitions I have encountered when raising this sort of question are: (1) "To lead is to take charge," (2) "Exercising leadership means getting things done," and (3) "Leading is the ability to get people to work together." Although there is nothing wrong with these descriptions, they do not provide a clear sense of what leadership is or what a leader does.

Why is it that concepts seemingly so easy to grasp on an intuitive level are so hard to explain? In large part, the difficulty arises from the fact that the concept of *leader* and the related concept of *leadership* are abstractions. And as such, they have many different referents. The greater the number of things to which a word can refer, the more problems experienced in attempting to define it. Does this suggest that the concepts of *leader* and *leadership* are therefore useless? Not at all. As I shall attempt to demonstrate in the remainder of this chapter, they represent important aspects of group life, and being aware of their relationship to a group's performance will not only help you to understand important sources of effectiveness and ineffectiveness in small group behavior, but also will provide a basis for becoming a better contributor in groups in which you can participate.[1]

### Concepts with which Leader and Leadership are Frequently Confused

The abstractness of the terms *leader* and *leadership* often results in a confusion with other concepts applying to groups. Perhaps the three most notable of these are *popularity, status,* and *power.* In identifying a leader or those who have exercised leadership in a small group, you can point to that individual who is most well-liked, who is viewed as the most important member, or who has the greatest amount of authority. Although it is frequently the case that a leader is well liked, is viewed as more important than the average member in some sense, or possesses more authority than other group members, there is no necessary relationship between these attributes and leadership or being a leader as such.

Leadership, as I hope to demonstrate, implies purposeful activity of a certain kind. Popularity, status, and power may derive as a consequence of such activity. However, there is no guarantee that performing as a leader culminates in the acquisition of these qualities. (In fact, leadership sometimes contributes to their denial or loss.) Nor is there any reason to assume that the possession of such attributes predisposes a person to act as a leader or, if you will, to exhibit leadership. In some instances, the possession of popularity, status, or power will even inhibit a person's willingness to perform the functions of leadership. The reasons for separating popularity, status, and power from the concepts of leader and leadership should become more apparent as we examine more concretely what each represents.

#### *Popularity*

In any small group, some individuals possess or exhibit personal traits that contribute to their being more well liked than others. Sociologists refer to the resulting rank order as the sociometric structure of a group and the individual's position in this ordering as his or her sociometric standing or rank.[2] A group member can achieve high standing and, hence, popularity with others for any number of reasons, including physical attractiveness, sense of humor, past achievements, a specific skill or ability, external notoriety, and general demeanor. Such sources of popularity are often completely unrelated to the serious work of a group. Sometimes, of course, increased popularity stems from contributions, but the attainment of high sociometric standing does not uniformly require that a person be actively involved in helping a group achieve its goals.

If asked to identify their leader, the members of a group may point to the most popular or well-liked member. Being acknowledged as a leader, however, is not the same thing as being a leader in many cases. Popularity would be a good index of leadership if a person could achieve high sociometric rank only—or even usually—as a result of certain types of contributions I shall later more specifically identify. Inasmuch as the sources of popularity are so frequently related to factors other than contributions, to equate being well liked with leadership is a mistake. In confusing popularity with leadership and thereby placing a popular person in a formal position of leadership, more than one group has had the misfortune of discovering the mistake too late.

### Status

The confusion of popularity with leadership is probably less common than the tendency in this society to think of leadership in terms of status. Before it is possible to appreciate the need to disentangle these two concepts, however, it is necessary to have a clear understanding of what status signifies in relationship to membership in a group.

The nature of groups is such that that individual members at some point begin to specialize their contributions in some way. That is, they contribute in ways that others do not and/or are not expected to contribute. This type of differentiation we think of as the role structure of a group.[3] In some cases, a role is prescribed or assigned—for instance, the role of treasurer among the elected officers of an organization or club. When a role is clearly defined and specified, we ordinarily use the term *position* to apply to it. In other instances, a role develops as a result of others' response to how a person behaves and their coming to expect a consistent pattern of such behavior. Among these more informal, evolving sorts of roles, one finds such designations as deviant, peacemaker, humorist (perhaps, more perjoratively, clown), facilitator, and critic.

Even when roles are formally designated and specified, they may undergo some degree of evolution. Hence, two people with identical positions may nevertheless have different roles by virtue of what they do in interpreting the requirements of their position. Therefore, it is useful to retain the label of *position* for the more restricted situation of assigned or specifically delineated responsibilities.

Whether using the term *role* in the narrow sense of a person's position or in the broader sense, it is clear that no one enacts a particular role 100 percent of the time. Still, individual group members are distinguishable from one another in respect to certain patterns of behavior that they typically exhibit and are eventually expected to display.

Different roles are seen as having corresponding differences in value or importance to a group, and the term *status* is used to represent these differences. As Shaw has suggested, status is the "rank accorded {a} position by the group members—the prestige of the position."[4] In the case of a group having a formal role structure, a certain amount of status derives from mere occupancy of the most highly valued positions. The role of chairperson, for example, carries a certain amount of prestige regardless of the person so designated. In less formally structured groups, status develops in relation to the evolution of a person's role. In this sense, a person earns or acquires status by virtue of contributions that other members perceive to be of value or importance to the group.

Because the role of leader in a group is so often highly valued, leadership can easily be thought of in terms of status. Not all highly valued roles entail leadership, however. The recording secretary in a group performs important functions and, as a result, occupies a position of reasonably high status, but the level of status accorded the position does not accrue from acts of leadership, or even their expectation. It is also possible to engage in acts of leadership without acquiring gains in status. The individual who finds it necessary to play the role of opponent to the majority to prevent a group from pursuing a foolish or unwise course of action shows leadership, but rather than being recognized for the value of his or her effort, might just as well be f1viewed as a nuisance or obstructionist. Roles such as these seldom if ever are highly valued and can actually limit the prospects for achieving status.

On some occasions, a person's status can serve as a deterrent to leadership. As in the case of sociometric standing, once an individual has acquired some degree of status, he or she is likely to want to maintain it. Leadership, however, may require a person to behave in ways that others will find objectionable. The subsequent conflict, then, results from a desire to protect status and the need to do what serves the interest of successful completion of a task. When a conflict of this type is resolved in favor of the maintenance of status, the individual involved is not acting as a leader.

Since persons of high status do not necessarily engage in leadership, one concept should not be taken as an index of the other. This is not to suggest that acts of leadership never result in the acquisition of status or that group members having the most status do not engage in leadership. The essential point of this discussion is simply that there is no necessary relation between a person's status in a group and the likelihood of his or her functioning as a leader.

*Power*

A third concept with which leadership is often confused is power. Power is usually defined in terms of influence or potential for influence. We think of a powerful person as one who is able to elicit the compliance of others.[5] Because we are prone to conceive of a leader as the individual who has the most influence on how a group performs, it is understandable that leadership and power are sometimes viewed as interchangeable concepts. As was true of popularity and status, however, the differences between power and leadership exceed the similarities.

To speak of a group member's power is most fundamentally to refer to the authority associated with his or her position and the possession of resources to reward compliance and to punish noncompliance. Authority is a right or freedom to take actions on behalf of a group or otherwise to determine what other members are permitted or not permitted to do. This authority is often invested in a position by the group, but in other instances results from the ability to make interaction rewarding or punishing.[6] Whatever the source of authority, its possession does not assure its use. This is the first crucial sense in which power differs from leadership. To exist, leadership must be displayed. It has no meaning apart from actual behavior. Power, on the other hand, can exist merely as a capacity or potential.

A second important distinction is that when power is manifest in actual behavior, the ends toward which it can be directed are considerably more encompassing than those ordinarily associated with leadership. Whereas leadership involves particular functions related to desired outcomes—namely, the achievement of a group's goals—the use of power can be motivated by any number of concerns. A powerful group member can use power simply to remind others that he or she has it. Power can even be used to prevent a group from achieving its goals, especially if they conflict with those of the powerful member.

It should not be inferred from this discussion that group members possessing power consistently work at cross purposes with the rest of the group. The point is that power represents an entitlement. It gives the holder freedom to determine what a group will do and how it will do it. Leadership does not carry freedom to influence. Power is a possession. Leadership is activity. Sometimes the two work in tandem; sometimes they work in opposition. Whatever the case, they are not the same thing.

## General Perspectives on Leaders and Leadership

Up to this point, I have been focusing primarily on what leaders and leadership are not. If a leader is not consistently the most popular, prestigious, or powerful member of a group, and if leadership is conceptually distinct from the concepts of popularity, status, and power, then how should leaders and leadership be conceived of? Although it has been acknowledged that there are nearly as many conceptions of leaders and leadership as people who write about them[7], we can most usefully examine these concepts from three perspectives. We can think of leadership as behavior associated with a position (role in the narrow sense of the term) and a leader as the person given the position. We can also think of leadership as a role (in the broader sense of the term) and a leader as the individual who enacts the role.[8] Finally, we can conceive of leadership as a process in which goal-directed acts have intended consequences and leaders as the individuals who perform these acts.

### The Positional Perspective

Many groups have in their internal makeup a set of positions that individual members fill. This is especially true when a group is a subset of a larger collection of people and serves as their representatives. Executive committees, some boards of trustees, and the officers of various clubs and organizations are common examples. Occupancy may come as a result of either appointment or election. In some cases, the number of different positions in a group can equal the size of the membership; for instance, the executive committee of an organization might consist of four people: the president, vice-president, secretary, and treasurer. Not all groups, of course, are so formally structured. At the very least, however, most task-oriented groups have a minimum of two positions: chairperson and committee member.

Groups with designated positions typically are hierarchically arranged. This means that at least one person has greater responsibility than others for assuring that certain functions have been performed. This individual is ordinarily called the chairperson and is often considered to be the group's leader. His or her duties are usually prescribed and include such activities as preparing the agenda, convening meetings, guiding discussion through the agenda, assigning subtasks to individual members, coordinating group products (reports, decisions, recommendations, etc.), and serving as the group's chief spokesperson.

To the extent that the occupant of this position executes the designated responsibilities, he or she is functioning as a leader and can be viewed as exercising leadership. Under such conditions, the quality of leadership is assessed by the degree of conformity the chairperson's (or equivalent term, such as *presiding officer's*) behavior shows to the expectations associated with the position. A chairperson who fails to perform the functions required by the position he or she holds will be viewed as a poor leader and, if the pattern persists, can be replaced.

The positional perspective on leadership represents a limited view of the concept and is probably most useful in relation to groups having a formal structure and clearly delineated expectations for various members. For many task-oriented groups, however, the perspective is too restrictive and leaves open the question of how well or poorly particular functions are performed and the attendant successes and failure of leadership. Additionally, even in groups with a formal structure of positions, the set of assigned or prescribed responsibilities of the leader do not exhaust the possible needs for leadership or cover all of the problems that can and do arise in the execution of a task. For these reasons, a broader view is often necessary.

### The Role Perspective

If the positional perspective were fully adequate for assessing leadership in groups and the behavior of leaders, in principle, successes and failures could be completely explained in terms of whether those in positions of leadership have performed the functions assigned to them. Not all task groups have a designated leader, however, nor in those that do is it always possible to observe consistency between the group's performance and the behavior of its leader. A designated leader can be doing an absolutely miserable job of discharging his or her responsibilities, and yet, somehow the group manages. In such cases, it might be discovered that someone else has either performed functions expected of the designated leader (taking up the slack, as it were) or has been responsive to needs that the presumed leader is ill-equipped to meet. For these reasons, it is sometimes preferable to think of leadership as a role that emerges as a consequence of situations that arise in the course of a group's execution of a task. From this perspective, a leader is any member who addresses the needs of a group as they relate to its ability to achieve desired or expected outcomes. That person may or may not be the designated leader.

Insofar as group interaction is concerned, the positional perspective on leadership assumes a relatively static and passive pattern of behavior on the part of the leader. The role perspective envisions much more dynamic and active involvement. These differences are evident in a number of respects. From the positional perspective, leadership derives from an assignment. From the role perspective, it derives largely from the contingencies of the situation. From the positional perspective, leadership is a duty or set of responsibilities. From the role perspective, it is primarily a response to a felt need. From the positional perspective, leadership is more or less routine. From the role perspective, it is highly variable. From the positional perspective, the leader of a group is a single individual. From the role perspective, leadership can reside in one or more individuals.

Thinking of leadership as a role that evolves in relationship to particular needs and of leaders as the persons who enact this role, expands considerably the scope of activities to which the concept applies. A leader in this frame of reference is a sort of troubleshooter who can encounter a substantial variety of problems. In addition to many of the task-related functions mentioned in the discussion of the positional perspective, a leader can find him or herself having to deal with many different social and emotional needs of the group. Among these are managing interpersonal conflicts, maintaining morale, developing cohesiveness, challenging questionable judgments, pointing out procedural irregularities, coping with disruptive members, and, in general, attempting to counteract the effects of inhibiting influences. In another essay, I have gone so far as to define leadership as the art of counteractive influence, since so much of what the leadership role entails has to do with problematic situations.[9]

When someone speaks of the "absence of leadership" in a small group, whether consciously or not, he or she is reflecting the role perspective. What such an observation suggests is that certain needs have arisen, and no one in the group has taken steps to address them. This further suggests that the quality of leadership and the skill of those who enact the role is to be judged primarily in terms of effort. In other words, does some member (or members) of a group attempt to deal with needs and related problems that occur in the execution of a task? If so, then leadership has been exhibited, and there is at least one person appropriately deserving of the title of leader. When leadership is judged in terms of effort, this leaves one in the sometimes enigmatic situation of seeing a good deal of leadership displayed, but still little in the overall performance of a group that would cause him or her to comment favorably. This paradox is apparent in the treatment accorded some athletic coaches with losing records. An oft heard justification for dismissal is, "Well, we couldn't very well fire the team." The statement is tantamount to saying that the role has been performed, but the results are unacceptable.

Although an improvement, the role perspective suffers from a limitation similar to that of the positional perspective. Specifically, it treats leadership as something separate from other aspects of the performance of groups. That is, leadership is something brought to or added to a group's interaction. If the quality of a group's performance—that is, the achievement of goals and the ease with which they are achieved—could be accounted for strictly in terms of the absence, presence, and number of leadership acts, then leadership as roles and leaders as the individuals who enact them would be adequate conceptualizations. Inasmuch as the absence, presence, and number of leadership acts are not sufficient to explain variations in the quality of group performance, however, we need to explore yet another perspective.

### The Process Perspective

In addition to its being thought of as position and role-related behavior, leadership can also be viewed as a process. From this perspective, to speak of leadership as particular types of acts without reference to the responses those acts elicit is rather like labeling as conversation a communicative event in which only one party has participated. A conversation, by definition, requires the joint participation of two or more individuals; hence, a conversation cannot have occurred unless this condition is satisfied. The mere presence of others is insufficient. Similarly, for leadership to occur, acts must elicit certain types of responses. It is these responses, moreover, that determine whether the acts arousing them constitute leadership and whether the persons initiating these acts are functioning as leaders. The idea that an act cannot be classified independently of its consequences may be difficult to accept at first, but for those who consider leadership as a process, the concept is otherwise meaningless.

From the process perspective, neither the intention of the actor nor the past history of similar acts provide warrant enough to identify any given act as an instance of leadership. As an illustration, consider the situation in which a person approaches another and says, "Good morning. How are you?" Most of us would be inclined to consider this bit of ritualistic behavior as a simple greeting. But suppose the response were something like, "I regard that question as an invasion of my privacy, and I strongly resent it." Far from serving the function of a greeting, the initial statement in the illustration has proved to be a provocation. Admittedly, it would be highly unusual to respond to a simple formality of human relations in the manner described. Nevertheless, I hope the example serves the point of demonstrating the difficulty of inferring from the characteristics of an act alone the classification to which it appropriately belongs.

Lest the preceding illustration seem too contrived, let me review an actual occurrence that relates much more directly to the discussion of leadership. A university committee on basic-skills education was discussing the possible introduction of a new course for students experiencing difficulty with a remedial English course. The remedial course was originally designed for students who, at the time of admission, lack adequate preparation for passing the university's regularly required English composition course. A certain percentage of students taking the remedial course were not doing very well, however. As a result, the suggestion being entertained was that the university create a preremedial course for these students. One particpant observed that prior to the creation of such a course, it would be useful to try to determine if the lack of success in the current remedial course were a function of inadequate preparation or ability below the level necessary to master the content of the more-advanced required course.

The observation apparently was intended to have other group members question an assumption that had gone unexamined and, thereby, to provide a cautionary note to those otherwise prepared to support a recommendation that might later prove to have been misdirected. As such, the observation was consistent with the notion of leadership implicit in the role perspective. That is, an initiative arose in response to a felt need to have the group address a relevant issue before endorsing a potentially ineffective solution to a problem. The first response to this initiative, however, was, "I don't know what the point is. We can't measure true native ability, and I don't think we should try." The comment was immediately reinforced by several other group members.

Given the immediate negative reaction to the observation, a person would be hard pressed to conclude that leadership had been exercised in the preceding example. The response of other committee members determined what the act in question was, and in this particular instance it was, for the moment at least, something other than leadership. Under the circumstances, it would be more appropriate to call the act something like "unintentional antagonism." One might even be inclined to think of it as an act of "futility." Had other members of the committee responded favorably and expressed a willingness to defer action on the recommendation until other information had been explored, the precipitating act could legitimately be construed as one of leadership.

By now, it should be clear that from the process perspective, leadership is more than a response to needs of the moment and to problematic or potentially problematic situations. It assumes a certain level of correspondence between the intention behind an act and its consequences. The process perspective further assumes a developmental character to leadership.[10] Rarely would one who subscribes to this perspective assess leadership in terms of discrete pairs of communicative acts. To do so would be equivalent to subtracting all unsuccessful acts from all successful ones and using the remainder as the net index of leadership. Experience tells us that some acts are more important than others and that initial failures can stimulate other, subsequently successful acts.

In the case of the basic skills committee, the person making the original observation about the need to avoid assuming that failure in the remedial English course was necessarily a result of inadequate preparation could easily have dropped the matter when confronted by a series of nonsupportive reactions. Instead, he chose to pursue it. In responding to the alleged impossibility of determining "true native ability," he tried to clarify his point by saying, "I wasn't suggesting that we assess native ability. My concern is that we attempt to determine if those who would qualify for preremedial instruction would have any greater likelihood of succeeding in such a course than they do now in the one in which they presently enroll. If not, then on what grounds can we justify the addition of the proposed course?" At this point, previously silent members of the committee began agreeing with the expressed concern, and those who earlier had been most rejecting began to acquiesce. As a result of the exchanges that occurred, the committee decided to couple its support for the recommendation to establish a preremedial course with caveats about the need for further evidence regarding probable success as well as the need for careful tracking of those who enroll.

### The Merits of Competing Perspectives

Of the three views of leadership we have been examining, which is the best one to adopt? There is no absolute answer to this question, since the very notion of "perspective" implies that different ways of viewing an object of attention have varying value under varying circumstances. If you are interested only in what the individuals we ordinarily think of as group leaders do or are expected to do, then the positional perspective appears to be adequate. On the other hand, if your interest lies in accounting for differences in the performance of small groups and in the outcomes they achieve, the role and process perspectives would seem to be more fruitful. Of these, the process perspective is probably better for most purposes. The role perspective focuses on what an individual (or set of individuals) does in response to conditions in a group and views as leadership attempts to deal with problematic or potentially problematic situations. Intent and effort become the yardsticks by which you assess leadership. The process perspective entails similar considerations but has the added restriction that the consequences of given acts correspond to their underlying intent. This addition takes us one step further in being able to understand and explain the successes and failures of groups. To be sure, the process perspective does not permit a full accounting for the performance of groups; but to the extent that leadership is a relevant factor, conceiving of it as a process has greater explanatory value.

The process perspective on leadership also has greater value than its counterparts for anyone interested in becoming a more influential participant in groups. I say this for a number of reasons. First, the perspective suggests that leadership is not the special province of any single group member. The role perspective also has this virtue, but nonetheless unfortunately encourages the identification of leadership with particular individuals, namely, those who respond most frequently to certain kinds of situations. The process perspective, in contrast, places the focus of interest sharply on acts that have intended consequences. As a result, the process perspective sensitizes us to the need for careful thought about the ways in which we attempt to deal with needs and related problems. Finally, the perspective steers away from formulae for success and in the direction of an expanded awareness of and appreciation for flexibility, adaptability, and persistence. It encourages the view of group interaction as complex and, therefore, recognizes that efforts to deal with problems must take cognizance of this complexity. Problems of leadership are not amenable to simplistic solutions. They are difficult to resolve, and this realization is most evident in the behavior of those who approach leadership from the process perspective.

### Qualities Supportive of Leadership

Subscribing to the process perspective on leadership at first may appear to have little practical significance. It could easily be inferred from the examination of leadership to this point that the process is so situationally bound that there is little of hope of ever being able to develop appropriate skills. If by *skills* we mean a set of techniques that invariably produce desired outcomes, or even a set of guidelines on which we can consistently rely, the observation is probably correct. The leadership as process perspective, however, requires us to think about the phenomenon in a somewhat unconventional way. In this context, skill is not so much a matter of technique and strategy as it is a matter of understanding—understanding of what factors contribute to problematic situations, the relative appropriateness of different responses to them, and the probability that any particular response will have the desired effect. When we begin to think in these terms, the implications of the process perspective have considerable practical significance.

For purposes of illustration, consider a problem-solving group in which all but one of the members have come to the conclusion that Alternative A provides the best solution to a problem. The holdout prefers Alternative B. Assume that for some reason it is important to the group to have consensus. Under these conditions, a common tendency is for the group's majority either to pressure the deviant member to yield or to convince the member that he or she is wrong. Acquiescence, were it to occur in the situation described, might well be reluctant, with the resulting consensus being less than genuine. A more desirable approach to the difficulty might be to invite the disagreeing member to provide reasons for his or her believing that Alternative B offers the better solution. At least two things could happen as a result of this open-handed gesture. First, the holdout might discover that he or she cannot articulate very good reasons for preferring the rejected alternative, in which case he or she could more willingly shift to the majority position. Second, the majority might discover that there are, in fact, very good reasons for rejecting the initially preferred alternative in favor of the other. In either case, the approach to the problem would have produced movement rather than increased resistance or a tenuous consensus.

The contributory act in the preceding example represents leadership. Moreover, it is illustrative of the kind of diagnostic and analytical capability the process perspective assumes. Common experience ought to tell us that more often than not, a person resents being pressured and that when he or she perceives such pressure as a threat to freedom of thought and action, he or she can become almost impervious to social influence.[11] An individual sensitive to this possibility would, therefore, be more inclined to adopt an approach that limits the likelihood that others will feel threatened.

Understanding the factors that create problems for groups, the relative appropriateness of responses to these factors, and the odds that a given response will have the desired effect—as critical as it may be—is not fully adequate for successful leadership. Yet other personal qualities are helpful. Two that appear to be especially important are objectivity and considerateness.

As an ideal state, objectivity is a quality that none of us is likely to attain, but most of us undoubtedly are capable of behaving in a more objective fashion than we are often prone to do. The person who is attempting to resolve a group's difficulties is more apt to be successful if he or she addresses them as objectively as possible. Objectivity contributes to one's credibility[12] and appears to affect the ease with which leaders elicit consensus.[13] (see Gouran, 1969; Hill, 1976) Group members find objective participants more trustworthy than unobjective ones and, hence, are more susceptible to their influence.[14]

In the case of task-related problems, objectivity involves greater reliance on facts and accumulated knowledge than on personal opinions and feelings. A dispute concerning whether a proposed dues increase is desirable, for instance, might be more easily resolved in a meeting of officers by reference to an organization's anticipated expenses and projected income than by their injecting opinions about the likely reactions of other members.

When the difficulty in a group stems from interpersonal relationships, objectivity is more a matter of trying to minimize the influence of a person's personal feelings on his or her responses to the problem at hand. As an example, many times a group member will refrain from expressing disagreement, even though it is warranted, because he or she does not wish to hurt another participant's feeling. When disagreement is necessary to prevent the ineffective execution of a task, objectivity requires that it be voiced. In this sense, objectivity represents a participant's willingness to do what is necessary rather than what may be merely expedient.

In addition to the degree of objectivity a person displays in his or her efforts to deal with a group's needs and related problems, the manner in which a person interacts with others can be of critical importance. Tolerance, respect for others' rights and opinions, a willingness to listen, openness to competing ideas, and acknowledgement of the merit of other group members' contributions are all indices of the quality of considerateness. In the earlier-mentioned example of the conflict created by a holdout, the invitation to offer reasons for supporting the less-preferred alternative could be extended in a variety of ways. One that surely would have a low probability of success is, "OK, if your solution to the problem is so good, prove it." Taking this "Show me" posture would undoubtedly be offensive and, therefore, represents an extremely poor way of trying to manage a conflict. If anything, such a statement might well serve to intensify it.

A failure to consider the manner in which a person responds to problematic situations can and does render potentially useful contributions completely ineffective. The value of considerateness, therefore, should not be underestimated. To display the civility other group members are due seldom, if ever, reduces chances for resolving the problems a group faces and, in general, will improve them. As James MacGregor Burns concluded at the end of a massive historical study of effective leaders, "In real life, the most practical advice for leaders is not to treat pawns as pawns, nor princes like princes, but all persons as persons."[15] We would all do well to remember this in trying to surmount the challenges that the problems of leadership present.

## Notes

1. I should point out here that most of my discussion deals with task-oriented groups, but many of the issues raised apply equally well to informal and social groups.
2. P. V. Crosbie, "Sociometric Structure," in *Interaction in Small Groups* ed. P. V. Crosbie (New York: Macmillan, 1975), pp. 115-24.
3. Bruce Jesse Biddle and Edwin John Thomas, *Role Theory: Concept and Research* (New York: John Wiley & Sons, 1966).
4. M. E. Shaw, *Group Dynamics: The Psychology of Small Group Behavior*, third ed. (New York: McGraw-Hill, 1981), p. 271.
5. D. Kipnis, The Powerholders (Chicago: University of Chicago Press, 1976).
6. H. H. Kelley and J. W. Thibaut, *Interpersonal Relations* (New York: John Wiley & Sons, 1978), p. 31.
7. J. M. Burns, *Leadership* (New York: Harper & Row, 1978).
8. From this point forward, I shall use the term *position* to refer to an assigned role for which a clearly specified set of responsibilities has been identified.
9. D. S. Gouran, "Principles of Counteractive Influence in Decision-Making and Problem-Solving Groups," in *Small Group Communication: A Reader*, fourth ed., R. S. Cathcart and L. A. Samovar, eds. (Dubuque, Iowa: William C. Brown, (1984), pp. 166-81.
10. B. A. Fisher, "Leadership as Medium: Treating Complexity in Group Communication Research," *Small Group Behavior* (1985), vol. 16, pp. 167-96.
11. J. W. Brehm. A *Theory of Psychological Reactance* (New York: Academic Press, 1966).
12. H. C. Russell, *An Investigation of Leadership Maintenance Behavior*, unpublished Ph.D. dissertation, Indiana University, Bloomington, Indiana.
13. D. S. Gouran, "Variables Related to Consensus in Group Discussions of Questions of Policy," *Speech Monographs* (1985), vol. 36, pp. 387-91; and T. A. Hill, "An Experimental Study of the Relationship Between Opinionated Leadership and Small Group Consensus," *Communication Monographs* (1976), vol. 43, pp. 246-57.
14. G. Lumsden, "An Experimental Study of the Effects of Verbal Agreement on Leadership Maintenance in Problem-Solving Discussions," *Central States Speech Journal* (1974), vol. 25, pp. 270-76.
15. Burns, *op. cit.*, p. 462.

# 27

# Corporate Quality Circles: Using Small Groups in Organizations

*Susan A. Hellweg* and *Kevin L. Freiberg*

In recent years increasing interest in the quality circle concept has been shown by United States corporations. In line with this increase, scores of books and trade journal articles have appeared describing step-by-step techniques for implementing quality circles and documenting success stories of their use in corporations around the globe.

The purpose of this paper is to examine theoretical and pragmatic extensions to the quality circle concept in view of the following questions: (1) Do they simply represent a "passing fad," or do they have long-range potential that can contribute to the widely known productivity declines in United States corporations and to the human relations aspects of organizational life? (2) To what degree have they been empirically tested by academic scholars? (3) What are the communicative implications of quality circles, particularly in the context of small group theory as it applies to organizations?

## Rudimentary Elements of the Concept

Quality circles can be regarded as a form of organizational intervention strategy to enhance productivity and product quality through employee participation. Operationally, quality circles are small groups of individual employees who normally work together; they voluntarily meet regularly to identify problems relating to productivity and product quality, discuss them, identify and analyze the causes of these problems, recommend solutions to management, and subsequently monitor the results.

## Historical Development of Quality Circles

In 1950 an American expert in statistical quality control, William Deming, introduced the quality circles concept in Japan, as part of the

World War II reconstruction effort. The JUSE (Japanese Union of Scientists and Engineers), as well as the Japanese Government, reinforced the concept by making quality a national goal. In 1954 Juran, another American quality control expert, introduced the idea of managerial participation in quality control activities in Japan. From Deming's statistical orientation to quality control and Juran's concept of managerial involvement in the process, Japan revolutionized its industries. To further inculcate quality control into the minds of the labor force, training programs focused on the concept blossomed and soon became widespread, as did regular magazine publications such as Quality Control for Foremen.

Deming's contribution centered on rigorous statistical methods to diagnose quality control problems and so monitor the production process. Juran emphasized the need for the involvement of managers and workers, not just quality control engineers, in a company in the quality control arena.

### Prevalence of Quality Circles

In 1974 the quality circles concept was first introduced in this country, at Lockheed's Space and Missile Unit in Sunnyvale, California. The initial diffusion of quality circles in the United States, according to Wood, Hull, and Azumi took place mainly in large corporations, particularly quality-conscious ones, such as those in the aerospace and defense industry; or in ones experiencing significant productivity difficulties, such as the automotive industry.[1] It is interesting to note that several of the Lockheed managers originally involved in the adoption of quality circles in United States industry subsequently organized the International Association of Quality Circles (IAQC), which still exists today to provide an institutionalized forum for discussing and promoting the quality circles concept.

According to Barra, there are approximately 1,200,000 quality circles present in corporations on a worldwide basis, involving a membership of approximately 12,000,000 employees.[2] The author cites the following figures for the number of quality circles in various countries around the globe:[3]

| | |
|---|---|
| Japan | 1,000,000 |
| Korea | 50,000 |
| Taiwan, China, Philippines, Thailand, Malaysia, and Singapore | 50,000 |
| South America (mostly Brazil) | 50,000 |

| United States | 25,000 |
| Canada | 2,500 |
| Mexico | 1,000 |
| France | 1,000 |
| United Kingdom, Belgium, Germany, Netherlands, Denmark, Sweden, and Norway | 1,500 |

## Relationship of the Quality Circles Concept

According to Nishiyama, the purposes of a quality circle are to (1) identify job-related problems; (2) improve production methods; (3) improve production skills among circle members; (4) enhance worker morale and motivation; and (5) stimulate teamwork within organizational groups.[4]

The quality circle facilitator functions, according to Wood, Hull, and Azumi are (1) to promote and help implement the corporate quality circle program; (2) to train members in the quality circle meetings; (3) to guide the initial quality circle meetings; (4) to solve any problems which emerge within the functioning of the circle group; and (5) to serve as a liaison between the circle group and organizational personnel who control informational resources required by the group.[5]

The quality circle leader, who directs the discussion that takes place, is often the supervisor to whom the workers in the circle normally report. Since the quality circle leader is typically expected to be supportive, nondirective, and nonevaluative, there is often a significant role shift required from that of work supervisor.

Quality circles are normally convened on a voluntary basis on company time. Leaders and members are provided training in various problem-solving techniques (cause-effect analysis, Pareto analysis, force field analysis, histograms) and group process techniques (nominal group techniques, brain-storming).

## Adoption of a Japanese Work Concept to American Firms

At the core of evaluating the feasibility of the Japanese-originated quality circles concept in United States firms must be the consideration of the implications of cultural differences between the two countries and, in particular, ones affecting organizational management orientations.

Fitzgerald and Murphy point to five such differences: United States organizational values stress individualism, competition, profits and growth, minimization in decision making, and high reliance on status lines, in contrast to Japanese organizational values that stress collectivism, collaboration, human competence, maximization in decision making, and low reliance on status lines.[6]

Nishiyama[7] and Ramsing and Blair[8] point to other important cultural variations: (1) a tolerance for a certain level of product defects in United States companies; (2) the adversarial role of unions in the United States in contrast to a nonadversarial role in Japan; (3) the presence of a relatively homogeneous population in Japan, such that workers are less individualistic and more team-oriented than are their counterparts in the United States; and (4) guarantees of job security and lifetime employment within companies in Japan.

## Strengths of and Potential Problems with Quality Circles

Aside from the primary purpose of quality circles to enhance product quality and production process effectiveness, a number of by-products are possible, given that the circles operate as they are designed to and the conditions are optimal:

1. product quality consciousness raising among employees is likely to occur;
2. organizational output measurement may become further refined;
3. employees learn new problem-solving skills, and the organization places an increasing emphasis on training and development;
4. members become sensitized to cost-reduction orientations;
5. team building within work groups can be stimulated, as well as pride in the outcomes of their efforts;
6. organizational planning and streamlining are made a priority among a greater number of employees;
7. the potential of various employees can be realized;
8. a collaborative spirit among workers can emerge;
9. potential organizational solutions are presented on the basis of thorough analysis;
10. communication flows become restructured between management and workers;
11. organizational change can become easier; and
12. workers receive greater feedback on task outcomes through group functioning.

Various problems can emerge with the adoption of the quality circles:

1. an initial decline in productivity can take place due to the orientation and problem-solving time required by the circles and contingent upon the ability of the circles to function effectively;
2. a considerable investment of time and personnel is involved in

implementing and operating the quality circles in an organization, as well as in providing the necessary training for leaders and members;
3. a threat to existing lines of authority is possible, since employees become participants in identifying system problems and providing recommendations for solutions;
4. initial confusion can prevail in the setting up of quality circles and the involving of employees in the process;
5. proposals rejected by management can dampen circle member morale; and
6. lower- and middle-management personnel can feel threatened by quality circle activity, since outcomes can be submitted directly to higher level management.

### Conditions for Effective Quality Circle Functioning

Quality circles cannot possibly be operationally effective unless management is willing not only to invest time and human resources into the process, but also to deal with recommendations coming through circle activity which can challenge traditional forms of operational procedures, policies, and relationships.

Quality circle groups must have significant concerns on which to concentrate their activity; inconsequential concerns will undermine the motivational thrust of the group. In addition, worker problems do not always fit into the quality circle concept; ones that do not need to be isolated and channeled through other means of resolution.

Because quality circles are driven in part by a concern for product quality, they are probably most effective in situations where human factors are a primary consideration in production efforts. In addition, the more product-quality oriented the firm, the more appropriate quality circles become as an intervention strategy. Quality circles can also be more useful with blue-collar workers than with white-collar workers where performance measures are more difficult to pinpoint and individualistic orientations become more prevalent.

### Empirical Research on Quality Circles

Although a number of conceptual papers have been written on quality circles,[9] few empirical studies have appeared testing the viability of the quality circles concept, specifically in terms of desired organizational outcomes or communicative implications of their operation.

Stinnett and Perrill conducted a study of quality circles in a circuit board factory.[10] The unit tested was separated from the main plant. Pre- and post-measures were made in regard to the ninety-seven employees participating in the factory quality circles. Baseline productivity measures were taken. No control group was utilized in the study.

Personal assessments were made specifically with regard to the following: product quality (importance of producing a quality product), work measures and feedback, reward, leadership, organizational structure effectiveness, participation, communication effectiveness, satisfaction, peer relationships, and group process. Six months intervened between the pre- and post-measures. In addition to the perceptual assessments, product quality data were collected in terms of the following: boards scrapped, boards passing first inspection, and boards passing final inspection. Correlational tests were run between employee ratings of the quality circle process and the outcome measurement components.

Although the researchers made no attempts to produce any causal claims from the data collected in the study, they did uncover intriguing results that deserve validation in other organizational settings.

Jenkins and Shimada conducted a controlled field experiment on the impact of quality circle training procedures and activities on worker performance in an electronics company.[11] Significant improvements were demonstrated with regard to specific performance parameters relating to product quality. Specifically, worker gross output rates were not found to change significantly, but the work quality was shown to improve. Workers were found to commit fewer errors, and the errors that they did commit were found to be less expensive to rectify.

## Pragmatic Evaluation of Quality Circles

Wood, Hull, and Azumi (1982) developed the following criteria and indicators for the pragmatic assessment of quality circle programs:[12]

1. Productivity
   - group/departmental performance rates
   - individual performance rates
   - standardized unit costs
2. Product Quality
   - reject rates
   - client evaluation
3. Cost Savings
   - materials/labor costs
   - machine maintenance costs
   - wastage costs

4. Worker Morale
   - satisfaction with supervision
   - satisfaction with coworkers
   - satisfaction with work content
   - satisfaction with organization
   - satisfaction with QCs
5. Attendance
   - absenteeism
   - turnover
   - attendance at QC meetings

For either empirical or pragmatic evaluation of quality circles, several typical research issues must emerge: (1) the need for pre- and post-measurements; (2) the isolation of moderating variable effects; (3) the need for comparison groups, specifically control versus treatment groups; (4) the realization of potential temporal effects in the implementation of quality circles, such as novelty effects at their inception; and (5) the need for multiple measurement forms.

### Future Empirical Directions for Quality Circles

The concept of quality circles, as Stinnett and Perrill suggest, provides considerable potential for organizational communication scholars for empirical research.[13]

Jablin[14] and Putnam[15] have argued for the influx of field research in group communication in the organizational context to balance out the myriad of laboratory studies that have been conducted, primarily out of the organizational context. Quality circles can provide organizational communication researchers with a useful outlet to perform such studies.

Downs and Hain[16] and Hellweg and Phillips[17] have described problems that exist in the literature that addresses establishing a link between communication and productivity or performance. Some of the difficulties involved are centered in developing meaningful and consistent definitions and operationalizations of constructs and variation in measurement techniques. Quality circles, once again, can serve as a useful outlet for organizational communication scholars to pursue this area of endeavor further.

From a pragmatic view, Ramsing and Blair point to the following questions about quality circles which could in some variation be put to empirical test: (1) How would the quality circle approach measure up to socio-technical intervention techniques? (2) Would United States corporations benefit more through automation expenditures than through the development of quality circles? (3) Are quality circles best implemented into ongoing workgroups? (4) Are quality circles more effective when introduced as a second intervention strategy after solid management-employee relationships have been established? (5) Is the quality circles approach superior to other intervention techniques such as team building, where the focus is on the improvement of interpersonal relations within the work group and in the supervisor-subordinate dyad?[18]

Quality circles from an empirical viewpoint might lend themselves well to a number of studies utilizing variables important to communication functioning within organizations:

1. Small group studies on cooperative and competitive orientations, group history, group size, leadership strategies, individual versus group contributions, problem-solving processes.
2. Motivational studies, specifically in regard to intrinsic and extrinsic forms of motivation, rewards and behaviors, presence of social cues.
3. Role conflict and role ambiguity studies.
4. Organizational socialization studies.
5. Organizational and communication climate studies.
6. Supervisor-subordinate studies to assess upward distortion effects, supervisor communication style, semantic information distance effects, perceptions of supervisor-subordinate credibility and homophily (as a function of quality circle participation), effects of various forms of perceived power on quality circle interaction, effects of quality circle interaction on perceptions of supervisor satisfaction.
7. Feedback studies (utilization of immediate and delayed forms of feedback, group versus individual feedback, quality and quantity of feedback).

The purpose of this paper has been to examine the quality circles concept as an organizational intervention strategy in view of their communicative implications, both empirically and pragmatically.

Future research needs to test further the specific effects of quality circles in various organizational contexts on organizational functioning and the individual employee to (1) learn the degree to which they can be a successful intervention strategy, given the cultural differences from the country in which they originated; and (2) assess the conditions under which they operate most effectively.

### Notes

1. Robert Wood, Frank Hull, and Koya Azumi, "Evaluating Quality Circles," paper presented at the Academy of Management Convention, New York City, August 1982.

2. Ralph Barra, *Putting Quality Circles to Work: A Practical Strategy for Boosting Productivity and Profits* (New York: McGraw-Hill, 1983).
3. *Ibid.,* p. 165.
4. Kazuo Nishiyama, "Japanese Quality Control Circles," paper presented at the International Communication Association Convention, Minneapolis, Minn., May 1981.
5. Wood et al., *op. cit.*
6. Laurie Fitzgerald and Joseph Murphy, *Quality Circles: A Strategic Approach* (San Diego, Calif.: University Associates, 1982).
7. Nishiyama, *op. cit.*
8. Kenneth D. Ramsing and John D. Blair, "An Expression of Concern about Quality Circles," paper presented at the Academy of Management Convention, New York City, August 1982.
9. E.g., Nishiyama; Ramsing and Blair; and Wood et al., *op. cit.*
10. William D. Stinnett and Norman K. Perrill, "Quality Circles, Attitudes, and Productivity in a Circuit Board Factory," paper presented at the International Communication Association, Boston, May 1982.
11. Kenneth M. Jenkins and Justin Y. Shimada, "Effects of Quality Control Circles on Worker Performance: A Field Experiment," paper presented at the Academy of Management Convention, Dallas, August 1983.
12. Wood et al., *op. cit.,* p. 27.
13. Stinnett and Perrill, *op. cit.*
14. Fredric M. Jablin, "Groups with Organizations: Current Issues and Directions for Future Research," paper presented at the Central States Speech Association Convention, Chicago, April 1980.
15. Linda L. Putnam, "Understanding the Unique Characteristics of Groups Within Organizations," paper presented at the Academy of Management Convention, Dallas, August 1983.
16. Cal Downs and Tony Hain, "Productivity and Communication," in *Communication Yearbook 5,* ed. Michael Burgoon (New Brunswick, N.J.: Transaction Books, 1982), pp. 435-53.
17. Susan A. Hellweg and Steven L. Phillips, "Communication and Productivity in Organizations," *Public Productivity Review* (December 1982), vol. 6, no. 4, pp. 276-88.
18. Ramsing and Blair, *op. cit.*

# Part VIII

# ALTERNATIVE FORMS OF CONFERENCING

# 28

# Assets and Liabilities in Group Problem Solving: The Need for an Integrative Function[1]

*Norman R. F. Maier*

A number of investigations have raised the question of whether group problem solving is superior, inferior, or equal to individual problem solving. Evidence can be cited in support of each position so that the answer to this question remains ambiguous. Rather than pursue this generalized approach to the question, it seems more fruitful to explore the forces that influence problem solving under the two conditions. It is hoped that a better recognition of these forces will permit clarification of the varied dimensions of the problem-solving process, especially in groups.

The forces operating in such groups include some that are assets, some that are liabilities, and some that can be either assets or liabilities, depending upon the skills of the members, especially those of the discussion leader. Let us examine these three sets of forces.

## Group Assets

### Greater Sum Total of Knowledge and Information

There is more information in a group than in any of its members. Thus problems that require the utilization of knowledge should give groups an advantage over individuals. Even if one member of the group (e.g., the leader) knows much more than anyone else, the limited unique knowledge of lesser-informed individuals could serve to fill in some gaps in knowledge. For example, a skilled machinist might contribute to an engineer's problem solving and an ordinary workman might supply information on how a new machine might be received by workers.

### Greater Number of Approaches to a Problem

It has been shown that individuals get into ruts in their thinking. Many obstacles stand in the way of achieving a goal, and a solution must circumvent these. The individual is handicapped in that he tends to persist in his approach and thus fails to find another approach that might solve the problem in a simpler manner. Individuals in a group have the same failing, but the approaches in which they are persisting may be different. For example, one researcher may try to prevent the spread of a disease by making man immune to the germ, another by finding and destroying the carrier of the germ, and still another by altering the environment so as to kill the germ before it reaches man. There is no way of determining which approach will best achieve the desired goal, but undue persistence in any one will stifle new discoveries. Since group members do not have identical approaches, each can contribute by knocking others out of ruts in thinking.

### Participation in Problem Solving Increases Acceptance

Many problems require solutions that depend upon the support of others to be effective. Insofar as group problem solving permits participation and influence, it follows that more individuals accept solutions when a group solves the problem than when one person solves it. When one individual solves a problem he still has the task of persuading others. It follows, therefore, that when groups solve such problems, a greater number of persons accept and feel responsible for making the solution work. A low-quality solution that has good acceptance can be more effective than a higher-quality solution that lacks acceptance.

### Better Comprehension of the Decision

Decisions made by an individual, which are to be carried out by others, must be communicated from the decision-maker to the decision-executors. Thus individual problem solving often requires an additional stage—that of relaying the decision reached. Failures in this communication process detract from the merits of the decision and can even cause its failure or create a problem of greater magnitude than the initial problem that was solved. Many organizational problems can be traced to inadequate communication of decisions made by superiors and transmitted to subordinates, who have the task of implementing the decision.

The chances for communication failures are greatly reduced when the individuals who must work together in executing the decision have participated in making it. They not only understand the solution because they saw it develop, but they are also aware of the several other alternatives that were considered and the reasons why they were discarded. The common assumption that decisions supplied by superiors are arbitrarily reached therefore disappears. A full knowledge of goals, obstacles, alternatives, and factual information is essential to communication, and this communication is maximized when the total problem-solving process is shared.

## Group Liabilities

### Social Pressure

Social pressure is a major force making for conformity. The desire to be a good group member and to be accepted tends to silence disagreement and favors consensus. Majority opinions tend to be accepted regardless of whether or not their objective quality is logically and scientifically sound. Problems requiring solutions based upon facts, regardless of feelings and wishes, can suffer in group problem-solving situations.

It has been shown that minority opinions in leaderless groups have little influence on the solution reached, even when these opinions are the correct ones.[4] Reaching agreement in a group often is confused with finding the right answer, and it is for this reason that the dimensions of a decision's acceptance and its objective quality must be distinguished.[5]

### Valence of Solutions

When leaderless groups (made up of three or four persons) engage in problem solving, they propose a variety of solutions. Each solution may receive both critical and supportive comments, as well as descriptive and explorative comments from other participants. If the number of negative and positive comments for each solution are algebraically summed, each may be given a *valence index*.[6] The first solution that receives a positive valence value of 15 tends to be adopted to the satisfaction of all participants about 85% of the time, regardless of its quality. Higher quality solutions introduced after the critical value for one of the solutions has been reached have little chance of achieving real consideration. Once some degree of consensus is reached, the jelling process seems to proceed rather rapidly.

The critical valence value of 15 appears not to be greatly altered by the nature of the problem or the exact size of the group. Rather, it seems to designate a turning point between the idea-getting process and the decision-making process (idea evaluation). A solution's valence index is not a measure of the number of persons supporting the solution, since a vocal minority can build up a solution's valence by actively pushing it. In this sense, valence becomes an influence in addition to social pressure in determining an outcome.

Since a solution's valence is independent of its objective quality, this group factor becomes an important liability in group problem solving, even when the value of a decision depends upon objective criteria (facts and logic). It becomes a means whereby skilled manipulators can have more influence over the group process than their proportion of membership deserves.

### Individual Domination

In most leaderless groups a dominant individual emerges and captures more than his share of influence on the outcome. He can achieve this end through a greater degree of participation (valence), persuasive ability, or stubborn persistence (fatiguing the opposition). None of these factors is related to problem-solving ability, so that the best problem solver in the group may not have the influence to upgrade the quality of the group's solution (which he would have had if left to solve the problem by himself).

Hoffman and Maier found that the mere fact of appointing a leader causes this person to dominate a discussion.[7] Thus, regardless of his problem-solving ability a leader tends to exert a major influence on the outcome of a discussion.

### Conflicting Secondary Goal: Winning the Argument

When groups are confronted with a problem, the initial goal is to obtain a solution. However, the appearance of several alternatives causes individuals to have preferences and once these merge the desire to support a position is created. Converting those with neutral viewpoints and refuting those with opposed viewpoints now enters into the problem-solving process. More and more the goal becomes that of winning the decision rather than finding the best solution. This new goal is unrelated to the quality of the problem's solution and therefore can result in lowering the quality of the decision.[8]

## Factors That Serve As Assets or Liabilities

### Disagreement

The fact that discussion may lead to disagreement can serve either to create hard feelings among members or lead to a resolution of conflict and hence to an innovative solution.[9] The first of these outcomes of disagreement is a liability, especially with regard to the acceptance of solutions; while the second is an asset, particularly

where innovation is desired. A leader can treat disagreement as undesirable and thereby reduce the probability of both hard feelings and
innovation, or he can maximize disagreement and risk hard feelings in
his attempts to achieve innovation. The skill of a leader requires his
ability to create a climate for disagreement which will permit innovation without risking hard feelings. The leader's perception of disagreement is one of the critical factors in this skill area.[10] Others involve
permissiveness,[11] delaying the reaching of a solution,[12] techniques for
processing information and opinions,[13] and techniques for separating
idea-getting from idea-evaluation.[14]

### Conflicting Interests versus Mutual Interests

Disagreement in discussion may take many forms. Often participants
disagree with one another with regard to solutions, but when issues
are explored one finds that these conflicting solutions are designed to
solve different problems. Before one can rightly expect agreement on
a solution, there should be agreement on the nature of the problem.
Even before this, there should be agreement on the goal, as well as on
the various obstacles that prevent the goal from being reached. Once
distinctions are made between goals, obstacles, and solutions (which
represent ways of overcoming obstacles), one finds increased opportunities for cooperative problem solving and less conflict.[15]

Often there is also disagreement regarding whether the objective of
a solution is to achieve quality or acceptance,[15] and frequently a stated
problem reveals a complex of separate problems, each having separate
solutions so that a search for a single solution is impossible.[17] Communications often are inadequate because the discussion is not syn-
chronized and each person is engaged in discussing a different aspect.
Organizing discussion to synchronize the exploration of different aspects of the problem and to follow a systematic procedure increases
solution quality.[18] The leadership function of influencing discussion
procedure is quite distinct from the function of evaluating or contributing ideas.[19]

When the discussion leader aids in the separation of the several
aspects of the problem-solving process and delays the solution-mind-
edness of the group,[20] both solution quality and acceptance improve;
when he hinders or fails to facilitate the isolation of these varied
processes, he risks a deterioration in the group process.[21] His skill thus
determines whether a discussion drifts toward conflicting interests or
whether mutual interests are located. Cooperative problem solving can
only occur after the mutual interests have been established and it is

surprising how often they can be found when the discussion leader makes this his task.[22]

### Risk Taking

Groups are more willing than individuals to reach decisions involving risks.[23] Taking risks is a factor in acceptance of change, but change may either represent a gain or a loss. The best guard against the latter outcome seems to be primarily a matter of a decision's quality. In a group situation this depends upon the leader's skill in utilizing the factors that represent group assets and avoiding those that make for liabilities.

### Time Requirements

In general, more time is required for a group to reach a decision than for a single individual to reach one. Insofar as some problems require quick decisions, individual decisions are favored. In other situations acceptance and quality are requirements, but excessive time without sufficient returns also represents a loss. On the other hand, discussion can resolve conflicts, whereas reaching consensus has limited value.[24] The practice of hastening a meeting can prevent full discussion, but failure to move a discussion forward can lead to boredom and fatigue-type solutions, in which members agree merely to get out of the meeting. The effective utilization of discussion time (a delicate balance between permissiveness and control on the part of the leader), therefore, is needed to make the time factor an asset rather than a liability. Unskilled leaders tend to be too concerned with reaching a solution and therefore terminate a discussion before the group potential is achieved.[25]

### Who Changes

In reaching consensus or agreement, some members of a group must change. Persuasive forces do not operate in individual problem solving in the same way they operate in a group situation; hence, the changing of someone's mind is not an issue. In group situations, however, who changes can be an asset or a liability. If persons with the most constructive views are induced to change, the end-product suffers; whereas if persons with the least constructive points of view change, the end-product is upgraded. The leader can upgrade the quality of a decision because his position permits him to protect the person with a minority view and increase his opportunity to influence the majority position. This protection is a constructive factor because a minority viewpoint influences only when facts favor it.[26]

The leader also plays a constructive role insofar as he can facilitate communications and thereby reduce misunderstandings.[27] The leader has an adverse effect on the end-product when he suppresses minority views by holding a contrary position and when he uses his office to promote his own views.[28] In many problem-solving discussions the untrained leader plays a dominant role in influencing the outcome, and when he is more resistant to changing his views than are the other participants, the quality of the outcome tends to be lowered. This negative leader-influence was demonstrated by experiments in which untrained leaders were asked to obtain a second solution to a problem after they had obtained their first one.[29] It was found that the second solution tended to be superior to the first. Since the dominant individual had influenced the first solution, he had won his point and therefore ceased to dominate the subsequent discussion which led to the second solution. Acceptance of a solution also increases as the leader sees disagreement as idea-producing rather than as a source of difficulty or trouble.[30] Leaders who see some of their participants as troublemakers obtain fewer innovative solutions and gain less acceptance of decisions made than leaders who see disagreeing members as persons with ideas.

### The Leader's Role for Integrated Groups

*Two Differing Types of Group Process*

In observing group problem solving under various conditions it is rather easy to distinguish between cooperative problem-solving activity and persuasion or selling approaches. Problem-solving activity includes searching, trying out ideas on one another, listening to understand rather than to refute, making relatively short speeches, and reacting to differences in opinion as stimulating. The general pattern is one of rather complete participation, involvement, and interest. Persuasion activity includes the selling of opinions already formed, defending a position held, either not listening at all or listening in order to be able to refute, talking dominated by a few members, unfavorable reactions to disagreement, and a lack of involvement of some members. During problem solving the behavior observed seems to be that of members interacting as segments of a group. The interaction pattern is not between certain individual members, but with the group as a whole. Sometimes it is difficult to determine who should be credited with an idea. "It just developed," is a reponse often used to describe the solution reached. In contrast, discussions involving selling or persuasive behavior seem to consist of a series of interpersonal interactions with each individual retaining his identity. Such groups do not function as integrated units but as separate individuals, each with an agenda. In one situation the solution is unknown and is sought; in the other, several solutions exist and conflict occurs because commitments have been made.

### The Starfish Analogy

The analysis of these two group processes suggests an analogy with the behavior of the rays of a starfish under two conditions; one with the nerve ring intact, the other with the nerve ring sectioned.[31] In the intact condition, locomotion and righting behavior reveal that the behavior of each ray is not merely a function of local stimulation. Locomotion and righting behavior reveal a degree of coordination and interdependence that is centrally controlled. However, when the nerve ring is sectioned, the behavior of one ray still can influence others, but internal coordination is lacking. For example, if one ray is stimulated, it may step forward, thereby exerting pressure on the sides of the other four rays. In response to these external pressures (tactile stimulation), these rays show stepping responses on the stimulated side so that locomotion successfully occurs without the aid of neural coordination. Thus integrated behavior can occur on the basis of external control. If, however, stimulation is applied to opposite rays, the specimen may be "locked" for a time, and in some species the conflicting locomotions may divide the animal, thus destroying it.[32]

Each of the rays of the starfish can show stepping responses even when sectioned and removed from the animal. Thus each may be regarded as an individual. In a starfish with a sectioned nerve ring the five rays become members of a group. They can successfully work together for locomotion purposes by being controlled by the dominant ray. Thus if uniformity of action is desired, the group of five rays can sometimes be more effective than the individual ray in moving the group toward a source of stimulation. However, if "locking" or the division of the organism occurs, the group action becomes less effective than individual action. External control, through the influence of a dominant ray, therefore can lead to adaptive behavior for the starfish as a whole, but it can also result in a conflict that destroys the organism. Something more than external influence is needed.

In the animal with an intact nerve ring, the function of the rays is coordinated by the nerve ring. With this type of internal organization the group is always superior to that of the individual actions. When the rays function as a part of an organized unit, rather than as a group that is physically together, they become a higher type of organization—a single intact organism. This is accomplished by the nerve ring, which in itself does not do the behaving. Rather, it receives and processes the data which the rays relay to it. Through this central organization, the responses of the rays become part of a larger pattern so that together they constitute a single coordinated total response rather than a group of individual responses.

### The Leader as the Group's Central Nervous System

If we now examine what goes on in a discussion group we find that members can problem-solve as individuals, they can influence others by external pushes and pulls, or they can function as a group with varying degrees of unity. In order for the latter function to be maximized, however, something must be introduced to serve the function of the nerve ring. In our conceptualization of group problem solving and group decision,[33] we see this as the function of the leader. Thus the leader does not serve as a dominant ray and produce the solution. Rather, his function is to receive information, facilitate communications between the individuals, relay messages, and integrate the incoming responses so that a single unified response occurs.

Solutions that are the product of good group discussions often come as surprises to discussion leaders. One of these is unexpected generosity. If there is a weak member, this member is given less to do, in much the same way as an organism adapts to an injured limb and alters the function of other limbs to keep locomotion on course. Experimental evidence supports the point that group decisions award special consideration to needy members of groups.[34] Group decisions in industrial groups often give smaller assignments to the less gifted.[35] A leader could not effectually impose such differential treatment on group members without being charged with discriminatory practices.

Another unique aspect of group discussion is the way fairness is resolved. In a simulated problem situation involving the problem of how to introduce a new truck into a group of drivers, the typical group solution involves a trading of trucks so that several or all members stand to profit. If the leader makes the decision the number of persons who profit is often confined to one.[36] In industrial practice, supervisors assign a new truck to an individual member of a crew after careful evaluation of needs. This practice results in dissatisfaction, with the charge of *unfair* being leveled at him. Despite these repeated attempts to do justice, supervisors in the telephone industry never hit upon the notion of a general reallocation of trucks, a solution that crews invariably reach when the decision is theirs to make.

In experiments involving the introduction of change, the use of group discussion tends to lead to decisions that resolve differences.[37]

Such decisions tend to be different from decisions reached by individuals because of the very fact that disagreement is common in group problem solving and rare in individual problem solving. The process of resolving difference in a constructive setting causes the exploration of additional areas and leads to solutions that are integrative rather than compromises.

Finally, group solutions tend to be tailored to fit the interests and personalities of the participants; thus group solutions to problems involving fairness, fears, face-saving, etc., tend to vary from one group to another. An outsider cannot process these variables because they are not subject to logical treatment.

If we think of the leader as serving a function in the group different from that of its membership, we might be able to create a group that can function as an intact organism. For a leader, such functions as rejecting or promoting ideas according to his personal needs are out of bounds. He must be receptive to information contributed, accept contributions without evaluating them (posting contributions on a chalk board to keep them alive), summarize information to facilitate integration, stimulate exploratory behavior, create awareness of problems of one member by others, and detect when the group is ready to resolve differences and agree to a unified solution.

Since higher organisms have more than a nerve ring and can store information, a leader might appropriately supply information, but according to our model of a leader's role, he must clearly distinguish between supplying information and promoting a solution. If his knowledge indicates the desirability of a particular solution, sharing this knowledge might lead the group to find this solution, but the solution should be the group's discovery. A leader's contributions do not receive the same treatment as those of a member of the group. Whether he likes it or not, his position is different. According to our conception of the leader's contribution to discussion, his role not only differs in influence, but gives him an entirely different function. He is to serve much as the nerve ring in the starfish and to further refine this function so as to make it a higher type of nerve ring.

This model of a leader's role in group process has served as a guide for many of our studies in group problem solving. It is not our claim that this will lead to the best possible group function under all conditions. In sharing it we hope to indicate the nature of our guidelines in exploring group leadership as a function quite different and apart from group membership. Thus the model serves as a stimulant for research problems and as a guide for our analyses of leadership skills and principles.

## Conclusions

On the basis of our analysis, it follows that the comparison of the merits of group versus individual problem solving depends on the nature of the problem, the goal to be achieved (high quality solution, highly accepted solution, effective communication and understanding of the solution, innovation, a quickly reached solution, or satisfaction), and the skill of the discussion leader. If liabilities inherent in groups are avoided, assets capitalized upon, and conditions that can serve either favorable or unfavorable outcomes are effectively used, it follows that groups have a potential which in many instances can exceed that of a superior individual functioning alone, even with respect to creativity.

This goal was nicely stated by Thibaut and Kelley when they

> wonder whether it may not be possible for a rather small, intimate group to establish a problem solving process that capitalizes upon the total pool of information and provides for great interstimulation of ideas without any loss of innovative creativity due to social restraints.[38]

In order to accomplish this high level of achievement, however, a leader is needed who plays a role quite different from that of the members. His role is analogous to that of the nerve ring in the starfish which permits the rays to execute a unified response. If the leader can contribute the integrative requirement, group problem solving may emerge as a unique type of group function. This type of approach to group processes places the leader in a particular role in which he must cease to contribute, avoid evaluation, and refrain from thinking about solutions or group *products.* Instead he must concentrate on the group *process,* listen in order to understand rather than to appraise or refute, assume responsibility for accurate communication between members, be sensitive to unexpressed feelings, protect minority points of view, keep the discussion moving, and develop skills in summarizing.

## Notes

1. The research reported here was supported by Grant No. MH-02704 from the United States Public Health Service. Grateful acknowledgment is made for the constructive criticism of Melba Colgrove, Junie Janzen, Mara Julius, and James Thurber.
2. See reviews by L. R. Hoffman, "Group Problem Solving," in *Advances in Experimental Social Psychology,* vol. 2, ed. L. Berkowitz (New York: Academic Press, 1965), pp. 99-132; and H. H. Kelley and J. W. Thibaud, "Experimental Studies of Group Problem Solving and Process," in *Hand-*

*book of Social Psychology* ed. G. Lindzey (Cambridge, Mass.: Addison Wesley, 1954), pp. 735-85.

3. K. Duncker, "On Problem Solving," *Psychological Monographs* (1945), vol. 58, no. 5 (whole no. 270); N. R. F. Maier, "Reasoning in Humans. 1. On Direction," *Journal of Comparative Psychology* (1930), vol. 10, pp. 115-43; and M. Wertheimer, *Productive Thinking* (New York: Harper, 1959).

4. N. R. F. Maier and A. R. Solem, "The Contribution of a Discussion Leader to the Quality of Group Thinking: The Effective Use of Minority Opinions," *Human Relations* (1952), vol. 5, pp. 277-88.

5. Maier, *Problem Solving Discussions and Conferences: Leadership Methods and Skills* (New York: McGraw-Hill, 1963).

6. L. R. Hoffman and N. R. F. Maier, "Valence in the Adoption of Solutions by Problem-Solving Groups: Concept, Method, and Results," *Journal of Abnormal and Social Psychology* (1964), vol. 69, pp. 264-71.

7. Hoffman and Maier, "Valence in the Adoption of Solutions by Problem-Solving Groups: II. Quality and Acceptance as Goals of Leaders and Members," unpublished manuscript, 1967.

8. *Ibid.*

9. Hoffman, "Conditions for Creative Problem Solving," *Journal of Psychology* (1961), vol. 52, pp. 429-44; L. R. Hoffman, E. Harburg, and N. R. F. Maier, "Differences and Disagreement as Factors in Creative Group Problem Solving," *Journal of Abnormal and Social Psychology* (1962), vol. 64, pp. 206-14; Hoffman and Maier, "Quality and Acceptance of Problem Solutions by Members of Homogeneous and Heterogeneous Groups," *Journal of Abnormal and Social Psychology* (1961), vol. 62, pp. 401-07; Maier, *The Appraisal Interview* (New York: Wiley, 1958); Maier, *Problem Solving Discussions and Conferences: Leadership Methods and Skills* (New York: McGraw-Hill, 1963); Maier and Hoffman, "Acceptance and Quality of Solutions as Related to Leaders' Attitudes toward Disagreement in Group Problem Solving," *Journal of Applied Behavioral Science* (1965), vol. 1, pp. 373-86.

10. Maier and Hoffman, "Acceptance and Quality," *op. cit.*

11. Maier, "An Experimental Test of the Effect of Training on Discussion Leadership," *Human Relations* (1953), vol. 6, pp. 161-73.

12. Maier and Hoffman, "Quality of First and Second Solutions in Group Problem Solving," *Journal of Applied Psychology,* vol. 44, pp. 278-83; Maier and Solem, "Improving Solutions by Turning Choice Situations into Problems," *Personnel Psychology* (1962), vol. 15, pp. 151-57.

13. Maier, *Problem Solving Discussions, op. cit.;* Maier and Hoffman, "Using Trained 'Developmental' Discussion Leaders to Improve Further the Quality of Group Decisions," *Journal of Applied Psychology* (1960), vol. 44, pp. 247-51; and N. R. F. Maier and R. A. Maier, "An Experimental Test of the Effects of 'Developmental' vs. 'Free' Discussions on the Quality of Group Decisions," *Journal of Applied Psychology* (1957), vol. 41, pp. 320-23.

14. Maier, "Screening Solutions to Upgrade Quality: A New Approach to Problem Solving Under Conditions of Uncertainty," *Journal of Psychology* (1960), vol. 49, pp. 217-31; Maier, *Problem Solving Discussions, op. cit.;* and A. F. Osborn, *Applied Imagination* (New York: Scribner's, 1953).

15. Hoffman and Maier, "The Use of Group Decision to Resolve a Problem of Fairness," *Personnel Psychology* (1959), vol. 12, pp. 545-59; Maier, "Screening Solutions," *op. cit.;* Maier, *Problem Solving Discussions, op. cit.;* Maier and Solem, "Improving Solutions," *op. cit.;* and Solem, "1965: Almost Anything I Can Do, We Can Do Better," *Personnel Administration* (1965), vol. 28, pp. 6-16.
16. Maier and Hoffman, "Types of Problems," *op. cit.*
17. Maier, *Problem Solving Solutions, op. cit.*
18. Maier and Hoffman, "Using Trained 'Developmental' Discussion," *op. cit.;* and Maier and Maier, *op. cit.*
19. Maier, "An Experimental Test of the Effect of Training on Discussion Leadership," *Human Relations* (1953), vol. 6, pp. 161-73; and Maier, "The Quality of Group Decisions as Influenced by the Discussion Leader," *Human Relations* (1950), vol. 3, pp. 155-74.
20. Maier, *The Appraisal Interview, op. cit.;* Maier, *Problem Solving Solutions, op. cit.;* and Maier and Solem, "Improving Solutions," *op. cit.*
21. Solem, "1965," *op. cit.*
22. Maier, *Principles of Human Relations* (New York: Wiley, 1952); Maier, *Problem Solving Solutions, op. cit.,* and N. R. F. Maier and J. J. Hayes, *Creative Management* (New York: Wiley, 1962).
23. M. A. Wallach and N. Kogan, "The Roles of Information, Discussion and Concensus in Group Risk Taking," *Journal of Experimental and Social Psychology* (1965), vol. 1, pp. 1-19; and M. A. Wallach, N. Kogan, and D. J. Bem, "Group Influence on Individual Risk Taking," *Journal of Abnormal and Social Psychology* (1962), vol. 65, pp. 75-86.
24. Wallach and Kogan, *op. cit.*
25. Maier and Hoffman, "Quality of First and Second Solutions," *op. cit.*
26. Maier, "Quality of Group Decisions," *op. cit.;* Maier, *Principles of Human Relations, op. cit.;* Maier and Solem, "Improving Solutions," *op. cit.*
27. Maier, *Principles of Human Relations, op. cit.;* and Solem, "1965," *op. cit.*
28. Maier and Hoffman, "Quality of First and Second Solutions," *op. cit.;* Maier and Hoffman, "Group Decisions in England and the United States," *Personnel Psychology* (1962), vol. 15, pp. 75-87; and Maier and Solem, "The Contribution of a Discussion Leader," *op. cit.*
29. Maier and Hoffman, "Using Trained 'Developmental' Discussion," *op. cit.*
30. Maier and Hoffman, "Acceptance and Quality," *op. cit.*
31. W. F. Hamilton, "Coordination in the Starfish, III. The Righting Reaction As A Phase of Locomotion (righting and locomotion)," Journal of Comparative Psychology (1922), vol. 2, pp. 81-94; A. R. Moore, "The Nervous Mechanism of Coordination in the Crinoid *Antedon rosaceus,*" *Journal of Genetic Psychology* (1924), vol. 6, pp. 281-88; Moore and M. Doudoroff, "Injury, Recovery and Function in an Aganglionic Central Nervous System," *Journal of Comparative Psychology* (1939), vol. 28, pp. 313-28; and T. C. Schneirla and Maier, "Concerning the Status of the Starfish," *Journal of Comparative Psychology* (1940), vol. 30, pp. 103-10.
32. W. Z. Crozier, "Notes on Some Problems of Adaptation," *Biological Bulletin* (1920), vol. 39, pp. 116-29; and Moore and Doudoroff, *op. cit.*

33. Maier, *Problem Solving Discussions, op. cit.*
34. Hoffman and Maier, "The Use of Group Decision," *op. cit.*
35. Maier, *Principles of Human Relations, op. cit.*
36. Maier and Hoffman, "Group Decision in England," *op. cit.;* and N. R. F. Maier and L. F. Zerfoss, "MRP: A Technique for Training Large Groups of Supervisors and Its Potential Use in Social Research," *Human Relations* (1952), vol. 5, pp. 177-86.
37. Maier, *Principles of Human Relations, op. cit.;* Maier, "An Experimental Test," *op. cit.;* Maier and Hoffman, "Organization and Creative Problem Solving," *op. cit.;* Maier and Hoffman, "Financial Incentives," *op. cit.;* and Maier and Hoffman, "Types of Problems," *op. cit.*
38. Thibaut and Kelley, *The Social Psychology of Groups* (New York: Wiley, 1961), p. 268.

# 29

# Audio Teleconferencing versus Face-to-Face Conferencing: A Synthesis of the Literature[1]

*Gene D. Fowler*
*Marilyn E. Wackerbarth*

## Introduction

Technological advances in communication make it possible to unite individuals and groups in distant locations through the use of audio conferencing systems. As audio conferencing is used more frequently in private and public organizational settings, it becomes important to examine a range of variables that are relevant to a comparison of the traditional face-to-face and the newer audio mode of conferencing. The purpose of this review is to examine and compare process and outcome variables that may be affected by the medium of communication. The substitution of audio conferencing for face-to-face meetings is attractive because audio conferencing appears to save participant travel time and expenses incurred in face-to-face meetings.[2] However, additional behavioral variables which may be affected by communication mode require examination before a choice between audio conferences and face-to-face meetings can be made.[3]

Early research concerned with the extent to which audio mediated meetings may be substituted for face-to-face meetings indicated that only 3% of the civil servants interviewed felt that their business meetings could have been conducted satisfactorily by telephone. However, the particular tasks or types of meetings that were involved in the substitution were not specified. Later research using management personnel concentrated on describing tasks which could successfully be conducted via the telecommunication mode: (1) discussion of ideas; (2) conflict; (3) information seeking; (4) disciplinary interviews; (5)

problem solving; (6) presentation of report; (7) forming impressions of others; (8) delegation of work; (9) negotiations; (10) policy decision making; and (11) giving information to keep people in the picture.[4]

Williams made estimates of successful substitutions based on these specific types of meetings to be held.[5] With reference to research relevant to each of the eleven types of tasks, Williams estimated that 12% to 41% of these meetings could have been conducted effectively using an audio-only telecommunication system, and that 0% to 37% of the meetings actually required face-to-face communication.

A subsequent survey conducted by the Communications Studies Group in 1973 gathered more representative data from 115 office establishments.[6] Based on this information, Williams revised his earlier estimates with the conclusion that 24% to 52% of the meetings surveyed could have been held effectively using audio-only communication, and that 17% to 30% would have required face-to-face communication.[7] Although the potential for substitution may not be precisely specified, it seems clear that audio teleconferencing is often a viable alternative to face-to-face meetings.

According to the literature on teleconferencing, no general statements of superiority can be made for either mode; each has positive and negative aspects which may be important for various tasks in different settings. In order to clarify this body of literature and to enable potential users of audio conference systems to make informed decisions as to the practicality of the system for specific tasks, this review outlines research on several important variables, including: (1) task-information exchange, problem solving, bargaining and negotiation, and interviewing; (2) group processes—leadership and coalition formation; (3) interpersonal dynamics—person perception and communication climate; and (4) affective responses to each medium.

Recently published reviews of experimental comparisons of face-to-face and mediated communication support the present selection of major variables.[8] The present review expands upon earlier ones by including reports from field trials and users of currently operational audio conferencing systems. This review adopts a dichotomous structure focusing on the strengths and weaknesses for each communication mode as used by the Institute for the Future in "The Camelia Report."[9] In an expanded discussion of field and laboratory research findings such a structure should provide a clear explanation of the strengths and weaknesses of each mode for specific tasks and settings.

The use of laboratory experiments in evaluating the utility of telecommunications media is a relatively recent and valuable research innovation. Short advocates the use of laboratory experiments because they provide methods of control necessary for measuring the relative effectiveness of different media for various tasks.[10] Short also believes that field research cannot accurately measure effectiveness, but is most useful for measuring the acceptability of new media.

Williams argues that the methodological problems of laboratory research and the need for subsequent validation of research findings make field experiments and quasi-experiments a necessary part of the empirical study of communications media.[11] The research reported in this review incorporates a number of different methodological approaches. Consequently, problems of validation, control and comparability may exist where research findings have not been tested in both settings.

Comparisons of audio and face-to-face conferences are limited in many ways. Researchers have not, as yet, established methodological procedures that promote systematic analyses of audio mediated meetings. Research comparing face-to-face conferences with audio conferences consistently reports that people generally prefer the face-to-face condition. Face-to-face conferencing is the normal, accepted mode; thus, there are few reports which criticize it. Further research must be completed before audio conferencing can be evaluated on its own merits without being compared to the traditionally acceptable face-to-face mode.

This review is divided into three sections: (1) Audio Teleconferencing Strengths and Weaknesses; (2) Face-to-Face Conferencing Strengths and Weaknesses; and (3) Conclusion. The discussion of each category provides a description of structural and psychological variables which either enhance or detract from the utility of a particular communication mode; the conclusion includes general propositions of audio and face-to-face strengths and weaknesses that are consistently supported by the reported research.

### Audio Teleconferencing Strengths and Weaknesses

*Strengths*

There is a popularly held belief that communication via telephone is inferior to face-to-face communication.[12] Research findings do not support this simplistic notion; in many respects audio communication is equal, if not superior, to face-to-face communication. Comparisons of the two modes in diverse settings show audio teleconferencing to be an effective means for a variety of tasks.

*Problem Solving.* In a study of information transmission, Champness observed pairs communicating either face to face, through an opaque screen, or by telephone.[13] In each case one member of the pair dictated a letter to the other who had to recall various critical items. No differences in the number of transactions or the accuracy of scores were found.

Cooperative problem solving by telephone or face to face was the task for pairs of civil servants in a study by Champness and Davies.[14] Utilizing a human relations problem, the authors found that the agreed solution and the participants' satisfaction with their solution did not differ between the modes. Because the nature of this task made scoring difficult, Davies conducted two additional studies in which pairs of subjects, communicating face to face or by telephone, attempted to solve a business problem concerning the export performance of factories.[15] No significant differences were found in the accuracy of the solution, although it was arrived at more rapidly by telephone in both studies. Similarly, in a bargaining task, Champness found that when teams communicated face to face or by audio only, the outcome of the bargaining was not affected by medium.[16]

According to Remp, audio conference calls can be successfully implemented for use during public discussions and voting on a public issue.[17] The evaluation of sixteen conference call discussions indicated that participants were quite pleased with the conduct and efficiency of the audio conference meetings: access to the floor was easy; attention was good; participation eager; participants felt more attentive to what was being said in the audio mode; and a majority of participants found the audio meetings to be congenial. However, members felt less interpersonal influence in the audio than in the face-to-face meeting; they reported less perceived pressure to go along with group opinions and more ease in changing their options and positions. From these results, Remp suggested that a mass participatory system can be used to provide wider involvement in decision making processes in our society.

Albertson compared communication efficiency across three media (face to face, videophone and telephone) for a variety of communication tasks including transmission of verbal data, message acceptance, transmission of statistical information, and cooperative problem solving.[18] The communicators' perceptions of each other and attitudes toward the medium were also compared. The initial assumption that face-to-face communication would be the most efficient with telecommunications media acting as substitutes was not justified by the findings; communication was not always more efficient with the presence of a visual channel, and the telephone was the most accurate medium for conveying objective information.

An ongoing research program on interactive communication led by Chapanis compared communication across a wide range of media.[19] Chapanis typically required two-person teams to solve credible "real world" problems such as a geographic orientation problem, an equipment assembly problem or a library information retrieval problem. Subjects were either randomly assigned to communication mode and problem or they participated in all modes with a different problem for each. The dependent measures in this series were: (1) time to solution; (2) number of messages sent; (3) number of total words and words per message; and (4) behavioral measures of activities engaged in by the participants. Two consistently observed results were: (1) there was no significant difference between face to face and audio modes in the amount of time required to solve a problem; and (2) face-to-face communication was not superior to audio communication for factual problem solving.

*Bargaining and Negotiation.* In three experiments studying cooperation and competition across media, Short paired subjects who argued bargaining and negotiation problems via telephone and face to face.[20] In the first experiment, thirty pairs argued a management-union dispute; half argued face to face, and half argued via telephone. The telephone conversations led to more complete breakdowns in negotiation and to relatively greater success for the "union" side, which had a stronger case. A follow-up experiment changed the task to a bargaining problem about staff reductions in a government research laboratory, with equally strong arguments for both sides. Thirty-two pairs engaged in two versions of the task, one face to face and one by telephone. No media differences in the solution, or the method of arriving at the solution, were detected.

The conflicting findings of these two studies were explained with reference to the different tasks. The strength of the cases was asymmetrical in the first study and symmetrical in the second. In order to determine the relationship between media effects and strength of case, a third study, which included asymmetrical strength of arguments, was conducted. Forty-eight pairs communicated either face to face, by closed circuit television, or by audio only as they attempted to reduce business costs by cutting specific expenses. Half of the participants were allowed to choose the priorities for which they argued, while the other half were required to argue the opposite priorities. The individual who chose the order of priorities did relatively better, in terms of agreed outcome, in the face-to-face condition, while the individual who argued a "brief" was more successful over audio. This result suggests that the degree of personal involvement in negotiation was an important mediating variable affecting the influence of communication medium on the outcome.

A later study by Short measured the differences between audio and face-to-face media for resolving conflicts of opinion simulated with attitude change tasks.[21] Members of pairs argued controversial issues on which they disagreed. When "real disagreement" existed, there was more attitude change after an audio discussion; if a "contrived disagreement" existed, then the face-to-face condition benefited the member arguing his or her true beliefs. In two replications of this study, Short and Young confirmed earlier findings that audio led to more attitude change than face to face.[22]

One explanation of the occurrence of greater attitude change by audio may be found in the work of Wilson who used the same task to measure the influence of medium of communication on speech content.[23] He found face-to-face meetings to be more extreme in emotionality (more expressed hostility and friendliness), and telephone conversations seemed better for resolving the disagreements.

In a final experiment in this series, Short employed the same two conditions:[24] in one, subjects argued a controversial issue on which they disagreed; in the other they were given opposing briefs to argue on a neutral issue. Seventy-two pairs participated, each arguing via two of four available media: face to face, audio, and two different video systems. In the "real disagreement" condition, the finding of greater attitude change in audio was supported. No medium effect appeared in the neutral bargaining condition, nor did medium affect subjects' perceptions of each other.

According to Short's findings, audio meetings offered subtle advantages to some participants. In negotiations, Short found that the side with the strongest case was more successful in audio than in face to face. His task was a modification of an earlier one by Morley and Stephenson, who simulated a management-union wage negotiation in which one side was given a stronger case to argue.[25] The same interaction of media with strength of case was noted in each of these studies. Morley and Stephenson interpreted their results as indicating that the more constrained telephone channel favors an objective appraisal of the case, while the richer face-to-face mode permits the weaker side to enhance its position through personal appeal.

It appears that in bargaining and negotiation via audio, effective communication is less dependent on interpersonal than on substantive considerations; a visual image may actually be distracting to the substantive proceedings.[26] Continuing this line of reasoning, objectivity may be more easily maintained in an audio only condition where personal involvement is limited by a single channel. The findings of Short can be interpreted to support the proposition that an individual who is not personally involved (who maintains an objective position) is likely to be relatively more successful in negotiations in an audio condition.[27]

*Person Perception.* In a replication of earlier studies, Short paired ninety-six civil servants in discussions of controversial issues in audio, video, and face-to-face conditions.[28] Half of the subjects were in "real disagreement"; for the other half, one person had the task of convincing the other. The only positive media effect observed was on the rating of trustworthiness of the partner: Audio partners were rated as more trustworthy than those in the video or face-to-face conditions.

*Interviews.* Dyadic interaction observed in various types of interviews have provided the basis for many comparisons of audio and face-to-face communication. Generally, audio communication can be used as effectively as face-to-face communication in many interview situations. In a study of eighty interviews with strangers, Janofsky analyzed three dependent variables: (1) interviewees' total self-references; (2) interviewees' total affective self-references; and (3) the ratio of interviewees' affective self-references to total self-references.[29] She found that there were no significant differences for the three variables, and that interviewees were as willing to talk about their feelings over the telephone as in a face-to-face interview.

Young conducted an exploratory study of the effect of telecommunicated interviews on the perception of personality.[30] Interviewers each met three different interviewees, one face to face, one by audio-video, and one by audio only. The interviews were open-ended and aimed at discovering the interviewee's vocational interests. Comparisons of the ratings of the interviewee's personality (rated by both interviewer and interviewee) allowed for the assessment of accuracy of perception. Accuracy was not affected by medium of communication and audio was perceived as more revealing of personality than video or face to face.

In a controlled field experiment by Rogers, comparisons of telephone and face-to-face modes provided positive support for telephone interviews.[31] City residents responded to a fifty-minute interview which covered: (1) knowledge and attitudes; (2) family income; (3) voting behavior; and (4) educational level. Results indicated that the quality of data obtained via telephone and in-person interviews was comparable. The interviewer's style, whether judged "cool" (task-oriented) or "warm" (person-oriented), appeared to intrude somewhat on the qual-

to-face mode led to more positive evaluations of the conversation and partner than either video or telephone. A second finding indicated that audio communication was perceived as less "personal" than in person.

In one of a series of three experiments focusing on the effects of visibility on dyadic interaction, Argyle, Lalljee, and Cook paired subjects who role played either an interviewer or an interviewee in one of four conditions of visibility: only eyes visible; only face visible; only body visible; and no vision.[39] After the interview, subjects rated comfort, enjoyment of the encounter, and ease of perceiving the other's personality, emotions and reactions to self. Tape-recordings were analyzed for quantity of interruptions and total length of pauses.

Ratings of perception and comfort were not directly affected by the conditions of visibility; pauses were affected by conditions of visibility, with more pauses in face-only than in no-vision; and the least number of pauses were in the body-only and eyes-only conditions. Interruptions were slightly affected by the experimental conditions, with the most occurring under no vision and the least in eyes-only. One conclusion of this study was that visual feedback was needed to determine reactions of others, and the face was the most useful area to see.

*Problem Solving and Communication Climate.* Weston, Kristen, and O'Conner conducted a field experiment investigating the levels of task accomplishment and the nature of interpersonal relationships across three communication modes: audio-only teleconferencing, audio-video teleconferencing, and face-to-face conferences.[40] Subjects were asked to discuss all aspects in a communication course and make recommendations for implementation of changes and improvements in the course. This task was chosen as being credible for the participants, potentially complex, and permitting communication behaviors that would generalize to other groups and tasks. Analyses were performed on data collected from more than eleven hours of speaker-identified verbatim transcripts of the conference sessions and post-session questionnaires were compared with the objective analysis of the transcripts.

Overall, fewer words were spoken in the audio sessions. Audio groups spent less time in task-related discussion than face-to-face groups, but more time in developing and maintaining organization. Audio groups discussed the constraints of the technological system about three times as much as did video groups; audio participants spent less time developing and exploring various dimensions of the task situation. Discussion prior to making a recommendation was less complex in audio, with a greater tendency to treat task dimensions individually rather than in combination. The audio groups made far fewer recommendations and adjusted their recommendations considerably less than the other groups.

The interpersonal environment was measured according to the following categories: positive social-emotional, negative social-emotional, social-emotional uncertainty, social-emotional neutrality, and addressing behavior. The audio groups devoted less of their communication to simple agreement. Although audio group members reported *more* uncertainty about the conference situation, they expressed these feelings of uncertainty much *less* frequently during the sessions. Of the three modes, individuals in the face-to-face condition were the most willing to ask for help, understanding or interpretation; those in the audio condition regularly sought confirmation that an individual or group was still psychologically present. The audio mode members were the least willing to make statements of disagreement with others, and audio group members deflated the importance of the task about three times as often as did those in video or face-to-face conferences.

Overall, in this complex and interpersonally involving task, the audio-only medium generated a task environment that was much less productive and more hostile. The authors concluded that the audio-only medium appeared to seriously affect group performance in meetings held for the purpose of comprehensive decision making. For such tasks, audio conferencing was an undesirable choice.

*Interviews.* A comparison of telephone and face-to-face interviews conducted in a mental health survey found differences in reporting mental health symptoms.[41] Respondents to telephone interviews reported fewer symptoms of poor mental health and a greater number of socially desirable responses on topics of moderate privacy. The authors concluded that respondents were reluctant to reveal very personal information in either mode. With topics of intermediate privacy, the personal interview elicited greater reporting than the telephone interview.

*Leadership.* In the complex interaction of small groups, leadership is often a critical influence on group outcomes. Williams conducted a study in which small groups met either face to face or by an audio conference link.[42] In half of the groups a chairperson was appointed and given special instructions. After a thirty-minute discussion of ideas, it was found that the audio groups showed more move to consensus although face to face was preferred. Also, a chairperson seemed to improve the face-to-face groups, but was, if anything, detrimental for the audio groups.

According to Strickland and associates, the emergence of a leader from an undifferentiated discussion group may also be affected by communication mode.[43] Summary of the results of an experiment with ongoing discussion groups participating in face-to-face or video mediated modes indicated the following: (1) a behavioral hierarchy emerged and maintained itself significantly more often in face-to-face groups; and (2) attributions of idea quality and attractiveness were related to behavioral measures of interaction quantity in face-to-face groups but not in mediated groups. The authors speculated that mediated communication reduced interpersonal cues to the extent that the individuality of each group member was also reduced. Additionally, the formality of the mediated communication imposed restraints on communication which increased the participants' focus on task and decreased attention to interpersonal processes. Potential leaders may have found it more difficult to exert interpersonal influence in an audio as well as a video mediated group setting.

### Summary of Audio Strengths and Weaknesses

The general findings of the literature on audio strengths indicate that audio conferencing may be effective for information exchange, discussion of ideas, problem solving, some negotiations, and interviewing. Both laboratory experiments and field trials of audio conferencing support the substitution of audio for face-to-face meetings. Because audio conferences have long been assumed to be inferior in many respects to face-to-face meetings, this review has interpreted findings of comparability of the two modes as positive indications for the future use of audio conferencing.

An additional body of research indicates some weaknesses in audio conferencing which are related to certain tasks. For tasks which are of a complex nature, or which involve interpersonal factors, the audio mode may not be the most satisfactory choice. In some task situations, audio-only communication may create an impersonal, unproductive, and hostile communication environment.

Based on a series of experiments which separate visual contact from physical presence, Ritter and Stephenson concluded that comparisons of audio and face-to-face communication may be incompletely specifying elements of face-to-face communication.[44] The authors state that visual contact and physical presence provide different sets of cues that interact in a face-to-face meeting. Audio-only communication is without these cues which leads to depersonalized, task-oriented discussions.

### Face-to-Face Conference Strengths and Weaknesses

### Strengths

*Information Exchange and Problem Solving.* For intense interpersonal communication tasks face-to-face communication may be more suitable than audio-only. Support for this finding is presented by Champness in a study in which participants were asked to assess the utility of several media for four types of tasks: factual information exchange; general discussion; conflict; and interpersonal relations.[45] Three media, face-to-face, audio-video, and audio-only, were considered equally satisfactory for the first two tasks, but for conflict and interpersonal relations, face to face was significantly more satisfactory than either audio or video. Williams found face-to-face conversations elicited more positive evaluations of both the conversation and the conversation partner than did the telephone conversations.[46] In addition, he found that face-to-face communication was preferred in a "free discussion" task, while audio was preferred in a "priorities" task.

Favorable evidence for face-to-face communication involving other kinds of tasks has been established in several studies. In an investigation comparing communication efficiency across three media (face to face, videophone, and telephone) for a variety of communication tasks, Albertson found that for the transmission of statistical information, the face to face and videophone conditions took less time.[47] Subjects were shown a graph and given a set of four questions based on the data presented. In the telephone condition, the data were transmitted by the speaker as a series of twelve points in a standard time of sixty seconds. Two measures of communication efficiency were used: (1) accuracy of receiving the transmitted data; and (2) speed of assimilating that data. Although the telephone and face-to-face conditions were found to be equally efficient with respect to accuracy, subjects in the telephone condition took longer to assimilate the data than in the two visual conditions. Measures used in other tasks including transmission of verbal data, message acceptance, and cooperative problem solving, generally found the telecommunications media to be equal or superior in efficiency to the face-to-face condition.

In one of several studies comparing communication over various media, two-person teams were asked to solve real-world problems for which computers could be of assistance.[48] Teams communicated in four different modes: typewriting, handwriting, voice, and natural, unrestricted communication. Time to solution and measures of various behavioral and verbal activities were compared across modes. Subjects in the two oral modes solved problems much faster than did those in the two hard-copy modes, and there was no significant difference in time to solution between voice and face-to-face modes. Further, the face-to-face mode produced over a hundred more messages than the voice mode. Summarizing the results of his numerous studies, Chapanis reported consistent and repeated findings that more messages are exchanged in face-to-face communication, in a given amount of time, than via other media.[49]

The results of a field experiment conducted by Weston, Kristen, and O'Conner concluded that face-to-face meetings promoted greater information exchange than audio or video.[50] Less time was spent developing and maintaining group organization in face-to-face sessions than in audio or video sessions resulting in more specific task-related discussion in the face-to-face mode.

*Affective Response in Different Media.* A major consideration relevant to a decision to use teleconferencing or face-to-face conferencing is the attitudes of people toward each communication mode. Champness studied the utility of the media for a variety of tasks and asked participants in an experiment to rate each of three communication modes (face-to-face, audio, and video) for specific kinds of tasks.[51] Face-to-face was considered significantly more satisfactory for "conflict" and "interpersonal relations" tasks, and all modes were rated equally satisfactory for general, objective tasks.

In a subsequent experiment which studied attitudes toward three media (face to face, loudspeaking audio, and closed circuit television), pairs of managerial civil servants participated in discussions via each medium and completed a media-attitude questionnaire.[52] Significant effects of the media upon three factors of aestheticism, evaluation, and privacy were found, with the majority of these effects due to differences between audio and the other two media. Audio was seen as less important, less sensitive, and less reputable than either face to face or video. Additionally, face to face was rated as more sociable, true, sensitive, successful, and good than either audio or video.

Similarly, Ryan investigated users' reactions to audio, video, and face-to-face conferencing modes.[53] Civil servants were assigned to groups and given a personal problem to solve. After proceeding through the three media treatment conditions they responded to scales measuring the aestheticism, evaluation, privacy, potency, and activity of the medium. Face-to-face conferencing was perceived as more aesthetically pleasing and was evaluated more positively than the audio teleconferencing.

Utilizing an interview situation, Reid investigated confidence in perceptions of others over two media.[54] Civil servants interviewed a role-playing interviewee by telephone or face to face, rated the interviewee on twelve scales and gave their confidence in their ratings. There were no differences in the actual ratings, but interviewers were more confident of their ratings after the face-to-face meeting.

## Weaknesses

*Information Exchange.* Although face-to-face conferences are generally preferred, they may not necessarily be better than audio conferences, an unrecognized distinction leading to resistance to using mediated communication links. Christie and Elton indicated that face-to-face conferencing is overused, that only about 30% of all business meetings actually require face-to-face contact.[55] For some tasks, face-to-face meetings may actually be less desirable than audio mediated meetings. An experiment conducted by the New Rural Society paired subjects who were either strangers or acquaintances in audio or face-to-face conditions.[56] The results of an information sharing task supported the general hypothesis that acquainted subjects using an audio system perform better than acquainted subjects meeting face to face. The explanation offered was that for acquainted individuals a face-to-face meeting was redundant as it involved information which may have been distracting.

### Summary of Face to Face Strengths and Weaknesses

In general, evidence suggests that tasks for which interpersonal communication factors are a consideration are best conducted face to face. Additionally, face-to-face meetings tend to promote greater information exchange and are generally preferred to audio meetings.

The primary weakness of face-to-face conferencing is the expense involved in gathering a group of people together. Travel time should be a consideration in evaluating the desirability of a face-to-face meeting. If for any reason conference participants cannot attend a face-to-face meeting, valuable input may be lost; audio conferences often allow for easier access to individuals and could result in greater benefits for an organization.

## Conclusion

The literature reviewed in this article supports the following general propositions:

### Audio Teleconferencing: Strengths

1. Simple problem solving can be conducted via audio communication.
2. Meetings which emphasize "information seeking" and "discussion of ideas" can be effectively conducted via audio.
3. There is no difference in output quantity or quality of ideas in audio brainstorming sessions and face-to-face brainstorming sessions.

4. Audio communication can be used effectively in interviews for the purpose of gaining information and in psychiatric interviews.
5. In negotiation, the side with the strongest case is more successful in audio than in face to face.
6. More opinion change occurs in conflict situations via audio than face to face.
7. Participants feel that they are more attentive to what is said using an audio-only system of communication than face to face.
8. Audio teleconferencing is cost-effective.

### Audio Teleconferencing: Weaknesses

1. For getting to know someone, people who meet via the telephone are judged less favorably than people who meet face to face.
2. Audio is perceived as less personal than face to face.
3. Audio-only communication may be less productive, produce more hostility, and require more time for maintaining group organization than the face-to-face mode.
4. For complex tasks, the audio mode is an undesirable choice.

### Face-to-Face Conferencing: Strengths

1. Face to face is better than audio for interpersonal relations and in conflict situations.
2. Face to face is better than audio for presentation of statistical information.
3. Time spent for maintaining group organization is less in face to face than in audio.
4. More messages are exchanged face to face than via audio in a given amount of time.
5. Face to face is generally rated more favorably than audio.
6. People are generally more confident in their perceptions of others based on face-to-face meetings than those based on audio-only meetings, though they are not necessarily more accurate.

### Face-to-face Conferencing: Weaknesses

1. Only about 30% of all business meetings actually require face-to-face contact.
2. In some task situations, face-to-face contact may create visual distractions which reduce participants' concentration.

Implications for the substitution of audio meetings for face-to-face meetings may be drawn from these propositions, although it is clear that no simple statement of superiority for either mode is possible. The clearest statement which can be made is that the single most important factor to be considered when choosing between meeting via audio or face to face is the nature of the task which necessitates the meeting.

This review has delineated the types of tasks for which audio meetings are as effective as, or superior to face-to-face meetings, and has detailed those for which face-to-face meetings are more effective.

Organizations may question the necessity of having participants invariably meet face to face when a telephone conference call might be as effective for handling routine business meetings and would, most assuredly, save participant travel time and costs. While individuals may initially resist the substitution of audio conferences for the preferred face-to-face mode for routine meetings, experience and familiarity with the audio medium should soon overcome this initial reaction.

## Notes

1. This material is based upon research initially supported by the National Science Foundation under the following grant: Jerome R. Corsi, Principal Investigator, "The Use of Teleconferencing in Administrative Fair Hearings," National Science Foundation Grant No. APR77-15516, starting date July 15, 1977, supplemented by National Science Foundation Grant No. DAR77-15516, funded on February 16, 1979. Any opinions, findings and conclusions or recommendations expressed in this article are those of the authors and do not necessarily reflect the views of the National Science Foundation. For a report of the Fair Hearing Project research to date see Jerome R. Corsi and Thomas L. Hurley, "Pilot Study Report on the Use of the Telephone in Administrative Fair Hearing," *Administrative Law Review* (1979), vol. 31, pp. 485-524.
2. Roger Pye and Ederyn Williams, "Teleconferencing: Is Video Valuable or is Audio Adequate?" *Telecommunications Policy* (1977), vol. 1, pp. 230-41.
3. Lawrence H. Day, "An Assessment of Travel/Communications Substitutability," *Futures* (1973), vol. 5, pp. 559-572; Ederyn Williams, "Teleconferencing: Social and Psychological Factors," *Journal of Communication* (1978), vol. 28, pp. 125-31; Lesley A. Albertson, "Telecommunications as a Travel Substitute: Some Psychological, Organizational, and Social Aspects," *Journal of Communication* (1977), vol. 27, pp. 32-43.
4. Roger Pye, Brian Champness, Hugh Collins and Steve Connell, *The Description and Classification of Meetings,* Communications Studies Group Report #P/73160/PY (London: University College, 1973).
5. Ederyn Williams, *Brainstorming and Coalition Formation Over Telecommunication Media,* Communications Studies Group Report #E/74003/WL (London: University College, 1974).
6. Steve Connell, *The 1973 Office of Communications Survey,* Communications Studies Group Report #P74607/CH (London: University College, 1974).
7. Williams, *Brainstorming and Coalition Formation Over Telecommunications Media.*
8. Williams, "Experimental Comparisons of Face-to-Face and Mediated Communication: A Review." *Psychological Bulletin* (1977), vol. 84, pp.

963-76; Williams, "Teleconferencing," pp. 125-31; and Albertson, "Telecommunications."

9. Robert Johansen, Jacques Vallee, Kathleen Spangler and R. G. Skirts, *The Camelia Report,* research report conducted under a grant from the Charles F. Kettering Foundation (Menlo Park, California: Institute for the Future, 1977).

10. John A. Short, *The Use of Laboratory Experiments in the Evaluation of the Effectiveness of Telecommunications Meetings as Substitutes for Face-to-Face Meetings,* Communications Studies Group Report #P/72150/SH (London: University College, 1972).

11. Williams, "Coalitions Formation Over Telecommunications Media," *European Journal of Social Psychology* (1975), vol. 5, pp. 502-07.

12. Champness, "Attitudes Toward Person-Person Communication Media," *Human Factors* (1973), vol. 15, pp. 437-447; James H. Kollen and J. Garwood, *Travel Communications Trade-offs: The Potential for Substitution Among Business Travelers* (Montreal: Business Planning Group, Bell Canada, 1975).

13. Champness, *The Efficiency of Information Transmission: A Preliminary Comparison Between Face-to-Face Meetings and the Telephone,* Communications Studies Group (London: University College, 1970).

14. B. Champness and Martin Davies, *The Maier Pilot Experiment,* Communications Studies Group Report #P/71030/CH (London: University College, 1971).

15. Davies, *Cooperative Problem Solving: An Exploratory Study,* Communications Studies Group Report #E/71159/DV (London: University College, 1971); Davies, *Cooperative Problem Solving: A Follow-up Study,* Communications Studies Group Report #E/17252/DV (London: University College, 1971).

16. Champness, *Bargaining at Bell Laboratories: An Experiment Involving Automated Measurement of Speech Patterns in Four-way Conversations, via Three Different Communications Media,* Communications Studies Group Report #E/71270/CH (London: University College, 1971).

17. Richard Remp, "The Efficacy of Electronic Group Meetings," *Policy Sciences* (1974), vol. 5, pp. 101-15.

18. Albertson, "The Effectiveness of Communication Across Media," TS (1973), Telecom Australia Research Laboratories, Melbourne.

19. Alphonse Chapanis, "Prelude to 2001: Explorations in Human Communications," *American Psychologist* (1971), vol. 26, pp. 946-61; Chapanis, "The Communication of Factual Information through Various Channels," *Information Storage and Retrieval* (1973), vol. 9, pp. 215-31; Chapanis, "Interactive Human Communication," *Scientific American* (1975), vol. 232, pp. 36-42; A. Chapanis, Robert B. Ochsman, Robert N. Parrish, and Gerald D. Weeks, "Studies in Interactive Communication: 1. The Effects of Four Communication Modes on the Behavior of Teams During Cooperative Problem Solving," *Human Factors* (1972), vol. 14, pp. 487-509; A. Chapanis, R. Parrish, R. Ochsman, and G. Weeks, "Studies in Interactive Communication: 2. The Effects of Four Communication Modes on the Linguistic Performance of Teams During Cooperative Problem Solving," *Human Factors* (1977), vol. 19, pp. 101-26; R. Ochsman and A. Chapanis, "The Effects of Ten Communication Modes on the Behavior of Teams

during Cooperative Problem Solving," *International Journal of Man-Machine Studies* (1974), vol. 6, pp. 579-619; G. Weeks and A. Chapanis, "Cooperative Versus Conflictive Problem Solving in Three Telecommunication Modes," *Perceptual and Motor Skills* (1976), vol. 42, pp. 879-917; G. D. Weeks, Michael J. Kelly and A. Chapanis, "Studies in Interaction Communication: 5. Cooperative Problem Solving by Skilled and Unskilled Typists in a Teletypewriter Mode," *Journal of Psychology* (1976), vol. 94, pp. 13-26; Kelly, *Studies in Interactive Communication: Limited Vocabulary Natural Language Dialogue*, dissertation, Johns Hopkins, 1975; Parrish, *Interactive Communication in Team Problem Solving As A Function of Two Educational Levels and Two Communication Modes*, dissertation, Johns Hopkins, 1973.

20. Short, *Bargaining and Negotiation—An Exploratory Study*, Communications Studies Group Report #E/71065/SH (London: University College, 1971); Short, *Conflicts of Interest and Conflicts of Opinion in An Experimental Bargaining Game Conducted Over Two Media*, Communications Studies Group Report #E/71160/SH (London: University College, 1971); Short, *Conflicts of Interest and Conflicts of Opinion in An Experimental Bargaining Game Conducted Over Three Media*, Communications Studies Group Report #E/71245/SH (London: University College, 1971).

21. Short, *Medium of Communication, Opinion Change, and Solution of Problem Priorities*, Communications Studies Group Report #E/72245/SH (London: University College, 1972); Ian Young, *Understanding the Other Person in Mediated Interactions*, Communications Studies Group Report #E/74266/YN (London: University College, 1974).

22. *Ibid.*

23. Chris Wilson, *An Experiment on the Influence of the Medium of Communication on Speech Content*, Communications Studies Group Report #E/74350/CW (London: University College, 1974).

24. Short, *The Effects of Medium of Communication on Persuasion, Bargaining, and Perception of the Other*, Communications Studies Group Report #E/73100/SH (London: University College, 1973).

25. Ian E. Morley and George M. Stephenson, "Interpersonal and Interparty Exchange: A Laboratory Simulation of an Industrial Negotiation at the Plant Level," *British Journal of Psychology* (1969), vol. 60, pp. 543-45; I. Morley and G. Stephenson, "Formality in Experimental Negotiations: A Validation Study," *British Journal of Psychology* (1970), vol. 61, pp. 383-84.

26. Morley and Stephenson, "Interpersonal and Interparty Exchange," and "Formality in Experimental Negotiations."

27. Short, *The Effects of Medium of Communication on Persuasion, Bargaining and Perception of the Other*.

28. Short, *Medium of Communication and Consensus*, Communications Studies Group Report #E/72210/SH (London: University College, 1972).

29. Annelies I. Janofsky, *A Study of Affective Self-References in Telephone vs. Face-to-Face Interviews*, dissertation, University of Oregon, 1970.

30. Young, *Understanding the Other Person in Mediated Interactions*.

31. Theresa F. Rogers, "Interviews by Telephone and In Person: Quality of Responses and Field Performance," *Public Opinion Quarterly* (1976), vol. 40, pp. 51-65.

32. Robert J. Simon, Joseph L. Fleiss, Bernice Fisher, and Barry J. Gurland, "Two Methods of Psychiatric Interviewing: Telephone and Face to Face," *Journal of Psychology* (1974), vol. 88, pp. 141-146.

33. David T. Antonioni, *A Field Study Comparison Counselor Empathy, Concreteness and Client Self-Exploration in Face-to-Face and Telephone Counseling During the First and Second Interviews,* dissertation, University of Wisconsin, 1973.

34. Bruce Christie, *The User's Evaluation of Teleconferencing and of the NRS Project's Union Trust Field Trial,* Task Report to the Department of Housing and Urban Development under Contract No. HR-2104R (Fairfield, Connecticut: Fairfield University, 1974).

35. Hilary B. Thomas and E. Williams, *The University of Quebec Audio Conferencing System: An Analysis of User's Attitudes,* Communications Studies Group Report #P/75190/TH (London: University College, 1975).

36. Williams, *Coalition Formation in Three-Person Groups Communicating via Telecommunications Media,* Communications Studies Group Report #E/73037/WL (London: University College, 1973).

37. Williams, "Coalitions Formation Over Telecommunications Media."

38. *Ibid.*

39. Michael Argyle, Mansur Lalljee and Mark Cook, "The Effects of Visibility on Interaction in a Dyad," *Human Relations* (1968), vol. 21, pp. 3-17.

40. J. R. Weston, C. Kristen, and S. O'Conner, *Teleconferencing: A Comparison of Group Performance Profiles in Mediated and Face-to-Face Interaction,* The Social Policy and Programs Branch, Department of Communications Report #3, Contract #OSU4-0072 (Ottawa, Canada: Department of Communications, 1975).

41. Ramon Henson, Charles F. Cannell, and Aleda Roth, "Effects of Interview Mode on Reporting of Moods, Symptoms, and Need for Social Approval," *Journal of Social Psychology* (1978), vol. 105, pp. 123-29.

42. Williams, *Chairmanship in Audio-Only Teleconferencing,* Communications Studies Group Report #E/76310/WL (London: University College, 1976).

43. Lloyd H. Strickland, Paul D. Guild, John C. Barefoot, and Stuart A. Paterson, "Teleconferencing and Leadership Emergence," *Human Relations* (1978), vol. 31, pp. 583-96.

44. D. R. Rutter and George M. Stephenson, "The Role of Visual Communication in Social Interaction," *Current Anthropology* (1979), vol. 20, pp. 124-25.

45. Champness, *The Perceived Adequacy of Four Communication Systems for a Variety of Tasks,* Communications Studies Group Report #E/72245/CH (London: University College, 1972).

46. Williams, "Coalitions Formation Over Telecommunications Media."

47. Albertson, *The Effectiveness of Communication Across Media.*

48. Chapanis, "The Communication of Factual Information through Various Channels."

49. Chapanis, "Interactive Human Communication: Some Lessons Learned from Laboratory Experiments," paper presented at a NATO Advanced Study Institute on "Man-Computer Interaction," Mati, Greece, 1976.

50. Weston, Kristin, and O'Conner, *Teleconferencing: A Comparison of Group Performance Profiles in Mediated and Face-to-Face Interaction.*

51. Champness, *The Perceived Adequacy of Four Communications Systems for a Variety of Tasks,* Communications Studies Group Report #E/72245/CH (London: University College, 1972).
52. Champness, "Attitudes Toward Person-Person Communication Media."
53. Michael G. Ryan, "The Influence of Teleconferencing Medium and Status on Participants' Perceptions of the Aestheticism, Evaluation, Privacy, Potency, and Activity of the Medium," *Human Communication Research* (1976), vol. 2, pp. 255-61.
54. Alex Reid, "Comparisons Between Telephone and Face-to-Face," in *Human Factors in Telecommunications: Proceedings of the Fifth International Symposium* (London, 1970).
55. B. Christie and M. Elton, *Research on the Differences Between Telecommunication and Face-to-Face Communication in Business and Government,* Communications Studies Group Report #P/75180/CR (London: University College, 1975).
56. Christie, *The User's Evaluation of Teleconferencing and of the NRS Project's Union Trust Field Trial.*

# 30

# Telecommunications as a Travel Substitute: Some Psychological, Organizational, and Social Aspects

*Lesley A. Albertson*

> *Travel and telecommunications are better seen as interrelated elements in a social context which they help create.*

> *Well before the year 2000 dawns the city office worker won't have to get up every morning to take the polluting commuter trail. He could be doing his job just as effectively from his living room at home. . . .*
> *Break through the travel barrier with Confravision, the inter-city conference service at your door. . . .*

In each of these statements, one taken from a discussion of the "home office"[1] in the popular press,[2] the other from a British Post Office brochure advertising its teleconference[3] facility, it is assumed that video telecommunications are capable of replacing physical travel.

A number of writers in the fields of transportation and urban development, as well as telecommunications, make the same assumption. Dickson and Bowers[4] devote a chapter to the effects on transportation of substituting video telephony for business travel, but do not attempt to justify their assumption that such substitution is possible, other than by commenting that it has been "frequently suggested."

As one future urban form, the LUTSANC study proposed a "cluster city," in which advanced telecommunications systems replace travel between nodes of population distributed over a wide area.[5] Day discusses travel/telecommunications substitutability from several points of view, including the "behavioral reasons" for travel.[6] In none of these cases, however, is it debated whether technologically-mediated interaction is a psychologically acceptable substitute for face-to-face communication, or whether using telecommunications devices over long periods of time might also have behavioral or social consequences.

In view of the importance to several areas of planning of the possibility that telecommunications could reduce the need for travel, it is surprising to find that such questions have been neglected, even by telecommunications specialists. This article therefore is concerned with developing a social psychological perspective on the use of telecommunications as a travel substitute, using the home office and video teleconferencing as focal points.

The absence, until recently, of any research into the question of whether video telecommunications allow business to be conducted as effectively as it is face-to-face is partly explained by the long-held belief of many telecommunications engineers that video telephony would provide "total communication." Those who accept this view argue that any differences observed between the two are a function of the limitations of present technology and, as this argument underlies the notion of substitution, it merits consideration in some detail.

Certainly some of the communication difficulties experienced using present video telecommunications are at least partly attributable to technological limitations. Surveys of teleconference users, for example, consistently report that "getting to know someone" is difficult over a video medium[7]. Reid[8] has suggested that when only a voice channel is available, communicators create an image of the person speaking, which, while it may not accurately represent that person, is complete in itself. A low-definition video representation may be sufficient to interfere with the formation of such an image, while being too ambiguous to create a satisfactory image in its own right. "Maintaining friendly relations" is reported in these surveys as being less difficult, suggesting that the video image is sufficient to act as a reminder stimulus if the person is already known, although people using teleconference for regular meetings still experience the need to meet face-to-face about once in every three or four meetings.[9] If Reid's explanation is correct, improving the quality of the video image could be expected to reduce this ratio.

But, if we imagine video technology as moving towards its ultimate state, with perhaps colored, life-sized holographs projected at the culturally appropriate communication distance, would there be a corresponding reduction in the perceived difference between the mediated exchange and an actual encounter? Although no empirical comparisons have been conducted, there are some *a priori* grounds for predicting that the relationship between technological improvement and the subjectively experienced quality of the communication medium is not so simple.

Conrath and Thompson[10] point out that when only a voice channel is used, the communicators share a common auditory space. With the introduction of a video channel, each communicator must present himself and part of his environment to the other. The inability of the communicators to share the visual environment or to move around in the other's environment could be partly overcome by designing a system which allowed camera control from the remote location. However, it seems likely that the feeling of discontinuity between the two environments would be increased as the visual image became increasingly lifelike.

Another problem which is often overlooked because of the strongly visual orientation of present Western culture is that telecommunications can only represent the auditory and visual dimensions, although our total sensory awareness also includes tactile, gustatory, and olfactory dimensions. Removing these dimensions obviously precludes some activities which are often associated with business meetings, such as shaking hands or sharing a meal; and although research in the area is limited, nonverbal communication theory[11] provides some basis for expecting that the absence of these dimensions may explain some of the difficulty experienced in getting to know someone over a video link. Although ingenious substitutes for some of these activities have been proposed, such as the hydraulically-controlled glove for remote handshaking, it seems unlikely that these dimensions can be telecommunicated in a psychologically meaningful way. Thus, improvement in the visual and auditory dimensions is likely to increase awareness of interdimensional perceptual discrepancies, the problem which Seyler has termed "cross-modal mismatch."[12] The other person may be observed drinking coffee or smoking a cigarette, but the accompanying stimuli in other modes (such as smell and tactile sensations) are absent.

Although the importance of these factors in communication effectiveness has not yet been empirically established, they are sufficient indication that even the ultimate in video communications cannot be assumed to be identical with face-to-face communication, and that there may be an optimum point beyond which technological improvement is self-defeating.

On one series of studies conducted by this group[13] persons were asked to use different media (usually telephone, closed-circuit television, or face-to-face) to perform a range of communication tasks. Such tasks included exchanging information, interviewing, problem-solving, persuasion, and negotiation. Perhaps the most important conclusion to emerge from these studies was that a communication medium as a whole cannot be located on a continuum of effectiveness in any simple manner. It was found that for less complex tasks, such as information exchange, the measured outcomes did not vary significantly with the medium of communication; a voice channel was found to be as effective as any other medium for this type of communication. In fact, one study found that information recall was significantly better using the telephone than when the medium was either videophone or face-to-face communication, which leads to the conjecture that a visual image may act as a distractor under some circumstances.[14]

However, for those tasks which involve interpersonal influence, such as persuasion or negotiation, outcomes were sensitive to the communication medium used. Morley and Stephenson found that when simulated management-union negotiations were conducted over the telephone, the side with the case which had previously been rated as stronger was significantly more successful,[15] a finding which was replicated by Short.[16] The outcomes of studies of persuasion have been less consistent. The combination of four laboratory studies of persuasion[17] resulted in the finding that the greatest opinion change occurs in the audio-only condition. Video outcomes were intermediate between the audio-only and face-to-face conditions, but were more similar to the former than to the latter. Thus, although it seems that the physical presence of another person reduces the emphasis on communication content which occurs when only a voice channel is available, a video image (at least of the commercial quality used in these experiments) does not have the same effect.

These findings, however, do not provide any obvious basis for ranking media in terms of their effectiveness for interpersonal tasks, as this would involve a subjective judgment of which outcome was preferable. Evidence from teleconference users indicates that both audio and video telecommunications are perceived as less satisfactory for tasks such as negotiation than for simpler tasks such as information exchange.[18] There is also evidence that attitudes towards communications media differ, independently of the purpose for which they are used. One study found that video systems are regarded as more "public" on a public-private dimension than either an audio system or face-to-face communication.[19] This result is interpreted as indicating that the video medium creates a psychological sense of intrusion rather than a distrust of its actual security, as the only change between the video and audio condition in this experiment was that the video picture was turned off in the latter case.

The inherent problems of laboratory studies, such as the artificiality of subjects role-playing a situation in order to satisfy experimental demands and their short exposure to the medium, make it hazardous to generalize from these results to the real-life situation of remote working. But, even if it is accepted that it is possible to predict how effectively a series of tasks can be performed using a video medium, or how psychologically comfortable people are likely to be in doing so, the possibility of the home office also raises basic questions about the nature of work.

Professionals, managers, and office workers are the groups for whom the home office is usually seen as most appropriate. However, the work of many of these people is directly concerned with interpersonal communication. Managers in one large company were found to spend an average of 59 percent of their time in communicating with people, mainly face-to-face[20], a result which is within the range reported from similar analyses. As even the laboratory studies have shown that communication tasks involving interpersonal influence are sensitive to the communication medium, it is doubtful whether this part of a manager's work could be effectively conducted over a videophone. In addition, the extent to which this general category of "communication" can be adequately represented as a series of tasks is open to question. Mortenson comments that to do so is to "reduce the complex and delicate process by which man somehow fashions a deluge of impressions into an orderly system . . . to the level of work habits required for laying bricks or digging foundations in a rainstorm."[21]

However, some writers have recognized that this social context has a number of important functions which are relevant to both work performance and satisfaction. Carne comments that "managers see their presence at the office as essential for direction, motivation and morale,"[22] and Harvey that "the social organization of the workplace is the means by which people enhance their self-esteem as persons of competence, and satisfy their needs for companionship, affiliation and belongingness."[23] Glover interviewed a small group of people who had experienced working from home under present conditions and found that, in addition to the undoubted benefits, such as avoiding rush-hour travel and being able to complete projects without interruption, working in isolation from a social group also caused many of the drawbacks mentioned by interviewees. These included difficulties in making business contacts, the absence of fertilization of ideas or feedback, professional anonymity, and lack of social contacts.[24]

Sophisticated telecommunications systems could be used to alleviate the difficulty of making social contacts, particularly if schemes such as a computerized method of meeting new people or video morning-coffee clubs were introduced. Nevertheless, the inherent limitations of the video medium, combined with the fact that telecommunications are primarily adapted to direct person-to-person communication, make it likely that under remote working conditions the other members of the organization would become less salient as a social group than is the case with face-to-face working.

This would have far-reaching effects on the nature of organizations. One consequence would be the erosion of corporate identity and the expectation that organizations have continuity over time. With employees' lessened affiliation with the work group and, as changing jobs would not involve a physical move, staff turnover could be expected to be much higher than at present. At the same time, organizations could be more flexible than at present; freed from the necessity to provide accommodation, organizations could tailor the number of people employed to meet changing needs, and conditions would be suitable for the formation of *ad hoc* organizations or task forces for carrying out particular projects. The removal of the social context would also mean that work would center around individual performance of tasks, which would present increased problems of coordination and control for the organization. Given the more fluid employment situation and the difficulties of using hours of work as a basis for payment, it seems likely that many people would work under relatively short-term contracts, with payment on the completion of specified projects.

More attention would necessarily be devoted to work definition, measurement, and evaluation. It is also likely that such organizations would become a more important source of the person's sense of competence and professional identity. But, as it is doubtful whether an organization as large as a union would be able to fully satisfy the need for a meaningful social context, remote working would place sudden additional demands on both the family and the community.

Although working from a home office is, in one sense, a modern version of the situation which obtained before the industrial revolution, the social changes which accompanied industrialization preclude any simple "return" to the society of that time. Modern families are smaller, and an increasing proportion of people live alone. At the same time, partly as a result of material self-sufficiency, families have become more isolated from the community. For these reasons alone, the capacity of telecommunications to provide an adequate sense of interpersonal relating could become a crucial issue if remote working is not to result in psychological stress and a society in which people are increasingly alienated from each other.

Another important difference is that, in contrast to a lifestyle in which work and family were closely integrated, the two contexts are now not only physically separate, but give rise to distinctly different role behaviors which may have very little in common.[25] The journey to work at present provides time in which the transition between roles can be accomplished smoothly, a transition which is assisted by appropriate changes in role symbols, such as dress. Performing both roles in the same context is likely to bring the two into sharp conflict, and much could depend on their successful integration. The possibility of the work role, with its requirement for "functional expertise and impersonal, detached attitudes"[26] invading the home role, in which the person's relationships are typically warmer and more relaxed,[27] presents the danger of people losing touch with an important aspect of reality. However, the alternative possibility that working from home would result in a basic change in work role behavior is also likely to have enormous social consequences; even if Zijderveld's view that "modern bureaucracy is the general cohesive force in pluralistic society that keeps this society together as a functionally integrated whole"[28] is perhaps overstating the case, work roles are undeniably a major organizing principle in modern society.

Thus, although remote working holds out a promise for a new principle of social organization based on greater integration of work and home roles and a renewed sense of community based on contacts with other people, the inherent social dangers in making the transition from the present system are also great. In view of the magnitude of the changes which remote working would initiate, it is clear that decisions concerning the implementation of the home office cannot be made by considering only travel and telecommunicating. The changes in the nature of work and organizations, in individual lifestyles and in society which would result from remote working, would also change communication needs and travel patterns to such an extent that to argue the substitution issue within an otherwise static social system is necessarily invalid.

Teleconference systems are now operating in a number of countries, including Britain, Canada, the United States, Japan, and Australia. As all these systems are relatively new, the most effective ways to use and market them are still being explored. Substitution for travel to existing meetings is an obvious application, and this possibility has received renewed attention as a result of recent public concern with the issues of energy conservation and pollution. The existing links have been used mainly for real meetings since, unlike the desktop videophone, they have been made available as point-to-point facilities and hence do not involve the expense of installing a network. As a result, research has emphasized acceptability to the users, rather than experimental studies of their effectiveness.

Surveys have typically reported that more than 90 percent of users profess to be highly satisfied with such facilities.[29] Nevertheless, relating satisfaction to subsequent use of the system, or to preferences for telecommunicating rather than traveling, has proved problematical. One reason is that the base for comparison is not necessarily an equivalent face-to-face meeting. Questionnaires completed by over 400 teleconference users showed that although 92 percent of users "liked" the system, and 98 percent stated that they would like to use it again, 39 percent also considered that their teleconference was less effective than a face-to-face meeting would have been (although it should also be noted that 11 percent rated it as *more* effective).[30] And, whereas some teleconference systems receive regular use, similar systems elsewhere are used seldom or not at all.[31] Attempts to explain this finding include: attitudes towards travel, such as avoidance of long-distance travel to routine meetings[32] or a liking for travel and its associated "frills";[33] the perceived unsuitability of the system for particular types of meetings;[34] or the territorial implications of where the facility is located.[35] In addition, the costs of video systems are generally high and are often greater than travel costs between the conference locations. But while these explanations may be correct in particular cases, a survey of more than 9000 businessmen traveling by air, road, and rail found that none of these or other explanations typically advanced in the research literature were significantly related to the respondent's reported decision to substitute telecommunications for the present trip.[36] After finding no correlations large enough to usefully predict substitution, the researchers concluded that "either the decision to substitute may be an idiosyncratic one which the present study did not tap," or that "conceptualizing substitution of telecommunications as a *replacement process* rather than as a supplement to travel is ill-conceived."

Evidence from teleconference users concerning the relationship between their teleconference and travel lend partial support to this conclusion. In the survey previously quoted,[37] although the majority of users (72 percent) considered that the option was "travel to a face-to-face meeting," not all the participants in the teleconference would have attended such a meeting. Twenty-two percent replied that they would not personally have been present, and a further 11 percent were uncertain. In 15 percent of cases, the exchange would not have occurred at all, and, with the exception of 5 percent who would have used a multi-party telephone call, the other alternatives involved a series of exchanges (for example, letters and telephone calls) rather than a meeting. Some of the face-to-face meetings would also have involved a multi-step process, such as a local meeting followed by sending a delegate to the remote location. These results suggest that, as well as replacing some existing travel, teleconferencing is also emerging as a communications medium in its own right; a greater number of simultaneous meetings occur than would otherwise have been the case, and many more people are directly involved in the communication than if traveling had been necessary.

However, these results represent only the initial phase of teleconference use. Other evidence suggests that if teleconferencing were used for a series of meetings between groups, the interrelationship between telecommunicating and travel would become more complex. One reason is that effective teleconferencing appears to require a proportion of face-to-face communication between the conferees; if they are not previously acquainted, teleconference users report that they need to speak more redundantly to ensure that the information is getting across,[38] and even those who are acquainted feel the need for periodic face-to-face meetings.[39] In addition, teleconferencing is not perceived as suitable for more complex interpersonal tasks such as persuasion and negotiation.[40] A determined substitutionist who prohibited all travel would find that teleconferencing would become, if not less effective, certainly less satisfactory to the participants.

Thus, even if it is assumed that the total number of meetings remained constant, the involvement of more people in the meeting would also mean that whereas some people would travel less than at present, this would be to some extent counterbalanced by the fact that the additional conferees would need to travel occasionally if their participation were to be effective. However, there is little reason to assume that the total number of meetings will remain constant. Factors such as the multi-disciplinary approach to solving problems of various kinds, demands for union participation in management decision-making, and even the pressures for more open planning at all levels of government are likely to increase the need for meetings. But in addition to serving a proportion of the growing need for inter-group communication, the survey results quoted above suggest that the availability of teleconference facilities makes long-distance communication between groups more feasible, and hence is likely to result in more communication. And this, in turn, will generate a proportion of trvel.

Although this conclusion may at first appear surprising, it is in fact consistent with the pattern of development of previous communication innovations. The opening of the transatlantic cable, for example, resulted in an enormous increase in both telecommunications traffic and travel across the Atlantic, partly because of the role of telecommunications in making transport systems safer and more efficient, and also because reliable communications made international operations a real possibility for the first time for many organizations. And, despite the conventional wisdom, television has not replaced other broadcast media in any simple sense, although overall use of the mass media has declined recently, at least in the United States.[41]

But while substitution has not been the general rule, communications innovations have sometimes induced qualitative changes in the existing media, with the old and the new polarizing toward what each does best. Television, for example, has probably influenced program innovations in radio, such as audience "talkback," and cinema's increasing exploitation of its large screen size. By analogy, it would be expected that since transport cannot compete with teleconferencing as far as speed is concerned, travel advertising is likely to increasingly emphasize other advantages, such as the importance of "real" face-to-face communication, the possibility of useful encounters or the opportunity to relax away from the office.

Teleconferencing also provides new communication opportunities for organizations. However, the mere availability of teleconference facilities does not ensure that these will be taken up. In particular, teleconferencing is not likely to have a great impact on organizations if the facilities are provided mainly on a shared basis. Under these conditions their use is inhibited both by practical difficulties, such as the time required to travel to the studio and the need to make advance bookings, and by psychological factors, such as the territorial implications of where it is located[42] and forgetting about its existence.[43] Even if it is assumed that organizations will gradually acquire their own facilities, introducing teleconferencing into organizations involves more than acquiring the technical apparatus or learning the most effective ways to conduct meetings over the system. If the new possibilities are to be exploited, teleconferencing needs to be integrated into the organization's functioning. This would require an analysis of the organization's patterns of communication, and how these relate to its aims, structure and functions. As a result of such an analysis, the constraints to the organization's aims which arise from existing communication patterns could be identified, and this would point to the specific ways in which teleconferencing would help these aims to be achieved more effectively.

Although the possibilities would vary with the particular organization, in general terms, teleconferencing could remove some of the gaps which result from the multi-step communication processes which are often necessary at present. And, by involving more people in direct communication, teleconferencing would increase dissemination of information throughout the organization, which would in turn improve job satisfaction and increase organizational cohesion and member identification with the organization's aims.[44]

Thus, although teleconferencing would not have the major impact of the home office, it has the potential of subtly influencing the nature of organizations and the direction of their development.

In conclusion, while it is certainly true that video telecommunications can be used to replace travel in particular instances, there is no convincing evidence that such systems are likely to provide a departure from the positive relationship which has previously existed between telecommunications use and travel. Substitution provides an inadequate picture of the overall relationship between the two, partly because the medium itself is not subjectively experienced as the same as face-to-face contact, but, more importantly, because major communication innovations, particularly those of the order of the home office, would themselves initiate such vast organizational and social changes that it is inherently untenable to see communication needs as remaining static, with only the travel/telecommunications ratio changing. Travel and telecommunications are better seen as interrelated elements in a social context which they help create. In the case of teleconferencing, placing limitations on travel would not automatically increase telecommunications use by an equivalent amount; the more probable long-term effect would be that organizations would function in a more localized manner. Conversely, extensive teleconference use would not necessarily reduce the need for travel, although it would provide new opportunities for communication which could initiate changes in organizational functioning. And, while a decision to implement remote working could obviously reduce travel to a central business district, the need for an alternative social context to that presently provided by the workplace would generate travel which does not occur under present conditions.

Therefore, not only is consideration of the social implications of telecommunications innovation part of responsible planning, but the changes in communication patterns which result from such innovation are so intricately linked with the process of organizational and social change that it is virtually meaningless to debate the question for travel substitution independently of this context.

## Notes

1. Usually depicted as a complex of telecommunications systems based on the video telephone, and including such additional facilities as a keyboard, computer terminal, a unit for the visual display of information and a facsimile device for hardcopy printouts.
2. *Australian National Times,* March 11-16, 1974.
3. "Teleconference" is used in this essay to include all telecommunications facilities which allow meetings between groups of people at two or more locations. These facilities may be audiovisual or audio-only.
4. E. M. Dickson and R. Bowers, "The Video Telephone, A Preliminary Technology Assessment," report prepared for National Science Foundation, Cornell University, June 1973.
5. Land Use/Transportation Structure Alternatives for New Cities (LUTS-ANC), "New Structures for Australian Cities," report prepared for the Cities Commission under the direction of Maunsell and Partners Pty., Ltd., Canberra, February 1975.
6. L. H. Day, "An Assessment of Travel/Telecommunications Substitutability," *Futures* (December 1973).
7. L. A. Albertson, *A Preliminary Report on the Teleconference User Opinion Questionnaire* (Melbourne: Australian Post Office, 1974); A. E. Casey-Stahmer and M. D. Havron, "Planning Research in Teleconferencing Systems," report by Human Sciences Research, Inc., Virginia, for the Department of Communication, Ottawa, September 1973; and E. Williams, "The Bell Canada Conference Television System: A Case Study," Communications Studies Group, Joint Unit for Planning Research, University College, London, 1973.
8. B. G. Champness, "Attitudes towards Person-Person Communications Media," *Human Factors* (1973), vol. 15, pp. 437-48.
9. Casey-Stahmer and Havron, *op. cit.*
10. D. W. Conrath and G. B. Thompson, "Communications Technology: A Societal Perspective," *Journal of Communication* (1973), vol. 23, no. 3, pp. 47-63.
11. M. Argyle, *The Psychology of Interpersonal Behavior* (Harmondsworth: Penguin, 1967).
12. A. J. Seyler, "On Some Fundamental Aspects of Teleconferencing," unpublished report, Australian Post Office, Melbourne, 1974.
13. Dickson and Bowers, op. cit.
14. Albertson, *A Comparative Study of Communication Effectiveness Across Media,* (Melbourne: Australian Post Office, 1974).
15. I. E. Morley and G. M. Stephenson, "Interpersonal and Inter-party Exchange: A Laboratory Simulation of an Industrial Negotiation at the Plant Level," *British Journal of Psychology* (1969), vol. 60, no. 4, pp. 543-45.
16. Communications Studies Group, "Interim Report, May 1972," Commu-

nications Studies Group, Joint Unit for Planning Research, University College, London, 1972.

17. J. Short, "The Effects of Medium of Communication on Persuasion, Bargaining, and Perception of the Other," Communications Studies Group, Joint Unit for Planning Research, University College, London, 1973.

18. Albertson, "A Preliminary Report"; Short, "A Report on the Use of Audio Conferencing Facility at the University of Quebec," Communications Studies Group, Joint Unit for Planning Research, University College, London, 1973; and Williams, *op. cit.*

19. Champness, *op. cit.*

20. P. L. Link, "Future Communications Systems in Australian Business Organizations," unpublished master's thesis, Monash University, Melbourne, 1973.

21. C. D. Mortenson, *Communication: The Study of Human Interaction* (New York: McGraw-Hill, 1972).

22. E. B. Carne, "Telecommunications: Its Impact on Business," *Harvard Business Review* (1972), vol. 50, no. 4, pp. 925-33.

23. L. V. Harvey, "Interpersonal Communication," paper presented at the annual conference of the Australian Psychological Society, 1973.

24. J. Glover, "Long Range Social Forecasts: Working from Home," Long Range Intelligence Bulletin No. 2, Telecommunications System Strategy Department, British Post Office, 1974.

25. M. Argyle and B. R. Little, "Do Personality Traits Apply to Social Behaviour?" *Journal for the Theory of Social Behaviour* (1972), vol. 2, no. 1, pp. 2-32.

26. A. C. Zijderveld, *The Abstract Society* (Harmondsworth: Penguin, 1973).

27. Argyle and Little, *op. cit.*

28. Zijderveld, *op. cit.*

29. Albertson, "A Preliminary Report"; J. P. Duncanson and A. D. Williams, "Video Conferencing: Reactions of Users," *Human Factors* (1973), vol. 15, pp. 471-86; and E. Williams, *op. cit.*

30. Albertson, "A Preliminary Report."

31. Communications Study Group, "Interim Report, May 1972."

32. Short, "A Report on the Use of Audio Conferencing Facility at the University of Quebec," Communications Studies Group, Joint Unit for Planning Research, University College, London, 1973.

33. Day, *op. cit.*

34. Short, "A Report on the Use of Audio."

35. Casey-Stahmer and Havron, *op. cit.*

36. J. H. Kollen and J. Garwood, "The Replacement of Travel by Telecommunications," paper presented at the Psychology and Telecommunications Symposium, 18th International Congress of Applied Psychology, 1974.

37. Albertson, "A Preliminary Report."

38. Casey-Stahmer and Havron, *op. cit.*

39. Casey-Stahmer and Havron, *op. cit.*; and Short, "A Report on the Use of Audio."

40. Albertson, "A Preliminary Report"; and E. Williams, *op. cit.*

41. R. Maisel, "The Decline of Mass Media," *Public Opinion Quarterly* (Summer 1973).
42. Casey-Stahmer and Havron, *op. cit.*
43. E. Williams, *op. cit.*
44. L. V. Harvey, *op. cit.*

# 31

# The Computer Conference: An Altered State of Communication

*Jacques Vallee, Robert Johansen,*
*and Kathleen Spangler*

Most of us communicate intuitively. We greet each other every morning without any thought of the contracting muscles of our vocal cords, the atmospheric support of sound vibrations, or the semantic intricacies of our language—all of which are necessary for our natural, face-to-face communication process. Suppose, however, that we had to explain face-to-face communication to someone who had never experienced it. How would we explain, for example, the necessity to be within vocal and visual range of other people? What about the possibilities for "body language," for interpreting all of the subtle visual cues, which accompany the vocal symbols of face-to-face communication? And how would you introduce vocal symbols to a person who has never depended on them to communicate? How do the social demand for immediate responses and our limited ability to remember words which vanish in the air define the nature of our communication?

Clearly, the task of explaining a communication process is staggering. Yet this is the task which we face in exploring the computer conference. Most of our intuitions about face-to-face interaction simply do not apply to this new and unusual form of communication. In computer conferencing, time and distance are dissolved. Visual cues no longer exist. Each person's "memory" of what has been said is accurate and complete. And everyone may speak at once or listen at leisure. With such features, it is not surprising that computer conferencing might actually establish an altered state of communication in which the realities of face-to-face communication are distorted and entirely new patterns of interaction emerge. Our research team at the Institute for the Future in Menlo Park, California, has often experienced this altered state of timeless, placeless, remote communication during the past two years, as we developed and experimented with a family of conferencing programs. Our computerized communication system, known as FORUM,[1] functions as an interpersonal medium for a variety of activities, including planning and forecasting, group conferencing, joint writing projects, electronic notepads (in which messages are stored in a computer instead of on paper), social simulations, and questionnaires. The system allows geographically separated people to communicate either simultaneously or on a delayed basis. We call these two basic usage modes "synchronous" and "asynchronous" conferencing. Participants do not need any technical expertise or even previous experience with computers, though they use a standard computer terminal. All of these characteristics combine to create social conditions that differ from face-to-face communication in at least three important ways: (1) the physical environment; (2) fewer time and space limits; and (3) the various communication structures which are allowed.

## An Altered Physical Environment

Unlike face-to-face gatherings, FORUM gatherings are characterized by physical isolation of each participant. Alone with his terminal, each computer conferee depends on an unseen computer to communicate with his colleagues. All "conversation" must be typed on a computer terminal with a standard typewriter keyboard. As a result, accessibility and reliability of terminals, typing skills, and writing skills—factors which are not even considered in face-to-face meetings—all influence communication in a computer conference. For example, a slow or uncertain typist will probably become more selective in the questions he answers and in making his own contributions. On the other hand, many users have found that typing allows them to "give more consideration and focus" to their statements. Expressing ideas through a keyboard is not always a negative factor. Ernest Hemingway reportedly preferred a typewriter for developing dialogues even though he returned to longhand for narratives and descriptions.

The remote keyboard situation hints at some interesting changes in the ritual of "meeting" people. In a computer-based conference, there are no gestures, facial expressions, or vocal cues like pitch, intonation, pauses, or stress. In face-to-face communication, these cues often regulate the flow of a discussion; they also convey emotional feelings and attitudes toward other participants. FORUM greatly narrows this field of information, and many emotional messages simply seem to disappear.

When the sole context for "meeting" someone is through an impersonal keyboard and an equally impersonal printout, the person at the other end might seem inaccessible—a mere extension of the machine. Fortunately, this is not entirely true. Many of the messages ordinarily expressed in body movement or voice tones are translated into written form, either implicitly or explicitly. One conferee reported that "relationships were established easily, personalities came across, conversations could be established." In short, people can become recognizable personalities, even when their only means of expression is the printout of a computer terminal.

The computer itself is invisible in the communication process, but it may intrude upon the discussion in a couple of ways. First, a heavily loaded computer network may transmit messages irregularly. The resultant delay can be frustrating and confusing, since satisfactory communication usually depends on rapid feedback. This frustration is minimal, however, compared to the experience of a system "crash," when the computer stops and the terminal automatically prints out a message such as "DRUM FULL" or "HOST DEAD." (The "HOST DEAD" message created considerable shock among many of our users who attended computer conferences for the first time. A British researcher pointed out to us that a more gentle announcement, such as "HOST PASSED AWAY," might be less traumatic.) Unfortunately, we have had no control over network access or reliability.

Computer system failures are always annoying, but a failure in the middle of a conference dealing with intellectual and emotion-charged issues is devastating. Each person is suddenly and totally isolated in midstream; frustration is intense. A comparable situation in face-to-face communication might be the violent disruption of an assembly by armed bandits, or a sudden collapse of the building.

## Alterations of Time and Space

When people in widely separated locations can interact at any time of day or night, their "real world" concepts of time and space are drastically altered. Most people have already had their sense of distance altered by the telephone, but FORUM further reduces the consciousness of distance since it typically costs no more to "talk" across thousands of miles than across ten feet.

Even more striking is the unique "suspended time" of a computerized conference. Participants may enter and leave the discussion at will, without risk of losing touch with the meeting. Time zones disappear since discussion can proceed without regard to the fact that one user is about to eat his supper in London, while a California user has just arrived at his office. If the London colleague unexpectedly joins the discussion while our Californian is busily entering his ideas, this "presence" suddenly adds a dimension of intimacy which restores the awareness of space and time.

Freedom from the constraints of time and distance can naturally reduce the obligation to communicate. No one is physically present, demanding a response. No ringing telephone demands an answer. There is only the knowledge that a conference is in progress and is available, at will, through the terminal. There are, of course, a number of motivations for joining: a need for information, the need to solve a problem, a professional sense of duty, or simply the desire to "be in touch."

Clearly, there are both advantages and disadvantages to such "self-activated" communication. A participant who is asked a question feels less pressure to respond immediately than he would in face-to-face discussion. He can take time to consult a library, review his own thinking, and present a well-prepared response. Still, this same lack of pressure may be an annoyance for someone who is eager to pursue a topic with an indifferent or preoccupied colleague; however, we have found that direct questions through FORUM have generally received prompt replies. And conference growth curves, which measure the number of entries, show that the majority of conferences have constantly or positively accelerated growth rates—an indication that the momentum of the conference can generate pressure to communicate. Nevertheless, the balance between motivation and lack of demand is strikingly different from face-to-face interaction. Thus, the communication might also evolve quite differently.

## Altered Structures in Communication

Computer-based conferencing allows a great deal of control of communication structures. For example, users may send *public* messages, which are entered into the transcript and available to all, or *private* messages, which are sent to specific individuals and seen only by them. Functionally, the private message enables colleagues to "whisper" in the midst of a discussion without any breach of etiquette. In content, the public messages tend to be more formal than private messages, and more closely related to the discussion topic, while private messages include more personal interaction, sometimes quite unrelated to the main topic of group discussion.

Anonymous messages permit participants to state their views without divulging their identities—a possibility which does not exist in face-to-face meetings. Conferees have used this feature to express unpopular opinions, voice grievances, or make jokes in a way which is usually not possible.

A FORUM conference can vary from an open-ended discussion in which the topic is simply introduced and the discussion evolves without prescribed direction to a carefully preorganized discussion. In these more structured conferences, the FORUM program becomes a many-roomed meeting hall, dividing the conference into activities according to topic. For still more structured needs, FORUM will administer questionnaires or secret ballots and report the results.

In some ways, even the most unstructured computer-based conferences are more structured than face-to-face communication. FORUM discussions have been characterized by what appears to be a narrower range of topics, less diversion from the subject, and more explicit decision-making than in face-to-face conferencing. On the other hand, it is difficult to compel a FORUM user to direct his comments. It is impossible to shout down or interrupt any other person in the "meeting." All participants may "talk" at the same time; the computer simply records the entries according to the time at which the user began typing.

### Mapping the Altered State

We have now begun to "map" the altered state of communications that arises from the special characteristics of a computer conference—physical isolation, dependence on the computer, suspension of time and space, reduced obligation to communicate, and a new set of communication structures. Each communication medium is a unique instrument with characteristics all its own. Because we are most familiar with face-to-face voice communication, we tend to make it a standard by which to measure other media. But we must be careful not to overlook the innovative patterns and opportunities of a new medium by clinging to our preconceptions of what communication really is. Just as it would be unfair to judge a piano by the narrow range of the human voice, it is misleading to evaluate computer conferencing as a simple substitute for face-to-face communication.

The social aspects of communications media have rarely been evaluated, and starting points are not easy to find. Perhaps as many as 50 researchers in the world are doing work on the social effects of different media in at least ten different locations. The theoretical basis for this work is rich, but scattered. The computer conferencing medium itself provides two powerful analytic tools for evaluating its social characteristics: (1) an up-to-date machine-readable transcript of every computer meeting is always available and (2) the computer can unobtrusively map interpersonal interactions to reveal patterns of communication among individuals, groups, and subgroups. Each of these points deserve elaboration.

1. A complete transcript of every computer conference is always available, current, and machine-readable. This transcript is automatically recorded exactly as it is typed, and members can review the record by subject, author, and date—during and after the conference. The possibilities for analyzing the content of the discussion are thus greatly improved over most other media. Using one analytic technique, we have classified entries by content, identifying them as regulatory comments dealing with the group process, comments on the substantive topics in the conference, humor, novel ideas, and similar classifications. In this way, we can evaluate a group's ability to focus on a particular task, and we can also determine where the time actually went (see Fig. 31.1).

    The transcript also makes it possible to track specific discussion topics over time. We have thus identified a strong tendency for "threads" or "chains of thought" to occur in the conference transcript. These topic threads are frequently labeled ("re comment 13"), but the tie is sometimes only implicit, requiring readers to review the earlier proceedings to find out what has been said on a particular topic. The review process is supported by the FORUM program: a participant can, for example, request the computer to search for any entries which mention a particular word, such as "energy." In general, our analysis of the topic threads shows that it is possible to discuss several topics at the same time, occasionally dropping one thread and then picking it up again later.

    In addition to tracking the content of discussions, topic threads enable us to analyze the role that the different participants play. We find that some persons tend to introduce many new ideas, while others are best at developing them; still others function as synthesizers. The roles can vary greatly among persons and conferences, but we have noticed an apparent tendency for the "provocative" and "synthesizing" roles to be mutually exclusive. The provoker seems to push the discussion forward into new areas of thought, while the synthesizer ties the loose strands together. By examining the patterns of a FORUM conference, one can easily identify both the key persons and the key ideas.

2. The computer itself can unobtrusively map many dimensions of the interaction that may or may not be evident from the transcript. The ability to map these interaction patterns within a conference may be the most powerful analytic tool inherent in any communications

## 1. PROCEDURAL

## 2. SOCIAL

(195)  Lipinski  FRI  1 FEB 74  1:47 PM
Good bye all, have a nice weekend.  I am going to do some work in
the garden.

(196)  Johansen  FRI  1 FEB 74  2:24 PM
I hope that 195 does not mean that this will be taken as a 9-5,
Monday-Friday conference.  Actually, the machine is usually quite
pleasant to use on weekends; and everyone is free to continue use
in an asynchronous fashion as we have been doing.

(198)  Kollen (Chairman)  FRI  1 FEB 74  2:43 PM
It would be appreciated if participants who are logging into the system
would be so kind as to offer comments concerning the agenda of this
conference (the five points set down for discussion) and remarks about the
discussion of the present point 1.  Thank you.

(199)  Johansen  FRI  1 FEB 74  2:57 PM
I am not sure what was meant by 198, Jim.  Does this mean you don't think we
are sticking to the topic, or does it mean you wish more people would make
comments?

(201)  Johansen  FRI  1 FEB 74  5:32 PM
Several people have suggested that we develop an easy to use channel for
collecting responses to FORUM conferencing as we go - something like a
"gripe Mode".  At present we need to set up a separate part of the conference to do this, and I would rather not do this for this conference.
However, if you do have comments/criticisms of FORUM as we go, how about
sending them to me in the form of private messages?

(202)  Johansen  FRI  1 FEB 74  5:38 PM
As a reminder, the procedure for sending a private message is contained in
entry 41, or you can just hit a ?.

(206)  Johansen  SAT  2 FEB 74  11:29 AM
If I could make another procedural suggestion:  since we are now working
with a basic agenda, it might be helpful to review entries 93 and 62, which
describe that agenda.
I am sure our chairman will keep reminding us when the discussion gets off
the track.  Please let me know if anyone is having any trouble with the
review process in FORUM.

**Fig. 31.1**
Excerpts from the transcript of an actual computer conference. Participants
discussed several topics simultaneously, occasionally dropping one topic "thread"
and picking it up later. The communications shown here can be classified as
procedural, social, or substantive.

# 3. SUBSTANTIVE

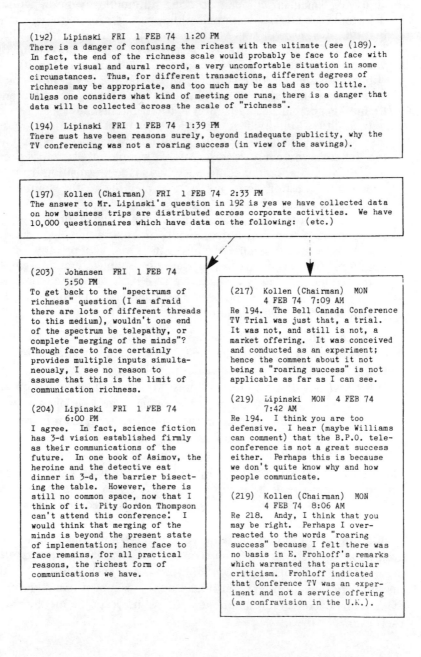

(192)  Lipinski  FRI  1 FEB 74  1:20 PM
There is a danger of confusing the richest with the ultimate (see (189)).
In fact, the end of the richness scale would probably be face to face with
complete visual and aural record, a very uncomfortable situation in some
circumstances.  Thus, for different transactions, different degrees of
richness may be appropriate, and too much may be as bad as too little.
Unless one considers what kind of meeting one runs, there is a danger that
data will be collected across the scale of "richness".

(194)  Lipinski  FRI  1 FEB 74  1:39 PM
There must have been reasons surely, beyond inadequate publicity, why the
TV conferencing was not a roaring success (in view of the savings).

(197)  Kollen (Chairman)  FRI  1 FEB 74  2:33 PM
The answer to Mr. Lipinski's question in 192 is yes we have collected data
on how business trips are distributed across corporate activities.  We have
10,000 questionnaires which have data on the following:  (etc.)

(203)  Johansen  FRI  1 FEB 74
        5:50 PM
To get back to the "spectrums of
richness" question (I am afraid
there are lots of different threads
to this medium), wouldn't one end
of the spectrum be telepathy, or
complete "merging of the minds"?
Though face to face certainly
provides multiple inputs simultaneously, I see no reason to
assume that this is the limit of
communication richness.

(204)  Lipinski  FRI  1 FEB 74
        6:00 PM
I agree.  In fact, science fiction
has 3-d vision established firmly
as their communications of the
future.  In one book of Asimov, the
heroine and the detective eat
dinner in 3-d, the barrier bisect-
ing the table.  However, there is
still no common space, now that I
think of it.  Pity Gordon Thompson
can't attend this conference.  I
would think that merging of the
minds is beyond the present state
of implementation; hence face to
face remains, for all practical
reasons, the richest form of
communications we have.

(217)  Kollen (Chairman)  MON
        4 FEB 74  7:09 AM
Re 194.  The Bell Canada Conference
TV Trial was just that, a trial.
It was not, and still is not, a
market offering.  It was conceived
and conducted as an experiment;
hence the comment about it not
being a "roaring success" is not
applicable as far as I can see.

(219)  Lipinski  MON  4 FEB 74
        7:42 AM
Re 194.  I think you are too
defensive.  I hear (maybe Williams
can comment) that the B.P.O. teleconference is not a great success
either.  Perhaps this is because
we don't quite know why and how
people communicate.

(219)  Kollen (Chairman)  MON
        4 FEB 74  8:06 AM
Re 218.  Andy, I think that you
may be right.  Perhaps I over-
reacted to the words "roaring
success" because I felt there was
no basis in E. Frohloff's remarks
which warranted that particular
criticism.  Frohloff indicated
that Conference TV was an experiment and not a service offering
(as confravision in the U.K.).

medium. This capability of the FORUM program means that the detailed coding and painstaking observation of interpersonal communication that social psychologists must typically carry out in analyzing small groups can be done automatically here, without disturbing the normal communication process. Comparative participation rates, growth curves, daily activity, and other related indicators create new dimensions for assessing group interaction. Private message statistics, for example, may indicate the formation of subgroups, cliques, or coalitions. Such statistics even allow us to trace individual participation characteristics from one conference to another, perhaps as a function of topic and task.

In addition to individual characteristics of participation, we can also evaluate group characteristics with growth curves. When plotted for the content categories, for example, these curves can indicate if and when the conference has made a transition from the procedural questions inherent in any meeting to the solution of substantive issues.

It is difficult to think of another medium in which an analysis of group interaction can be automatically and unobtrusively generated with this level of detail. At the same time, the privacy of the conference is not violated. The statistics about interaction can be compiled independently of the content of the conference; conferees must grant their permission before we can make any comparison of personal interaction and content.

We have evaluated over 25 conferences using these and more traditional analytic techniques (including interviews and questionnaires). In general, our user groups have had the following characteristics: (1) little familiarity with computer systems; (2) a genuine need to communicate with each other; (3) group sizes ranging from 3–20, but averaging about 5; (4) tasks which were relatively unstructured; (5) time periods averaging several weeks; and (6) primarily asynchronous communication. After 5,000 conference hours with these groups, we are convinced that long-running field tests—as opposed to laboratory experiments—provide the most realistic environment for fully exploring conference styles and usage. FORUM was designed to be learned quickly, so that new users would be able to master its features after an introductory period of about 15 minutes. However, the styles of usage could vary greatly after persons and groups are more familiar with computer conferencing and with their own abilities to present themselves in the medium. In long-term tests, attitudes can be sampled over time, and evaluations become more credible as users integrate the medium with their everyday lives.

### Implications for the Future

A scant 100 or so persons throughout the world now use computerized conferencing on a regular basis. But the time may be fast approaching when far more people will be conferring through computers and we will begin to view computer conferencing as a "natural" way to interact.

In this new environment, "invisible colleges" may develop, since this medium can introduce and coordinate groups of people who may or may not have been in touch previously. Scholars, businessmen, and government officials would be able to interact outside the normal limits of time and space; they would no longer need to spend so much time exchanging journal articles, memos, and reports, arranging meetings, or traveling to conventions in distant places. (See Fig. 31.2).

Perhaps we can enhance group creativity through a new communications style, forged in the computer conference. With everybody at a conference thinking and expressing his thoughts in multiple streams, we might observe a process of "fast thinking" that would enhance our

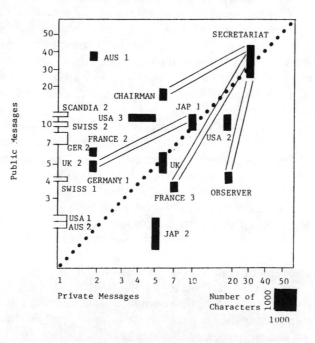

**Fig. 31.2**
**Participation map for a simulated computer program[2]**

collective abilities to resolve conflicts, deal with crises, or improve decision-making capability. Or perhaps computer conferencing will spawn new types of poetry or literature.

From a practical viewpoint, a portable computer terminal may be hooked up to any standard telephone line, enabling persons immobilized with illness, or away from the office for any reason, to continue many of their regular duties. Computer conferencing also has great potential in providing handicapped persons with a channel to the outside world.

The "coolness" of the medium may also prove useful for such activities as encounter sessions, counseling, and discussions of personal values. Psychotherapy may also find uses for the medium: for instance, the altered environment for self-presentation may help in defining self-concepts (for example, in relating to persons of the opposite sex or of other races). Certainly a detailed analysis of self-presentation processes is possible in FORUM, and the FORUM communication environment may also be potentially less threatening than a face-to-face group. The major question is how such an environment could be used therapeutically to obtain results which could be transferred effectively to more "normal" communication situations.

On the other hand, we are not oblivious to the potential negative impacts of computer-based conferencing. Though costs are already encouraging (about $15 per terminal hour on a commercial computer network, with further cost reductions anticipated), computer conferencing is not yet a medium for the masses. And a type of electronic elitism is certainly a possibility as long as terminals and network access remain the privilege of a few.

Could computer communications replace much—or all—face-to-face contact? At present, "human contact" usually means being together "in person." For some people, the mere thought of a communication medium in which human bodies (or even voices) are irrelevant is frightening. Isaac Asimov, in his novel *The Naked Sun,* and E. M. Forster, in his 1929 story *The Machine Stops,* offer nightmarish projections of a future in which electronic communication replaces human contact as we now know it. Our research team has examined computer-based conferencing as a supplement to face-to-face communication, not as a replacement, but long-term negative possibilities deserve attention, if only so they can be avoided.

Our studies to date indicate that computer conferencing has unique potential for enhancing the exchange of ideas among people. In current field tests, we are exploring its usefulness in bargaining and negotiation, conflict resolution, crisis management, and some educational applications. However, as should be clear from this article, our work should only be viewed as a foot placed in an interesting door. We are convinced that this medium will change quickly and that it should not be evaluated by narrow criteria. We believe as well that the potential of computer-based communication remains largely unexplored.

## Notes

1. The FORUM system has been developed by a team composed of Roy Amara, Hubert Lipinski, Ann McCown, Richard Miller, Thad Wilson, and the authors of this article. This research is supported by the Department of Computer Research at the National Science Foundation (under Grant GJ-35 326X). The authors wish to thank Arthur Hastings for suggesting that computer conferencing might represent an "altered state." PLANET-1, a simpler version of FORUM, is now available on the TYMSHARE, Inc. computer network.
2. Figure 31-2 was constructed with statistics *gathered directly* in a simulation of a computer-based international conference. In this test, the work of an International Telephone and Telegraph Consultative Committee Study Group was simulated by 18 graduate students at San Jose State University, assisted by several technical experts. The students played the roles of eight national delegations from which previous position papers were available. An analysis of user behavior with respect to negotiation and information exchange was then conducted. Rectangles represent each participant, indicating the number of private messages and public messages each has sent. The sides of the rectangles are proportional to the verbosity, defined here by the average length (in characters) of messages in private and public mode. This type of map can help define roles of participants; it also enables us to observe coalitions and subgroups and to track individual participation characteristics from one conference to another.

# Part IX

# CREATIVE PROBLEM SOLVING

# 32

# Creative Problem Solving

*Stephen L. Ross*

> *The more Philosophy and Science I tried to bring on problem solving, the more I came to realize that even together they can assure us no more than adequate solutions to problems. They cannot provide exciting solutions, ones that we call "beautiful". Only the kind of problem solving that involves art can do this. And art implies creativity.*
>
> —Russel L. Ackoff *The Art of Problem Solving*

Creativity is something that we normally associate with the arts. We may look for it in writers, painters, sculptors, dancers; but rarely expect to find it in the business or administrative world. Sometimes we do hear of someone who parlays a novel idea into a profitable business venture or who comes up with an innovative solution to a long-standing organizational problem, but such creativity is often viewed as a somewhat haphazard occurrence, a fortuitous event that we may wish for, or wait for, but not as something that we can do much about.

Though creativity in itself is difficult to define or explain, most writers in the field of creative thinking seem to agree on the following principles:

- Creativity is necessarily involved in the generation of new ideas.
- Creative ideas are to be valued as essential ingredients for change and progress.
- Traditional linear thinking processes, Western logic, and bureaucratic methods do not foster, but rather inhibit creative thinking. Indeed, the human mind is not normally very good at creative thinking.
- Creativity is not an end product; it is a process.

- Techniques exist to enhance the likelihood of generating creative ideas, and these techniques can be taught.

Problem solving generally involves three stages: the generation of new ideas, the formulation of a solution using the new ideas, and the implementation of the solution. Given a willingness to be innovative, the second and third stages can be approached using traditional logic and accepted organizational procedures. It is the first step, the generation of new ideas, that seems to be so difficult to effect through traditional methods; yet we tend to rely almost completely on linear thinking and traditional logic in the problem-solving process. We become locked into traditional approaches, expecting that solutions that worked before will work again, and that perfect logic can produce perfect solutions. This latter idea, de Bono[1] tells us, leads to smugness and arrogance. He argues that the answers derived by logic are correct but only in terms of the starting concept and only if all necessary information is available when we start. The logic processing may be perfect, but we still may end up with a less-than-perfect solution if our starting concept package is inappropriate, or if new information is added as we proceed.

Why are creative solutions so difficult? Indeed why does creativity itself seem so rare? Traditionally, creativity has been viewed as an innate ability; one either has it or one doesn't have it. Some argue that we all are born with a certain innate creativity that most of us lose along the way. Children certainly seem to be naturally imaginative and creative, and many people credit our educational practices with the stamping out of these imaginative and creative tendencies, long before adulthood is reached. Some argue that creativity is more prevalent in the arts than in business or the sciences, simply because only in the arts is creativity accepted and allowed to exist, let alone nurtured. Factors often identified as tending to diminish the likelihood of creative responses are the nature of the mind, the functions of the brain, traditional logic, and the "Scientific Method." Even the language we use as a tool for thinking tends to lead us in linear, step-by-step thought processes, rather than into nonlinear creative thinking.

The pattern-creating nature of the mind itself seems to make creative thinking more difficult. The mind incorporates all previous experience. Our thinking with regard to any new experience is coloured by past experience and the satisfactory or unsatisfactory results of these experiences. The mind forms what de Bono[2] calls concept patterns. If we had completely and consciously to analyse all the information that enters the mind with each new experience before we could act, we would never get through the average day. But the mind tends to organize the incoming information or stimuli into patterns and match them with patterns created from previous experience, thus enabling us, often unconsciously, to assess each experience and react successfully to meet it. This pattern recognition ability, combined with the procedures we establish to maintain the smooth running of our lives or businesses, serves us very well in our normal routine, but it can fail us in several ways. We come to rely on this ability and fail to recognize when it is inappropriate. When changed circumstances demand novel approaches or solutions, we have difficulty restructuring or escaping from these restricting patterns. Whether or not we accept de Bono's terminology, we can appreciate that it is easy to become trapped in thinking and response patterns and fail to realize when a new response is in order.

Research has shown that the human brain is divided into two hemispheres with separate and unique functions. The left brain handles language, linear, analytical type of thinking and right-hand dominance. The right brain is more involved with integrative and intuitive, rather than deductive thinking. For most of us the left brain seems dominant, and with this left brain dominance comes the propensity for giving more attention to linear, logical approaches to problem solving rather than the intuitive, integrative, creative approaches of right-brain thinking. It has been suggested that truly left-handed people are naturally more intuitive and creative than right-handers, because their right brain is dominant. Peter suggests that it is left-brain dominance that explains why, "within bureaucracies and other rigid hierarchies, some individuals are much more prone to the methodical, compartmentalized, ritualistic kinds of behaviour for which bureaucrats are so famous."[3]

Analytic thought, under whichever name we choose to call it, is no doubt responsible for much of the success that Western civilization has experienced, but our emphasis on this mode of thought has tended to submerge or even discourage other modes of thinking. Analytic thinking differs from creative thinking in several ways. Rawlinson[4] suggests that analytic thought uses logic, arrives at unique, or few, answers, and is convergent and vertical (or hierarchical). Creative thinking, on the other hand, uses imagination, produces many possible answers or ideas, is divergent, and lateral (a de Bono term) rather than vertical in approach. Analytical thinking tends to be exclusive, constantly narrowing down possibilities until the "best answer" is found, Creative thinking is inclusive and tries to produce numerous ideas from which a solution can be selected.

Even one's own self-concept can be a barrier to creative thinking. We have been conditioned since youth to be serious and logical and consequently are often reluctant to suggest innovative, imaginative ideas for fear of being regarded as frivolous. Yet frivolous and even "far out" ideas often lead to valuable insights in the problem-solving process. Creative problem solving encourages farfetched suggestions that logic might reject, and many initially frivolous suggestions lead eventually to innovative solutions to vexing problems.

Proponents of creative problem-solving techniques do not denigrate the contributions of logical, analytical thought, but they do point out the pitfalls that exclusive use of analytic methods can lead us into. Given the rapid pace of change, the complexity of our institutions and problems, and today's competitiveness in ideology and commerce, it is the elegant solution that can provide the competitive edge, reduce confrontation or improve the quality of our lives.

Whatever the differences in approach, all creative problem-solving techniques have as their aim the breaking down of the barriers to creative thinking that we have described.

## Brainstorming

Brainstorming is probably the most familiar and widely used creativity technique. The idea was originated by Alex Osborne. It is a group process intended to be used to analyse problems and generate large numbers of potential solutions. Suspension of judgment is of prime importance and farfetched suggestions are encouraged, based on the assumption that it is often the apparently absurd idea that initiates a train of events leading to a creative breakthrough. Hundreds of ideas are normally generated in the course of a brainstorming session.

Traditionally, a brainstorming group is made up of six to a dozen people. It is thought that the group will be most effective if the persons involved possess a variety of experience and expertise and if the group includes the people who will be involved in the implementation of any solutions generated. If the brainstorming group is seen as being an elite think tank dreaming up new problems for the rank and file, then cooperation in the implementation phase may be difficult to obtain.

J. Geoffrey Rawlinson[5], a creativity and brainstorming consultant, defines brainstorming as "a means of getting a large number of ideas from a group of people in a short time" and suggests six stages in the process. These are as follows:

- State the problem and discuss
- Restate the problem—How to—
- Select the basic statement and write it down, "In how many ways can we—
- Warm-up session
- Brainstorm
- Wildest idea . . .

Throughout the session all ideas are recorded since, of the enormous number generated, some may be forgotten. Often, as much as one-third of the time spent by the consultant or coordinator is devoted to explaining the barriers to creativity and the means used to overcome these barriers. David Oates describes the four major rules under which brainstorming is conducted as follows: suspend judgment, generate ideas in quantity rather than quality, allow the mind to "free-wheel," and cross-fertilize ideas. Suspending judgment prevents the participants from criticizing each others suggestions, eliminating many promising ideas before they are able to lead to something worthwhile.[6]

### Synectics

Synectics is similar to brainstorming in that it tries to stimulate groups to generate creative solutions to problems. The approach is more methodical, introducing some degree of evaluation of the ideas generated. A greater attempt is made to see that the group chosen includes the most appropriate people to shed light on the problem under discussion. Participants are not encouraged to completely suspend judgment, but each person is forced to come up with at least one positive response to any ideas generated before they are allowed to express any reservations they might have about them. This assures that apparently wild ideas are not dismissed out of hand. Also, this rule encourages the individual to make novel suggestions, knowing that the initial response of his colleagues will be positive rather than critical. Synectics however, unlike brainstorming, focuses on the quality of the ideas generated, as well as the quantity. As do all creativity techniques, synectics encourages one not to immediately dismiss any idea, to challenge existing assumptions, and to try to look at realities in an entirely different way. An often heard phrase connected with Synectics is: "making the strange familiar and making the familiar strange."

### Lateral Thinking

The term Lateral Thinking was coined by Edward de Bono, a British creativity expert and is intended to imply a distinction from logical or hierarchical thinking. De Bono states that his procedures are intended to foster right-brain thinking rather than the left-brain thinking that has become prevalent in our society, particularly in business, science and educational institutions. As stated earlier, De Bono claims that logical thinking encourages a blind arrogance. One tends to believe, "My logic is perfect, therefore my solution must be perfect." De Bono argues that this attitude creates a blindness, encourages one to accept an adequate solution when an elegant solution might be available, and limits the ideas and hence the potential solutions that might be found. He enjoys peppering his writings with illustrations of perfect logic that has produced perfectly silly solutions. He greatly admires the imaginative responses of children and in his demonstrations often uses children to illustrate that, unhampered by the barriers to creativity that burden most adults, children often amaze observers with the imaginativeness, quantity and quality of their solutions.

De Bono's techniques are aimed at helping us escape the logic traps, concept packages, and sequential traps that we have been conditioned to accept. One of his techniques is the introduction of the magic word *PO*. *PO* is a word introduced to any communication to signal that we should stop at this point, dismiss our assumptions, and try to look at the situation in a new and different light. He claims that "yes" and "no" (especially "no" are the functional words in logic. Logic is an excluding methodology. It must continually narrow down, exclude, say "no" to stated hypotheses. De Bono counteracts this "no" with *PO*. He says, "*PO* really has but a single function and that is to generate new ideas. There are, however, two aspects to this single function. The first is the provocation of new ideas. The second aspect is the escape from old ideas. This second aspect involves challenging the unique validity of any current idea."[7]

Another device he has created is the *think tank*. A *think tank* is no more than a globe filled with a random assortment of words. One draws a word out of the globe and uses this word, via analogy for example, to stimulate ideas related to the problem at hand. It is normally and most effectively used with groups, but it can also be used alone. "The *think tank* device makes it possible for any person to hold a brainstorming session with himself. With its random words, the *think tank* provides the stimulation that would normally be provided by the other people in a brainstorming session. No longer does one have to wait to get together a group of people before beginning to generate new ideas."[8]

The above descriptions of creativity methods touch only upon a sampling of creativity techniques and do justice to none of them. It is hoped that these brief descriptions of some of the barriers to creative thinking and some of the techniques used to break down these barriers may intrigue the reader and stimulate further research, perhaps starting with the readings listed in the bibliography.

## Utilization

Reports indicate that many of the most progressive and fastest-growing companies in the United States successfully use some form of creativity techniques to bring about improvements in organization performance. These are not intended in themselves to replace the judgment of experienced and expert management, but rather to make available to the decision maker greater diversity of ideas and possible solutions. Effective implementation may depend on the following conditions:

- The activity should be fully endorsed and supported by senior administration.
- The makeup of the problem-solving group should be such that the group contains the necessary diversity of expertise and experience to successfully address the problem faced; the group should likewise be well integrated into the organization.
- The group should include people who will be involved in the implementation of the solution.
- The organization should be open to creative solutions and novel ideas. Companies organized along rigidly hierarchical and bureaucratic lines may not be comfortable with creative people and nontraditional solutions.

Creative problem-solving techniques offer value to organizations and to individuals. For organizations, these techniques can be used to improve the quality of the decision-making process. Such improvements can give a competitive edge over organizations who rely completely on traditional decision-making practices. For nonprofit organizations, improved decision making should result in more efficient and better-quality service. For the individual, even one working in an inflexible organization that does not encourage creativity or innovation, such creativity techniques can help improve performance on the job and greatly enhance decision making in the context of the individual's personal life.

## Notes

1. Edward de Bono, *PO: A Device for Successful Thinking* (London: McGraw-Hill, 1971).

2. de Bono, *Lateral Thinking for Management* (London: McGraw-Hill, 1971).
3. Lawrence J. Peter, *Why Things Go Wrong or the Peter Principle Revisited* (Toronto: Bantam, 1984).
4. Geoffrey J. Rawlinson, *Creative Thinking and Brainstorming* (Westmead: Gower, 1981).
5. *Ibid.*
6. David Oates, "The Boom in Creative Thinking," *International Management* (December 1972).
7. de Bono, *Lateral Thinking,* p. 136.
8. de Bono, *THINK TANK: A Tool for the Mind* (Toronto: Think Tank Corporation, 1973), p. 51.

## Bibliography

Ackoff, Russell L. *The Art of Problem Solving* (Toronto: John Wiley and Sons, 1978).
de Bono, Edward. *Lateral Thinking for Management* (London: McGraw Hill, 1971).
———. *THINK TANK: A Tool for the Mind* (Toronto: Think Tank Corporation, 1973).
———. *PO: A Device for Successful Thinking* (London: McGraw Hill, 1971).
———. *Atlas of Management Thinking* (Harmondsworth: Penguin, 1983).
Fulmer, Robert M. *The New Management* (New York: Macmillan, 1974).
May, Rollo. *The Courage to Create* (New York: Norton {Bantam Edition}, 1976)
Mueller, Robert Kirk. *The Innovation Ethic* (American Management Association Inc., 1971).
Oates, David. "The Boom in Creative Thinking," *International Management* (December 1972).
Peter, Lawrence J. *Why Things Go Wrong or The Peter Principal Revisited* (Toronto: Bantam, 1984).
Rawlinson, Geoffrey J. *Creative Thinking and Brainstorming* (Westmead: Gower, 1981).
Summers, Irvin and White, Major David E. "Creativity Techniques: Toward Improvement of the Decision Process," *Academy of Management Review* (April 1976).
Webber, Ross A. *Management: Basic Elements of Managing Organizations* (Homewood, Illinois: Irwin, 1975).

# 33

# Using Nominal Grouping to Improve Upward Communication[1]

*Thad B. Green* and *Paul H. Pietri*

Communicating with subordinates is one of the most crucial activities of a manager. Its importance is rivaled only by its difficulty. Particularly troublesome is the manager's need to feel the pulse of that part of the organization which functions under his leadership.

In examining the internal communication system of an organization, one generally finds greater managerial dedication to downward, rather than upward, communication. Much of this undoubtedly stems from the obvious importance of downward communication. No organization could function efficiently without the downward flow of objectives, policies, rules, and work assignments. Unfortunately, however, many managers visualize the upward communication function narrowly. They view it in terms of how well their downward communications have been followed. Are objectives being met? Are policies and rules being adhered to? Are assignments being carried out? Although it is frequently overlooked, there should be an upward flow of additional information. Upward communication may include information about such things as subordinates' feelings and attitudes toward their jobs, special problems encountered in performing work activities, and ideas for alleviating these problems. Normally, communicating downward is facilitated by a number of formal media. Subordinates are bombarded from above by devices such as bulletin boards, policy statements, conferences, company newspapers, pay inserts, and formal addresses. Yet, the only formal upward communication mechanisms that frequently exist are the ancient suggestion system and a so-called open door policy.

This article investigates the widespread potential of the relatively new nominal grouping technique or process as a communication tool. The idea of using nominal grouping as a communication technique is new, but it is rapidly gaining acceptance. It is one of those rare approaches that does not have to be sold. It is eagerly being bought on its own merits—simplicity and intuitive soundness. Management practitioners generally are not familiar with nominal grouping, but once aware of it, they become successful users. Among communication experts there is not a widespread awareness of nominal grouping either. In fact, an extensive survey of the literature reveals only a single source suggesting the use of nominal grouping in a communication context.[2] But the technique is being advertised and publicized—by word of mouth among satisfied customers.

The authors are aware of the use of nominal grouping as a communication tool in a wide variety of organizations including General Motors, the U.S. Department of Agriculture, Wachovia Bank, Mississippi Medical Center, CECO Corporation, a number of state employment agencies, and in colleges and administrative offices of several major universities.

## What Is Nominal Grouping?

Nominal grouping is a technique formulated through the collection of diverse, proven features embodied in a variety of research on small group dynamics, including brainstorming and "pooled individual effort." The nominal grouping procedure described here is a modification of a model first identified in 1970 as a technique for program planning.[3]

Nominal grouping is a method in which several assembled individuals (usually five to ten) follow a highly structured, noninteracting format to achieve an assigned goal. It is this noninteracting characteristic from which nominal grouping derives its name; *nominal* means "in name only." Relative to the operating mode of a typical group, a nominal group is indeed a group in name only. The process begins with the grouper[4] asking each person to respond, in writing, to a specific question designed to generate the desired information, such as any of the following hypothetical queries:

- What changes do you feel should be made to improve your working environment?
- What solution approaches do you see for the departmental morale problem?
- What problems exist in the organization that deserve special attention?
- What is the general employee attitude regarding unionization?

Regardless of the nature of the question and the extent of controversy it may provoke, discussion is not permitted during the listing phase in which each person generates a personal list of items in response to the question presented.

A recording phase follows after a specified time limit (usually twenty minutes is adequate). The grouper calls on someone to read the first idea from his written list. The grouper records this verbatim on a large sheet of paper in full reading view of all group members (taped to the wall, for example). Each successive person is called upon to read an item for recording, with this process continuing in round-robin fashion until all items from each group member's list have been read and recorded.

A voting phase follows to obtain a consensus regarding items of greatest importance. Having the group collectively identify the five most important items, for example, enhances the utility of the total information set.

A set of instructions for the grouper describing the nominal grouping process in greater detail is shown in Exhibit 1. The highly structured yet simple format facilitates the ease with which it is employed. This structural feature coupled with the absence of discussion enables the grouper to perform effectively in the absence of the special, but seldom present, leadership skills so essential in typical discussion groups.

The quotes which follow are typical of those that might originate in almost any organization. They contain a common thread: upward communication is being suppressed for one reason or another. Properly used, nominal grouping offers a valuable opportunity to help alleviate these and other upward communication problems that are difficult to solve. Nominal grouping lubricates the machinery of upward communication by providing subordinates with a vehicle for expression that cuts across the maze of red tape and standard operating procedures, and even closed doors. The extent and value of information received from subordinates is limited only by management's lack of ingenuity in developing topics to be handled in a nominal grouping session. These quotes are typical:

> Boy, does the old man have a temper! He asks for an honest opinion on the new sales control reports which my salesmen have to fill out each day, so I tell him what I think. Boy, did he ever hit the ceiling! Accused me of undermining top management. You can believe me that I'll never make the mistake of telling him something that he doesn't want to hear. It's not worth it!

> My boss is an o.k. guy, if you know what I mean. He gives you a job to

do and you do it well and you get treated fairly. He's always asking my feelings about things in the plant and my ideas about how the company could be doing better, but to tell you the truth, I always agree with him. Oh, I've got some pretty good ideas, but I just don't think it's my place to tell him how to run things. He gets paid for that. I don't think my people should be having to give me ideas that I'm paid to come up with either. The whole nature of a manager's job is to make decisions for other people, otherwise you have no business being in a manager's position. That's what you're paid to do.

## EXHIBIT I

### Instructions for Nominal Groupers

---

#### Listing Phase
1. Arrange subjects, including yourself, to sit in a circle.
2. Discuss the purpose of the meeting, emphasizing that the organization is genuinely interested in getting ideas from individuals.
3. Indicate to the group that they will be working with a technique called *nominal grouping*. Briefly describe nominal grouping by outlining how the group will operate in each of the three phases (listing, recording, voting).
4. Request that everyone be concise in his or her written responses during the listing phase, using short phrases or key words rather than complete sentences. For example, in a group that was identifying management problems, two persons identified the same problem. One stated it as "The company does not do an adequate job of training employees." The other simply stated "inadequate training." The meaning of the short statement is as clear as the longer statement, but is much easier and faster to record.
5. Point out to the group that there is to be no discussion during the listing phase.
6. Indicate the time period to be allowed for the listing phase. (Usually fifteen to twenty minutes is sufficient.)
7. Hand out to each person a sheet of paper which specifically states the task he is to address. (This should be a concise statement of the "purpose of the meeting" which was generally described in step two above.) Read the statement aloud, then allow time for those who may have questions.
8. Request group members to write their responses on the sheet distributed to them, and encourage each person to generate a list as long as possible— "the more items the better."
9. Ask if there are any final questions, then begin the recording phase.

#### Recording Phase
1. Have the group stop writing, and prepare to record the items by writing them on a chalkboard or large sheets of paper taped to the wall in full view of all group members. (Recording on paper usually is preferred since it provides a permanent record of all that is recorded.)
2. Indicate that no discussion is allowed during this phase.
3. Impress upon the group the need to record all items listed, regardless of how trivial they may seem.
4. Have an individual read aloud the first item he has listed so it may be

recorded. Write it verbatim unless the item is too long. If necessary, ask the reader to condense it; don't help condense and don't allow anyone else to help. Place a check mark by the item for each member who has essentially the same item listed on his sheet. (Simply ask for raised hands to determine this.) If some member of the group does not understand the item and needs clarification, the reader of the item should offer clarification. But there is to be no discussion of the item.

5. Have the next individual read aloud his first item for recording, following the same procedure as in step four above.
6. Proceed in this round-robin fashion until all items are recorded.

### Voting Phase

1. Distribute voting ballots to the members, asking them to assign priorities (the top five, the top ten, or whatever is deemed appropriate) to the items that have been recorded. They should ask themselves "What is the most important item on the list? The next most important?" and so forth.
2. Remind the group that no discussion is allowed.
3. Collect the ballots and terminate the session.
4. Any number of methods can be used to tabulate the votes, a simple one being to give five points for a first place vote, four points for a second place vote, and so forth, to the "top five" items.

---

### Keep the Boss Out

One way nominal grouping facilitates upward communication is related to the homogeneous composition of the group. The groups should be composed of individuals of equal rank and authority. This homogeneity neutralizes the role of formal authority and status, two factors which research has shown will strongly mitigate against free, honest, and upward communication in organizations.[5] Face-to-face communication with the boss may be perceived as risky by the subordinates; anonymous conveyance of information is far more acceptable.

Communicating in a noninteracting way and in the absence of superiors depersonalizes individual inputs and reduces the fear of reprisal by one's superior. Not only does a homogeneous group mitigate against the need to withhold distasteful information, but the absence of superiors reduces the need to communicate what the boss "expects" to hear. One member stated after his initial nominal grouping session:

> You know, we came in here with definite reservations about this. We were probably each wondering about how honest other members sitting in our group would be about listing their real feelings on the subject. But man, we came out with things that we never would have told the boss to his face. Face to face you have a tendency to tell him about how well things are going along down here. But there are a heckuva lot of

problems that he ought to know about, but doesn't. Our group really told it like it was, and it's a good feeling to know you've gotten some of these things out in the air. I only hope the boss takes these things in the right manner and not personally. But I guess that he wouldn't have done this unless he wanted to hear it like it really was.

### Group Meeting with No Discussion

At first glance, the fact that nominal grouping does not allow a discussion of individual inputs appears to be inconsistent with *good* communication practice. However, this is not the case. It has been long recognized that "two heads are better than one," yet research indicates interaction among group participants often has a damaging effect on both creativity and productivity.[6] Nominal grouping is structured to bring a group of individuals together, but discussion is not permitted. This is a way of eliminating factors which otherwise inhibit group performance. A variety of inhibiting forces are overcome with the "no discussion" feature of nominal grouping. Richard C. Huseman suggests three sources which are subdued: (1) with no criticism allowed, participants are more willing to share ideas that are not yet well developed; (2) since there is no discussion, the nominal groups do not fall in a rut by focusing on one particular train of thought; and (3) because contributions are not evaluated, the nominal group can concentrate all of its time and energy on the specifically assigned task.[7] Beyond this, (4) nominal grouping prevents dominance of strong personalities (formal or informal group leaders) since they have no persuasion opportunity.[8] Also, (5) the expression of minority opinions and ideas is encouraged since criticism is not allowed.[9] Finally, (6) incompatible, conflicting ideas are more likely to be expressed because feelings of inferiority or defensiveness among group members are minimized.

### The Ultimate Goal Is Information

Another characteristic of nominal grouping which contributes to effective communication is the ultimate goal of the group. The expected group output is information. Such an objective has a forcing effect upon group members to communicate feelings and ideas that might ordinarily have little opportunity or probability of being communicated through normal organizational channels. When management brings a nominal group together, it is essentially saying to the group: "You have some valuable inuts which we'd like to have. Will you please give them to us?"

Some typical upward communication barriers which retard normal upward communication flow and which the "forcing" effect of nominal grouping helps overcome are:

- tendency of managerial authority to suppress accurate upward communication;
- lack of availability for interpersonal communication. Many managers simply do not make themselves available for interpersonal contacts by their subordinates;
- the fact that many subordinates don't ordinarily view upward communication as part of their normal work role;
- poor listening habits by managers. Because of listening ineptness, managers discourage subordinates from communicating upward. Poor listening habits might include lack of concentration or attention; extreme ego protection or defensiveness; and the tendency to become overly emotional when receiving unpleasant information.

If a manager can recognize his own limitations as well as those of his subordinates, the nominal grouping approach can provide a valuable source for information which might have little chance to pass through normal communication channels.

### Who Can Use It?

Nominal grouping can be an important tool for improving communication at all levels in an organization. The attractiveness of the process is reflected by its potential use by any individual manager. As shown in Fig. 33-1, manager A can use the technique to receive valuable information from his immediate subordinates, $B_1$, $B_2$ and $B_3$. Moreover, $B_1$ can use the technique with his own subordinates, $C_1$, $C_2$ and $C_3$. Managers $B_2$ and $B_3$ can also employ the process with their own subordinates.

In addition to two-level usage, nominal grouping can be utilized more comprehensively to include any number of lower level inputs. For example, a higher level manager (manager $A$ in Fig. 33-1), may employ the process on a multi-level basis (see dashed line in Fig. 33-1) when:

1. He strongly suspects that important information from lower levels (Level $C$ in Fig. 33-1, for example) is being "filtered" by intervening managerial levels (such as Level $B$ in Fig. 33-1).
2. He feels that a number of managers within his jurisdiction ($B_1$, $B_2$ and $B_3$, for example) have negative attitudes toward upward communication which discourage lower levels (such as Level $C$) from communicating relevant information.

3. He suspects that adverse conditions exist between various levels (between Levels *B* and *C*, for example) or within subunits that fall under his jurisdiction (such as within units $C_1$, $C_2$ and $C_3$).
4. He feels that an occasional "purging" is necessary to allow short circuiting of formal organizational channels so that information can be received directly from lower levels (*C*).

When a manager decides to employ nominal grouping on a multiple level basis, several important factors must first be considered. Among them is determining which organizational subunits will be included in the sessions. How many levels of the organization should be involved? Which particular subunits should be included? Who will be charged with conducting the sessions? Will the nominal groups be conducted by the manager who makes the decision to utilize the process, by an appointee or staff assistant, or even by an outside consultant?

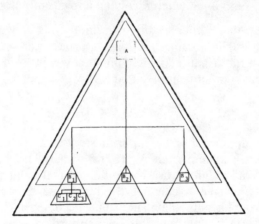

**Fig. 33.1**
**Nominal grouping as a tool for individual managers**

Another important decision to be made concerns the disposition of the data generated. Will they be made available to all levels of management (including the by-passed levels) or shared only among a few managers? Answers to this question undoubtedly depend upon the given purpose of the sessions, and the nature of the data received.

### A Technique for Multi-Directional Communication

Nominal grouping is a technique for multi-directional communication. When subordinates meet together for the purpose of communicating upward, lateral communication unavoidably takes place. The information items which participants generate and read aloud in the recording phase are a reflection of their interests, attitudes, and concerns; also, perhaps, an indication of their perceptiveness and intelligence. This kind of idea sharing among peers often goes beyond the typical degree of lateral communication. Nominal grouping also allows for downward communication if the total information sets generated by superiors are made available to subordinates. In the same way, diagonal communication, whether downward or upward, can also be a planned by-product advantage. Deliberate, overt action is necessary to achieve the downward and diagonal communication, and circumstances dictate the procedure of doing so. However, lateral communication is a natural, unavoidable by-product of the technique.

### Information Is Generated

Nominal grouping can do more than simply facilitate the communication of existing knowledge. One principal advantage emanates from its utilization for the purpose of "idea generation." For example, the process may be used in this way to identify various solution approaches for a specific problem. The purpose here goes far beyond the simple role of communication. It embraces the creativity/information-generation function. Evidence indicates that the nominal grouping environment is highly conducive to the intense, searching pattern necessary for "idea generation."[10]

### Participation Par Excellence

Nominal grouping is a vehicle for participative management. Conducting the sessions per se is a form of participation, but the way and extent to which the process is employed dictates the degree to which participative management is operationalized. Asking several groups of five to ten employees to communicate with management by means of the nominal group setting is a minimal form of participation. Participation can be maximized, however, by using the same people to identify problem areas and to decide (by voting) which ones are to receive attention first, and further allowing them to identify problem solutions and to decide which are to be implemented.

With either approach, however, employees are participating, and the simple act of using the technique is a demonstration of management's interest and confidence in its subordinates (a form of downward communication). For many individuals, this results in an increased feeling of importance, an enhanced self-image and a greater level of self-confidence. For some peer groups, the effect may be stronger group identification and cohesion, and an eager, excited, productive attitude. A general feeling of "at last, respect from our superiors and the opportunity to really be involved and to contribute" may well be generated. This is summarized by Huseman who notes that the use of nominal grouping "creates a type of 'Hawthorne Effect' with the employees involved." The authors have experienced this same display of enthusiasm by participants in a wide variety of nominal grouping situations.

Nominal grouping can be used to provide the necessary impetus to overcome the status quo. For example, if employees are asked to identify problem areas in their work environment, the inference is that management intends to resolve them. This creates an "expectation for change" on the part of employees (that is, an environment conducive to change), and serves as a productive stimulus for management actions.

Another by-product advantage which almost invariably results from the use of nominal grouping is the identification of training needs. Almost any nominal grouping session in which problems are identified (communication inadequacies, managerial problems, and so forth) provides indications of training needs.[11]

Although many of the problems are best solved through managerial decisions and action, others often can be resolved only by providing the employees with appropriate kinds of training. Designing training programs from this informational base results in a program more nearly tailored to specific individual needs.

### It Is Not "Something for Nothing"

For the potential user of the technique, several caveats are in order. Utilization of nominal grouping gives birth to the expectation for action, and the process should not be used if positive change is not desired. Nominal grouping is a commitment to action and the information communicated in the sessions may open a "can of worms." The process has no place where management is not interested in identifying and solving problems. Nominal grouping is perceived as a threat to some employees, and should not be used if identifying and strengthening weaknesses is not considered beneficial. Using the process for multi-level purposes may mean re-channeling communication and by-passing superiors. If the value of this improved communication does not exceed the detriment of a by-passed link in the chain of command, then the process should not be used in a by-passing way. Finally, nominal grouping does require time—about one and one-half hours per session. But this is a nominal cost in absolute terms and especially relative to other techniques (such as discussion groups) and to the value of the information generally communicated.[12]

## Notes

1. This article is based on a paper originally presented at the annual meeting of the Southern Management Association, 9 November 1973, in Houston, Texas.
2. Richard C. Huseman, "Defining Communication Problems within the Organizational Setting," *Journal of Organizational Communications* (Summer 1972), pp. 19-20.
3. Andre L. Delbecq and Andrew Van de Ven, "Nominal Group Techniques for Involving Clients and Resource Experts in Program Planning," in *Academy of Management Proceedings* ed. T. J. Atchison and J. V. Ghorpade (San Diego, California: Academy of Management, 1970), pp. 208-27.
4. The leader of a nominal group is called a *grouper,* rather than leader, since he does not assume a typical leadership role.
5. Chris Argyris, *Personality and Organization* (New York: Harper and Row, 1957), pp. 159-60.
6. Donald W. Taylor, Paul C. Berry, and Clifford H. Block, "Does Group Participation When Using Brainstorming Facilitate or Inhibit Creative Thinking?" *Administrative Science Quarterly* 3 (1958), pp. 23-47; and Marvin D. Dunnette, John Campbell, and Kay Jaastad, "The Effect of Group Participation on Brainstorming Effectiveness for Two Industrial Samples," *Journal of Applied Psychology* (1963), vol. 47, pp. 30-37.
7. Huseman, "Defining Communication Problems," p. 20.
8. Andrew Van de Ven and Andre L. Delbecq, "Nominal versus Interacting Group Process for Committee Decision-Making Effectiveness," *Academy of Management Journal* (June 1971), p. 207.
9. *Ibid.*
10. *Ibid.*
11. Thad B. Green, "The Utilization of Nominal Grouping To Determine Needs," paper presented at the thirty-fourth annual meeting of the *Academy of Management,* August 1974, Seattle, Washington.
12. For additional references on research and applications of nominal grouping see Thad B. Green, "An Empirical Analysis of Nominal and Interacting Groups," *Academy of Management Journal* (forthcoming); Donald C. Mosley and Thad B. Green, "Nominal Grouping As An Organization Development Intervention Technique," *Training and Development Journal* (March 1974), pp. 30-37; and H. William Vroman and Thad B. Green, "The Application of Nominal Grouping to Health Care Distribution Systems," paper presented at the first annual Miami Conference on Progress and Prospects in Health Care Distribution Systems, Miami, Florida, November 1974.

# 34

# The Delphi Technique: A Long-Range Planning Tool

*Richard J. Tersine* and *Walter E. Riggs*

Group decisions are necessary when the scope of a problem is such that no individual has sufficient expertise and knowledge to effect a solution. Group processes are also functional in disseminating information and providing instruction. However, grouping "experts" together causes a number of hindering side effects. Emergent leaders (high status, expressive or strong individuals) tend to dominate activities either because of their knowledge or informal influence. Personalities and organizational status affect decisions because credibility is influenced by perceptions of the person offering an idea, or his position. Generally, *compromise* decisions are obtained as opposed to *consensus* decisions.[1] Group processes often leave participants exhausted, discouraged and frustrated because of endless meanderings and a lack of resolution.

## Advantages of Delphi

In an effort to eliminate these negative side effects, the RAND Corporation developed a technique called *Delphi,* to be used in long-range technical forecasting where a group of experts from diverse backgrounds is called upon to make decisions. Delphi is a method to systematically solicit, collect, evaluate and tabulate independent opinion without group discussion. This quasi-objective, or subjective, technique replaces direct debate with a carefully designed program of individual interrogations, usually conducted by a series of questionnaires. The control of interaction among respondents is a deliberate attempt to avoid the disadvantages of the more conventional use of experts via round table discussions, committees and conferences. The experts are not identified to each other in any way, and there is usually a greater flow of ideas, fuller participation and increased evidence of problem closure.

Delphi has many advantages over more conventional means of gathering opinions on matters not subject to precise quantification. Most of these advantages are the result of keeping the identities of the participants unknown, to eliminate bias. A participant finds it much easier to change his mind if he has no ego involvement in defending an original estimate (only he knows if he changes his mind). He is less subject to the *halo effect,* where the opinions of one highly respected man influence the opinions of others. Also reduced is the *bandwagon effect* which encourages agreement with the majority. A significant advantage of Delphi is that it forms a consensus of opinion by requiring justification for any significant deviation from the group average.

Since Delphi does not require the participants to meet at a common time in a common location, geographical dispersion presents very little difficulty and fewer demands are put on panel members. In face-to-face groups, full participation by individuals is restrained as the size of the group increases. Delphi imposes no such limitations and there is no restriction on the number of participants. Delphi encourages individual thinking, forces a panel to get on with the business at hand, and forces respondents to move towards a consensus, unless strong convictions to the contrary are held.

### Eliminates Confrontations

The central idea is to eliminate any direct confrontation of the experts and to allow their projections to reach a consensus based upon increasingly relevant information. A series of questionnaires are distributed or interviews are conducted with each participant. After the initial response, individuals are asked to request any information they need or specify what information they have which can aid others in the decision process. Opinions are left out and only facts are considered relevant to the entire group. Following tabulation of each questionnaire, the participants are given the information that other participants contributed. The process is continued through an iterative number of rounds until there seems to be sufficient convergence of opinion.

The last step is to apply a correction process to the results to bring into line those responses that may be the result of inappropriate assumptions or misinterpretations of data. Therefore, the results are based upon not only a consensus of end product, but a consensus of assumptions and uniform interpretations of the importance and effect of the data.[2]

Although in actual application the specific procedures of Delphi vary, the following example is typical: A forecast is initiated by a questionnaire which requests estimates of a set of numerical quantities (dates by which specific technological events will occur, probabilities of occurrence by given dates, event desirability and feasibility, and the like). The results of the first round are summarized, and the median and interquartile range of the responses is computed and fed back to the respondents with a request to revise their first estimates where appropriate. On succeeding rounds, those individuals whose opinions deviate greatly from the majority (outside the interquartile range) are requested to give the reasons for their extreme opinions. A collection of these reasons is presented to each participant, along with a new median and interquartile range, and participants are given another opportunity to reconsider and revise earlier opinions or estimates. The process is continued until a consensus is reached. Instead of starting with a preconceived list of questions, sometimes preliminary question-naires are used to select and develop questions for which estimates can be obtained.

### Wide-Ranging Uses

The Delphi technique has been applied to a variety of problems. The most predominate use has been for long-range technological forecasting. It was originally developed in the early 1950s and applied to problems of a military nature, but nonmilitary applications were developed in the 1960s.

One of the first reported corporate applications was to explore a firm's future external environment and to analyze evolutionary product lines. Delphi has been used to predict likely inventions, new technologies and product applications. In education, it has been used to design a new curriculum and to predict the impact of socioeconomic developments on future school systems. In retailing, Delphi was used to indicate future changes in department stores. Other applications of the method have been to predict the impact of a new land use policy; information systems relative to development planning; and to identify problems, set goals, establish priorities and obtain solutions in health care programs. Delphi has become a multiple-use tool, and has proved to be an effective method of forecasting future events in both business and government. Cities and municipalities are just beginning to adopt the technique and it is likely they could become its largest user.

### The Procedure

The steps of the Delphi technique can vary somewhat based on the intended application, but a basic diagram of the process is shown in Fig. 34.1.

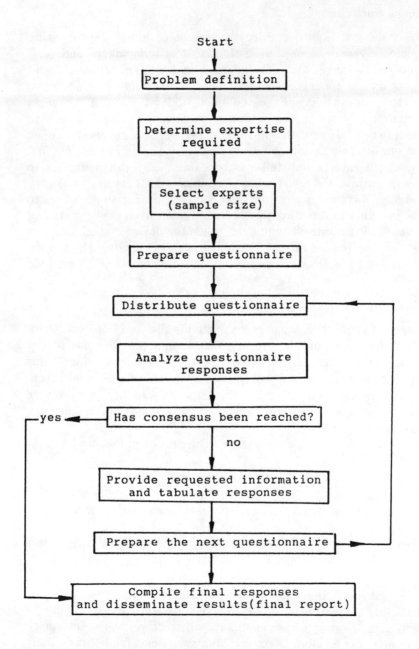

**Fig. 34.1**
**Delphi technique**

### Forming a Work Group

Before the questionnaire process begins some initial steps must be completed. A work group consisting of decision makers and staff members must be selected. The decision makers are individuals who must act on the conclusions of the study; they should play an active role in the process to insure their complete understanding of the events leading to the consensus. The staff members are the professionals who conduct the Delphi process; they do the typing, sending and receiving of the questionnaires and make a preliminary analysis of the results. The decision makers and staff members must work in conjunction to analyze, appraise and revise the questionnaires in succeeding rounds.

The staff members must interview each of the decision makers to determine what information should be obtained from the experts and how that information will be utilized. Then the design and structure of the questionnaires can be developed. This step is very important to the success of the undertaking, and plenty of time should be allowed for this process.

### Selecting Experts

A second group which must be selected is the panel of experts, or respondents. These are the people whose judgments are being sought and who agree to answer the questionnaires. The composition of this group is critical in determining the effectiveness of the Delphi technique. Respondent selection is very important to the value of the process, and five basic criteria should be considered in choosing participants:

They must have a basic knowledge of the problem area and be able to apply that knowledge.

They must have a good performance record in their particular areas.

They must possess a high degree of objectivity and rationality.

They must have the time available to participate to the conclusion of the program.

They must be willing to give the amount of time and effort to do a thorough job of participation.[3]

The composition of the respondent group must also be considered, and will vary with the nature of the problem. If the problem is highly specific and technical, all of the respondents should have technical expertise. If the problem is general and abstract, a team of interdisciplinarians might be more effective.[4] Many problems fall between these extremes, so a balance of specialists and generalists may be desirable. Also, a proper balance of theoreticians and pragmatists should be sought. The knowledge and composition of the panel will depend on the nature of the forecasting problem.

The sample size is the next major item for consideration, and will vary with the homogeneity of the respondent group and the amount of work the staff can adequately handle. If the group is homogeneous, between ten and fifteen respondents should be sufficient to generate effective results. However, as the degree of homogeneity declines, a larger number is necessary to achieve reasonable quality. The University of Virginia used 421 respondents in one study, and achieved workable results.[5] The general feeling is that the sample size should be the minimum necessary, thereby avoiding much administrative staff work, but there are no specific guidelines for determining the optimum number of panel members to use.

Contacting the respondents is the next step in the process. The nominator or panel of nominators who initially chose the respondents should convey to them the following points: the purpose of the study, the primary question/problem to be analyzed, the part they will play in reaching a solution, the importance of a concerted effort on their part to successful results and the uniqueness of their abilities in the total effort. As is usually the case in such processes, some will decline to participate and additional new respondents will have to be chosen.

## The First Questionnaire

There are two conceptual approaches to the development of the first questionnaire. First, if the primary question or problem is of such a nature that it can be stated in specific terms, it should be set forth in the greatest detail possible. In this case, each response will contain one opinion about the primary question, the respondent's reasoning, the facts which he considered important and his requests for additional information needed to make future responses.

The second approach is used when the primary question or problem is stated in general terms, thus requiring further specification. The questionnaire will then contain one or more open ended questions that will attempt to better define the problem. Also included will be questions regarding reasoning, facts and additional information requests.

Regardless of which approach is followed, a short cover letter should accompany the questionnaire, explaining the instructions and thanking the respondents for their participation. Include a self-addressed stamped envelope for returning the response, and set a specific completion date deadline.

Upon receipt of the completed questionnaires, the tabulation process will begin. The staff will examine each questionnaire to determine the areas of agreement and disagreement. The items requiring clarification and additional information will be identified and summarized, creating the material for the next questionnaire.

## Subsequent Questionnaires

A composite of responses to the first questionnaire, along with an explanation of any misconceptions on the part of any respondents, will form the base of the second questionnaire. Usually some measure of central tendency, such as the mean or median response, and some measure of dispersion, such as the interquartile range, are provided to the respondents. Each participant will be asked to revise his opinion based upon the new data and responses of his peers. If an expert's response falls outside the interquartile range, it is customary to have him give the reasons for his extreme position. These justifications are summarized and distributed in succeeding rounds so that other group members can take exception to a stated position. The purpose of information feedback is to produce more precise predictions and to encourage opinion convergence. The tabulation procedure is repeated in a similar manner for subsequent questionnaires until convergence is obtained. The number of questionnaires varies, but generally a minimum of three is necessary to achieve a reasonable consensus of opinion.

## The Correction Process

The final step in the Delphi process is the correction phase, which takes many different approaches. The RAND Corporation took the median of the responses as the consensus and then gave some consideration to the trend of responses.[6] A weighted average of the component estimates has also been used with the weighting factor being the relative expertise of the individual participant.[7] A final report should summarize the goals, processes and final results of the study.

## Extensions of the Technique

There are several extensions and modifications of the Delphi technique. One modification is known as cross-impact analysis. This process takes into consideration the impact of the occurrence of one event on a subsequent event when several events are interrelated. Usually the analysis will develop a series of conditional probabilities for events.

An iterative process helps to insure the elimination of contradicting predictions.

Another modification is called System for Event Evaluation and Review (SEER). SEER modifies the process by establishing an initial list of forecasts that have been constructed through a series of interviews prior to the beginning of the Delphi process. It can reduce the number of questionnaire rounds, thus saving time. Also, participants can be asked to answer questions in only their area of expertise. This aids in eliminating possible distorted responses caused by lack of knowledge in a particular area.[8]

Although Delphi tends to be futuristic, it can also be used to investigate opinions about the past. As a form of cybernetic arbitration, experts could be placed at terminals on-line to a computer so that the time of the Delphi process could be reduced considerably.

## Limitations

Several limitations to Delphi deserve discussion. First, the crucial step in the entire process involves the selection of the participants. The mechanics of the Delphi can be completely negated by poor panel selection and poor motivation. The length of time required for the analysis also presents a problem—it can take several weeks for a three round Delphi. If the results do not come quickly, participant motivation can wane. Adequate time must be available to use the technique.

Delphi should not be considered for routine decision making. Its use is for issues requiring wide and representative input. When aggregate, individual judgments are desirable, it can be most helpful, but the following issues must be resolved during the process: whether to use open-ended or structural questions; how many questionnaires are required; the number and design of feedback reports needed; guidelines for aggregation of panel judgments.

Delphi compares favorably to other group processes on such items as number of working hours required, cost of utilizing committees and the proximity of group participants. It usually requires the least amount of time for participants. However, the calendar time required to obtain judgments from respondents can be a disadvantage. (On long range considerations, calendar time to decision is not usually that relevant.)

The final problem lies in the action that is taken as a result of the forecast. Executives will generally assign a rather low priority to events likely to occur far in the future due to their concern for more immediate problems. Implementation of results can be a problem, but it is not exclusive to Delphi.

## Validation

The validation or testing of the accuracy of Delphi predictions is difficult particularly when the events will not take place for many years. There are two approaches to Delphi validation. The first compares Delphi predictions with actual occurrences. A study of eight groups of 20 people satisfactorily predicted 32 out of 40 short-range questions in a two round Delphi.[9] Experimental results indicate that Delphi is at least a "good" predictor with predictions relatively close to actuality.[10]

The second approach compares Delphi predictions with those of conventional confrontation methods. One study that compared Delphi and direct confrontation groups found Delphi more accurate in thirteen of sixteen cases, less accurate in two cases, and in one case the two methods were equal, indicating that Delphi was more accurate than direct confrontation.[11] Unfortunately, comparison studies are practically nonexistent at this time, but it appears that Delphi is at least as good as, if not superior to, other long-range forecasting techniques.

Long-range planning has been a constant source of difficulty for many organizations. Because of the interrelated factors which must be considered in decisions of major magnitude, it becomes necessary to rely on group decision making. The problems associated with traditional methods are well known. Delphi eliminates some of the more glaring difficulties, particularly those associated with personality domination and status of the contributors.

The Delphi technique is a general methodology for achieving a reliable consensus of opinion from a group of experts concerning the impact or implications of some unknown or uncertain future event. It is accomplished through the use of a series of intensive questionnaires interspersed with controlled opinion feedback. The process is based on the notion that single experts may hold incorrect opinions regarding future occurrences, but increased accuracy is achieved by collecting the opinions of a number of experts. That is, the collective opinion corrected for individual biases and misinformation will result in a more reliable forecast or estimate.

Long-range forecasting has increased substantially in organizational importance. Realizing that survival in the future depends on effective planning, organizations are adopting more elaborate and sophisticated forecasting approaches and it is timely and appropriate that the Delphi technique be considered an effective approach to such long-range predictions since judgmental decisions are best facilitated by judgmental techniques.

## Notes

1. Andre F. Delbecq and Andrew H. Van, *Techniques for Program Planning* (Glenview, Ill.: Scott, Foresman, and Co., 1975), pp. 83-107.
2. Norman Dalkey and Olaf Helmer, "An Experimental Application of the Delphi Method to the Use of Experts," *Management Science* (April 1963), pp. 458-467.
3. Richard N. Farmer and Barry M. Richman, *Corporate Management and Economic Progress* (Homewood, Ill.: Irwin, 1965), pp. 328-59.
4. *Ibid.*
5. Frederick R. Cypert and Walter L. Gant, "The Delphi Technique: A Case Study," *Phi Delta Kappan* (January 1971), pp. 272-73.
6. Dalkey and Helmer, pp. 458-67.
7. Farmer and Richman, pp. 328-59.
8. Alan R. Fusfeld and Richard N. Foster, "The Delphi Technique: Survey and Comment," *Business Horizons* (June 1971), pp. 63-74.
9. N. C. Dalkey, "Comparison of Group Judgment Techniques with Short-Range Predictions and Almanac Questions," (New York: RAND Corporation, R-678, May 1971).
10. Robert C. Judd, "Delphi Method: Computerized 'Oracle' Accelerates Consensus Formation," *College and University Business* (September 1970), pp. 30-34.
11. John Pfeiffer, *New Look at Education* (New York: Odyssey Press, 1968), pp. 154-55.

# Part X

# MANAGING CONFLICT AND CHANGE

# 35

# Conflict: An Overview

*Olga L. Crocker*

*Conflict*—the word conjures visions of disagreement, strikes, picket lines, fighting, and a host of other negative images. It results when two or more incompatible forces meet. Each party, through its behavior and actions, attempts to win, to defeat or suppress an opponent and to create an imbalance in power in favor of itself.

Although each of us has experienced conflict, we have great difficulty in understanding it, managing it, and resolving it. Behavioral scientists provide limited help. The study of conflict involves problems of timing. The observer must be in the midst of the action, privileged to the inside story and the thoughts and feelings of the parties. He or she must not become involved; involvement provides vision through biased spectacles. Unfortunately, from an observer's point of view, an audience changes the actions of the participants. They become intimidated; they grandstand; they become more reasonable or exhibit other behaviors atypical of the unobserved situation.

Nonetheless, we do know a few things about conflict. We know, for example, the parties to a conflict and the sources of the problem. We can analyze whether conflict is functional or dysfunctional for each of the parties. We are beginning to know something about those factors that increase and decrease conflict. This article will discuss each of these points in turn.

## Parties to Conflict

Conflict may be classified according to the individuals who are involved: (a) the individual personally (intrapersonal or internal), (b) two individuals (interpersonal), (c) the individual within the group, or (d) two or more groups.

### Internal Conflict

The inner struggle an individual experiences is attributable to role conflict and role ambiguity.

Role ambiguity results when the individual is uncertain what actions and behaviors are expected. This uncertainty results from a lack of clarity about responsibility, a lack of knowledge about how a task is to be performed, and a lack of knowledge regarding the standards and expectations that will be applied in deciding whether satisfactory performance has occurred.

Role conflict, on the other hand, is generally categorized into four types: inter-role, intra-role, person-role, and role overload. *Intersender* or inter-role conflict results when pressure is exerted by different senders who perceive the individual's role from different viewpoints. A professional woman, for example, must not only be a leader, but she must often be a wife, a mother, and a housekeeper. Satisfactory performance of one role makes the other one difficult or impossible to perform. *Intra-role* conflict is the product of conflicting or contradictory demands made by one person or a given situation. Who has not experienced the three-day task and the words of the boss who wants no efforts spared in performing an exceptionally good job—by tomorrow morning! *Person-role* conflict results when action is required that violates the codes and standards by which the person prefers to live. At times, a clash occurs between a desire for personal independence and the authoritarian demands of the organization or group to which we belong. There may also be a clash between obligations incurred because of friendship or kinship and obligations to society at large. The last type of role conflict, *role overload,* is the consequence of too many expectations. Each expectation may be legitimate and compatible; together, they are impossible to complete within the given time restrictions.

A certain amount of inner conflict that results from role ambiguity and role conflict tends to increase an individual's effectiveness. If these levels become too high, however, productivity and physical and emotional health may be affected.

### Interpersonal Conflict

Conflicts between individuals are what movies are made of. Two heroes fight over the same heroine. Two girls argue about the rules of a game. An editor and a reporter argue the merits of a story. Four men vie for the presidency of an organization. Two executives disagree on where a new computer installation should be located, each desiring it for his own department. Spiderman fights for his life against one of his innumerable foes. Conflicts between individuals are familiar and legendary.

### Individual Within a Group

When an individual first joins a group or an organization, many negative aspects appear to dominate. He or she is not accepted and does not fit within the group. After some time, the individual learns the argot of the group, the tricks of the trade, and the social skills required to be part of the group. Conflict has subsided and socialization has occurred. The group has influenced the individual to accept its goals and values.

The individual may also be in conflict with the group when an attempt is made to gain influence, leadership, or power over the group. In that case, the individual is resisting the socialization process that the group is attempting to impose.

### Group Conflict

Within groups and organizations a law of interorganizational conflict appears to exist—i.e., every group is in partial conflict with every other group. Israel and Egypt, line and staff people, vice-presidents of different departments, the hard sciences and the social sciences at the university, labor and management; all these groups are in conflict with each other. Conflicts occur because different groups have different goals and values, because they share resources, and becuase they must depend upon each other to accomplish their own goals.

## Sources of Conflict

Basic to any conflict episode are at least one of three causes: (a) the desire for power, (b) communication, and (c) unresolved prior issues. Power or the desire to change the power structure includes differences attributable to values and ideologies, goals and methods, and interdependencies. Communication can cause problems because the receiver and the sender do not perceive information in the same way, because words do not have the same meaning, and because different importance is attached to the same facts. Unresolved prior issues are the unsolved problems and residual of feelings each party brings to the present relationship. They result from previous interfaces between the two parties.

### Power as a Source of Conflict

The control of people and the ability to direct money and other resources to desired ends or goals is the essence of power. It is for this reason that there is conflict over the setting of goals and over the means to achieve these goals. Power conflicts arise in the value differences of people and because they are dependent on others to achieve their goals.

*Ideologies and Values.* The desire for power begins in the ideological or value base of individuals. Some people have a strong need to be liked and accepted and would avoid conflict if possible. Others have a strong need to excel and achieve and, therefore, might ignore conflict. For a third group of individuals, the strongest need involves a desire to control the environment and others within that environment; in other words, a need for power.

A factor in power conflict is attributable to racial differences, especially if one group feels that there is a superiority of particular genes. During World War II, the Nazis in Germany perceived themselves as the superior people of the world. In the southern States, South Africa and Rhodesia, the superiority of whites was an unquestioned ideology for many decades.

Conflicts over power are the result of differences in value orientations. Each person perceives the world in terms of personal experience, training, and background. This uniqueness means that different aspirations and different types of tangible and intangible goods are valued by different people. Within organizations these values translate to different expectations of the same leader, to differences in time perspectives, and a desire for the same organization to assume different forms of structure.

In other words, some people within the organization prefer tall hierarchies and autocratic leaders who lay down the law and expect to be followed. Others value the lower, flatter organization with its greater participation and the opportunity to be consulted and to share in the decision processes.

University students are at least somewhat future-oriented; they look for situations in which they will reap generous rewards in the not-too-distant future. Young people born and living in a ghetto want their rewards here and now; they have little faith and trust in an uncertain future.

Conflicts result when the organization cannot satisfy, to an equal degree, the values and expectations of all these different kinds of people because of their differences in attitudes, tolerances, and ideas of justice.

*Interdependencies.* Interdependencies exist not only within the organization, but also in interpersonal relationships. Others have power to the extent that there is a dependency on them to fulfill needs or to the extent that common resources are shared. Power is the right to give commands and expect obedience, to reward, and to punish. Power is the extent to which an individual has knowledge that is needed and the extent to which the individual is admired. The need exists for this admiration to be reciprocated.

Where no dependencies exist, there is no power and no potential for conflict. The president of a university has considerable power, but his power over students in a particular class is much less than that of the professor who teaches them. The professor, on the other hand, treads lightly in the presence of the departmental secretary. When a dependency exists, when individuals have to share resources or wait for the outcome that another can provide, the power exerted and the potential for conflict is considerably increased.

*Goals.* Goals are the expression of intentions. They serve as targets of behavior; they provide motivation; they determine the direction of expenditures and efforts; and they decide how resources will be utilized.

One might think that the goals of a group or an organization are very simple to identify—to make money, to heal people, to provide welfare. A look at the concept of profit shows the difficulty in determining goals. What is profit? Is it cash in the bank? Is it the money value of the items sold? Is it the margin on each item? What if it costs more in overhead to sell one item than it does another? What about turnover of goods? Is profit dependent on the number and kinds of units produced or on the number and kind of units sold? Would the production department, the sales department, and the credit department agree on one definition? The production department wants to minimize costs. This is accomplished by minimum shut-downs and minimum retooling and by producing large quantities of a few products. Salesmen require a great variety of products, some of which are loss leaders (the company loses money on these but produces them to retain customers), and very liberal credit terms. The credit department must collect accounts; they want minimal credit and then only to A-1 customers.

Surely the goal of healing people in a mental hospital is more easily defined! Are drugs and shock to be used in healing? Is it to be therapy? Both? In what quantity? Would the psychosomaticist and the psychotherapist perceive the solution in the same way? If therapy requires that the patient spend a portion of time working with normal people outside the walls of the institution, would everyone agree? Is the goal of the mental institution to protect society by confining these people? What about the ward aide? How does he or she translate patient progress and healing? By the patient's display of individualism? By his or her challenge to authority? Or is the ward aide's life easier if the patient is subdued and submissive?

And so it goes. The perception of organizational or group goal differs, depending on the role one has in attaining that goal.

Goals also depend on the vantage point of the individual. A senior leader might look outward—to profits, public acclaim, re-election, or growth. At the operational levels, the important goals are units per hour or survival in a hostile world. These two types of goals are not generally compatible. That individual who is close to the power source, who controls the goals or objectives of the organization and the methods by which these will be achieved, controls the people and resources of the organization. This situation invites conflict.

### Communication as a Source of Conflict

Conflict results because the communication transmitted is misunderstood or does not reach the individual who could best influence the conflict situation. This occurs because the message is (a) distorted by the sender; (b) distorted, suppressed, or unintentionally dropped while it is being transmitted; or (d) distorted or misunderstood by the receiver.

The communication process has at least four elements: the sender, the message, the channel, and the receiver. The sender brings to the situation certain values, experiences, training, background, and an emotional and cognitive state. The message is translated into physical, semantic, and symbolic forms—i.e., into some type of vocabulary, body language, gestures, and facial expressions. It travels through a channel as verbal, written, and/or visual symbols. These forms are retranslated and interpreted by a receiver who has his or her own values, experience, training, background, and cognitive and emotional states of mind. This individual transmits a reaction to the interpretation of the message by other symbolic or physical forms (by ignoring it, by smiling, by frowning, by a rigid posture, etc.). With each element of the communication process, the potential exists for increasing or decreasing the degree of conflict.

The clarity of the message depends on the motivation and communication skills of the sender. The sender may condense the message (because of a desire for brevity) or distort it to retain power. (The possession of required information gives the holder expert power over others.) In transmitting the message, the sender may state a personal view as if it were a certainty—i.e., he or she may attempt to obtain closure by making the information appear to be more precise and definite than it is. Of course, some individuals are more competent at communicating; others are less so. Conflict may be increased because the sender cannot or does not adequately convey the intended message, and the intent of the communication is misunderstood by the receiver.

Situations may exist where a message is lost in transmittal. This can occur intentionally or unintentionally. Within groups and organizations, gatekeepers exist who assume the responsibility of filtering and interpreting information. At other times, the loss may be unintentional—the message was not read, was not salient and thereby ignored, or was only partially heard or understood. Some unintentional filtering occurs as a result of specialization. Specialists interpret the message in terms of their area of expertise, omitting or not understanding the significance of those elements that appear inconsistent with their experience and knowledge.

The receiver is also important in the communication process. He or she filters the message because of differences attributable to perceptions and the interpretation of words used. A denial or selectivity process may be used so that mental choices established earlier and personal cognitive consistency are maintained.

There is, however, an additional problem. Although the correct message may reach the receiver and all aspects may be correctly understood, it may come so rapidly or in such quantity that information overload occurs. When overload results, conflict may be prolonged or aggravated because the receiver (a) is unable to process the information and omits all or a portion of it; (b) processes it incorrectly; (c) mentally files the received information, hoping to use it later; and (d) stereotypes or is influenced by a dominant characteristic of the opponent. This overload leads to a distortion, not only of information but also of the motives and the attributes of the opponent.

An example from a labor-management negotiation situation, which the author had the opportunity to witness, may help indicate the importance of communication in the abatement or exacerbation of conflict. In this instance, the labor negotiator prided himself on being tough and hard. Frequently he mentioned that "schoolin" was unnecessary, that he had become a leader in spite of his minimal educational level. The management negotiator who sat across from him had never worked on the shop floor. This man was equally proud—that he had been university educated, that he had received a law degree.

The labor negotiator spoke of factory problems in the vernacular of the plant. The lawyer did not share this vocabulary. Other factors also may have influenced this man's perceptions. He may have been listening selectively, hearing and seeing only that which he understood or wanted to hear. He may have been evaluating the message in terms of his opponent and basing this opinion not on the leadership and negotiating qualities displayed, but on the lack of education and the coarseness of behavior exhibited. Certainly the lawyer might have had personal problems; perhaps he was thinking that he himself would not have a job if he did not drive a sufficiently hard bargain.

Time after time, the management negotiator misunderstood and misinterpreted what was being said. Each time he would reiterate the company position. And each time, the labor negotiator would explain the problems and the solution. Ironically, both men were saying the same thing: the company was in financial difficulty; it was mandatory that it remain in business; some improvement in wages and conditions would be necessary so that the employees would not leave the company.

A number of factors contributed to the conflict. There was a lack of common background, an inability or unwillingness to recognize this lack of commonality, a reluctance to express feelings and bring them into the open, and an introduction of many smoke screen issues. The tendency to speak in shop floor vernacular, in generalities, or in legalese presented a barrier to meaningful communication and heightened conflict to almost nonreconcilable levels. Both parties recognized the same goals, were satisfied with the prevailing power balance, and were willing to compromise on the same settlement. In spite of the fact that there was no basis for conflict, conflict did exist; neither man could understand what the other was saying!

### Residual Issues as a Source of Conflict

The third source of conflict is residual issues. The relationship that existed between the parties in the past affects the present relationship. To understand this concept, it is necessary to understand the process of conflict and its seven elements—i.e., latent conditions, perceptions of these conditions, a felt injustice, action, retaliation, resolution, and residual or aftermath.

Before conflict can occur, undesirable conditions must exist (latent conditions) within the environment or in the relationship between two individuals or groups. At least one party must perceive that this injustice exists and experience some emotional discomfort regarding the situation. Conflict begins when action is taken to right the injustice and a retaliation results.

Resolution of the conflict leads to an "aftermath." At the time of resolution, some issues are solved, others are not. Feelings and emotions that were developed in the course of the conflict are retained by both parties. These three outcomes are the "aftermath" or residual issues that are carried over into the future relationship between the two parties.

The potential that this carry-over has for future conflict depends on the type of solution reached. In a problem-solving situation, both parties may attempt to resolve future mutual problems jointly. In a domination or annihilation, one party will be supreme; the other will either not dare to challenge or will be unable to challenge. If a temporary truce is reached, one or both of the parties will likely retrench to gather forces and attack again. The potential for future conflict is heightened if the struggle was bitter, if the solution for at least one party was unsatisfactory, and if an opportunity for retaliation exists. The perceptions and feelings aroused in the prior conflict and the outcomes in terms of resolved and unresolved issues are carried over and affect the parties in future relationships.

### Functional or Dysfunctional

Contrary to popular belief and the impression that may have been given in this article, conflict is neither good nor bad. It merely leads to functional or dysfunctional results.

Conflict is functional to the extent that it increases effectiveness. This can occur in a number of ways. Conflict can prompt a search for new facts and solutions. It can act as a safety valve. If small problems can surface and be resolved satisfactorily, a major blow-up may be prevented. Conflict can increase the motivation and energy that is available. It can increase group cohesiveness and performance. During conflict, members tend to close ranks to achieve a superordinate goal or to defeat the superordinate enemy. Conflict can also decrease group cohesiveness. It can promote a circulation in leadership and a reevaluation of goals. Last, but not least, conflict provides an easy measure of an individual's or group's own power relative to the opponent.

Whether conflict is dysfunctional depends on the viewpoint of the participants. Within the group or organization, it is dysfunctional if it decreases effectiveness. It is dysfunctional to the organization, for example, when superiors deliberately create dissension so they can gain stature in the eyes of constituents when they solve the problem. The individuals concerned, however, would view this dissension as functional; it achieved the purposes desired. Conflict used as a cover for empire building can be viewed in the same way. Conflict is dysfunctional to all parties involved, however, if it becomes personalized. When this occurs, individuals direct more energies to self-defensiveness than they do to solving the real problems and issues. Conflict is dysfunctional also to the extent that it rigidifies the group and to the extent that it leads to gross distortions of reality.

Whether the results are favorable or unfavorable depends upon the measures and actions used in resolving the conflict, on the attitudes of the opponents toward each other, and the values and orientations of the party making the judgment. It is not unusual for conflict and the outcomes of conflict to be viewed favorably by one party and unfavorably by another party.

## Factors Affecting the Resolution of Conflict

Whether conflict can be resolved and the quality of that solution depend upon (a) the attitude of the parties towards conflict itself, (b) the environmental component, and (c) the personalities of the parties involved.

### Attitude of the Parties toward Conflict

Three attitudes toward conflict exist: avoidance, management, and interactionist.

*Avoidance.* The earlier scientific management view (which is still used in many organizations) stated that conflict must be avoided at all costs. It is dysfunctional for the organization. It is used as a cover for empire building; it becomes personalized and results in bitterness; it rigidifies the groups; it leads to distortions of reality; it undermines the control management has on employees. In short, it threatens the existing situation and power structure.

Managers who believe that conflict must be avoided take precautions to ensure that it does not exist or is not acknowledged. These leaders are of two types—those who rule with an iron hand (dispensing justice at the slightest deviation) and those who "bury their head in the sand." No matter what occurs in the organization, they do not wish to know about it. When this is the dominant view of conflict, it is the responsibility of subordinates to resolve the problem by whatever method they can and to keep it from surfacing.

*Management.* The management view of conflict is at the same time a complement and a contradiction to the human relations point of view, which recognized that conflict was inevitable within the organization. Minor dissensions would always surface, and they should be controlled. The role of the manager under this system is to manage conflict and control people. Performance is judged by how well participants are manipulated and by the minimal disruptions that occur to the organization as a result of these minor scrimmages.

Under this view, managers learn not only human relations skills—how to be leaders, how to motivate workers, and how to use communication channels—but a multitude of survival tactics best described a number of centuries ago in Machiavelli's *The Prince*.

*Interactionist*. Higher levels of education and an introduction of employees to differing philosophies and methods of supervision have made functioning difficult for those who would control and channel conflict. These two aspects have led to the interactionist approach, which states that conflict should be brought into the open.

This approach sees conflict as good for the organization. Conflict acts as a pop-off valve, prompts a search for new solutions, increases group cohesiveness, provides a measure of power, provides a means for settling a participant's own internal conflict, and promotes a reevaluation of goals and a circulation of leadership. Conflict can provide entertainment and a release from tension as well. There are those who enjoy the challenge of battle and those who enjoy watching the sweetness of success and the bitterness of defeat. In short, conflict keeps the organization viable and striving.

For interactionists, conflict is an organizational process. They utilize it in brainstorming, in Delphi techniques, in conferences, and at every opportunity within the organization.

To effectively use the interactionist approach, organizations must be ready to effect change. When the black rights movement began, for example, the blacks wanted change—a change in leadership and a change in goals and values. The institutions they sought to influence wanted to maintain the status quo; conflict would not serve that purpose. For the interactionist approach to be used effectively, a change in mental attitudes on the part of all participants is necessary.

### The Environmental Components

The surroundings and the physical and social structure often work to determine if and to whose advantage a conflict situation will be resolved. Basically, home territory, room and seating arrangements, and the presence of time limits act as moderators. The presence of an audience also influences the conflict relationship.

*The Physical Environment*. Home territory generally provides the host with an advantage. Control can be exerted over the physical arrangements in such a manner as to offset any advantage the opponent may have, or as a compensator for lack of status, ability, or personal power. Home territory also gives the host a psychological advantage.

It is not known why, but at least three reasons have been suggested. Since the host knows the home territory, it is expected that he or she will look after details and the guest will accept these arrangements graciously—whether he or she likes them or not! The guest may retain a fear and distrust that the host will use the knowledge of home territory to personal advantage. This puts the guest on the defensive; energies are channeled, not toward the conflict, but toward being alert to the possibility of fouls or of displaying this defensiveness in an overt manner. In familiar situations, there is a tendency for the individual to become more assertive and to win more frequently.

Seating arrangements can influence the relationship between the parties. Close arrangements (right angles, side by side) force opponents to look at each other and to interact. This makes it more difficult to tell a lie or to bluff, and it makes conflict resolution easier. Distant seating arrangements (across the ends of a long table, for example) make it more difficult for the opponents to see and hear each other. Under these circumstances, it is easier to avoid direct visual contact and intimate interaction. For the same reasons, round tables tend to increase the informality and the closeness; long oblong tables tend to decrease the opportunity for communication and thus increase the coldness and the formal nature of the conflict resolution process.

The use of artistic objects, such as flower vases and abstract sculptures, tends to facilitate informality and affiliation; the use of books and magazines tends to inhibit these processes.

The presence of time limits can often affect the resolution of conflict because it places pressure on the participants to settle their differences or accept the consequences. If the consequences are sufficiently severe, each party will lower the least favorable terms under which it is willing to settle and lower its expectations of what it can obtain as a result of the conflict.

*Social Environment.* Research in social psychology indicates that the individual's judgments, perceptions, attention, and motivation become different when he or she is watched or is a member of a group. Groups make riskier decisions and are more willing to take riskier action. At the same time, there is greater peer pressure to conform to the norms and expectations of the group, and the individual directs more effort toward pleasing others and being positively evaluated by the group and by onlookers. This issue becomes particularly crucial in situations when an individual involved in a conflict represents or is accountable to constituents. Energies become directed, not toward solving the problem, but toward gaining or retaining the approval of constituents.

### The Role of Personality in Conflict

Personality is an illusive variable. Some people are pleasant; some are aggressive; some are introverts; some are neurotics; and some provoke conflict everywhere they go. When it comes to specifying the characteristics of these individuals, however, the task is more difficult. It appears that there are four types of individuals who are generally the focal point of conflict.

The first type is the group of people who are very sensitive to threatening clues within their environment and reveal this sensitivity in a negative manner. This tends to invite hostility and aggression from others. These individuals may lack self-esteem, may be insecure, or may be personally aggressive.

A second group of individuals who invite conflict are those who are dogmatic and authoritarian. Because of their rigidity and inflexibility, they do not listen and cannot hear arguments that differ from their own point of view. It is not unusual for these people to continue to argue at length and often beligerently after a point has been conceded by their opponent.

A third group of individuals who are generally in the midst of conflict are those who perceive the world and the behavior of others with distrust and suspicion. This attitude has, of course, its own self-fulfilling opportunity. If we expect people to act suspiciously, we will look and find indications of this behavior. Having found these indications, we confirm our original suspicions, and the cycle continues to escalate. When these feelings and perceptions are telegraphed to others, they respond with hostility and self-defensiveness, thus confirming the original suspicions.

The last group of individuals who provoke conflict exhibit none of the characteristics named above. Indeed, these people may be exactly the opposite. The energy, the creativity, the assertiveness, the nonconformity, and the independence of these individuals may trigger resentment and aggression in others. Too frequently these people elicit a feeling of guilt in others and are perceived as a threat, either from a materialistic or a self-image point of view.

A great many studies of other personality traits and how they affect conflict have been carried out. Unfortunately, these studies are often contradictory in their findings. It appears that personality is not a variable that can be studied separate from the environmental world in which it exists. There appears to be an interaction between personality and the physical and social aspects within which an individual functions.

## Concluding Remarks

This overview of conflict has examined the parties to the conflict; three sources of conflict (power, communication, and residual issues); how differences in ideologies and values, interdependencies, and goals act to increase conflict; whether conflict is functional or dysfunctional; and some of the factors that determine how readily a conflict might be resolved or escalate.

Much of what has been stated is based on laboratory experiments, on observations, and on conjecture. Conflict is difficult to observe and more difficult to analyze. Perhaps the time will come when behavioral scientists have the ability to examine inner thought processes; we then may find a more precise method of learning about conflict, its true causes, and all of its outcomes.

## Bibliography

1. Crocker, Olga L. "Precipitators of Job-Related Stress," M.B.A. thesis, Edmonton, Alberta, University of Alberta, 1974.
2. Filley, Alan C. *Interpersonal Conflict Resolution.* Glenview, Illinois: Scott, Foresman and Company, 1975.
3. French, J. R. P., and Raven, B. H. "The Bases of Social Power." In Dorwin Cartwright, ed. *Studies in Social Power.* Ann Arbor: University of Michigan Press, 1959.
4. Hall, Richard H. *Organizations, Structure and Process.* Englewood Cliffs, N.J.: Prentice-Hall, Inc., 1972.
5. Pondy, Louis R. "Organizational Conflict: Concepts and Models." *Administrative Science Quarterly* (September 1967): 296-320.
6. Robbins, Stephen P. *Managing Organizational Conflict. A Nontraditional Approach.* Englewood Cliffs, N.J.: Prentice-Hall, Inc., 1974.
7. Rubin, Jeffrey Z., and Brown, Bert R. *The Social Psychology of Bargaining and Negotiation.* New York: Academic Press, 1975.
8. Webber, Ross A. *Management. Basic Elements of Managing Organizations.* Homewood, Illinois: Richard D. Irwin, 1975.
9. Wieland, George F., and Ullrich, Robert A. *Organizations: Behavior, Design and Change.* Homewood, Illinois: Richard D. Irwin, 1976.
10. Winter, D. G. *The Power Motive.* New York: Free Press, 1973.

# 36

# Managing Conflict and Stress[1]

*Maryruth K. Nivens*

Growing up in a famous Western mining town, I observed some pronounced differences between male and female styles of conflict and stress management. Men in conflict would invite each other out into the streets, throw more than a few punches, then with their arms around each other return indoors for some liquid refreshment. I decided these male encounters were more on the order of skirmishes than battles. Women, on the other hand, would hold in their anger for months on end, seldom revealing its true source even when they could no longer contain it. Nor was the conflict over in a short time. Sometimes the interpersonal stress lasted until one of the parties died. These encounters seemed to me more like true wars, and I wondered, as a child, if the wrong sex were not sent into combat.

Women seemed more capable of making a conflict last, and wars *are* endless wastes whose true motivation is rarely made public.

However sexist these evaluations may sound, they are observable in the environment and represent learned behaviors. There are exceptions in both sexes but our socialization processes encourage these male and female stereotypes. Fortunately most learned behaviors can be modified and/or extinguished.

Many women have been socialized to "behave nicely," to develop a facade of passive behaviors which mask any anger we experience. Women's behaviors are controlled by words and phrases like "dumb broad," "bitch," "Southern Belle," "castrating female," "ding-a-ling," "Queen Bee." Our language is emotionally charged with words that help to create a mold, a way to be. Indeed, most of the insults directed toward or about men are merely reflections of their mothers' sexual behavior, as in "son of a bitch" and "bastard." Strongly negative female models have been reinforced and institutionalized through language and no matter how personally able an individual female may be, she struggles to but cannot avoid the negative connotations of the language in her environment.

The emotional power of words can be so intimidating that these sounds serve as agents of control which maneuver and limit women's conflict resolution strategies. Ironically this manipulation by language becomes a self-fulfilling prophecy whereby women do act ineffectively, are pushy, manipulative (especially with tears) or aggressive (hence castrating).

We, as women, need an understanding of how we contribute to the maintenance of our negative stereotypes—how we behave so that those of us under forty-five can be dismissed with the comment that "it must be that time of the month" and those over forty-five can be discounted by the remark that "she's probably going through the change." Biology *is* destiny, even among managerial women, if we cannot effectively handle conflict.

Fantasize with me that you are coming down a hall from which there is no escape. You are about to meet that person with whom you are currently most in conflict. Keep in mind how you feel, what happens in terms of physical sensation, what you want to say or do, as we consider some alternative ways of coping with conflict. Some common coping strategies are avoidance, diffusion, and confrontation.

If during your fantasy you chose avoidance, you may have pretended that nothing was wrong by repressing your true feelings. Translated to the work setting, that approach is exemplified by quitting your job, transferring, moving away, having a headache or other physical symptoms so that you can plead illness, taking longer lunch breaks, making medical appointments during business hours, and doing your work after hours or on weekends to have the office to yourself. Avoidance behavior contributes to the age old female stereotype of "Southern Belle" or "poor little ole me."

If diffusion was your choice, you used delaying tactics, letting the problem grow by refusing to deal with the issue. You rationalized, made excuses for yourself or the other party without checking the veracity of your rationalizations. You engaged in back biting to release your own feelings about the conflict to everyone except those involved. You confused the issue, dickering about minor details or peripheral concerns. You may have dredged up the past, talked about other past infractions in order to build your case, then assigned blame, seeing conflict as something to which you are subjected but certainly do not cause. The stereotypes for the diffusor are "dumb broad" or "ding-a-ling."

Moving on our continuum to the area of confrontation, we will examine two types of confrontation, power and negotiation. Power confrontations involve the use of physical force, bribery (as in the use of tears), providing favors (including sexual activity), pouting, and punishment. Punishment includes keeping score of wins and losses, inducing guilt and engaging in work slow downs. Power also involves manipulation, the undercutting of the other person's credibility with the rest of the staff, dealing with personality rather than issues. Power plays include demands for special consideration. Statements like, "I don't have to work so I won't do such and so" or, "I'm a single parent or sole survivor or whatever" so that the other person seems to be taking unfair advantage. These and similar behaviors reflect the stereotypes of the "Queen Bee" and "bitch." Power confrontations generally cause hostility, anxiety, and alienation in the loser, and there is always a loser.

All of the previous behaviors in the categories of avoidance, diffusion and power confrontation might be described as short sighted goals. These short term, short sighted goals may make you feel better for a little while, but if you have really won the battle (rather than merely silenced your opponent), you have lost the war.

One primary difference between men and women in their approach to conflict resolution lies in this matter of short term, short sighted goals (often employed by women) versus long range plans (the usual male approach). This difference also seems apparent in the area of career choices. Men as little boys plan careers. Females plan something to do until they are married to someone who has a career.

If we explore the negotiating aspect of confrontation, we see that one basic aspect of negotiation involves diagnosing the nature of the problem, of being able to at least keep ourselves in hand by making our part of the interaction rational. Anne Russianoff, New York psychologist, believes that one reason women experience more stress in conflict situations than men is that women tend to "catastrophize"; to see every mistake as larger, more intense, and of deeper significance than it is actually. To analyze a situation accurately is to approach it calmly.

Several writers in the field of conflict management suggest that women tend to view their jobs less globally than do men. Many women take deadend jobs because they already have the skills to do well in that particular job or they believe, initially, that their job is secondary to that of their spouse. Women who are unable or unwilling to move to another location may not examine their existing skills to determine if these talents could be utilized toward upward mobility in a career. This partitioning off of one's job as sufficient in and of itself, while temporarily satisfying, finally becomes a source of conflict, especially when that job becomes a financial or emotional necessity and the woman plans to work until retirement age.

The match between your values and those you observe in your organization will indicate the ease with which you can enter into a psychological contract with that organization. When there is a "bad fit" your choices are 1) to try to change the organization, 2) to limit your involvement, or 3) to allow yourself to feel trapped. Entrapment has been identified as a primary source of conflict for many career women.

An accurate diagnosis, then, suggests the need for a second skill in conflict resolution, initiation of action. Interpersonal responses may be designated as passive, assertive or aggressive. These terms derive from a model by Pat Jakubowski and A. J. Lange.[2] Although we did not use those labels, much of our previous discussion has focused on passive and aggressive behaviors, feelings, and attitudes. We will now discuss assertive behavior, the use of constructive feedback, and the levels of assertiveness attached to this model of communication styles.

Feedback is a process by which you and I determine how things are in our world. If we did not have the expressions on the faces of our friends and family, if no one ever really told us anything, we would be locked into repeating old and inappropriate behaviors until finally, because we had no responses, we would become withdrawn, depressed, and possibly even suicidal. For many of us, feedback is synonomous with combat, not a pleasant experience; but constructive feedback, while not always pleasant, concerns itself with information that is always useable and sometimes combative.

Let me describe here some of the salient aspects of constructive feedback. 1) Feedback, to be constructive, must be timed. Feedback should be as close to the described event as possible. Of course, common sense indicates that if a robber enters your home tonight, you need not tell him how that makes you feel. 2) Useful feedback tells another person something over which the person has some control. You might say that you would like me better if I were taller, thinner, younger, and had black hair. My response to such a feedback is "too bad about you." I diet regularly, albeit unsuccessfully. I am not going to dye my hair, and I can't do anything about those other two items. I may resent you for bringing my age and my height to my attention in a negative way. 3) Useful feedback is information the listener may either choose to do something about or disregard. But given the feedback, the listener has a choice that was not available until you cared enough to share your thoughts and feelings. 4) The most useful feedback is concrete, specific, more a description of behavior than of guessing why something happened. Moreover, feedback, especially that which evokes a highly emotional response from the listener, can be discredited unless you as a speaker make your messages congruent. Please don't smile and call me a bitch or frown and say how much my work has improved. I will be confused as to which signal merits my response. Mixed signals often destroy the entire feedback process. Finally, check with your listener to be sure that the message sent was the message received. We perpetuate misunderstandings and disrupt communication with vague or misunderstood messages.

Assertiveness differs from passivity and aggression, both of which are part and parcel of diffusion and avoidance, in that assertiveness opens up the possibility of increased dialogue. Note that I said "increased dialogue," not "guaranteed happy ending." Aggressiveness and passivity control the outcome of a given situation by shutting off the other person. Of the three approaches, assertiveness requires the highest level of initial risk-taking behavior but carries with it a greater possibility of satisfaction with one's part in an interaction. When a person is effectively assertive, there is no need to replay a given interaction or to wish you had done things differently.

To initiate a negotiating confrontation, approach the other person with respect for that person. We respect others even as we disagree with a particular behavior or decision.

Our statements reflect a position of self-respect as well as concern and are not accusatory. "I am disappointed that I was not promoted" is quite a different statement from "You treated me unfairly by promoting Jean." In being assertive, we own our feelings as in "I am disappointed." In initial or subsequent levels of assertiveness, we speak in the first person singular, always giving the other person some wiggle room. Without accusation, the listener need not become defensive and can explain or even apologize, if actually in error. Assertive statements are not, however, magic one-liners. The more our assertive statements match linguistically our regular speech patterns, the more likely it is that this communication tool will work for us. Often a well phrased assertive statement allows the listener to respond in such a way that we can then proceed toward a conciliation.

Sometimes our first statement is not understood, either because our behavior is new, or the other person has chosen not to listen. We would then proceed to another level of assertiveness. This middle level includes a statement of how we feel or perceive the situation and a statement of what we want the other to do about the problem. "I feel disappointed that I was not promoted, and you may be able to help me understand why I was passed over." Again we have taken steps to keep the level of defensiveness low for all participants in this interaction.

Should this middle level not generate a satisfactory response, we move to a higher level of assertiveness with a statement of this type; "I am disappointed, and you could help me. If you do not wish to give me an explanation, I will make an appointment to discuss this tomorrow with Mrs. G." This level of assertiveness repeats the initiator's original stance (I am disappointed), adds a request for assistance from the listener (You could help explain this), and incorporates a course of action that the initiator is both willing and able to take (I will make an appointment to discuss this tomorrow with Mrs. G.). Unfortunately, many of us begin at the last stage first. This leaves us nowhere to go once we have made a threat that we didn't mean or our listener reacts defensively to the intensity of our approach. And there goes our credibility!

The skills of active listening will be extremely helpful if we elect to engage in a negotiating form of confrontation. We must hear not just the tone of voice but also the other person's words so that we can restate in condensed form what we hear. Reiteration is vital as it prevents further misunderstandings. Both participants may then move toward solution during the interchange by either 1) collaborating, working jointly once you both discover more points of agreement than disagreement; 2) replacing the goal of winning with the goal of problem solving; 3) compromising, making concessions without totally abandoning either person's values or major premises; 4) accommodating, absorbing some of the other person's ideas, then enlarging and expanding to other areas of agreement.

Would you now take a few moments and re-do your original fantasy? Do you see alternatives to avoidance, diffusion, angry confrontation?

Finally you may want to remember that conflict is a challenge, not an annoyance or a contest. Leaping to conclusions is not a healthful form of exercise, and the best skills of conflict resolution may be having the good sense to be aware of the complexity of human interaction.

In closing let me quote George Bernard Shaw from an 1891 essay on women:

> "If you believe that the natural place of women is the kitchen and the nursery, you are like English children who consider the cage as the natural habitat of the parrot, having seen one nowhere else. Oh, there may be docile parrots who are content to remain in the cage provided there is enough hemp corn and water, and there are those missionary parrots who feel it is their lot in life to keep a family contented by

whistling Pretty Polly—but the only parrot worth anyone's genuine concern is the parrot who demands to be released from the cage as a condition of becoming agreeable.''

The business world is not a high school dance. We are no longer little girls. We can handle our own conflicts. So let's not get all dressed up, professionally speaking, to sit on the sidelines waiting for our male colleagues to ask us to tango.

## Notes

1. Speech delivered at "Up the Managerial Ladder, a Conference for Women," Nov. 2, 1979, Auburn University at Montgomery.
2. Arthur J. Lange and Patricia Jakubowski, *Responsible Assertive Behavior: Cognitive/Behavioral Procedures for Trainers* (Champaign, Illinois: Research Press, 1976).

# 37

# The Consultant-Client Relationship and Organizational Change

*Barry J. McLoughlin*
*James R. McLoughlin*

*The consultant-client relationship is critical to the organizational decision-making process. How that relationship is developed and managed will determine the nature and scope of change in the organization.*

In an age of "down-sizing," the shift to leaner organizations has resulted in increased contracting-out of consultant services. At the same time, internal support units such as personnel administration and public affairs have increasingly moved to a "consultative" role in an effort to clarify their relationships to line management. In this chapter we shall focus on the nature of the consultant-client relationship and its effects on organizational change.

## The Consultant-Client Relationship

### Working Definitions

*Client:* The person who has designated decision-making authority in an organization.

*Client Group:* The superiors, peers, or subordinates of the client, who are directly or peripherally related to the consultation.

*Consultant:* One who exercises a range of skills and knowledge in helping others to solve their problems. An agent of change or a facilitator whose services are contracted by a client for a specific project. The primary consultant is responsible for establishing the client relationship and ensuring completion of the assignment to the client's satisfaction.

*Problem:* A condition that needs to be changed.

## The Role of the Consultant

At the core of a successful consultant-client relationship is the realization that consultant expertise must be delivered and applied in a collaborative mode. Consultant expertise lies in the field of problem identification and solution and must never be confused with decision–making, which is solely in the client's territory.

The consultant is usually engaged whenever the resolution of an issue or problem is perceived by the clients to be beyond their organizational competence at a given time. Logically one might assume that the decision to engage a consultant implies that the client has a reasonable understanding of the nature and scope of the proposed project. However, in practice, experienced consultants will regard the client's initial description of the problem as "provisional" and thus subject to potential future modification. Acceptance of the tentative nature of the problem definition becomes a vital issue when the terms of the contract are being negotiated.

Another logical assumption is that the client's decision to engage a consultant has been made free of undue pressure from others. Identifying possible pressures, however, will help the consultant to determine the role he or she is expected to assume. Examples of possible roles are as follows:

• Honest broker
• Neutral "expert"
• Partisan "scrapper" (on the client's behalf)
• Fall guy
• Traffic cop

The consultant's skill in the successful introduction of a required change in a politicized organizational climate is linked to the role he or she is expected to play. As the old song goes, though, "it's not where you start, it's where you finish." Thus, as the project proceeds, the consultant must shape the role in such a way that he or she has the most potential to effect the desired change.

The consultant must be sensitive to the complexity of factors that have to be countered or engaged to achieve a desired outcome. Once the consultant has identified and evaluated these factors, he or she is better able to renegotiate the initial project description articulated by the client at the outset.

With this initial clarification phase completed, the task of "engaging" the client in seeking the mutually agreed-upon goal can commence.

## Consultant's Goals

Central to the success of the consultant-client relationship is the achievement of four goals that consultants set for themselves in most contracts:

1. To get their expertise used
2. To have leverage over a situation in which they have no direct control
3. To solve the client's immediate problems
4. To enable the client to solve problems independently when they recur.

Meeting these goals requires a shared responsibility between the client and the consultant. (Fig. 37.1)

## Establishing Shared Responsibility

A consultant operates at two levels:

### Content

What is being *talked* about—the issues, problems, solutions, etc. This is the *cognitive* part of the relationship.

---

| Consultant | 50:50 | Client |
|---|---|---|

SHARED RESPONSIBILITY CONTINUUM

**Fig. 37.1**
**Shared responsibility continuum**

*Process*

What is going on *between* the client and consultant; the feelings about one another; the level of tension; supportive or confrontational mode of interchange; this *interpersonal* part of the relationship which involves the critical skill of developing with the client a shared responsibility for the desired outcome.

## The Internal or Staff Consultant

The contracting process can be extremely complex for the internal or staff consultant in the organization where disparity in the status of client and consultant militates against a shared responsibility relationship.

Organizational traditions too often place essential power and authority with senior executives and responsibility for project success or failure with lower hierarchical levels. Where organizational policies do not explicitly spell out the role of staff consultants, the essential element of shared responsibility must be negotiated.

In addition, the internal staff person must contract with his or her own manager, who has a different stake in satisfying the client's needs. This stake often involves securing a reputation with senior management, regardless of the staff member's priorities or professional judgment. Thus, many staff or internal consultants must strive to serve the needs of the client, while at the same time furthering their boss's hidden agenda.

This extra dimension facing the staff consultant can also be relevant to the external consultant's situation. In either case, a second contract beyond the consultant-client relationship must be negotiated, and that is the contract between the consultant and his or her boss.

As illustrated in Figure 37.2, two primary contracts must be negotiated: (1) between the consultant and the client and (2) between the consultant and the consultant's boss. In both relationships, the consultant faces certain expectations and demands—whether verbalized or not. In order to address adequately the requirements of the situation, the consultant must seek an articulation and clarification of the position of both parties.

In the consultant relationship rectangle depicted in Figure 37.3, we can see the pressures on the consultant-client relationship once the client's boss enters the picture. With this added variable, the potential impact of a failure to achieve a satisfactory conclusion becomes even more significant for the client and perhaps for the organization.

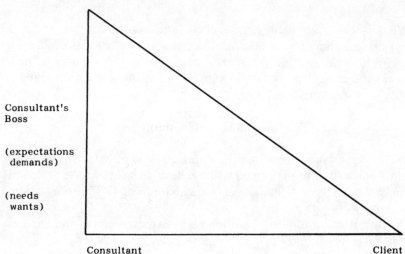

Consultant's
Boss

(expectations
 demands)

(needs
 wants)

Consultant                                    Client
(needs, wants)              (expectations, demands)

**Fig. 37.2**
**The consultant triangle**

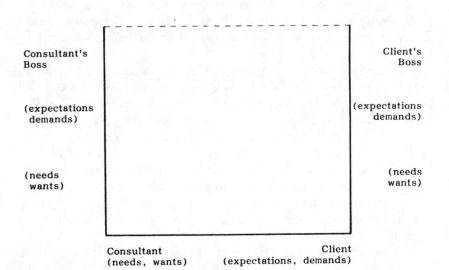

Consultant's                                              Client's
Boss                                                      Boss

(expectations                                         (expectations
 demands)                                                  demands)

(needs                                                     (needs
 wants)                                                     wants)

Consultant                            Client
(needs, wants)        (expectations, demands)

**Fig. 37.3**
**The Consultant Relationship Rectangle**

The consultant must be aware of the relationship between the client's boss and the client (and the accompanying expectations and demands).

The relationship between the consultant's boss and the client's boss may be unarticulated; nevertheless, its existence can significantly affect both the process and the eventual outcome of the contract.

### The Consultant's Contract with the Boss

The contract between the consultant and his or her boss is crucial to the successful outcome of a project. The consultant must fulfill a range of expectations and demands from the boss, whether or not these are actually verbalized in the relationship. Typically these expectations include the following:

- No matter what, get the job done.
- Don't upset or antagonize the client, and (especially) the client's boss.
- Stay long enough to do the job, but don't stay too long: time is money.
- Convince the client to do what you recommend; sell the "company way."
- Every problem can be solved.
- Every client can be "reached" if the consultant is really on the ball.
- Be loyal to your own (consulting) organization.
- Don't wash your dirty linen in public.
- Never admit a mistake to a client.
- Contracts with clients should be flexible; don't box yourself in.
- Don't make any commitments for future work.
- Ensure openness and feedback.
- Keep your boss informed.

### The Client's Contract with the Client's Boss

As with the foregoing expectations and demands that relate to the consultant and his or her boss, the client must address similar types of expectations and demands. These might include the following:

- Keep a lid on our problems, don't let too much "out of the bag."
- Keep a close eye on the consultant.
- Make as few commitments as possible regarding our response to the consultant's work.
- Don't be too positive in your response to the consultant's work; it might cost us more.
- Wring every cent of work out of the consultant; if we're going to go elsewhere for help, let's get our money's worth.

- Remember you're the boss; don't let the tail wag the dog.
- Every problem can be solved.
- No matter what, get the job done.
- Be loyal to your own organization.
- Never admit a mistake to a consultant.
- Contracts with consultants should be very flexible.
- Keep your boss informed.

Into this scenario steps the consultant!

If these peripheral sets of expectations and demands are strong enough, they can seriously impede the consulting process. The primary goal is to have these conflicting demands articulated and ameliorated, both from the consultant's position and from the client's, so that the contract can proceed in an atmosphere of mutual trust.

Unreasonable expectations lead to unrealistic contracts.

### Elements of a Successful Consultant-Client Relationship

There are two broad elements essential to the successful negotiation of a productive consultant-client relationship.

#### Mutual Consent

Both sides must enter the agreement freely and of their own choice.

#### Valid Consideration

It is essential to focus on the needs of the client. After all, the *raison d'être* for a consultant is to serve these needs. At the same time, the needs of the consultant must not be neglected. The consultant must make known his or her needs and wants and negotiate valid consideration of these needs, which include the following elements:

> *Operational Partnership in the Project*    i.
> This means having influence over what happens during the project and being made aware of significant organizational events as they occur.
>
> *Access to People and Information in the Client Organization*    ii.
> There must be freedom of movement to pursue issues and data that seem relevant to the consultant.
>
> *Time of People in the Client Organization*    iii.
> A major cost to most consulting projects is the time of the client personnel. Often the consultant is given an assignment with the proviso that contacts with client's personnel must be kept to a minimum. Such a proviso signals that the consultant's needs will not be given valid consideration.

*Opportunity to be Innovative*                                    iv.
Consultants often want to be creative and innovative. They should
test this possibility during precontract negotiations.

Consultants undermine their influence or leverage if their own needs
and wants are ignored or undervalued from the outset. A productive
bond between client and consultant requires valid consideration of the
needs of both.

## Definition of a Contract

A contract is the set of expectations people have when they work
together to attain a common objective. A contract should evoke mutual
consent and consideration, clarifying the roles of the consultant and
the client; their expectations of each other; the responsibilities of each;
and the ground rules affecting their transactions. If the situation
changes, the contract must change.

### The Outcome of the Consultant-Client Relationship: Effecting Organizational Change

Once the contract is negotiated and the consulting work is underway,
the consultant faces two broad opportunities to effect organizational
change: (1) during the consultative process, or (2) in the clarification
of the client's objectives. Let us briefly examine the nature of organizational change and its implications and opportunities for the internal
or external consultant.

## The Nature of Organizational Change

Organizations tend to change for one of three reasons: (1) The
environment in which the organization operates changes, and the
organization responds to fit its perception of the changing marketplace.
For example, a steel company diversifies through acquisitions or shifts
its product line to specialized metals. (2) Key players in the organization change the focus or direction of the organization to conform to
their personal vision. For example, the new president of a company as
a consequence of his past experiences decides to shift the company
product line into a new direction. (3) The company changes incrementally and without real intent; it drifts and changes for lack of leadership.
For example, an old family chain of jewelry and china stores gradually
changes its character over time, broadening its product line into
housewares, furniture accents, and interior design services. No plan

or vision is apparent; instead, these lines are added piecemeal, according to the proprietor's fancy of the moment.

In all three scenarios, a consultant has an opportunity to effect positive organizational changes in direct proportion to the willingness and the power of the client to implement or respond to the consultant's input.

The consultant's input may take the form of (1) *asking critical questions* about the client organization's mission, goals, market perceptions, technology, strategies, operational plans, policies, procedures, communications activities, personnel practices, management-employee relations, information systems, etc; (2) *analyzing the environment* within which the organization operates—the problems, opportunities, and challenges facing it; (3) *assessing the performance* of the organization against objective criteria and benchmarks; (4) *developing options* for the organization to consider; and (5) *making recommendations* for action.

In order to accomplish these ends, the consultant requires from the client (1) an open unthreatening *climate* where the "political" acceptability of questions, answers, and observations is not a major impediment to discovery and analysis; (2) the *authority* for the consultant to test the responses from the client group and to challenge their validity, accuracy, and consistency within the client organization; and (3) *support* when the consultant must pursue difficult issues and meets resistance from significant others in the organization.

### Change Potential

> *The ability of the consultant to effect organizational change is in direct proportion to the client's ability to develop the climate for change and to provide the authority and support for the consultant to effect change.*

In this situation, one or more of the following organizational characteristics must be present: (1) The key people in the organization must be open to change. The consultant must be able to identify major influences. Experienced consultants know that the organization chart does not always clearly depict organization power sources. These key players should be consulted as the project progresses. (2) Changes must be tied in to existing systems, unless the efficiency or effectiveness of these systems is at stake. (3) Changes must be implemented incrementally in the development process. In every organization, evolution is more saleable than revolution. (4) The consultant must have a champion in a leadership position. When a proposal is being floated through an organization, it must have a strong proponent—preferably one who has few enemies and is widely respected. (5) There must be a general recognition that change is needed; otherwise, there is little hope for success. If the key players are satisfied with the way things are going, then change can be only cosmetic at best. A sound sampling of organizational opinion can be most effective in changing executive opinions of needed change.

## The Challenges to the Consultant

Change should be packaged in such a way that there are as few losers as possible in the proposed scenario. There should be something for everyone, so long as it doesn't hurt the overall objective. The more "winners" in the process, the greater the chances of success in acceptance and implementation.

It is important to reduce, as much as possible, the element of "threat" in the consultant's work. Most people are threatened by change. Combine this fact with poor communication, and you have a recipe for disaster. Keep communication channels constantly open.

It is also important to realize ultimately that the client, not the consultant, must live with the change. Therefore, the responsibility for the change proposals must be transferred as quickly as possible to the client organization. If the consultant fails to accomplish this transfer at the end of the consultation, there is a strong likelihood that the change, even when accepted, will not be successfully implemented.

## Conclusion

The consultant is an "agent of change," or a facilitator, not the "doer."

Many resources for change already exist in most organizations. The aim of the consultant must be to identify and mobilize these resources.

A consultant must maintain his or her objectivity, testing and challenging assumptions not only of the client but also those underlying his or her own approaches.

In effecting organizational change, a consultant must offer objectivity. Once consultants cross the line into advocacy, they threaten their own effectiveness.

The most useful tool in a consultant's kit to effect organizational change is not a sledgehammer, but a mirror.

# Part XI

# ASSESSING COMMUNICATION IN THE ORGANIZATION

# 38

# Assessing Information Load

Designing communication systems that efficiently meet the needs of organizations and institutions has been the concern of policy makers since the evolution of organizations. Whether the communication system involves the moving of information or the moving of things or people, the problem is in many ways the same.

Consider the difficulty of designing a mass transit system in a city like London. Literally millions of people have to be transported in the morning and evening rush hours. The problem is to have sufficient service to fill the peak demand, but not too much for the rest of the day. The same kind of problem is reflected in the sliding scale of telephone charges for off-peak times and in the reduced utility rates in some areas for late night use.

These examples demonstrate the concepts of overload and underload. When the system cannot reasonably meet the demands made on it, we have overload; and when the system is grossly underutilized, we have underload. Both of these states are clearly inefficient.

Information systems are also subject to underload and overload. For the purposes of clarity and organization, information load can be discussed at two levels—in terms of how the system copes, as above, and in terms of how the individual within the system copes.

### How the Individual Copes

An example often used to illustrate information overload is the Japanese attack on Pearl Harbor. It is said that the attack was successful not because the Americans did not have enough information on the likelihood of such an attack, but because they had too much information and were unable to differentiate between the significant information and the trivia!

The Pearl Harbor example introduces two important concepts in communication and information theory. The first of these concepts is *noise*, and the second is *pattern recognition*. In communication theory, *noise* refers to any part of a transmitted message that does not contribute to the transfer of the *intended* meaning in the communication. This noise could be static or mechanical or electrical distortion. Noise could also be symbolic content, such as superfluous or distracting information.

Contained in this second aspect of noise is our second concept of pattern recognition. The information theorist (or learning theorist) looks at information as being made up of packages of building blocks. The smallest unit or block is called a bit. Collections of related bits are known as chunks.[1] When information is assembled in a library, or in a computer memory bank, or in an individual's cognitive data bank, it is brought together in packages of related bits. For instance, the library will group its data by subject and author, and experience in using the card index can bring a searcher to the right shelf very quickly. Another network is accessible through reference to bibliographical notes or through subject indices; and by a series of associated steps, it is possible to locate data of a very precise nature.

Computer information is stored in a similar way and is retrived on the presentation of *descriptors*. These descriptors are words that describe the contents of certain packages, or chunks. When a package of information is stored, it is given a number of descriptors; and when a search is called and one of these descriptors is fed into the computer, the package will be drawn. The usefulness of the data bank will depend on the skill with which descriptors are initially *assigned* and on the skill with which the descriptors are *used* by the searcher.[2]

Anyone who has done any research work in the Library of Congress will understand the meaning of information overload. It is of little comfort to the uninitiated to know that he is in one of the most comprehensive libraries in the world if he does not know how to locate the material he needs. Whether the individual regards the situation as presenting chaotic information overload or an abundance of useful information will depend on his ability to locate and to extract from the vast array of information available the precise information he requires. Overload then is a characteristic of the individual reacting with information, rather than of the information itself.

The individual assembles his personal information program in a way very similar to the librarian or the computer programmer. Experiences and impressions are categorized and stored in chunks and bundles of related chunks. They are recallable under the stimuluation of trigger signals similar to the descriptors the computer uses. An individual stores his information and makes connecting cross-reference networks. The skill with which he assembles and activates the appropriate networks is what we generally regard as his level of intelligence.[3]

The more networks are utilized, the more accessible they become.

They may indeed become so accessible that they can be drawn on and used without conscious effort. This is what is known as learned or reflexive response. The instantaneous response to an emergency situation, which we generally call reflexive, is far from a mindless response. Indeed, it is a demonstration of the mind working at the highest level. The reflexive response demonstrates a lesson so well learned that it can be applied instantly without the need for conscious step-by-step analysis. Conscious analysis would generally involve so much time that it would be difficult, if not impossible, to drive an automobile or to type a letter at any reasonable speed if only conscious awareness were involved.

To relate these points to the subject of this chapter, the learner-driver who finds that he does not have enough feet, hands, or eyes to fulfill the demands that the machine and the environment are making on him is suffering from information overload. The experienced driver, on the other hand, may choose to drive, rather than take a plane or train, so that he can relax or have some time to think out a solution to a problem. The situation in both of these instances is the same; but the load is heavy or light depending on the individual's capabilities, which in turn are dependent on his past experience and training.

An individual who is a specialist in some field will have organized his information according to context, and he will have arranged various contexts according to some priority scale. Fitting a concept to the appropriate context is what we mean by pattern recognition. The non-specialist being confronted with a total cargo of information on a subject may be confused by the seeming lack of form or the seemingly contradictory nature of some of the information.

The problem-solving techniques used by an electronics engineer illustrate this distinction. Faced with a non-functioning piece of equipment, the engineer enters the problem through a series of steps that move from the very general to the very specific. First he will check for power at the wall outlet and then test the supply cord to note whether or not the power is reaching the equipment—two steps that any intelligent person would take. The next step, however, will distinguish the specialist from the non-specialist. The non-specialist will remove the back of the piece of equipment and look inside at the mass of intimidating wires, resistors, capacitors, and transistors (after the fashion of those perplexed bodies we see on the shoulders of highways, peering under gaping car hoods), hoping for some divine inspiration. The specialist, on the other hand, will seek out a diagram of the system and study it. Given the schematic, he sees sets of subsystems assembled according to principles he is familiar with. These subsystems are linked together in dependent ways. Following the chain of dependency and checking on successive subsystems leads the specialist to the faulty subsystem. Once he has located the faulty subsystem, he tracks down the faulty component in the same way.

The schematic on which the specialist depends would probably serve only to intimidate the non-specialist. The procedure followed by the engineer is dependent on his information *chunking* background. These successive processes operate on the same principle as the parlor game of twenty questions. The series of answers to yes-no questions can either answer twenty questions or, by elimination, reduce over half a million possible questions to one yes-no question. The specialist, by the use of a series of dependent chunking decisions, moves very rapidly to a decision. The non-specialist does not have the chunking ability and so, in effect, asks twenty questions randomly out of a possible universe of half a million questions.

In short, a person's capacity to organize the information that is impinging on him will depend on his ability to recognize the appropriate context to which the information belongs. Only by having an understanding of various patterns of context will a person recognize whether a piece of information is vital or trivial. Without the capacity to recognize vital clues, all information must be regarded as vital, and thus we have a Pearl Harbor situation of overload.

Whether an individual in an organization has a high or low load potential is important or not important depending on his function in the system. If he is a linking agent between two subsystems, then it could be imperative that he have a high level of chunking ability to be able to isolate the essential elements of communication. Failing to do so, he may transfer noise instead of information from one subsystem to another.

It would seem to be futile to try to prescribe ways an individual may cope with overload. Acquisition of chunking skills is a long-term process dependent on background, education, experience, and in many regards, on personality. A more fruitful approach may be to examine how the system deals with the problem through its control of load and its placement of individuals in the system. The second part of this article will address itself to these issues.

## How the System Copes

It has been said that the primary function of organizational structure is to restrict communication.[4] By so doing, the organization can control information load on members of the system. Restricting flow to formal channels and placing gatekeepers in strategic positions are fundamental to maintaining control. Gatekeepers serve an important screening function. They act as checks against the inundation of management by irrelevant information, information that would constitute overload. As liaison figures, it is essential that persons acting in gatekeeper capacities be able to adapt to high load work demands. If they fail to do so, the work load on other members of the organization may result in unnecessarily chaotic conditions.

Other strategies the organization may use in its efforts to cope with overload are working to rule, queuing or assigning priority to certain categories of messages during high load periods and delaying handling others, hiring additional assistants to help those on whom the heaviest load falls (especially those in linking capacities), adopting self-service techniques, subcontracting extra load, creating branch offices, and reducing service standards and/or performance standards.[5]

Many of these strategies have the potential to generate bad morale among employees and ill will among customers. In implementing strategies designed to avoid problems of information overload, the organization brings other problems upon itself.[6] It is generally agreed that any person who handles and transmits information modifies it in some way. Thus, information that must pass through different layers in an organizational hierarchy will change in character as it is passed from one individual to the next. In some cases, the changes will be intentional; in other cases, unintentional. Either out of self-interest or because the gatekeeper does not recognize the significance of an information item, he may omit or distort some part of a messge. In so doing, he may be inhibiting the flow of information essential to the well-being of the organization. It is sometimes proposed, and only part in jest, that by virtue of his office, the President of the United States is among the least well-informed people on earth. Because of the vast amount of information relevant to his position and because of the enormous bureaucracy that he heads, the President's information may well be more characteristic of the gatekeepers through which it has passed than of the information events in question.

Everett and Rekha Agarwala-Rogers discuss the 1968 My Lai massacre of Vietnamese civilians by American troops as an example of the distortion that can occur with messages flowing through the formal hierarchy:

> Newspaper reporters in Vietnam at the time observed that Army orders tended to be interpreted quite broadly, and frequently with distortion, as they passed from echelon to echelon down the chain of command.

For instance, a war correspondent was present when a hamlet was burned down by the United States Army's First Air Cavalry Division. Inquiry showed that the order from division headquarters to the brigade was: "On no occasion must hamlets be burned down."

The brigade radioed the battalion: "Do not burn down any hamlets unless you are absolutely convinced that the Vietcong are in them."

The battalion radioed the infantry company at the scene: "If you think there are any Vietcong in the hamlet, burn it down."

The company commander ordered his troops: "Burn down that hamlet."[7]

Most organizations recognize the possibilities for distortion, omission, and bad morale inherent in attempts to monitor and control information flow in the system. Attempts to compensate may take the form of 1. redundancy, or repetition of a message in more than one form or through more than one channel or at different times, 2. verification, or checking out the accuracy of a message by reference to additional persons or documents, and 3. bypassing individuals who act as gatekeepers in the organizational chain or authority. Such bypassing may be encouraged by an organization's expressed commitment to an open door policy, use of suggestion boxes, and/or employment of ombudsmen who function as independents in a liaison capacity, hearing complaints from employees and resolving differences between employees and administration.[8]

The difficulty with these approaches is that the solution again becomes the problem. While redundancy, verification, and bypassing procedures help the organization to cope with distortion, omission, and the potential for low morale, these practices generate more messages and new information overload problems. Bypassing individuals in the organizational chain of authority can also undermine the self-image of supervisory staff.

Figure 38-1 illustrates the cyclical nature of overload coping strategies.[9]

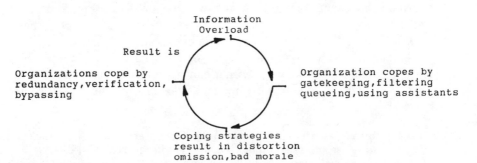

```
                        Information
                          Overload
          Result is

Organizations cope by                    Organization copes by
redundancy,verification,                 gatekeeping,filtering
bypassing                                queueing,using assistants



            Coping strategies
            result in distortion
            omission,bad morale
```

Viewed from this perspective, it is clear that any strategy employed by the organization has its price, and the organization's successes in coping with information load will always be costly ones. The choices the organization makes in its efforts to set policies for dealing with information load will, in many regards, reflect the basic values of the organization.

## Notes

1. Information theory is described in Claude E. Shannon and Warren Weaver, *The Mathematical Theory of Communication* (Urbana, Ill.: University of Illinois Press, 1964).
2. For development of the computer analogy, see Allen Newell, Herbert A. Simon, and John C. Shaw, "Elements of a Theory of Human Problem Solving," in *Readings in the Psychology of Cognition,* ed. Richard C. Anderson and David P. Ausubel (New York: Holt, Rinehart and Winston, Inc., 1965), pp. 136–37.
3. For further discussion of ideas, see Carl I. Hovland, "Computer Simulation of Thinking," *Psychology of Cognition,* pp. 158–64.
4. Everett M. Rogers and Rekha Agarwala-Rogers, *Communication in Organizations* (New York: The Free Press, 1976), p. 91.
5. Richard V. Farace, Peter R. Monge, and Hamish M. Russell, *Communicating and Organizing* (Reading, Mass.: Addison-Wesley Publishing Company, 1977), pp. 115–24, discuss various strategies that they classify as minimal effort, moderate effort, and major effort strategies for coping with information overload. They credit these strategies to Campbell (1958), Meier (1972), Weick (1970), J. G. Miller (1960), Galbraith (1973), Prince (1970), Dearden, McFarlan, and Zani (1971).
6. Rogers and Rogers, pp. 93–94.
7. *Ibid.,* p. 93.
8. *Ibid.,* pp. 93–94.
9. The ideas presented in the diagram derive from a discussion by Everett Rogers and Rekah Agarwala-Rogers, *Communication in Organizations* (New York: The Free Press, 1976), pp. 90–95.

# 39

# The Functions of a Communication Audit

The term *communication audit* was first used by G.S. Odiorne in 1954. The name was later applied to an organizational communication measurement system developed in the 1970s by some 150 researchers from different countries. This research was sponsored by the organizational communication division of the International Communication Association (ICA). Following five years of development and pilot testing, the audit instrument was implemented in nineteen organizations in the United States and Canada. By 1979 some 8,000 people had participated in ICA audits.[1]

Individuals to whom particular credit has been given for their role in the development of the audit are Harry Dennis and Gary Richetto.[2] Some of the most complete acccounts of the history and use of the audit have appeared in articles and books by Goldhaber;[3] Yates, Goldhaber, Porter, Lesniak, Dennis, and Richetto;[4] Goldhaber and Krivonos;[5] and Goldhaber and Rogers.[6]

The ICA Communication Audit, included in the appendix, is comprised of the following five measurement tools, capable of being administered independently or in any combination: questionnaire surveys, interviews, network analysis, communication experiences, and communication diary. Original computer programs were developed to assist in analysis of all data except the interviews.

The final reports of audits typically include "organizational profiles of communication events, practices, and relationships; a map of the operational communication network; verbal summaries of successful and unsuccessful communication experiences; an organizational and individual profile of actual communication behaviors; and a set of recommendations."[7]

An audit project similar to the ICA Communication Audit was pursued in Finland in this same time period. Osmo A. Wiio and Martti Helsila of the Helsinki Research Institute for Business Economics evolved a system that became known as the LTT Communication Audit Procedure. The first LTT audit was implemented in 1973; and by 1977, more than twenty-three organizations and 6,000 people had been subjects of this audit.[8]

The LTT was refined and eventually replaced by the Organizational Development (OCD) Procedure, which by 1980 had been implemented in six organizations involving a sample of 1,600 organization members.[9]

Goldhaber, Dennis, Richetto, and Wiio suggest that rather than competing, the ICA and the LTT/OCD audits complement each other:

> The LTT/OCD technique is a simple single instrument procedure for a quick analysis of the perceived organizational and communication climates. The ICA Audit is a multi–instrument research system for detailed analysis of organizational communication problems.[10]

The various audits can take anywhere from a month to six months to administer and to process and analyze the data. Many consider the audit systems as a major "methodological breakthrough" in the study of organizational communication, which makes it possible for the first time to study organizations over time, using reliable techniques. As of 1984, over 13,000 individuals in forty-eight organizations from three countries had participated in one of these three audit types.[11]

In their book *Auditing Organizational Communication Systems: The ICA Communication Audit,* Goldhaber and Rogers discuss the kinds of questions about communication that any audit should be able to answer. According to these two writers, audits should seek to answer questions about 1. the existing communication system, 2. communication between the individual and the organization, 3. integration between organizational units, and 4. transactions between the organization and the environment.[12]

The following excerpt addresses these points.*

## Information Needs

What kinds of information does the manager need? First, the manager needs factual information. This type of information is descriptive in character. This information describes the organization, its structure, its operations, its activities, its units, its people, its problems, its strength, its goals, its resources, its needs, etc. This information also describes the organization's environment, its supporters, its enemies, its competitors, its community, its threats, its opportunities, its potential resources, etc. Second, the manager needs value information. This

---

*From Goldhaber-Rogers: *Auditing Organizational Communication Systems.* Copyright c 1979 by Kendall/Hunt Publishing Co. Used with permission.

type of information is judgemental in character. This information evaluates the organization's effectiveness, the performance of its functions, the achievement of its goals, the acceptance of its responsibilities, the satisfaction of its members, the value of its activities, and the quality of its relations (with community, government, business, educational, and family "others"). Third, the manager needs policy information. This type of information is tactical in character. This information suggests what options are available, what actions can be taken, what changes can be made, what activities can be eliminated, what consequences can be expected, what results can be achieved, what problems can be encountered, etc.

Dennis (1973) as part of the ICA Audit Project developed a list of the kinds of questions of fact (describing the system) and value (appraising the system) which can be important to a manager in formulating policy. An outline of those questions follows:

Part One: **The Existing Communication System**

I.  *Description*
    A.  Is there an established policy statement concerning a communication program?
        1.  What value is placed on communication?
        2.  What functions are attributed to communication?
        3.  What are the premises underlying the communication program?
        4.  Is there a Director of Communication?
        5.  Is there an on-going communication program?
        6.  How "open" is the communication system?
    B.  What structural factors affect the system?
        1.  Organizational design?
        2.  Interdependence of organizational units?
        3.  Are channels clearly defined?
        4.  Are roles clearly defined?
        5.  Are both goals and sub-goals defined?
        6.  Are expectations clear at each level?
        7.  Is the flow of information clearly defined and easily followed?
        8.  Are expectations of vertical and horizontal communications clearly defined?
        9.  Does the structure allow for informal networks?
    C.  Are components for implementation of the system adequate?
        1.  What forms and means of communication are available?
        2.  What evaluating mechanisms exist?
        3.  What facilitating mechanisms exist?

II. *Appraisal*
   A. How much of an organization's resources are allocated for communication?
      1. How much manpower and media?
      2. Training programs?
   B. Does the program reflect human values?
      1. Are managers and subordinates aware of shared values?
      2. Do managers and subordinates understand the mission of the total enterprise?
      3. Do employees feel involvement in the organizational goals?
   C. Do employees understand the relationship of their work to the overall goals of the organization:?
   D. Do employees have a clear understanding of existing communication channels?
   E. Do employees have a clear understanding of their roles and the roles of others?
      1. Do managers and subordinates agree on expectations?
   F. Do employees feel that they get timely and adequate information to carry out their tasks?
   G. Do employees feel that the organizational structure facilitates communication?
   H. How do the employees respond to various media and forms of communication?
   I. Does the organization evaluate and adjust its communication program?
   J. Does management recognize the multiple functions of communication and evaluate accordingly?

### Part Two: Communication Between Individual and Organization

I. *Description*
   A. Is the communication related to both organizational and individual goals?
   B. Do mechanisms exist for upward communication?
   C. Do mechanisms exist for grievances?
   D. What kinds of information are transmitted to subordinates and to superiors?
   E. Are channels of communication identified as open?
   F. What mechanisms exist for interaction at all levels?
   G. Do employees have a voice in their own destiny and in the way work is carried out?
   H. What is the nature of performance-appraisal procedures?
   I. What role do the employees play in decision-making?
   J. How many levels of management exist?
   K. What are the assumptions behind communication directed to employees?

    L.  Is the employee looked upon as a human resource that can be developed?

    M. How well does management know its people?

II.  *Appraisal*

    A.  Do employees understand organizational goals and their attitudes toward those goals?

    B.  How do employees perceive the interest of management toward their (employees) individual goals and needs?

    C.  Do employees feel that effective upward communication exists?

    D.  What disparities exist between management and subordinate perception of effective communication?

    E.  Do employees feel that they can air grievances and suggestions without retaliation by others?

    F.  Do employees feel that they are "recognized" by the communication transmitted?

    G.  Do superiors feel that they receive the bad news as well as well as the good?

    H.  Are all levels of organization involved in communication activities? (meetings, etc.)

    I.  Does management acknowledge and act on communication from subordinates?

    J.  Is "negotiation" between organizational levels a reality and perceived as such by employees?

    K.  Do employees feel that their communication means something in terms of having a voice in the way work is carried out?

    L.  Do employees feel that effective communication takes place in performance-appraisal procedures?

    M. Do employees feel that they have an opportunity to be heard in the decision-making process?

    N.  Do employees feel that the communication directed toward them is designed to help them "grow" in their jobs?

    O.  What types and content of messages are absent according to employees?

    P.  To what degree does the system meet stated communication desires of employees?

    Q.  What values are reflected by the communication program?

    R.  Do employees feel that they get the right information at the right time?

    S.  What is the perceived communication competence of managers by subordinates?

## Part Three: Integration Between Organizational Units

I.  *Description*

    A.  What relationships exist between groups in terms of interdependence?

B.  What role does each group play in organizational goals?
C.  How differentiated are the various units of the organization?
D.  How cohesive are the groups?
E.  Is there planned interaction between groups?
F.  How much integration is required between units?
G.  What mechanisms exist to deal with conflict?

II.  *Appraisal*
A.  Are groups aware of interdependence?
B.  Do groups understand their role and relationship to other groups?
C.  Do groups feel that there is adequate exchange between units?
D.  Do groups have a perspective on sub-group and organizational goals?
E.  Do groups interact on an informal basis as well as formal?

## Part Four: Transaction Between Organization and Environment

I.  *Description*
A.  What type of organization is being examined?
B.  What information from the environment is necessary for organizational survival?
C.  What kind of communication is being sent to the external environment and for what reason?
D.  What types and forms of communication are used to communicate externally?
E.  Does the organization recognize change in the environment and convey such knowledge to its members?
F.  Does the organization monitor the effects of external communication?
G.  Is relevant information from the external environment conveyed to the proper internal units?
H.  Does the organization have the capacity to change on the basis of environmental information?
I.  Does the organization serve and diverge clientele with its communication?
J.  What image does the organization attempt to project?

II.  *Appraisal*
A.  Are all members of the organization aware of the external messages being sent?
B.  Do members of the organization feel that the external communication represents an accurate and desirable point of view?
C.  Do members of the organization have knowledge of the ele-

II. *Appraisal*
  A. Do employees understand organizational goals and their attitudes toward those goals?
  B. How do employees perceive the interest of management toward their (employees) individual goals and needs?
  C. Do employees feel that effective upward communication exists?
  D. What disparities exist between management and subordinate perception of effective communication?
  E. Do employees feel that they can air grievances and suggestions without retaliation by others?
  F. Do employees feel that they are "recognized" by the communication transmitted?
  G. Do superiors feel that they receive the bad news as well as well as the good?
  H. Are all levels of organization involved in communication activities? (meetings, etc.)
  I. Does management acknowledge and act on communication from subordinates?
  J. Is "negotiation" between organizational levels a reality and perceived as such by employees?
  K. Do employees feel that their communication means something in terms of having a voice in the way work is carried out?
  L. Do employees feel that effective communication takes place in performance-appraisal procedures?
  M. Do employees feel that they have an opportunity to be heard in the decision-making process?
  N. Do employees feel that the communication directed toward them is designed to help them "grow" in their jobs?
  O. What types and content of messages are absent according to employees?
  P. To what degree does the system meet stated communication desires of employees?
  Q. What values are reflected by the communication program?
  R. Do employees feel that they get the right information at the right time?
  S. What is the perceived communication competence of managers by subordinates?

Part Three: **Integration Between Organizational Units**

I. *Description*
  A. What relationships exist between groups in terms of interdependence?

case, many hundreds of instruments are available to the communication consultant, often on a commercial basis. Others choose to develop their own instruments. In broad terms, these instruments can measure *personal, relational,* or *organizational* variables, or any combination of the above.[15]

Goldhaber and colleagues cite examples of tests that measure *personal* variables, such as the cognitive stretch test (to assess managerial cognitive styles in solving problems and making decisions); the Clary organizational script checklist (to help managers determine their self-image in relationship to their organization); the Kirkpatrick supervisory inventory on communication (to give a manager feedback on his or her listening, speaking, and writing skills); the communication apprehension report form developed by Scott, McCroskey, and Sheahan (to measure the degree of apprehension a manager feels toward communicating in general and at work in particular); Rokeach's dogmatism scale (to measure individual differences in the degree of openness or closedness of belief systems); and a similarity–dissimilarity test developed by Daly, McCroskey, and Falcione (to measure the similarity or dissimilarity of the attitudes and values of employees and those of their supervisors).[16] Other instruments used to assess personal communication style or variables are listening tests, creativity tests, and Fiedler's leadership style questionnaire (included in the chapter on human resource theory).

A communication consultant may also want to measure *relational* communication variables (for example, dyad and group interactions). Some of the examples cited by Goldhaber and Rogers that illustrate tests designed to measure relational variables are disparity tests (to suggest the amount of disparity between a manager's estimate and his or her subordinates' estimates of their authority, responsibility, and problem-solving ability), accuracy tests (to determine the extent to which employees receive and/or understand their jobs and company policies and procedures), readability formulas such as the Flesch test (to assess the relative difficulty of comprehending any given text), credibility tests such as those developed by McCroskey and by Falcione (to measure subordinates' perceptions of the credibility of their immediate supervisor), and communication climate measures such as those developed by Dennis (to measure the degree of supportiveness, trust, confidence, openness, and frankness evidenced in an organization).[17] Other examples of tests that might be administered to measure relational variables are small–group leadership or participant questionnaires.

The following questionnaires offer examples of instruments used by communication specialists to measure personal or relational variables:

## Personal Report of Communication Apprehension (PRCA-24)*

Directions: This instrument is composed of 24 statements concerning your feelings about communication with other people. Please indicate in the space provided the degree to which each statement applied to you by marking whether you 1. Strongly Agree, 2. Agree, 3. Are Undecided, 4. Disagree, or 5. Strongly Disagree with each statement. There are no right or wrong answers. Many of the statements are similar to other statements. Do not be concerned about this. Work quickly, just record your first impression.

_____ 1. I dislike participating in group discussions.

_____ 2. Generally, I am comfortable while participating in a group discussion.

_____ 3. I am tense and nervous while participating in group discussions.

_____ 4. I like to get involved in group discussions.

_____ 5. Engaging in a group discussion with new people makes me tense and nervous.

_____ 6. I am calm and relaxed while participating in group discussions.

_____ 7. Generally, I am nervous when I have to participate in a meeting.

_____ 8. Usually I am calm and relaxed while participating in meetings.

_____ 9. I am very calm and relaxed when I am called upon to express an opinion at a meeting.

_____10. I am afraid to express myself at meetings.

_____11. Communicating at meetings usually makes me uncomfortable.

_____12. I am very relaxed when answering questions at a meeting.

_____13. While participating in a conversation with a new acquaintance, I feel very nervous.

_____14. I have no fear of speaking up in conversations.

_____15. Ordinarily I am very tense and nervous in conversations.

_____16. Ordinarily I am very calm and relaxed in conversations.

_____17. While conversing with a new acquaintance I feel very relaxed.

_____18. I'm afraid to speak up in conversations.

_____19. I have no fear of giving a speech.

_____20. Certain parts of my body feel very tense and rigid while giving a speech.

---

*James C. McCroskey, *An Introduction to Rhetorical Communication*, 4th ed. (Englewood Cliffs, N.J.: Prentice-Hall, 1982). The instrument may be reprinted and used for research and instructional purposes without additional authorization of the copyright holder. Uses for which there is expectation of profit, including publication or instruction outside the normal college or school environment, is prohibited without written permission of James C. McCroskey.

_____21. I feel relaxed while giving a speech.

_____22. My thoughts become confused and jumbled when I am giving a speech.

_____23. I face the prospect of giving a speech with confidence.

_____24. While giving a speech I get so nervous, I forget facts I really know.

### Interpersonal Communication Satisfaction Inventory*

The purpose of this questionnaire is to investigate your reactions to the conversation you just had. On the next few pages you will be asked to react to a number of statements. Please indicate the degree to which you agree or disagree that each statement describes this conversation. The 4 or middle position on the scale represents "undecided" or "neutral," then moving out from the center, "slight" agreement or disagreement, then "moderate," then "strong" agreement or disagreement.

For example, if you strongly agree with the following statement you would circle 1;

The other person moved around a lot.

Agree:  1  :  2  :  3  :  4  :  5  :  6  :  7  : Disagree

1. The other person let me know that I was communicating effectively.
2. Nothing was accomplished.
3. I would like to have another conversation like this one.
4. The other person genuinely wanted to get to know me.
5. I was very *dis*satisfied with the conversation.
*6. I had something else to do.
7. I felt that during the conversation I was able to present myself as I wanted the other person to view me.
*8. The other person showed me that he/she understood what I said.
9. I was very satisfied with the conversation.
10. The other person expressed a lot of interest in what I had to say.
11. I did *NOT* enjoy the conversation.
12. The other person did *NOT* provide support for what he/she was saying.
13. I felt I could talk about anything with the other person.
14. We each got to say what we wanted.
15. I felt that we could laugh easily together.

---

*From Michael L. Hecht, "The Conceptualization and Measurement of Interpersonal Communication Satisfaction," *Human Communication Research* (Spring 1978), vol. 4, p. 259; reprinted with permission of the International Communication Association and the author.

16. The conversation flowed smoothly.
*17. The other person changed the topic when his/her feelings were brought into the conversation.
18. The other person frequently said things which added little to the conversation.
19. We talked about something I was *NOT* interested in.

*Communicator Competence Questionnaire\**
*The Subordinate Version Is Provided; Substitution of the Word Supervisor Throughout Will Provide the Supervisor Version*

In this series of questions we would like you to describe how your subordinate communicates. Think about his/her behavior in general, rather than about specific situations.

In responding to the statements below, please use the following scale:

*YES!* = very strong agreement    *NO!* = very strong disagreement
YES = strong agreement    NO = strong disagreement
yes = mild agreement    no = mild disagreement
                    ? = neutral feelings or don't know

1. My subordinate has a good command of the language.
    *YES!*    YES    yes    ?    no    NO    *NO!*
2. My subordinate is sensitive to others' needs of the moment.
    *YES!*    YES    yes    ?    no    NO    *NO!*
3. My subordinate typically gets right to the point.
    *YES!*    YES    yes    ?    no    NO    *NO!*
4. My subordinate pays attention to what other people say to him or her.
    *YES!*    YES    yes    ?    no    NO    *NO!*
5. My subordinate can deal with others effectively.
    *YES!*    YES    yes    ?    no    NO    *NO!*
6. My subordinate is a good listener.
    *YES!*    YES    yes    ?    no    NO    *NO!*
7. My subordinate's writing is difficult to understand.
    *YES!*    YES    yes    ?    no    NO    *NO!*
8. My subordinate expresses his or her ideas clearly.
    *YES!*    YES    yes    ?    no    NO    *NO!*
9. My subordinate is difficult to understand when he or she speaks.
    *YES!*    YES    yes    ?    no    NO    *NO!*
10. My subordinate generally says the right thing at the right time.
    *YES!*    YES    yes    ?    no    NO    *NO!*

---

*From Peter R. Monge, Susan G. Bachman, James P. Dillard, and Eric M. Eisenberg, "Communicator Competence in the Workplace: Model Testing and Scale Development," *Communication Yearbook* (1982), vol. 5, p. 510; reprinted with permission.

11.  My subordinate is easy to talk to.
     *YES!*      YES      yes      ?      no      NO      *NO!*
12.  My subordinate usually responds to messages (memos, phone
     calls, reports, etc.,) quickly.
     *YES!*      YES      yes      ?      no      NO      *NO!*

## Interpersonal Communication Inventory*

This inventory offers you an opportunity to make an objective study of the degree and patterns of communication in your interpersonal relationships. It will enable you to better understand how you present and use yourself in communicating with persons in your daily contacts and activities. You will find it both interesting and helpful to make this study.

### Directions

The questions refer to persons other than your family members or relatives.

Please answer each question as quickly as you can according to the way you feel at the moment (not the way you usually feel or felt last week).

Please do not consult anyone while completing this inventory. You may discuss it after you have completed it. Remember that the value of this form will be lost if you change your answer during or after this discussion.

Honest answers are very necessary. Please be as frank as possible, since your answers are confidential.

Use the following examples for practice. Put a check (√) in one of the three blanks on the right to show how the question applies to your situation.

|  | Yes (Usually) | No (Seldom) | Some-times |
|---|---|---|---|
| 1.  Is it easy for you to express your view to others? | _____ | _____ | _____ |
| 2.  Do others listen to your point of view? | _____ | _____ | _____ |

The Yes column is to be used when the question can be answered as happening most of the time or usually.

The No column is to be used when the question can be answered as seldom or never.

---

*Copyright 1971, Millard J. Bienvenu, Sr.; reprinted with permission of the author.

The Sometimes column should be marked when you cannot answer definitely Yes or No. Use this column as little as possible.

Read each question carefully. If you cannot give the exact answer to a question, answer the best you can but be sure to answer each one. There are no right or wrong answers. Answer according to the way you feel at the present time. Remember, do not refer to family members in answering the questions.

| | Yes (Usually) | No (Seldom) | Some-times |
|---|---|---|---|
| 1. Do your words come out the way you would like them to in conversation? | | | |
| 2. When you are asked a question that is not clear, do you ask the person to explain? | | | |
| 3. When you are trying to explain something, do other persons have a tendency to put words in your mouth? | | | |
| 4. Do you merely assume the other person knows what you are trying to say without your explaining what you really mean? | | | |
| 5. Do you ever ask another person to tell you how he or she feels about the point you may be trying to make? | | | |
| 6. Is it difficult for you to talk with other people? | | | |
| 7. In conversation, do you talk about things which are of interest to both you and the other person? | | | |
| 8. Do you find it difficult to express your ideas when they differ from those around you? | | | |
| 9. In conversation, do you try to put yourself in the other person's shoes? | | | |
| 10. In conversation, do you have a tendency to do more talking than the other person? | | | |
| 11. Are you aware of how your tone of voice may affect others? | | | |
| 12. Do you refrain from saying something that you know will only hurt others or make matters worse? | | | |
| 13. Is it difficult to accept constructive criticism from others? | | | |
| 14. When someone has hurt your feelings, do you discuss this with him or her? | | | |
| 15. Do you later apologize to someone whose feelings you may have hurt? | | | |

16. Does it upset you a great deal when someone disagrees with you?
17. Do you find it difficult to think clearly when you are angry with someone?
18. Do you fail to disagree openly with others because you are afraid they will get angry?
19. When a problem arises between you and another person, can you discuss it without getting angry?
20. Are you satisfied with the way you settle your differences with others?
21. Do you pout and sulk for a long time when someone upsets you?
22. Do you become very uneasy when someone pays you a compliment?
23. Generally, are you able to trust other individuals?
24. Do you find it difficult to compliment and praise others?
25. Do you deliberately try to conceal your faults from others?
26. Do you help others to understand you by saying how you think, feel, and believe?
27. Is it difficult for you to confide in people?
28. Do you have a tendency to change the subject when your feelings enter into a discussion?
29. In conversation, do you let the other person finish talking before reacting to what he or she says?
30. Do you find yourself not paying attention while in conversation with others?
31. Do you ever try to listen for meaning when someone is talking?
32. Do others seem to be listening when you are talking?
33. In a discussion, is it difficult for you to see things from the other person's point of view?
34. Do you pretend you are listening to others when actually you are not?
35. In conversation, can you tell the difference between what a person is saying and what he or she may be feeling?
36. While speaking, are you aware of how others are reacting to what you are saying?

37. Do you feel that other people wish you were a different kind of person?  _____  _____  _____
38. Do other people understand your feelings?  _____  _____  _____
39. Do others remark that you always seem to think you are right?  _____  _____  _____
40. Do you admit that you are wrong when you know that you are wrong about something?

*Total Score*

### Thomas-Kilmann Conflict Mode Instrument*

1. A. There are times when I let others take responsibility for solving the problem.
   B. Rather than negotiate the things on which we disagree, I try to stress those things upon which we both agree.
2. A. I try to find a compromise solution.
   B. I attempt to deal with all of his/her and my concerns.
3. A. I am usually firm in pursuing my goals.
   B. I might try to soothe the other's feelings and preserve our relationship.
4. A. I try to find a compromise solution.
   B. I sometimes sacrifice my own wishes for the wishes of the other person.
5. A. I consistently seek the other's help in working out a solution.
   B. I try to do what is necessary to avoid useless tensions.
6. A. I try to avoid creating unpleasantness for myself.
   B. I try to win my position.
7. A. I try to postpone the issue until I have had some time to think it over.
   B. I give up some points in exchange for others.
8. A. I am usually firm in pursuing my goals.
   B. I attempt to get all concerns and issues immediately out in the open.
9. A. I feel that differences are not always worth worrying about.
   B. I make some effort to get my way.
10. A. I am firm in pursuing my goals.
    B. I try to find a compromise solution.
11. A. I attempt to get all concerns and issues immediately out in the open.
    B. I might try to soothe the other's feelings and preserve our relationship.
12. A. I sometimes avoid taking positions which would create controversy.

---

*Thomas-Kilmann Conflict Mode Instrument, copyright 1974 by Xicom, Inc., Sterling Forest, Tuxedo, NY 10987.

    B. I will let the other person have some of his/her positions if he/she lets me have some of mine.

13. A. I propose a middle-ground.
    B. I press to get my points made.

14. A. I tell the other person my ideas and ask for his/hers.
    B. I try to show the other person the logic and benefits of my position.

15. A. I might try to soothe the other's feelings and preserve our relaticnship.
    B. I try to do what is necessary to avoid tensions.

16. A. I try not to hurt the other's feelings.
    B. I try to convince the other person of the merits of my position.

17. A. I am usually firm in pursuing my goals.
    B. I try to do what is necessary to avoid useless tensions.

18. A. If it makes other people happy, I might let them maintain their views.
    B. I will let other people have some of their positions if they let me have some of mine.

19. A. I attempt to get all concerns and issues immediately out in the open.
    B. I try to postpone the issue until I have had some time to think it over.

20. A. I attempt to immediately work through our differences.
    B. I try to find a fair combination of gains and losses for both of us.

21. A. In approaching negotiations, I try to be considerate of the other person's wishes.
    B. I always lean toward a direct discussion of the problem.

22. A. I try to find a position that is intermediate between his/hers and mine.
    B. I assert my wishes.

23. A. I am very often concerned with satisfying all our wishes.
    B. There are times when I let others take responsibility for solving the problem.

24. A. If the other's position seems very important to him/her, I would try to meet his/her wishes.
    B. I try to get the other person to settle for a compromise.

25. A. I try to show the other person the logic and benefits of my position.
    B. In approaching negotiations, I try to be considerate of the other person's wishes.

26. A. I propose a middle ground.
    B. I am nearly always concerned with satisfying all our wishes.

27. A. I sometimes avoid taking positions that would create controversy.

    B.  If it makes other people happy, I might let them maintain their views.

28.  A.  I am usually firm in pursuing my goals.

      B.  I usually seek the other's help in working out a solution.

29.  A.  I propose a middle ground.

      B.  I feel that differences are not always worth worrying about.

30.  A.  I try not to hurt the other's feelings.

      B.  I always share the problem with the other person so that we can work it out.

## Power Base Inventory*

1.  A.  They think I am much smarter about these things.

    B.  They have to agree with the facts that I use for support.

2.  A.  They accept my formal right to decide matters.

    B.  They have a general sense of goodwill towards me.

3.  A.  They believe that I may do something for them in return for their assistance.

    B.  They realize that, beyond a certain point, noncompliance might not be tolerated.

4.  A.  They enjoy doing what they can for me.

    B.  They are impressed with my greater competence.

5.  A.  They believe that my official status allows me to settle these issues.

    B.  They know that I will try to make their cooperation worthwhile for them.

6.  A.  If we disagree, I demonstrate to them how they are wrong.

    B.  If things got out of hand, they know I would have to be firm with them for the good of the organization.

7.  A.  They are impressed with my greater competence.

    B.  They feel formally responsible for following my instructions.

8.  A.  They comply because they care about me and like to make me happy.

    B.  They perceive that I will reward them for helping me out.

9.  A.  They know they would have to be punished if they violated important directives.

    B.  They put less stock in their own powers of judgment than in mine.

10.  A.  They understand my reasoning and are persuaded by it.

      B.  I have some rapport with them.

11.  A.  They believe that I could be hard on them if they deserved it.

      B.  They believe that it is their duty to obey me.

12.  A.  They see that I provide positive incentives for their contributions.

---

*Power Base Inventory, copyright 1985 by Xicom, Inc., Sterling Forest, Tuxedo, NY 10987.

B. I show them how to properly interpret and deal with the situation, so that we agree.

13. A. They comply because they care about me and like to make me happy.
    B. They are aware that if they persisted in defying me, I might have to take corrective action for everyone's sake.

14. A. They believe that my official status allows me to settle these issues.
    B. They have to agree with the facts that I use for support.

15. A. They trust my skills and abilities much more than their own.
    B. They realize that conscientious cooperation will merit some form of compensation.

16. A. If we disagree, I demonstrate to them how they are wrong.
    B. They think I am much smarter about these things.

17. A. They enjoy doing what they can for me.
    B. They realize that I have been delegated the power to make these judgments.

18. A. If things got out of hand, they know I would have to be firm with them for the good of the organization.
    B. They perceive that I will reward them for helping me out.

19. A. I have established a reputation with them for making good decisions.
    B. I have developed a good working relationship with them.

20. A. They know I will try to repay them for their good work.
    B. They believe that my official status allows me to settle these issues.

21. A. If things got out of hand, they know I would have to be firm with them for the good of the organization.
    B. They have to agree with the facts that I use for support.

22. A. They respect the fact that the organization has empowered me to determine such matters.
    B. They believe that I am considerably more qualified to make good decisions.

23. A. They see that I provide positive incentives for their contributions.
    B. They enjoy doing what they can for me.

24. A. They think I am much smarter about these things.
    B. If things got out of hand, they know I would have to be firm with them for the good of the organization.

25. A. They follow my example because they feel positive about me.
    B. I am able to get them to see why I am right.

26. A. They do my bidding because of my superior rank.
    B. They think that I could be tough with them if I had to.

27. A. They have to agree with the facts that I use for support.
    B. They know I will try to repay them for their good work.

28. A. They believe that I could be hard on them if they deserved it.

   B.  They go along with me because they have some affection for
       me.
29.  A.  They are forced to go along with the overwhelming evidence
        which I marshal for support.
     B.  They believe in my official right to tell them what to do.
30.  A.  They perceive that I will reward them for helping me out.
     B.  They think I am much smarter about these things.

## *Measuring Organizational Communication*[20]

- How free do you feel to discuss with your immediate superior the
  problems and difficulties you have in your job without jeopardizing
  your position or having it "held against" you later?
- In general, how much do you feel that your immediate superior can
  do to further your career in this organization?
- How important is it for you to progress upward in your present
  organization?
- How desirable do you feel it is in your organization to be in contact
  frequently with others at the same job level?
- While working, what percentage of the time do you spend in contact
  with superiors?
- While working,, what percentage of the time do you spend in contact
  with subordinates?
- While working, what percentage of the time do you spend in contact
  with others at the same job level?
- When receiving information from the sources listed below (superior,
  subordinate, peers), how accurate would you estimate it usually is?
- When transmitting information to your immediate superiors, how
  often do you summarize by emphasizing aspects that are important
  and minimizing those aspects that are unimportant?
- Of the total amount of information you receive at work, how much
  do you pass on to your immediate superior?
- Do you ever feel that you receive more information than you can
  efficiently use?
- Put a check under the face that expresses how you feel about
  *communication* in general, including the amount of information you
  receive, contacts with your superiors and others, the accuracy of
  information available, etc.?
- Of the total time you engage in communications while on the job,
  about what percentage of the time do you use the following methods:
- Written
- Face-to-face
- Telephone
- Other

Finally, a consultant may wish to measure *organizational* variables
such as communication load on key individuals, networks utilized by
organization members, direction of communication flow, or most fre-

quent media or channels used for message exchange. Organizational communication theory suggests that networks in organizations perform four primary kinds of functions: (1) *regulatory* (exemplified by policy statements, procedures, and rules to assure conformity to organizational goals), (2) *innovative* (suggestion systems and participative problem–solving meetings that ensure that the organization recognizes and adapts to changes in the internal and relevant external environments), (3) *integrative* or *maintenance* (illustrated by the grapevine, performance–appraisal meetings, and the employee newsletter—all of which work to relate the employee to the organization, while at the same time influencing employee morale), and (4) *informative-instructive* (the corporate magazine, bulletin–board notices, and training activities intended to enable the organization member to better execute his or her job). The consultant can choose to analyze the efficiency with which the different networks are functioning.[18]

Rather than considering the purposes served by networks, the communication specialist can decide instead to examine the *direction* of communication flow in the organization. If the latter is his or her aim, he or she can look at the frequency, quality, and/or quantity of upward, downward, or horizontal communications to see dominant trends that characterize the organization.

In 1952 Keith Davis developed Episodic Communication Channels in Organizations (ECCO) analysis techniques to track a particular messasge or set of messages as it/they move through the organization. By following the message's path through the organization, a consultant can map out networks, determine the time necessary for the message to make its way through all levels of the organizational hierarchy, assess the degree of distortion that occurs in the message, and see the extent of redundancy in the networks (i.e., how many times does one person receive the same message but from different people).[19]

Computer analysis techniques developed by William Richards and reviewed in a subsequent chapter of this book illustrate still more sophisticated tools for examining communication networks in organizations.

The I.C.A. Communication Audit, included in the appendix, offers a comprehensive instrument for assessing *personal, relational*, and *organizational* communication variables. A data base is available to help the consultant to interpret the results he obtains with the I.C.A. audit.

### Notes

1 Gerald M. Goldhaber, Harry S. Dennis III, Gary M. Richetto, and Osmo A. Wiio, *Information and Strategies: New Pathways to Management*

*Productivity* (Norwood, N.J.: Ablex Publishing Corporation, 1984), PP. 313 and 335.

2 *Ibid.*, p. 313.

3 Gerald Goldhaber, "The ICA Audit: Rationale and Development," paper presented to the Academy of Management, Kansas City, 1976; cited in Goldhaber, Dennis, Richetto, and Wiio, *Information Strategies,* p. 358.

4 M. Yates, G. Goldhaber, P. Porter, R. Lesniak, H. Dennis, and G. Richetto, "The ICA Communication Audit System: Results of Six Studies," paper presented to the International Communication Association, Portland, Oregon, 1976; cited in Goldhaber.

5 G. Goldhaber and P. Krivonos, "The ICA Communication Audit: Process, Status and Critique," *Journal of Business Communication* (Fall 1977) vol. 15, pp. 41–56.

6 Gerald Goldhaber and Donald P. Rogers, *Auditing Organizational Communication Systems: The ICA Communication Audit* (Dubuque, Iowa: Kendall/Hunt, 1979).

7 Goldhaber, Dennis, Richetto, and Wiio, *op. cit.*, p. 337.

8 This system was described in Osmo Wiio, "Auditing Communication in Organizations: A Standard Survey LTT Communication Audit." Paper presented to the International Communication Association, New Orleans, 1974. Also Osmo Wiio and Martti Helsila, "Auditing Communication in Organizations: A Standard Survey LTT Communication Audit," *The Finnish Journal of Business Economics* (1974), vol. 4, pp. 303–315; cited in Goldhaber, Dennis, Richetto, and Wiio, *op. cit.*, p. 336.

9 Goldhaber, Dennis, Richetto, and Wiio, *op. cit.*, p. 336.

10 *Ibid.*

11 *Ibid.*, p. 338.

12 Goldhaber and Rogers, *op. cit.*, pp. 3–6.

13 *Ibid.*, pp. 35–53.

14 See Myron Emanuel, "Auditing Communication Practices," in *Inside Organizational Communication,* ed. Carol Reuss and Donn Silvis (New York: Longman, 1981).

15 These categories of discussion were used by Goldhaber, Dennis, Richetto, and Wiio in their revised edition of *Information Strategies, op. cit.*.

16 *Ibid.*, pp. 219–27.

17 *Ibid.*, pp. 228–37.

18 See Howard H. Greenbaum, "The Audit of Organizational Communication," in *Readings in Interpersonal and Organizational Communication,* 3rd ed., ed. Richard C. Huseman, Cal M. Logue, and Dwight L. Freshley (Boston: Holbrook Press, Inc., 1977), pp. 139–141, for a discussion of these network functions.

19 Keith Davis, "Methods for Studying Communication in Organizations," *Journal of Communication* (1978), vol. 28, pp. 117–23.

20 Sample questions from an instrument designed by Karlene H. Roberts and Charles A. O'Reilly III, reported in "Measuring Organizational Communication," *Journal of Applied Psychology* (1974), vol. 59, p. 323; copyright 1974 by the American Psychological Association; reprinted by permission of the authors.

# 40

# Steps in Performing a Communication Audit[1]

*Michael Z. Sincoff, Dudley A. Williams,*
and
*C. E. Tapie Rohm, Jr.*

As managerial thought has evolved, the result has been the continual redefinition, expansion, and description of a growing number of functions identified as responsibilities of the modern manager.[2] According to many management professionals,[3] the manager today is responsible not only for facilitating effective and efficient operation of each functional area, but also for insuring their timely and continual mutually supportive interrelation within an organization.

Nearly 70 years ago Frederick W. Taylor, the founder of the school of scientific management, identified the primary functions of a manager as planning, organizing, controlling, scientifically selecting the right man for the right job, and facilitating cooperation between employee and employer.[4] Since that time, the conception of management has enlarged Taylor's list of functions to include planning, organizing, staffing, coordinating, controlling, investigating, communicating, formulating goals and objectives, directing, motivating, evaluating, innovating, decision-making, listening, and administering.[5]

Associated with the widening scope of managerial functions has been an increasing awareness that communication is a key function among the others, and is, in fact, the "linkage" binding the other functions.[6] As that linkage, communications is depicted as having the objective of interrelating and providing the mutual support among the other functions within an organization.

As the significance of the communicative function emerges, common sense and logic indicate that management must accept the inherent responsibility to become personally involved with communication activities.[7] The effectiveness of an organization's communication is directly related to implicit and explicit organizational objectives and accomplishment of the organizational mission.[8] The very important relationship among managerial functions is allowed and provided for through communicative activity and the resultant organizational cohesiveness.

In the past, top management through its supervision and direct involvement in selective functional areas, has initiated studies, inquiries, reviews, financial audits, or analyses to determine organizational problem areas. Unfortunately, such investigations usually focused upon the dominantly recognized managerial functions and excluded communication. When communication appeared to be involved in the area of scrutiny, then the communication activity was included within the scope of the study, but generally only as a component or subelement of the more traditional system. Since the proper instrumentation to conduct research in, on, or about communication systems had not been developed and refined, communication was the lesser part of any particular analysis.

Only recently has a technique begun to be developed and tested to permit thorough and accurate evaluation of the effectivenss of communications systems and activities within the organization. The technique is the *communication audit*. Previously, managers used questionnaires, interviews, administrative logs, flow-charts, ECCO analysis, card sorts, participant-observation, content analyses, or any number of research techniques adapted to investigate separate functions and their particular problems. While any of these research techniques can be used to determine communication variables within an organization, until the recent advent of the communication audit, no single integrated and standardized procedure had been developed. Partial approaches generally focused on previously discovered problems and their impact. Seldom did these approaches address either the effectiveness of the organization's communication climate as a whole, separately, or by component. The currently developing communication audit technique provides a sophisticated approach for the capability of determining communication effectiveness.

This paper reviews current knowledge of the procedures for preparing for and conducting a communication audit so that managers, management, and outside consultants can become aware of the audit as a key supportive activity, how it is accomplished, and what benefits develop from its proper use.

The concept of the communication audit is explained best through a schematic (see Fig. 40.1) which depicts the stages of the audit from initiation to completion. The flow chart and accompanying text address the communication specialist since he, either as a member of the particular organization, or as a member of an outside organization specializing in audit services, must obtain the permission and support of top management in an organization, conduct the audit, and evaluate data obtained.

The schematic traces the major steps from inception to conclusion of the audit: introductory contacts between the auditor and management, the conduct of the audit, and final evaluations of communication effectiveness as revealed by the audit. Comments are general, since no two organizations are identical, and as such will require some special planning and tailoring of the audit. Both auditor and client must be able to conceptualize the audit within the special areas and environmental characteristics of the respective organizations.

## Approach to Organizational Problems

### Choosing the Potential Client

To establish potential target markets for implementation of the communication audit, consideration of several factors is necessary. They include: 1. Determination of any restrictions to be placed on the market; for instance, if the target market encompasses an industrial, governmental, or religious organization, an essential requirement is to identify the specific levels and communication activities that the audit will address. Legal and political considerations must also be included in selection criteria if these pose operational constraints within which the audit must be conducted. 2. Establishment of restrictions as to size, geographical location, industrial limitations, or number of employees. 3. Clearly establishing the relationship between the term "communication"/"communication audit" and the organization(s) under consideration. 4. Establishment of an operational definition for the terms "communication" and "communication audit." Attending to the criteria above will facilitate the selection of target markets, or of those segments of the available population with which the communication audit will be concerned.

### Determining Approach Methodology

Upon the selection of a prospective client and a particular segment of the client population, a final decision must be made concerning what initial approach(es) will be taken to reach him. Alternatives include: Contact through advertisement mail and/or brochures containing an attractive outline of the proposed audit; telephone; interview; personal appearance; referral; or, any combination of the above. The financial

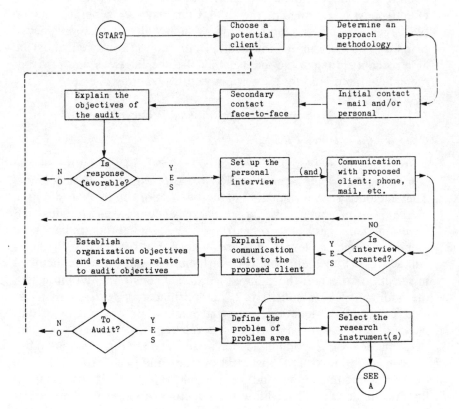

**Fig. 40.1**
**Schematic of communication audit**

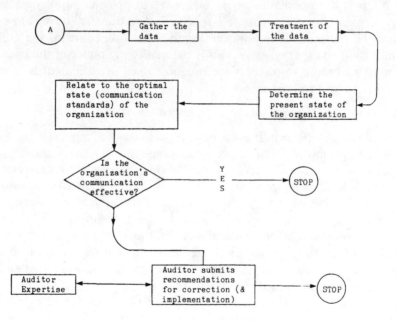

**Fig. 40.1**
**Schematic of communication audit (cont.)**

cost of contact incurred by the auditor should be considered, however, before any meaningful decision along these lines is implemented.

### Secondary Contact

Due to the lack of any established contact at the outset, the initial contact is a critical step in the entire contact/sell approach in the audit business. Therefore, in the secondary contact, care should be taken to expand on the theme which was utilized in the approach campaign; e.g., if a brochure were received by the prospective client, the auditor, in his follow-up contact, would take care to provide supplementary information about the materials received. Additionally, he would expand the concept, definition, and operational procedure of the communication audit. Obviously, this is the marketing phase of the operation, since failure to impress the organizational management is likely to elicit an unfavorable response.

### Explaining the Objectives of the Communication Audit

A communication audit must have objectives. An important part of the sales promotion of the pre-audit phase is the establishment of objectives in a clear, concise manner to which management can relate. Several objectives for conducting a communication audit are: 1. assessing the effectiveness of the organizational communication system; 2. mapping the communication flows within an organization; 3. pinpointing weak and/or undesirable areas in the system; 4. ascertaining whether or not the appropriate elements are present within the existing organizational structure; 5. assembling information through data gathering instruments, in order to measure and compare that information within standards previously set by the organization, and, 6. developing recommendations for the correction of apparent deficiencies and preparing plans for implementation of these recommendations.

### Is Response Favorable?

If the response from the prospective client is unfavorable, then the auditor must begin the whole process again, i.e., repeat the initial and secondary contact procedures.

### Setting Up the Personal Interview and the Communication Form Used

If the response from the prospective client is favorable, then the auditor needs to set up an interview in order to explain what a communication audit is, and how it will benefit the particular organization. Several alternatives are suggested to set up the personal interview: a personal telephone call, a letter, a face-to-face interaction, referral, or any combination thereof.

### Is the Interview Granted?

If the interview is not granted, this would necessitate starting at the beginning of the diagrammed procedure.

Once the appointment for the interview is arranged, the auditor should intensify his research of the organization (i.e., obtain general knowledge of it, perhaps through its public financial statement, annual report, and/or any published listing of a given organization's characteristics) and establish his approach for the interview, before the next contact can be made. Preparation for this sales interview requires a complete analysis of the client organization. Since this interview determines whether or not permission is granted to conduct the audit, the client must be convinced of the need for, and benefits derived from the audit, along with the compatability of organizational objectives and those of the audit. How well the auditor analyzes the particular organization and the problem will largely determine his chance for success in the coming interview. This is the critical point where all excellent principles of interviewing should be appropriately chosen and executed.[9]

### Explaining the Communication Audit

Answers to the following questions should be provided by the auditor: What is the communication audit? What can a communication audit do for the organization in question to help identify and solve some of its problems? How can a communication audit check for potential problems in the organization?

Goldhaber explained: "A communication audit is a research procedure which assesses the effectiveness of the organizational communication system according to a set of standards.[10] When explaining the audit, the auditor should include mention of areas where communication problems are frequently encountered: horizontal,[11] vertical,[12] and diagonal communication;[13] the grapevine;[14] bypassing, allness, and frozen evaluation;[15] and, specific formal and informal communication patterns.[16]

### Showing Alignment of Organizational Objectives With Audit Objectives and Establishing Standards

As the interview takes place, the auditor should elicit management's organizational objectives and determine what the organization's communication standards are. At this time a joint decision is made by client and auditor to proceed with the audit.

### Definition of the Problem

At this stage in the pre-communication audit strategy, attention is directed toward identification of specific area(s) within the organization to be audited through specially selected instruments and methods chosen by the audit team (auditor and associates).

Within the framework, further definition of the problem occurs. Having some idea of the number and classification of employees who will be informants in the audit will allow for further specification of instruments and techniques useful in obtaining the information desired. Should the focus of the audit be in a production department, for example, only foremen might be made aware of the presence of an audit team, and a participant observer will be used to collect data. If the informants are vice-presidents or directors perhaps an information-giving interview should be chosen as one means of gathering data. Because many types of information-gathering devices are used in communication auditing, the audit team should have some knowledge of the number and types of employees who will be serving as informants in the study in order to select the most appropriate methods and instruments.

In addition to numerical and geographic information, the audit team must also be aware of the current communication climate within the area involved.[17] Whether or not the atmosphere is one that would facilitate or hinder honest open communication is an extremely important factor in determining the methods to be used for information gathering.[18] Tensions and jealousies must be taken into consideration in an analysis of communication climate. Previous exposure to communication surveys and reactions to them by the client sample are appropriate data to obtain.

### Selection of the Instruments

Following definitions of the audit objectives, the auditor should select the data gathering instruments(s), a process involving three phases: 1. Determination of the instrument's relevance to a particular purpose; 2. estimation of cost factors (temporal and monetary) which are involved in using the particular instrument; and 3. evaluation of the strengths and weaknesses of each instrument.

Since a variety of data gathering instruments are available, the auditor has to decide which ones will provide the desired information about the problem under study. The auditor should determine the scientific usefulness of the instrument considered, i.e., its reliability and validity. Since many instruments (commercially prepared questionnaires) neither consistently nor accurately measure the constructs they purport to measure, determining reliability and validity of the instrument becomes a critical step. Relative cost factors must be considered when determining the extent to which reliability and validity need to be demonstrated.

Having narrowed the selection of data gathering instruments, the auditor compares the strengths and weaknesses of the remaining instruments by looking for answers to the following questions: 1. Can the instrument be easily used? 2. Is it objectively scored? 3. Is it available for use? 4. Is is easily explained? Some common weaknesses of which the auditor should be aware are biased or leading questions, subjectivity in scoring, and data which are subject to only unfamiliar forms of statistical procedures. These and other comparisons will lead the auditor to choose the optimum data gathering instruments.

Although many instruments can be employed in the communication audit, most of them are representative of one of the three major types of data gathering techniques: the questionnaire, the interview, and observation. Since the auditor needs to be familiar with all three if he desires proficiency in his task, they are explained here briefly.

### The Questionnaire

The questionnaire is a written instrument which attempts to secure information concerning an individual's attitudes, knowledge and perceptions on a particular topic or activity. In most cases, the questionnaire is self-administered—the individual providing information completes the questionnaire without assistance from the auditor.

The ease with which the questionnaire is administered is one of its main advantages. Other inherent advantages are its flexibility, low cost, the wide variety of information obtainable, and the relatively short period of time necessary for its administration.

The major disadvantages of the questionnaire include low, unrepresentative return rates (especially for mailed questionnaires), biased responses due to inadequate alternative responses or leading questions, and difficulty in coding open-ended questions. Often the questionnaires tend to incorporate cultural biases, especially in language use.

To guard against these problems, the following precautions should be taken during the construction of the questionnaire: (1) The respondent's identity should be anonymous, (2) items included should be free of bias, and (3) there should be only one way to interpret the question asked in each item.

### The Interview

The interview ". . . is the most powerful and useful tool of social scientific society research."[19] Essentially, the interview is "a form of oral communication involving two parties, at least one of whom has a preconceived and serious purpose, and both of whom speak and listen from time to time."[20] Although many authors make little distinction between the questionnaire and the interview, there are some important differences.

The interview is much more versatile than the questionnaire. In addition to serving as the main instrument of the research, the interview also functions as an explanatory device as well as a supplemental aid to other research methods. Moreover, the interview has the distinct advantage of being an immediate and direct communication exchange between the parties involved. While this format enables the interviewee to explain his answers more fully, it gives the interviewer insight into both the conscious and preconscious attitudes, beliefs, and perceptions of the respondent.

Besides having certain advantages over the questionnaires, the interview also possesses some disadvantages not found in the questionnaire, specifically 1. it requires a great deal of time and money; and 2. bias can result from the interaction between the parties and/or subjective interpretation of the informant's reponses by the interviewer. An auditor experienced in the various approaches and techniques of interviewing can eliminate (or at least minimize) some of the interview's weaknesses.

### Observation Methodology

The third overall methodology useful in the communication audit is observation. It is "collecting information-in-society first-hand by maintaining alert attention, with maximum use of the observer's complement of perceptual abilities and sensitivities, to all the accessible and relevant interpersonal and intrapersonal events going on in the immediate field situation through a period of time."[22] The phases of the observation technique are 1. observing, 2. recording, and 3. analyzing.

In the observational phase, achieving and adapting to the situation are crucial to the methodology. The establishment of rapport is important throughout the course of the audit, first to enter the organization, and second to maintain cooperation from its members. Rapport between the observer and the observed influences the quality of data which are obtained, since the person observed will not behave in his usual manner unless he trusts the observer. Achieving rapport is an ongoing process that necessitates the observer's concern with dress, nonverbal symbols, intimacy of relations, conformity, eavesdropping, and revealing information about the audit to be observed.

Adaptations are essential to the maintenance of rapport and by extension to the success of the study, i.e., characteristics of the person being observed who would assure the success or failure of gathering observation data. Adaptation to the environment discourages contamination of observation and encourages social interaction. Cues given by the observed guide the observations of the observer and prepare him for role adjustments or unanticipated events. Such flexibility in approach is a major advantage of observation methodology. Another advantage is that the auditor not only observes the actual communication patterns of specific individuals, but also has the opportunity to question them about their behavior as soon as it occurs.

The major disadvantage of this methodology is that it tends to disrupt the normal activities and functions of the individuals being observed. Thus, the observed behaviors are not necessarily routine behaviors, but possibly reactions to the presence of the observer, a form of the Hawthorne effect. A further disadvantage of observation is that the observer is limited to the number of places in which he can be at one time to observe, and by the number of detailed observations he can make. The technique is also time consuming and the accuracy of observations is contingent upon rapport establishment. In addition, lack of attention to the situation and subjectivity in data interpretation are problems inherent to observation methodology.

### Application of Techniques

Once selected, the auditor has to decide how he wants to employ the research instruments. This decision requires the auditor to examine the operational factors or procedures inherent in the use of a particular research method. The term *operational factors* refers to the mechanics involved in using each instrument. Since each instrument has its own operational factors, attention is focused here on the three principal information gathering categories: the questionnaire, the interview, and observation.

If a questionnaire is going to be included as part of the audit, some operational procedures to be considered are administration, time, and collection. *Administration* consists of determining: 1. whether the questionnaire is self-administering, 2. whether the directions are easy to follow, 3. if the items apply to all respondents, 4. whether the respondents have to take the test at the same time or location, and 5. if special instruments such as lead pencils are needed to complete the form. *Time* encompasses both the completion and scoring of the questionnaire. Finally, the auditor investigates the procedures involved in *collecting* the questionnaire. One method of collection requires the auditor to retrieve each form personally. While assuring a high return rate, it is also very time consuming. An alternative method permits the respondents to return the questionnaire to stations conveniently located. Unfortunately, the percentage rate of return declines sharply when this procedure is employed.

## Treatment of the Data

Beyond the cursory discussion of data treatment specifically designed for each instrument, the auditor should be aware of the general steps in data treatment while maintaining alertness to his purpose: He is seeking a frequency of occurrence, percentage of the total, difference between groups, average of time or number, pictorial representation of a process, or illustrative details. This, in turn, will determine if the data he gathered must be qualitative—such as flow-chart, nondirective interview, or sociometric technique analyses—or quantitative— such as a highly structured questionnaire elicits.

The auditor must also determine if his data are categorical: can they be portioned into appropriate classes? Often qualitative data can be converted into quantitative units for analysis through such categorization. Generally, the more highly structured the research instruments, the more easily classifiable are the data obtained.

In constructing categories, the auditor should keep the following rules in mind: 1. Categories are set up according to the research problem; 2. the categories are exhaustive; 3. the categories are mutually exclusive and independent; 4. each category is derived from one classification principle; 5. any categorization scheme must be one level of discourse.[22] Another rule which might be added is that it is usually better to have too many separate categories which can be combined at a later date, than too few.[23]

Similar procedural decision have to be made when the interview is used in the communication audit; the auditor again analyzes the administrative and time factors involved, deciding what approach he will use—directive or nondirective. He also selects his informants and determines the sequence in which they will be interviewed. Depending on whom he interviews, the auditor also decides if he needs to modify his appearance or language so that it will be more compatible with that of the interviewee. Finally, the auditor must also determine the best physical location for the interview.

If the auditor selects observation methodology to supplement other data gathering techniques, he still has to make some decisions before taking on the role of an observer: 1. He decides at which sub-unit in the organization he will begin; 2. he selects the type of observation best suited to his purpose—be it participant observation, observer as participant, or complete participant; 3. he finds the most subtle and effective way of recording the observed behavior; and 4. he considers how much time needs to be spent in collecting information.

Having evaluated the operational factors of the instrument he intends to use, the auditor has to examine the environmental factors particular to the organization under study. Upon completion of this task, the auditor applies his instrument, gathers his data, and treats it using the appropriate analytical method.

Once the data have been categorized, the form of statistical presentation is determined. The simplest and most commonly used type of statistical presentation is frequency distribution, or the number of cases or distribution of cases falling into different categories. Primary presentation is descriptive, while secondary analysis consists of comparing frequencies and percentages.

Often the auditor may wish to present a visual representation of the data gathered. Graphs, tables, and figures are especially helpful here. For information on their construction and uses, one may refer to available style manuals.

## Evaluation of Communication Effectiveness

### Determine Present State of the Organization

Having analyzed the data, the auditor looks for patterns, familiar elements, relationships, and trends which they show, making inferences about the state of the organization at the present time. The second step is to determine the optimal state of the organization.

### Optimal State of the Organization

Information about the optimal state of the organization is derived from the organization's statements of its objectives (regarding the ideal or desired state of the organization's communication and obtained in the initial and secondary contact interviews).

### Is Present State Optimal?

The third step in audit evaluation is the actual comparison of the present state of the organization as determined by the audit, with the optimal state as determined in the pre-audit inquiries. This phase requires the auditor to compare the data he has collected and the conclusions he has drawn from them with the statements made by his organizational contact persons regarding its desired state or standard of communication. If the auditor determines that the present state of the organization is in line with the organization's optimal state, then no further work is necessary.

### Making Recommendations

If the auditor determines that the present state of the organization fails to meet the communication standards of the client, then he may make recommendations proposing ways that the organization can achieve its goals and objectives through corrective action of communicative behavior.

### Expertise of the Auditor

In making recommendations, the auditor draws on his own knowledge, training and experience. He is, for example, aware of specific techniques that may be employed to alleviate certain communication problems. He knows of communication and organizational models whose application may prove helpful to the client. Furthermore, he has acquired experience in applying certain methods in real life situations, and is expected to know how well or to what extent those methods have worked in the past. The auditor should bring to bear on the problem the sum total of his knowledge and experience.

### Conclusion

The auditor must be thoroughly trained and experienced in understanding the communication characteristics of organizations. He must develop an understanding of the organizational characteristics of the firm being considered for an audit. Repeated contacts, primarily of a face-to-face nature between audit personnel and top management representatives, are mandatory to establish the foundations for thorough and mutual understanding. Optimum planning must be an objective of both parties. Data must be evaluated against communication standards previously set by the organization and not the audit team. Top management's support of the audit and announcement interest must be evident from the initial contact through completion.

The communication audit is relatively new to the management environment. While any given audit will be tailored to fit a particular organization, there will be universalities which lend themselves to all organizations.

## Notes

1. This paper is based on a research report submitted in partial fulfillment of the requirements in the course Interpersonal Communication 746: "Communication Process in Organizations" conducted during the Winter Quarter, 1975, School of Interpersonal Communication, Ohio University, Athens, Ohio. Participants in the research were: Robert Edmunds, Craig Harter, R. A. Iglowski, Craig Inabnet, John Nolan, Jean Rahrig, C. E. Tapie Rohm, Jr., William Rossiter, Geraldine Simone, Leah Vaughan, Holly Ann Wellstead, Dudley A. Williams, and James W. Wright.
2. D. A. Wren, *Evolution of Management Thought* (New York: Ronald Press, 1972).
3. J. B. Miner, *The Management Process* (New York: Macmillan, 1973); and W. Weisman, *Wall-to-Wall Organizational Communication,* third rev. ed. (Huntsville, Ala.: Walter Weisman, 1974).
4. Miner, *op. cit.*
5. Koontz and O'Donnell (1964) [author queried for fuller documentation]; W. C. Redding, *Communication Within the Organization* (New York: Industrial Communication Council, Inc. 1972); and P. F. Drucker, *Management* (New York: Harper & Row, 1974).
6. T. Haimann and W. G. Scott, *Management in the Modern Organization* (New York: Houghton-Mifflin, 1970); and Weisman, *op. cit.*
7. L. A. Townsend, "A Corporate President's View of the Internal Communication Function," *Journal of Communication* (December 1965), vol. 15, pp. 208–15; and W. Weisman, "Management's Toughest Job—Organizational Communication," *Defense Management Journal* (1969), vol. 6, pp. 33–37.
8. W. C. Redding and G. A. Sanborn, *Business and Industrial Communication: A Source Book* (New York: Harper & Row, 1964).
9. R. Goyer, W. C. Redding, and J. Rickey, *Interviewing Principles and Techniques,* rev. ed. (Dubuque, Iowa: Wm. C. Brown, 1968).
10. G. M. Goldhaber, *Organizational Communication* (Dubuque, Iowa: Wm. C. Brown, 1974).
11. Townshend, *op. cit.*
12. A. Chase, "How to Make Downward Communication Work," *Personnel Journal* (1970), vol. 48, pp.478–83.
13. J. Hulbert and N. Capon, "Interpersonal Communication Marketing," *Journal of Marketing Research* (February 1972), vol. 9, pp. 27–34.
14. K. Davis, "The Organization That's Not on the Chart," *Supervisory Management* (1961), vol. 6, pp. 2–7.
15. W. V. Haney, *Communication and Organizational Behavior* (Homewood, Ill.: Richard D. Irwin, 1967).
16. A. Bavelas and D. Barrett, "An Experimental Approach to Organizational Communication," *Personnel* (March 1951), vol. 27, pp. 366–71.

17. Redding, "The Empirical Study of Human Communication in Business and Industry," in *The Frontiers in Experimental Speech–Communication Research,* ed. P. E. Reid (Syracuse, N.Y.: Syracuse University Press, 1966), pp. 47–81; G. T. Hunt, "Communication, Satisfaction and Decision-Making at Three American Colleges," unpublished Ph.D. dissertation, Purdue University, 1972; and H. A. Dennis, "A Theoretical and Empirical Study of Managerial Communication Climate in Complex Organizations," unpublished Ph.D. dissertation, Purdue University, 1974.
18. M. Z. Sincoff, "An Experimental Study of the Effects of Three 'Interviewing Styles' upon Judgment of Interviewees and Observer Judges," unpublished Ph.D. dissertation, Purdue University, 1969.
19. F. Kerlinger, *Foundations of Behavioral Research,* second ed. (New York: Holt, Rinehart & Winston, 1973), p. 412.
20. Goyer, Redding, and Rickey, p. 6.
21. B. Junker, *Field Work* (Chicago: University of Chicago Press, 1960), p. 14.
22. Kerlinger, p. 137.
23. J. Madge, *The Tools of Social Science* (New York: Doubleday, 1953), p. 259.

# 41

# Network Analysis in Organizations

*William D. Richards, Jr.*

The importance of communication in organizations is fundamental. Without communication, there could be no organizations. There would be no hospitals, no corporations, no universities, no societies. The process of communication not only *allows* people to work together for common goals; it is necessary for the development and sharing of those goals. It allows people to share their feelings and to coordinate their actions. It has been described as the "thread" that holds organizations together, as the "glue" that bonds people together in relationships, and as the "force" that allows groups of people to take on their own identity. Clearly, the process of communication is fundamentally important to any activity that requires more than a single person.

As the number of people working toward a common goal increases, as the complexity of that goal increases, so does the importance of communication increase; the more people there are, the more important it becomes to keep everyone informed and the more important it becomes to efficiently coordinate the actions of the people. The more complex the task of the organization, the more important that everyone knows his or her job and the more important an efficient information flow. It follows, then, that the importance of an understanding of the communication networks in organizations rises along with the importance of the organization, whose very existence depends on the continued flow of communication.

Where other approaches to communication focus in abstract terms on the process itself, on the coding system and the message, or on the relation between the "source" and the "receiver" and all their characteristics, the network approach looks at the whole set of relationships that exists in functioning, ongoing systems. The network approach allows us to make statements about organizations, rather than about individual people or individual communication transactions, because it takes a systems approach to situation analysis. It focuses on the relationships among the people in the system and looks at all the relationships at once, without isolating the people from each other or from the relationships between them. The network approach not only looks at the system as a whole to see how it is structured; it also looks at the way each individual person fits into the larger structure. This becomes crucial when very large systems are involved, as people come to play specialized roles in the communication networks of these systems, and as poorly organized networks can lead to very serious problems for the organization as a whole.

The network approach rests on some concepts that come from a systems perspective on organization. The central concepts are all connected with the fact that (to paraphrase Gerard.)[1]

> The more interaction there is between the individual members of a social system, the more does the system itself become an individual in its own right, with characteristics belonging to itself as a whole, rather than to the individuals of which it is composed.

Let us explore the meaning of this statement. It implies, first, that a set of people who *do not* communicate with one another is the same as the sum of the people in the set. In this case the whole is *equal* to the sum of the parts. Here we would learn more by studying the individual people than by studying the set of people.

Second, the statement implies that a set of people who *do* communicate with one another is, somehow, more than the sum of the people in the set. Here the whole is *greater* than the sum of the parts. A set of interacting people will behave as an individual unit in its own right. This unit will have new characteristics—new properties—that none of the individual people had. Some of these properties *won't even make sense when they are considered in the context of a single person. These properties of the system are called emergent* properties, because they "emerge" when we shift our perspective from the individual person to the group of communicating people.

But what is the source of these emergent properties? Since the only difference between the set of *independent* people (the ones who do not communicate) and the set of *interdependent* ones (those who do comunicate) is the presence or absence of communication, the emergent properties must result from the communication relationships that bind the individual people together into a larger unit.

Some examples will help to make these points more clear. Consider a set composed of ten people selected at random from all the people whose birthdays fall on 17 December. The only point of commonality is an arbitrary (and rather silly) criterion of birthdays. The set of people has no organization. Each person is independent of all the others. The actions of each person are unrelated to the actions of the others. The set can be described only in terms of the individuals of which it is composed.

Now consider a set of ten scientists working together in a research laboratory. Each scientist has a specified role, and the scientists are coordinated in such a way that the group depends on the continued contributions of the whole group. These people are highly interdependent. Because their communication relations allow them to coordinate their actions, they can work together as a group; and the group can accomplish more than the individuals could even consider.

The main difference here is the existence of *organized relationships* that tie the individuals together into a single coordinated unit. Not only are these relationships made possible through communication, they are dependent on communication for their continued existence.

It is more than the existence of communication relationships that allows organizations to perform highly complex tasks. *Organization* is necessary as well. This is why the phrase "organized relationships" was used above instead of just the word "relationships." It is possible to have a group of people who communicate with one another but not in an organized way. For example, the people at a cocktail party can communicate with one another; but since they are not organized in any particular way, they don't work together as a unit. What seems to be as important as the presence or absence of communication relationships is the presence or absence of order or pattern—organization—in the set of relationships. In other words, the *relationships* among people are themselves *interdependent*. The relationship between one pair of individuals is dependent on or influenced by the other relationships in which those people may be involved.

The network approach to communication in organizations is based on these theoretical notions. In order to understand either the behaviour of the whole system or the way the whole influences any single person in the system, it is necessary to examine the organization of the relationships that bind the individual people together into the larger unit. It is this focus on organization that makes the network approach a systems approach.

This approach to the study of organizational communication is relatively new. For this reason both the research techniques and the theory of communication networks are relatively primitive. The ideas described in the rest of this paper are therefore only the beginning of what promises to become an important area in communication.

The remainder of this article is divided into three sections. The first, loosely called "Theory," introduces and briefly discusses several theoretical issues related to communication networks. The second section describes the methods that are used in network research, and the third presents some of the research findings. Although the material has been divided into three apparently discrete categories, the actual development of the area has progressed in a much more integrated fashion. While discussions of this sort seem naturally to begin with theory and move toward findings, such clear progressions are not seen in practice. Rather, it seems that all three areas—theory, methodology, and findings—advance in parallel. Since a historical recounting would thus be confusing and difficult to follow, the arbitrary (and possibly misleading) category system of theory, methods, and findings will be used here.

## I. THEORY

### A. The Form of Communication Networks: The Structural Model

The goal of the network approach is to gain an understanding of the organization of communication networks and to learn how other phenomena are related to charateristics of networks. In a sense, then, the starting point for this approach is the identification of the types of organizational pattern found in communication networks. The basic model that is seen most frequently in the literature is a hierarchical one. At the lowest level are individual people. At the next level are groups of individuals who have most of their interactions with one another. Then there are groups of groups, and so on, up to the level of the whole system.

Support for the validity of this model can be seen in a diverse range of organizations. Both human-information processing theory and organization theory suggest that the optimum size for efficient work groups is from seven to twelve people. This is within the range of the effective span of control limits that restrict supervisors. In larger groups so much effort must be spent in coordination that the performance of the group suffers. In very large organizations, groups can be arranged in a hierarchy of departments or divisions, which make up additional levels between the whole system and the work group. As we shall see in Section Three, the data support this basic model.

Of course, there must be some way to coordinate the actions of the groups. The first way of accomplishing this goal involves direct contacts between members of different groups. The individuals connected by these *bridge links* are sometimes called *bridges*. Second, there will be individuals who serve as *liaisons,* providing communication channels between the groups. Obviously there is greater need for both bridges and liaisons in very large systems, where there are many groups.

So far nothing has been said that goes beyond classical models of organizational structure. Indeed, the basic model outlined above worked well for many years. It was not until the development of computerized network-analysis techniques in the early seventies that more explicit formal definitions were put forth. In fact, it was the nature of the computer that required more advanced definitions to be developed.

The analysis of communication networks by traditional methods required very large expenditures of time and effort. It took hundreds of hours to do a single network analysis for what are now considered to be medium-sized organizations—about 300 people. Work was begun on the development of computer programs that would speed the analysis sufficiently to make it possible to study many networks. Computers, however, require very explicit and complete instructions, and the network models in use at the time were relatively vague, as well as unclear and sometimes inconsistent.

*1. Network Roles.* This situation led to the advancement of a more sophisticated network model. (Fig. 41.1) The new model was based on the old one, but it was more precise about the concepts it included in its definition. The concept of group was retained, but it was made much more explicit. Where the old definition simply said "a set of people who interact with each other more than with non–members," the new definition put forward several criteria that had to be met:

a. There must be at least three members.
b. Each member has more than half of his or her interaction with other members.
c. There must be some path, lying entirely within the group, from each member to every other member.
d. It must not be possible to split the group into disconnected parts by removing a small set of members.

The first two criteria are straightforward. The third was introduced to prevent situations in which completely separated subsets would be identified as single groups; and the fourth prevents cases in which two or more groups, connected by a single communication link, are identified as one group.

Under this definition, a *group member* would be a person having more than half of his or her interaction with other members of the same group.

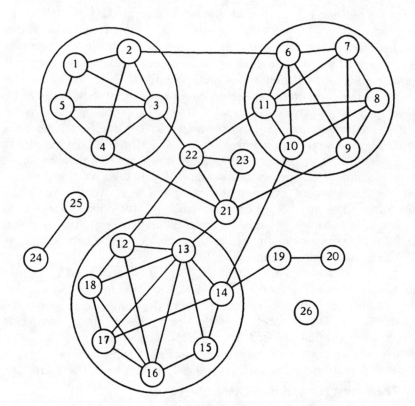

| Group Members | | Linkers | | Non-Participants | |
| --- | --- | --- | --- | --- | --- |
| Group A: | 1,2,3,4,5 | Direct | | Isolate Type 1: | 26 |
| Group B: | 6,7,8,9,10,11 | Liaisons: | 21,22 | Isolate Type 2: | 20 |
| Group C: | 12,13,14,15, | Indirect | | Tree Node: | 19 |
| | 16,17,18 | Liaison: | 23 | Isolated Dyad: | 24,25 |

**Fig. 41.1**
**Network roles**

Individuals functioning as specialized *linkers* are divided into two categories—those having most of their interaction with members of groups (but not with members of any *single* group), and those having the majority of their interaction with non–members (i.e., with other liaisons). The first category of linkers are called *direct liaisons;* the second are called *indirect* or *multi–step* liaisons. Direct liaisons provide direct links between groups, and indirect liaisons provide indirect links by connecting the liaisons who have contacts with groups.

In most organizations there are some individuals who do not participate in the communication flows through the network in the same way that group members and liaisons do. To differentiate them from the *participants*, they are called, simply enough, *non participants*. This class is divided into several types of *isolates*, including both those who have no links whatsoever to anyone in the network and those who have only one link to participants.

*2. Relationships.* The concept of *link* was elaborated at the same time network roles were made more explicit. Because the communication relationship itself was so basic to the model, it was one of the first concepts to be specified. The following three characteristics of relationships are commonly used in the description of communication networks: *function* or *content*, *strength*, and *symmetricality*.

The *function* of a relationship refers to the particular type of information that is communicated. For example, one strategy divides all interaction into two types—*formal* and *informal*. Another scheme uses three types—*production, innovation*, and *maintenance*. Production is defined as communication about matters related to getting the job done. Innovation refers to communication about the new ways of doing things, and maintenance is information communication about social or emotional matters.

The *strength* of the relationship most often refers to the amount of time spent in interaction, the frequency of communication, or some other idea that gets at the magnitude of the relationship.

Finally, the relationship might be *symmetrical,* where information or influence flows in both directions; or *asymmetrical,* where the influence goes in one direction only.

*3. Conceptual vs. Operational Terminology.* Most of the terms mentioned so far refer to the conceptual part of the network model. These conceptual terms must be related to operational procedures that can be used to build a model of the system in the form of data. This translation is accomplished by the specification of *operational definitions* and *measurement* procedures.

For example, while we speak of people in the organization, we use the term *nodes* in network analysis. Similarly we use *links* to represent *relationships*. While people in the organization are connected by relationships, nodes are connected by links. The link *is not* the relationship; it indicates that there is a relationship between the people corresponding to the nodes it connects. This may seem to be a useless philosophical complication, but it is important to keep the distinction clear.

If we conceptualize the relation as symmetrical, then whenever A is related to B, B should also be related to A. In other words, the data should show a link from node A to node B as being *reciprocated*. This means there will also be a link from node B to node A. If this is not the case—if the link from A to B is not reciprocated—we know there is a problem. Perhaps we were wrong when we conceptualized the relationship as symmetrical. Perhaps the person corresponding to node B forgot about the person corresponding to node A. Perhaps a status difference is leading to systematic bias in the data. Examining the relationship between the conceptual model and the data can make it possible to uncover problems of this sort before it is too late to correct them.

  *4. Useful Measures of Network Characteristics.* It is useful to define precise quantitative measure of certain network characteristics. Perhaps the most useful of these measures are *integrativeness* at the ·individual level, *density* at the group level, and *structuring* at the whole–system level.

  a. The concept behind *integrativeness* has a long history of use in network studies. For example, Granovetter's famous "Strength of Weak Ties" article used this concept to explain underlying causes of important aspects of large–scale societal structure.[2] The original, relatively informal definition of integrativeness was "the degree of interconnection of the individual in the network" or the "social fit" of the individual.

  A more recent, explicit definition captures part of the meaning in these earlier versions: A person's integrativeness is defined as the degree to which the person's contacts are linked to one another. This value is calculated by dividing the actual number of links among the person's contacts by the maximum possible number of such links. The obtained value varies from zero to one, where zero indicates minimal integration and one indicates maximal integration. When this concept is applied to a network of friendship relations, an individual whose friends are friends of one another would have a high integrativeness score. Danowski describes these people as having *interlocking* networks.[3] An individual whose friends are not friends of one another would have a low integrativeness score. Danowski's term for this kind of network is *radial*. In formal organizations, the concept has quite a different use: Individuals with radial networks provide the only direct link between the people with whom they have links. These individuals are thus important for the continued flow of information through the network. Individuals with interlocking networks, on the other hand, add redundancy to the network, since the people with whom they connect are already linked to one another.

b. A group's *density* is defined to the actual number of within-group links divided by the maximum possible number of links. This value also runs from zero to one in principle, although it never reaches zero. Density can also be calculated for the whole system, where it has many statistical applications. Density is a rough index of the total amount of interconnection among a set of individuals.

c. *Structure* is the amount of order or organization in a network. Whereas density is the degree of interdependence among *individuals,* structure is the degree of interdependence among the *relationships* linking the individuals. It is defined as a deviation from complete chaos, so that a value of zero would indicate that the system is essentially random, and a value of one would indicate total constraint or maximum order. While a highly organized network shows very clear differentiation into groups, a random network is not organized; it does not break down into clear groups. Rather, it appears as a more or less homogeneous web. For this reason the structure measure can be used as an index of differentiation in the network.[4]

The characteristics and relationships described so far are all internal *structural* properties of networks. When these issues are examined by themselves (i.e., without being related to the social context in which the network exists), the research approach is called *structural* analysis. This type of analysis is appropriate when relations between various structural properties are of interest. If the goal of research is to understand how networks influence and are influenced by other issues, however, a different type of analysis is required. Because it examines networks in the context of other social variables, this type of analysis is called *contextual* analysis. Where structural analysis focuses on the form of the network, contextual analysis looks at the content or meaning of the network. The next section describes some examples of contextual network research.

## B. The Context of Communication Networks

The network approach has been used in numerous applications. Both theoretical and empirical connections have been drawn between various aspects of communication networks and individual, organizational, and social life. For example, there have been studies of personality characteristics of individuals with radial and interlocking networks, the relation between network position and attitudes, the kinds of relationships that connect people in different levels of organizations, managerial style and network characteristics, the relation between network characteristics and content or purpose of interaction, the relation between network structure and task characteristics, and the relation between an organization's environment and network characteristics. Several examples of this research are briefly described here.

*1. The Relation between the Individual and the Network.*

a. We have already seen how the limits on the amount of information any single person can process put limits on the size of efficient work groups. For this reason we would expect groups to have between seven and twelve members. Furthermore, we would expect larger groups to be less densely connected than smaller groups. In situations where precise coordination of the actions of members is important, the need for all members to communicate with one another would lead us to expect to find small, highly connected groups, where each person is tightly integrated into the group.

b. Since the members of groups spend most of their time interacting with one another, rather than with nonmembers, we would expect them to have similar attitudes toward their jobs. Since much informal communication takes place when people work closely, we would expect the similarity of ideas and attitudes to go beyond work–related matters.

Members of different groups, however, do not exchange ideas or opinions on a regular basis, and we would therefore expect different groups to have different views on a variety of topical areas.

These similarities and differences are more likely to be significant when the communication density of groups is high and when there are few connections between groups. This would especially be the case in very large organizations where most of the coordination of groups is carried out through liaisons, who do not belong to groups themselves. This is, perhaps, a source of alienation for the majority of organization members, who feel primary loyalty to their work groups and often a sense of impersonal mechanistic relations to the organization as a whole.

c. Because of the different communication relations they have with others in the organization, occupants of different network roles will have different kinds of interpersonal environments. Group members can be contrasted to liaisons, for example, in terms of their levels of integrativeness. Whereas group members will be more integrated into their groups (the people with whom they communicate also communicate with each other), this is not the case for liaisons. In fact, the very function of liaisons is to provide connections between parts of the network that would not otherwise be connected. Liaisons are therefore likely to be forced to relate to a wider variety of types of people than are group members.[5]

These important individuals are therefore likely to develop more complex views of the organization and of issues related to its functioning.[6] This derives in part from the exposure of liaisons to many different situations in which a variety of viewpoints and attitudes, often contradictory, are expressed. There are thus fewer opportunities to verify socially any particular idea or set of ideas than would be the case in the context of a highly connected group.

Isolates may be contrasted with participants in much the same way, with the difference here being that, whereas both group members and other participants have several links to the network, isolates have either no links at all or only one link. Isolates thus tend to have only a low degree of social integration into the system. Along with isolation comes a sense of alienation, a feeling that is supported by the fact that isolates, to a degree, are "outsiders." Other characteristics associated with isolation include low degrees of trust in other members of the organization, an absence of willingness to share information with others, and low degrees of commitment to the organization. It is important to notice that it is not clear whether a particular type of person becomes an isolate or whether people who are put into isolated positions adopt the characteristics noted above.

d. The relative positions of a pair of people in the network can have significant effects on the nature of the relationship between the people. For example, traditional organization theory suggests that vertical relationships (i.e., relationships between people of different status levels) differ from horizontal ones (relationships between people at the same status level) in many ways. Compared with the high–status person, the low–status person tends to see interactions with the high–status person as being more important and more frequent. Similar patterns are seen in many circumstances where there is a real or perceived difference in status, such as age, seniority, education, or occupation.

Other sources of discrepancy have also been examined. For example, some individuals regularly tend to report more communication than do the individuals with whom they interact. The study of over– and under–estimators promises to provide much information about the way individuals relate to others in the network.

*2. Networks and Organizational Information Needs.* Using other theoretical approaches, we can relate the structure of the network to the functioning of the organization. With these approaches, we are concerned with the relation between the organization of the network and basic information needs of the organization. At least three of these perspectives seem promising.

a. We can take what might be called a "basic communication theory" approach to networks, based on a set of assumptions about communication that we believe to hold in general. We then apply these assumptions to the particular network in question; drawing conclusions about its overall efficiency, identifying parts of the network that are likely to give rise to a variety of problems, and developing suggestions that would allow the organization to be modified in such a way as to reduce the problems.

The basic assumptions might be as follows:

1. Individual people have limited capacities for information processing.
2. The more links a message goes through, the greater the chance that errors or distortion will creep into the message.
3. The more links a message must go through, the longer it will take to reach its destination.
4. Accurate communication is more likely in horizontal (equal–status) relationships than in vertical (different–status) relationships.

Problem areas would be identified as situations involving the following:

1. Individuals having very large numbers of links, especially when the integrativeness of these individuals is low. These will be cases in which the individual in question provides the only direct connection between the others.
2. Long chains of links connecting parts of the network that should be in direct contact for reasons of either accuracy or speed.
3. Chains of links involving many vertical links where alternate routes, using only horizontal links, could be substituted.

Although this brief example seems very simple, the use of this approach can lead to significant benefits for both the managers and the participants in organizations.

b. A second general approach would be one that centers on the overall problem of coordination. Here we would be concerned with problems that are especially important in very large organizations. It has been pointed out that, because of practical limitations, the optimum size for work groups ranges from seven to twelve. As the size of the organization increases, coordination of the activities of the increasing number of groups becomes a more important problem. An analogy is provided by the examination of the role of elevators in tall buildings. In many ways, elevators are much like liaisons in networks: They provide links between the different floors of the building, much as liaisons provide links between the various groups. It is impractical to build very tall, narrow buildings, because more elevators are needed as more floors are added. This is due both to the increased volume of traffic and the large numbers of floors. In very tall buildings it is not practical to have elevators that stop at all floors. Imagine going to the ninety-second floor on an elevator that stops fifty or sixty times on the way up. One solution is to have express elevators that go relatively large distances to selected floors and local elevators that pick passengers up at the drop–off points of the express elevators and deliver them to narrower ranges of floors. With this kind of system, the overall average length of elevator rides is several minutes shorter than it would be with only local floor to floor service. Very large organizations can assure the same kind of hierarchical connection by providing special people whose function it is to connect the liaisons, who in turn have links with members of groups. This approach to networks would lead us to expect greater proportions of the participants in larger organizations to be linkers.

c. A general systems theory approach to networks centers on yet another set of variables and issues. For example, the type of task the organization performs is related in fundamental ways to the overall structure of the communication network. A production system, where the task is highly structured and involves standardized processes repeated with little variation, can be compared to a research and development firm, where the task is highly variable and unstructured. In the first case, one expects the information needs to be highly structured and regular, much as is the task of the organization. In this kind of situation, the communication network for production information can be highly "tuned" to maximize efficiency, since information needs are regular and predictable. We expect a high degree of structural differentiation in this kind of system. Flexibility is unnecessary. In fact, flexibility may be unwanted, because it will lower efficiency and cause error and delays.

Since the task of the research and development organization is both variable and unpredictable, we expect the information needs to reflect these characteristics. In other words, communications networks in this kind of organization will be less structured and more flexible. Each individual will have more options, and the network as a whole will be less differentiated and less organized. Flexibility in this situation is necessary if the organization is to survive.

The index of structural differentiation described in an earlier part of this paper was designed to be able to measure this kind of structuring. High values on this index indicate high degrees of organization, while low values mean that the network is less constrained and more flexible.

## II. METHODS

It is impossible within the constraints of this discussion to give a complete description of all the methods used in the analysis of communication networks. Therefore, I will present a brief summary of the most-often–used methods in order to show the general trends. I will begin with a description of the data–collection methods most frequently used in this kind of research. The rest of the section will be devoted to a review of the major analytic techniques in use at this time.

### A. *The Data for Network Analysis*

In order to do a network analysis, we need to know who is in the network and where the relationships are. When we are interested in a formal organization, it is easy to identify the members. In other situations, such as studies of communication about illegal drugs or the network of social connections through which a disease like AIDS spreads, it is more difficult to identify the boundary of the relevant social system. What is needed is a clear unambiguous criterion for determining whether or not a particular person is a member. In addition, there must be some way of ascertaining the relationships that tie the members to others in the system.

Relationships can be identified in several different ways. Sometimes it is possible to have observers who report on the interactions among the members of the system. Sometimes available records provide the same information. Telephone companies, for example, record numbers called by each of the customers in a particular community or service area. More often, though, the researcher must collect new data.

Most network studies rely on one of two basic methods for collecting the data. The first, called the *diary method,* requires the individuals to record all interactions in which they are involved. The second, called the *recall method,* requires them to remember their interaction patterns and record them on a specially designed form. Since the recall method is used more than the diary method, it will be worthwhile to explain in more detail how it works. (Many of the comments will apply also to the diary method.)

In studies involving fewer than a thousand people, the researcher prepares a *roster,* or list of all the people in the system. After each person's name are spaces used to record:

1. how often the respondent communicates with the individual,
2. how important the interaction is, and
3. the purpose or content of the interaction.

(The last category—content—is not used in many studies.)

Each respondent is asked to provide this information for every other person in the system. A sample communication network form is shown in Figure 41.2.

In studies involving large numbers of people, a roster format can be impractical because of its length. In these situations, respondents are asked to supply the names of the people with whom they interact. There are theoretical and pragmatic arguments both for and against the roster technique and the *open–ended method*.

The result of the measurement will be a list of communication links for each member of the system. The task of analysis is to create from this data a useful description of the system in terms of groups, network roles, and various indicators of structural characteristics of the network. If the study is contextual, additional data describing the characteristics of the individuals will be collected and utilized in the analysis.

### B. Analytic Methods

Before I describe the methods of analysis, it will be useful to define some concepts important to understanding what the methods do.

We begin with the *adjacency matrix*,[7] in which there is one row and one column for each member of the network. In the *binary* version, a "1" is placed in row $i$, column $j$, whenever Person $i$ reports a link with Person $j$. All the other entries in the matrix are set to zero. This is also called the "Who-to-Whom" matrix, because it indicates who is linked to whom. A small network, together with a binary adjacency matrix, is shown in Figure 41.3.

In the *scalar* version of the adjacency matrix, a number indicating the strength of the relationship is used instead of a zero or a one, which merely indicates the absence or presence of a relationship. Obviously, the scalar version is a more precise representation of the real situation.

A second useful concept is the *distance matrix*. Here again there is a row and a column for each individual in the network, but the entry in row $i$, column $j$ is the number of links in the shortest path from $i$ to $j$. The distance from any node to itself is zero. The shortest distance between any two nodes is one; and the longest is $n-1$, where $n$ is the number of people in the group. The distance matrix is obtained by performing an algebraic operation on the adjacency matrix.[8] Because there is no way of incorporating the strengths of links in the calculation of this type of distance matrix, calculations are done with the binary form of the adjacency matrix.

Please indicate by circling the appropriate numbers which people you talk to, how often you talk to them, and how important the interaction usually is. Use the coding system shown here.

FREQUENCY

1 = once/month
2 = once/week
3 = once/day
4 = several times/day

IMPORTANCE

1 = slightly important
2 = moderately important
3 = very important
4 = crucial to survival

| NAME | FREQUENCY | IMPORTANCE |
|---|---|---|
| John Jones | 1 2 3 4 | 1 2 3 4 |
| Emily Stuart | 1 2 3 4 | 1 2 3 4 |
| Tony Roberts | 1 2 3 4 | 1 2 3 4 |
| Linda Hall | 1 2 3 4 | 1 2 3 4 |
| Mark Smith | 1 2 3 4 | 1 2 3 4 |

Please indicate how often you talk to the following people about each of the three topic areas. Use this system for coding your responses.

1. Once a month
2. Once a week
3. Once a day
4. Several times a day

| NAME | PRODUCTION: GETTING MY JOB DONE, DAY-TO-DAY MATTERS | INNOVATION: NEW IDEAS FOR WAYS OF DOING THINGS | SOCIAL RELATIONS, INFORMAL FRIENDSHIP CONVERSATIONS, ETC |
|---|---|---|---|
| Harry | 1 2 3 4 | 1 2 3 4 | 1 2 3 4 |
| Timothy | 1 2 3 4 | 1 2 3 4 | 1 2 3 4 |
| Maude | 1 2 3 4 | 1 2 3 4 | 1 2 3 4 |
| Jenny | 1 2 3 4 | 1 2 3 4 | 1 2 3 4 |
| Donald | 1 2 3 4 | 1 2 3 4 | 1 2 3 4 |
| Michael | 1 2 3 4 | 1 2 3 4 | 1 2 3 4 |

Shown here are examples of two different data collection "instruments". The one on the top provides information on both frequency and importance. The one on the bottom provides information for three different content areas.

**Fig. 41.2**
**Data collection instruments**

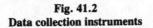

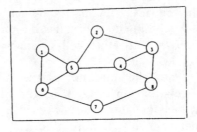

BINARY FORM

DISTANCE FORM

At the top of this figure is shown a hypothetical eight-node network. The matrix directly below the network is a binary version of the network. In this matrix, each node has a row and a column. The i,j entry of the matrix is 1 if node i is linked to node j.

The matrix on the right is the distance matrix for the same network. The entry in the i,j element of the matrix is the number of links in the shortest path from node i to node j.

**Fig. 41.3**
**Binary and distance matrices**

## IMAGINARY DATA ILLUSTRATING
### THE MATRIX MANIPULATION PROCEDURE

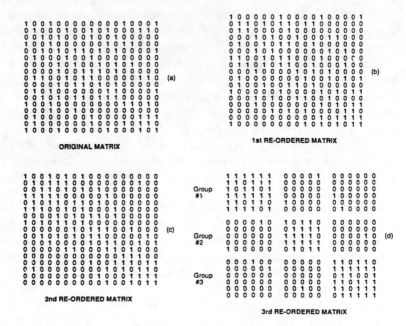

(a) shows the original sociomatrix ; (b), (c) and (d) are the matrices resulting from successive re-orderings of rows and columns of the original matrix. In (d) the groups are identified as blocks of non-zero entries on the main diagonal.

**Fig. 41.4**
**Imaginary data illustrating the matrix manipulation procedure**

We now turn to a description of the methods. It should be noted here that the discussion throughout this section is necessarily limited. Many important points and limitations are not included. Furthermore, the methods described are only a sample of the many available methods.[9]

*1. The Sociogram.* The sociogram is both the most intuitive and the most limited of the methods of analysis. In a sociogram, individuals are represented by points and communication relationships *between* individuals by lines drawn between the corresponding points. (A sociogram is illustrated in Figure 41.1.) In examining the sociogram for a given network, it is possible to determine the structure of the system, in terms of cliques or clusters of people who communicate primarily with each other—the "groups" in the definition used in this chapter.

The introduction of the sociogram was a major advance for the field, offering for the first time a concrete way of representing systems of interacting individuals. The process seemed quite elegant and was operationally very simple. The graphical representation of group structures provided by sociograms proved to be useful to both practitioners and theoreticians alike. For small simple systems, the sociogram seemed to be the ideal tool. Despite these good points, however, there were problems with this method. As the size of the system increased, so did the difficulty of analysis; so that for systems having over a hundred members, the method was practically worthless. It is virtually impossible to "comprehend" a sociogram for a system with as many as 200 members. This problem was further aggravated by the lack of systematic procedures that produce replicable results. Two independent investigators, using the same data, seldom arrive at sociograms that are even vaguely similar.

*2. Matrix Manipulation.* This technique is named after the method used to prepare the data prior to identification of groups. In this process, rows and columns of the adjacency matrix are simultaneously permuted in such a way as to move as many of the nonzero entries as possible close to the main diagonal of the matrix. If there are any groups, they will be visible as clusters of nonzero entries, as shown in Figure 41.4. Groups are the sets of nodes whose columns and rows comprise these clusters. They are loosely defined as sets of people who interact more with one another than with those outside the group. Since group detection and identification are accomplished by visual inspection of the permuted matrix, this approach is also subject to error, although perhaps not as much as the sociogram method.

*3. Matrix Multiplication.* The binary adjacency matrix specifies which individuals are connected by direct (one–step) links. Call this matrix "$A$." When this matrix is multiplied by itself, the result, $A^2$, specifies which individuals are connected by two–step links. $A^2$ multiplied by $A$ gives $A^3$, which specifies which individuals are connected by three–step links. The matrix multiplication method detects groups by using $A$, $A^2$, $A^3$, $A^4$, etc. Utilizing both direct and indirect links to the rest of the system, this process allows an individual's integration into the system to be assessed. Although this method detects the presence or absence of groups, the technique does not enable specification of the number of groups or their membership. The concept of "group" is not clearly defined here, since groups are only detected— not identified—by this method. In spite of its limitations, the matrix multiplication technique is important because it made the tools of matrix algebra familiar to network researchers.

*4. Factor Analysis.* Two techniques employing factor analysis have been used—direct factor analysis of sociometric data and factor analysis of a correlation matrix constructed from the raw sociomatrix. Both factor–analysis methods construct new dimensions corresponding to variance patterns, where successive dimensions or factors account for as much of the remaining variance as is possible, using linear combinations of the variables (which are people in the network). Each factor then becomes a group, once an appropriate arbitrary cutting point is chosen to discriminate between members and nonmembers (people loading highly or people not loading on a given factor).

There are many problems with the use of factor analysis in the network situation. Although it is not possible to discuss these problems in depth, it is enough to point out that they are so severe that this method is not used when alternatives are available. Factor analysis is mentioned here because its use marked the beginning of the application of powerful computer programs to the analysis of network data.

*5. Multidimensional Scaling Methods.* Multidimensional scaling techniques (both metric and nonmetric) attempt to identify groups from the sociomatrix by employing measures of the "distance" between points in a "sociometric space". (There is no single agreed–on method of measuring "distance" between people in network terms. Many long–standing disagreements with regard to the use of these methods have stemmed from this problem.) To use these methods, we must determine first the "minimum dimensionality" of the "space" and second, the projections of each observation onto the dimensions. Since the data must take the form of "distances" between persons, the dimensional axes will represent characteristics of the members of the cliques rather than actual communication behaviours. Groups, then, are based on the projections of original observations onto the new dimensions.

Neither the groups produced by factor analysis nor the ones produced by multidimensional scaling will satisfy the definition of *group* presented in this chapter, for in borrowing analytic techniques originally developed for other uses and attempting to apply them to the network situation, both methods also borrow the definitions and assumptions associated with those techniques.

*6. SOCK and COMPLT.* These computer programs, some of the earliest ones designed specifically for network analysis, work together as a package. They use only binary symmetrical data, where each person must choose a specified number of others in the network. The results produced by this method include a family of groups defined in graph–theoretical terms that are mathematically elegant but not necessarily theoretically relevant for communication networks.

*7. Blockmodeling Techniques.* These methods try to identify "blocks" of *structurally equivalent* individuals. Structural equivalence means that the members of any particular block have similar patterns of interaction with members of the other blocks. Blocks are unrelated to groups as we have defined them in that there is no implication that the members of a block cooperate or coordinate with one another. In fact, the members of a block need not be connected at all in any way. The most well–known blockmodeling program is CONCOR.

*8. NEGOPY.* NEGOPY is a computer program for network analysis based on the definitions described earlier in this chapter. It begins with the data describing the relationships of each person in the system. The results of analysis include a specification of the network structure, in terms of groups and their members, liaisons, isolates, and so on. The output also identifies patterns of connection between groups, as well as relationships between each individual and the rest of the network. Besides the structural information, a variety of statistics and numerical indicators of different aspects of the network are provided. The results produced by NEGOPY fit directly into the theoretical discussion presented earlier in this chapter.

More comprehensive comparisons appear in the literature, and several articles written by the developers of the various methods appear in the bibliography at the end of the chapter.

## IV. RESULTS OF NETWORK RESEARCH

Many network studies have been completed in the last fifteen years. The most important basic findings are reviewed in the following discussion. The organization of this section parallels the organization of the section on theory. Findings about basic structural characteristics appear first, followed by findings relating individuals to the network. Finally, studies related to the major communication theory and systems approaches are described.

### A. Basic Structural Characteristics

The structural model of groups connected by bridges and liaisons has been supported in almost every communication system that has been studied. Although group size varies from one system to another, all large systems that have been studied, from banks to school systems to naval fighter squadrons to Korean villages, break down into a structure of connected groups. Only data from random systems or data generated by the use of random number tables fails to be organized in this way. The fact that we *find* groups when we look is important. Some analytic methods *impose* their models on the data. These methods would *create* groups, even if the data did not contain the kind of patterns we have identified in our definition of groups. However, when we use analytic methods that are consistent with the theoretical model described in this chapter, we will not find groups where they do not exist.

### B. Relations Between Individuals and the Network

Nodes have between five and fifteen links on the average, regardless of the type of network or the content area being studied. Groups have between five and twelve members in most cases, although larger groups are seen in some networks.

In studies of the relationship between group membership and attitudes, it has been found that the members of each group are similar to one another and different from the members of other groups in terms of their attitudes. In fact, one study was fairly successful in predicting group structure on the basis of attitudinal information alone.

In studies comparing liaisons and isolated with group members,[9] some interesting differences have been found. For example, liaisons report more feelings of alienation than do group members, and believe that the information they receive about matters related to getting their jobs done is insufficient and of low quality. Group members, on the other hand, are more satisfied with the information they get.

Isolates have a greater tendency to withhold information or to feel generally dissatisfied with communication than do participants. Furthermore, isolates tend to report greater use of written or telephone messages than do participants, who feel that most of their communication has taken place in face–to–face verbal exchanges. A general conclusion is that communication participation is associated with perceptions of increased information flow, more redundancy, and greater general satisfaction with communication.

### C. Research Relating Networks to Other Theoretic Approaches

It has been suggested that larger organizations require a greater proportion of linkers than do smaller ones. A comparison of data from three network studies[10] supports this hypothesis: The percentage of linkers was 9.5 for a network with 120 members, 19.9 for a network with 239 members, and 31.9 for one with 973 members. Although these numbers come from only three networks, they are in the direction we would expect.

Other preliminary studies indicate that both the type of organization and its communication needs can affect the degree of structuring or organization in the network. For example, groups are more clearly differentiated in formal production networks than they are in social maintenance ones. The same kind of difference is seen in comparisons of established networks in standard production situations with networks in either newly formed organizations or with networks in nonstandard task environments.

These findings suggest an important relation between the information needs of the members of the system and the amount and type of organization. The network will be more organized when the needs have been established over time, especially in predictable environments, than in cases where either the organization is relatively new or where the needs are not predictable because of the nature of the task. In other words, networks will be less structured and more flexible where information needs are more variable and uncertain.

### V. SUMMARY

It is clear that the network approach to the study of communication flows provides a uniquely useful perspective, integrating the communication flow into the larger context of the communication system of which the individual person is a member. In so doing, this approach provides a means by which we can begin to study and understand the relation between the process of communication and the structure of social systems to which we belong. Furthermore, the network approach allows us to relate these organizational phenomena to environmental demands and constraints and to see how these influences come back to change both the way the individual relates to the communication system and the way the individual views the world in which he or she lives.

The network approach is new. Modern analytic capabilities have been available for only a few years. There have not been enough studies done to allow us to make confident statements about relations between communication networks and other aspects of the world. We do have some preliminary findings, however, and I have tried to indicate their implications. It is clear that the area is fertile; it is also clear that much work needs to be done if we are to benefit from this approach.

### Notes

1. H. Gerard, "Units and Concepts of Biology," in *Modern Systems Research for the Behavioral Scientist,* ed. W. Buckley (Chicago: Aldine, 1968), p. 53.
2. Mark S. Granovetter, "The Strength of Weak Ties," *American Journal of Sociology* (1973), vol. 78, pp. 1360–80.
3. J. A. Danowski, "Personal Network Integration: Infographic, Psychographic and Demographic Characteristics," paper presented to information/systems division, International Communication Association, San Francisco, May 1984.
4. The actual computational procedures used to measure structure are too complex to describe here. See W. D. Richards, Jr., "Network Analysis in Large Complex Organizations: Theoretical Basis; The Nature of Structure; Techniques and Methods—Tools," four papers presented to the International Communication Association, New Orleans, 1974; Richards, "A Coherent Systems Methodology for the Analysis of Human Communication Systems," unpublished dissertation, Stanford University, 1976; and Richards, "Getting Data for Network Analysis II: Developing the Measurement Instrument," paper presented at the International Communication Association, Chicago, May 1986.
5. E. Rogers, in his book *The Diffusion of Innovations* (Glencoe, Ill.: Free Press, 1962), speaks of change agents—rural extension service workers— as being more *cosmopolitan* than the people with whom they work. This is because it is the job of change agents to bring new ideas to the farmers, who would not otherwise learn of them. In order to do this, the extension agents must be in contact with people who are likely to live and work in urban areas. They tend to be more educated and have less traditional ideas about life in general. Most importantly, they are more open to change.
6. Danowski *op. cit.,* found that liaisons:
   —want more input into the decision–making process, don't think their ideas are considered enough;
   —are less likely to participate in a "rubber stamp" vote to approve a proposal;
   —consult more formal information sources about the external work environment;

—read employee publications less;
—are asked more often for their opinion;
—are more independent, have greater self–control, and value their independence more;
—have more education;
—have higher incomes.

7. The term "adjacency" comes from a branch of mathematics known as "graph theory." Graph theory deals with sets of points and "edges" which connect some of the points to others. A pair of points connected by an edge are said to be "adjacent" to one another. The adjacency matrix therefore shows which points are adjacent to one another.

8. The calculation requires the adjacency matrix to be raised to successively higher powers. The $i,j$ element in the distance matrix is set to the number of the power on which the $i,j$ element of the adjacency matrix becomes nonzero.

9 See the studies by Roberts & O'Reilly and Roberts et al. in the bibliography.

10. See Richards, "A Coherent Systems Methodology For the Analysis of Human Communication Systems," *op. cit.*

## Bibliography

Alba, R. D. "COMPLT: A Program for Analyzing Sociometric Data and Clustering Similarity Matrices." *Behavioral Science* (1972), vol. 17, pp. 566–67.

Alba, R. D. "A Graph–Theoretic Definition of a Sociometric Clique." *J. Math. Soc.* (1973), vol. 3, pp. 113–26.

Alba, R. D. and M. P. Guttman. *SOCK: A Sociometric Analysis System* (New York: Columbia University Report, 1974).

Alba, R. D. and G. Moore. "Elite Social Circles." In R. S. Burt and M. J. Minor (eds.), *Applied Network Analysis* (Beverly Hills, CA: Sage, 1983).

Allen, T. J. and S. I. Cohens. "Information Flow in Research and Development Laboratories." *Administrative Science Quarterly* (1969), vol. 14, pp. 12–20.

Alt, J. E. and N. Schofield. "CLIQUE: A Suite of Programs for Extracting Cliques from a Symmetric Graph." *Behavioral Science* (1975), vol. 20, pp. 134–35.

Arabie, P. (1977). "Clustering Representations of Group Overlap." *J. Math. Soc.* (1977), vol. 5, pp. 113–28.

Arabie, P. "Clustering Representations of Group Overlap." *J. Math. Soc.* (1977), vol. 5, pp. 113–28.

Auron, P. E., W. P. Rindone, C. P. H. Vary, J. J. Celentano, and J. N. Vournakis. "Computer aided prediction of RNA secondary structures." *Nucleic Acids Res.* (1984), vol. 10, no. 1, pp. 403–19.

Barney, J. B. "Dimensions of Informal Social Network Structure: Toward a Contingency Theory of Informal Relations in Organizations." *Social Networks* (1985), vol. 7, pp. 1–46.

Barney, J. B., and W. G. Ouchi. "Efficient Boundaries." Unpublished paper, Graduate School of Management, UCLA.,

Berkowitz, S. D. *An Introduction to Structural Analysis* (Toronto: Butterworths, 1982).

Berkowitz, S. D. and B. Wellman (eds.). *Structural Sociology* (Cambridge, England: Cambridge University Press, 1983).

Berlo, D. K., R. V. Farace, P. R. Monge, and J. A. Danowski. "An Analysis of the Communication Structure of the Office for Civil Defense." Technical Report. (East Lansing: Michigan State University Department of Communication, 1972).

Bernard, H. H. and P. D. Killworth. "Some Formal Properties of Networks." Technical Report. (Arlington, Va. ONR (Contract No. N00014-73-A-0417-0001-117-949, 1975).

Breiger, R. L. "Career Attributes and Network Structure: A Blockmodel Study of a Biomedical Research Speciality." *Am. Soc. Rev.* (1976), vol. 41, pp. 117-35.

Breiger, R. L., S. A. Boorman, and P. Arabie. "An Algorithm for Clustering Relational Data with Applications to Social Network Analysis and Comparison with Metric Dimensional Scaling." *J. Math. Psych.* (1975), vol. 12, pp. 328-83.

Burns, J. and G. M. Stalker. *The Management of Innovation* (London: Tavistock, 1961).

Burt, R. S. "Positions in Networks." *Social Forces* (1976), vol. 55, pp. 106-31.

Burt, R. S. "Cohesion Versus Structural Equivalence as a Basis for Network Subgroups." *Soc. Methods & Res.* (1978), vol. 7, pp. 189-212.

Burt, R. S. "Relational Equilibrium in a Social Topology." *J. Math. Soc.* (1979), vol. 6, pp. 211-52.

Burt, R. S. "Actor Interests in a Social Topology: Foundations for a Structural Theory of Action." *Soc. Inquiry* (1980), vol. 49, pp. 107-32.

Burt, R. S. *Toward a Structural Theory of Action: Network Models of Stratification, Perception and Action in a System of Actors* (New York: Academic Press, 1981).

Carrington, P. J. and G. H. Heil. "COBLOC: A Hierarchical Method for Blocking Network Data." *J. Math.Soc.* (1981), vol. 8, pp. 103-32.

Carrington, P. J., G. H. Heil, and S. D. Berkowitz. "A Goodness of Fit Index for Blockmodels." *Social Networks* (1980), vol. 2, pp. 219-34.

Carroll, J. D. and P. Arabie. "Multidimensional Scaling." *Annual Review of Psychology* (1980), vol. 31, pp. 607-49.

Carroll, W., J. Fox and M. Ornstein. "The Network of Directorate Interlocks Among Largest Canadian Firms." *Can. Rev. Soc. & Anth.* (1982), vol. 19, pp. 44-69.

Cartwright, D. and F. Harary. "Structural Balance: A Generalization of Heider's Theory." *Psychological Review* (1956), vol. 63, pp. 277-93.

Crane, D. *Invisible Colleges: Discussion of Knowledge in Scientific Communities* (Chicago: University of Chicago Press, 1972).

Danowski, J. A. "An Information Processing Model of Organizations: A Focus on Environmental Uncertainty and Communication Network Structuring." (New Orleans: International Communication Association, 1974).

Danowski, J. A. "Personal Network Integration: Infographic, Psychographic and Demographic Characteristics." Paper presented to information/systems division, International Communication Association, San Francisco, May 1984.

Davis, J. A. "Clustering and Structural Balance in Graphs." *Human Relations* (1967), vol. 20, pp. 181-87.

Davis, J. A. "Sociometric Triads as Multi-Variate Systems." *J. Math. Soc.* (1977), vol. 5, pp. 41–60.

Davis, J. A. and S. Leinhardt. "The Structure of Positive Interpersonal Relations in Small Groups." In J. Berger, M. J. Zelditch, and B. Anderson (eds.), *Sociological Theories in Progress,* Vol. 2 (New York: Houghton-Mifflin, 1972).

Delattre, M. and P. Hansen. "Bicriterion Cluster Analysis." *IEEE Transactions on Pattern Analysis and Machine Intelligence,* PAMI-2 (1980), pp. 277–91.

Devereux, J., P. Haeberli, and O. Smithies. "A comprehensive set of sequence analysis programs for VAX." *Nucleic Acids Res.* (1984), vol. 12, no. 1, pp. 378–95.

Dill, W. R. "Environment as an Influence on Managerial Autonomy." *Administrative Science Quarterly* (1958), vol. 2, pp. 409–43.

Doreian, P. "Linear Models with Spatially Distributed Data: Spatial Disturbances or Spatial Effects." *Soc. Methods & Res.* (1980), vol. 9, pp. 29–66.

Doreian, P. "Maximum Likelihood Methods for Linear Models: Spatial Effect and Spatial Disturbance Terms." *Soc. Methods & Res.* (1982), vol. 10, pp. 243–70.

Dubin, R. and S. Spray. "Executive Behavior and Interaction." *Industrial Relations* (1964), vol. 3, pp. 99–108.

Edwards, J. A. and P. R. Monge. "The Validation of Mathematical Indices of Communication Structure." *Communication Yearbook* (1977), vol. 1, pp. 183–94.

Eisenberg, E. M.; R. V. Farace; P. R. Monge; E. P. Bettinghuis; R. Kurchner-Hawkins; K. Miller; and L. Rottman: "Communication Linkages in Interorganizational Systems: Review and Synthesis." *Progress in Communications Sciences* (1985), vol. 6, pp. 236–61.

Farace, R. V. and D. Johnson. "A Comparison of Selected Network Characteristics Across Six Organizations." Paper presented to annual meetings of International Communication Association, New Orleans, 1974.

Farace, R. V. and T. Mabee. "Communication Network Analysis Methods." In P. R. Monge and J. N. Cappella (eds.), *Multivariate Techniques for Human Communication Research* (New York: Academic Press, 1980), pp. 365–92.

Farace, R. V., P. R. Monge, and H. M. Russell. *Communicating and Organizing* (Menlo Park, Calif.: Addison-Wesley, 1977).

Farace, R. V. and M. Pacanowsky. "Organizational Communication Role, Hierarchical Level and Relative Status." Paper presented to the Academy of Management Association, Seattle, 1974.

Felling, A. J. A. "A Graph-Theoretical Approach to the Structure of Local Elites." *Zeitschrift fur Soziologie* (1975), vol. 4, pp. 221–33.

Felling, A. J. A. and T. van der Weegen. "Programmer's Notes for Main Program NCLIQUE" (Nijmegen, Netherlands: Mathematical Soc. and Research Technical Department, University of Nijmegen, 1976).

Fienberg, S. E. *The Analysis of Cross-Classified Categorical Data* (Cambridge, Mass.: MIT Press, 1979).

Foster, C. C. and W. J. Horvath. "A Study of a Large Sociogram. III. Reciprocal Choice Probabilities as a Measure of Social Distance." *Behavioural Science* (1971), vol. 16, pp. 429–35.

Freeman, L. C. "On Measuring Systematic Integration." *Connections* (1978), vol. 2, no. 1, pp. 13–14.

Friedkin, Noah. "University Social Structure and Social Networks among Scientists." *Am. J. Soc.* (    ), vol. 83, pp. 1444–65.

Frost, P. A. and R. D. Whitley. "Communication Patterns in a Research Laboratory." *J. Research and Development Mgmt.* (1971), vol. 1, pp. 71–79.

Gerard, H. "Units and Concepts of Biology." In W. Buckley (ed.), *Modern Systems Research for the Behavioral Scientist* (Chicago: Aldine, 1968).

Gleason, T. C. and D. Cartwright. "A Note on a Matrix Criterion for Unique Colorability of a Signed Graph." *Psychological Biometrika* (1967), p. 32.

Goad, W. B. and M. I. Kanehisa. "Pattern-recognition in nucleic acid sequences. I. A General Method for Finding Local Homologies and Symmetries." *Nucleic Acids Res.* (1984), vol. 10, no. 1, pp. 247–63.

Guttman, L. "A General Nonmetric Technique for Finding the Smallest Coordinate Space for a Configuration of Points." *Psychometrika* (1968), p. 33.

Hallinan, M. "Comment on Holland and Leinhardt." *Am. J. Soc.* (1972), vol. 77, pp. 1201–05.

Hallinan, M. and D. Felmlee. "An Analysis of Intransitivity in Sociometric Data." *Sociometry* (1975), vol. 38, pp. 195–212.

Hansen, P. and M. Delattre. "Complete-Link Cluster Analysis by Graph Coloring." *J. Am. Statistical Association* (1978), p. 73.

Heil, G. H. and H. C. White. "An Algorithm for Finding Simultaneous Homomorphic Correspondences Between Graphs and their Image Graphs." *Behavioral Science* (1976), vol. 21, pp. 26–35.

Hinrichs, J. R. "Communications Activity of Industrial Research Personnel." *J. Personal Psych.* (1964), vol. 17, pp. 193–204.

Holland, P. W. and S. Leinhardt. "The Structural Implications of Measurement Error in Sociometry." *J. Math. Soc.* (1973), vol. 3, pp. 85–111.

Horan, P. M. "Information-Theoretic Measures and the Analysis of Social Structures." *Soc. Methods & Res.* (1975), vol. 3, pp. 321–40.

Jablin, F. M. "Organization Communication Theory and Research: An Overview of Communication Climate and Network Research." In D. Nimmo (ed.), *Communication Yearbook,* 4 (Beverly Hills, Calif.: Sage, 1980), pp. 327–47.

Jacobson, A. B., L. Good, J. Simonetti, and M. Zucker. "Some simple computational methods to improve the folding of long RNA's." *Nucleic Acids Res.* (1984), vol. 12, no. 1, pp. 45–52.

Jennings, H. H. "Sociometric Choice Process in Personality and Group Formation." In J. L. Moreno (ed.), *The Sociometry Reader* (Glencoe, Ill.: Free Press, 1960).

Kanehisa, M. I. and W. B. Goad. "Pattern-recognition in nucleic acid sequences. II. An efficient method for finding locally stable secondary structures." *Nucleic Acids Res.* (1984), vol. 10, no. 1, pp. 265–77.

Killworth, P. D. "Intrasitivity in the Structure of Small Closed Groups." *Social Science Res.* (1974), vol. 3, pp. 1–23.

Killworth, P. D. and H. R. Bernard. "CATIJ: A New Sociometric and its Application to a Prison Living Unit." Tech. Rep. No. 192–73. Arlington, VA: ONR (Contract No. N00014–73–A–0417–0001, 1973).

Klemmer, E. and F. Snyder. "Measurement of Time Spent Communicating." *J. Communication* (1972), vol. 22, pp. 142–58.

Kochen, M. "The Structure of Acquaintance Nets and Rates of Societal Development." *Social Networks* (1985), vol. 7, no. 4, pp. 323–39.

Krippendorf, K. "Clustering." In P. R. Monge and J. N. Cappella (eds.), *Multivariate Techniques for Human Communication Research* (New York: Academic Press, 1980), pp. 259–308.

Kroger, M. and A. Kroger-Block. "Simplified computer programs for search of homology within nucleotide sequences." *Nucleic Acids Res.* (1984), pp. 193–213.

Kruskal, J. B. and M. Wish. *Multidimensional Scaling* (Beverly Hills, Calif.: Sage, 1978).

Lankford, P. M. "Comparative Analysis of Clique Identification Methods." *Sociometry* (1974), vol. 37, pp. 287–305.

Laumann, E. O. *Bonds of Pluralism* (New York: Wiley Interscience, 1971).

Lesniak, R., M. P. Yates, G. M. Goldhaber, and W. D. Richards, Jr. "NET-PLOT: An Original Computer Program for Interpreting NEGOPY." Paper presented to the International Communication Association, Berlin, 1977.

Levine, S., P. E. White, and B. D. Paul. "Community Interorganizational Problems in Providing Medical Care and Social Service." *Am. J. Public Health* (1963), vol. 53, pp. 1183–95.

Lingoes, J. "The Guttman-Lingoes Nonmetric Program Series" (Ann Arbor, Mich.: Mathesis Press, 1973).

MacRae, Jr., D. "Direct Factor Analysis of Sociometric Data." *Sociometry* (1960), vol. 23, pp. 360–71.

McFarland, D. D. and D. J. Brown. "Social Distance as Metric: A Systematic Introduction to Smallest Space Analysis." In E. O. Laumann (ed.), *Bonds of Pluralism: The Form and Substance of Urban Social Networks* (New York: Wiley, 1973), pp. 213–53.

McQuitty, L. L. "Elementary Linkage Analysis for Isolating Orthogonal and Oblique Types and Typal Relevancies." *Ed. & Psych. Measurement* (1957), vol. 17, pp. 207–29.

Meyer, M. W. "Size and the Structure of Organizations: A Causal Analysis." *Am. Soc. Review* (1972), vol. 37, pp. 434–41.

Miles, R. *Macro Organizational Behavior* (Santa Monica, Calif.: Goodyear, 1980).

Monge, P. R., K. K. Kriste, and J. A. Edwards. "A Causal Model of the Formation of Communication Structure in Large Organizations." paper presented at International Communication Association, New Orleans, May 1974.

Mullins, N. C. "The Distribution of Social and Cultural Properties in Informal Communication among Biological Scientists." *Am. Soc. Review* (1968), vol. 33, pp. 786–97.

Murray, Stephen O. and R. C. Poolman. "Strong Ties and Scientific Literature." *Social Networks* (1982), vol. 4, no. 3, pp. 225–32.

Ornstein, M. D. "Interlocking Directorates in Canada." *Social Networks* (1982), vol. 4, pp. 3–25.

Pattee, H. H. *Hierarchy Theory* (New York: Braziller, 1973).

Pfeffer, J. and G. E. Salancik. *The External Control of Organizations: A Resource Dependence Perspective* (New York: Harper & Row, 1978).

Phillips, D. P. and R. H. Conviser. "Measuring the Structure and Boundary Properties of Graphs: Some Uses of Information Theory." *Sociometry* (1972), vol. 35, pp. 235–54.

Porter, L. W. and K. H. Roberts. "Communication in Organizations." Tech. Rep. No. 12. Arlington, VA: ONR, ERIC (microfiche) ED–066–773, 1973.

Pugh, D. S., D. F. Hickson, C. R. Hinnings, and C. Turner. "Dimensions of Organizational Structure." *Admin. Science Quarterly* (1968), vol. 13, pp. 65–104.

Reid, W. "Interorganizational Co-ordination in Social Welfare: A Theoretical Approach to Analysis and Intervention." In R. Kramer and H. Specht (eds.), *Readings in Community Organization Practice* (Englewood Cliffs, NJ: Prentice-Hall, 1967).

Reitz, K. P. "Using Log Linear Analysis with Network Data: Another Look at Sampson's Monastery." *Social Networks* (1982), vol. 4, pp. 243–56.

Rice, R. E. "Investigations into the Validity and Reliability of NEGOPY: A Computer Program for Network Analysis." Paper presented to International Communication Association, Philadelphia, 1979.

Rice, R. E. "Communication Networking in Computer Conferencing Systems: A Longitudinal Study of Group Roles and System Structure." In M. Burgoon (ed.), *Communication Yearbook*, 6 (Beverly Hills, Calif.: Sage, 1982).

Richards, Jr., W. D. "Network Analysis in Large Complex Organizations: Theoretical Basis; The Nature of Structure; Techniques and Methods—Tools." Four papers presented to the International Communication Association, New Orleans, 1974.

Richards, Jr., W. D. "A Coherent Systems Methodology for the Analysis of Human Communication Systems." Unpublished dissertation, Stanford University, 1976.

Richards, Jr., W. D. "Getting Data for Network Analysis II: Developing the Measurement Instrument." Presented at International Communication Association, Chicago, May 1986.

Richards, Jr.. W. D. "The NEGOPY Network Analysis Program." Department of Communication and Laboratory for Computer and Communications Research, Simon Fraser University. LCCR TR 87–3, 1986.

Roberts, K. H. and C. A. O'Reilly, III. "Failures in Upward Communication: Three Possible Culprits." Tech. Rep. No. 1. Arlington, VA: ONR, April (Contract No. N000314–69–A–0200–1054, 1973). Revised version published in *J. Academy of Mgmt*, (1974), vol. 17, p. 205.

Roberts, K. H. and C. A. O'Reilly, III. "Empirical Findings and Suggestions for Future Research on Organizational Communication." Tech. Rep. No. 6. (Arlington, VA: ONR [Contract No. N000314–69–A–0200–1054], 1974).

Roberts, K. H. and C. A. O'Reilly, III. "Organizations as Communication Structures: An Empirical-theoretical Approach." Technical Report on ONR Research Project, University of California, Berkeley, 1975.

Roberts, K. H. and C. A. O'Reilly, III, G. Bretton, and L. W. Porter. "Organizational Theory and Organizational Communication: A Communication Failure." Tech. Rep. No. 3 (Arlington, VA: ONR, May [Contract No. N000314–69–A–0200–1054], 1973). Revised version published in *Human Relations*, (1974), vol. 27, pp. 501–24. 1973.

Rogers, E. *The Diffusion of Innovations* (Glencoe, Ill: Free Press, 1962).

Rogers, E. M. and D. L. Kincaid. *Communications Networks: Toward a New Paradigm for Research* (New York: Free Press, 1981).

Rosengren, W. R. "Structure, Policy, and Style: Strategies of Organizational Control." *Administrative Science Quarterly* (1967), vol. 12, pp. 140–64.

Russell, H. "Communication Network Study." Memorandum to Department of Agriculture, Victoria, Australia, 11 October, 1974.

Sailer, L. D. "Structural Equivalence: Meaning and Definition, Computation and Application." *Social Networks* (1978), vol. 4, pp. 117–45.

Schwartz, D. F. "Liaison Roles in the Communication Structure of a Formal Organization: A Pilot Study." Paper presented at annual meeting of National Society for the Study of Communication, Cleveland, 1969.

Schwartz, J. E. "An Examination of CONCOR and Related Methods for Blocking Sociometric Data." In *Sociological Methodology* (ed.), D. R. Heise (San Francisco: Jossey-Bass, 1976), pp. 255–82.

Seidman, S., and B. Foster. "SONET-1." *Social Networks* (1979), vol. 2, pp. 85–90.

Seidman, S. B. and B. L. Foster. "A Graph-Theoretic Generalization of the Clique Concept." *J. Math. Soc.* (1978), vol. 6, pp. 139–54.

Shapiro, B. A., J. Maizel, L. E. Lipkin, K. Currey, and C. Whitney. "Generating Non-overlapping Displays of Nucleic Acid Secondary Structures." *Nucleic Acids Res.* (1984), vol. 12, no. 1, pp. 75–100.

Shaw, Jr., W. W. "Statistical Disorder and the Analysis of a Communmication Graph." *J. Am. Society for Information Science* (1983), vol. 34, pp. 146–49.

Shepard, R. N. *Multidimensional Scaling* (New York: Seminar Press, 1972).

Sondquist, J. and T. Koenig. "Interlocking Directorates in the Top U.S. Corporations: A Graph Theory Approach." *Insurgent Sociologist* (1975), vol. 5, no. 3, pp. 196–229.

Thomason, G. F. "Managerial Work Roles and Relationships: Part 1." *J. Mgmt. Studies* (1966), vol. 3, pp. 270–84.

Thompson, J. D. "Authority and Power in 'Identical' Organizations." *Am. J. Soc.* (1956), vol. 62, pp. 290–301.

Tryon, R. C. and D. E. Bailey. *Cluster Analysis* (New York: McGraw-Hill, 1970).

Warner, W. L., D. B. Unwalla, and J. H. Trimm (eds.). *The Emergent American Society: Large-Scale Organizations* (New Haven: Yale Univ. Press, 1967), pp.121–57.

Wasserman, S. "Analyzing Social Networks as Stochastic Processes." *J. Am. Statistical Association* (1980), vol. 75, pp. 280–94.

Watanabe, K., K. Yasukawa, and K. Iso. "Graphic Display of Nucleic Acid Structure by a Microcomputer." *Nucleic Acids Res.* (1984), vol. 12, no. 1, pp. 801–56.

Webber, R. A. "Perceptions of Interactions between Superiors and Subordinates." *Human Relations* (1970), vol. 23, pp. 235–48.

Weick, K. *The Social Psychiatry of Organizing* (Reading, Mass.: Addison-Wesley, 1969).

Weineke, P. R., E. Mansfield, D. A. Jaffe, and D. L. Brutlag. "Rapid Searches for Complex Patterns in Biological Models." *Nucleic Acids Res.* (1984), vol. 12, no. 1, pp. 263–80.

Whitley, R. D. and P. A. Frost. "Authority, Problem Solving Approaches,

Communication and Change in a British Research Laboratory." *J. Mgmt. Studies* (1972), vol. 9, pp. 337–61.

Wickesberg, A. K. "Communications Networks in the Business Organization Structure." *Academy of Mgmt. J.* (1968), vol. 11, pp. 253–62.

Wigand, R. T. "A Dynamic Model of Interactions among Complex Organizations within an Organization-Set." *Progress in Cybernetics and Systems Research*, Vol. 5. R. Trappl *et al.* (ed.) (Washington, DC: Hemisphere Publishing, 1978).

Wigand, R. T. "The Communication Industry in Economic Integration: The Case of West Germany." *Social Networks* (1982), vol. 4, pp. 47–79.

Zaenglein, M. M. and C. Smith. "An Analysis of Individual Communication Patterns and Perceptions in Hospital Organizations." *Human Relations* (1972), vol. 25, pp. 493–504.

Zucker, M. and L. Steigler. "Optimal Computer Folding of Large RNA Sequences Using Thermodynamics and Auxilliary Information." *Nucleic Acids Res.* (1984), vol. 9, no. 1, pp. 133–48.

# 42
# Small World Research Techniques

In much the same way that the physiologist can enhance his or her understanding of biological systems by following the progress of a radioactive isotope introduced into an organism, the social scientist can gain an improved understanding of social organization and interaction by studying the patterns of information flow. Stanley Milgram has proposed small–world research techniques as one way of gaining these insights.

## Origins of Small
## World Research Methods

The term "small world" was first employed in the social sciences by Ithiel de Sola Poole and Manfred Kochen in 1958.[1] Small world studies ask the question, "Given any two individuals in the world, what is the probability that they will know one another?" Or "Given any two individuals X and Y, how many intermediate acquaintance linkages are needed to connect the two persons?"

Stanley Milgram stated the problem in this way:

> "There are two general philosophical views on the small world problem. Some people feel that any two people in the world, no matter how remote from each other, can be linked in terms of intermediate acquaintances, and that the number of such intermediate links is relatively small."[2]

This view sees personal *radial* networks permitting flow of information from one social grouping to another through a series of connecting links. The contrasting view of *interlocking* networks sees unbridgeable gaps between various groups:

> "Given any two people in the world, they will never link up, because people have circles of acquaintances which will not necessarily intersect. A message will circulate in a particular cluster of acquaintances, but may never be able to make the jump to another culture. This view sees the world in terms of isolated clusters of acquaintances."[3]

Ithiel de Sola Poole of M.I.T., working with Manfred Kochen of IBM and assisted by Michael Gurevitch, predicted mathematically that while there is only about one chance in 200,000 that any two Americans chosen at random will know each other, there is better than a fifty-fifty chance that any two people can be linked up by *two intermediate* acquaintances. Poole's study dealt with mathematical odds, based on each person knowing roughly 500 other people.[4] In actual fact, many of the 500 friends of any individual can also be "friends of the friend;" so that there will not necessarily be a continually widening net of acquaintances: "Although poor people always have acquaintances, it probably turns out that they tend to be among other poor people, while the rich speak mostly to the rich, according to Milgram,[5] who suggests that society is not built on the random connections that Poole's results presuppose, and that connecting two randomly selected individuals may take more than the number of links that a mathematical formula suggests.

The following discussion explains Milgram's small world techniques. Milgram sent out letters of solicitation to residents in two midwest cities—Wichita, Kansas, and Omaha, Nebraska—requesting volunteers to participate in a study of social contact in United States society. The persons who volunteered came from varied walks of life. Each was designated as a "starter" and was given the name, address, and a few pertinent details about a "target" person (a person chosen at random and living somewhere in the United States). While many starters (the volunteers who initiated the process of sending the message) were used, only two "targets" were used. One target individual was the wife of a Divinity School student living in Cambridge, Massachusetts; the second was a stockbroker who worked in Boston and lived in Sharon, Massachusetts.[6]

Each of the volunteer starters was asked to move a message toward the designated target person, using only a chain of friends and acquaintances known on a first-name basis. Each volunteer could transmit the message to *one* friend or acquaintance more likely than he/she to know the target person. The message to be transmitted was a document containing a. the name of the target individual, as well as certain information about the person; b. a set of rules for reaching the target person, with the most important being that you must pass the folder on to someone whom you know on a first-name basis; c. a roster on which the recipient of the document affixes his name, in order to prevent endless looping of the document through participants who have been earlier links in the chain; and d. a stack of fifteen postcards to be filled out and returned to the researchers. These information postcards gave the researchers relevant sociological characteristics of the sender and receiver of the messages and also gave continuous feedback on the progress of the chains.[7] (see figure 42.1)

From these studies Milgram and his colleagues learned that completed chains involved from 3 to 10 intermediate acquaintance links, with the median at 5.5. In the Nebraska study, 160 persons acted as starters in an effort to reach a stockbroker in Sharon, Massachusetts; 42 chains were completed.[8]

These completed chains yielded some interesting information. For example, the Kansas study found subjects more than three times as likely to send the folder to someone of the same sex as to someone of the opposite sex.[9] Out of 74 females, 56 sent the folder to another female; only 18 sent the folder to a male. Fifty-eight of the 71 males sent the folder to other males, while 13 sent the folder to females.[10]

In the Kansas study, 123 cards were sent to friends and acquaintances, while only 22 were sent to relatives. In United States society, where extended kinship links are not maintained, particularly in urban areas, acquaintance and friendship links seemed to be the main basis for reaching the target person. It could be speculated, however, that within certain ethnic groups in the United States, a higher proportion of familial links might be found.[11]

The study also concluded that not all acquaintances constitute equally important bases of contact with the larger society. Some acquaintances appear to be more important than others, possessing wider circles of acquaintances and more far-reaching networks, as compared to other, more isolated friends.[12]

Finally, Milgram concluded that social communication is sometimes restricted less by physical distance than by social distance. For example, messages often traveled very quickly and with few intermediaries to the city and even the immediate locale of the target, only to die without ever making contact with the target. In some cases, messages floundered and failed only a few hundred feet from the target person's house.[13]

This last finding prompted Milgram to call for research that would draw the starting person and the target person from different socioeconomic backgrounds, examining the relative likelihood of chains being completed. He also suggested applying the small world method to subgroups in society to investigate to what extent racial and ethnic lines influenced the transmissions and to what extent information flowed between group. Is flow easier in some parts of the country than in other areas?[14] In later studies, Milgram tried to answer some of these questions himself.[15]

## Small World Techniques
## Applied to Organizations

Some of the questions that small–world research can answer within an organizational context are the following: 1. What are the characteristics of liaisons or cross–over links who act as information brokers between professional, cultural, or other elite groups within an organization? 2. To what extent do links extend between upper management and lower levels of the organization? Between men and women in the organization? Between women? Between different departments and units? Between more senior and less senior employees? Between older and younger employees? 3. What are the characteristics of "funnels," or the individuals who act as the last linking agents in the completion of an interpersonal communication chain? Do these funnels give us additional insights into how information is transferred within the organization?

The small world study is designed to gain insight into information flow paths; it is, by the nature of its design, concerned with liaisons who act sometimes as linking pins and sometimes as gatekeepers. Because an item is passed physically along a chain and is monitored, like an isotope, at each point of departure, there is a level of objectivity that is not present in some of the more usual survey–type studies. An examination of the existence or nonexistence, and relative effectiveness of linkages should tell us something concrete in much the same way that a glance at a roadmap quickly distinguishes between arterial and secondary or tertiary systems.

The first question on the characteristics of liaisons is fundamental to the broader issue of organizational identity. Participation in or identification with a social organism is dependent on effective intercommunication between the many subsystems of which the culture is composed. In other words, the linking, bridging, or liaison agents are the means whereby definition of organizational culture becomes possible. Understanding the characteristics of these liaison figures can help us to understand further how information is passed between subunits within the organization. Knowledge of the social status of these individuals, their affiliations, and subgroups to which they belong can help us to identify access points in networks through which information may be disseminated.

The answers to the second set of questions indicate to what extent people at various levels of the organization are involved and connected to each other. Are some subgroups more or less involved than others?

# COMMUNICATIONS PROJECT
322 Emerson Hall   Harvard University
Cambridge  Massachusetts  02138

We need your help in an unusual scientific study carried out at Harvard
University.  We are studying the nature of social contact in American
society.  Could you, as an active American, contact another American citizen
regardless of his walk of life?  If the name of an American citizen were
picked out of a hat, could you get to know that person using your network
of friends and acquaintances?  Just how open is our "open society"?  To answer
these questions, which are very important to our research, we ask for your help.

You will notice that this letter has come
to you from a friend.  He has aided this study
by sending this folder on to you. He hopes that
you will aid this study by forwarding this folder
to someone else.  The name of the person who sent
you this folder is listed in the Roster at the
bottom of this sheet.

| TARGET PERSON |
| --- |
| Name, address, and |
| information about the |
| target person is |
| placed here. |

In the box to the right you will find the name and
address of an American citizen who has agreed to
service as the "target person" in this study.  The
idea of the study is to transmit this folder to the
target person using only a chain of friends and
acquaintances.

Remember, the aim is to move this folder toward the target person using only a
chain  of friends and acquaintances. On first thought you may feel you do not
know anyone who is acquainted with the target person. This is natural, but at
least you can start it in the right direction! Who among your acquaintances
might conceivably move in the same social circles as the target person?
The real challenge is to identify among your friends and acquaintances
a person who can advance the folder toward the target person. It may take
several steps beyond your friend to get to the target person, but what counts
most is to start the folder on its way!  The person who receives this folder
will then repeat the process until the folder is received by the target person.
May we ask you to begin?

Every person who participates in this study and returns the postcard to us
will receive a certificate of appreciation from the Communications Project.
All participants are entitled to a report describing the results of the study.

Please transmit this folder within 24 hours.  Your help is greatly appreciated.

Yours sincerely,

Stanley Milgram, Ph.D.
Director, Communications Project

## Fig. 42.1
### Communications project.

(From Stanley Milgram, "Interdisciplinary Thinking," in *Interdisciplinary Relationships in the Social Sciences,* ed. by M. Sherif and Carolyn W. Sherif.
Chicago: Aldine, 1969. Reprinted with permission.)

```
┌─────────────────────────────────────────────────────────┐
│              HOW TO TAKE PART IN THE STUDY                │
├──────────────────────────────┬──────────────────────────┤
│ 1    ADD YOUR NAME TO THE    │ 3    IF YOU KNOW THE TARGET│
│      ROSTER AT THE BOTTOM OF │      PERSON ON A PERSONAL  │
│      THIS SHEET, so that the │      BASIS, MAIL THIS      │
│ next person who receives this│ FOLDER DIRECTLY TO HIM     │
│ letter will know who it came │ (HER).  Do this only if you│
│ from.                        │ have previously met the    │
│                              │ target person and know each│
│                              │ other on a first name basis│
├──────────────────────────────┼──────────────────────────┤
│ 2    DETACH ONE POSTCARD,    │ 4    IF YOU DO NOT KNOW THE│
│      FILL IT OUT AND RETURN  │      TARGET PERSON ON A    │
│      IT TO HARVARD UNIVERSITY│      PERSONAL BASIS. DO NOT│
│ No stamp is needed.  The     │ TRY TO CONTACT HIM DIRECTLY│
│ postcard is very important.  │ INSTEAD, MAIL THIS FOLDER  │
│ It allows us to keep track of│ (POSTCARDS AND ALL) TO A   │
│ the progress of the folder as│ PERSONAL ACQUAINTANCE WHO  │
│ it moves toward the target   │ IS MORE LIKELY THAN YOU TO │
│ person.                      │ KNOW THE TARGET PERSON.    │
│                              │ You may send the folder on │
│                              │ to a friend, relative, or  │
│                              │ acquaintance, but it must  │
│                              │ be someone you know on a   │
│                              │ first name basis.          │
└──────────────────────────────┴──────────────────────────┘
```

PLEASE FILL IN THE FOLLOWING INFOR-
MATION ABOUT THE PERSON TO WHOM YOU
ARE SENDING THE FOLDER

HIS (HER) NAME _____
_____

HIS (HER) ADDRESS_____
_____

HIS (HER) OCCUPATION_____
_____

APPROXIMATE AGE_____  SEX_____

NATURE OF RELATIONSHIP TO YOU_____
_____PLEASE EXPLAIN IF
A FRIEND, ACQUAINTANCE, RELATIVE,ETC.

PLEASE FILL IN THIS
INFORMATION ABOUT YOURSELF

MY NAME_____

MY ADDRESS_____
_____

MY OCCUPATION_____

AGE_____          SEX_____

DETACH ONE POSTCARD FILL IT OUT AND
RETURN IT TO HARVARD UNIVERSITY

```
┌─────────────────────────────┐
│            ROSTER           │
├──┬──────────────────────────┤
│ 1│                          │
│ 2│                          │
│ 3│                          │
│ 4│                          │
│ 5│                          │
│ 6│                          │
│ 7│                          │
│ 8│                          │
│ 9│                          │
│10│                          │
│11│                          │
│12│                          │
│13│                          │
│14│                          │
│15│                          │
├──┴──────────────────────────┤
│     SIGN YOUR NAME HERE     │
└─────────────────────────────┘
```

Research indicates a strong connection between involvement and commitment and between commitment and quality of performance.

The third question relating to "funnels" is very important in understanding how information makes its way through networks. Not all persons in any group or organization are equally likely to receive a message. The old concept of the information flow in a society being a matter of percolation from the top down through the social pyramid has been discarded. If the pyramid model ever was appropriate, it was a very long time ago. Modern society and modern organizations are too complex to accommodate such a model. What may be a more appropriate communication model looks somewhat like a collection of family tree diagrams, with links connecting each. If a message is passed vertically, horizontally, or diagonally through the system from one initiating individual to a specific target individual, the pathway is made through a number of links. Alternative routes to the target may be available but the closer one gets to the target, the fewer the alternatives. The process is in some regards similar to getting from one address to another. A person has a choice of numerous ways of reaching the destination. Some paths are more logical and efficient than others. However, the closer the individual gets to the destination, the fewer the available choices. In interpersonal networks, the message can pass through several intermediate agents; research suggests that whether a message actually reaches target sections of the population will depend in large measure on whether the information happens to be acquired by one of the individuals who act as a "funnel" for other individuals. Understanding more about these funnel persons is important in knowing how information moves in society.

### Literature Review

Three major areas of study in the literature have relevance for the particular questions being pursued. Relevant to the crossover aspect of small–world studies is related research on liaisons and gatekeepers that appears in communication network theory, in political and anthropological/sociological theory, and in organization theory. Relevant to group membership concepts is the sociological literature on urbanism and social network formation. Most germaine to the funneling concepts are related communication network theories.

*Research on liaisons and gatekeepers.* When confronted with the task of understanding patterns of social interaction, the sociologist tries to draw a map of the linkages. This map can take the form of a sociogram or network analysis. A sociogram can give valuable information; however, this technique is generally limited to the study of relatively small numbers of subjects. With a study population of more than one hundred, the possible permutations of interaction become extremely large, and the sociogram technique becomes cumbersome and very costly.

While what is often most interesting in sociograms is the *frequency* of interaction between individuals in small interlocking networks; in larger network studies such as diffusion of innovations, researchers attempt to study the flow of communication through ever-widening arteries branching out through the population in a radial fashion. What is often most interesting in these studies is the difference between subcultural or elite groups and the characteristics of the liaisons or agents who link the groups.

Someone acting as a broker on the basis of his ability to make bridges of common interest between different groups will be an influential figure. The social science literature suggests that the bulk of communication with a group will be ritualistic and of low information content.[16] The more entrenched the individual is within the group or the stronger his or her bonds of kindship with other members of the group, the more rare his or her access to information other than in–group transactions. Conversely, the "weak" link (the link to the outside) will have much greater information access. Everett Rogers and Rekha Agarwala—Rogers noted:

> Human communication typically entails a balance between novelty and similarity. Communication research on personal networks has dealt with an issue that has come to be called "the strength of weak ties" (Liu and Duff 1972; Granovetter 1973; Rogers 1973). This research is summarized in the statement that *the information strength of dyadic communication relationships is inversely related to the degree of homophily (and the strength of the attraction) between the source and the receiver*. Or, in other words, a new idea is communicated to a larger number of individuals, and traverses a greater social distance, when passed through weak sociometric ties (in radial personal networks) rather than strong ones (in interlocking personal networks). There is little informational strength, then, in interlocking personal networks. "Weak ties" enable innovations to flow from clique to clique via liaisons and bridges.[17]

In 1951, Jacobson and Seashore found in their investigation of communication patterns in the Office of Naval Research that "some individuals appear to function as 'liaison' persons between groups, and characteristically have many, frequent, reciprocated, and important contacts that cut across the contact group structure."[18] Numerous scholars have given attention to these linking agents, or liaisons. In 1957, Robert Merton used the term "cosmopolite" to describe the liaison function in the process of a society's shift from the traditional to the urban society.[19] Rensis Likert coined the term "linking pin" in 1961 to describe the liaison in organizational structure.[20]

In diffusion of innovation studies, scholars such as Everett Rogers[21] and Daniel Lerner[22] found liaisons to be extremely important figures in situations of accelerated culture change. An individual caught between two cultures, the liaison helps to explain social change in terms that are not threatening to the people for whom the liaison acts as interpreter. By virtue of his role, the liaison can acquire a certain prestige and, in some cases, acquires leadership status.[23]

Elihu Katz and Paul Lazarsfeld, in developing the construct of the two–step information flow, used the term "opinion leader" to describe the role of the liaison in information–diffusion and opinion–formation processes.[24] Keith Davis speaks of the role of the liaison in rumor processes.[25] Richard Farace, Peter Monge, and Hamish Russell point out that, of all the communication roles that have been studied, the liaison role has attracted the most interest and research.[26]

It is not surprising that so much attention has been given to the liaison role. In large part, the level to which a social organization can develop is controlled by the effectiveness of its communication linkages. When the liaison function in an organization, for example, is weak or nonexistent in places where it is needed, information fails to pass through the system and overload is the consequence for certain individuals. The liaison function is a critical one. (See the earlier chapter on information load.)

In a small world study involving passage of information between racial groups, Charles Korte and Stanley Milgram set out to discover where and when the message would cross the racial barrier. They also sought to identify the liaison–gatekeepers responsible for transmitting chains between racial groups. They anticipated that the chain with White starters would gain access to Black networks via gatekeepers and then travel within the Black community until contact with the target was made.[27]

The results of their study indicated that of the 540 chains originated with White starters in Los Angeles, 123 (or 22 percent) reached their targets in New York City. Of these 123 chains that reached their destination, 88 (or 33 percent) of those with White targets completed; while only 35 (or 13 percent) of the chain with Black targets completed. The all–White chains were two and one-half times more likely to complete than the White–Black crossover chains.[28] Of the chains that did reach their targets, the difference in total intermediaries was not significant (5.5 intermediaries for all–White chains and 5.9 intermediaries for White–Black chains); however, the dropout rate was significantly higher for White–Black chains.[29]

The study did reveal some new information on who acts as liaison-gatekeepers between these two racial groups in the United States. Korte and Milgram found that where acquaintanceship ties succeeded in crossing racial lines, the gatekeepers between the two cultures (both the White senders and the Black receivers) were predominantly males of professional status. Also represented were managers, officials, and sales–clerical personnel, while lower–and working–class gatekeepers were practically nonexistent.[30] (There is a hint in these findings confirming the idea presented by authors such as Paul Fussell, *Class: A Guide through the American Social System,* of the "disconnected masses" or the "invisible" part of the population.) Typically, the White gatekeeper forwarding the message to the Black recipient termed the recipient as a "friend" or "acquaintance" (71 percent) rather than as a "business or work friend" (23 percent). However, the most common reason given for selecting the recipient was occupational similarity (43 percent).[31]

Korte and Milgram also compared the gatekeepers in completed chains with gatekeepers in chains that made the crossover but did not complete. Their results were summarized in this way:

> Forty–two per cent of eventually successful white gatekeepers were professional service people (doctors and lawyers predominated), while this category comprised only 9% of the eventually unsuccessful white gatekeepers, who had a greater preponderance of managers and officials. In the nature of relationship data, the biggest differences occurred with reference to the *friend* and *role reciprocal* categories. Compared with eventually unsuccessful white gatekeepers, those eventually successful defined the relationship with the Negro as friend with much less frequency (25% versus 51%) and as role reciprocal (e.g. employers–employees, doctor–patient) with much more frequency (14% vs. 0%). In stating why the Negro recipient was chosen to receive the booklet, eventually successful whites gave far greater prominence to occupational similarity with target as a reason than did those eventually unsuccessful (63% versus 38%).[32]

Examining the 35 chains with Black targets that completed also revealed that in 23 out of 35 chains the *recipient* of the crossover message was also the *target* individual. In another seven chains, the crossover recipient was the final link to the target. Thus in only five instances, or 14 percent of the successful completions, was there more than one linking agent between the Black gatekeepers and the target.[33] The study demonstrated that the most effective way of reaching between the two racial groups was to chain White acquaintances until the target was within striking distance.

Studying the incomplete message–transmission chains reveals very clearly the inadequacy of communication networks between White starters and Black targets:

> Of the 187 chains that failed to reach their Negro targets, 148 or 79%, stopped with white terminals. Even if one were to consider as completed those Negro–target chains that had made contact with a Negro but were still short of the target himself, the Negro completion rate would not match that obtained with white targets. Thus, Negro–target chains either succeeded in making contact via an essentially white acquaintanceship network, or else were exhausted within the white community without ever making a first contact with Negro networks.[34]

Eighty percent of the uncompleted Black target chains never crossed the racial barrier. Many potential channels of communication were never used.[35]

These studies showed that most chains run themselves down over a fixed number of removes. Unless the target is reached in this number of removes, he or she probably won't be reached:

> Thus the *efficiency* with which the target is reached is what chiefly determines the number of completions. Each choice in forwarding the document can be efficient in so far as it reduces the number of steps to the target by the greatest possible amount, rather than leaving the number of steps unchanged or increased.[36]

This fact can be important to groups or individuals attempting to disseminate information. These studies imply that while formal networks can be highly efficient in moving information (as rumour studies have frequently demonstrated), beyond a certain fairly limited number of intermediaries, a chain will die. Evidence to support this conclusion can also be found in classic studies by Keith Davis, who traced the passing of information on informal networks in organizations.[37] Other message diffusion studies reported by Melvin DeFleur and Edith Rainboth found 93 percent of the persons who eventually knew about a message acquired the information on the first day.[38] Thus, it is essential to choose well the initial starting point for information.

In summary, Korte's and Milgram's study seemed to indicate that occupational similarity offers an important basis for choosing recipients of information and that information chains typically experience status descent at the target. The study concluded that the best way of getting a message to the final individual or group target is to advance it toward the persons and networks that "have surveillance over the occupational and affiliative domain in which the particular target is located."[39] Advancing the message to persons lower in status than the *target* or to a peer of the target are less efficient means of reaching the target. The lower-status person can be separated by physical and institutional barriers, and passage between peers often necessitates using higher-status intermediaries who have better coverage of the *total* setting or institution. Lerner's studies found that the person acting as liaison in a traditional society typically conforms to the anthropological concept of the pariah as innovator, as in the case of the grocer who is not a member of the cultural group among whom he or she lives but is an extracultural link by virtue of his or her job.

In summarizing the research on the liaison communication role, Farace, Monge, and Russell noted that liaisons tend to have higher formal status in the organization and to be more senior members than are nonliaisons. They are more likely to serve as first sources of information and to be aware of their communication contacts in the organization. Liaisons perceive themselves to have greater influence, more numerous contacts, and easier access to information than do nonliaisons. Others seem to agree that the liaison figures are more influential, more competent, better informed, better connected with others in the organization, and more powerful.[40] (See Table 42.1)

*Social Network Formation.* Jean Piaget's writing on socialization of the individual, where the self-perception evolves from awareness of self through the various stages from family and peers to the larger society, describes the process of social network formation.[41] Claude Fischer also describes the ever-widening process of network formation in the following way:

> Individuals' personal networks are sometimes embedded within a single subculture—as might be the case with an actor whose entire social life revolves around the theatre—or sometimes bridge two or three subcultures—as might be the case with a second-generation immigrant, half of whose ties are with professional colleagues and half with people in her old ethnic community. In either instance, the relations within any individual's personal networks are part of larger social networks—subcultures—that, linked together, define the society. It is through these ramified interconnections (as well as through more bureaucratic institutions such as unions and courts) that any individual is integrated into society, first by bonds with individuals in his or her personal network, through them to a particular subculture, and through that to society as a whole.[42]

Studies on mental health make the connection between mental illness and poorly developed or nonexistent interpersonal networks,[43] and

**Table 42.1**

**Summary of research on the liaison communication role.**

*Actual*
1. Liaisons have higher agreement (between themselves and others they talk with) about the identity of their contacts than do nonliaisons.
2. Liaisons are more likely than others in the organization to serve as first sources of information.
3. Liaisons have higher formal status in the organization than do nonliaisons.
4. Liaisons have been organizational members for longer periods of time than have nonliaisons.
5. The levels of formal education and the ages of liaisons are similar to those of nonliaisons.

*Liaisons' perception of themselves*
1. Liaisons perceive themselves to have greater numbers of communication contacts in the organization.
2. Liaisons perceive themselves to have greater amounts of information with respect to the content dimensions upon which their role is defined.
3. Liaisons perceive the communication system as more "open" —information is seen as more timely, more believable, and more useful.
4. Liaisons perceive themselves to have greater influence in the organization.

*Others' perceptions of liaisons*
1. Liaisons are perceived by others to have greater numbers of communication contacts in the organization.
2. Liaisons' communication contacts are seen as having a wider range throughout the organizational structure.
3. Liaisons are perceived as having more information on the content dimensions on which the network is defined.
4. Liaisons are perceived as having more control over the flow of information in the organization.
5. Liaisons are perceived to have more influence over the "power structure" of the organization.
6. Liaisons are perceived to be more competent at their organizational activities.

Henri Pirenne[44] and George Duby[45] speculated that the breakdown of communication between the cities of Western Europe in the Dark Ages contributed to the disintegration of society. Communities were isolated from each other, and people had little contact with anyone living outside their immediate place of residence.

Much of the personal network literature grew out of the studies of urbanization and urbanism. The early Chicago school of urban sociology headed by Robert Park studied networks in cities. Cities provided a convenient setting in which to examine networks, by virtue of there being large numbers of people in a small area, sufficiently large numbers to contain a wide variety of distinct networks. The old Chicago school that grew out of the European tradition of Max Weber and Emile Durkheim saw urbanization and modernization as largely dehumanizing influences.[46] The proposition of anomie and alienation have dominated the thinking through to recent times. David Riesman's concept of the lonely crowd echoes the traditional thinking.[47] However, more recent sociology is not so pessimistic; and Fischer, himself a product of Chicago, regards urbanism as offering variety by enabling individuals with minority interests to find kindred spirits and to form subcultural networks, a possibility nonexistent in a more dispersed population arrangement. Well-defined, readily available, easily accessible, and seemingly relevant networks help to explain the positive experience of many people in cities. As communication technology advances, the differences between urban and rural network access become less marked. Marshall McLuhan's global village may still be in the distant future, but the trend is toward the *geselschaft*.

*Funneling*. Funneling was strongly evident in Milgram's studies. In the case of the stockbroker who lived in Sharon, Massachusetts, and worked in Boston, a total of 62 messages reached him, 38 at work and 24 at his place of residence. Within Sharon, messages from 16 different correspondents were passed to the stockbroker by a Mr. Jacobs, a clothing merchant in the town. Jacobs apparently served as the principal intermediary between the target person and the larger world, a fact that came as a shock to the stockbroker. At his place of work in a Boston brokerage firm, ten of the chains passed through a Mr. Jones and five through Mr. Brown, business associates. In fact, 48 percent of the chains that were completed reached the target through three men—Jacobs, Jones, and Brown. While one man served as a main transmission point for residential contact, two others were popular channels in the work area, indicating some differentiation among the commonly used channels. This same phenomenon occurred in a number of the message transmission chains studied by Milgram.[48]

In a second study that compared White and Black target chains, Milgram and Korte found that funneling appeared to be more common to Whites than to Blacks.[49] The most extreme case of convergence involving White targets showed the final links of eleven completed messages for one target funneled through two individuals.[50]

Korte and Milgram reached the following conclusion:

> The chains had two predominant paths to the target, either by the way of his occupational setting or by way of his residential setting. The former route, that is occupational contacts, proved the more efficient

(i.e. short-chained) of the two. There was also a distinct 'funneling' or 'common pathways' phenomenon, a decrease in the number of different persons who were involved in the chains as they approached the target. The target person appeared to be surrounded by 3 key persons whom the chains would reach first before being completed to the target.[51]

As we earlier noted, it is interesting that in the Milgram study many of the chains were formed across considerable distances but died within a few hundred yards of the target because an appropriate final link was not found. It seems that propinquity, or closeness, is not of itself sufficient to ensure communication.[52]

Korte and Milgram also discovered some of the characteristics of people who act as funnelers. Summarizing points previously stated, they found that the final link to the target typically occupied a higher status than the target individual. In sixty-two percent of the cases of chain completion, the final contact person had a professional status, whereas the target had professional status in only twenty-seven percent of the cases.[53]

Communication network theory deals with a related phenomenon under the term "zone size." The term is used to designate the extent of an individual's linkages with others in his or her network. Farace, Monge, and Russell clarify the concept in the following way:

> A first–order zone contains all members with whom the individual has direct contact. A second–order zone extends this to include all individuals who have direct contact with members of the first–order zone, but who are not already in that zone. A third–order zone extends this concept still further to include all individuals having direct contact with members of the third–order zone, without, of course, being in the second– or first–order zone. Zone size can be extended to any number of steps removed from the focal member.[54]

As one moves from fifth–order zones in toward a target individual, graphically depicted the phenomenon is cone–shaped, with first–order individuals being candidates for funnels, as shown in figure 42.2.

## Conclusion

Application of small–world techniques to organizations could yield interesting results. Studying the extent to which women, for example, are linked to higher echelons of the organization could prove informative. Discovering the distance between upper and lower levels of the organization and comparing results obtained in United States organizations, Japanese organizations, and United States–based Japanese

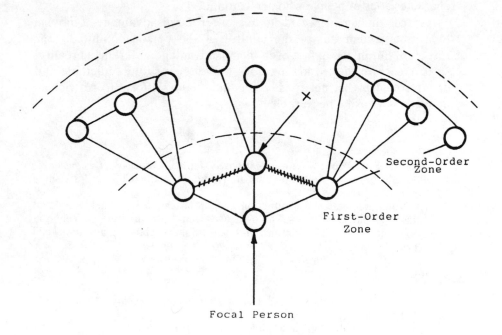

**Fig. 42.2**
**First and second-order network zones for selected focal persons.**

(From *Communicating and Organizing,* by Richard V. Farace, Peter R. Monge and
Hamish Russell. Copyright © 1977 by Richard V. Farace, Peter R. Monge and
Hamish Russell. Reprinted by permission of Random House, Inc.)

subsidiaries could offer new insights in the cross–cultural field. Past application of small world techniques to public– and private–sector organizations has been extremely limited; yet the technique offers a unique approach to acquiring data on how information moves in society. How connected, for example, are people at the grass–roots level to those in authority positions in city, state and national governments? Is social distance greater under Democratic leadership or Republican leadership? Under Tory or Liberal leadership in Canada? What are characterizing features of the people who link different groups to the larger society? What are the personal and demographic characteristics of people who act as funnels?

It is true that small world studies suffer the disadvantage of moving to a great extent out of the control of the person conducting the research, but in actual fact even this disadvantage well reflects reality. In the real world, information does move on very unpredictable and uncontrolled paths, not readily accommodating efforts to restrict its flow and not easily measurable.

## Notes

1. Ithiel de Sola Pool, "Communication Systems," *Handbook of Communication,* ed. Ithiel de Sola Pool, *et al.* (Rand McNally College Publishing Company, 1973).
2. "A Nonmathematical Introduction to a Mathematical Model," undated mimeo, Department of Psychology, Massachusetts Institute of Technology. Cited by Stanley Milgram, "Interdisciplinary Thinking and the Small World Problem," in *Interdisciplinary Relationships in the Social Sciences* ed. M. Sherif and Carolyn W. Sherif (Chicago: Aldine, 1969,), p. 104.
3. *Ibid.*
4. *Ibid.*
5. Stanley Milgram, "The Small World Problem," *Psychology Today* (1967) vol. 1, p. 63.
6. Milgram, "Interdisciplinary Thinking," *op. cit.* p. 109.
7. *Ibid.*
8. *Ibid.,* p. 112.
9. *Ibid.,* p. 114.
10. Milgram, "The Small World Problem," *op. cit.* p. 65.
11. Milgram, "Interdisciplinary Thinking," *op. cit.* p. 114.
12. *Ibid.,* p. 115.
13. *Ibid.,* p. 117.
14. *Ibid.,* p. 117–118.
15. Charles Korte and Stanley Milgram, "Acquaintance Networks between Racial Groups: Application of the Small World Method," *Journal of Personality and Social Psychology* (1970), vol. 15, pp. 101–108.
16. Everett M. Rogers and Rekha Agarwala-Rogers, *Communication in Organizations* (New York: Free Press, 1976), p. 115.

17. *Ibid.*
18. E. Jacobson and S. Seashore, "Communication Practices in Complex Organizations," *Journal of Social Issues* (1951), vol. 7, pp. 28–40.
19. Robert Merton, "Patterns of Influence: Local and Cosmopolitan Influentials," in *Social Theory and Social Structure*, ed. R. Merton (New York: Free Press, 1957).
20. Rensis Likert, *New Patterns of Management* (New York: McGraw-Hill, 1961).
21. Everett M. Rogers. *Diffusion of Innovations* (New York: Free Press of Glencoe, 1962).
22. Daniel Lerner, *The Passing of Traditional Society* (New York: Free Press, 1958).
23. Stewart Ferguson and Sherry Ferguson, "The Role of Liaison in Culture Change," paper presented at the annual meeting of the International Communication Association, Intercultural Division, Chicago, 1978. Also Stewart Ferguson, "Satellite Television: Change Agent for the Third World," unpublished dissertation, Indiana University, 1976.
24. Elihu Katz and Paul F. Lazarsfeld, *Personal Influence* (New York: Free Press, 1955); also Elihu Katz, "The Two-Step Flow of Communication: An Up-to-date Report on a Hypothesis," *Public Opinion Quarterly* (1957), vol. 21, pp. 61–78.
25. Keith Davis, "A Method of Studying Communication Patterns in Organizations," *Personnel Psychology* (1953), vol. 16, pp. 301–12; also Keith Davis, "Management Communication and the Grapevine," *Harvard Business Review* (1953), vol. 31, pp. 43–49.
26. Richard V. Farace, Peter R. Monge, and Hamish M. Russell, *Communicating and Organizing* (Reading, Mass.: Addison-Wesley Publishing Company, 1977), p. 187.
27. Korte and Milgram, *op. cit.* pp. 101–02.
28. *Ibid.*, p. 103.
29. *Ibid.*, p. 104.
30. *Ibid.*, p. 105.
31. *Ibid.*
32. *Ibid.*, p. 105–06.
33. *Ibid.*, p. 106.
34. *Ibid.*
35. *Ibid.*
36. *Ibid.*, p. 107.
37. Davis, "Management Communication and the Grapevine," *op. cit.*, p. 43–49.
38. Melvin L. DeFleur and Edith D. Rainboth, "Testing Message Diffusion in Four Communities: Some Factors in the Use of Airborne Leaflets as a Communications Medium," *American Sociological Review* (December 1952), vol. 17, pp. 734–37; see also Melvin L. DeFleur, "A Mass Communication Model of Stimulus Response Relationships: An Experiment in Leaflet Message Diffusion," *Sociometry* (March 1956), vol. 19, pp. 12–25.
39. Korte and Milgram, *op. cit.*, p. 107.
40. Farace, Monge, and Russell, *op. cit.*, p. 191.
41. Jean Piaget, *The Psychology of the Child* (New York: Basic Books, 1969); see also Richard Isadore Yuans, *Jean Piaget: The Man and the Ideas.*

42. Claude S. Fischer, *To Dwell Among Friends: Personal Networks in Town and City* (Chicago: University of Chicago Press, 1982), p. 7.
43. *Ibid.*, p. 149.
44. G. Duby and R. Mandron, *Histoire de la civilisation francaise* (Paris: Colin, 1958); cited in Milgram, "Interdisciplinary Thinking," *op. cit.*, p. 105.
45. Henri Pirenne, *Medieval Cities: Their Origins and the Revival of Trade* (Princeton, N.J.: Princeton University Press, 1925); cited in Milgram, "Interdisciplinary Thinking," *op. cit.*, p. 105.
46. Cited in Fischer, *op. cit.*, p. 10.
47. David Riesman et al., *The Lonely Crowd: A Study of the Changing American Character* (New Haven, Conn.: Yale University Press, 1950).
48. Milgram, "the Small World Problem," *op. cit.*, p. 66.
49. Korte and Milgram, *op. cit.*, p. 105.
50. *Ibid.*
51. *Ibid.*, p. 102.
52. Milgram, "Interdisciplinary Thinking," *op. cit.*, p. 117.
53. Korte and Milgram, *op. cit.*, p. 105.
54. Farace, Monge, and Russell, *op. cit.*, p. 200.

# Part XII

# APPENDIX AND CASE STUDIES

# Appendix A

### QUESTIONNAIRE SURVEY*
by
### The International Communication Association

*Instructions*

Please mark all your responses on the enclosed answer sheet. Please use the pencil supplied, as ink or hard lead pencils will not be recorded. Also, please carefully erase any stray pencil marks. Please answer all questions since each is important for possibly improving the operation of your organization. If there are any questions which do not apply to you, leave them blank. If there are questions which you do not understand, please ask us about them. We appreciate your patience for this important survey.

PLEASE MARK ONLY ONE RESPONSE TO EACH QUESTION

You may find the following definitions useful as you answer the questions on this survey:

[A client-specific glossary of key terms goes here if necessary.]

### Receiving Information from Others

*Instructions for Questions 1 through 26*

You can receive information about various topics in your organization. For each topic listed on the following pages, mark your response on the answer sheet that best indicates: (1) the amount of information you *are* receiving on that topic and (2) the amount of information you *need* to receive on that topic, that is, the amount you *have* to *have* in order to do your job.

---

*From Goldhaber-Rogers: AUDITING ORGANIZATIONAL COMMUNICATION SYSTEMS. Copyright (c) 1979 by Kendall/Hunt Publishing Company, Dubuque, Iowa. Used with permission.

| | This is the amount of information I receive now | | | | | | This is the amount of information I need to receive | | | | |
|---|---|---|---|---|---|---|---|---|---|---|---|---|
| **Topic Area** | | Very Little | Little | Some | Great | Very Great | | Very Little | Little | Some | Great | Very Great |
| How well I am doing in my job. | 1. | 1 | 2 | 3 | 4 | 5 | 2. | 1 | 2 | 3 | 4 | 5 |
| My job duties. | 3. | 1 | 2 | 3 | 4 | 5 | 4. | 1 | 2 | 3 | 4 | 5 |
| Organizational policies. | 5. | 1 | 2 | 3 | 4 | 5 | 6. | 1 | 2 | 3 | 4 | 5 |
| Pay and benefits. | 7. | 1 | 2 | 3 | 4 | 5 | 8. | 1 | 2 | 3 | 4 | 5 |
| How technological changes affect my job. | 9. | 1 | 2 | 3 | 4 | 5 | 10. | 1 | 2 | 3 | 4 | 5 |
| Mistakes and failures of my organization | 11. | 1 | 2 | 3 | 4 | 5 | 12. | 1 | 2 | 3 | 4 | 5 |
| How I am being judged. | 13. | 1 | 2 | 3 | 4 | 5 | 14. | 1 | 2 | 3 | 4 | 5 |
| How my job-related problems are being handled. | 15. | 1 | 2 | 3 | 4 | 5 | 16. | 1 | 2 | 3 | 4 | 5 |
| How organization decisions are made that affect my job. | 17. | 1 | 2 | 3 | 4 | 5 | 18. | 1 | 2 | 3 | 4 | 5 |
| Promotion and advancement opportunities in my organization. | 19. | 1 | 2 | 3 | 4 | 5 | 20. | 1 | 2 | 3 | 4 | 5 |
| Important new product, service or program developments in my organization. | 21. | 1 | 2 | 3 | 4 | 5 | 22. | 1 | 2 | 3 | 4 | 5 |
| How my job relates to the total operation of my organization. | 23. | 1 | 2 | 3 | 4 | 5 | 24. | 1 | 2 | 3 | 4 | 5 |
| Specific problems faced by management. | 25. | 1 | 2 | 3 | 4 | 5 | 26. | 1 | 2 | 3 | 4 | 5 |

## ICA COMMUNICATION AUDIT COMMUNICATIVE EXPERIENCE FORM

While you were filling out the previous section, the questions may have brought to mind a recent work-related experience of yours in which *communication* was particularly ineffective or effective. Please answer the questions below and give us a clearly printed summary of that experience.

A.  To whom does this experience primarily relate? (circle *one*)

    1. Subordinate   2. Co-worker   3. Immediate supervisor

        4. Middle management   5. Top management

B.  Please rate the quality of communication described in the experience below (circle *one*):

    1. Effective   2. Ineffective

C.  To what item in the *previous section* does this experience *primarily* relate? _____(Put in the item number)

Describe the communicative experience, the circumstances leading up to it, what the person did that made him/her an effective or ineffective communicator, and the results (outcome) of what the person did. PLEASE *PRINT*. THANK YOU.

_____

_____

_____

_____

_____

_____

_____

_____

_____

_____

_____

_____

_____

### Sending Information to Others

*Instructions for Questions 27 through 40*

In addition to receiving information, there are many topics on which you can send information to others. For each topic listed on the following pages, mark your response on the answer sheet that best indicates: (1) the amount of information you *are* sending on that topic and (2) the amount of information you *need* to send on that topic in order to do your job.

| | This is the amount of information I send now | | | | | | This is the amount of information I need to send now | | | | |
|---|---|---|---|---|---|---|---|---|---|---|---|
| **Topic Area** | Very Little | Little | Some | Great | Very Great | | Very Little | Little | Some | Great | Very Great |
| Reporting what I am doing in my job. | 27. | 1 | 2 | 3 | 4 | 5 | 28. | 1 | 2 | 3 | 4 | 5 |
| Reporting what I think my job requires me to do. | 29. | 1 | 2 | 3 | 4 | 5 | 30. | 1 | 2 | 3 | 4 | 5 |
| Reporting job-related problems. | 31. | 1 | 2 | 3 | 4 | 5 | 32. | 1 | 2 | 3 | 4 | 5 |
| Complaining about my job and/or working conditions. | 33. | 1 | 2 | 3 | 4 | 5 | 34. | 1 | 2 | 3 | 4 | 5 |
| Requesting information necessary to do my job. | 35. | 1 | 2 | 3 | 4 | 5 | 36. | 1 | 2 | 3 | 4 | 5 |
| Evaluating the performance of my immediate supervisor. | 37. | 1 | 2 | 3 | 4 | 5 | 38. | 1 | 2 | 3 | 4 | 5 |
| Asking for clearer work instructions. | 39. | 1 | 2 | 3 | 4 | 5 | 40. | 1 | 2 | 3 | 4 | 5 |

## ICA COMMUNICATION AUDIT COMMUNICATIVE EXPERIENCE FORM

While you were filling out the previous section, the questions may have brought to mind a recent work-related experience of yours in which *communication* was particularly ineffective or effective. Please answer the questions below and give us a clearly printed summary of that experience.

A. To whom does this experience primarily relate? (circle *one*)

    1. Subordinate   2. Co-worker   3. Immediate supervisor

       4. Middle management   5. Top management

B.  Please rate the quality of communication described in the experience below (circle *one*):

1.  Effective    2.  Ineffective

C.  To what item in the *previous section* does this experience *primarily* relate? _____(Put in the item number)

Describe the communicative experience, the circumstances leading up to it, what the person did that made him/her an effective or ineffective communicator, and the results (outcome) of what the person did. PLEASE *PRINT*. THANK YOU.

_____

_____

_____

_____

_____

_____

_____

_____

_____

_____

_____

_____

_____

### Follow-up on Information Sent

*Instructions for Questions 41 through 50*

Indicate the amount of *action* or *follow-up* that *is* and *needs* to be taken on information you send to the following:

| Topic Area | | This is the amount of follow-up now | | | | | | This is the amount of follow-up needed | | | | | |
| --- | --- | Very Little | Little | Some | Great | Very Great | | | Very Little | Little | Some | Great | Very Great |
| Subordinates | 41. | 1 | 2 | 3 | 4 | 5 | | 42. | 1 | 2 | 3 | 4 | 5 |
| Co-workers | 43. | 1 | 2 | 3 | 4 | 5 | | 44. | 1 | 2 | 3 | 4 | 5 |
| Immediate supervisor | 45. | 1 | 2 | 3 | 4 | 5 | | 46. | 1 | 2 | 3 | 4 | 5 |
| Middle Management | 47. | 1 | 2 | 3 | 4 | 5 | | 48. | 1 | 2 | 3 | 4 | 5 |
| Top Management | 49. | 1 | 2 | 3 | 4 | 5 | | 50. | 1 | 2 | 3 | 4 | 5 |

## ICA COMMUNICATION AUDIT COMMUNICATIVE EXPERIENCE FORM

While you were filling out the previous section, the questions may have brought to mind a recent work-related experience of yours in which *communication* was particularly ineffective or effective. Please answer the questions below and give us a clearly printed summary of that experience.

A. To whom does this experience primarily relate? (circle *one*)

    1. Subordinate  2. Co-worker  3. Immediate supervisor

    4. Middle management  5. Top management

B. Please rate the quality of communication described in the experience below (circle *one*):

    1. Effective  2. Ineffective

C. To what item in the *previous section* does this experience *primarily* relate? _____(Put in the item number)

Describe the communicative experience, the circumstances leading up to it, what the person did that made him/her an effective or ineffective communicator, and the results (outcome) of what the person did. PLEASE *PRINT*. THANK YOU.

_____

_____

_____

_____

_____

_____

_____

_____

_____

_____

_____

_____

_____

### Sources of Information

*Instructions for Questions 51 through 68*

You *not only* receive various kinds of information, but can receive such information from *various sources* within the organization. For each source listed below, mark your response on the answer sheet that best indicates: (1) the amount of information you *are* receiving from that source and (2) the amount of information you *need* to receive from that source in order to do your job.

|  | This is the amount of information I receive now | | | | | | This is the amount of information I need to receive | | | | | |
| --- | --- | --- | --- | --- | --- | --- | --- | --- | --- | --- | --- | --- |
|  |  | Very Little | Little | Some | Great | Very Great |  | Very Little | Little | Some | Great | Very Great |
| **Sources of Information** | | | | | | | | | | | | |
| Subordinates (if applicable) | 51. | 1 | 2 | 3 | 4 | 5 | 52. | 1 | 2 | 3 | 4 | 5 |
| Co-workers in my own unit or department | 53. | 1 | 2 | 3 | 4 | 5 | 54. | 1 | 2 | 3 | 4 | 5 |
| Individuals in *other* units, department in my organization | 55. | 1 | 2 | 3 | 4 | 5 | 56. | 1 | 2 | 3 | 4 | 5 |
| Immediate supervisor | 57. | 1 | 2 | 3 | 4 | 5 | 58. | 1 | 2 | 3 | 4 | 5 |
| Department meetings | 59. | 1 | 2 | 3 | 4 | 5 | 60. | 1 | 2 | 3 | 4 | 5 |
| Middle Management | 61. | 1 | 2 | 3 | 4 | 5 | 62. | 1 | 2 | 3 | 4 | 5 |
| Formal management presentations | 63. | 1 | 2 | 3 | 4 | 5 | 64. | 1 | 2 | 3 | 4 | 5 |
| Top management | 65. | 1 | 2 | 3 | 4 | 5 | 66. | 1 | 2 | 3 | 4 | 5 |
| The "grapevine" | 67. | 1 | 2 | 3 | 4 | 5 | 68. | 1 | 2 | 3 | 4 | 5 |

## ICA COMMUNICATION AUDIT COMMUNICATIVE EXPERIENCE FORM

While you were filling out the previous section, the questions may have brought to mind a recent work-related experience of yours in which *communication* was particularly ineffective or effective. Please answer the questions below and give us a clearly printed summary of that experience.

A. To whom does this experience primarily relate? (circle *one*)

     1. Subordinate    2. Co-worker    3. Immediate supervisor

         4. Middle management    5. Top management

B. Please rate the quality of communication described in the experience below (circle *one*):

         1. Effective    2. Ineffective

C. To what item in the *previous section* does this experience *primarily* relate? _____(Put in the item number)

Describe the communicative experience, the circumstances leading up to it, what the person did that made him/her an effective or ineffective communicator, and the results (outcome) of what the person did. PLEASE *PRINT*. THANK YOU.

_____

_____

_____

_____

_____

_____

_____

_____

_____

_____

_____

_____

**Timeliness of Information Received from Key Sources**

*Instructions for Questions 69 to 74*

Indicate the extent to which information from the following sources is usually *timely* (you get information when you need it—not too early, not too late).

| | | Very Little | Little | Some | Great | Very Great |
|---|---|---|---|---|---|---|
| Subordinates (if applicable) | 69. | 1 | 2 | 3 | 4 | 5 |
| Co-workers | 70. | 1 | 2 | 3 | 4 | 5 |
| Immediate supervisor | 71. | 1 | 2 | 3 | 4 | 5 |
| Middle Management | 72. | 1 | 2 | 3 | 4 | 5 |
| Top Management | 73. | 1 | 2 | 3 | 4 | 5 |
| "Grapevine" | 74. | 1 | 2 | 3 | 4 | 5 |

## ICA COMMUNICATION AUDIT COMMUNICATIVE EXPERIENCE FORM

While you were filling out the previous section, the questions may have brought to mind a recent work-related experience of yours in which *communication* was particularly ineffective or effective. Please answer the questions below and give us a clearly printed summary of that experience.

A. To whom does this experience primarily relate? (circle *one*)

1. Subordinate   2. Co-worker   3. Immediate supervisor

4. Middle management   5. Top management

B. Please rate the quality of communication described in the experience below (circle *one*):

1. Effective   2. Ineffective

C. To what item in the *previous section* does this experience *primarily* relate? _____(Put in the item number)

Describe the communicative experience, the circumstances leading up to it, what the person did that made him/her an effective or ineffective communicator, and the results (outcome) of what the person did. PLEASE *PRINT*. THANK YOU.

_____

_____

_____

_____

_____

_____

_____

_____

_____

_____

_____

_____

_____

_____

### Organizational Communication Relationships

*Instructions for Questions 75 through 93*

A variety of communicative relationships exist in organizations like your own. Employees exchange messages regularly with supervisors, subordinates, co-workers, etc. Considering your relationships with others in your organization, please mark your response on the answer sheet which best describes the relationship in question.

| Relationship: | | Very Little | Little | Some | Great | Very Great |
|---|---|---|---|---|---|---|
| I trust my co-workers | 75. | 1 | 2 | 3 | 4 | 5 |
| My co-workers get along with each other | 76. | 1 | 2 | 3 | 4 | 5 |
| My relationship with my co-workers is satisfying | 77. | 1 | 2 | 3 | 4 | 5 |
| I trust my immediate supervisor | 78. | 1 | 2 | 3 | 4 | 5 |
| My immediate supervisor is honest with me | 79. | 1 | 2 | 3 | 4 | 5 |
| My immediate supervisor listens to me | 80. | 1 | 2 | 3 | 4 | 5 |
| I am free to disagree with my immediate supervisor | 81. | 1 | 2 | 3 | 4 | 5 |
| I can tell my immediate supervisor when things are going wrong | 82. | 1 | 2 | 3 | 4 | 5 |
| My immediate supervisor praises me for a good job | 83. | 1 | 2 | 3 | 4 | 5 |
| My immediate supervisor is friendly with his/her subordinates | 84. | 1 | 2 | 3 | 4 | 5 |

| | Very Little | Little | Some | Great | Very Great |
|---|---|---|---|---|---|
| My immediate supervisor understands my job needs | 85. 1 | 2 | 3 | 4 | 5 |
| My relationship with my immediate supervisor is satisfying | 86. 1 | 2 | 3 | 4 | 5 |
| I trust top management | 87. 1 | 2 | 3 | 4 | 5 |
| Top management is sincere in their efforts to communicate with employees | 88. 1 | 2 | 3 | 4 | 5 |
| My relationship with top management is satisfying | 89. 1 | 2 | 3 | 4 | 5 |
| My organization encourages differences of opinion | 90. 1 | 2 | 3 | 4 | 5 |
| I have a say in decisions that affect my job | 91. 1 | 2 | 3 | 4 | 5 |
| I influence operations in my unit or department | 92. 1 | 2 | 3 | 4 | 5 |
| I have a part in accomplishing my organization's goals | 93. 1 | 2 | 3 | 4 | 5 |

## ICA COMMUNICATION AUDIT COMMUNICATIVE EXPERIENCE FORM

While you were filling out the previous section, the questions may have brought to mind a recent work-related experience of yours in which *communication* was particularly ineffective or effective. Please answer the questions below and give us a clearly printed summary of that experience.

A. To whom does this experience primarily relate? (circle *one*)

    1. Subordinate   2. Co-worker   3. Immediate supervisor

    4. Middle management   5. Top management

B. Please rate the quality of communication described in the experience below (circle *one*):

    1. Effective   2. Ineffective

C. To what item in the *previous section* does this experience *primarily* relate? _____(Put in the item number)

Describe the communicative experience, the circumstances leading up to it, what the person did that made him/her an effective or ineffective communicator, and the results (outcome) of what the person did. PLEASE *PRINT*. THANK YOU.

_____

_____

_____

_____

---
---
---
---
---
---
---
---
---

### Organizational Outcomes

*Instructions for Questions 94 through 106*

One of the most important "outcomes" of working in an organization is the *satisfaction* one receives or fails to receive through working there. Such "satisfaction" can relate to the job, one's co-workers, supervisor, or the organization as a whole. Please mark your response on the answer sheet which best indicates the extent to which you are *satisfied* with:

| Outcome | | Very Little | Little | Some | Great | Very Great |
|---|---|---|---|---|---|---|
| My job | 94. | 1 | 2 | 3 | 4 | 5 |
| My pay | 95. | 1 | 2 | 3 | 4 | 5 |
| My progress in my organization up to this point in time | 96. | 1 | 2 | 3 | 4 | 5 |
| My chances for getting ahead in my organization | 97. | 1 | 2 | 3 | 4 | 5 |
| My opportunity to "make a difference"—to contribute to the overall success of my organization | 98. | 1 | 2 | 3 | 4 | 5 |
| My organization's system for recognizing and rewarding outstanding performance | 99. | 1 | 2 | 3 | 4 | 5 |
| My organization's concern for its members' welfare | 100. | 1 | 2 | 3 | 4 | 5 |
| My organization's overall communicative efforts | 101. | 1 | 2 | 3 | 4 | 5 |
| Working in my organization | 102. | 1 | 2 | 3 | 4 | 5 |
| My organization, as compared to other such organizations | 103. | 1 | 2 | 3 | 4 | 5 |
| My organization's overall efficiency of operation | 104. | 1 | 2 | 3 | 4 | 5 |
| The overall quality of my organization's product or service | 105. | 1 | 2 | 3 | 4 | 5 |
| My organization's achievement of its goals and objectives | 106. | 1 | 2 | 3 | 4 | 5 |

## ICA COMMUNICATION AUDIT COMMUNICATIVE EXPERIENCE FORM

While you were filling out the previous section, the questions may have brought to mind a recent work-related experience of yours in which *communication* was particularly ineffective or effective. Please answer the questions below and give us a clearly printed summary of that experience.

A.  To whom does this experience primarily relate? (circle *one*)

    1. Subordinate   2. Co-worker   3. Immediate supervisor

      4. Middle management   5. Top management

B.  Please rate the quality of communication described in the experience below (circle *one*):

    1. Effective  2. Ineffective

C.  To what item in the *previous section* does this experience *primarily* relate? _____(Put in the item number)

Describe the communicative experience, the circumstances leading up to it, what the person did that made him/her an effective or ineffective communicator, and the results (outcome) of what the person did. PLEASE *PRINT*. THANK YOU.

_____

_____

_____

_____

_____

_____

_____

_____

_____

_____

_____

_____

_____

## Channels of Communication

*Instructions for Questions 107 through 122*

The following questions list a variety of channels through which information is transmitted to employees. Please mark your response on the answer sheet which best indicates: (1) the amount of information you *are* receiving through that channel and (2) the amount of information you *need* to receive through that channel.

| Channel: | This is the amount of information I receive now | | | | | This is the amount of information I need to receive | | | | |
|---|---|---|---|---|---|---|---|---|---|---|
| | Very Little | Little | Some | Great | Very Great | Very Little | Little | Some | Great | Very Great |
| Face-to-face contact between two people | 107. 1 | 2 | 3 | 4 | 5 | 108. 1 | 2 | 3 | 4 | 5 |
| Face-to-face contact among more than two people | 109. 1 | 2 | 3 | 4 | 5 | 110. 1 | 2 | 3 | 4 | 5 |
| Telephone | 111. 1 | 2 | 3 | 4 | 5 | 112. 1 | 2 | 3 | 4 | 5 |
| Written (memos, letters) | 113. 1 | 2 | 3 | 4 | 5 | 114. 1 | 2 | 3 | 4 | 5 |
| Bulletin Boards | 115. 1 | 2 | 3 | 4 | 5 | 116. 1 | 2 | 3 | 4 | 5 |
| Internal Publications (newsletter, magazine) | 117. 1 | 2 | 3 | 4 | 5 | 118. 1 | 2 | 3 | 4 | 5 |
| Internal Audio-Visual Media Videotape, Films, Slides) | 119. 1 | 2 | 3 | 4 | 5 | 120. 1 | 2 | 3 | 4 | 5 |
| External Media (TV, Radio, Newspapers) | 121. 1 | 2 | 3 | 4 | 5 | 122. 1 | 2 | 3 | 4 | 5 |

## ICA COMMUNICATION AUDIT COMMUNICATIVE EXPERIENCE FORM

While you were filling out the previous section, the questions may have brought to mind a recent work-related experience of yours in which *communication* was particularly ineffective or effective. Please answer the questions below and give us a clearly printed summary of that experience.

A.  To whom does this experience primarily relate? (circle *one*)

    1. Subordinate   2. Co-worker   3. Immediate supervisor

       4. Middle management   5. Top management

B. Please rate the quality of communication described in the experience below (circle *one*):

1. Effective   2. Ineffective

C. To what item in the *previous section* does this experience *primarily* relate? _____(Put in the item number)

Describe the communicative experience, the circumstances leading up to it, what the person did that made him/her an effective or ineffective communicator, and the results (outcome) of what the person did. PLEASE *PRINT*. THANK YOU.

_____

_____

_____

_____

_____

_____

_____

_____

_____

_____

_____

_____

### Background Information

This section is for statistical purposes only and will be used to study how different groups of people view your organization. We do not want your name, but would appreciate the following information.

123. How do you receive most of your income from this organization?
   1. Salaried
   2. Hourly
   3. Piece work
   4. Commission
   5. Other

124. What is your sex?
    1. Male
    2. Female

125. Do you work:
    1. Fulltime
    2. Parttime
    3. Temporary Fulltime
    4. Temporary Parttime

126. How long have you worked in this organization?
    1. Less than 1 year
    2. 1 to 5 years
    3. 6 to 10 years
    4. 11 to 15 years
    5. More than 15 years

127. How long have you held your present position?
    1. Less than 1 year
    2. 1 to 5 years
    3. 6 to 10 years
    4. 11 to 15 years
    5. More than 15 years

128. What is your position in this organization?
    1. I don't supervise anybody
    2. First-line supervisor
    3. Middle management
    4. Top management
    5. Other (Please specify:_____

129. What was the *last* level you completed in school?
    1. Less than high school graduate
    2. High school graduate
    3. Some college or technical school
    4. Completed college or technical school
    5. Graduate work

130. What is your age?
    1. Under 20 years of age
    2. 21 to 30 years of age
    3. 31 to 40 years of age
    4. 41 to 50 years of age
    5. Over 50 years of age

131. How much training to improve your communicative skills have you had?
    1. No training at all
    2. Little training (attended 1 seminar, workshop, training activity or course)
    3. Some training (attended a few seminars, workshops, training activities, or courses)
    4. Extensive training (attended a great number of seminars, workshops, training activities, or courses)

132. How much money did you receive from this organization last year?
    1. Less than $9,000
    2. $9,000 to $11,999
    3. $12,000 to $17,999
    4. $18,000 to $25,000
    5. Over $25,000

133. During the past ten years, in how many other organizations have you been employed?
    1. No other organizations
    2. One other organization
    3. Two other organizations
    4. Three other organizations
    5. More than three others

134. Are you presently looking for a job in a different organization?

    ⎯⎯ Yes

    ⎯⎯ No

# Case Study 1
## (Coordinated with Chapter 1)

### Exonidair Airlines

Exonidair Airlines was a small but growing regional airline serving the eastern part of the United States. Because the airline had been expanding rapidly in recent years and had decided to add services in some of the smaller communities it had not previously served, Exonidair was hiring new employees. One of the changes involved the consolidation of reservation services in one central location in Buffalo, New York. Although some employees agreed to move in order to retain employment with Exonidair, on the whole the change of location required a new contingent of reservation clerks.

The personnel department took charge of interviewing and hiring the new employees, and the company set up a six-week training program designed to initiate the new employees into the company, to acquaint them with its management philosophy, and to instruct them in the particulars of reservation work.

A member of the administrative staff, a man with many years of experience in the airline industry and a friendly accommodating manner, conducted many of these training sessions. The general atmosphere was relaxed, and the trainees displayed an enthusiastic attitude toward their new jobs.

The training period ended with a photography session and a new write-up on the new employees in the company magazine. The thirty-plus new employees began work on a full-time basis in a reservations office that included another ten to fifteen employees of longer-term standing with the company. The average age of the longer-term employee was thirty-five years. The average age of the new employee was twenty-five. With the exception of four young men in the class, the remainder of the trainees were women; and all of the previously existing reservations staff were women. The average education level was high school graduate, with a half dozen of the trainees having some university training.

The administration of the reservations staff involved three female supervisors, one scheduled for each eight-hour shift, to whom the reservations personnel answered. These supervisors were in their mid-to-late thirties. They had an average of six to ten years experience with the airline. Appointed head of the entire reservations area was William Andrews, a man twenty-nine years of age who had been with the airline for three years as a counter reservations clerk at the Syracuse airport. Before that he had two years experience with a small travel agency.

The airline reservations office was located away from the main airport. The clerks who worked in the reservations division of Exonidair Airlines never saw the public that they served. Nonetheless, a uniform dress code was part of the general airline policy, and this code was made to apply to the reservations clerks also. The clerks wore institutional gray, light wool suits and white shirts, which they were required to purchase themselves.

Work shifts varied from week to week, with seniority determining the priority of requests. For the large number of employees who shared the same employment starting dates, age was established by upper management as the basis for determining request preferences. In actual practice, however, Bill Andrews arbitrarily decided the weekly shift schedules. There was no rotational scheme of which the employees were aware, leading employees to feel that gaining favor with Andrews was the only sure way of avoiding the unpopular graveyard shifts.

The physical layout of the offices included long rows of tables furnished with telephones and headsets. The tables faced a front area that offered daily flight information, weather data, maps, etc. Individual work stations were designated by small partitions on the desks themselves, giving partially protected work areas but no seating privacy. Because the changing shifts entailed working with different people on different days and there were more employees than desks, no employees had his/her own private work station.

At the back of the reservations workroom was an elevated area that overlooked the individual work tables. Here the first level supervisor sat while on her eight-hour shift. A large electronic switchboard allowed her to access any individual operator's telephone conversations as part of her supervisory duties. The operator would not be aware of the intrusion. The reservation clerks sat with their backs to this supervisor, a fact that deemphasized her presence as an overseer.

To the immediate left of the reservation desks was the middle supervisor's office, separated from the rest of the room by a glass partition. None of the employees was ever quite sure what Bill Andrews did, apart from designating the weekly shift schedules and occasionally reprimanding an employee for tardiness or an unpressed suit.

The relations between the reservations clerks and their immediate supervisors were good. The three women who oversaw the other clerks were friendly and accessible. The best adjective to describe them, however, was "unobtrusive." They rarely intervened in the day-to-day functioning of the office, and their roles as supervisor seemed more token than operational. Nonetheless, they did offer assistance on occasions when, for example, an individual needed to locate a replacement for a shift he/she could not make. As the onus for finding a substitute was on the person seeking the replacement, this service was generally appreciated.

Relations between employees were sometimes strained. This seemed to be particularly the case with the new employees, who formed cliques and spent a fair amount of time gossiping. The older employees, who had been with the company for some time, took less interest in the informal groups but approached their jobs in a very perfunctory way, putting in their hours and carrying out their duties, but displaying little enthusiasm for their work.

No one had any sense of this particular job leading any higher in the organization. Unless one of the supervisors quit or was fired, there was no place to go within the reservations unit. Occasionally, a reservations clerk applied to become a hostess or a counter clerk at an airport office, but this was a horizontal rather than vertical move. The employees' only contact with upper management came in the form of bimonthly visits by one of the company's vice-presidents to the reservations office; but this visit was not viewed by anyone as official, a view that was reinforced by the VP's light flirtations with the female employees.

Although logs were kept of the number of calls received, reservations made, and queries answered by each employee, the employees were never given feedback on their performance. Pay increases were based on time employed. After the initial training period, no input was requested from employees. Rules were outlined, and the employees were expected to conform. Employees punched a time clock when they arrived and left each day. Personal calls at work were against the rules, but everyone made them anyway, particularly those on late-night shifts; and the first-level supervisors tacitly accepted the noncompliance.

Within the first six months after the new employees were inaugurated into Exonidair Airlines, one-third had resigned their jobs, some without notice, and a number of others were looking for alternative job opportunities. Middle manager Bill Andrews was angry and frustrated, feeling that the high turnover reflected badly on him. Personnel was concerned about the financial implications since they had invested a large sum of money and resources in training the new employees, and they felt that their investment was lost. The head of personnel, John Matthews, decided to undertake a study of the situation which included interviews with the remaining employees and with the supervisors.

1. In what way did the physical environment at the Exonidair Airlines reservations office manifest signs of a scientific management orientation?
2. What policies were symptomatic of this particular management philosophy?
3. What employee behaviors indicated that the airlines faced a major personnel problem in its reservations office? Who would you hold accountable for the problem?
4. Do you think that the rather dramatic change of management style from the training sessions to the actual work situation had any effect on employees' attitudes and expectation?
5. Suggest alternative solutions to Exonidair's problems, and recommend the one you would support.

# Case Study 2
## (Coordinated with Chapter 2)

### Alexander's Girls

Philip Alexander walked into the lounge and paused. A large number of his female employees were relaxing, enjoying their morning coffee break.

"Hi girls!"

"Hello, Mr. Alexander."

"How are you doing, Jeanne? Has your sister had her baby yet?"

"No, and she's getting really anxious. We've been picking out clothes and a new crib."

"I see you're wearing a new sweater, Mary. That one you knitted yourself?"

"Yep." Mary smiled.

"I like it."

"Would you like some coffee, Mr. Alexander?" Jeanne asked.

"Yes, don't bother. I'll get it. Anyone need a refill?" Philip responded, moving toward the coffee urn.

"We haven't seen you for the last couple of weeks. Have you been out of town?" Mary asked her boss.

"No, just busy. A lot of important meetings. Priority items. I know I've ignored some of your memos, but I trust you to keep the shop going when I'm not around."

"How did your seminar go, Mr. Alexander? It was this past weekend, wasn't it?" Mary asked.

"It was. And I found it very interesting. I'd like to set up one for all of you to attend sometime. Maybe bring in a consultant to conduct the sessions," Philip responded with some enthusiasm.

"What was the seminar about?" Milly asked.

"It's called a sensitivity session."

"I've heard of those," Mary said with a grimace. "You tell your boss and colleagues what you think of them on Saturday, and then you have to face them at morning coffee on Monday."

The other employees smiled.

664

"Sounds awful," Milly seconded. "I don't think I'd have the nerve."

"That's the confrontation part of the sessions. But there's more to it than that. Being able to reveal your feelings is important. I hope all of you girls realize that I'm here for you anytime you have a problem. I want you to know that I appreciate your commitment and your loyalty to this company." Philip paused, looking directly at each of his employees.

An awkward silence followed. Then Milly spoke, "We know that, Mr. Alexander." (Several of the women exchanged glances.)

"Good. Well, I just wanted to say it again. By the way, Milly, do you think you can have that financial report to me by noon today? I'll be circulating it at an afternoon board meeting. I know it's not much notice, but anything's possible for a good cause, isn't it?"

Milly (looking down at her watch) responded, "Sure. Well, guess I'll see you guys later."

"Natalie, Jim in advertising called me about an hour ago. He needs someone to help him this evening with a layout. I told him I was sure you wouldn't mind." Philip looked quickly around the room to locate Natalie.

"Mr. Alexander, you know I have a problem with babysitters in the evening. I don't mean to be uncooperative, but I honestly don't know who to call at such a late time. All my babysitters are in school now." Natalie looked questioningly at her boss, obviously hoping for a reprieve.

"I'm sure you'll find someone. We count on you, Natalie. You're one of our most dependable workers, always there when we need you. I would offer to come in myself but my son has a baseball game this evening. You know how that is."

Alexander's employees began making motions of leaving. Alexander turned to the one closest to him and spoke in a somewhat lower voice.

"I need to talk to you later today about some problems I see with your latest report. I've made up a list of suggested changes. Maybe if you check with me more often while you're writing up the report, we can avoid the rewrites."

"I did try to check with you last week, but you were out. I thought you liked the last report, Mr. Alexander," Randy said, displaying some frustration.

"I did appreciate your effort. I gave you a bonus for the extra time you put in, didn't I? There's no need to get emotional. I know you'll agree we get a lot more accomplished when we approach things in a cool calm manner."

"I realize I experimented with the format of this report and changed the presentation of the graphs, but I thought the changes added to the readability of the report. I put a lot of effort into this project. In fact, I got so interested in the subject that I worked through the weekend. I don't expect overtime pay, but I had hoped you might give me more independence and responsibility on the next project." Randy paused for breath, and Alexander interrupted her monologue.

"Cooperation, being part of a team, that's what it's all about, Randy. If you're having trouble finishing your projects on time, perhaps you and Mrs. Wilson should be working together on this next one. I just don't really have the time for individual problems. Our company is at a turning point this year, and I have to be concerned with the larger picture. You understand. I'll speak with Mrs. Wilson next week. Just a minute, Randy. Girls, don't forget that our bowling tournament begins Monday. I expect to see you all there in team shirts. Sure I'll drop in. Got to show the company spirit!"

1. Is there anything in this case study that particularly signals to you the presence of a human relations management philosophy in this organization? Be specific.
2. What were the strengths and weaknesses of early organizational development techniques such as sensitivity sessions? Given the situation described in this case study, how likely is it that (1) Alexander's employees would level with him in such a session, (2) that any changes effected would be long-lasting?
3. In what way do the early t-group and sensitivity group techniques differ from more contemporary team-building approaches? What is problematic about Alexander's concept of team work? There are similarities in this case study with the Japanese approach, but also differences. Discuss the similarities and differences.
4. To move Alexander from the category of a "human relations" manager to a "human resources" manager, what would be required?

# Case Study 3
## (Coordinated with Chapter 3)

*Braxton University*

Braxton University is located in the town of Braxton, Ontario. The economic base of the community is predominantly manufacturing of heavy industrial equipment, household appliances, and an increasing amount of high tech development. The cultural make-up of the town is diverse, with almost equal numbers of Anglophone and Francophone Canadians and with almost equally large Italian, Ukrainian, and Spanish immigrant communities. The support and maintenance work force of the university represented a cross-section of the cultural mosaic of the larger community.

The university grew with the town, having originally been a church school set up in the nineteenth century. It graduated to its present status by way of having been, in turn, secondary school, seminary, teacher training college, and community college. In the 1950s, the school was granted university status as part of the government's policy to invest in education as a means of stimulating industrial and economic development.

The late 1950s and the 1960s saw an expansion of the curriculum beyond the traditional humanities and philosophy base on which the school had been built. The new curriculum included faculties of law, business, medicine, sciences, and engineering. Several of the disciplines—notably social science, law, and engineering—earned international recognition, drawing noted scholars to their faculties.

Enrollment at the university grew several fold in the course of twenty years and settled around 10,000 students. Over the years, the university acquired a reputation for attracting large numbers of students from Asia; and these students eventually accounted for over 15 percent of the student population.

The education boom tapered off toward the end of the 1960s; and by the beginning of the 1970s, the days of unlimited dollars were gone. However, throughout the 1970s there continued to be development within various faculties, particularly in the sciences and professional fields.

As a consequence of an economic recession toward the end of the 1970s, university enrollment in all but the major universities in the country declined significantly, and many of the students that the university would have expected to attract were lost to the vocational schools. This trend was interpreted by some university faculty as indicating a public feeling that the university curriculum was neither relevant to the social environment nor useful in preparing students to enter the economic mainstream of society.

The advocates of this point of view suggested that, since the vocational colleges were attracting students that the university would have expected to recruit, the university should counter by emphasizing programs of seeming relevance to the needs of the job marketplace. This was generally translated to mean an emphasis on professional training and on the sciences, particularly the applied sciences as distinct from the theoretical sciences. Furthermore, argued the proponents of this approach, these were the faculties that were already attracting the highest numbers of students; and so these areas should be developed in preference to the traditional humanities, classics, and philosophy arms of the university.

Another group maintained that the purpose of a university was not to provide vocational training as such, but rather to provide the student with an education that was broader and at the same time deeper than that defined by vocational skills training. These proponents argued that competing with the community colleges on their terms undercut the justification for a university education. In other words, if universities set out to achieve the same goals as did vocational colleges, why have universities? They argued that, in times of economic recession, universities have to strive to be more like universities and not less. In such a climate of economic recession and difficulty, the need for an improved economic base could best be realized by strong innovative leadership and scientific and technical advances spawned in idea-oriented universities. Solutions to the society's underlying problems would not come from generating increased numbers of people competing for the very jobs that were already scarce.

Two years after the marked fall in enrollment, the pendulum swung in the other direction, and enrollments reached unprecedented levels. The second group took this to be proof of the validity of their position. They interpreted the swing to indicate a failure of the vocational schools to meet the promise that students had seen them as offering.

However, soon after the enrollment upswing, the university budgets, which had been hardening under government restraints, were cut even more severely. Also a federal commission, set up to make recommendations on the future of universities, put forward a proposal that smaller universities be absorbed into the larger institutions and that a faculty be supported only if it could demonstrate that it offered facilities not already available in other institutions.

These events resulted in the earlier debate being renewed with even more intensity. The board of governors, on which the university president served, instructed the president to set up an investigative committee with two principal objectives. The first of these was to make recommendations on long-range goals, and the second was to devise a strategical plan for attaining the goals. As part of the second objective, the committee would search for ways of attracting support from the private sector so that important university programs, particularly research programs, would not be so dependent on government funds in the future.

The president announced a public meeting to address the topic "The Future of Your University." Advance notice of this meeting appeared in the press, on radio and television, and in posters. It was said that the purpose of the meeting was to inform the public of the problems confronting the university and to invite the assistance of all concerned in developing an action plan.

The announcements stressed that input was sought from the general public, students, faculty, university workers of all levels, the private sector, and the media.

At the public meeting, the president made a very brief opening announcement and welcomed the audience. He then turned the meeting over to the past president of the university, who had earned strong public support as a result of over thirty years of service to the university and to the community.

Retired President John McIver stressed that the object of the meeting was to find the best solution for the community, and he outlined a proposal for making a start. In brief, the plan involved the assembly of a working group with members drawn from all sectors of the community and the university—the faculty, the local labor force, ethnic and minority groups, cultural organizations, industry, etc.

These liaisons with the larger community would in turn call for volunteers to join subcommittees that they would chair. These subcommittees would meet as frequently as they considered to be necessary, reporting periodically to the full working group scheduled to meet on the second Thursday of each month. The meetings of the full working group would be carried on the local community television channel.

The plan was to operate in this way for nine months, at the end of which the working group would submit to the president a report outlining their findings and recommendations. The president would take these recommendations into account in the preparation of his report to the governing body.

Former President McIver stressed the need to include representation of non-salaried workers from the university and the community and the need to consider innovative approaches.

1. How does Braxton University's plan for deciding its future course of action reflect open systems theory? Characterize an alternative approach the university could have taken that would have demonstrated a closed systems approach.
2. How do you think the advocates for a more vocational emphasis in the university curriculum would justify their case as conforming to systems theory? What arguments could the traditionalists use in justifying their approach as a systems approach?
3. In your opinion, which of the above views regarding the function of a university is more likely to result in entropic rundown? Give reasons.
4. Using your knowledge of the role of liaisons and cosmopolites, what would you say would be the ideal characteristics of the committee members?
5. In what ways would the socioeconomic and cultural diversity of the university's clientele exert a positive or negative influence on the search for answers to its dilemma?
6. Do you think that the relevant influences operating on Braxton came more from within the boundaries of the organization or from outside? How is the term *external accountability* more appropriate to some organizations than to others?

# Case Study 4
## (Coordinated with Chapter 4)

*Julie Mitchell*

### The Littletown Gas Company

The Littletown Gas Company boasts of overall efficiency within its various departments. Nevertheless, the Property and Security Department is experiencing a problem with its space-planning section. This section affects the functioning of the whole company, since it is responsible for laying out offices and work areas.

Since the company employs an open-space concept, it is easy to change the size and shape of work areas and thus create much work for the space-planning section. Various sections and entire departments make frequent demands for reshaping to fit their needs, and the space-planning section has to keep up with these demands. The section supervisor who receives the requests then assigns the work to the space-planning technicians under his supervision.

Section manager Paul Lortie receives the initial requests. He then reports the requests to Nick Fulton, supervisor of the space-planning technicians. It is Fulton's responsibility to keep Lortie informed as to the status of each work request. Once Lortie has received confirmation that the work can go ahead, he sets moving dates and books movers, informing all the concerned parties. In the meantime, Fulton's group must produce the plans for the respective deadlines.

The first sign of problems arose when Fulton's group failed to submit its plans on time, creating an embarrassing situation for Lortie, who had already sent out memos to relevant parties regarding their moving dates. Some groups, disrupted by the rescheduling of moves, complained to the director, Mrs. Garrett, who was shocked that her Property and Security Department was not functioning as efficiently as she had thought. She called a meeting with Lortie to discover exactly what was happening within her department.

In his meeting with Garrett, Lortie claimed that he had allotted sufficient time for the plans to be drawn up and could not understand why Fulton and the space-planning technicians had not met his dead-lines. He assured Garrett that he would speak to the space-planning supervisor to rectify the situation.

When Lortie later met with Nick Fulton, he discovered that Fulton was dealing with an attitude problem among the space-planning tech-nicians. Fulton claimed that on numerous occasions, he had had to reprimand his technicians for sloppy work. Furthermore, some of the technicians were complaining that they could not possibly do all the work that was coming to them.

Lortie, for his part, could not understand why Fulton's group was so slow at drawing up the plans; however, if the jobs were going to have to be delayed, why had Fulton not given him greater advance notice?

To this point, Fulton responded that he had notified his technicians of the deadline dates and was not aware there would be problems until it was too late to give Lortie the advance notice that he wished. In concluding the discussion, Lortie requested that Fulton meet with his people to try to uncover the source of the problems.

In response to Lortie's request for a solution to the problem, Fulton set up a meeting with one of his senior space-planning technicians. Fulton had not had much time in recent months to meet with his technicians. So many other duties occupied his day such as ordering furniture, allocating work assignments, and discussing requests with office managers. He had noticed that the technicians were complaining and irritable but felt they were lazy and a heavier work load wasn't a bad thing. In a period of time when many companies were having to lay off employees and cut wages, the Littletown Gas Company had offered secure steady employment. Fulton felt that his subordinates did not properly appreciate their good fortune in being employed by Littletown Gas.

The senior space-planning technician, Norma Williams, stated her own complaints first when Fulton called her into his office. She felt inundated with work, and she felt that her reward for good work was more work. She would not mind the extra load if someone showed some appreciation for her achievement of the impossible. Further-more, Williams said, "Who is Lortie to say when our work should be accomplished? After all, he has no idea what our work entails. When does he ever visit our shop to see what we do? When does he ever ask our opinion?"

Williams turned out to be a wealth of information concerning em-ployee dissatisfaction. Working with the other space-planning techni-cians allowed her to overhear their conversations, and often the technicians confided in her. Most of them did not feel they could approach Fulton with their problems; and even if they could, he was rarely available to approach. Also Williams complained that her group often required additional information about the reshaping of work areas, information that only Fulton could provide. Williams revealed that the technicians resented Fulton's insensitivity to their need for privacy in their interactions with him. For example, on more than one occasion, Fulton had reprimanded a technician in his open-concept office made up of partitions. The other technicians were able to hear the entire exchange.

Fulton rejected this last complaint, explaining that if he and the person to be reprimanded had gone to a separate meeting room, the others, in any event, would have known that the person was going to be reprimanded.

Nonetheless, Williams continued, the lack of privacy created problems. On one occasion, for example, Fulton had inadvertently referred to some of the space-planning technicians as junior draft persons. According to Williams, these people looked on themselves as professionals and resented the implication that they were mere draftsmen.

Fulton responded, "If these people want to be referred to as professionals, then they should start acting like professionals and get their work done."

Williams next raised the issue of career planning and promotions. Some of the technicians were upset that others had received promotions over them. The technicians who had received the promotions had less seniority and less experience. No one had explained the grounds for the promotions. Furthermore, none of the technicians had any sense of where their careers were leading them. No one ever discussed goals or career progress with them. The annual performance appraisals were perfunctory and uninformative.

Fulton defended himself by saying that those who had worked hard and were deserving of promotions had received them, and all employees made a good salary. Obviously, those who were not promoted had not displayed a hard-working attitude. As for career planning, that was not the responsibility of the company. The employees should have the initiative to make their own career plans.

In closing, Fulton asked Williams to collect a list of complaints from the technicians and also suggestions for improving the efficiency of their section.

Williams laughed. "You've never considered any of our ideas before, so why should we think you'd start now?"

Fulton countered that good ideas had never been turned down.

Williams left his office, muttering that obviously nobody had ever had any good ideas.

When Lortie later asked Fulton if he had sorted out the attitude problem among the technicians, Fulton said that it would take a few days to study the list of complaints that his senior technician was compiling for him. He figured that the best approach to solving the efficiency problem was to supervise his employees more closely, as they appeared to be unable or unwilling to work without his guidance. He assured Lortie that the efficiency of the section would be improved.

Feeling more confident that the problem had no bearing on his own job performance, Lortie now approached the director, Mrs. Garrett, to inform her that the problem had been found in the attitude of the technicians and that Fulton was moving quickly to rectify the situation.

1. How well does the Littletown Gas Company appear to be fulfilling the needs of its employees in the Property and Security Department? Relate Maslow's, McClelland's, and Herzberg's ideas to your discussion.
2. Do you think that the Littletown Gas Company is relying too much on traditional motivators? If so, how might a different approach better respond to the needs of these employees?
3. How does Nick Fulton's attitude exemplify a Theory X approach to management?
4. Does this case study illustrate any of the principles discussed by Vroom in his expectancy theory? Do you think that management by objectives might be appropriate in this particular instance? Explain.
5. Do you think that the performance of the employees in Fulton's space-planning division can be part of a self-fulfilling prophecy? How?

# Case Study 5
## (Coordinated with Chapter 4)

### CBM's Ron Lipman[1]

Harry Rhodes was a technical representative with Abel Electronic Data Systems, Incorporated, before he joined Corporate Business Methods (CBM) as head of their technical sales force. He had been with Abel for seven years, having joined the company as a technician. Two years later, he was given the position of technical representative. Harry decided to apply for the job at CBM because he felt that he had little chance for further advancement at Abel. Company policy at Abel was to bring in graduates from management schools to staff the administrative positions.

Before joining CBM, Harry did some research into the company and found that it was rated as third in the field and predicted to be the leader in a few years time. CBM also had a reputation for rapid promotion on the basis of contribution to the company rather than on formal qualifications.

Ron Lipman, who was the VP in charge of the Indianapolis plant, had a reputation throughout the industry as the man to work for if you wanted to be groomed for senior management. Some of the most successful executives in the field had been trained by Ron; and as a consequence, Harry had to compete with many other applicants for the job as technical sales head. The Indianapolis plant was also the most productive and profitable of the North American operations.

At the initial interview, which was conducted by a small panel chaired by Ron Lipman, Harry was surprised that no one asked any questions on sales. He had in fact spent a fair amount of time brushing up on sales techniques, since he felt that this was the weakest part of his background. Instead, Lipman concentrated his questions on Harry's technical background. Even then, the questions did not seem to be designed to measure technical competence but rather reflected a curiosity regarding how Harry came to be interested in electronics and what he thought the future trends in technology would be.

Harry's first encounter with Lipman after joining the company was

675

not quite what he had expected. He went to see Lipman, ostensibly to get advice on a new sales strategy that he had been developing. In fact, he was really using the opportunity to make contact, as a large factor in his decision to join CBM was the prospect of becoming the protégé of Lipman.

He met Lipman outside his office and greeted him by saying, "Hi Ron, I'm having some problems with the new sales policy."

"Good," said Lipman, "come and tell me when you've solved them." Lipman smiled and went into his office, leaving Harry confused and unsure of whether to follow.

Harry looked at Lipman's secretary, who smiled in a half-sympathetic, half-reassuring way.

"What did I do wrong?" he asked.

"You didn't do anything wrong. Why don't you wait until the Wednesday afternoon meeting and let *him* explain how he works. But you should listen carefully, since Mr. Lipman doesn't like repeating himself. He will take some time to put you in the picture, since that will be your first Wednesday meeting."

The Wednesday afternoon meeting was Lipman's idea for coordinating the company's affairs. Wednesday was chosen because it was midweek, sufficiently far from the beginning and the end of the week to leave time for preparation before or action after the meeting. At the meeting, managers and supervisors reported on problems that had arisen since the last meeting or on the progress of ongoing projects.

Any problems brought to the meeting had to be accompanied by proposed solutions. Lipman was insistent that his job was not to solve other people's problems but to help others to find ways to solve their own problems. This did not mean that an individual was discouraged from seeking information and advice from his colleagues. In fact, such cooperative activity was encouraged. In deciding merit increases and promotions, he placed much emphasis on the contribution individuals had made to the solution of their colleagues' problems through assistance, advice, or information offered. For this reason and to further a cooperative spirit, Lipman required that anyone reporting problem solutions must credit those who contributed to the solution.

Wednesday's meetings were not chaired by Lipman. The chairman was chosen on the basis of his or her record of contributions to the problem solutions of others. To Lipman, the person to whom others turned most often for help was the natural choice for leader. As the meeting-leader position was considered to be grooming for senior management, it did not take long for the team members to learn that contribution to the success of the company as a whole was valued above individual performance.

Lipman attended all Wednesday meetings, but his contribution was largely to supply information that could be useful to his subordinates. He maintained that he could make the maximum contribution only if he was freed from the day-to-day decisions that, in any case, others were paid to make.

Lipman refused to interfere with decisions on problem solutions, even when he was confident that the proposed solution approach would fail. He considered that failure was a more expedient, and certainly more memorable, way of learning than through lectures. So long as the immediate cost to the organization was not too great, he felt that over the long term the organization would come out ahead. Besides, there was always a chance that he would be wrong in his evaluation. The fact that Lipman headed CBM's most profitable plant appeared to confirm the wisdom of this approach to employee learning.

The Wednesday meeting was the only regular company activity to which Lipman had a stated commitment. He said that by refusing to do other people's work, he freed himself to do his own work, which he saw as establishing direction and long-range policy for the company. He regarded the leader's job to be that of philosopher, thinking in terms that transcended the department and organization. Only by moving into a more global environment could a person see how the organization fitted into the larger scheme of things.

To accomplish this end, Lipman maintained that he had to have time to read and to think, and more important, time to do nothing. He was a prodigious reader, both in terms of professional literature and literature in general. Lipman also spent a lot of time curling. As he put it, the temperature of ice rinks and the pace of the sport were conducive to the contemplative metabolism. During the season, Lipman flew all over the continent to take part in competitions or just to watch them, the only condition being that the competition not fall on Wednesday afternoon. He was also active in city affairs, having served on the town council and various civic committees. Typically, he answered his own telephone and was available without appointment to anyone who walked into his office, whether colleague, subordinate, or member of the community.

Harry didn't have to wait until the Wednesday meeting to get Lipman's briefing. Lipman dropped into Harry's office in a very casual way the morning after the encounter outside his office and started a conversation that developed into an explanation of his approach to running an organization. Although Lipman's style of presentation was informal and friendly, what he said showed that he had given the subject a great deal of thought and that he was completely committed. Nothing was said about the exchange of the previous day, but Harry took the visit to be a gesture to soften the impact of Lipman's seeming brusqueness. Harry concluded that the need to instill self-reliance was so fundamental to Lipman's approach that no concessions were to be made, even at the expense of civilities.

1. From the information given above, would you say that Lipman's assumptions about what motivates people conform with McGregor's Theory X or Theory Y? Explain.
2. Using Livingston's theoretical propositions on managerial expectations, how would you account for the superior performance and achievements of Lipman's team members?
3. In what ways does Lipman's operating style conform to or contradict the definitions of leadership offered by Bennis, Anshen, and Zaleznik? Would you characterize him as a manager or a leader?
4. Do you think that Lipman conforms to or departs from Argyris' findings on the typical CEO?
5. Is there enough information given in the above description to indicate whether Lipman would be classified by leadership theorists as people-centered or task-centered? If so, explain. If not, what further information is required?
6. Would you consider the Lipman approach to be compatible with the systems school approach? With Japanese concepts of leadership? With human resource theories in general? Explain.

## Note

1. This fictional case study was inspired by a longer description of an actual study. The latter study by Arthur Elliott Carlisle is described in "MacGregor," *Organizational Dynamics* (Summer 1976), pp. 50–62. The case is also depicted in a film titled "Thinking Smarter, Not Harder."

# Case Study 6
## (Coordinated with Chapter 4)

*Gabrielle Scheler*

### Cocktail Hour at the Rosewood Hotel

The Beverage Section of the Rosewood Hotel is a small department within the larger Banquets and Catering Division. "Beverage" is made up of three full-time and seven part-time bartenders who work on a regular basis. During a busy season, such as Christmas, the hotel has casual workers who come in from time to time when needed. Until recently the bartenders were under the supervision of Don Walker, the Beverage manager. The Beverage Section's function is to provide bartending services to receptions, conventions, dinner dances, state dinners, etc., organized by the Banquets and Catering Division of the hotel.

Before each function, the Beverage Section has one hour to set up the portable bars and to stock them with the required liquor, ice, garnishes, soft drinks, beer, and juices. Once the bars are stocked, the bartenders roll them out to the various designated areas in the hotel where bars will be required. It is also the bartenders' responsibility to ensure that there is a table stocked with an adequate supply of glassware at each portable bar station.

Naturally, with every function, the locations of the portable bars and length of time they will be required is different. For instance, a client may want the bar directly in the room where the function is to be held, or he or she may want the bar outside the room in the foyer or hallway. The client may only want the bar for a half hour before a meeting, or he or she may request that the bar stay open all night. The client makes all these particulars known to the Banquets Section or to the hotel's sales department. As soon as Banquets has the necessary information, they notify Walker.

If there are ten bars, all required for the same time, that one hour beforehand can be very hectic! Under Walker's supervision, however, the bars were always ready on time. Walker ran what he would call a tight ship. He had supervised the Beverage Department since the hotel's opening one year earlier, and he had personally hired and trained all his staff. Walker's subordinates regarded him as a good supervisor who knew his job and provided his staff with firm leadership and guidance.

The bartenders admitted that Walker's strong supervisory style didn't leave much room for individuality, but they recognized the necessity for this approach in assuring that the bars would be ready in the one hour allowed for their preparation. As one bartender said, "There are so many things to be done, and often there are last-minute changes; so it's better if there's only one person in charge who can tell everybody what to do and when to do it."

Each afternoon prior to the bartenders reporting for work, Walker studied the function sheets from Banquets to familiarize himself with the specific requirements of each function. Subsequently, as each bartender reported for duty in Walker's office, he or she was assigned a specific job. For instance, the employee might be responsible for putting ice in all the bars, or for cutting the fruit and garnishes required for each bar, or for ensuring that the bars were stocked with the proper liquors, beers, and wine. As a result, everyone had specific duties to perform within the team, guaranteeing that the bars would be ready on time.

When questioned about his leadership style, Walker observed that, given the nature of the job, strict supervision was essential. "I've built a good team, and I'm proud of them. However, things can get hectic, and something new always comes up at the last minute. There must be strict supervision at all times to get the job done. Once the bars are ready and rolled out, then the bartenders are pretty much on their own. Of course, if they have problems, as with a customer drinking too much, I'm always there to lend a hand. But during that one hour beforehand, I don't pay my employees to think; I pay them to work. My team has always abided by these rules and, as far as I can see, they're happy in their jobs."

In an industry where correct timing is crucial and last-minute changes are the norm, Walker's department was regarded as a model of efficiency. At least, that was the case until recently. Approximately one month ago, Walker was promoted; and Jim Roscoe, manager of sales, was transferred to Beverage to take Walker's place. Walker spent several days familiarizing his replacement with the position, and then Roscoe was on his own.

Roscoe was well aware of the enviable reputation Walker's department had enjoyed, and he felt confident that things would continue to run as smoothly as before. On his first night on the job, there were several large functions requiring a total of twelve bars. Roscoe received from the Banquets Department the function sheets outlining the details of each function such as its duration, designated location of the bar, type of alcohol to be served, etc. After reading the sheets quickly, he tacked them on the office bulletin board.

As soon as all the bartenders arrived in the office to receive their instructions, Roscoe smiled at them. "I'm very impressed by the record of efficiency this department has enjoyed. Mr. Walker spoke highly of all of you. There are the function sheets. Take a look at them, see what needs to be done, and let's get started!" With that he turned back to his desk and resumed his paperwork.

There was some hesitation and uncertainty among the bartenders, and one of them approached Roscoe to ask, "So, what would you like each of us to do?"

Roscoe replied somewhat impatiently, "I trust your judgment. Just do what you always do, but you'd better hurry. You've got forty minutes left to prepare those bars."

What followed was complete confusion, as everybody tried to do everything at once. As a result, the bars weren't ready on time; and some clients got very angry. Over the next two weeks, this situation recurred several times and was eventually brought to the attention of the Director of Food and Beverage, Mrs. Barker. Surprised at the sudden dramatic loss of efficiency in the Beverage Department, she called Roscoe to her office for a meeting.

Asked what was going wrong, Roscoe replied, "I don't understand it. The staff worked well under Mr. Walker; so they're obviously competent. But now when they come to work, they're always looking to me for specific instructions and step-by-step guidance. However, I don't feel it's a manager's duty to lead his staff by the hand. They're intelligent enough to think for themselves and contribute their own initiative and judgment. It seems the more freedom I give them to organize their own duties, the more confused things become. This leaves the staff, me, and especially the customers very frustrated. I never had this problem with my sales staff; they always worked well on their own."

1. How does this particular case study illustrate the relevance of contingency theory?
2. Do you think that Walker's leadership style suited his job as manager of the Beverage Section? How about Roscoe's style?
3. Did Roscoe's style of management better suit his first position as

sales manager? Do you think that Walker's style of management would have been appropriate for a sales manager?

4. Do you think that the employment of casual workers has an impact on the appropriateness of a given leadership style in an organization?

5. What are alternative courses of action that might be pursued by Mrs. Barker, the Director of Food and Beverage, to resolve her department's problems? What might be the preferable course of action, taking Fiedler's ideas into consideration?

# Case Study 7
## (Coordinated with Chapter 4)

*Robert Laliberte*

### The Axeman and OBS

Once upon a time there was a government agency known as the Office for Buying and Selling. Quite naturally, it had two major operating components, one for buying and one for selling. For most of its history, OBS had been run by two deputy heads, one for selling and one for buying, both of whom reported to the same cabinet member. Each deputy had his own establishment, budget, programs, and administration.

One fateful day, however, as a result of a government economy drive, OBS's two components were amalgamated under the single stewardship of Jamieson K. Ferguson—also known as the Scottish Axeman, a nickname earned as a result of this thrift, his proclivity for cutting waste, and his track record of ruthlessly eliminating those who opposed his ideas. Ferguson had been the Deputy of Buying before amalgamation and so was well known to OBS's management cadre.

True to his record and reputation, within five minutes of being appointed the sole deputy of OBS, the Axeman replaced all three assistant deputies of selling (one fired and two retired), closed two of the Selling Department's directorates, and put the rest of Selling on notice that henceforth it would have to "profit or perish." Ferguson left Buying virtually untouched. By the end of his first month, Ferguson had struck twenty-three more executives from the office ranks, twenty-two of them from Selling.

To establish his leadership further, Ferguson put in place a Management Review Committee that had responsibility for reviewing all matters of substance in OBS operations. Ferguson chaired MRC, set its agenda, and held a veto over all its final decisions. Submissions to MRC seeking approval for operational and organizational changes had to clear the secretary of the committee, Ferguson's executive assistant.

To this management control Ferguson added an operating style that

$67.6 million profit the previous year. The company is expecting a small profit for 1986–87.

1. This case study, which describes actual events, illustrates some of the most fundamental tenets of Japanese management philosophy. What are these basic principles?
2. Contrast JAL's reaction to the airline crash with behavior that would characterize a United States airline.

## Notes

1. This case study is based on an account by Peter McGill that appeared in *Maclean's,* March 23, 1987, p. 12a.
2. *Ibid.*

# Case Study 9
## (Coordinated with Chapter 7)

### Kawasaki

Kawasaki Motors Corporation, headquartered in California, was a subsidiary of Kawasaki Heavy Industries Ltd. of Japan. Kawasaki decided to extend its United States operations to the Great Plains, where a Nebraska-based plant would manufacture motorcycles, three-wheeled rough-terrain vehicles, and jet skis.[1]

Kawasaki hired Americans for most of the top Administrative positions and drew on the local labor force to staff other positions such as welders, painters, shipping and packing clerks, assembly line workers, and first-line supervisors. The latter they sent to an Askashi, Japan, plant to learn production and fabrication techniques so that they would then be able to train those working under them. At the same time, welders and other specialists traveled to Nebraska to instruct the new employees. Production was underway by January of 1975. Peak employment at the plant was 700 employees in the 1976-to-1981 period.

Operating in a United States context, Kawasaki was faced with several challenges. The Japanese subsidiary had to translate lifetime employment into the nearest United States equivalent, job security. It did so by emphasizing the long term. The company had to encourage flexibility in its employees, a task it accomplished through job rotation practices. Kawasaki undertook long-range career planning for its employees to assure full skill development.

The firm set out to make the workers feel personally responsible for producing high-quality work, but without using the quality circle concept. The workers were given running statistics throughout their work shift, which provided them with immediate feedback on how well they were meeting daily quotas and allowed the opportunity to make adjustments. Where problems were encountered, the workers could decide by themselves about necessary actions, thus minimizing conflicts with first-line supervisors. Recognizing that United States workers don't like overtime, management tried to hold such practices to a minimum.

A relatively flat organizational structure facilitated rapid inter-changes between line supervisors, staff specialists, and workers. Communication networks were well developed, making use of suggestion systems, bulletin boards, letters to employees and their families, and face-to-face meetings, both formal and informal. Production requirements were displayed throughout the plant, with daily, weekly, and monthly comparisons of output. Social activities outside of work hours encouraged a sense of family. Management adopted a policy of being open, candid, and available. An employee faced with an urgent problem could fill out a green card and get immediate attention.

Kawasaki was soon a popular employer. Absenteeism was low. When asked to fill out a form listing what they liked and disliked at the plant, 431 employees who returned the form listed positive points, and only 112 listed any negative points. Positive comments made reference to the nature of the work, good benefits, and job security. Negative comments mentioned environmental conditions, job grade determinations, and overtime.

The quality of the work produced at the Nebraska subsidiary was acknowledged to be on a par with or better than Japanese imports. Output at the plant increased with time.

When Kawasaki first started its Nebraska operation, the firm established its salary scales on the basis of an employee's age, education, and length of service. Subsequent merit increases were to be given at regular intervals. Because many workers felt that this system was unfair (probably as much as anything else because of its administration by a relatively young and inexperienced supervisory staff), management changed in 1979 to a seniority-based merit system. Rather than using the typical Japanese bonus system, the company gave regular pay increments and established a 1 percent skill bonus that was tied to job grade and added to a worker's hourly rate. The response to this revised pay system was much more favorable.

The Nebraska plant adopted the "just-in-time" inventory system whereby required parts were delivered on a daily basis rather than being held in stock. The savings in storage space and labor costs allowed payment of the skill bonuses.

The company did well until 1981 when, faced with a United States recession, demand for Kawasaki products declined. Rather than lay off or terminate employees, however, Kawasaki loaned the city of Lincoln a number of employees for city projects such as building, renovation, and furniture repairs. A condition of the loan was that no regular city employees would be laid off as a consequence of the additional help. Learning of the project, U.S. President Ronald Reagan sent a telegram to Kawasaki, complimenting the firm on its efforts to maintain employment.

When Kawasaki was eventually forced to reduce its staff numbers, it did so on a seniority basis and voluntarily added severance pay. By reassigning workers to plant-maintenance jobs and creating work-sharing and housekeeping duties, the company attempted to keep the layoffs to a minimum.

1. Which Kawasaki policies suggest that the company is governed by a Theory Z management approach?
2. Which policies are reminiscent of a United States-style management, and which are reminiscent of a Japanese style?
3. If Kawasaki's problems continue despite all its economy measures, the company will need to take additional action. Consider alternatives that would be in line with a Theory Z approach.

### Note

1. This case study is based on a description by William D. Torrence, "Blending East and West: With Difficulties Along The Way," *Organizational Dynamics* (Autumn 1984), vol. 13, pp. 23–34.

# Case Study 10
## (Coordinated with Chapter 10)

*Sandra M. Ketrow*

### Nonverbal Communication in Organizations

*Monolith Construction Company*

It is 4:25 p.m. on Thursday, August 25. A meeting, hastily called to begin at 4:15 p.m., has been called to order in the small office of an administrator for the Monolith Construction Company. Four department heads were called in following an unscheduled (but occasionally expected) inspection from a state inspector of safety. The inspector is new, but highly competent, and has found numerous violations of important state safety regulations. Three of these supervisors are talking loudly and boisterously about their softball team, and one is just walking in the door. All are dirty and sweaty, wearing well-worn heavy work clothing and boots.

Although the inspector waited as long as possible to make her report, she has decided to speak, clearing her throat loudly several times. The administrator sits behind a dirty desk cluttered with paper stacks and various building samples. He positions the inspector in a chair at the side of the desk facing the department heads, where she can see everyone. Taking care not to get dirty or touch anything, she sits down, although stiffly upright. In a fashionable but conservatively tailored navy suit, the inspector tries hard not to ruin her suit or her matching navy high-heeled pumps. The supervisors are seated on old straight chairs in a rough semi-circle, although the late person has to stand in a corner of the small and crowded office. It takes a few minutes for the department heads, who are male, to quiet.

They listen for forty-five minutes, although one continually opens his mouth saying "Uh," and leans forward; another slouches in the chair with legs sprawled in front of him and looks around the room. The inspector loosens her tie as she continues reading her long list. When the inspector finishes speaking at 5:30 p.m., one supervisor attacks her qualifications; another begins making excuses; and the others generally join in the chaos.

After the department heads leave, the administrator and the inspector compare their ideas about the results of the meeting and its effectiveness. They decide that the meeting was ineffectual in identifying safety problems and determining solutions. The safety inspector states that she must put the company on report to her bureau, an action that could result in heavy fines for the company.

*Just Add Water Boats, Inc.*

You and your two coworkers in a small boat/marine sales, supply, and service center have been asking your boss (who is the sole owner of the company) to adjust the vacation/sick leave policy. There is no set system for taking time off. Each of you has three weeks per year to use as you see fit, with the stipulation that you be frugal about taking off on Saturdays and never two weeks at a time (especially in the spring and summer). However, you and your colleagues feel that you often work long hours above and beyond the call of duty without compensation or notice. Your owner, Bob Skipper, believes that you all abuse your time off, and he often makes you feel guilty about taking a day off in the same week that you take a sick day. He agreed to meet with you alone (you often function as a store manager) about this issue this morning at 9 a.m. before the store opens for business at 10.

Your discussion begins in the small office located behind (and entered from) the store area. Seated at his antique semi-circular desk in a corner of the office, Skipper leans back with legs out under the desk, hands locked behind his head. You are seated behind your small metal office desk, positioned roughly perpendicular to Skipper's desk, although your desk faces the office door squarely. You have in front of you a written sheet that lists the issues and a record of time taken, as well as regular and extra time worked. You check off each point with a flourish as you proceed.

As the discussion heats up, you get upset and rise, walking around to lean standing against the front of your desk. You have your arms folded, and your chin juts forward; you glare steadily at your boss. Skipper pulls his legs back, feet under the chair. With his head lowered and hardly looking at you, he begins to shuffle the neat stacks of paper on his desk. Since he does not seem to accept your point about actual time off versus time worked, you walk behind his desk and place the sheet in front of him on his desk. Placing one hand on his shoulder, you lean over him to point at one of the figures.

As you corner Skipper on this crucial point, he abruptly gets up, pushing past you to walk briskly out into the store area. Moving behind the chest-high sales counter and still looking down, he begins to straighten magazines and other displays while you trail behind him. You loudly ask him what he intends to do. A customer enters the unlocked front door; you both look at her; and Skipper smiles and asks, "What can I do for you today?" The official day is under way, and the issue seems tabled by mutual unspoken consent.

1. What function(s) does nonverbal communication perform in each case?
2. Identify the *classes* of nonverbal communication that affect organizational functioning and effectiveness.
a. Which one(s) seem to have the most impact in each situation?
b. Which one(s) seem absent, minimally present, or have limited effect on the situation outcomes?
3. In a functional analysis of kinesics and proxemics, which dimension(s) is/are involved in the Monolith Construction Company meeting? In the Just Add Water case? How is this/are these exhibited?
4. How might you manipulate or change these nonverbal factors to enhance organizational and/or relationship effectiveness?
5. There is much not described in each case. What other nonverbal communication "facts" are not included here, but could be important?

# Case Study 11
## (Coordinated with Chapter 11)

*Richard McCarron*

### Torcelli Ski Repairs

The town of Mace, Alberta, lies in the midst of the Canadian Rockies among some of the most spectacular scenery found anywhere in the world. The permanent population is quite small at around four thousand; however, each year in November an influx of several thousand more people occurs, all of whom come to enjoy the wide range of winter activities that life in the mountains has to offer. Although the majority of these people come to ski, they cannot be labeled tourists as such, since they usually work at seasonal jobs to support their winter activities.

Most of these transient workers remain as long as the snow; therefore, they are not regarded with high esteem by those residents whose year-long efforts go into making a real livelihood over the profitable winter months. In fact, there exists a very definite antagonism on the part of the locals (permanent residents) toward the young people (usually from the East) who supply labor for the ski season. A high annual employee-turnover rate and the unskilled nature of the work performed combine to give local residents the attitude that these people are a dime a dozen and thus easily replaced if they get out of line. Also, most of the businesses are small, family-run operations whose hiring and firing policies are not affected by the usual union regulations.

Torcelli Ski Repairs was one such family-run business, and Antonio was the sole owner and manager. Each year, he hired four people from the many applicants who knocked on his door, to assist him in the supply and repair of skis. Antonio serviced thousands of tourists who brought their business to him each year. Although Antonio was considered to be one of the more fair employers, employee Danny Carruthers did not feel that the hours Antonio demanded of his employees in return for the money he paid could be described as equitable.

693

Danny was the senior worker at the ski shop, having been employed there the two previous winter seasons. He had decided to return to Mace each winter, and he hoped eventually to make the town his home. He spent his summers in Toronto, Ontario, at a job where he earned enough to support him through the low-paying winter months.

Despite the poor pay, Danny kept returning to the same ski shop each winter because he believed that Antonio was tiring of dealing directly with the tourists. Antonio had spoken many times of leaving the place to a competent manager, if one could be found. Danny held hopes of becoming that manager, a position that would allow him to reside permanently in Mace.

The third season for Danny began early in November with the preparation of all the skis required for the winter season. Normally this job (being so dirty) was designated to the most junior worker; but this year Antonio had contacted Danny early to request his assistance, since the season promised to be an unusually heavy one. Danny did not really mind doing these favors (it was not the first time he had arrived early or stayed later than normal), since he believed that this would be the year when his responsibilities would increase beyond the tedious work usually given to the transient workers. After all, he had shown loyalty to Antonio by returning year after year; and he was a competent worker.

The first two months passed quickly since there was so much to be done. It was not until the quiet period after the Christmas holiday rush that Danny began to have uneasy feelings about his relationship with the ski shop. Even though he was an experienced employee, he was still receiving treatment no different from that of any other transient worker. His hours remained as long as those of the other employees. His pay was only a fraction higher. Most importantly, he was given no increase in responsibility. On the days that Antonio took off work, he brought in a local resident to open the doors, look after the cash, and lock up at the end of the day. Danny felt angry that he was not trusted, despite all of the favors he had done for Antonio, as well as the loyalty he had shown by returning to the same work for three years.

Although he was hurt, Danny decided to remain the winter at the shop and make known his frustrations to Antonio. He still hoped that things could be worked out. Nonetheless, he had no intention of continuing indefinitely in a job that held no prospects for the future.

The winter for Danny finished in the same manner it began. He was still working long hours at the usual mindless tasks, with no additional responsibilities. His approach to Antonio had been met with little or no reaction, and he realized that he was still regarded as a transient worker who could be easily replaced. Danny left early in March and returned to Ontario, feeling that he had been unjustly treated and also feeling that Antonio had lost a very competent worker, even if he didn't realize it.

1. If Antonio had wanted to keep Danny as an employee, what might he have done to sustain Danny's motivation?
2. Considering Maslow's hierarchy of needs, how many of Danny's needs were being fulfilled by his winter work with Antonio?
3. In what way did Danny's self-expectancies differ from Antonio's expectations of him as an employee?
4. Is it possible that cultural differences based on age, ethnic, or regional affiliation could have influenced the discrepancy between Danny's and Mr. Torcelli's view of the situation? Elaborate, constructing possible characteristics of each individual based on lifestyle, previous experiences, group identities, and expectations.

# Case Study 12
## (Coordinated with Chapter 12)

### A New Job with Carrington Sportswear

Elizabeth examined the possibilities in her wardrobe. Hired for the position of executive sales manager of swimwear for Carrington's Sportswear, Elizabeth felt that the image she presented on her first day was important.

She hesitated, touching a navy blue silk suit. Her eyes flitted to a mauve jersey dress, then back again. No, maybe the jersey was too feminine. Something more businesslike, at least for first impressions, was required. She drew the suit from its hanger.

With three men under her supervision, all older than she, Elizabeth felt that it was important to appear authoritative and controlled in her initial meeting with them. She selected a soft cream-colored shirt and a scarf to add color to her outfit. High heels were out. Something more functional seemed appropriate. Elizabeth pulled a lower-heeled pair of shoes from her closet.

At that moment, Elizabeth's young daughter entered the room. "May I call you today when I get home, Mother? Mrs. Tanner says you have to say it's ok."

Elizabeth hesitated. She felt torn. Leaving Alisha to go back to work had been difficult. She knew that her daughter was going to miss having her at home in the afternoons when she returned from school. But a neighbor had offered to watch her. Elizabeth didn't want to tell Alisha that she couldn't call, but neither did she want to appear to her office help to be burdened by family responsibilities.

"Why don't you have Mrs. Tanner ring me. Then you can get on the phone afterwards." Somehow adults calling never seemed so personal. "Have a good day, honey, and don't forget your lunch. It's on the table."

"Bye, Mom."

Thinking ahead to her day, the young female executive considered the specifics of her planned approach with her staff:

8:00—Meeting with immediate subordinates, the three assistant sales
    managers. Agenda: set schedules and announce new policies.
9:30—Tour plant, meeting other staff members.
11:00—Review financial statements for last year with administrative
    secretary.
12:00—Lunch with V.P of sales and marketing.
2:00—Meeting with designers for briefing on the new look in spring
    swimwear.
3:00—Meeting with marketing director to discuss sales strategies.
4:15—Answer correspondence.

Elizabeth's day began as planned. She met with Thomas, Mitchell, and Gregory, outlining to them certain changes in procedure that she wished to effect. She was careful to seat herself behind her desk, deliberately adding social distance to the encounter.

During the course of the meeting, Elizabeth noticed that the men were very quiet, but she attributed their silence to their lack of previous acquaintance. In closing, she asked if they had any questions. She rose from her desk and walked around closer to the men.

"I hope you'll feel free to come and talk with me about any contributions you might wish to make to our new action plan. I'll distribute the plan next week. In the meantime, please discuss the plan with your employees and get their feedback."

"Will we be meeting again soon?" Mitchell asked.

"Do you think we should?" Elizabeth asked in return.

"Perhaps not. We used to have weekly meetings, to coordinate our efforts." Mitchell paused at the door.

"Did you find the meetings useful?" Elizabeth wondered if Mitchell was trying to tell her something.

"Well, Jim usually wanted our input, but I guess that's a matter of personal style," Mitchell answered.

"Yes." Elizabeth looked directly at Mitchell for a moment. Was he trying to tell her that he didn't like her management style? For a moment, she had doubts about whether she had gone overboard with her attempt at impersonality. The men seemed nice enough—quiet, but nice.

Gregory took the pause as an opportunity to add, "We're getting together for drinks at 5:00, in the downstairs pub. Would you like to join us? Might be an opportunity to get to know each other better." He smiled at her in a warmer, more friendly fashion.

Elizabeth bristled. No, she had been right. Distance was important. The first day in the office, and she was already being invited out for drinks. What nerve to assume she would go out to a bar with them! All Elizabeth's fears surfaced. The stereotypes of women that she had been working so hard to overcome crowded into her thoughts. Her first sign of unsureness had been interpreted as weakness.

"No, thank you," she said coldly. She looked away quickly.

"Another time perhaps," Gregory said to her, with a faint smile. Elizabeth thought that he looked a bit hurt. Well, it served him right. He shouldn't have assumed that she would accept such an invitation.

Thomas, the oldest of the three assistant managers, rose last from his chair, a little too slowly and deliberately, Elizabeth thought. She wondered if his age was going to pose any problems. Obviously, he had been passed over for promotion, and he was bound to resent her appointment. The fact that she was a woman in a male-dominated area must have added salt to the wound.

Thomas stopped, as if he intended to say something to her, but he didn't. Instead, he patted her on the shoulder, smiled and started toward the door, leaving Elizabeth feeling totally confused and flustered. On a rational level, she knew she should feel insulted by Thomas' paternal pat on the shoulder; yet she didn't feel insulted or angry, just confused and unsure how to respond.

She turned to watch him leave the room. For an assistant sales manager, Elizabeth thought, he was dressed rather casually, with a well-worn grey cardigan sweater and suede shoes. He had a somewhat rumpled, tired look. She wondered if he drank. She'd heard that salesmen spent so much time entertaining people that they often became heavy drinkers. Elizabeth wondered if her background as a designer of sportswear had adequately prepared her for this job. It was certainly going to pose challenges. One male chauvinist, one alcoholic, and one manager who obviously had strong loyalties to his former boss.

That afternoon as she was finishing her memos, Elizabeth looked up to see Sally, her administrative assistant, standing at the door.

"Are you joining us downstairs?" Sally asked in a friendly fashion.

"I'm sorry, what do you mean?" Elizabeth looked puzzled.

"Oh, I don't guess you know. It's office tradition to meet Friday afternoons at 5:00 for cocktails. Husbands and wives invited. We're so busy during the week that we don't have much time for socializing, and it gives us a chance to unwind. You'll have a chance to meet our new female Vice-President."

"Mrs. Jennings?" Elizabeth asked, startled at the news that one of the company's top executives would be there.

"Susan rarely misses a Friday. And her son often drops in too. She's a great cook. We have a pot luck dinner once a month, and she makes fantastic perogis." Sally looked at Elizabeth's shocked expression and laughed. "You look surprised. Just wait until you get to know everyone. We have a very special group here. You'll love Thomas, but you won't see him today. He just got a call from the place where he works as a volunteer. He helps out at a shelter for runaway kids. Sometimes if they're short on help, he doesn't even make it to bed at night. If he looks scruffy on occasion, it's because he doesn't always make it home to change. Last year the company gave him the award for most valuable employee."

"For community service?" Elizabeth asked.

"For community *and* company service," Sally responded. "You won't find a more dedicated man—or woman. You know, he turned down your job on two occasions because he felt he couldn't accept the responsibility. He didn't want to give up his volunteer work. Just between you and me, he's good friends with the president of the company; and he pushed hard to get you this position. A few people were worried that you didn't have enough management experience. Others thought you were a bit young. But Thomas was behind you all the way."

Elizabeth gulped in embarrassment at her earlier thoughts. "Sally, I just remembered. I'd like to book another meeting with Thomas and the others on Tuesday. Could you put it on my agenda? And if you'll give me ten minutes, I'd like to join you downstairs."

1. In trying to escape from stereotypical female behavior, do you think Elizabeth is acting out another stereotype? Explain your answer.
2. In what ways does Elizabeth reveal her insecurities to others? Do you think that her first day's agenda is an appropriate one? If not, what would be a better agenda for her first day at work?
3. Why do you think she fears showing her femininity? Do you think her fears are valid in this situation? Does experience show them to be valid for most women in similar situations?
4. Do you think Elizabeth's actions would, in most work settings, be interpreted as assertiveness or aggressiveness?
5. Does it appear to you that Elizabeth is comfortable in her managerial role? If not, how might she modify her behavior to become more comfortable? To what support systems or networks might she turn for help?
6. It is said that perception and self-concept, as well as one's beliefs, attitudes, and values are all learned. If this is true, what conclusions might you be able to draw about experiences that can be influencing Elizabeth's present behavior patterns?

# Case Study 13
## (Coordinated with Chapter 17)

### Amplex Paper

Cire Nosugref was a chemical engineer who worked for a large paper manufacturing plant based in Twin Forks, Mississippi. Twin Forks is a town with a population of 10,000, most of whom are either directly employed by Amplex Paper Products or earn a living by providing services for the plant employees.

Nosugref joined Amplex as a junior chemist in 1972 and worked his way up to the position of chief chemist. He was married with two young children. His younger child suffered from a severe respiratory disorder. Because she displayed symptoms at a very early age, the family doctor told the Nosugrefs that the child's condition was probably congenital. However, two years before she had spent the summer with her grandparents in Oregon; and over the two month period, her symptoms disappeared. Shortly after returning to Twin Forks, her respiratory problems returned.

Nosugref concluded that his daughter's condition was being generated by some environmental factor; and since Amplex Paper was the only industrial plant within fifty miles, he began a search for the cause of her condition by analyzing the effluents from the plant smokestacks.

The work cycle at the paper plant was arranged so that stack emission was kept to a minimum during daylight hours; but the stacks were opened from 2 a.m. to 6 a.m., during which time there was heavy emission. The stacks were over 100 feet high; and the plant was located on the northeast side of town, with the prevailing wind blowing from the southwest. The plant had always been a source of unpleasant odor; but since the smell was most noticeable when the wind was from the north and since the plant was the town's chief source of revenue, residents felt that the odor was a small price to pay. In fact, the local residents referred to the effluent as "the smell of prosperity."

Nosugref conducted his tests privately, because he did not want to be an alarmist or to seem to be biting the hand that fed him. Nonetheless, it soon became apparent to Nosugref that the sulphur content in the effluent was far in excess of environmental standards; and he was even more worried to discover a significant level of mercury and traces of asbestos in the emission. Still, Nosugref was reluctant to make his findings known until he had investigated what was involved in removing the toxics from the effluent.

Further investigation revealed that, in order to bring the toxic emission down to acceptable levels, gas-scrubbing equipment would have to be installed; and the estimated cost of such an installation was between five million and seven million dollars. Nosugref was concerned for the health of his family and for the community as a whole. He decided to tell his immediate supervisor of his findings and to ask him to bring them to the notice of the board of directors.

When consulted, Nosugref's supervisor agreed to discuss the matter with senior management but asked Nosugref to keep the matter confidential in the meantime.

After two weeks, Nosugref asked his supervisor if there were any developments. The supervisor indicated that he had not had an opportunity to raise the matter.

After several similar inquiries provided the same response over the next two months, Nosugref decided that his immediate supervisor was not going to do anything. He arranged for an interview with the plant director and told the director of his findings. The director requested that Nosugref write a confidential report detailing the results of his investigation.

Immediately before filing his report, Nosugref received notice from his supervisor that he had been given an unsatisfactory performance evaluation for the previous six-month period. The evaluation contained a warning that if this unsatisfactory performance continued, he might be fired. Nosugref interpreted this report as an admonition that he should drop his allegations against the company. As distressing as he found the company's response, he felt a moral and ethical obligation to follow through in filing his report.

A month after submitting his report to senior management, Nosugref received notice of termination of his employment. No reason was given for his dismissal. He consulted his professional association and was told that he would have to take legal action if he wished to contest dismissal. The association cautioned that this action would be very costly, with no guarantee that he would win.

Nosugref decided to make his findings public and wrote a letter to the press. The day after the press published the story, Amplex countered with the accusation that Nosugref had been fired for incompetence. The company officials also made public a report that had been prepared by one of their consultants. The report ran contrary to every finding of Nosugref, and the company claimed that Nosugref had concocted his report of dangerous levels of toxic waste out of maliciousness when he was warned that he was to be fired.

1. In what ways does Nosugref's case conform to the model of the typical whistle-blowing incident? In what regards is it different?
2. According to whistle-blowing theory, is it more likely that Nosugref's immediate supervisor passed up the information to his boss but did not tell Nosugref or that he kept the information to himself?
3. Do you think that an ombudsman would have been useful in this particular case?
4. How much support do you think Nosugref will get from the local townspeople? If he challenges his dismissal in court, is he likely to win?
5. According to Stewart, who loses more from an "abusive discharge," the employer or the employee?

# Case Study 14
## (Coordinated with Chapter 24)

*Robert Laliberte*

### Boar's Head and Regent Palace

The Boar's Head Inn hotel and restaurant chain has had a long and successful history. Its Inns and fine restaurants, spread throughout the United Kingdom, cater principally to the upper classes and well-to-do, although there are small eateries in each hotel to meet the needs of the less sophisticated.

Until recently, the company has grown consistently and profitably for most of its 112-year history. In the past two years, however, the Boar's Head company has begun to encounter financial problems. Five of its twenty inns are losing money and the profits from the other fifteen are down sharply. While the company is in no danger of imminent collapse, it has had to curtail operations and shelve plans for an ambitious expansion into Europe and the United States.

The company is run by a small group of English lords, with ancestral ties going back for hundreds of years. The present owner group hasn't changed for over a quarter of a century. Each owner lord inherited his position and an equal share in the company from his father. All the lords (known in business circles as "The Nine") attended the same colleges, albeit at slightly different times. They each belong to the most important and appropriate clubs and hold positions of trust in those that are of most relevance and interest to the company.

The various posts on the Board are held on a rotational basis for a period of not less than three years, subject to renewal for another three years. Each lord has held at least four different posts in the executive of the company, as preparation for Board responsibility. They have all assumed at least three different Board positions over the past twenty-five years.

Each lord has one vote in all Board matters. Decisions are agreed to by a simple majority vote, except in cases of appointment to executive positions in the company. For executive appointments, a two-thirds vote is required—both on hiring and firing.

According to an article in the financial section of the *London Daily Times,* the Boar's Head's recent difficulties can be traced directly to an "upstart" operation from the United States—Regent Palace Hotels. In less than five years, this publicly traded, highly profitable company with its "rapacious business-school dropout" CEO, Stanely Smythe (formerly Smith), has managed to build or buy out hotels on sites in direct competition with all the inns of the Boar's Head chain.

The article outlined to readers that the Regent's board of directors was comprised of "inexperienced, under-age 'whiz kids,' MBAs with marketing skills, the inevitable industrial engineer, a chef (of questionable French credentials), and turncoat aristocrats, along with assorted 'fast guns' hired to clear out the opposition." The article further indicated that Regent's profits came in large part from having "velour parading as velvet, plaster in place of wood, plastic in place of stained glass and thinly disguised 'burgers and fries' and 'kiddie plates' masquerading as proper cuisine."

The *Daily Times* article was written by a second cousin of the lord in charge of Marketing at the Boar's Head—Lord Forthwain. It was the subject of quiet discussion at the weekly Board meeting of "The Nine."

*Lord Bathshaw:* "I say Charles (Lord Forthwain) . . . I thought we'd agreed not to take on this Regent fellow Smythe. We agreed he's no problem to us. It's the economy, my man . . . the economy. Can't go around writing stuff like this, you know. It just isn't cricket, old man. Now we may have stirred up interest in this fellow. Damned nuisance, wot?"

*Lord Forthwain:* "I realized we agreed. Just thought we should do something, you know. After all, Smythe is making money and we're not. Damned inconvenient, but there it is."

*Lord Montenoy:* "Now hold on here a moment, Charles. That Smythe fellow is no bother to us. Plenty of room in the market. Why, the British people will see that his outfit is a rank fake . . . the people who count will see. Why, it would be obvious to a blind man that Regent just isn't up to snuff. What does Smythe know about the British and Britain? Certainly, there are a few problems with our operation. We need to make a few changes. Perhaps replace a manager here or a chef there. But fundamentally, Charles, we're sound. Now let's stay together on this, Charles. We all agree that we just have to settle in and ride out this blasted economic downturn . . . nothing for it really . . . just ride it out."

*Lord Bathshaw:* "Here, Here! Stout thinking indeed! Not to panic.

No more mattering about this Smith/Smythe fellow. The good will come through. Always have . . . always will. We hold tight and weather the storm. Agreed?''

*Nine Lords:* ''Agreed!''

At the same time, at the biweekly meeting at Regent Place, Stanely Smythe was discussing the *Daily Times* article with his Board and Executive.

*Smythe:* ''Ladies and gentlemen . . . I presume you have all read the *Daily Times* piece. Good. I'd like your suggestions on what we should do with it; but before I open the floor for comments, there are a few things I want to say to some of you individually.

Jackson (public relations), I'd like you to look into options for dealing with the image and other problems the *Times* is trying to create here. We're not faking anything and they know it. So, we have to find out why they printed this piece, whether it's done us any damage, and how we can minimize the effects. You lead the project, Jackson. Get a team together and see what the damage is. Report back to the board at the next meeting and give us ten to fifteen suggestions on how we should proceed.

Second . . . ah yes . . . Lord Marion (Finance). As one of the ''turncoat aristocrats,'' I'd like you to pull together a report on British feelings, sentiments and culture, and the type of market constraints or opportunities they present to us. I realize we had a full-blown market study done five years ago, but it's time for another look. I'm particularly interested in your perceptions as a member of the society, class, and network we aim at in Britain. Michael James from research and analysis will help you with the technical part. Call on any of us if you need anything further.

As well, I think we should put together some in-house groups and bring in an outsider to see what we can do to avoid this type of problem in future. Perhaps we can discuss the specifics for these task forces over the next few meetings; but right now I'm interested in what ''The Nine'' think, where they're going, what their strategy is, their strengths and weaknesses . . . the whole picture. I don't want to be caught short if this article turns out to be the opening salvo in some sort of war between them and us. All right . . . Let's have any suggestions any of you may have . . . the floor's open . . .''

*Jackson:* ''Well, Stan, I think we may be overreacting a bit here. Let's not go overboard on this. I'll check out their connections with the *Daily Times* . . . could be they're just running scared of us. As well, I can pull together some feature pieces for the paper on the advanced materials we use.''

*Lord Marion:* ''Hold it, Jackson. Not to be too conservative, but that isn't what's important here. Better to push on the fit that Regent tries to make between heritage and the best in building, on the tradition and craftsmanship we keep alive by renovating the great hotels we buy

. . . all these types of things. Fast, modern, efficient, big . . . that may be great for the U.S.; but here, for this market, we need to show our concern with tradition, heritage, and class.''

*Jackson:* ''O.K., I'll buy that, but I'm not sure I want to go too far down tradition road. We do have a market to serve and it's not all that hidebound. I'll pull something together and run it past you. I'll use some of the local talent to help balance the perspective out . . . OK?''

*Lord Marion:* ''Agreed. Now what about you, Michaels? What do you and the rest think about what we should be doing?''

1. Which of the two companies do you think will be successful in reaching the market they both share? Why?
2. What do you think of the strategy of ''The Nine'' to use the ''old boy'' network of the *Daily Times*? Will it be successful?
3. The two companies demonstrate very different decision-making processes and styles. Which style do you think would be more effective in responding to ongoing problems? To crisis situations? Why?
4. You have reviewed materials on groupthink and other types of decision-making process difficulties. Which company do you feel has the more effective decision-making process? Why?
5. What elements do you feel exist in both companies to promote or inhibit problems of communication relative to decision processes?

# Case Study 15
## (Coordinated with Chapter 25)

### Executive Decision Making at Thomas Discount Enterprises

Jerry Thomas was the prototype of the successful self-made man. He formed his own company six years out of high school. His enterprise grew from a small discount clothing store to a chain of discount stores that claimed clientele across three southern United States states—Texas, Louisiana, and Mississippi.

Nominally, Thomas Discount Enterprises was governed by the decisions of a board of directors that Thomas chaired, with three vice-presidents in charge of the tristate regional operations. In actual fact, however, Thomas himself made all important decisions, leaving the day-to-day running of the company to the vice-presidents.

In the past, no one had argued with Thomas' managerial style. As the founder of the company and a man acknowledged by associates and competitors to be of impeccable character, Thomas was admired by those who worked under him. On many occasions, he had demonstrated that his strong, personal, intuitive-based decision-making style worked. The company had grown and prospered under his leadership.

After thirty-five years as president of Thomas Discount Enterprises, Thomas had made the decision to retire from the presidency, while still retaining the title of chairman of the board. Having decided to retire, Thomas was faced with the need to choose his successor, a right that he had retained.

Thomas Discount Enterprises was a family business. Two of the regional vice-presidents, Matthew Thomas of the Mississippi region and James Elridge of the Louisiana region, were related to Thomas. Matthew Thomas was a younger brother, and James Elridge had married Jerry Thomas' youngest daughter.

Elridge had displayed a keen interest in the family business for the fifteen years that he had been a part of the Thomas family. It was generally believed that Thomas was well-disposed toward Elridge, often having him over for weekend gatherings and asking advice on many matters requiring executive decisions.

Like Jerry Thomas, Elridge's entry into the business world came after a high school education and several years experience in a sales position with a retail shoe store chain. Since coming to Thomas enterprises, he worked his way from assistant merchandising manager to regional vice-president of the Louisiana division. The stores under his control showed consistent but unspectacular profits. He had a solid reputation as a family man and a loyal Thomas supporter.

A third vice-president, Louis Melville, who headed the prestigious Texas operation, bore no relation to the family but had gained the respect of Jerry Thomas in his ten years with the company. Prior to joining Thomas' firm, Melville had worked for a competitor, Willow-dale Discount Company, as an advertising executive. Since coming to work for Thomas, he had compensated for a somewhat abrasive and direct personality with an unprecedented profit record. Melville's failure to conceal a certain contempt for the casual way in which decisions in the company were made and his resentment of what he felt to be undue influences by the family members did not contribute to his popularity with the other two vice-presidents. He did, however, have a working relationship with David Wilson, nephew to Jerry Thomas and the youngest of the contenders for the presidency.

Wilson held a master's in business administration from Harvard University. His aggressiveness and ambition had contributed to his being hired as director of marketing for Texas, the largest and most profitable state operation. Some in the company felt that he had been strategically placed under Melville to be prepared for later executive status.

Other influential positions in the company were held by legal counsel Stephen Shepherd; personnel director William Marsh; and advertising head for the Louisiana-Mississippi regions, Richard Davis. Of these three, only Shepherd could have been considered as a serious contender for the future presidency of Thomas Discount Enterprises.

Thus, the contingent that qualified for consideration for the presidency included family members James Elridge, David Wilson, and Matthew Thomas. Nonfamily members included Louis Melville and Stephen Shepherd. Matthew Thomas had disqualified himself, claiming that with only a few years before retirement himself, he did not want the added responsibilities.

While not everyone who attended the meeting to discuss Jerry Thomas' impending retirement regarded himself as an equal or even serious contender for Thomas' job, all held opinions and favoured certain persons over others. Therefore, more than one hidden agenda was being pursued at the meeting. The following typifies the exchange that took place:

*Jerry Thomas:* As you know, the purpose of this meeting is to consider the question of a new president for Thomas Enterprises. Although I reserve the right to make the final decision, I am interested in hearing your views on the subject. That's the reason I've called you together. I consider this group as the management core of Thomas Enterprises, and I have a deep respect for your opinions.

*Elridge:* I think you know we all appreciate what you've contributed to the company and to us over the years, but I would just like to formally say so now. It's going to be tough replacing you.

(Murmurs of agreement come from around the table.)

*Jerry Thomas:* I'll be the first to admit that we've been experiencing some problems in recent years. The downturn in the economy has affected most firms in North America. We've had to trim the fat off some of our operations. But we're still showing a profit, and things will probably pick up again in a year or two. Nonetheless, both the choice of a new president and the support that all of you can give him in the coming months will be important. We're at a critical point in the growth of the company. Some important decisions will have to be made, questions about diversifications and investments. Not like when I started out. Specialization's out, and diversification's in.

*Marsh:* I was having a casual discussion with our financial advisor the other day, Jerry. He says we need to move quickly on some investments.

*Davis:* I personally don't think this is the time to buy. We've had some serious outlays in recent months, and some of Hodgkin's suggestions have not panned out.

*Shepherd:* Maybe we should consider another financial advisor rather than giving up investing.

*Melville:* I'm inclined to agree. Profits in my region are up 20 percent over last year. We've got extra cash. It's time to take some risks.

*Jerry Thomas:* Maybe I'm just growing more conservative as I get older, but I think Richard has a point. I remember when I first started out this company. Millicent and I had so much to do just keeping the day-to-day operations of the company going that we didn't have time to argue about where to invest next. An opportunity came up, and we took it; or we didn't take it. But we didn't plan so far ahead. Maybe I'm wrong. I don't know. That'll be something for the new president to decide.

*Matthew Thomas:* I think we're getting a bit off track, Jerry. Maybe we should get back to the topic of choosing a new president.

*Jerry Thomas:* Agreed. You've reminded me, Matthew. I'd like to have a chance to sit back and listen. I'd like to ask you to take over chairing the discussion.

*Matthew Thomas:* Ok, I think first we've got to decide "Do we want the position to be filled from inside or outside the organization?"

*Elridge:* I don't know how the rest of you feel, but I think, "What's the point in working hard for a company and giving your loyalty over a lifetime if somebody else can just come in and take over?''

*Davis:* I agree.

*Elridge:* The people in this company are as good as anyone we're going to get from outside.

*Marsh:* I think we shouldn't completely discount the idea of someone from outside. Jerry's done a great job of guiding this company, but maybe it's time for some new blood. You said yourself, Jerry, we're at a critical point. Profits have dropped in the last few years. Maybe a fresh outside point of view would be what the company needs.

*Melville:* I disagree. I think more openness within the company is what we need. A lot of people feel that too many decisions are made in living rooms.

*Elridge:* At family gatherings?

*Melville:* You said it.

*Shepherd:* I think there is some feeling that you don't have the same opportunity to have your opinions considered if you aren't present at the time that the decisions are made.

*Jerry Thomas:* Hold on, now. I consider all of you as family. You've all been in my home. I respect you all. I ask your advice.

*Melville:* Some more than others. Excuse me, Jerry, but that's how I feel.

*Matthew Thomas:* Things are getting a bit heated up here. Reminds me of the old joke about the pot-bellied stove whose owner said, ''I think you've been eating a bit too much.'' The stove replied, ''I need the energy.'' Let's get back on track here. I think most agree that the first criterion for president should be ''member of the company.'' Any other suggestions?

*Elridge:* Yes, good family man.

*Marsh:* I think that in today's marketplace—no offence intended, Jerry—that a sound educational background is important.

*Jerry Thomas:* I think we shouldn't define education too narrowly. The school of hard knocks can teach you a lot.

*Matthew Thomas:* Maybe we could say a ''demonstrated sound knowledge of the present business climate.'' I think everyone would agree with that definition.

*Melville:* I personally would like to clarify whether anyone outside the family is going to be considered for the presidency.

*Elridge:* I don't think Jerry has any intention of suggesting that you or anyone else in this room wouldn't be considered.

*Matthew Thomas:* Let's not get upset.

*Melville:* I think we should get our feelings out in the open. Let's call a spade a spade.

*Shepherd:* I think Louis has a valid point. I too would appreciate a word from Jerry on this question.

*Jerry Thomas:* I certainly do have something to say. I said before, and I will say again, I haven't made any decision at this point. I'm open to all points of view.

*Shepherd:* And to all people?

*Jerry Thomas:* And to all people.

*Wilson:* Getting back to criteria, I'd like to add a point, Matthew. "Energetic." A president in 1980 has to be energetic.

*Melville:* And aggressive. I agree, David. I'd like to add "Willing to take risks." You can't be afraid to get out there and do battle.

*Elridge:* I think "moral" is a word that still has importance. Thomas Enterprises was built on the solid reputation of Jerry Thomas. A man of integrity, loyal to his friends and his family.

*Jerry Thomas:* Millicent and I would never have thought thirty years ago where we would be today. We had our dreams. We all have our dreams. But it's a different world now. Maybe it was easier to be a family man then. Families stayed together. Not like the divorce rates today.

*Elridge:* A company still has to think of its image. You certainly know that as well as anybody, Richard. In advertising you don't sell the company. You sell the company's image.

*Matthew:* Let's see. I've got down "loyal" as the last point. Anything else?

*Wilson:* I would like to suggest a new direction for the discussion. I think we've expressed our views on some of the most important criteria for a new president. I think we should also consider "What should his role be?" I'd like to hear some of your opinions on this topic.

*Shepherd:* That's a good point, David. What do you think?

*Wilson:* I think a president should have a visionary role today. For example, he should think of where we want to be ten years from now.

*Shepherd:* A long-range planner?

*Wilson:* Yes, but he should be more than that. He should be a leader, not a manager. He should trust those under him to carry out the day-to-day operations of the firm and should himself be a link with the external environment. I think Jerry was this kind of leader. I think that's been his key to success. He claims to have made impromptu decisions on many occasions, but I don't think there was a day that Jerry didn't think of where he wanted to be five years or ten years ahead.

*Jerry Thomas:* Like I said, we always had our dreams, and I'm pleased to say most of them happened.

*Elridge:* A good thing for all of us, I'd say!

*Shepherd:* Expanding on what you've said, David, I'd like to add that developing an inner advisory group would probably be useful, one that could coordinate the efforts of the three state operations. Many times I feel that we don't talk enough to each other. What do the rest of you think?

*Marsh:* More meetings would probably be useful.

*Melville:* I'm not opposed to that. I do think it's important though not to lose the distinctiveness of approaches that characterizes our different state operations. Texas isn't Mississippi, and vice-versa. We cater to a different clientele.

*Marsh:* I have to admit, I feel a bit worried. We've had such high turnover in the lower ranks of the organization in recent months. I've been personally feeling that there's something wrong that I can't quite identify.

*Matthew Thomas:* What do you mean?

*Marsh:* Well, here we are talking about a new president for Thomas Enterprises, but most of the employees out there could care less. They don't identify with anyone beyond their immediate supervisor. And I don't know what to say to middle management anymore, what to tell them to do about the high rates of absenteeism and turnover. Personally, I feel unable to cope. I want to help, but I don't know how to.

*Elridge:* We know you're trying, Bill. That's all we expect.

*Jerry Thomas:* I'd say we're coping very well. We're showing a profit when many other companies aren't.

*Wilson:* I think we all sympathize with you, Bill, and we should consider your problem at one of our future meetings. Today, however, we're pressed for time, and maybe we should go on.

*Melville:* I agree. We seem to be getting nowhere fast.

*Matthew Thomas:* I think we were considering the role of the new president. Does anyone else have a contribution to make? It's important that we all feel comfortable with our decisions today. We don't want injured feelings and conflict. David?

*Wilson:* I myself feel there is a relationship between some of the qualities we listed as ideal ones for a president and the role he will be expected to play. Maybe we should try to tie some of these points together. And I personally would like to hear more from you, Jerry. You've been rather quiet today, and I think I speak for all of us when I say we'd like your views too.

1. Identify some of the communication roles played by members of the executive committee.
2. Who played group maintenance roles?
3. Were there any clearly identifiable dysfunctional roles?
4. What hidden agendas were operating? How were these evidenced in the dialogue that took place at the meeting?

# Case Study 16
## (Coordinated with Chapter 30)

### Telecommuting

Elissa David was employed by Kalif Insurance Company of Chicago when she became pregnant with her second child. At seven months, Elissa took a six-month maternity leave, three months paid and three months unpaid.

When her baby was four months old, Elissa resumed work at Kalif. Her job entailed examining computer records of insurance claims to determine the eligibility of claimants for benefits.

Living in a suburb of the city, Elissa found that she had to begin her day at home at 5:30 a.m. in order to reach work by 8:00 a.m. She had to rise early enough to feed and dress her two children, take the baby to the next-door neighbor and the five-year-old to her mother who lived three blocks away. Her husband and she then drove together into the city, a drive that often took as long as forty-five minutes from time of departure to parking the car in an urban lot.

Sitter and parking charges were high, and sometimes Elissa wondered if the money left after paying the extra costs was worth the effort she expended.

Evenings were no less hectic. At 4:15 p.m. each day, Elissa and her husband Jeff met at the parking lot that was located halfway between their two offices. They generally stopped at a grocery store on the way home to pick up last-minute items before collecting first five-year-old Susan and then baby Melissa.

Preparing the evening meal, feeding the children, and clearing the dinner dishes consumed the next two hours for Elissa, while Jeff took over the after-dinner care and night baths of the children. By 8:30 p.m. both children were in bed, and Elissa and Jeff had a short reprieve before organizing clothes and lunches for the next day.

For eight months, Elissa pursued this schedule before making the decision to discuss telecommuting and part-time work with her boss, Jim Edwards. Initially she met with resistance, since the company had not experimented with alternative work styles; but Elissa's determination and the quality of her work as an employee eventually combined to convince Edwards that it was worth a try.

Elissa set up her computer at home and agreed to a four-hour work day, with the understanding that she would work overtime when necessary. She arranged to keep her children with her until 11:00 a.m. each day and to pick them up again at 4:00 p.m., allowing an unrushed four hours for carrying out her business activities.

In the first week that Elissa began her new work schedule, she discovered a number of advantages but also some unexpected disadvantages to her new employment program.

1. What would have been some of the advantages of Elissa's new work program, from the point of view of Elissa and Kalif Insurance?
2. What could have been some of the disadvantages, both for Elissa and for her employer?

# Case Study 17
## (Coordinated with Chapter 32)

*Jenepher Lennox*

### Odessy Communications

Odessy Communication Systems is a company specializing in the distribution of computer software programs. The company was established six years ago by Colin Bright and Jessica Thom, two friends who had studied together in the University. In its first year, Odessy had grown to a staff of eight. Six of the original members were still with the company; and two new members, Stacey Ratton and Brad Broad, had joined a year before.

The management philosophy shared by all members of Odessy was that frequent group discussions, participatory decision making, and an open and supportive climate would allow Odessy to grow and prosper. To promote the philosophy, the following policies were created in the initial stages of Odessy's development:

- Weekly meetings would allow consideration of problems, airing of grievances, and discussion of new ideas.
- Consensus would be reached on all major decisions.
- To create an open climate, activities such as sports, social gatherings, and membership in a software club would be encouraged. Also, a comfortable, informal dining area would be created; and offices would be bright and comfortable, easily accessible by everyone.

Six months ago, Odessy introduced a new line of software called "Dear John," a collection of prewritten letters in various styles and for a variety of occasions. The user simply had to fill out a series of questions on the requirements for the letter; and the software, drawing from its collection, would automatically compose a letter.

At first, the software had received good publicity and had produced good profits; in the last several months, however, Odessy had received many complaints from dissatisfied users. Apparently, the software was creating letters that did not meet the needs of its users.

A discussion session was called, to be attended by all staff members. Two members, Jim and Sheila, entered the meeting together.

*Jim:* I don't know what could be wrong with "Dear John." It's the most exciting new software on the market since we designed "Filer" two years ago.

*Sheila:* I know. We spent so much time conceptualizing and designing it.

*Jim:* I'm sure that the trouble is with the retailers. Their attempts to demonstrate and sell the products are a farce. Even without real sales experience, I know that any of us could do a better job of selling.

The rest of the staff was seated; so all turned their attention to Colin, who began to outline the problem.

*Colin:* I guess you've all heard that "Dear John" is generating some complaints and receiving some pretty bad publicity. I've brought the complaints report and the press clipping file so that we can all take a look to see what the problem is.

*Amanda:* Well, I've read the complaints report, and I can pretty well summarize it for all of you. People don't feel that the letters written by "Dear John" are meeting their needs. The tone and working don't match the occasion.

*Tony:* The press clippings mainly say the same thing. The critics say that the letters that come out of "Dear John" are too much the same from one to the next. They claim that anyone receiving a "Dear John" feels like it's the same letter that everyone else got. (Everyone laughs)

*Jessica:* OK, so it sounds like a problem of poor PR. The customers just aren't being shown how individual each letter is. They need to be convinced that "Dear John" is a necessary and valuable tool in their work.

(Nodding heads, several voices of agreement)

*Brad:* Isn't it possible that "Dear John" is just lacking in originality? If it's the tone and working that people don't like, how will better publicity change that?

(Several members voice their disagreement)

*Jim:* We all know it's a super product. We did numerous tests; we did consumer surveys; and we're the only company marketing anything like "Dear John."

*Amanda:* You agreed that it was great, Brad, when we were doing the original tests. Product promotion has a huge effect on how the product is perceived by consumers; so if "Dear John" is not getting the right kind of marketing, we can't blame the software for the lack of positive response.

*Jessica:* Right. Now, we have to decide how to market "Dear John" so that consumers will appreciate it as the useful product it is. Any suggestions?

*Jim:* What if we invest in some quality advertising on television and in the newspaper? If we hire a good ad agency, we'll get the message across.

(Nodding heads, murmurs of agreements)

*Brad:* Before we embark on an ad campaign, don't you think that we should decide whether the product should be modified, or even withdrawn? I mean, we can't ignore the fact that there are more than superficial problems with it.

*Amanda:* Are you kidding? After the months we've all spent working on "Dear John," designing it, testing it, perfecting it, and finally putting it on the market? We can't just forget all that work and abandon the whole project!

*Jim:* Yeah, we know it's good. If we put out a couple of thousand dollars to really promote the product, show people its good qualities, then we won't have to worry about a few letters of complaint. Besides there are always a few people who don't like a product, no matter how good it is. You know, those natural complainer types.

*Brad:* No way, you can't ignore the facts and try to camouflage the product under a glossy ad campaign. You have to look at the problems in "Dear John" and correct them.

*Colin:* You know, Brad, every time we get started on some good ideas, you break in with your negative attitude. If you can't suggest anything constructive, then don't waste time arguing and criticizing.

Nodding in agreement, the other group members began discussing the ad campaign. The group reached consensus on the final plans, although Brad avoided participating in the planning sessions. After the meeting, Jim and Sheila left together.

*Jim:* Well, I can't wait to see the results of the ad campaign. The public can't help but be persuaded to buy the product after being exposed to this campaign.

*Sheila:* Yes, it does look good. I was thinking though about what Brad was saying, that there may be problems with the product itself. We didn't really examine that question. I wonder if some of those consumer complaints may be valid. I didn't want to mention my doubts, though, because everyone else seemed to feel so strongly about "Dear John." I didn't want to seem pessimistic.

*Jim:* No, it's a good thing you didn't say anything. There was no need. It would have put people on edge and maybe hurt some feelings. Oh, are you meeting us for a baseball game at lunch tomorrow?

*Sheila:* You bet I will!

They parted, waving, contented with their accomplishments and another successful day at Odessy Communication Systems.

1. How does this case study illustrate the phenomenon of "group-think"?

2. Two of the symptoms of groupthink are said to be an illusion of unanimity and an illusion of invulnerability. How does the Odessy group display these symptoms?
3. What approach might the group employ that would better exemplify creative problem-solving techniques? Rewrite this case study to illustrate one such technique.

# Case Study 18
## (Coordinated with Chapter 35)

*David Thorne*

### Trouble on the *Merrimac*

Like other traditional Canadian industries, Great Lakes shipping has suffered its fair share of labor problems. These problems have been aggravated by factors unique to the marine industry. In particular, one ship, the five-year-old, seventy-million-dollar *Merrimac,* belonging to Clark Central Marine Ltd., was being plagued by labor problems. These problems resulted in slowdowns in loading and reduced tonnage carried. In addition, the ship itself had been damaged in an unusually high number of minor collisions during the shipping season.

"I don't understand it," said Clark's Shore Captain, Nathan Cormier, speaking to the company's labor relations officer. "That ship is almost brand-new, with the latest technology. It should have the fastest loading time on the lakes. Captain Danforth has had an excellent record up until now; there is no reason why she (the ship) should be hitting lock walls and docks so hard. The repair bill during the winter lay-up will be astronomical! And those pesty union officials keep sending grievances on behalf of the unlicensed crew."

"There may be something to that," replied Sam Beckworth, the labor relations officer. "I see there is a high turnover rate in the crew. Many have quit. Others have been fired."

"Well, Sam, I'd appreciate it if you could look into the matter and come up with some recommendations. If she doesn't move more cargo faster, Head Office will be on my back."

At that, Sam packed his bags and joined the ship in the Welland Canal where she was downbound toward Port Cartier, Quebec. He took the spare cabin on the unlicensed crew's deck in preference to the Captain's guest quarters. He wanted to project the image of a nonpartisan observer instead of a "company man."

The next day, while the ship crossed Lake Ontario, Sam observed the deckhands working under the supervision of the Second Officer,

719

Charlie Merkle. When work began at eight o'clock in the morning, there was an intense discussion between Second Officer Merkle and the deckhands about how to accomplish the day's assigned task.

"Charlie," said the deckhand to his Second Officer, "why don't we just take the hoses into the holds and clean the hatches from the top of the ore piles, instead of wasting time taking off each hatch separately?"

"No," said the Second Officer, "we'll do it the way we've always done it."

The exchange quickly turned into a heated argument with the deckhand stomping away, muttering under his breath in frustration.

Charlie Merkle turned to Sam.

"Some of these unlicensed crew think they know everything. None of them can obey a simple order without questioning it," he said.

Later in the day, Sam ran into the deckhand, still furious over the morning's incident.

"I hate it when Charlie puts in overtime by supervising us. Usually the First Officer allows us to do a job our way. As long as the job gets done and done right, he doesn't care how it's done. I like when we're allowed to do things on our own without them breathing down our necks," said the deckhand. "I'm tempted to quit and see what jobs there are around the union hall," he added.

Despite the deckhand's obvious discontent, Sam noticed the seaman proudly wore the same company coveralls all the time, while his coworkers wore the standard department-store green. Another crew member noted to Sam that the deckhand had been on this particular ship since it had been launched. While there had been a tremendous turnover in crew, he had remained.

As the ship continued down the seaway, Sam had many occasions to observe Captain Danforth and his officers at work on the bridge, as well as relaxing in their off-duty hours. Despite company regulations forbidding alcohol on board ship, it seemed a ubiquitous commodity from the Captain down to the unlicensed crew. The Captain openly invited Sam to his cabin for drinks, and Sam joined a few boisterous parties with the other crew members.

At one small "get together" involving off-duty engine and deck officers, Sam had a chance to talk to the First Officer, Hank O'Reilly, a tired-looking, greying, middle-aged man.

"You know, Sam," said Hank, "this business isn't the same anymore. These new ships and technology have changed sailing since I was a young man. The company is always on my back about loading time and tonnage carried. I liked working on the old boats. Loading and unloading was at a relaxed pace, usually supervised by someone on shore. The First Officer didn't have to be on deck all the time.''

"But you get more overtime," responded Sam.

"Who cares about the money! With this pressure, I'll be lucky to make it to retirement," countered Hank as he swallowed his drink.

After Hank left the room, his Second Officer said, "Hank's losing it. He's treading water until retirement. He's weak, let's the crew do what they want. If the Chief Engineer and I didn't have any backbone, the crew would get away with murder with no fear of losing their jobs.''

"You think so?" said Sam.

"Well, you saw that deckhand the other morning. He's going next. I don't care what Hank says about how hard he works and the fact he is the only permanent unlicensed crew member. You have to take a hard line with these people—and their union. Those union officials are always coming on board and waving the contract in our faces.''

The next day, the ship arrived in Port Cartier without incident, and Sam caught the first plane back.

1. How has changing technology affected workers in the marine industry? Are the changes perceived as negative or positive by the seamen? Do you think there is a resistance to change?
2. What is the nature of the conflict in this case study? What are its sources?
3. Do you think the conflict is functional or dysfunctional?
4. What factors are likely to affect attempts to resolve the conflict?
5. Characterize the management styles in this case study. Whose style appears best-matched to the situation?
6. What would be appropriate recommendations for Sam to make to senior management? Think about Fiedler's ideas in your consideration of this case study.

# Case Study 19
## (Coordinated with Chapter 35)

*Darlene Bruzzese*

### The Unhappy Elves

The Top Hat, a very successful restaurant in San Diego, California, hosts as many as 1,200 guests per day during its peak season from June to September. Its appeal is its location atop one of the tallest buildings in the city. The restaurant revolves, giving a magnificent view and adding to its drawing power as a tourist attraction. Because of its success and profits, the operation of the restaurant is highly ordered and tightly supervised.

Those employed directly in the restaurant are kitchen staff (approximately fifteen during the peak season), a head chef, and an assistant who acts in his absence. The restaurant itself, which seats 200, is divided into five sections, each manned by three waiters (one captain and two assistant waiters). Leonard Savoie, head maître d', is responsible for the entire restaurant management. He also has two assistant maître d's who act in his absence.

The restaurant elves, the hostesses, are the workers most taken for granted but essential to the restaurant's effective operation. The women are responsible for "greeting and seating" the customers at their preassigned table. Because the restaurant is circular and constantly revolving, the hostesses are indispensable. There are usually four working at any given time, standing alert in their two-inch (no more, no less) red patent leather pumps and cream and red dresses, exactly two inches below the knee. The hostesses are allowed one fifteen minute break in a five–six hour work day or one half-hour break in a work day involving seven or more hours. Amanda Wilson, who is directly in charge of the hostesses, works downstairs in the office. As a consequence, she rarely sees the girls when they are working. The maître d' and the head hostess are in constant supervision of the hostesses.

During peak season, when tension and the constant pressure to perform superhumanly hang like a cloud, the restaurant becomes a jungle with everyone fighting to survive. "The customer is always right" and "money, money, money" are the mottos held by the management. The most anyone hears of management is "Mr. Big is coming for inspection; pass it on."

Arriving to work late, or showing up with your top button undone usually results in a very bad day. Joyce, one of the new hostesses, almost broke in tears when she was openly reprimanded by Paul, the assistant maître d', for going into the kitchen to get an ashtray for one of the guests. He promptly informed her that it was not her place to do so. She felt that she was only trying to please the customer, behavior consistent with her orientation instructions. Another day, Joyce overheard a hostess being "asked" not to wear "that type of jewelry" and being informed that her hair was a "bit overdone."

By mid-July, obvious feelings of resentment and lack of commitment began to surface among the hostesses. They were quitting at steady intervals; the last to quit did so after being publicly reprimanded twice in the same day by the head chef and Paul, the assistant maître d'. The chef loudly told her that the hostesses were able to have this soup, not that one, and that employees were allowed only one dinner roll. Later that day, Paul screamed at her for answering the phone in the maître d's office. The previous night, the head maître d' scolded her for not answering the call.

The waiters were not without their problems. The continual lack of supplies (silverware, tablecloths) often resulted in verbal, as well as fist, fighting in the kitchen. The chef told the waiters to stay away from the kitchen, while the maître d' sent them to the kitchen to wait for their orders. The waiters complained that their captains, who distributed the tips as they saw fit at the end of the night, were cheating them.

With two solid months left in the peak season and inadequate numbers of staff, management decided to make an appearance to investigate the unhappiness and conflict.

1. Analyze the nature of the conflict in this case study. Who are parties to the conflict? What are its sources?
2. If you were a member of the Top Hat management team, what recommendations might you make to help management solve its employee problems?

# Case Study 20
## (Coordinated with Chapter 36)

*Doretha L. Murphy*

### Kontral Pharmaceuticals

Martin Smith is the director of the legal department of a large corporation, Kontral Pharmaceuticals. He manages a staff of ten lawyers, three paralegals, and nine secretaries. Martin sometimes speculates as to whether the company has not deliberately structured the department in such a way as to allow advancement only to those lawyers willing to take on administrative duties. Reflecting on his three long years in the position and the numerous petty problems with which he has had to deal, he wonders if private practice might not be preferable to the frenetic pace of his present job.

"Yes, Mrs. Bush. What is it?"

"I'm sorry to disturb you, sir, but I wanted to talk to you about the company's new parking policy."

"What about it? It won't affect my parking spot, will it?"

"No, sir. But it is causing a great deal of dissension among the staff, particularly the lawyers."

"Well, what seems to be the problem?"

"As you know, sir, for years the lawyers have automatically been given parking spaces; and the leftover spaces have gone to the support staff to fight over. The lawyers feel that, being professionals, they should not have to worry about parking. However, the new company policy dictates that the thirteen parking spaces be allocated on the basis of need and on the basis of distance from the office to the residence."

"Let me guess, Mrs. Bush. Some of the lawyers are upset that they are going to lose their parking. Am I right?"

"Yes, sir. You are."

"I can understand how the lawyers feel. They should have parking. After all, they often work late and the buses aren't running their regular schedules then. They also work on weekends quite often. They should have access to parking.''

''Yes, sir. I agree with you, Mr. Smith.''

''On the other hand, I know that most of the lawyers live within a healthy walking distance from the office.''

''That's right, sir.''

''And a number of the secretaries live outside the city and have small children to drive to a day-care center or a sitter. They would certainly find getting to work easier if they could drive straight to work and find parking.''

''That's right, sir.''

''But then they have been managing all right so far. Have they complained of not being able to get to work because of lack of a parking space?''

''No, sir. You are right. They have been managing all right so far.''

''Well, Mrs. Bush. I understand your problem. Thank you for drawing it to my attention.''

''Yes, sir.''

''By the way, Mrs. Bush, it's that time of year again and I've had to do your performance evaluation. Here, take a moment and read it over.''

Martin put the final touches on a brief that he required the next day while Sarah Bush read her yearly evaluation. Martin was annoyed that he was producing an important document so close to the deadline. Before he had administrative duties to handle, he was always on top of everything, so much so that he did not always feel pressured by deadlines. Maybe he could get Mrs. Bush to work overtime tonight; otherwise he might not have the document typed in time for his court date the next day. He knew he could have come in the previous day to finish the brief, but it was such a beautiful day and he hadn't had much time this summer to enjoy his new cottage. Besides, he had promised his family that he would set Sundays aside for them.

''May I ask a few questions, Mr. Smith? There are some points I don't understand.''

''By all means. That's what I'm here for. But let's move along quickly and not get hung up on anything; we've got to get this brief typed. By the way, could you stay late tonight?''

''Not tonight. This is Monday and I always have rehearsals on Mondays. We have a show in two weeks time; and if I miss a rehearsal, I won't be allowed in the show. It's an important show, too. The guest conductor is world renowned. I'm looking forward to working with him.''

"And I, Mrs. Bush, am looking forward to getting this document completed. You know the consequences of missing a deadline. And we've had other conversations regarding the nature of legal work. The work must come first. Everything else is second. That's the nature of the beast. Sometimes work is slow, and I have no problem with your outside activities then. But when we have a deadline to meet, as I've told you before, everything else has to be put aside."

"Mr. Smith, I work harder than anyone else here! I never take a coffee break; I often work through my lunch hour; and when I can, I stay and work overtime when you ask. I don't complain about not having coffee breaks and missing some lunch hours, because it has been my decision to give them up. Nor have I claimed overtime for the extra work. And what good has it done me? No one ever acknowledges the extra effort I put in to meet deadlines. The only things you see about me are the negative things."

"That's not true, Mrs. Bush! And lest we forget our place, I believe you had a question before we were to start on this urgent and important work?"

"I simply question how you arrive at an evaluation of "marginally satisfactory" when every single one of my previous supervisors has rated me "superior" for performing the same type of work?"

"Obviously there is a difference of approach in completing the performance evaluation, and there must be a difference in expectations. I wouldn't worry about it if I were you. With the ratings I gave you, you still get your annual increment. Nobody pays attention to these evaluations anyway. As you can see, all they do is cause problems. Are you ready to get started?"

"Yes, I suppose so." Sarah accepted the manuscript in quiet frustration and anger, more determined than ever to start searching for another job. She reminded herself that she had never really intended this job to be a permanent one. It was a stopgap, a chance to pay off family bills and allow her husband and herself a few extras. Somehow, however, the family seemed to have become more reliant on the second income as time went by. They had purchased a second car. Her children's expenses grew as they got older. Sarah suddenly realized that she felt trapped and out of control. Let's face it! She had to work, at least for a while longer, and she wasn't confident that her next situation would be better than her present one. Maybe it was her fault for expecting too much. Other people certainly had worse jobs, more physically demanding and not so well paying. Maybe wait-and-see was the best attitude. Take a few days sick leave next week to relax and catch up at home. Why not? She couldn't get a performance appraisal much worse than "marginally satisfactory," and Mr. Smith said himself no one paid any attention to the evaluations. If nobody else cared, why should she?

1. In what ways does this case study illustrate some of the principles discussed under "managing conflict and stress"?
2. How well is Sarah handling the negative feelings she is experiencing? Are these indications that Sarah's boss, Martin Smith, may also be experiencing the situation as one of tension and conflict?
3. Does Sarah conform to one of the stereotypes in which women are sometimes cast? If so, which one? How does this stereotype tend to deal with conflict?
4. Did Sarah at any point confront her boss? If so, what kind of confrontation was it? Did her confrontation resolve her problems?
5. How much responsibility does Sarah bear for her current dilemma? How might she change her behavior to break present patterns and effect a different outcome?
6. Construct a dialogue between Sarah and her boss wherein Sarah manifests a more assertive personality. Be careful not to confuse assertiveness with aggressiveness.

# Case Study 21
## (Coordinated with Chapter 37)

### A Lost Contract for Quennel Consultants

Thad Quennel puzzled over a recent development affecting his company, Quennel Consultants of Houston, Texas. In the fifteen years that he had been in business, the company had never had a more profitable year; yet his firm had just lost a bid for a major project to a small and relatively unknown competitor. The state government had awarded a $50,000 contract to the Perkins Agency of Austin.

Thad called in one of his top consultants, Robin Mallory. "Robin, I wonder if you could shed any light on what happened with the public works contract that we recently lost to the Perkins Agency."

"I'll try, Thad. It goes back a long way, I'm afraid." Robin hesitated, looking somewhat uneasy.

"What do you mean?" Thad queried.

"About a year and a half ago, we did some work for the State Health Department. We conducted a training-needs analysis that involved a number of local clinics and made quite a few far-reaching suggestions for changes in their operation."

"Yes, I remember. I thought our study was well received," Thad responded.

"It was, by most people. But it was very much resented by a few persons. It seems that some of the training directors interpreted our recommendations as criticism of their work. One director was particularly upset by the report."

"I don't recall that we intended the report to be a critical commentary on the way the clinics were being run," Thad said.

"Of course not," Robin replied, "but you know how sensitive people can be to someone coming in from outside and appearing to be telling them what to do."

"Ok, but what does this have to do with our losing the contract to the Perkins Agency?" Thad tapped his pen nervously, anxious to get to the point.

"As I told you, Thad. It's rather complex. One of the people who was offended by the report was Lisa O'Neil, the training director for the northeast Texas region.''

"She gave us some problems when we were setting up initial interviews, didn't she?'' Thad queried.

"She certainly did. She didn't want us speaking to the clinic heads in her jurisdiction. She wouldn't give us access to the necessary files. She was altogether uncooperative,'' said Robin, remembering her feeling of annoyance at the time that she had had to deal with O'Neil.

"How did we handle the situation?''

"Not very well,'' Robin admitted. "We eventually bypassed her and went directly to her superior in Austin. O'Neil was reprimanded, and we were given access to employees and records.''

"Doesn't sound too good. Did you discuss this last decision with me before you took action against O'Neil? You know it's our policy to negotiate such situations. We can't afford to antagonize possible future clients.'' Thad was clearly uncomfortable with his consultant's actions.

"We did consult you, but you were very busy and never recommended alternatives to us,'' Robin responded to Thad's accusations in a defensive manner.

"Mmh.'' It was Thad's turn to look embarrassed. "Did you sense at the time that there was any internal conflict between the O'Neil woman and her Austin colleagues? Could her lack of cooperation have signaled some more deep-rooted problems or insecurities?''

"I think you're right, Thad. But we were so frustrated by her uncooperative attitude that it was difficult to get past that point.''

"You think maybe someone wanted to get at her, and we were one way of doing so?'' Thad asked.

"It may be that her boss wasn't getting the results she desired, and we were brought in from outside to confirm the existence of problems,'' Robin said.

"Who employed us? The central office?'' Thad wanted to get to the root of the problem.

"That's correct. Our contract was with Austin,'' said Robin. "Some of the details are coming back to me now. I remember that you needed us to move on to another couple of projects that had urgent status, and we just didn't have time to cajole and negotiate. We did what we had to do to finish the job,'' Robin explained.

"Were our recommendations initiated?'' Thad asked.

"I have no idea,'' Robin responded. "I do know, however, that O'Neil left the department a few months later, and this point leads us to our present problem.''

"Yes?" Thad leaned forward, anticipating Robin's explanation.

"Lisa O'Neil is now chief of training for the Public Works Department." Robin looked closely at her boss to assess his reaction to this news.

"O'Neil was the one who gave the Perkins Agency the contract?" he groaned.

"That's right. She was one of three people involved in the decision, but she obviously played an influential role."

"So we solved a short-term problem and created a long-term one?" Thad looked purposefully at Robin.

"I'm afraid so. Is there anything we—I—can do to make amends? Should I try to speak with Mrs. O'Neil to reestablish relations?"

"Let me think about the problem, and I'll get back to you. Thanks, Robin."

Thad considered the potential future repercussions of his consultants' actions. Then he thought about his own failure to respond to *their* needs, his lack of availability, and the preoccupations that had shut them out. The present contract was lost, but for the sake of the credibility of his firm, Thad felt he should make an appointment to speak personally with Mrs. O'Neil at the first opportunity.

1. How does this case study exemplify some of the principles discussed in chapter 37 on the consultant-client relationship and organizational change?
2. How might the Quennel consultants have better handled the situation that developed with the regional training director?
3. How does this case study exemplify systems theory?

# Case Study 22
## (Coordinated with Chapter 38)

*Anne Bisson*

### Snowfield Public Library

The Snowfield Public Library serves the 35,000 citizens of Snowfield, Ontario. Once located in what was considered the heart of the city, the area around the library has been taken over by lawyers' and accountants' offices and by the public utilities companies.

The hub of the town has moved across the city, where a large shopping mall was built four years ago. Since then, the library has received less business.

One year ago the library building was completely renovated, but many of the people of Snowfield have not even seen the new facility. They remember the library as the gloomy place it used to be. The library also used to sponsor a bookmobile that traveled around the town, allowing people additional access to the library's resources. However, lack of funds terminated this service four years ago.

The price of a library card is fifty cents. Overdue fines are collected on books which are at least a week late, beginning with ten cents a day in the children's department. The fines are slightly more stringent in the adult and audio-visual departments. Also, the library has book sales for its discarded books every five years. Otherwise, the library's funds are supplied by taxes.

The library employs twenty-seven people, including the janitorial staff. The head librarian, Mrs. McCormick, has her office on the top floor. She does the hiring and the firing for the whole library. She retains final approval over scheduling, vacation time, and time off. Paychecks are given to the department heads; and after being hired, employees rarely see Mrs. McCormick. Most of the staff have a bad image of the head librarian. Her main channel of communication to her subordinates is the memo. She retains the authority to approve all orders, a fact that frustrates the department heads who feel as if they should know their department's needs and who resent the slow pace at which requests are processed.

Mrs. McCormick explained the reasons for this policy in the following way: "I have to answer to the board of directors for everything; so I'd rather make the decisions myself."

Adult services, which include the audio-visual and reference rooms, are located on the second floor of the library. Altogether, fifteen employees work in this area.

The children's department is in the basement and is headed by Mrs. Black, who has been a member of the library staff for nine years. The children's department has books for preschool children, children in the primary grades, and for young adults to the ages of fifteen or sixteen. This department is open nine to six weekdays and nine to five on Saturdays. Saturdays are quite busy, especially with junior high school students working on class projects. It seems that it is not practical for parents to drop off their younger children on weekends, since the library is so out of the way. During the week, especially during school hours, things are relatively quiet.

Four people work under Mrs. Black. Caroline is in her mid-fifties. After Mrs. Black, she has the most seniority. Her main task is to stay on the floor, ready to be of assistance to children or to parents looking for reference or reading material. She has been talking of quitting for several years now, but as of yet she has taken no action.

Claire is in her mid-thirties. However, she has only a year and a half less seniority than Caroline. Her main duty consists of checking books in and out and giving new library cards.

Jeanne is twenty-five. She has been at the library for three years. She has a dynamic personality but spends most of her time in the back room, covering books and performing related duties.

Paula is a high school student who comes in one day a week after school and all day Saturday. Her job is to reshelve books. Popular with the young crowd who come in on Saturdays, Paula is approached for help more often than is Caroline.

Caroline takes advantage of Paula's presence on the weekends to send her into the storage room to retrieve back issues of magazines that library patrons request. Paula has more than enough to do, but the library cannot afford to hire any other high school students.

The board of directors has been pressuring Mrs. McCormick to do something about the library's small patronage. In turn, Mrs. McCormick has been pressuring Mrs. Black to come up with a reading campaign or programs designed to attract young people to the library.

Mrs. Black has not asked her staff for help, however, and Claire complained to Jeanne about this oversight.

"She must think we're pretty dumb. I see the kids every day. Doesn't she think I'd have some ideas? Boy, I have plenty of ideas about making changes in this place."

The board of directors believe that if children enjoy visiting the library, their parents will bring them and browse upstairs for themselves. They also believe that if the children learn to use the library when they are young, they will continue to use it when they move to the adult department, eventually bringing their own children. There is no university in Snowfield, and the three high schools have their own libraries.

In spite of the small size of the library, surprisingly little communication goes on between the floors. There is no need really, since Mrs. McCormick makes all the decisions. It is not that the employees are unfriendly; it is just that they never see each other. Each floor has its own coffee break and lunch room facilities; so the three departments on the second floor interact, while the basement staff are isolated. The idea behind the design was that while some of the librarians had lunch, the others would never be far away if things got too busy, as was often the case on Saturdays.

Caroline is friends with the bookkeeper who works on the same floor as Mrs. McCormick. Consequently, Caroline often receives second-hand information about top decisions or plans, which she shares with her coworkers often before Mrs. Black officially announces them. It was in this fashion that Jeanne, Claire, and Paula heard eight months earlier that the library was going to get computers.

Beverly is in charge of the "overdues" for every department. Her job consists of keeping track of all late material and notifying borrowers by phone and then by mail. The job is sought after because it not only offers contact with the public; it also involves visiting every department to verify that the book in question has not been replaced on the shelf. Consequently, Beverly interacts frequently with all employees. She is the first to hear news of weddings, pregnancies, and trips, information that she good-naturedly shares with the whole library. She is jokingly known as the gossip; but, in fact, the rest of the staff relies on her to fill the missing social element in the library.

Unfortunately, Beverly has just announced that she is leaving Snowfield to accept another job. Mrs. McCormick has not yet decided who will replace her. The word is that Caroline will get the job because of her seniority. An indignant Claire confided to Jeanne.

"Surely a year and a half does not make her more qualified than me. Besides, she'd rather sit and let Paula do her running for her. How can they think she'll have enough energy to take the stairs between floors?"

Just the other day, Mrs. McCormick asked Claire to enter some new titles into the computer, since Jeanne was off sick. Not being used to working with the computers, Claire had some difficulty. She stomped into Mrs. Black's office, shouting in frustration:

"Why did you ever agree to these stupid computers anyway? It's taking me twice as long to enter the new books as it would to type up a few cards! You'd better wait until Jeanne gets back. She's the only one who understands the thing!"

1. Is the library a tall or flat organization? What effect does the structure have on its functioning?
2. Are employees experiencing information overload? If so, are the causes identifiable? Is hiring more employees the solution, or are there other factors which should be considered?
3. Are there sufficient liaison functions in the organization?
4. Which problems require long-term solutions, and which require only a short-term solution?
5. Is the grapevine operating as a positive or negative factor in the organization? Who are its members?
6. Consider the physical environment. Is there any way in which it can or should be changed?
7. Do you think the organization is suffering any motivation problems?
8. From a systems perspective, can the library afford to continue to ignore the needs of the people of Snowfield?
9. Would a communication audit serve a useful function?